PRAISE FOR
ASSIGNMENT TO H

"*Assignment to Hell* is a book every modern [...] should read. The 'assignment' is World War II, the largest event in the history of mankind, a war unlike any other before or since. The men who covered it on the front lines, in the air, and at sea were beyond brave and resourceful—and great company for each other. Those legendary journalists, Cronkite and Rooney among them, were the eyes and ears of a nation depending on them for stories that instructed, inspired, and entertained. I salute them all."   —Tom Brokaw, author of *The Greatest Generation*

"If one can say that reading a book titled *Assignment to Hell* was a delight, I say it now. The stories are so vivid and alive all these years later that I felt I was there with the legendary correspondents of World War II as they wrote their way from France to Germany."

—David Maraniss, Pulitzer Prize–winning author of
They Marched into Sunlight

"World War II was also fought by a free press. *Assignment to Hell* is a worthy story about great and adventurous reporters, my father among them, who flew in the bombers, jumped with parachutes, and ducked into foxholes to report news of the war home to America."

—Brian Rooney, former ABC news correspondent and
son of Andy Rooney

"Timothy Gay is a gifted, perceptive writer who succeeds in deftly weaving together journalism and military history. *Assignment to Hell* is a poignant human story that will move you deeply."

—John C. McManus, author of *September Hope*

continued . . .

"*Assignment to Hell* is racy reading—full of backstories, private lives, booze, and gossip about generals, reporters, and news organizations. It is also an important book, telling how five men became writers of the first draft of the history of World War II. A free press never had better allies, and Americans who prize democracy should know them, warts and all. Their kind of work keeps dictatorships at bay."

—Betsy Wade, former *New York Times* editor

"Tim Gay brilliantly tells the tale of five of the greatest reporters of World War II chasing the biggest story of their lives, filing the first draft of history with their newspapers while writing letters home to wives and girlfriends with the first version of lifelong family lore."

—Chip Cronkite, son of Walter Cronkite

"A sprightly synthesis of literature and history . . . unique [and] engaging."

—*Kirkus Reviews*

"This charming, wide-angle recap shows how the men who wrote history's first draft worked and played while in the line of fire."   —*World War II*

ASSIGNMENT TO HELL

✭

The War Against Nazi Germany

with Correspondents

Walter Cronkite, Andy Rooney, A. J. Liebling,

Homer Bigart, and **Hal Boyle**

✭

TIMOTHY M. GAY

NAL
CALIBER

NAL CALIBER
Published by the Penguin Group
Penguin Group (USA) Inc., 375 Hudson Street,
New York, New York 10014, USA

USA / Canada / UK / Ireland / Australia / New Zealand / India / South Africa / China

Penguin Books Ltd., Registered Offices: 80 Strand, London WC2R 0RL, England
For more information about the Penguin Group visit penguin.com.

Published by NAL Caliber, a division of Penguin Group (USA) Inc.
Previously published in an NAL Caliber hardcover edition.

First NAL Caliber Trade Paperback Printing, May 2013

NAL Caliber Trade Paperback ISBN: 978-0-451-41715-2

The Library of Congress has catalogued the hardcover edition of this title as follows:

Gay, Timothy M.
Assignment to Hell: the war against Nazi Germany with correspondents Walter Cronkite, Andy
Rooney, A.J. Liebling, Homer Bigart, and Hal Boyle/Timothy M. Gay.
p.   cm.
Includes bibliographical references and index.
ISBN 978-0-451-23688-3
1. World War, 1939–1945—Press coverage—United States. 2. World War,
1939–1945—Journalists—Biography. 3. World War, 1939–1945—Campaigns—Europe.
4. World War, 1939–1945—Campaigns—Africa, North. 5. War correspondents—United States—
Biography. 6. Cronkite, Walter. 7. Rooney, Andrew A. 8. Liebling, A. J. (Abbott Joseph),
1904–1963. 9. Bigart, Homer, b. 1907. 10. Boyle, Hal.   I. Title.
D799.U6G39   2012
070.4'49994053092273—dc23   2011049869

Printed in the United States of America
10 9 8 7 6 5 4 3 2 1

Set in Minion Pro
Designed by Ginger Legato

ALWAYS LEARNING   PEARSON

To my mother,

Anne Harrington Gay,

still going strong at eighty-five,

Civil Air Patrol volunteer, 1942–1944.

And to the memory of my aunt and uncle,

Ella Harrington Cashman (1910–2009) and William Maurice Cashman,

MD (1904–1989), U.S. Navy surgeon, 1941–1945.

The best of the best generation.

I know that it is socially acceptable to write about war as an unmitigated horror, but subjectively at least, it was not true, and you can feel its pull on men's memories at the maudlin reunions of war divisions. They mourn for their dead, but also for war.

—A. J. Liebling, 1962
Mollie and Other War Pieces

CONTENTS

★

AUTHOR'S NOTE

★

Despite all the books and movies, despite popular culture's genuflection to the Greatest Generation, it's still difficult for us to imagine the heartache that World War II exacted on our parents and grandparents. This story illustrates why.

In July 2011, my wife, Elizabeth, and I took our kids—Allyson, then twenty-one, Andrew, eighteen, and Abigail, eleven—on a World War II–inspired trip through England and France. While visiting the Normandy American Cemetery and Memorial at Colleville-sur-Mer, we wanted to pay our respects to the brother of Associated Press columnist Hal Boyle's sister-in-law, Radioman Second Class John N. Murphy of Kansas City, Kansas. Young Jack was killed D-Day evening on Omaha Beach. At the visitor's center, I approached the guide sitting behind the counter and asked for help in finding Jack's grave. One of Boyle's best columns was a tender tribute to Jack, written at Normandy a month after Murphy perished.

The guide turned out to be Anthony Lewis, a patient and gracious Brit. Lewis has bushy brown hair, a ready smile, and an enviable, Joe Liebling–

like facility for carrying on simultaneous conversations in English and French. He clearly enjoys helping people find the burial spots of family members and old friends of old friends on the bluff near Omaha Beach.

"Let's see," he said, squinting through wire-framed glasses at the database he'd called up on his computer screen. He scrolled through endless names. "John N. Murphy of Kansas City . . . John N. Murphy . . ."

After a few minutes, Lewis reckoned that *our* John Murphy was no longer buried at Colleville. Once the war had ended, Jack's family must have requested that his remains be repatriated; the bodies of more than half the Americans killed in Europe during World War II were eventually transferred back home, Lewis explained.

Lewis continued to eye his screen. He was "sad to report" that there were many other martyrs named John Murphy buried in the eleven cemeteries maintained around the world by the American Battle Monuments Commission (ABMC).

"Good heavens. How many?" I asked.

Eventually Lewis determined that there were twenty-seven John Murphys resting in ABMC gravesites: four in Margraten, Holland; three in Florence; two in Sicily; two in Normandy; two in Ardennes, France; one in Henri-Chapelle, Belgium; three in Honolulu; and ten in Manila.[1]

Twenty-seven?

World War II was so malignant that twenty-seven Americans named John Murphy are buried in ABMC cemeteries—and that doesn't even count the John Murphys, like *our* John Murphy, resting elsewhere?

Lewis pointed out that a Sergeant John P. Murphy of New York, a member of the 299th Engineer Combat Battalion, happened to be buried at Normandy, in Plot I, Row Five, Grave Eighteen. He'd been killed on D-Day, too, not far from *our* John Murphy.

So the five of us set out through those sacred grounds to find Sergeant John P. Murphy's gravestone. There's something about that immaculately landscaped lawn, those thousands of pristine and geometrically precise white markers, that envelops you, that makes you feel large and small at the same time.

While we stood over Sergeant Murphy's grave, I thought of Andy Rooney's lovely hymn to the men interred at Colleville: "Even if you didn't know anyone who died, the heart knows something the brain does not— and you weep."[2]

Too many of us still take the fight against Adolf Hitler and global Fascism for granted. We're so familiar with the war's ebb and flow—the "inevitable" Allied triumph over evil—that we've become inured to the sacrifice it demanded.

There was nothing inevitable about victory over Nazi Germany. It was accomplished against long odds through stirring leadership and incalculable suffering.

There was also nothing inevitable about the caliber of U.S. journalism in World War II. Much of the press coverage of America's earlier conflicts— the Spanish-American War of 1898 and the Great War of 1917–1918—had been tainted with "yellow," appallingly shallow and propagandistic, usually concocted a healthy distance from the front lines.

Most World War II correspondents were of a different breed: conscientious journalists who insisted on being close to the action and reporting something resembling the truth. Even with intrusive censorship, the journalism they practiced during the war helped propel their postwar craft— and spawned the greatest era of press independence and integrity in American history.

We know now that Hitler's blitzkrieg through France stopped soon after the Wehrmacht captured Paris. But the *New Yorker*'s A. J. Liebling didn't know that when, with Stuka dive-bombers still terrorizing the French countryside, he jumped into a tiny Citroën with two other correspondents and lit out for Lisbon.

We know now that enemy resistance to the Allied landings in Morocco was comparatively light. But the Associated Press' Hal Boyle didn't know that when, in the dank chill of a November morning, he joined other petrified young Americans in shimmying onto a landing craft.

We know now that the Nazis were eventually pushed off the high ground surrounding the beach at Anzio. But the *New York Herald Tribune*'s

Homer Bigart didn't know that as he spent two agonizing months on Anzio's beachhead, constantly diving for cover as enemy gunners peppered it with artillery.

We know now that, after weeks of gruesome combat, the Germans retreated from St.-Lô in Normandy. But Staff Sergeant Andy Rooney of the *Stars and Stripes* didn't know that when he was following GIs up savagely defended hills, dodging machine gun and mortar fire. Rooney's bravery earned him a Bronze Star.

We know now that Hitler's prized *Panzer* units eventually abandoned Holland. But United Press' Walter Cronkite didn't know that when his 101st Airborne glider crash-landed in Zon. The glider turned upside down as it slithered in a farm field, splintering in two. As Cronkite scrambled out, he could hear enemy artillery. It barely let up for weeks.

For every moment of joy in the struggle against Nazi Germany, there were dozens laced with profound grief. To be sure, covering the war to stop Hitler took journalistic skill. But mainly it took courage. It's been an honor to tell their story.

So to Andy Rooney, who sadly left us at age ninety-two just as the manuscript was nearing completion, and to his friends and family, to the friends and families of Walter Cronkite, A. J. Liebling, Homer Bigart, and Hal Boyle, to the families of the twenty-eight blessed John Murphys, and to the hundreds of other Allied heroes celebrated in these pages, the Gay family of Vienna, Virginia, would like to say thank you.

Timothy M. Gay
December 2011

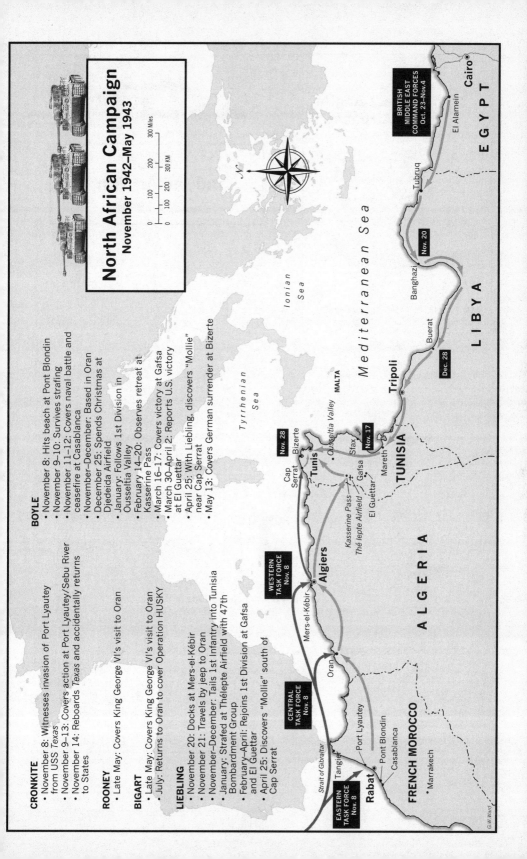

North African Campaign
November 1942–May 1943

CRONKITE
- November 8: Witnesses invasion of Port Lyautey from USS *Texas*
- November 9–13: Covers action at Port Lyautey/Sebu River
- November 14: Reboards *Texas* and accidentally returns to States

ROONEY
- Late May: Covers King George VI's visit to Oran

BIGART
- Late May: Covers King George VI's visit to Oran
- July: Returns to Oran to cover Operation HUSKY

LIEBLING
- November 20: Docks at Mers-el-Kébir
- November 21: Travels by jeep to Oran
- November–December: Tails 1st Infantry into Tunisia
- January: Strafed at Thélepte Airfield with 47th Bombardment Group
- February–April: Rejoins 1st Division at Gafsa and El Guettar
- April 25: Discovers "Mollie" south of Cap Serrat

BOYLE
- November 8: Hits beach at Pont Blondin
- November 9–10: Survives strafing
- November 11–12: Covers naval battle and ceasefire at Oran
- November–December: Based in Oran
- December 25: Spends Christmas at Djedeida Airfield
- January: Follows 1st Division in Ousseltia Valley
- February 14–20: Observes retreat at Kasserine Pass
- March 16–17: Covers victory at Gafsa
- March 30–April 2: Reports U.S. victory at El Guettar
- April 25: With Liebling, discovers "Mollie" near Cap Serrat
- May 13: Covers German surrender at Bizerte

FRENCH MOROCCO

ALGERIA

TUNISIA

LIBYA

EGYPT

Mediterranean Sea

Ionian Sea

Tyrrhenian Sea

MALTA

Rabat

Casablanca

Marrakech

Port Lyautey

Pont Blondin

Tangier

Strait of Gibraltar

Mers-el-Kébir

Oran

Algiers

Bizerte

Cap Serrat

Tunis

Ousseltia Valley

Sfax

Gafsa

Mareth

El Guettar

Kasserine Pass

Thélepte Airfield

Tripoli

Buerat

Banghazi

Tubruq

El Alamein

Cairo

EASTERN TASK FORCE Nov. 8

CENTRAL TASK FORCE Nov. 8

WESTERN TASK FORCE Nov. 8

Nov. 28

Nov. 17

Dec. 28

Nov. 20

BRITISH MIDDLE EAST COMMAND FORCES Oct. 23–Nov. 4

0 100 200 300 Miles
0 100 200 300 KM

G.W. Ward

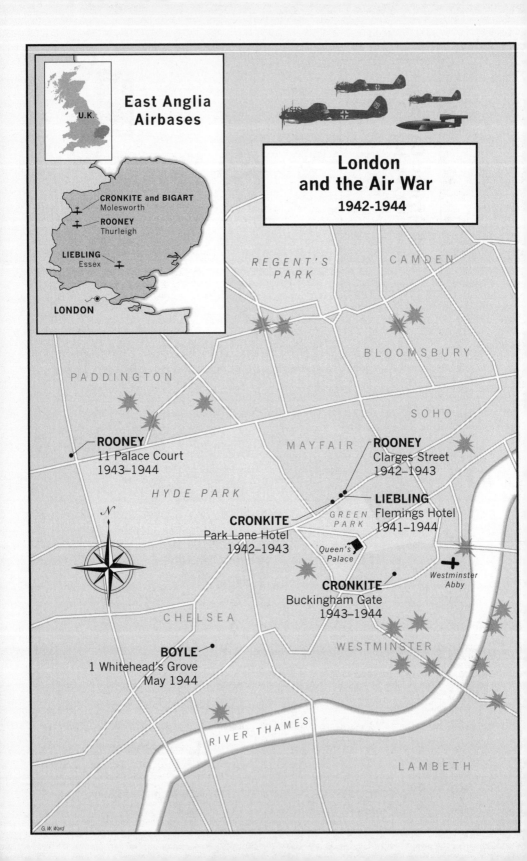

East Anglia Airbases

U.K.

CRONKITE and BIGART
Molesworth

ROONEY
Thurleigh

LIEBLING
Essex

LONDON

London
and the Air War
1942–1944

REGENT'S
PARK

CAMDEN

BLOOMSBURY

PADDINGTON

SOHO

MAYFAIR

ROONEY
11 Palace Court
1943–1944

ROONEY
Clarges Street
1942–1943

HYDE PARK

LIEBLING
Flemings Hotel
1941–1944

N

CRONKITE
Park Lane Hotel
1942–1943

GREEN
PARK

Queen's
Palace

CRONKITE
Buckingham Gate
1943–1944

Westminster
Abby

CHELSEA

WESTMINSTER

BOYLE
1 Whitehead's Grove
May 1944

RIVER THAMES

LAMBETH

G. W. Ward

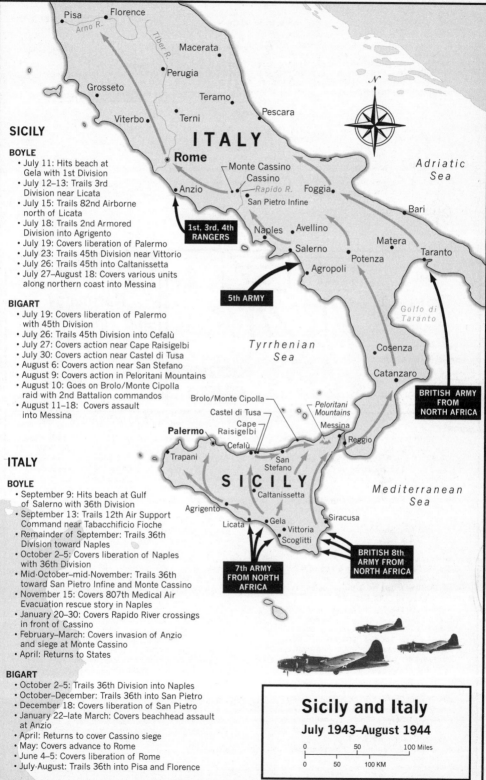

SICILY

BOYLE
- July 11: Hits beach at Gela with 1st Division
- July 12–13: Trails 3rd Division near Licata
- July 15: Trails 82nd Airborne north of Licata
- July 18: Trails 2nd Armored Division into Agrigento
- July 19: Covers liberation of Palermo
- July 23: Trails 45th Division near Vittorio
- July 26: Trails 45th into Caltanissetta
- July 27–August 18: Covers various units along northern coast into Messina

BIGART
- July 19: Covers liberation of Palermo with 45th Division
- July 26: Trails 45th Division into Cefalù
- July 27: Covers action near Cape Raisigelbi
- July 30: Covers action near Castel di Tusa
- August 6: Covers action near San Stefano
- August 9: Covers action in Peloritani Mountains
- August 10: Goes on Brolo/Monte Cipolla raid with 2nd Battalion commandos
- August 11–18: Covers assault into Messina

ITALY

BOYLE
- September 9: Hits beach at Gulf of Salerno with 36th Division
- September 13: Trails 12th Air Support Command near Tabacchificio Fioche
- Remainder of September: Trails 36th Division toward Naples
- October 2–5: Covers liberation of Naples with 36th Division
- Mid-October–mid-November: Trails 36th toward San Pietro Infine and Monte Cassino
- November 15: Covers 807th Medical Air Evacuation rescue story in Naples
- January 20–30: Covers Rapido River crossings in front of Cassino
- February–March: Covers invasion of Anzio and siege at Monte Cassino
- April: Returns to States

BIGART
- October 2–5: Trails 36th Division into Naples
- October–December: Trails 36th into San Pietro
- December 18: Covers liberation of San Pietro
- January 22–late March: Covers beachhead assault at Anzio
- April: Returns to cover Cassino siege
- May: Covers advance to Rome
- June 4–5: Covers liberation of Rome
- July-August: Trails 36th into Pisa and Florence

Sicily and Italy

July 1943–August 1944

0   50   100 Miles

0   50   100 KM

G. W. Ward

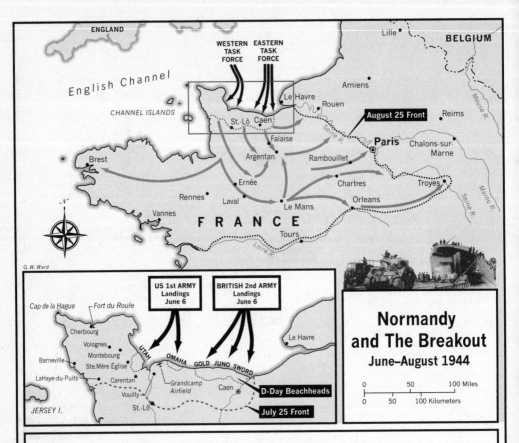

Normandy and The Breakout
June–August 1944

G. W. Ward

ROONEY
- June 10: Hits beach at Utah with 4th Division
- June 11–13: Covers action near Carentan
- June 14–15: Trails advance into Ste-Mère-Église
- June 15–26: Trails advance up Cotentin Peninsula to Montebourg and Valgones
- June 27: Covers liberation of Fort du Roule, Cherbourg
- June 28–30: Stays in Cherbourg with Liebling
- Early July: Stays at Grandcamp Airbase with Bede Irvin
- Early mid-July: Stays in Vouilly while covering action around St.-Lô
- July 15–17: Covers assault on Hills 192 and 122 outside St.-Lô
- July 18: Covers liberation of St.-Lô with 29th and 1st Divisions
- July 20: Covers Bradley's press conference at Vouilly
- July 25: Covers COBRA breakout
- August 3: Files story on F.F.I. action near Vannes
- August 15–18: Covers action at Falaise Pocket
- August 18–22: Stays at Bagnoles press camp
- August 23–25: Stays at Rambouillet
- August 25: Covers liberation of Paris with French 2nd Armored

LIEBLING
- June 24: Arrives in Normandy from England
- June 25–26: Covers F.F.I. on Cotentin
- June 27: Covers liberation of Fort du Roule, Cherbourg
- June 28–30: Stays in Cherbourg with Rooney
- Early July: Stays at Vouilly with Boyle and Rooney, covers action around St.-Lô
- July 8–9: Trails 79th Infantry into Barneville and La Haye-du-Puits with Boyle

- July 18: Covers liberation of St.-Lô with 29th Infantry
- July 20: Covers Bradley's press conference in Vouilly
- July 25: Covers COBRA breakout
- Late July–early August: Stays at Canisy press camp
- Mid August: Trails First Division artillery unit
- August 15–17: Covers action near Falaise Pocket
- August 18: Stays at Bagnoles press camp
- August 21: Covers Bradley's press conference at Laval
- August 22: Stays at Ernée
- August 24: Stays at Montlhéry outside Paris
- August 25–September 30: Covers liberation of Paris and aftermath

BOYLE
- June 27: Arrives in Normandy from England
- June 29: Covers surrender of Cap de la Hague
- July 8–9: Trails 79th Infantry into Barneville and La Haye-du-Puits with Liebling
- Early July: Stays at Vouilly with Liebling and Rooney, covering St.-Lô
- July 20: Covers Bradley's press conference in Vouilly
- July 25: Covers COBRA breakout
- August 3: Covers action around Rennes
- August 13: Trails 5th Division into Argentan
- August 14: Covers liberation of Chartres
- August 18: Stays at Bagnoles
- August 21: Covers Bradley's press conference in Laval
- August 22–24: Stays at Rambouillet
- August 25: Covers liberation of Paris
- August 29: Injured in motorcycle accident in Paris

CRONKITE
- June 13–September 17: Dodges V-1s in London

NORTH SEA

HOLLAND

The Hague

**Allied Front
Dec. 15**

Lek R.

Nijmegen

Overloon

**Allied Front
Sept. 15**

Venray

Eindhoven

**Allied Operation
Market-Garden
Dec. 15**

Antwerp

Dunkirk

Cologne

Rhine R.

Brussels Zon

Maastricht

Roetgen

BELGIUM

Liège

Aubel

GERMANY

Meuse R.

Malmedy

Stavelot

Dinant

Celles

**Allied Front
Dec. 24**

Bastogne

**Battle of the Bulge
German Counter Attack
Dec. 16**

Somme R.

LUX.

Luxembourg

FRANCE

Marne R.

Paris

N

Seine R.

Troyes

HOLLAND

CRONKITE
• September 17–18: Drops into Zon with 101st Airborne
• September–October 3: Covers action around
  Eindhoven with 101st Airborne
• October 3–5: Covers action around Nijmegen with
  82nd Airborne
• October 6–8: Covers Allied advance on Overloon
  and Venray

ROONEY
• September 21: Covers liberation of Maastricht

BOYLE
• September 20: Covers liberation of the Hague

BELGIUM/LUXEMBOURG

CRONKITE
• September 29–December 16: Covers Montgomery
  in Brussels
• December 16–25: Covers Bulge from Luxembourg City
• December 26–27: Covers Bulge from south of Bastogne

BOYLE
• October 15: Covers Aubel
• December 17: Covers Malmédy Massacre
  involving 285th Field Artillery
• December 20: Covers action near Stavelot
• December 28: Covers action near Celles

MARKET-GARDEN
and
the Battle of the Bulge
September 15–December 24, 1944

GERMANY

ROONEY
• September 20: Covers action in Roetgen with 1st Army

0   25   50 Miles
0   25   50 KM

G. W. Ward

PROLOGUE

✦

D-DAY FOR ALL THEIR LIVES

*I have D-Day now for all of my life . . . No one can ever
take [it] away from me, but nobody can give me another
D-Day, either.*

—A. J. LIEBLING, 1944
LETTER TO JOE MITCHELL OF THE *NEW YORKER*

The June sun had barely crept over the soggy English countryside when Captain Robert W. Sheets, his nine crew members, and their surprise guest began crawling through the belly of the B-17G Flying Fortress *Shoo Shoo Baby*. Launched at Molesworth, a Cambridgeshire airdrome sixty miles north of London, that morning's mission would mark the hellion pilot's twenty-first raid over enemy territory.[1]

Bob Sheets loved living on the edge. On a whim four years earlier, sans passport, he had ditched the University of Oregon to swab decks on a freighter bound for the Philippines. Right after Pearl Harbor he had enlisted, but balked when the Army groomed him toward tanks; instead, he insisted on enrolling in flight school.[2] Now, just six months removed from pilot training, the wiry towhead with the sly wit had become a balls-out bomber jock for the Eighth Army Air Force. Every time Sheets went wheels up, he was bucking survival odds—and he and his crew knew it.

His boys had come to believe their new "Fort" was a talisman; *Shoo Shoo Baby* was named after a bluesy and bittersweet tune by the Andrews Sisters about a serviceman kissing his girl goodbye. Painted on the nose's

1

starboard side was the obligatory "bomber gal" provocatively stretched out in a peignoir, her auburn tresses almost brushing the crude block lettering of SHOO SHOO BABY. Scrawled on the port side was their squadron's mascot, Warner Brothers wise guy Bugs Bunny, coolly munching a carrot while standing atop a plummeting bomb.[3]

Bugs, the temptress, and SHOO SHOO BABY[4] shooed away flak and checker-toothed Focke-Wulf 190s and Messerschmitt (Me) 109s and the twin-engine Me 110s—or surely that's what the men told themselves over pints of beer at Molesworth's Cross Keys tavern when, battered and bloodied, they made it back from the Third Reich while so many pals in less providential planes hadn't.

They were proud to belong to the 303rd Bomb Group, a rough-and-tumble outfit that defiantly called itself Hell's Angels. The men of the 303rd may have been hell in the air, but they knew how to operate on the ground, too. More than beer guzzling went on at Cambridgeshire pubs: Molesworth produced more marriages between Englishwomen and American servicemen than any U.S. air base in Great Britain.[5]

SHEETS AND HIS CREW HAD been introduced to their visitor at the preflight briefing precisely three and a half hours after midnight.[6] They found themselves shaking hands with a stoop-shouldered twenty-seven-year-old United Press (UP) correspondent with a husky baritone, a Gable-ish mustache, and a pair of mischievous eyes that missed nothing—especially if wire service competitors were lurking. His name was Walter Leland Cronkite, Jr., and he'd spent so much time at Molesworth he considered the dingy base his second home in England.

Around airmen, Cronkite was the soul of affability, often springing for the next round of ale and offering a sympathetic ear as he scribbled their accounts of clashes with the Nazi war machine. But in the company of rivals—reporters with Associated Press (AP) and the International News Service (INS)—he could be aloof, often curt.[7] Rats churned inside the young Cronkite; with a deadline looming, he suffered no fool gladly. Instead of sitting square to an Olivetti or a portable Hermès as he typed his dispatches, he tended to perch sideways, legs crossed, furiously puffing a pipe as his fingertips crashed over the keyboard. Literally every second counted when butting heads with the competition.

Two years into covering the war, Cronkite's waistline was thinning almost as rapidly as his hair. He complained in letters to his wife, Betsy, that the combination of round-the-clock reporting, food rationing, and dreadful English cuisine made it tough to keep on weight. Cronkite was just under six feet tall; his weight that spring had dipped alarmingly south of 160 pounds.[8] He was so haggard he looked "like hell," he confided to Betsy.[9] The faux officer's uniform commissioned by the U.S. military—a dark olive suit coat with WAR CORRESPONDENT stitched over the left breast pocket and on the left shoulder patch—now bagged around his neck like the blazers he had once borrowed from his dad for Chi Phi fraternity dances at the University of Texas.[10]

Cronkite may have been emaciated, but from the deft way he fastened his flak jacket and "Mae West" life preserver, then hoisted himself through *Shoo Shoo Baby*'s starboard-side waist hatch and wriggled past the ammunition box, the two waist-gun emplacements, the aperture to the Sperry ball-turret gunner's post, the radar and radio compartments with their wires jutting every which way, then negotiated the narrow metal beam that spanned the bomb bay, inched past the ladder to the top-turret gunner's perch, and—skirting the elevated cockpit—finally lowered himself into the Plexiglas nose with the bombardier and the navigator, it should have been apparent to his new friends that he was hardly a rookie.

Fifteen months earlier, on his first combat foray in a Flying Fortress, Cronkite had manned the starboard nose machine gun, hammering away at German fighter planes in clear violation of the Geneva Conventions governing the conduct of noncombatants. It seemed absurd, Cronkite later said, to observe the niceties of international law while being attacked by a malevolent enemy. He may not have wounded any Nazi fliers ("Boy, they came at you!" he remembered years later[11]), but as Cronkite climbed out of the B-17 he had the satisfaction of wading through hundreds of spent shells.[12]

By midwar, in fact, Cronkite had gone up in practically every crate the

Yanks and Brits had in their fleets—trainers and two-man fighters and medium and heavy bombers and reconnaissance rattletraps that hawked enemy *Unterseebooten* (U-boats) in Torpedo Junction, the treacherous waters surrounding the British Isles. In November of '42, desperate to outscoop a wire service foe, he'd even squeezed into a pontoon plane catapulted from the deck of the battleship USS *Texas*.[13]

Cronkite was proud to be a straitlaced Missourian, but he was ultracompetitive; part of him had always been a daredevil. Whether on a twolaner in Jackson County or a blacked-out country road in East Anglia, the future auto racing buff drove like a banshee.[14]

In the late '30s, with the specter of war looming, Betsy and Walter had signed up for the federal government's Civilian Pilot Training Program. Much to his chagrin, Walter had been washed out because of color blindness, but Betsy had earned her wings—and bragging rights for the rest of their lives together.[15]

The color-blind correspondent's penchant for going airborne elicited a rebuke from his UP superiors, who had already lost prized reporter Brydon Taves in a plane mishap and didn't want to lose another. In February 1944, after Cronkite returned from a B-26 Marauder operation against nascent enemy V-1 rocket sites along the Pas de Calais coast on the English Channel, he was told in no uncertain terms to forswear combat flights.[16]

Decades later, after "Uncle Walter" had succeeded Franklin Roosevelt and Dwight Eisenhower as paterfamilias—twentieth-century America's last (and best) surrogate dad—his CBS News underlings, astounded and a little put off by his doggedness and unflappability, dubbed him "Old Iron Pants." It was one of those exquisite nicknames meant to convey heartfelt respect and a hint of disdain all at the same time.

But the Cronkite who wedged himself between bombardier F. E. Umphress, Jr., (front right) and navigator Kenneth Olsen (back left) in the transparent nose beneath *Shoo Shoo Baby*'s cockpit wasn't wearing iron pants. Cronkite was plenty nervous, he later admitted. The UP reporter had been on the bombing beat for his entire tenure in England. He'd written tons of profiles about airmen like Umphress and Olsen, kid lieutenants who risked life and limb and braved subzero temperatures to take the fight directly to Adolf Hitler's Germany. Millions of American newspaper readers, anxious to learn more about their boys in battle, hung on every word.

Cronkite was never as pious as his public persona. With a good smoke and cocktail in hand, he loved to spin yarns about his dalliances in bookie joints and topless bars and the rest of Kansas City's steamy underbelly. Still, he'd once toyed with becoming an Episcopal minister. But he had a soft spot—and not inconsiderable envy—for hell-raisers. He was forever pulling his rakish London roommate, fellow UP reporter Jim McGlincy, out of barroom brawls and scrapes with the landlord.[17]

So Cronkite was bemused to learn that *Shoo Shoo Baby*'s Bob Sheets was one of the four B-17 pilots who'd gotten in Dutch the previous fall for buzzing Yankee Stadium during the first game of the 1943 World Series.[18] Members of the New York Yankees and St. Louis Cardinals weren't the only ones ducking for cover that afternoon as Sheets and his wing mates, completely unannounced, came thundering in low over the Bronx. Many in the sellout crowd of sixty-eight thousand–plus thought the city was under attack. Enraged, mayor Fiorello La Guardia wanted the miscreants court-martialed, but there was too great a demand for competent bomber pilots. Sheets, his buddy Jack Watson, and their two accomplices got away with mild reprimands and seventy-five-dollar fines.[19] Overnight, the Yankee Stadium quartet became legends in the hell-for-leather air corps.

Correspondents, especially wannabe pilot Cronkite, were in awe of flyboys: the bomber skippers who hustled the "swellingest gals";[20] the fighter hotshots who bragged about their duels with Luftwaffe aces over the North Sea; the bombardiers, radar technicians, radio operators, flight engineers, and navigators who, when not in their cups, would calmly dissect their planes' performance at five miles above the earth; and, most of all, the tail-, topside-, and ball-turret gunners, the eighteen-year-old kids who stared into their beer a little too long, hands trembling as they took another gulp.

Cronkite the correspondent may have been awed, but Cronkite the human being knew enough not to get too close. Indeed, among the first things he told Harrison Salisbury when the UP senior editor (and future *New York Times* sage) arrived in London in early '43 was to keep an emotional distance from the bomber boys. Too many wouldn't be coming back—or if they did, they'd be shot up, maybe crippled for life, Cronkite warned.[21]

No reporter understood the macabre metrics of air combat survivability better than Cronkite. *S for Sugar*, the Molesworth-based B-17 in which Cronkite had flown his first mission over the Reich, was one of eleven bombers shot down in January '44 while attacking an aircraft assembly plant in Oschersleben, Germany. The *S for Sugar* men were luckier than many Allied fliers that day: they bailed out and spent the rest of the war in a Luftwaffe-run stalag.[22]

Fully three-fourths of the American airmen who flew against Nazi Germany in 1943 and the first half of 1944 ended up as casualties of one kind or another,[23] apparitions that haunted the journalists who covered East Anglia airdromes, sharing beer and small talk with doomed young men. *Stars and Stripes* reporter Andy Rooney, Cronkite's friend and fellow air war writer, likened bombing missions to playing Russian roulette with a six-shooter.[24]

CRONKITE HAD BEEN AROUND MOLESWORTH for a lot of missions. But he'd never seen it as frenzied as it was on that early June morning. At the last minute the brass had added a horde of new targets and demanded extra sorties, exacerbating Molesworth's bedlam. Each of the thirty-four B-17s in *Shoo Shoo Baby*'s 427th Bomb Squadron was being loaded with a full complement of ten five-hundred-pound demolition bombs, believed to be the optimal weapons for the unprecedented low-altitude attack the squadron was being asked to undertake.

A few hours earlier, Cronkite had been alone in his London flat. Like virtually everyone in the south of England that evening, he'd heard the unstinting drone of Allied warplanes and figured something big was up. "The whole world knew that the [cross–English Channel] invasion was imminent," Cronkite remembered a half-century later. "The secret being guarded to the very death was exactly when and where."[25]

Over Cronkite's protestations, his bosses at UP that spring had dictated that once the assault began, he would stay in London, write the lead story, and coordinate transatlantic coverage. Their edict left him "broken-hearted," he wrote to Betsy on May 14. "I am safe and snug and hating it," he snarled.[26] Fewer than three dozen of the five hundred Allied war correspondents in England had been "assimilated" with invasion-day troops; Cronkite, despite his stature, wasn't one of them. Ironically, his party-boy roomie, McGlincy, was among the elite few.[27]

At his place on Buckingham Gate a couple of blocks from the royal palace, Cronkite was trying to nod off after midnight when he was startled by someone banging on his door. Standing there, red-faced and in full uniform, was Major Hal Leyshon, an Eighth Air Force public relations officer whom Cronkite had gotten to know from poker games and the occasional spree in Piccadilly. A postmidnight visit from Leyshon, then, was not all that unusual—but not with Hal wearing a uniform and a scowl.

A onetime New York newspaperman, Leyshon brusquely inquired about the whereabouts of McGlincy. Still half asleep, Cronkite explained that Jim was somewhere in the south of England, sequestered with an Army outfit "on maneuvers."[28] Still not satisfied, Leyshon stormed around the apartment, jerking open every closet door. "What in the devil are you doing, Hal?!" Cronkite demanded.[29]

Finally Leyshon growled, "Cronkite, you've drawn the straw to represent the Allied press on a very important mission. It will be dangerous. No guarantee you'll get back. But if you do, you'll have a great story. You can turn it down now, or you can come with me. And security is on—you can't tell your office!"[30]

Cronkite did not hesitate. "I'm in. I'm with you," he assured Leyshon.[31] Already rehearsing an alibi, he hurriedly climbed into his ill-fitting uniform. "I figured if I made it," he wryly recalled, "the UP would forgive me."[32]

Leyshon had a sedan and driver waiting. As they tore north on blacked-out country roads, the wily public relations officer stoked his friend's competitive fire. Leyshon promised Cronkite he'd have the hottest story in the European Theater of Operations (ETO) that day. Best of all, Cronkite would be back at UP's offices off Fleet Street before any Allied reporter—

including his nemeses at AP and INS—had even filed a story![33] Leyshon
knew his man: Cronkite was as vainly cutthroat as any correspondent in
England.

THEY PULLED INTO MOLESWORTH IN time for the premission briefing at
0330. Having been awakened ninety minutes earlier, the B-17 crew members were perched on chairs and benches, eager to learn their objectives.

G-2 intelligence officers wielding wooden pointers stood on a platform;
behind them was a huge map concealed by a drape. Every briefer in Britain
at that hour was smiling "like a skunk eating chocolate," one flier recalled.[34]
After calling the men to attention, the officers paused for dramatic effect—
then dropped the curtain.

Everyone hooted. Instead of a flight path taking them deep into the
Third Reich, the tacked-up ribbons foretold a brisk run across the Channel
into northern France. Colonel Kermit D. Stevens, commander of a 303rd
combat wing, marched to the front of the stage and bellowed, "This is the
day we have all been waiting for! Make 'em know it!"[35]

Along with scores of other Allied air units, the 303rd's mission was to
bomb enemy entrenchments and transportation arteries immediately behind the Calvados coast of Normandy—all aimed, they were told, at helping seaborne infantry gain a toehold on Normandy's beaches. *Shoo Shoo
Baby*'s squadron was given a daunting target: a bridge over the Orne River
and its parallel canal that, left intact, would enable the Germans to rush
reinforcements to the beaches. The bridge was some 10 miles inland, outside a village known as Caen.[36]

For weeks, Cronkite had groused about being sidelined. Now, thanks
to a lucky draw and a friendship forged over watered-down bourbon, he
would be an eyewitness to the twentieth century's most epochal moment.
On that day of days, Cronkite's Fort was one of 9,500 Allied warplanes that
saw action over the Channel. The Missouri daredevil was the only American correspondent that morning to fly on a bomber. During takeoff,
Cronkite parked himself in the B-17's plastic nose, the better to absorb the
full adrenaline rush.[37]

By the time *Shoo Shoo Baby* rumbled down Molesworth's mucky runway, jostling its men with each bump, the sun had been up for a while. Twenty-four thousand Allied paratroopers had already hurtled into the dank gloom all over Normandy. Before long Cronkite could glimpse through the clouds the "unbelievable" spectacle of vessels steaming across the Channel—so many, he wrote, that there "didn't seem to be room for another."[38] By now it was nearing 0700, Tuesday, June 6, 1944.

It was D-Day.

ONE OF THE BOATS THAT *Shoo Shoo Baby* barreled past at sixteen thousand feet was LCI(L)-88, a Landing Craft Infantry, Large, operated by the U.S. Coast Guard and carrying an elite band of demolitionists from the Sixth Amphibious Naval Beach Battalion. At that precise moment, LCI(L)-88 was hovering a mile or so off a beach Allied planners had christened Omaha.

Bracing themselves against choppy seas, LCI(L)-88's officers were standing on the bridge, peering through field glasses, trying to divine how the first wave of seaborne troops—infantrymen from the U.S. Army's Blue and Gray Division, the Twenty-ninth—was faring. From that distance it was tough to tell, but it didn't look good. Huge plumes of smoke billowed from German artillery and 88s, the deadly accurate antiaircraft and antitank guns. Every few seconds there was a concussive *whoosh!* as enemy gunners zeroed in on the boats in front of them. The splashes were getting closer and louder.

At exactly 0735—sixty-five minutes after H-Hour—LCI(L)-88's job was to clear a path for the next wave of invaders scheduled to hit the heart of Omaha. Its mission was to deposit the Navy demolition team, expert engineers who'd been trained to dismantle the insidious obstacles that German commander Erwin Rommel had planted to repel an attack. Allied planners called that section of the beach, apparently without irony, Easy Red.

Perched next to the officers was a rotund thirty-nine-year-old writer with thick wire-rim glasses named Abbott Joseph Liebling. Liebling, scion of a wealthy New York family, owned a set of binoculars so powerful that he loaned them to the LCI(L)'s captain that morning.

The essayist was A.J. to readers of the *New Yorker* magazine but Joe to his friends—and in five days on board the LCI(L), four of them spent docked at Weymouth, England, Liebling had made a lot of new friends. The Coast Guard and Navy men were tickled that an intellectual with an Ivy League pedigree could talk sports—especially prizefighting—with such relish. Liebling not only knew more about boxing than most cornermen, but loved to imitate his heroes, inducing howls as his chubby carcass pranced and jabbed, bobbed and weaved. He was also a dead-on mimic, the kind of guy who could eavesdrop on a snatch of conversation and instantly spoof both ends.

One of the crew members who got a kick out of Liebling was a chunky youngster from the District of Columbia. The other Coasties needled the D.C. kid about his habit of beginning every letter to a girl back home with "Well, Hazel, here I am again."[39] The Coast Guardsman who served as the LCI(L)'s coxswain—the swabbie who lowered the ramp and plunged into the water to secure the anchor—had aspirations to be a journalist.

Among the seamen in the Navy's amphibious force (or, as the Coasties kiddingly called it, the "ambiguous farce"[40]) was a twenty-two-year-old radioman from Kansas City, Kansas, named John Murphy. Young Jack was the kid brother of Associated Press columnist Hal Boyle's sister-in-law. During the North African campaign earlier in the war, Boyle and Liebling had become jeep mates and drinking buddies. Thanks to Jack and his cohorts, Normandy would soon reunite them.

Liebling was the least pretentious-looking correspondent in the ETO. Combat reporters weren't necessarily matinee idols, but most tried to dress the part, sporting an aviator's scarf or a tanker's jacket or some other item that projected a martial image. Fashion affectation, though, was lost on Liebling, whose military-issue slacks fit so loosely they flapped in the breeze. Three decades later, fellow correspondent Don Whitehead remembered that Liebling "managed to look like a large, uncomfortable sack of potatoes."[41]

The potato-shaped boxing aficionado had begged the Army for an invasion assignment with foot soldiers. Liebling wanted to coldcock Hitler's *Festung Europa* (Fortress Europe) with his First Division pals from

Tunisia—and had a personal invitation from the First's commanding general, Clarence Huebner, to hit the beachhead at Omaha.[42] Many of the men in the Big Red One, as the First Division was known, were native New Yorkers, ethnic guys with "Toidy-Toid Street" accents and attitudes to match—the streetwise cockiness that Liebling loved to celebrate in print.

After the Army press brass refused to honor Huebner's proffer, Liebling accused them of perpetrating reverse snobbery. Nobody wanted to hand a plum invasion spot to some fat egghead from a snooty rag, he crabbed. But Liebling was lucky: Two old friends, John Mason Brown, a once and future Broadway critic, and Barry Bingham, a prewar reporter with the *Louisville Courier-Journal*, were handling the Navy's invasion-day press relations. Lieutenants Brown and Bingham arranged for a berth for Liebling on LCI(L)-88, one of the first large landing crafts scheduled to hit Omaha.[43]

When Francophile Liebling, who was almost as enamored of northern France as he was of New York City, learned four days before the invasion that Normandy was the objective, he remembered feeling "as if, on the eve of an expedition to free the North from a Confederate army of occupation, I had been told that we would land on the southern shore of Long Island and drive inland toward Belmont Park."[44]

Liebling had no idea until he arrived at Weymouth that the boat was skippered by an acquaintance. Before the war, Coast Guard captain Henry Kilburn "Bunny" Rigg had been a prizewinning sailor; on occasion, Rigg would write up his seafaring adventures for none other than the *New Yorker*. Liebling didn't know Rigg well, but it's likely he viewed Bunny's presence as a heartening omen.[45]

Rigg's gangplank greeting was so nonchalant it was "as if we were going for a cruise to Block Island," Liebling wrote. But Rigg wasn't leading a pleasure outing: the Supreme Headquarters Allied Expeditionary Force (SHAEF) had made it clear to journalists that once aboard a boat bound for the Channel, there was no getting off. The LCI(L) was a marvel of design: Its flat bottom and collapsible ramp permitted it to run right onto a beach.

Liebling's prewar critiques of New York's dining scene had betrayed a weakness for the good life. He was both gourmet and gourmand, and the thin gruel of service chow took some getting used to. On his first night on LCI(L)-88, before sitting down to a repast of frankfurters and beans, Liebling made mental notes as Rigg and the commanding officer of the beach battalion rolled out a remarkably detailed map of Omaha, buttressed by reconnaissance photographs of Easy Red that showed where the Germans had dug in pillboxes and artillery guns. Rigg pointed out a blockhouse on the bluff overlooking the beach, saying they could expect menacing fire from that area.

Eleven months earlier, the captain and his crew had weathered their share of action during the dicey landing at Licata in Sicily. Liebling was also comforted by the knowledge that the Coast Guard and Navy men had, together, been rehearsing their movements for weeks.

LCI(L)-88's goal, Rigg chuckled, was to give the Navy boys a "dry-ass landing." Knowing that Liebling was worried about enemy guns as the craft maneuvered near the beach, the Navy commander, a Washington, D.C., attorney and Annapolis grad named Eugene Carusi, assured the writer that LCI(L)s tended "to make a fairly small target bow on."[46] Carusi was Liebling's kind of guy: He detested military chickenshit. His men loved him for it; they proudly called themselves Carusi's Thieves.[47]

RIGG KNEW THAT CARUSI'S THEORY would be tested as, staring through Liebling's binoculars at 0720, he sought the correct alleyway to Easy Red. If the team that had stealthily surveyed Omaha's attack routes before dawn had done its job, LCI(L)-88 would come across colored buoys marking its path through the underwater mines, iron barriers, and concrete blocks. Not much went according to plan that morning at Omaha. But remarkably, the painted buoys were bobbing almost exactly where Rigg had anticipated.

The Coast Guard captain turned to his staff and barked, "Mister Liebling will take his station on the upper deck during action." It was Rigg's felicitous way of telling his friend to stay the hell out of the way. Once topside, Joe watched Rigg send the craft surging toward the buoy-marked opening "like a halfback going into a hole in the line." Rigg had spotted, dead ahead, two "spider" mines attached to a block of sunken concrete. He slowed LCI(L)-88 to ensure that it didn't go anywhere near the tentacles sprouting out of the mines; the slightest brush would have been catastrophic.[48]

D-Day's beauty and pathos is distilled into what Liebling glimpsed that morning from his aerie on LCI(L)-88. After the boat sped back up, it soon encountered capsized vessels, a burning LCT (Landing Craft, Tank), and infantrymen floating in bloodied water, many with their heads submerged. Other GIs were struggling in water up to their necks. Fourteen years later, Liebling was to write of the men in the water off Easy Red: "They seemed as permanently fixed in time and space as those Marines in the statue of the flag-raising on Iwo Jima."[49]

Tracer bullets, each with a descending arc, were zinging all around as Rigg swung LCI(L)-88 to the right. With machine gun bullets battering the boat, Liebling found himself shoulder to shoulder with a pharmacist's mate. The two flattened their backs against the pilothouse and sucked in their guts. Artillery explosions were ripping into the water; it felt like at any second the boat would founder. Noxious smoke was everywhere; the noise was deafening.

Moments later Liebling felt the craft run aground. He craned his neck toward the bow and saw that the landing ramp somehow, miraculously, was already down; his pal, the coxswain, clad only in bathing trunks and a helmet, had leapt into the surf. In spite of the pandemonium, the Navy men were rushing forward, rifles and demolition equipment in hand. Liebling could hear an officer, probably Carusi, chanting, "Move along now! Move along!" as if, Liebling wrote, "he were unloading an excursion boat at Coney Island. But the men needed no urging; they were moving without a sign of flinching."[50] Much of the enemy firing, Liebling surmised, seemed to be coming from the blockhouse on the right that Rigg had singled out.

Something scratched at the back of Liebling's neck. Fearing the worst, he grabbed at it, and discovered that the ship's cargo rigging, knocked loose by machine gun fire, had fallen around his shoulders "like a character in an old slapstick movie about a spaghetti factory."[51] As Liebling rid himself of the rope, he glanced toward the stern. There he took in "a tableau that was like a recruiting poster." Three enlisted men, one of them a black wardroom steward, were manning a twenty-millimeter rapid-firing gun. Fluttering behind them was a crisp American flag that Rigg had broken out for the occasion.

Amid the din, Liebling heard the welcome rattling of the stern anchor being dislodged. Seconds later the boat was rocked by a blast. It was, Liebling later learned, a seventy-five-millimeter enemy artillery shell that tore through the bulkhead and smashed through the ramp winch, disabling it.

"Pharmacist's mates, go forward! Somebody's hurt!" an officer yelled. Liebling's pilothouse pal and another medic scurried below. A Coastie came running by and screeched in Liebling's ear: "Two casualties in bow!"[52] By now, they had swung clear of the beach and were chugging toward deeper water. Captain Rigg almost forgot about the spider mines as he yanked his craft away from danger; the LCI(L) limped toward a designated area mid-Channel where a hospital ship awaited.

To Liebling, whose ears ached and head throbbed, it had seemed like an eternity. But LCI(L)-88 had been anchored off Easy Red for just four excruciating minutes.[53]

As Liebling worried about which of his shipmates had been wounded, his chum and acolyte, Staff Sergeant Andrew Aitken Rooney of the military publication the *Stars and Stripes*, was also aboard a warship headed for Normandy. Over dinners together at Fleet Street eateries like The Lamb and Lark, the *New Yorker* essayist had taken a shine to the kid reporter.[54] The cocky Rooney must have reminded Liebling of the Irish pugs he loved to watch at Gleason's Gym in Brooklyn.

At 0739 on D-Day, though, Rooney was still closer to Britain than France. He was billeted with a Fourth Division infantry unit floating a few miles out in the Channel. Rooney and his *Stars and Stripes* colleague Charles Kiley had been embedded with the Fourth nearly a week prior to the invasion; for the first few days, they had stayed in a Bristol couple's home before transferring to the troopship in Bristol Harbour. Their British hosts, in a gesture that touched Rooney and Kiley, had scrimped on ration points to treat their Yank guests to morning coffee—which they mangled by making with milk, not water.

Although it was situated on the Atlantic, not the Channel, Bristol was nevertheless a major invasion staging area and embarkation point. To get to Normandy, ships launched from Bristol had to steam west around the promontory at Land's End before reversing course.

The men on Rooney's boat were scheduled to come ashore at the assault's westernmost beach, code-named Utah, on D-Day plus four. Rooney's section of Utah was some twelve miles west and south of where Rigg and Liebling had eluded Omaha's spider mines.

Like his friend Cronkite, Rooney had been covering the U.S. bombing campaign against Hitler almost from its outset. A former Colgate University lineman, Rooney was a pugnacious GI who had trouble keeping his lips zipped around superiors. Before being transferred to the *Stars and Stripes* in the fall of '42, his stint in the Army had been marked by one contretemps after another with higher-ups.

Upon receiving his draft notice in the summer of '41, Rooney had been assigned to an artillery unit that was eventually sent to North Africa. Fortunately for the upstate New York kid, by then he was in England carrying a steno pad, not in Tunisia hauling a howitzer.

Late in the evening of June 5, Allied planes flying wingtip to wingtip in magnificent V formations soared over Rooney's convoy. Rooney didn't know it, of course, but the planes were C-47 Dakota transports and gliders ferrying paratroopers of the U.S. 101st and 82nd Airborne Divisions to their drop zones behind Utah Beach—the very place where Rooney and his shipmates were headed.

A few days before, General Eisenhower's office had issued a directive urging reporters to be circumspect. There was "nothing threatening" about SHAEF's memo, Rooney remembered. "It assumed we knew a lot and Eisenhower was simply reminding us to be careful. It also assumed, which is what made it friendly, that we were all on the same side."[55]

In truth, Rooney didn't know a whole lot more about the nuances of D-Day than his Fourth Division pals did. The Army had given him his own jeep, which he spent hours weatherproofing, slapping thick grease onto its electrical connections, ignition, and generator. At the *Stars and Stripes'* insistence, the jeep was being transported across the Channel, too. When Rooney hit Utah, he was determined to drive it over the dunes and into the farmland beyond.

Rooney spent June 6 getting snatches of invasion news from the ship's radio, trying to avoid getting seasick as he stared across the waves and wondered at what point on French soil he and his jeep would have to begin dodging enemy fire. He'd been in the ETO for twenty-three months and had never been near a ground fight, although he'd earned an Air Medal for flying along on five combat missions.

The infantrymen huddled on the deck had a different persona than the flyboys Rooney had covered for so long. Infantry guys were less smug, a little less feisty. Yet the one thing that brought GIs and airmen together, Rooney realized, was the specter of imminent death.

"It's hard to see the big picture," he wrote, "and especially hard if you're in the picture."[56]

ONE CORRESPONDENT WHO THOUGHT HE understood Normandy's big picture was Rooney's prospective jeep mate, Harold V. "Hal" Boyle, a thirty-three-year-old reporter and columnist for the Associated Press. An Irishman who under normal circumstances was witty and gregarious, Boyle was, on the afternoon of D-Day, the "maddest man in England," a colleague remembered.[57] Along with a select group of reporters that included Cronkite's UP pal McGlincy, Boyle was supposed to be on board a landing craft hitting Omaha Beach. Things went so rough on day one at Omaha, however, that officials kept the press contingent "sitting on their prats" in England, Boyle complained.

Boyle was so frustrated, he wrote his wife, Mary Frances, that he wanted to jump off Waterloo Bridge—but punned that his protest "wouldn't make that big of a splash."[58] The last thing Army public relations officers (PROs) wanted was a household-name journalist like Boyle getting bloodied at Normandy, so he spent the next couple of days helping AP pry news out of the Brits' Ministry of War Information at the University of London.

Boyle by then was a grizzled veteran of amphibious landings, having witnessed four of them in the Mediterranean Theater. In November of '42, he nearly drowned in the waters off Casablanca when his craft got swamped on a coral reef. Members of General George S. Patton's armored corps fished him out. Boyle repaid the favor by praising Patton's men and (sometimes) their combative and controversial leader on two different continents.

Guys in the trenches loved swapping stories with Boyle. He had an Irish bartender's mug, an infectious smile, a big belly and a big belly laugh, pockets crammed with cheap cigars, chewing gum, and chocolate bars, and, most importantly, an omnipresent flask of rotgut that he was only too happy to share. He also knew how to deliver a profane punch line. His gift for salty language impressed even the most hard-bitten grunts. He was ruddy-faced and beefy, with a batch of brownish Hollywood hair that made him the envy of every aging correspondent in the ETO.

Boyle loved Big Red One infantrymen from the Big Apple as only a Midwesterner could, laboring to capture their banter in Leaves from a War Correspondent's Notebook, the popular column he started in late '42. Faithful readers of Boyle—and by June of '44 hundreds of papers back home were running his features—knew that the First Division had saved the Allies' bacon in Tunisia and later up the gut of Sicily.[59]

As he listened to briefing officers describe the stiff resistance that Allied invaders were likely to encounter in Normandy, Boyle braced himself for the worst. The seaborne landings in Morocco and Sicily had been relative cakewalks. But getting off Italian beachheads at Salerno and Anzio had proven nightmarish. For weeks following the Anzio invasion, enemy tanks and artillery operated so close in the nearby hills that binoculars weren't always needed to follow their movements.

WHILE BOYLE STEWED IN LONDON on June 6, his friend Homer William Bigart, a thirty-seven-year-old correspondent for the *New York Herald*

Tribune, was doing his own stewing eight hundred miles southeast. The dogged Bigart, almost never without a Lucky Strike stuck between oft-stammering lips, was another veteran of the siege at Anzio. Along with other journalists who had followed the dispirited campaign of Lieutenant General Mark Clark's Fifth Army, Bigart was in freshly liberated Rome. At that moment the *Trib* reporter was trying to make sense of Clark's curious decision to abandon pursuit of German field marshal Albert Kesselring's Army Group C, which was finally on the run after a long and bloody stalemate.

Bigart believed in covering war, a Shakespeare-loving colleague once said, "from the cannon's mouth."[60] In late May of '44, Bigart's bullheadedness nearly cost him his life. Cruising solo in a jeep, determined to score an exclusive, Bigart was trying to keep abreast of the Allies' breakout through the Alban Hills south of Rome. Careering around a bend, he suddenly found himself staring at the barrel of a hostile tank. The enemy soldiers were lolling outside, taking a lunch break. They scrambled for weapons as Bigart jammed the jeep into reverse and flew back down the hill. The hair on the back of Bigart's neck stood straight up, he admitted four decades later, until he got out of range.[61] Despite the near-death experience, Bigart got what he wanted, grabbing a story that day that trumped the *New York Times*.

A few nights later, on the evening of June 4, Bigart was following forward elements of Clark's army as they entered the Eternal City. In the rugged prose for which he was already renowned, Bigart wrote, "[It] was a moment of such wildly primitive emotion that even now, 12 hours afterward, it is impossible to write soberly of the nightmarish scene along the Via Nazionale, where jubilation gave way to frozen panic and sudden death." Nazi commanders, in a last-ditch effort to keep the Allies from crossing the River Tiber, hurled flak wagons—lethally armed half-tracks—into Clark's lead column, which at that instant was engulfed by delirious Romans.

"It was like a scene from the Russian revolution," Bigart continued. "The transition from exultation to paralyzing fear was not immediate—

there was that split second of astonishment when the throng merely stood agape, watching the tracers ricochet off the stone walls of the Palace of Rospigliosi."[62]

The next morning, June 5, it was Bigart's turn to stand agape as the squirrelly Clark insisted on posing for photographs on Capitoline Hill instead of chasing Kesselring. Clark's bearing was so imperious that, outside his earshot, staff officers called him Marcus Aurelius Clarkus.[63] When he arrived for a press conference called by his fifty-person public relations team, Clark feigned surprise that newsreel cameramen, photographers, and correspondents were waiting. The shutterbugs were strategically positioned so that they'd get shots of Clark's left profile, the general's "manlier" side—or so he believed.

To ensure that the photo opportunity remained an all-American affair, Clark's staff stuck military policemen at key Roman intersections to stymie any attempt by British officials to infiltrate. It was too bad, reporters sniggered, that the general hadn't expended that kind of energy in cutting off the enemy.

For months Clark had told the press that the aim of the Italian offensive was clear: to decimate Kesselring's forces. Now, suddenly, the campaign seemed to have a more cynical objective: to make Mark Clark a newsreel star and a hero in the pages of *Life* and *Look*. At one point during the session, Clark spread a map on an ancient balustrade and, nodding thoughtfully, pretended to point out something to his corps commanders, a couple of whom were so embarrassed they tried to avoid making eye contact with reporters.

Bigart, cigarette undoubtedly bouncing, exchanged incredulous looks with Paul Green of the *Stars and Stripes*, Eric Sevareid of CBS Radio, and other journalists. One correspondent, quite possibly the acerbic Bigart, notorious for his cut-through-the-crap quips, averred, "On this historic occasion, I feel like vomiting."[64]

On June 6 Mark Clark was still holed up in Rome, and so was the Fifth Army's media entourage. Reporters were at the makeshift press headquarters banging out copy when word came over the radio that the Allies had finally launched the cross-Channel invasion. The correspondents threw up their hands and pulled out their cigarettes. They knew they were missing the biggest story of the war.

AT ROUGHLY 0750 ON D-DAY, as LCI(L)-88 chugged out of range of shore guns, Joe Liebling went down to the well deck, hoping its injured seamen weren't seriously hurt. He stumbled onto a grisly scene. Permeating everything was a "shooting-gallery" stench. Since enemy shells had ripped into cases of rations, much of the deck was covered with food debris.

The news wasn't good. Bloody body parts were splattered all over; the coxswain, the aspiring journalist, never made it back onto the boat.[65] Two Coasties were gravely wounded; one of them was the D.C. youngster, Hazel's would-be boyfriend. The other injured man "lay on a stretcher on deck breathing hard through his mouth," Liebling wrote. "His face looked like a dirty drum-head: his skin was white and drawn tight over his high cheekbones. He wasn't making much noise."[66]

Fifteen miles offshore they linked up with the *Dorothea Dix*, a transport that had been converted into a hospital ship. LCI(L)-88's wounded men had to be lifted to the floating sick bay in wire baskets.[67]

At one point, a "Coast Guardsman reached up for the bottom of one basket so that he could steady it on its way up," Liebling wrote. "At least a quart of blood ran down on him, covering his tin hat [and] his upturned face. . . . He stood motionless for an instant, as if he didn't know what had happened, seeing the world through a film of red, because he wore eyeglasses and blood had covered the lenses."[68]

A decade after the war ended, Liebling admitted that the unnamed Coastie had, in fact, been himself. "It seemed more reserved at the time to do it this way," he wrote. "A news story in which the writer said he was bathed in blood would have made me distrust it."[69]

LCI(L)-88 clung to the transport area on D-Day morning, expecting at any instant to be ordered back to Omaha. But when no instructions came, Rigg and Liebling concluded, correctly, that the boys on Easy Red and all the rest were having too tough a time.

That afternoon, Liebling spotted an undamaged can of roast beef lying on the deck. "I opened it, but I could only pick at the jellied juice, which reminded me too much of the blood I had seen that morning, and I threw the tin over the rail."[70]

By early evening, the situation on Omaha had become less toxic; LCI(L)-88 soon began ferrying infantrymen from bigger boats to landing craft positioned closer to shore. Rigg and his men performed similar duties on D-Day plus one and plus two. On June 9, Liebling cadged a ride with a rocket-firing speedboat, which in turn transferred him to a Higgins craft that, fittingly enough, maneuvered onto Easy Red.[71]

When Liebling neared the top of the cliffs he spotted bilingual signs. Above crudely drawn skulls and crossbones they snarled, *"Achtung Minen!"* and *"Attention aux Mines!"* It amused Liebling that the Germans had been caught so flat-footed they hadn't had time to remove their own placards warning of minefields.[72]

Liebling had visited Normandy several times in his youth; he had always pictured the Channel a brilliant shade of blue. Now in his mind's eye it would forever remain a dull and depressing gray.

Four years earlier, Liebling had fled his precious Paris just before the Nazis goose-stepped down the Champs-Élysées. Liebling had long dreamed of a triumphant return. But now machine gun nests and pillboxes and *Panzer* tanks and half of Hitler's Wehrmacht stood in his way.

IT WASN'T ENEMY RESISTANCE THAT foiled the bombing run of *Shoo Shoo Baby* and its sister planes at 0715 on D-Day so much as the weather. The formation encountered only a few bursts of flak and sporadic rocket fire. But as squadron leader Lewis "Hoss" Lyle and the Flying Fortresses in the 427th arrived over Normandy, gunning toward the bridge at Caen, the cloud cover suddenly thickened.

Cronkite, who'd been nervously searching for Luftwaffe fighters that never materialized, now looked toward the ground and could see nothing. Neither, staring through his bombsight, could bombardier Umphress. It was such a blackout that Captain Bob Sheets and his copilot, Second Lieutenant Darwin Sayers, couldn't see the Forts flying on either side. "Any collision," Cronkite remembered, "would probably [have] set off a chain explosion, wiping out the squadron."[73]

Flying blind, the squadron zoomed over what should have been Caen, but no one could tell for sure. Then Lyle ordered a second pass, this time at a perilously low altitude, hoping there'd be a break in the clouds.[74] There wasn't. Lyle had no choice but to call off the attack.

Under normal conditions the bombers would have jettisoned their packages over enemy territory, but strict orders forbade that: D-Day planners didn't want bombs dropped anywhere near Allied paratroopers. Dumping their load over the Channel wasn't permitted on D-Day, either: There were too many Allied planes flying at too many altitudes; accidents would have been inevitable. So the squadron had no choice but to execute a big bank, climb many thousands of feet—no easy trick in zero visibility—and return to Molesworth. All of which meant Bob Sheets' worst nightmare: Setting down his plane on a fog-shrouded runway while armed with live ordnance. "Now, that was a hairy landing," Cronkite recalled.[75]

There was little time to exchange pleasantries with *Shoo Shoo Baby*'s crew: A quick photo was taken, then Cronkite raced back to London to file his story. His bosses at UP had been frantically searching for him, convinced, Cronkite recalled, that he'd "been up to no good in Londontown."[76]

"Where were you shacked up last night?!" they screeched as Cronkite rushed into the UP offices in the News of the World building on Bouverie Street off Fleet.[77] They calmed down when Cronkite informed them his ass had been over the Channel and back in a B-17.

Hal Leyshon, it turned out, had been mistaken: flashes about the Allied assault had already hit the wires. One of them was from Cronkite's archrival, Gladwin Hill of Associated Press—a turn of events that rankled him no end.

Cronkite had never been so disappointed, he confided a few days later to Betsy. "Why, we [*Shoo Shoo Baby*] didn't even get shot at," his letter grumbled. Not being able to drop bombs on Caen was "like taking only one drink on New Year's Eve."

HAL BOYLE DIDN'T GET ASHORE at Omaha until June 9, the same day as his buddy Liebling. Although both were angry that they'd been kept off invasion beaches, in truth, only a handful of correspondents had beaten them there. One was their friend Ernie Pyle, the sainted Scripps Howard columnist. Pyle's stature earned him a prize spot on the USS *Augusta*, the flagship of General Omar Bradley, the commander of U.S. invasion ground forces. On the morning of June 7, Pyle wangled a ride to shore.

Ernie's encomium to the men of Omaha Beach should be chiseled in the American pantheon of journalism. "As I plowed out over the wet sand of the beach on that first day ashore, I walked around what seemed to be a couple of pieces of driftwood sticking out of the sand. But they weren't driftwood," Pyle wrote. "They were a soldier's two feet. He was completely covered by the shifting sands except for his feet. The toes of his GI shoes pointed toward the land he had come so far to see, and which he saw so briefly."[78]

On D-Day plus three, as Boyle arrived at Omaha for a brief visit before returning to England, he could hear artillery fire unnervingly close. Among the first things Boyle spotted was the way the Germans had implanted concrete-encased guns on the bluffs that towered above the beach. Many of the enemy 88s, Boyle noticed, had bloated barrels; in midbattle, American attackers had bravely disabled the guns by jamming grenades down their mouths.[79]

Twenty-six days later, Boyle was back at Omaha. For a year, through two theaters of the war, he had been looking for Navy seaman and fellow Kansas Citian John Murphy, his brother's brother-in-law.

"Today I found him at last," Boyle wrote in a column that rivaled Pyle at his most powerful.

"John was stretched flat on his strong young back under five feet of Normandy soil. He was lying in Plot B, Row Five, Grave Eighty-four of the first American cemetery in France in World War II."

Radioman Second Class Murphy, Boyle learned in talking to a surviving member of the Sixth Naval Beach Battalion, had been killed some twelve hours after being dumped on Easy Red. Hauling his equipment in one hand and a tommy gun in the other, young Jack had eluded machine gun fire and mortar shells while pounding up the beachhead to set up his radio. Within minutes, he had established shore-to-ship contact so Navy artillery gunners could effectively concentrate their barrages. All day, amid Easy Red's mayhem, John raced from hot spot to hot spot, directing fire over his radio. At about seven o'clock that night, an 88 that hadn't yet been disabled found a foxhole in which Murphy and another radioman were dug in. Both were killed.

"That Murph was a popular Irishman," one of his buddies from the Sixth told Boyle. "Everybody liked him. He was a tall fellow and good-looking. Had a pink face. He was a helluva good ballplayer, too."

Of Murphy's thirty-five-man platoon that Joe Liebling had watched assault Omaha Beach on D-Day morning, five were killed and ten were wounded.

Seven years earlier, when Boyle's older brother Ed had married Monica Murphy, Jack was still in his midteens. Now, Boyle wrote, "there was a mound of earth above his body and in it was stuck a stake bearing his identifying "dog tag." And tangled in the wire which held his dog tag was a withered Normandy rose left there by French peasants who have put a flower over every one of the two thousand American graves in the cemetery."[80]

Back in Kansas City, Monica took the column as it appeared in the hometown *Star* and pasted it into a scrapbook she was lovingly keeping on the war. When she had started the album two years earlier, it had never occurred to her that her brother-in-law would someday write a eulogy to her brother.

ON JUNE 10, WHEN ANDY Rooney drove his greased-up jeep onto Utah Beach, there were scattered artillery salvos—but nothing that caused him to flinch; the nearest fighting was some two miles inland. Utah had been captured on D-Day without Omaha's horrific bloodshed. Yet signs of death were everywhere: The Graves Registration Unit had placed rows of dead GIs in the sand just above the high-tide mark.

"They were covered with olive-drab blankets, just their feet sticking out at the bottom. I remember their boots—all the same on such different boys," Rooney wrote in unwitting homage to Pyle.[81]

While sitting in his jeep that first evening in France, Rooney pulled out a notepad and scrawled a poem. His first verse imagined a future battleground guide lecturing a "bus-load of people about events that never happened in a place they never were."[82]

In the decades to come, Rooney would visit Normandy many times. As he watched visitors listening in a variety of languages to guides not yet born in 1944, he was struck by the prescience of his poem.

"Even if you didn't know anyone who died, the heart knows something the brain does not—and you weep," Rooney wrote of his pilgrimages. "If you think the world is selfish and rotten go to the cemetery at Colleville overlooking Omaha Beach. See what one group of men did for another on June 6, 1944."[83]

FIFTEEN MONTHS BEFORE D-DAY, WHEN Homer Bigart, joined by friends Andy Rooney and Walter Cronkite, flew on his first bombing mission, he used an inimitable Bigartism—"stoogeing around over a particularly hot corner of the Third Reich"[84]—to describe how their formation staggered in the skies over Lower Saxony before turning to attack a U-boat base. Together, the journalists celebrated in these pages stooged around some of the European war's hottest corners.

Beginning in London in late '42, their paths frequently intersected. Four of them covered the air campaign against the Nazis, taking the train out to East Anglia's airdromes and then, on the ride back to London, trying not to think about the young men who hadn't made it back. The reporters were stationed together in Britain for long stretches, appraising bomb damage and standing shoulder to shoulder at briefings conducted by Allied leaders. All five knew their way around blacked-out Piccadilly; often in the company of Army and Navy press officers, they closed down their share of pubs. In some capacity, they all covered the North African offensive, which for the first time threw American infantrymen into the fight against Hitler.

They often shared the same datelines, beachheads, and flasks of whiskey, covered the same horrific scenes, and tried to make sense of the same apocalyptic world. Sometimes they scribbled notes in the same trench or hovel; at other times they were separated by dozens or hundreds of miles, pursuing different story lines. Yet they dodged the same shrapnel, suffered the same heartache, battled the same censors, and spoke to the same anxious readers.

To be sure, our five weren't alone: Scripps Howard's Ernie Pyle; the *Los Angeles Times'* Tom Treanor; the *New York Times'* Harold Denny; CBS' Edward R. Murrow, Bill Downs, Charles Collingwood, and Eric Sevareid; AP's Don Whitehead, Noland "Boots" Norgaard, Ken Dixon, and Wes Gallagher; UP's Chris Cunningham and Hank Gorrell; the *Chicago Daily News'* Robert Casey; the *Chicago Daily Tribune's* Jack Thompson; *Life's* Margaret Bourke-White; *Collier's Weekly's* Martha Gellhorn and her (sort of) husband, Ernest Hemingway; the *New York Herald Tribune's* John "Tex" O'Reilly; and untold others made brilliant contributions to the journalism of World War II.

But there was a certain bond among the five men of this book; in many ways, they were a journalistic band of brothers. Cronkite, Bigart, and Rooney formed the core of the "Writing 69th," the coterie of reporters trained by the Army Air Force in early '43 to fly on bombing raids. Throughout much of the North African campaign, Liebling and Boyle traveled in the same jeep. Boyle and Bigart bunked in the same tents in Sicily and Italy. Boyle, Liebling, and Rooney were credentialed to cover the First Army after Normandy; they were together almost every day in the sweep across France. Boyle and Cronkite covered Operation Market Garden in Holland and later slogged through the bloody snows of the Ardennes. Rooney and Boyle together uncovered the horrors of Hitler's concentration camps.

Allied correspondents had to wrestle with constantly changing censorship rules; inevitably, especially given the wickedness of the enemy and the rightness of the Allied cause, their reporting at times bordered on propaganda. Yet they weren't vacuous cheerleaders; their copy was surprisingly pointed, sometimes irreverent. They ticked off their share of Allied commanders.[85]

The newspaper business that four of them had entered before the war was a provincial backwater: outlets for their owners' ideological breast-beating or parochial business agendas or just voyeuristic rags—or often, all three rolled into one. Each was determined to make journalism an honorable profession. To a remarkable degree in postwar America, they succeeded—at least for a time.

Four of the five started on the humblest rung of journalism's ladder: covering local news. It was training that served them well. "Any reporter who can do justice to a four-alarm fire can do well by a war, which is merely a larger fire affecting more people," Boyle once remarked.[86] Boyle did so much justice to World War II firefights that he earned a Pulitzer Prize. So did his friend Bigart.

All five were characters in their own F. Scott Fitzgerald saga, inventing themselves in an America stumbling toward greatness. A wartime colleague said of Boyle that he "had the drive of a locomotive"[87]—an appellation that applied to the other four as well.

IN FEBRUARY 1943, FOLLOWING THE Writing 69th's bombing raid over Nazi Germany, Bigart asked Cronkite if he'd thought through a lede. "I think I'm going to say," mused Cronkite, "that I've just returned from an assignment to hell, a hell at 26,000 feet above the earth, a hell of burning tracer bullets and bursting gunfire. . . ."

Bigart, who prided himself on his taut writing style, stared at Cronkite, incredulous that his colleague would resort to such purple prose. "You— you—w-w-wouldn't," Bigart stammered.[88] But Cronkite would. His story (the *New York Times* headlined it "Hell 26,000 Feet Up") got huge pickup in the States and dominated the British tabloids. It was so successful, in fact, that for the next half century Bigart and Rooney felt obliged to give their pal unmerciful guff about it.

"When I want to remind Cronkite that he is mortal man," Rooney wrote in the 1990s, "I quote him a few sentences from his United Press story that day."[89]

Over his esteemed career, Walter Cronkite issued millions of words for public consumption. But he never wrote or uttered a truer phrase. Covering the Allies' struggle against Nazi Germany was, indisputably, an "assignment to hell."

ON THE EVENING OF JUNE 6, 1946, the second anniversary of D-Day, A. J. Liebling was at the Palace Bar and Grill, a West Forty-fifth Street watering hole run by a cigar-chomping barkeep named Joe Braun. Liebling loved his saloon chum; Braun spoke Liebling's language, the gritty patois of "side-street New York."[90] The *New Yorker* writer had come alone to Braun's joint that night, beleaguered by thoughts of Easy Red and Normandy.

Liebling sat on a barstool and drank quietly. After a while he looked up and asked Braun, "Have you ever seen a deck awash with blood and condensed milk?" Braun didn't say anything and went off to chip ice and serve someone else. Liebling, thinking his friend callous, was irked.

But a few moments later Braun stood in front of Liebling, put his cigar on the bar, and said, "If you seen that, Joe, it will stay with you." Liebling, Cronkite, Rooney, Bigart, and Boyle "seen" much in the Allies' crusade to right a world gone hideously wrong—and it stayed with them.

A decade after the war ended, Liebling wrote that if you leave memories alone, "they'll come home, wagging their tails behind them. In time, they recur in forms so implausible that you must go back and make sure the events they represent were real."[91]

CHAPTER 1

✦

EARLY IMPRESSIONS

It is impossible for me to estimate how many of my early impressions of the world, correct and the opposite, came to me through newspapers.

—A. J. LIEBLING, 1947
THE WAYWARD PRESSMAN[1]

For a stubby man with flat feet, Joe Liebling was amazingly agile. Acquaintances in London during the war were startled to see him jogging through Hyde Park, a towel tucked inside his sweatshirt, tossing jabs and uppercuts, à la a boxer doing roadwork. While covering combat in North Africa and France, Liebling surprised reporter pals and platoon sergeants with his stamina and quickness afoot.

Still, whether at the Hotel Aletti in Algiers, Scott's Bar in Piccadilly, or a dumpy café in La Rive Gauche, Joe Liebling did some of his best work sitting on a barstool. It was in a gin joint near the *New Yorker* offices in the fall of 1939 that Liebling wheedled his way to Paris. Janet Flanner, the *New Yorker's* longtime Paris correspondent who wrote under the pseudonym Genêt, had a family situation that required her to return to the States. Liebling, who'd studied at the Sorbonne in 1926 and adored everything French, had always coveted the Parisian beat, especially now that his *héros* in the French army were, for the second time in two decades, facing down their foe from the east.

29

His immediate superior, fellow writer St. Clair McKelway, was impressed by anyone who could converse in a foreign tongue. So after Liebling plied him with alcohol and began not only babbling in French but also offering paeans to Gaulic culture and cuisine, McKelway, who'd been cool to the idea of his chubby thirty-five-year-old friend heading to Paris with Hitler's forces massed along the Maginot Line, crumbled.

But before Liebling could book passage on the Pan Am Clipper, the move had to be blessed by Harold Ross, the *New Yorker*'s irascible founder. Ross loved Liebling's writing but fretted that Joe's appetite for *ooh la la!* might do him in. "But for God's sake stay away from the low-life!" Ross barked as the ebullient Liebling plotted his return to the City of Light.[2]

In truth, it was Liebling's passion for New York's raffish underground that made him such an invaluable contributor to Ross' magazine. There was no shortage of *New Yorker* writers familiar with Manhattan's upscale haunts. But no one else at the journal knew the city's gambling dens and boxing havens and forbidden speakeasies.[3]

Indeed, it was a back-alley assignment that got Liebling hired in the first place. That and the fact that McKelway was almost as big a screwup—which, given Liebling's checkered academic and professional past, was saying a lot. McKelway, remembered *New Yorker* editor Katharine S. White, had been assigned a 1935 story about a black evangelical faith healer accused of bilking his flock. Although a gifted stylist, McKelway was a slipshod interviewer and note taker. Liebling, who could be methodical when he put his mind to it and had connections to bunko artists that could prove helpful, was signed on as McKelway's legman.[4] Their partnership worked beautifully, the story turned out edgy, and Liebling was given a job at the only publication in America suited to his tastes and talent.

His *New Yorker* colleague Brendan Gill marveled at one of Liebling's devastating interview techniques: Joe liked to sit in stony silence, his ovoid head cocked to one side, staring at the interviewee, until the poor thing cracked.[5] It was said of Ring Lardner, one of Liebling's sportswriting idols, that he talked in grunts. Liebling, wrote First Army public relations officer Lieutenant Roy Wilder, Jr., was the obverse: Joe talked in chuckles.

When provoked, however, chuckling Joe was prone to fisticuffs. One night at Bleeck's Artist and Writers saloon on West Fortieth, John Parsons O'Donnell, a lippy America Firster with the *New York Daily News*, loudly disparaged the Roosevelt Administration. Liebling unleashed a couple of haymakers before friends hauled him away.[6] Another night at Bleeck's he flattened a loudmouth—supposedly with one punch—who was spewing anti-Semitic garbage. It was one of Joe's prouder moments.

Katharine S. White, E.B.'s wife, was around Liebling for decades. She was astonished that, unlike the other temperamental writers in her orbit, Liebling never seemed to suffer from writer's block.[7] Liebling's colleagues, most of whom agonized over every word, would shake their heads as they walked past Joe's office with its clattering typewriter. Within minutes he'd be prowling the hallways, eager to show off his immaculate copy.

"I can write better than anyone who can write faster," Liebling once boasted. "And I can write faster than anyone who can write better."[8]

IT'S NOT THAT THE FAST-BUT-STILL-GOOD Liebling couldn't have been a successful newspaperman. It's that he chose not to. Of his two years studying at Columbia University's Graduate School of Journalism, Liebling wrote that it "had all the intellectual status of a training school for future employees of the A & P."[9]

As a cub reporter at the *Providence Journal and Evening Bulletin* and later a night deskman at the *New York Times*, he exhibited the same cheeky indifference that had gotten him thrown out of Dartmouth College as an undergrad in the early '20s. In Hanover he was dismissed for repeatedly cutting compulsory chapel service. At the *Journal*, he decided that covering civic meetings and petty crime in a provincial town was beneath him. But the clincher came at the *Times*, where Liebling was unceremoniously dumped for messing around on the overnight sports desk. Liebling somehow thought it would be clever to list the referees for high school basketball games as *Ignoto*, Italian for "unknown."[10] Once his recurring gag was uncovered, the *Times* bade him *arrivederci*.

He went on to work at the *New York World* (later the *World-Telegram*) in the early '30s, where, at least on occasion, he flashed lush writing and reportorial skills. But the daily grind of journalism bored him; in '35, when the *World-Telly* stiffed him on a raise, he quit.

Liebling's cockiness was rooted in a pampered childhood of nannies, private schools, and summering at Lake Como. His father, Joseph, although conspicuously nonobservant, achieved the dream of every Jewish immigrant. While still a young man, the Austrian émigré became *balabos far sich* (Yiddish for "one's own boss"[11]), striking it rich in the furrier trade and real estate. In a few short years, Joseph went from living hand to mouth in Manhattan's Bowery to basking on the Upper West Side. He married a socially prominent San Franciscan named Anna Slone, whose Judaism was almost as indifferent as his own.

Their first child, Abbott Joseph, born in the fall of 1904, would be raised only nominally Jewish. Abbott, as his parents insisted on calling him, harbored ambivalent feelings about his ancestry, never quite embracing it, but never quite repudiating it, either. "Even Hitler didn't make [Liebling] an intensely self-conscious Jew," his third wife, the writer Jean Stafford, remarked.[12]

Liebling was a pudgy kid who never backed down if a playground tough taunted him about his weight, or his girly name, or his thick glasses. Young Abbott was forever losing his specs when he took them off to mix it up in upper Manhattan or later in Far Rockaway on the Queens/western Long Island border, where the family moved in 1913.

For the rest of his life, Liebling remained an unrepentant New Yorker. Among his first books was a collection of pieces on his passion for life in the Big Apple. The charm of America's heartland eluded Liebling. "Friends often tell me of their excitement when the train on which they are riding passes from Indiana into Illinois, or back again," Liebling wrote in *Back Where I Came From*. "I am ashamed to admit that when the Jerome Avenue express rolls into Eighty-sixth Street Station I have absolutely no reaction."[13]

He almost never got the chance to extol New York's virtues. As an eleven-year-old, Liebling contracted typhoid fever. For six months he was confined to bed, a condition that left him delirious for a time but fueled a voracious reading habit. The infirm Liebling devoured what he later called the "literature of fact," developing a lifelong infatuation for the writing of

"Stendhal," Marie-Henri Beyle, the nineteenth-century Frenchman considered the father of literary realism. Liebling's French was so advanced that, as a teenager, he could appreciate Stendhal in the writer's native tongue. In his youth Liebling read a lot of fiction, mainly Charles Dickens, but never cared as much for make-believe. Years later, Liebling's efforts at crafting straight fiction proved frustrating, although he loved the detective stories of Frenchman Guy de Maupassant. Joe proudly became "my own Sherlock Holmes," he said.[14]

Young Liebling also followed the horrors of the Great War—the sinking of the *Lusitania*, the siege at Gallipoli, the early trench maneuvering at the Somme. By the time the French commander at Verdun issued his gallant vow *"Ils ne passeront pas!"* ("They shall not pass!"), Liebling had become a Francophile. He developed a scorn toward everything Germanic. Since his parents had hired a series of fräuleins, spiteful German nannies, to watch over Liebling and his younger sister, it didn't take much to persuade young Abbott that there was something inherently defective in Teutonic culture.

What Liebling loved most about his old man was that he was street savvy, a guy who talked pure "Noo Yawk," knew his way around a con game, and palled around with the shady characters Joe loved to call "boskos," or "gozzlers," or, most memorably, "Telephone Booth Indians." Liebling reveled in telling effete friends about how his father, with a well-timed contribution, had snookered Reverend Charles Parkhurst, an antivice crusader, into ridding a certain Manhattan neighborhood of prostitutes. Unbeknownst to the good preacher, as soon as the streetwalkers were ejected, a syndicate headed by Liebling senior swooped in to make a killing on the suddenly "clean" real estate.[15]

At roughly the same time, Homer William Bigart's father, Homer S., wasn't providing blood money to ministers or taking his clan on summer jaunts to Switzerland. Bigart senior, in fact, was barely getting by in Hawley, Pennsylvania, a factory and coal-mining hamlet perched in the Poconos between Scranton and the Delaware Water Gap. Old man Bigart made sweaters for a living, running a shop in which his bookworm son and two daughters toiled after school.

Young Homer, tall and pasty with stringy dark hair, was exceptionally bright but had a debilitating stutter. Homer senior and his wife, Anna Schardt Bigart, were devout parishioners at First Presbyterian, a few steps from their home on Church Street. His Calvinist upbringing, his harsh surroundings, and his social awkwardness all contributed to young Homer's combative personality, future colleagues surmised. Bigart's prickliness served him well in the newspaper business. Even his smiles bore traces of "wry exasperation," recalled Betsy Wade, who worked with Bigart at both the *Herald Tribune* and the *Times* and collected a book of Homer's best war correspondence.[16]

Not many sons of Hawley earned scholarships to the Carnegie Institute of Technology (now Carnegie Mellon) in the '20s, but Bigart did. He showed up in Pittsburgh with the intent of studying architecture. But within a few days it was apparent that Bigart couldn't draw; he not only withdrew from the architecture program but also dropped out of school.

In 1927, at age twenty, he rented a $3-a-week room in Brooklyn, took occasional English and journalism classes at New York University, and landed a job as a nighttime copyboy at the *New York Herald Tribune*.[17] The *Herald Tribune* may have had a distinguished history as Horace Greeley's abolitionist organ but Bigart was starting in its cellar. He earned the princely sum of $12 a week fetching coffee and cigarettes for the hard-bitten scribes on the *Trib*'s overnight city desk.

Year after year, Bigart performed menial tasks, hoping it would lead to a full-time reporting job. He even started a newsletter for entry-level cohorts, *Copy Boy's Call*.[18] In 1933, his perseverance was rewarded, sort of: At age twenty-six, he was made head copyboy—quite possibly the oldest copyboy in the *Trib*'s history. "On the job, [Bigart's] charges saw him as something of a tyrant; off it, they thought him almost a recluse," Richard Kluger wrote in *The Paper*.[19] Not only did Bigart's speech impediment make it difficult for him to communicate with newsroom staffers, he often wore a sarcastic smirk that did not endear him to superiors. Instead of hanging around Bleeck's, the *Trib*'s ground-floor saloon, Bigart liked to go home and devour books. Later, his eclectic knowledge and grasp of literature astounded Ivy-educated friends. In 1935, in fact, the *Trib* sent its Renaissance man to interview Thomas Wolfe when the *Look Homeward, Angel* novelist visited New York.[20]

Reading was one thing; reporting quite another. On those rare occasions when Bigart was given a chance to write an obituary or cover a church service or handle some other pedestrian assignment, his copy was full of cross-outs; it took him forever to compose even the simplest stories. Nevertheless, the *Trib* tried him out as a spot reporter at $25 a week.

Early on, he managed to screw up the unscrew-up-able when he was sent to Penn Station to cover the inauguration of a new New York–to–Miami line. He somehow ended up at the wrong track; worse, his article singled out the wrong outfit, angering a large advertiser. Bigart's gaffe earned a personal knuckle rapping from Helen Rogers Reid, the domineering wife of the *Trib*'s publisher.

But Bigart survived and, slowly but surely, began showing a gift for what Kluger called "sardonic observation." In March 1940, Bigart's front-page take on the city's annual St. Patrick's Day parade included this sparkling passage: "The snow lay an inch deep in the folds of the Mayor's large black felt hat by the time the County Kerry boys went by singing, 'The hat me dear old father wore.'"[21]

Moreover, by his early thirties, he'd figured out how to "use" his stutter. He perfected what became universally known as "Homer's All-American Dummy Act." Recognizing that people misconstrued his impediment as ignorance, Bigart would put on a theatrical stammer and ask the same basic questions over and over again. "And then w-w-what happened?" was a typical Bigart query, usually delivered from behind a Lucky Strike spilling ashes.

It drove colleagues and competitors to distraction, but interviewees tended to take pity on Bigart, often sharing information they had no business sharing because they felt sorry for him. In truth, Bigart was always two steps ahead of the competition because he'd done his homework.

"Homer didn't know anything—like a fox," his acolyte Andy Rooney chuckled a half century later.[22]

———

UNLIKE HIS MENTORS LIEBLING AND Bigart, Rooney never came up through the ranks of workaday journalism. He didn't have the chance: the pug-nosed kid, all of five-foot-eight with bushy brown hair and bushier brown eyebrows, was still a junior at Colgate University when he was conscripted into service.

Like a lot of college students in the '30s, Rooney, appalled by the Great War's hypocrisy, flirted with pacifism and conscientious objection. An iconoclastic economics professor, a Quaker, preached something that Rooney and his Colgate friends took to heart: "Any peace is better than any war."[23] It was a maxim Rooney would come to regret in April 1945 when he walked through the gates of Buchenwald.

But Rooney the undergrad paid a lot more attention to Colgate's nationally prominent football squad than he did to the spread of European Fascism. He was an undersized and scrappy mule who—in a prelude to the rest of his life—wasn't afraid to stick his nose into bigger guys.

He'd grown up in a comfortable upper-middle-class home, the son of a Williams College graduate who abhorred FDR. His dad was a successful enough salesman with the Albany Felt Company to send his son to private school and afford a vacation cabin on nearby Lake George.

Young Rooney showed some promise as a writer at the academy, crafting funny essays that caught an English teacher's fancy.[24] But his only brush with journalism was a brief apprenticeship as an intern/copyboy at the *Knickerbocker News* and a couple of letters—one advocating pacifism—published in upstate New York papers.[25]

Rooney always pooh-poohed his academic performance at Colgate, but he was more than a jock: He became a protégé of noted English professor Porter Perrin, a contributing editor of the student magazine, a member of the debate team, a faithful reader of E. B. White and the *New Yorker*, and a good enough after-dinner speaker to win an undergraduate competition two years running.

"Andy was a word man," his roommate Bob Ruthman remembered. "He enjoyed reading, writing, speaking, and conversing. His subjects were whatever he thought worth talking about. He never used profanities, slang, or told off-color jokes."[26]

Belying his later image of Everyman, Rooney could also be something of a snoot. Ruthman met Rooney at the "R" mailbox freshman year. "Andy asked where I lived and my prep school. 'I'm from Evanston, Illinois, and I went to Evanston High School,' I said. Andy seemed surprised. 'A high school—an elevated structure? And no prep school?'"

Ruthman remembered his "Room" (as they called one another) as fun to be around and an athlete who got the most out of his limited abilities. But Rooney could be stubborn to a fault.

Part of the hazing ritual at Sigma Chi, the fraternity they pledged together, was to tromp through the snow-covered hills of Madison County. Ruthman, an experienced wintertime hiker, owned a pair of sturdy, Iroquois-style snowshoes and urged Rooney to buy a similar pair. But Andy went cheap, getting snowshoes that constantly slipped off his feet.

"I had to pull his ass out of the snow the entire way," Ruthman laughed seven decades later.[27] But the two of them avoided frostbite and got into Sigma Chi.

The young Rooney sometimes rubbed people the wrong way, Ruthman allowed, coming across as "brash" and "impolitic"—the very qualities that in the years to come Rooney turned into his own cottage industry.

When his draft number was called in the spring of '41, Rooney mulled it over and concluded he wasn't introspective enough to be a conscientious objector. So off he went that July to Fort Bragg, North Carolina, where he developed an instant—and lifelong—disdain toward martinets in uniform. He also learned that if you popped off to a noncommissioned officer, reprisals would come fast.

Rooney was in one of the few places he could abide on a military base— the mess hall—on December 7, 1941, when news came over the radio that the United States was now at war.[28] Post–Pearl Harbor, his outfit, now known as the Seventeenth Field Artillery Brigade, put him to work cobbling together a weekly newsletter. One of the brigade's colonels came away from a conversation with Rooney convinced that the youngster was a Communist—or at least a serious subversive.

HAL BOYLE, ROONEY'S FUTURE FIRST Army jeep companion, was rebellious in his own way, too. His middle name, Vercingetorix, conveyed defiance: It came from a Gaul chieftain who gave the Roman Empire everything it could handle in 45 BC. Boyle eventually shortened the moniker to "Vincent." Even while covering a world war Boyle exhibited "Boston tea party tendencies," his great AP friend and editor Wes Gallagher wrote in 1944.[29]

But Boyle had reporting in his blood; as a student at Central High School in Kansas City, Missouri, he finagled a job as a copyboy at the local Associated Press office. More than four decades later he was still working for the same wire service. But instead of sharpening pencils he was penning a nationally acclaimed column—and had been for thirty years. His first real reporting assignment in Kansas City came in 1928 when AP sent him to cover a triple hanging.[30]

Boyle's old man was an Irish immigrant, one of seventeen kids from a hardscrabble coal-mining family. "Every Irish family is a staircase to heaven," Boyle was fond of writing.[31] In the case of the Kansas City Boyles of the 1920s and '30s, the stairwell was cluttered. His hard-drinking pop disliked imposing discipline over Boyle and his three male siblings. "He thought boys had to get a few bumps in the process of learning to pit their strength against life," Boyle wrote, "and he didn't think it paid to interfere or protect them too much."[32]

Hal's father was an ardent Democrat, a proud foot soldier for "Boss Tom" Pendergast, Kansas City's notorious political strongman.[33] Hal inherited much from his old man, including feistiness and a fondness for drink.

Boyle's mother was off the boat from County Mayo, a tart-tongued farm girl who provided her son with fodder for dozens of columns. She never got Mayo out of her blood; although they lived in the heart of Kansas City, all manner of farm animals wandered around the Boyles' backyard.

His dad ran a butcher shop where Hal and his brothers worked before and after school. Young Hal didn't care for the stench out back but loved the old-timers who stopped in to exchange wisecracks and talk politics and sports. His AP colleague and fellow Pulitzer Prize winner Don Whitehead once wrote of Boyle: "He gazes at the world through the eyes of a boy looking across the meat counter and finding the procession of customers interesting and exciting."[34]

In the summertime the Boyles liked to host big neighborhood gatherings, with tons of fried chicken, ham, watermelon, and cold beer.[35] But times weren't always rosy; at the height of the Depression, the Boyles were forced to shutter the meat shop at Twenty-third and Vine.[36]

As a kid Boyle became infatuated with Richard Harding Davis, the dashing *Harper's Weekly* correspondent who helped create the legend of Rough Rider Teddy Roosevelt during the Spanish-American War. When just twelve, Boyle told his mother he wanted to be a famous war reporter like Davis.

At Central High, he won various essay contests and was introduced to the joys of Emily Dickinson and other great poets. He was so taken with Dickinson that he named a collection of his columns after one of her classic verses: "A day! Help! Help! Another day!" He also mastered enough philosophy to one day be christened "The Pavement Plato" and the "Poor Man's Philosopher."

He spent a year at a local junior college before enrolling at the University of Missouri in Columbia. His Sigma Phi Epsilon fraternity brothers were floored by his off-the-wall political views and often flattened by him in late-night wrestling matches. "No Sig Ep," the *Kansas City Star* once wrote, "ever felt himself safe from the clutches of Boyle's steel-like arms." No matter the hour, Boyle celebrated his wrestling triumphs by shrieking like Tarzan.[37]

Around campus he became celebrated for witty—and usually obscene— limerick composition, plus an uncanny ability to commit chunks of poetry to memory. AP arranged for him to work out of its Columbia office, so through most of his college days he had dual responsibilities. He graduated on the same afternoon with degrees in both journalism and English and did so well he earned a scholarship to attend Missouri's Graduate School of Journalism. In 1934–1935, he completed his grad school course work but never finished the requisite thesis.

Boyle's farewell party in Columbia when he was promoted to AP's St. Louis office achieved such notoriety it was written up in the *Daily Tribune*. Thrown at the Log Cabin tourist camp, the soirée featured singing, dancing, and some drunken fisticuffs over a young lass, "but casualties were minor," the paper reported.[38]

In 1936, he was assigned to the Kansas City AP office as a full-time reporter. Boyle spent a week covering the tragic gas explosion in New London, Texas, that killed nearly three hundred people—many of them schoolchildren. It was a grisly story that riveted the country for weeks. Among the other reporters interviewing grieving New Londoners was his counterpart from United Press, a fellow Missourian named Walter Cronkite.

Back in Kansas City, Boyle met Mary Frances Young, a secretary and spitfire blonde who shared his passion for joie de vivre and, once they could afford it, travel. Frances followed Hal to New York in 1937 when he was transferred to the New York City AP office. They were shopping at Macy's one day when Boyle offered Frances the cheapest wedding ring in the jewelry department; she accepted the proposal but declined the ring: it would have busted their budget.[39]

In New York, Boyle worked his way up to nighttime city desk editor. The Boyles eventually moved into a snug apartment at 110 Waverly Place in Greenwich Village. They kept it through the war and for years after.[40]

CRONKITE WAS A KANSAS CITY kid, too, but his family moved to Houston, Texas, when he was eleven. What should have been a comfortable upbringing sadly went awry. He was the only child of Walter Leland Cronkite, Sr., a dental surgeon sent to the Great War's front lines with a Missouri artillery unit headed by Lieutenant (later Captain) Harry S Truman. The ghastly sights that Dr. Cronkite witnessed in the Argonne Forest contributed, his granddaughter believes, to post-traumatic stress and an enervating bout with alcoholism that ultimately broke apart his little family.[41]

Cronkite's mother was an arts devotee who doted on her only child. As her husband's drunkenness grew worse and the Depression deepened, her son was forced to grow up in a hurry. Young Walter became increasingly protective of his mother and began taking paternal care of the people who came into his orbit—a generosity of spirit that grew larger as the years went on.

Like Boyle, Cronkite was bitten by the journalism bug early in life. A retired newspaper reporter taught the fundamentals of reporting to students at San Jacinto High School. Young Walter showed so much promise that his teacher entered him in a newswriting competition sponsored by the Texas Interscholastic Press Association. Cronkite won the contest going away, dramatically ripping his copy out of the typewriter while other kids were still agonizing over their opening paragraphs.[42]

At the University of Texas in Austin, Cronkite wrote for the *Daily Texan* and broadcast sports scores for the campus radio station. KNOW couldn't afford a sports ticker, so a half hour before he was scheduled to go on the air, Cronkite would wander into a combination smoke shop/saloon. Afraid he'd get nabbed if he wrote anything down, he'd sip a three-point-two beer while feigning nonchalance as he glanced at the ticker a few feet from the bar. He'd yawn as the bartender posted scores on a blackboard. Then, a couple of minutes before airtime, Cronkite would sprint to the station, relying on his memory to relay that day's sports headlines. "It was one of the best bits of journalistic training I ever got," Cronkite recalled.[43]

One semester Cronkite announced scores at a "sports club" that turned out to be a thinly veiled bookie operation. Fearing that the cops would bust the joint, Cronkite eventually quit, but not before he pocketed some nice cash.

Not unlike Rooney a few years later, he flirted with a left-wing clique but was too busy to become a campus crusader in the mold of future CBS colleagues Eric Sevareid at the University of Minnesota or Ed Murrow at Washington State. Cronkite joined the Curtain Club, a thespian troupe whose leading light was Cronkite's fraternity brother (and future movie star) Eli Wallach. Cronkite didn't act in a lot of plays but learned how to project his baritone.

He also landed a part-time position with the Austin bureau of Scripps Howard's *Houston Press*, covering the state legislature and learning how to place gratis calls from a pay phone by inserting a hairpin instead of a nickel. When the *Press* offered him a full-time job in Houston, Cronkite leapt, leaving school before earning his degree. The country was caught in the vise of the Depression; his parents, struggling with Walter Senior's substance addiction and flagging dentistry practice, needed financial help.

In 1936, Cronkite returned to his boyhood home to take a job as a rookie broadcaster at Kansas City's KCMO Radio. The term always used to describe prewar Kansas City was "wide-open"—a euphemism that covered a variety of "forbidden" pursuits, from bootlegging and black jazz to strip clubs and illicit gambling—all of it enriching the coffers of Boss Pendergast. KCMO was owned by a crony of Boss Tom's; thanks to Pendergast's muscle, it enjoyed one of the Midwest's most powerful broadcast signals.

The station also insisted that its "talent" take stage names, so Cronkite became "Walter Wilcox," budding newsman and sportscaster. Cronkite-Wilcox was a jack-of-all-trades, handling copywriting and narration duties, too. It was while reading ad copy, in fact, that he summoned the courage to introduce himself to Betsy Maxwell, a lithe redhead and recent graduate of Hal Boyle's alma mater, the University of Missouri's School of Journalism. It appears to have been love pretty much at first sight. After two months of dating they drove out to Independence one lunch hour intent on eloping at the Jackson County Courthouse. But at the last second they got cold feet.

It would be another four years before they walked down the aisle, a period in which Cronkite bounced from radio announcing to reporting for United Press, back to radio as a play-by-play broadcaster for the University of Oklahoma football squad, and even to fledgling Braniff Airways as a public relations flack. While working for the airline, he scored a coup when he arranged for striptease artiste Sally Rand and her trademark naughty balloon to be pictured on the steps of a Braniff plane.

When he rejoined UP's Kansas City office, he often served as an overnight rewrite guy, embellishing stories in ways that made him wince in future years.[44] Cronkite loved doing offbeat features, especially pieces that allowed him to obliquely address the town's wicked ways. As the prospect of war loomed larger, he was interviewing a Kansas City burlesque performer named Hinda Wassau.

"What do you think, Miss Wassau, will be burlesque's part in maintaining wartime morale?" Cronkite queried. She grabbed him by his coat lapel and hissed, "Let me tell you something. The morales behind a burlesque stage are just as good as the morales at Radio City!"[45]

Betsy, meanwhile, became the Kansas City *Journal-Post*'s advice-to-the-lovelorn columnist. On the evening of September 1, 1939, her husband was working UP's overnight desk when the flash came across the wire that Adolf Hitler's troops were pouring en masse across the Polish border. Cronkite stayed up past dawn, hawking the latest developments and imagining himself covering the blitzkrieg from the front.

As the war spread in Europe in the spring of 1940, he begged UP for a foreign desk or overseas assignment. But none came; much to his disappointment, he stayed put in Kansas City for another eighteen months.

Walter and Betsy were at the Maxwell homestead in Kansas City for a family gathering when news came over the radio that the Japanese had attacked Pearl Harbor. Soon thereafter, Cronkite got his wish: he was transferred to UP's foreign desk in New York. Betsy and Walter found a little walk-up in Jackson Heights; Cronkite took the subway to UP's offices near Park Row in Manhattan.

Reading the dispatches of the *New York Times*' Robert Perkins Post from London and listening to the CBS broadcasts of Edward R. Murrow made Cronkite yearn to get to Europe and report on the war himself.

HAD CRONKITE BEEN IN PARIS with Joe Liebling in 1940 he might have been less eager to see Hitler's legions up close. Once Harold Ross gave his blessing in early October 1939, Liebling made plans to fly to Lisbon on the Pan American Clipper.[46]

Liebling left for Europe without his emotionally volatile wife. Ann Beatrice McGinn was a radiant but troubled redhead whom Liebling had met when she tore his ticket while working at the box office of a Providence movie house. The McGinns were shanty Irish; her father had died when she was three. She and her siblings were raised in a grim orphanage that left permanent scars.

Their courtship and marriage were as erratic as her psyche. At various points throughout the '30s she was institutionalized for behavior that was alternately diagnosed as manic-depressive or schizophrenic. The Lieblings were separated more often than not. Neither adhered to their vows of fidelity. Ann's condition steadily worsened; heavily sedated, she would often disappear for days at a stretch.[47] She apparently had a fixation for New York's Irish cops. Liebling caught Ann and one of Gotham's finest in flagrante delicto in his apartment one afternoon. "I don't mean no harm," the cop told Liebling, "but a piece of tail is a piece of tail."[48] For Liebling's part, getting three thousand miles away from his oft-suicidal wife must have been an attractive scenario.

Liebling's flight to Portugal was nearly deserted; after the seaplane docked at Lisbon Harbor, Liebling boarded a train that was detained by belligerent policemen at the Spanish border. It was Liebling's first exposure to Fascists, whom he described as "strutting sparrows of men."[49] He jumped aboard the blacked-out Sud-Express and pulled into Paris on October 12, checking into the Hôtel Louvois across the square from the Bibliothèque Nationale. The neighborhood had in abundance two Liebling must-haves: haute cuisine and hot prostitutes.

He had plenty of time to indulge in both. There wasn't much conflict to cover in late '39 and early '40. The Phony War, as coined by American skeptics, or la drôle de guerre, the Strange War, as the French called it, was at its apogee. Dug in behind the Maginot Line in France and the Siegfried Line in Germany, neither side had made much noise since Hitler's attack on Poland in September of '39. Many commentators believed that Hitler's passivity—it was scornfully labeled "sitzkrieg"—was a sign of weakness.

It may have been delusional, but Liebling, at least to a point, fell for it. Parisians, being Parisians, ignored the military's plea to black out their windows; the city's nightlife rolled on, almost unabated.

During the year-end holidays he traveled to Strasbourg to interview French soldiers staring down the Wehrmacht. "The mist on the river Christmas morning was so heavy that the French soldiers in the little redoubt on the Strasbourg side were hampered in their game of trying to see Germans through their machine gun sights," he wrote.[50] Liebling asked a

French officer if it would be all right to peek over the parapet at the German sentries patrolling the Kehl side of the bridge. The captain told Liebling to take off his tin helmet first. "If they think you are an Englishman they may fire," the officer warned. Bareheaded, Liebling gingerly craned his neck but couldn't make out any enemy soldiers.

Back in Paris, Liebling scrambled to make his dispatches, pegged as Letters from Paris, relevant. He interviewed French generals and German prisoners, trying to make the Allied armies look resolute and *les Boches* weak and venal.

One Sunday morning Liebling was strolling through Montmartre with a French acquaintance when they bumped into a musical panhandler bellowing into a megaphone. Roughly translated, the ditty went:

> *Hitler hasn't got one*
> *Not at all, not at all!*
> *Hitler hasn't got one*
> *Not even a little tip!*

Harold Ross was so prudish that he wouldn't permit the *New Yorker* to print the prurient riff. Liebling fans had to wait until the publication of *The Road Back to Paris* four years later to chuckle over the passage. It turned out, of course, that Hitler had much more than a little tip, at least in matters of war.

The French were indeed in denial that spring—and so was Liebling. In an April 27 article, Liebling told readers that the "great joke of the past fortnight" was Nazi propaganda minister Joseph Goebbels' claim that the Germans would be in Paris by the middle of June. A music hall comic that Liebling had seen that week drew howls of laughter by urging Parisians to learn German so they could chat with Hitler when he got to town.[51]

Liebling wrote his mother every few days, often on Hôtel Louvois stationery. Even after the Nazis launched their blitzkrieg across the Ardennes on May 10, Liebling was still sending his mother pie-in-the-sky accounts of French resolve.[52] Liebling so loved the French that it must have been impossible for him to conceive of their impotence. But by May 29 he conceded to his mother that "this has been a terrible month." French courage, he wrote, "is wonderful as ever, but for the first time, I am beginning to wonder if it will be enough."[53]

It wasn't. In a mid-May *New Yorker* piece he wrote:

> The new phase of the second World War was announced to Parisians at daybreak Friday. . . . With the dawn came the air raid sirens, startling a city that had heard no alerte during the daytime since the first week of the war. At once each of the innumerable residential squares in Paris took on the aspect of an Elizabethan theater, with tiers of spectators framed in the opened windows of every building. . . . All wore nightshirts, which, since the prosperity of tenants in a walkup is in inverse ratio to their altitude, appear considerably dingier on the sixth and seventh floors than on the second and third.

Soon antiaircraft guns began firing, their tracers illuminating the reddish sky. A few minutes later the *ack!-ack!* stopped and an enemy bomber was spotted so high, Liebling wrote, "that it looked like a charm-bracelet toy."[54]

The writing was quintessential Liebling: literate, witty, and irreverent: in fact, way *too* witty and irreverent for the circumstance. The City of Light was about to be overrun by Fascist storm troopers; it was no time for Liebling to be flippant about pajamas. He was trying to write about wartime Paris the same way he wrote about peacetime New York—and discovering that it didn't always translate. It wasn't until he began covering combat operations in North Africa two years later that Liebling learned to harness his rococo style.

He witnessed other bombing raids in early June, but assured his mother that "no bombs fell within miles of me, so cheer up. I am perfectly safe anyway as it seems that the bastards only kill children."[55] On the morning of June 9, along with other American correspondents, Liebling was interviewing Jean Prouvost, the French minister of information.

"From a military standpoint," Prouvost told reporters with a straight face, "it is improving steadily. Disregard reports of the Government quitting Paris." At which point Prouvost promptly bolted for Tours, where the French government was setting up emergency headquarters.

Within hours Paris was in full-scale panic. "I will return," Liebling told a French friend. "We can't let your country die."[56]

Liebling jumped into a tiny Citroën 11 with Waverly Root, a food critic, broadcaster, and occasional reporter with the *Chicago Daily Tribune*, and John "Tex" Elliott of the *New York Herald Tribune*. They made quite a threesome. Root, like Liebling, was a tubby glutton. Elliott, no shrimp himself, had broken his leg in a car accident a few weeks before and was still hobbled. With Root behind the wheel, Liebling weighing down the passenger seat, and Elliott trying to find room in the back to stretch his leg, they joined the onslaught of refugees streaming out of Paris. It took them eight hours to go seventy miles to Orléans.

Every spare inch of Orléans was occupied by a fleeing Parisian, including its park benches. The trio spent a miserable night in the Citroën. Whenever Root would drift off, his arm would whack the horn, waking them up all over again. At four a.m., Orléans' air raid siren went off. Liebling allowed that he wouldn't mind sticking around to see what would happen if the Luftwaffe did indeed attack. Root told Liebling that if he got out of the car he'd be wandering around Orléans solo. With that, they pushed off again. They spent three fitful days in Tours, praying that Hitler's blitzkrieg would somehow bog down. When it didn't, they got back in the car and, along with thousands of others, beat a retreat south toward Bordeaux. They spent one night in a village called Barbezieux. Liebling, streetwise in two languages, sweet-talked the town mechanic into allowing them to sleep in his house. Joe appealed to the Frenchman's patriotism by fibbing that Elliott had been injured on the front lines while covering the *armée*.[57]

Keeping a wary eye out for Stuka dive-bombers, Liebling made his way to the Spanish border. Then he took a train to Lisbon, where the *New Yorker* had booked passage home on the Clipper.

———

WHEN HE GOT BACK TO New York, the apathy and ignorance of friends stunned him. Some of his left-wing pals had the temerity to argue that British prime minister Churchill, a fiery Tory, was as big a threat as Hitler.[58]

Liebling had lunch one day with *New Yorker* contributor Dick Boyer, who'd just returned from Berlin, where he'd covered Hitler's depredations for the progressive newspaper *PM*. "I don't feel like a man from Mars but like a man from earth who has landed on another planet," Boyer commiserated. "Don't the damn fools know what is happening on earth?"[59]

Apparently the damn fools didn't. Liebling went to Washington in the fall of '40 to profile General George C. Marshall, the Army Chief of Staff. Liebling penned a *New Yorker* piece that lauded Marshall's foresight in preparing America for war. But after his article appeared, Liebling got the impression it hadn't made a ripple: His progressive friends didn't think much of professional soldiers.

When *McCall's* magazine commissioned him a few months later to write an essay on propaganda, Liebling used the platform to skewer the isolationist America First movement and its apologists among Wall Street chieftains and newspaper editors, chief among them right-winger Colonel Robert R. McCormick of the *Chicago Daily Tribune*. But in truth the America First movement was buttressed by left-wingers, too—a reality that depressed the liberal Liebling.[60]

France "represented for me the historical continuity of intelligence and reasonable living," Liebling reminisced after the war. "Nothing anywhere" would have meaning for Liebling until that continuity was restored.[61] A French friend who had escaped the Nazis vowed to Liebling in early '41: "We will awake from this nightmare."[62]

Despite his best efforts, Liebling couldn't wake up America. Whether liberal, conservative, or agnostic, Americans deceived themselves into thinking that the spread of Fascism was somebody else's problem.

CHAPTER 2

★

"ALL SORTS OF HORRORS"— CROSSING TORPEDO JUNCTION

> *This correspondent came over recently in a fast ship.*
> *He had carefully schooled himself for a nervous break-*
> *down by imagining all sorts of horrors: packs of sub-*
> *marines under foot; the sky darkened by the Luftwaffe*
> *after the second day out; breakfast of kippers, boiled*
> *potatoes at noon, brussels sprouts at night.*
>
> —HOMER BIGART, JANUARY 19, 1943
> *NEW YORK HERALD TRIBUNE*

In September 1941, just three months before the U.S. was catapulted into war, the future Supreme Allied Commander, Dwight David Eisenhower, was a colonel running training exercises at Fort Sam Houston, Texas. Prospective four-star general Omar Bradley had seen more action than Ike, his West Point classmate, but most of it had come while chasing the bandit Pancho Villa in the Army's quixotic 1916 incursion into Mexico.

Walter Cronkite in the autumn of 1941 was on the foreign desk of United Press' New York operation, editing stories filed by correspondents abroad while groveling to get overseas himself. The worldly future anchorman had never been east of Long Island.

Andy Rooney was still a buck private being trained as an artilleryman at Fort Bragg, North Carolina. Outside of Rooney's English classes at Colgate, the future commentator had never penned a commentary, let alone a who-what-where-why-when-how news article.

Hal Boyle was a rewrite guy on the Associated Press' night desk in New

York. The columnist who in the postwar years would travel the globe so extensively that the Overseas Press Club of America named an award in his honor, had never been outside North America.

Homer Bigart was a spot features writer for the city desk of the *New York Herald Tribune*. Bigart, too, had lived a parochial existence. Harrison Salisbury's portrait of the early-war Bigart as a "journeyman with no foreign language, no foreign experience, no more knowledge of war or foreign affairs than he could glean from the headlines"[1] accurately described the other three, as well. Just as World War II brought out the best in Eisenhower and Bradley, it stirred something within Cronkite, Rooney, Boyle, and Bigart that they may not have known they had.

Only Joe Liebling among the five had any background in European affairs or combat reporting. But Liebling hadn't witnessed much actual fighting in his first go-round as a war correspondent. The French and British armies had disintegrated so quickly in Hitler's onslaught that most of Liebling's spring 1940 bylines limned Parisians' weirdness as the Nazis grew closer.

The five men brought different perspectives and journalistic acumen to war coverage. Cronkite was a better writer than he gave himself credit for, but at heart he was a meatball journalist, a guy who learned his craft in no-nonsense newsrooms and wrote in a rat-a-tat style that he never completely abandoned, but later managed to adapt for broadcast. His métier during the war was telling the story of a clash through the eyes of one or two heroic combatants.

Boyle was raised in the same bare-bones wire service world but developed a creative technique that transcended it. Indeed, during the war Boyle's narrative helped redefine AP's services. Leaves from a War Correspondent's Notebook, Boyle's column, was second only to Ernie Pyle's dispatches in grassroots popularity; by midwar, Boyle's features had become a breakfast table fixture in millions of American homes. Boyle's copy rarely addressed the larger ramifications of an Allied offensive. Instead, Boyle plowed ground that Pyle was to make famous: profiling grunts in the trenches, always looking for the human side of the war. "The fellow who pulls the trigger on a gun is more interesting than what happens to the bullet," Boyle remarked in midwar.[2]

Rooney was a cub reporter tossed—untrained—into the biggest maelstrom in history. Through trial and error, he helped forge the *Stars and Stripes*, the wondrous "paper for Joe," the broadsheet that chronicled the bravery and struggles of American servicemen and servicewomen caught thousands of miles from home. By war's end, Rooney had saluted nurses, medics, motor pool mechanics, Red Cross hostesses, amateur thespians, truck drivers, cooks, tankmen, howitzer operators, air gunners, and incalculable numbers of GI Joes—not to mention Generals Eisenhower and Bradley and hundreds of field officers. But not General George Patton, for whom Rooney developed an instant—and lifelong—contempt.

Bigart, who had less classroom education than any of them, ironically became renowned for his facile grasp of geography and military tactics. No reporter in the ETO could recount a particular day's actions, then plug them into a larger strategic framework as powerfully as Bigart. Journalism is often called the first draft of history. In Bigart's case, and perhaps his alone among the ETO's workaday correspondents, it was literal. Any historian studying the nuances of the Allied air war, or the campaigns in Sicily, Italy, the Riviera, and later the eleventh-hour push toward the Japanese home islands, would do well to read Bigart's daily reportage.

Often Bigart's stuff was featured in the right-hand column on page one of the *Herald Tribune*. Despite his remarkable success during the war, Bigart the Depression kid never felt secure at the *Trib*. Every day, he believed he had to prove himself to demanding editors. Cronkite and Boyle had also been upended by the Depression; even after they achieved fame, their letters back home were full of worries about job security.

Liebling the rich kid and Times Square raconteur had been insulated from Depression anxiety. Joe became something very different from his colleagues during the war. Unconstrained by daily deadlines and usually unconcerned about a censor lurking over his shoulder, he could still indulge his passion for oddballs and eccentrics. But his narrative was leavened by a reverence for the Allied cause and a profound gratitude for the kids sacrificing their lives and limbs to liberate his beloved France. He pretended that combat bored him, but few could describe the bloody back-and-forth of a battle with Liebling's panache.

A YEAR BEFORE THE U.S. entered the war, the *New Yorker* had sent Liebling to London. Joe got the news about Pearl Harbor while returning for a holiday visit to the U.S. He was in the mid-Atlantic aboard a Norwegian trawler that escaped the sonar screens of U-boats. Joe toasted America's entry into the war with his new Scandinavian friends.

Liebling ultimately called the book he published in midwar *The Road Back to Paris.* In it, the boxing devotee divided his pieces into three chronological categories: The World Knocked Down, The World on One Knee, and The World Gets Up.

The others may not have known Liebling early in the war, but they certainly shared his zeal to grab a ringside seat for the most momentous fight in history. By early '42, Cronkite, Boyle, and Bigart had been hectoring their bosses to send them to a war zone. The three were also impelled by something besides a red-blooded yearning to catalogue the conflict: All three were young enough to be drafted. But the U.S. War Department had deemed that combat correspondents would be exempt from Selective Service.[3]

THE WORLD KNOCKED DOWN DOESN'T begin to describe the dire straits faced by the Allies in 1942. Adolf Hitler's empire, in the words of New Zealander historian Chester Wilmot, "stretched from the Mediterranean to the Arctic, from the English Channel to the Black Sea and almost to the Caspian. Between the Pyrenees and the Ukrainian steppes there was no other sovereign state but Switzerland." By mid-'42, *Panzer* armies had reached the Volga in their push against the Soviet Union and gotten precariously close to the Nile in their thrust against British forces in North Africa. "In three years of war," Wilmot wrote, "Hitler had been denied victory only in the sky above London and in the snow outside Moscow."[4]

Moreover, Hitler's Axis partner, General Hideki Tojo, emboldened by the success of his sneak attacks at Pearl Harbor and the Philippines, continued Japan's imperial conquest of Asia Pacific and sought to do the same in the lands bordering the Indian Ocean. Allied leaders fretted that, unless thwarted soon, Hitler and Tojo would inevitably join forces somewhere east of the Suez and west of the Ganges.

The war's geographic parameters may have eluded many Americans, but most were driven by two primal emotions: a desire for quick revenge against Japan and a deep-seated dread of German U-boats. One of Hal Boyle's first wartime articles, written aboard a troopship, described the disappointment a group of GIs felt upon learning that the convoy was heading toward the Mediterranean, not the Pacific. "We wanted to get the Japs first," a California private told Boyle while fingering the six-inch knife sheathed on his hip.[5] President Roosevelt gained some measure of vengeance against Tojo by correctly insisting—over the objections of his military advisors—on Lieutenant Colonel Jimmy Doolittle's bombing raid against Tokyo in April 1942. Doolittle's raiders inflicted only superficial damage on Japanese factories but did wonders for U.S. morale.

But in early '42 nothing struck fear into the hearts of Americans like the dastardly *Unterseebooten*. Unrestricted submarine warfare was a vestige of the Great War, the biggest reason that American public sentiment had turned against Kaiser Wilhelm's Germany. People who couldn't find Château-Thierry on a map still remembered the Germans' torpedoing the ocean liner *Lusitania*. Americans now feared, two and half decades later, that troopships carrying their children and grandchildren would suffer the *Lusitania*'s fate. Admiral Karl Dönitz, Hitler's U-boat commander, was unconscionable: After deadly attacks, Dönitz defied international conventions by instructing his captains to machine-gun survivors.

Americans' paranoia was well-founded. Since East Coast merchants stubbornly refused to impose blackouts, bright shore lights silhouetted freighters and tankers, turning them into sitting ducks. Horrified beachcombers from the Gulf Coast to New England watched as massive amounts of oil, cargo, and human debris washed up onshore. Losses quickly mounted: in May of '42, U-boats decimated three times the amount of Allied shipping that had been sunk in January.[6]

Churchill admitted that his lowest moments came while contemplating the appalling toll inflicted by German submarines. "The Battle of the Atlantic was the dominating factor all through the war," he wrote. "Never for one moment could we forget that everything happening elsewhere, on land, at sea, or in the air, depended ultimately on its outcome."[7]

"A SOLDIER ABOARD A TROOPSHIP has at least one advantage over a canned sardine—he comes out alive," Hal Boyle joked while crossing the Atlantic for the first time in the fall of '42. Although Private First Class Andy Rooney's sardinelike trip was involuntary, Rooney beat Boyle across the ocean by four months. Rooney's 17th Field Artillery Regiment, then stationed at Florida's Camp Blanding, got word in July 1942 that it was being transferred to Fort Indiantown Gap, Pennsylvania. The men didn't stay near the Susquehanna River for long: After being immunized with a series of shots, they were en route to New Jersey to catch a troopship.[8]

Just before they got on the train to north Jersey, the men were called in to have mug shots taken. Rooney's photo, he later conceded, accurately captured his attitude toward Army life. With snarling eyes and pursed lips, adorned with a sign strung around his neck that read, "A. A. Rooney, Pvt.," it made him look like he was a fugitive from justice.

None of the enlisted men in Rooney's outfit had a clue as to where they were headed. It could just as easily have been the Pacific, on a ship routed through the Panama Canal. Along with four thousand other men, Rooney was loaded on board a converted British cargo carrier, the *Orcades*. The men's sleeping quarters were crammed into the storage space down below; thousands of uncomfortable canvas hammocks hung from pipes.

Boyle later likened the crush of soldiers on a troopship to being along the rail at the Kentucky Derby.[9] Enlisted men killed time by reading pulp magazine fiction and murder mysteries while officers played checkers and chess and listened to "Lord Haw-Haw," the German radio mouthpiece, on the shortwave.[10] Worried about U-boats and nauseated by the smell, Rooney couldn't sleep, so he roamed around in the shank of the night, chatting up British galley mates and bakers. Poker and craps games were a popular pastime for other sleepless GIs, although lights were forbidden on deck. To escape claustrophobia, some guys dragged their bedrolls into the open air. But as the ship entered more dangerous waters, officers told them to go back below.[11]

Soon Rooney figured out the modus operandi that got him through the ten-day ordeal: he'd get shuteye during the daylight hours when most of the men—and their noxious odors—were up on deck, and explore the ship at night when it was easier to move around. The *Orcades* was part of a huge convoy that included battleships, cruisers, destroyers, and minesweepers; the flotilla followed a typical course for early '42 crossings, heading northeast to Halifax, Nova Scotia, then refueling and skirting Newfoundland and Iceland before arriving in the British Isles. Fortunately for Rooney and mates, the midsummer seas weren't especially rough; still, many of the men had trouble keeping down distasteful British food. It seemed to take forever, but eventually the *Orcades* and its escorts steamed into Liverpool; Rooney got his first glimpse of England, his home base for the next three years.

Rooney had no way of knowing it as he grabbed his gear and joined the mêlée headed toward Liverpool's train station, but the *Orcades* was damned. Less than three months later, while traveling unescorted on a secret mission to the Indian Ocean, it was torpedoed by a U-boat in the South Atlantic. The *Orcades* was one of the largest Allied troop carriers— one of the biggest Allied ships, period—sunk during the war.[12]

Reminded seven decades later that his troopship went down eighty days after he walked its plank, the ninety-two-year-old shrugged and said that a lot of ships were sunk during the war.

THE ILL-STARRED *ORCADES* WASN'T GIVEN much time to refuel or restock. Within days of getting back to New York from the Rooney mission, the transport was thrown into another convoy to the United Kingdom, this one even bigger. It would be witnessed by a wire service correspondent and future sailing enthusiast making his first-ever sea voyage.[13]

Transporting men and equipment and buttressing the Royal Navy's convoy protection were virtually the only combat roles America played in the first few months of the European war. As a result, a news-starved public wanted to learn as much as it could about the people and ships navigating what Allied sailors had come to call Torpedo Junction.

Walter Cronkite had been begging UP president Hugh Baillie and senior editors Harrison Salisbury and Virgil Pinkley to cover the Battle of the Atlantic from the deck of a warship. In early August '42, Cronkite was designated a Navy correspondent and authorized to cover a convoy.

Before Cronkite could jump aboard the World War I–vintage battleship USS *Arkansas*, then docked off Staten Island, he needed proper credentials and attire. The paperwork took several hours at the Navy's headquarters at 90 Church Street in New York. Cronkite was told to pack light: he'd be limited to a musette bag, a portable typewriter, and some carbon paper.[14]

"The United States military was as unprepared for handling the requirements of the press as it was for meeting the enemy," Cronkite remembered.[15] "They were ad-libbing as they went along."[16]

Ordered by Navy officials to get himself a proper uniform, Cronkite excitedly showed up at Brooks Brothers in Manhattan, only to discover that its tailors were as clueless as he was about what a correspondent's garb was supposed to look like. So Cronkite phoned the public relations office at Navy headquarters, asking for guidance. There was a long pause. Make it look a little like an officer's uniform, Cronkite was told.[17] So he did. Cronkite may have been the first ETO reporter to actually procure a dress uniform.

Eventually, the ad-libbers in the War Department determined that civilian correspondents would be given officers' privileges and field-grade uniforms without insignia of rank or branch of service.[18] At a quick glance, the drab olive outfits made them look like ersatz Army captains. Cronkite and other uniformed correspondents were startled when enlisted men began saluting them. It took repeated episodes before reporters learned to return the courtesy with an awkward gesture of their own. Wearing a uniform made the chubby Joe Liebling so uncomfortable that he felt he was "play acting."[19] UP insisted that Cronkite sit for a portrait shot; their twenty-five-year-old prodigy gazed beyond the camera with hardened eyes.

At first, the military dictated that correspondents' uniforms be augmented by a green brassard with a large white C on the left arm. But among the uninitiated, the undefined "C" created confusion. On one of his first days aboard the *Arkansas*, an officer in the wardroom surprised Cronkite by inquiring about his religious affiliation. When Cronkite, mystified, allowed that he was "sort of a jackass Episcopalian," it caused the officers seated around the table to exchange glances. After a few strained moments, a lieutenant queried, "Well, how did you happen to become a chaplain?"

A couple of weeks later, after the convoy docked along the Firth of Clyde, a kilted Scottish officer took umbrage at Cronkite enjoying the officers' club. "I say, old boy," he censured Cronkite, "is it customary in your army for cashiered officers to drink with the gentlemen at the officers' bar?"[20] The U.S. military eventually changed the lonely "C" to "War Correspondent," and directed that patches be sewn over the jacket's left breast pocket and shoulder. The gold-embroidered shoulder patch handsomely featured "War Correpondent" encircling "U.S."[21]

Cronkite didn't know it until midvoyage, but he was part of an immense task force charged with conveying thousands of Army Air Forces personnel, plus the USAAF's vital construction equipment, to the United Kingdom. A dozen troop carriers were escorted by the flagship *Arkansas*, a 555-foot behemoth christened in 1911; a phalanx of cruisers; and some fifteen U.S. and British destroyers.

To avoid collisions in poor visibility, each of the bigger ships, Cronkite explained in a diary he began keeping while aboard the *Arkansas*, would maintain a distance of a thousand yards port to starboard and a gap of six hundred yards fore to aft. Cronkite's journal was typewritten and edited by hand on a batch of Mackay Radio and Telegraph letterhead—the stationery on which many of his war dispatches to the UP wire would be composed. His wartime diaries and letters sat in a trunk in a closet of his Martha's Vineyard home; although known to exist, they were uncovered only after Cronkite's death.

Given just a few minutes' warning by the Navy, Cronkite arrived at Staten Island on August 3, 1942, two and a half days before the convoy was scheduled to shove off. The landlubber hurriedly kissed his wife goodbye on the dock and boarded a skiff to transport him out into the harbor, where the leviathan lay anchored. Cronkite "felt damn homesick that night," especially since Betsy remained close by at their Jackson Heights apartment.[22] "My god, [the *Arkansas*] looked a mess," Cronkite later recalled, with crates and debris strewn all over.[23]

The *Arkansas* crew made Cronkite a makeshift stateroom out of spare space near Captain (and future Rear Admiral) Carleton F. Bryant's cabin. Bryant was a soft-spoken, if occasionally flinty, Northeasterner whose patrician elocution over the ship's loudspeaker caused his men to titter.

Cronkite's setup was spare but sumptuous by Navy standards: a single bed, a wall chair, a strangely large chest of drawers, plus a tub and shower.[24] He learned the hard way that a metal beam ran a couple of feet over the head of his bed. Captain Bryant liked to have his men practice shooting their three-inch and fifty-millimeter guns at odd hours; their *wham-wham!* would cause the snoozing Cronkite to bolt upright, bashing his head on the beam.

"I must have hit that thing three times before I got smart enough to get up gradually. It was my first wound as a noncombatant," Cronkite laughed in 1995.

Captain Bryant didn't know what to do with Cronkite, so he ordered the ship's chaplain, a genial Unitarian named Irwin Stultz, to show the reporter around. When the junior officers with whom Cronkite and Stultz were dining the night before their departure learned that reveille would be at three bells, they greeted the news with stony silence, which Cronkite interpreted as a substitute for the moaning and groaning of seamen. Cronkite knew the captain meant business when he broke up the card and dice games in the wardroom before ten p.m. and told everyone to get a good night's sleep—they'd need it.

At precisely 0430, the task force went anchors aweigh, with Cronkite standing on the sky lookout above the captain's bridge, transfixed by how Bryant and his crew would navigate the channel's submarine nets. It didn't take long for Cronkite's heart to jump into his throat: just ten minutes out, the task force experienced its first scare.

The destroyer *Roe*, on the convoy's far left position as it exited the harbor, signaled to the *Arkansas* that its radar had detected an unidentified object underwater off Fire Island. Bryant sounded general quarters and ordered the entire convoy to execute an emergency starboard turn, no mean feat in a near blackout. He also instructed the destroyer to drop four depth charges on the suspicious bogey. The *Roe* wasn't sure what it uprooted—but it clearly wasn't a U-boat. A yellowy substance that Cronkite's diary described as "disagreeable" soon floated to the surface. It looked and smelled like lemon extract; in all probability, the *Roe* had unearthed an old cargo ship that had been at the bottom of the channel for eons.

After the *Roe* reported no danger, Bryant ordered the convoy back onto its prescribed course; the picket line of destroyers and cruisers was restored. In single file formation, they headed north; once they swung clear of land, the convoy assumed its regular "box" formation, screened on all four sides by destroyers.

Their destination was Halifax, where they were scheduled to refuel and pick up additional troops and escort ships. Army Air Forces bombers and Navy scout planes flew overhead as the convoy hugged the New England and then Canadian shore, scouring the sea for submarines. When the ocean was calm, the task force steamed at 20 knots—a handsome clip.

Reveille was at 0330 sharp, with the chow line queuing up immediately. Cronkite, who enjoyed a hearty breakfast and prided himself on his ability to move in a hurry, couldn't understand why so many men were beating him to the mess. Then he noticed facial hair on a lot of sailors; it occurred to him that guys must have been forgoing a shave until they had a break later in the day. Cronkite started doing the same and soon was among the first in line every morning. Correspondents marveled at how servicemen managed to eat in rough seas; Hal Boyle described the heaving tables and clattering dishes as pastiche from an old Mack Sennett movie. You could eat off six plates as they hurled past you, Boyle joked.

Once the sun came up, the *Arkansas'* Bryant kept crew members on their toes by constantly rehearsing various antisubmarine and antiaircraft drills. Each day, Bryant would throw out a different set of scenarios: a U-boat firing torpedoes off the port bow, enemy dive-bombers attacking from the starboard side, etc. Cronkite got a kick out of Reverend Stultz's

designated role during attack drills: the chaplain served as the *Arkansas'*
official historian, recording a blow-by-blow rundown of the action.

After a couple of days, Bryant took Stultz aside and told the preacher
that his correspondent friend was welcome to watch drills—but that
Cronkite had to remove his hands from his pockets. The captain didn't
want any seamen thinking that a uniformed "officer" had idle time. By
midvoyage, Cronkite wrote in his diary, he had created an attack drill task
for himself: When the bridge got too noisy, Cronkite would hand a megaphone to Bryant so that the captain's orders could be heard by officers and
men standing below. It might have technically violated Cronkite's noncombatant status, but at least it kept his hands occupied. Most of Cronkite's
days on the *Arkansas* were spent shooting the breeze with enlisted personnel, scribbling notes, and banging on his typewriter—a routine he would
continually repeat through the duration of the war.

It took two days for the flotilla to reach Nova Scotia, where it was
greeted with rough seas and a killer fog. The weather was so nasty that,
after refueling, the convoy's departure was delayed a day. They inched out
of Halifax Harbor in a pea-soup mist that demanded lookouts on every
bridge. As the *Arkansas* gingerly drew abreast of one troopship, a musical
combo of doughboys, wailing away from the top deck, saluted the seamen
with a screechy rendition of "Anchors Aweigh." The sailors hooted their
approval. "The music was not good," Cronkite noted in his journal, "but it
didn't have to be."[25] The seas stayed jagged for several days. But the captain
explained to Cronkite that bad weather helped keep U-boats at bay by
making the convoy tougher to track. The first night out of Nova Scotia, a
catapult plane from the light cruiser *Brooklyn* spotted several overturned
lifeboats, clearly from a sunken Allied ship. But the pilot waited until he
was back on board before quietly issuing his report. Had the pilot used
regular radio channels to describe the depressing scene, it would inevitably
have leaked to crew members, hurting morale, Cronkite explained.

No signs of life were visible, but even if there had been, the convoy
likely would not have stopped, officers told Cronkite. "To do so would risk
the lives of thousands in the convoy to perhaps save the life of one person

in the lifeboat," Cronkite typed that night. He was learning the unsparing arithmetic of world war.

By midocean the competitive Cronkite had proudly mastered a form of elementary backgammon called acey-deucy; he got so good at it he started drubbing senior officers, including the captain.

Every day seemed to bring at least one phantom enemy sighting; nerves were beginning to get frayed. Now that the convoy was approaching Great Britain, Cronkite sensed a change in Captain Bryant: he was chuckling less and dressing down underlings more. The thirty-two-year-old "Arky," as the men called the ship, was showing her age, gasping and shuddering. Cronkite couldn't wait to see land, especially when he learned from Bryant that their destination was Scotland.

Cronkite's task force essentially aped the same route as Rooney's convoy had taken the previous month. Instead of heading to Liverpool, however, Cronkite's fleet steamed to the Royal Navy base at Greenock, which had been turned into a major axis for transatlantic convoys. Greenock's train tracks came practically to the water's edge, then fanned north, south, and east. Cronkite was granted permission by the U.S. Navy to go ashore, but once there was told by British Admiralty officials that he couldn't use a telephone. Nor would he be permitted, in any article for publication, to describe the convoy's size, location, or purpose.

During his ten-day stay in the U.K., Cronkite got his first look at destruction wreaked by the Luftwaffe. Fifteen months earlier, in May 1941, the village of Greenock and its rail hub on the bluff overlooking the Firth of Clyde had been viciously attacked. Three hundred enemy planes, many of them lethal Heinkel (He) 111s, strafed and bombed anything in close proximity to the Royal Navy yard. Nearly three hundred people were killed and more than 1,200 injured.[26]

As Cronkite walked its cobblestone streets, the village still had a pockmarked look; many of its buildings remained bombed-out shells.

Cronkite got a three-day pass to visit London and boarded an overnight train, an experience he found intimidating. "It was a very great thrill" to visit the British capital, but "I didn't know my way around [London], and

I found the language peculiar."[27] He wandered through the city before showing up at the UP offices on Bouverie near Fleet Street, in the News of the World building.

His UP colleagues encouraged him to see London's bomb damage first-hand and to interview a few of its plucky souls. Cronkite was told that to clear censors, he would have to compose and file his articles at the British Ministry of War Information, set up in the Senate building at the University of London. He wrote a couple of pieces about the *Arkansas* convoy that, though toothless, were still stymied by censors—and stayed that way for a couple of months.

Cronkite arrived in London just as recriminations over the disastrous August 19 Dieppe raid on the English Channel were reaching a fever pitch.[28] Some blamed Churchill and his deputy, Lord Louis Mountbatten, the head of Combined Operations, for carrying out a doomed operation to placate Soviet premier Joseph Stalin on the one hand, and, on the other, to show Roosevelt and Marshall the perils of a cross-Channel attack. Others attributed the debacle to poor leadership, mainly Canadian, at the beachhead. Either way, nearly 3,400 Allied troops were killed or captured in a mission that had no chance to succeed.

Even if Cronkite had wanted to, he couldn't have filed a piece critical of Churchill's Dieppe planning; censors would never have allowed it. Saluting the gritty spirit of Londoners, however, was a different story.

In a bylined article that ran in the *Los Angeles Times* and other U.S. papers—the first of hundreds of London-based articles that Cronkite would file during the war—Cronkite noted that Brits "expect at least one more blitz" from the Luftwaffe "regardless of the course the war takes." The German bombing raids of two years before triggered a "fatalistic philosophy" among the British. "There is no sense being afraid of bombs," Cronkite quoted one Londoner. "Either they have your number on them or they haven't." German bombs had the numbers of forty-three thousand Britons during the nine-month Blitz of 1940–1941.[29]

Yet by the summer of '42, many Londoners weren't even bothering to seek shelter during air raids. "They glance at the sky and seeing no canopy of Swastika-marked bombers like those of September 1940, go about their business," Cronkite wrote.[30]

Except for the ubiquitous barrage balloons hanging over the city and fewer cars on the streets, it was difficult at first glance to know that London was at war. Gasoline rationing had virtually eliminated private vehicles, Cronkite noted, except those marked with signs "explaining their continued operation: 'Doctor,' 'Press,' 'Apothecary,' and the like."[31]

Cronkite observed that many of London's passenger cars were American vehicles that had been shipped across the Atlantic. These Detroit-made sedans were operated by "pretty girls"—chauffeurs with the British army, navy, and air force auxiliaries. Red placards were placed in the back windows of American vehicles that warned "Danger, Left-hand drive, No signals."[32]

After his quick trip to London, Cronkite hustled back to Greenock to rejoin the task force. The troop transports and most of the escort vessels departed in late August for their return voyage. Nine days later, as the U.S. coast loomed beyond the horizon, the flotilla gave Cronkite his first major scoop.

Cronkite was the only correspondent around when a converted luxury liner, the *Wakefield*, caught fire one evening and was the subject of a remarkable ocean rescue. The *Wakefield* hadn't been attacked by a U-boat or any enemy vessel; the conflagration, a Navy officer told Cronkite, was probably caused by sloppy disposal of cigarettes. It was carrying 1,600 passengers and crew, including several hundred U.S. military specialists and construction personnel who had been providing technical help to the British.

The skipper of the light cruiser *Brooklyn* courageously steered his bow against the burning ship and, along with several destroyers, saved all of the *Wakefield*'s passengers. Most of the *Wakefield*'s seamen stayed aboard and eventually managed to quell the blaze.

Cronkite had covered dozens of fires in Austin, Kansas City, and other places. He knew what readers wanted: a graphic description of the blaze coupled with a salute to the firefighters.

Datelined EAST COAST PORT, Cronkite's story earned him front-page bylines in newspapers all over the country. A note at the top of the article, no doubt scripted by Cronkite, acknowledged that "Walter Cronkite, United Press staff correspondent assigned to the Atlantic Fleet, was the only newspaperman to witness the burning at sea of the big naval transport Wakefield."

Cronkite's copy was consummate wire service stuff: crisp and evocative. "We have just brought home the flame-scarred hulk of the United States Navy transport Wakefield . . . victim of a fire which spouted from a passenger's cabin and raced across her decks as our convoy neared the end of what otherwise would have been a most successful journey.

"We also have brought home the Wakefield's 810 passengers and 750 brave crew members—all of them rescued by escort vessels which nosed so close to the stricken ship their paint was scorched and blistered by the intense heat and their hulls bruised from bouncing against the Wakefield."

Cronkite watched the inferno through his field glasses from a distance of a thousand yards. Fire hoses were soon turned loose. "But from where I watched, the water seemed only to feed the fire. Within 10 minutes the big ship was shrouded in smoke. Our vessel and the rest of the convoy, risking the danger of lurking submarines, circled the burning liner." To get to the *Brooklyn*, *Wakefield* passengers clambered over rope ladders and makeshift gangways.

He was surprised that an article describing the demolition of one of America's biggest troopships was approved by censors. "I had lucked in to early recognition as a war correspondent," he wrote.[33]

Having survived a benign baptism under fire, UP's new war reporter returned to New York to await his next assignment.

TWO MONTHS BEFORE CRONKITE'S CONVOY left Staten Island, Franklin Roosevelt by executive order had created the Office of War Information (OWI). Its mission was to enhance understanding of Allied war aims and policies. FDR appointed America's most esteemed radio journalist, Elmer Davis of CBS, to head OWI. Davis was a native of Indiana who, as a *New*

York Times reporter two decades before, had gained notoriety for his exposé of slippery evangelist Billy Sunday.

After Davis joined CBS in the late '30s, his soothing Hoosier baritone drew millions of ears to the network's evening news roundup. Without doubt Davis ran what could be described as a "propaganda" machine, producing radio shows, posters, documentaries, editorial commentaries, motion pictures, and museum exhibitions—many of which rankled congressional Republicans by celebrating FDR's "Four Freedoms."[34] One of OWI's centerpieces early in the war was director Frank Capra's series of films called *Why We Fight*. Capra was one of several great Hollywood directors who lent his talents to OWI and the Signal Corps. Later in the war, John Huston and William Wyler would film documentaries in close proximity to our five correspondents.

Despite today's popular misconception, OWI was never charged with "censoring" newspaper and radio coverage. Wartime censorship evolved more or less willy-nilly from service to service; early on, U.S. officials took their cues from the ultrastrict British Ministry of Information. While in a war zone, U.S. reporters in '42 and '43 were put through a wringer, forced to compose their stories in the presence of a censor who immediately blue-lined their copy, then usually submitted it to a second review from a superior public relations officer before allowing it to be relayed. It often took days—sometimes weeks—before the copy was fully approved and disseminated.

Cronkite's experiences at the Ministry's offices at the University of London were typical. Early in the war, censors encouraged reporters to draft stories the way they normally would. "Then your story went in to the censors, and the censors killed it, cut it, or did whatever they needed to do to it," Cronkite remembered. "And then they sent it back out to you, whether you wanted to file it that way or not. Sometimes, if you didn't care how they censored it but just wanted it to move as quickly as possible, you could mark it, 'Read and File.' This meant for them to censor it and then send it to your office in the censored form. It might not make much sense, but you would feel that your office would get enough of the story out of it."[35]

Back home, away from the war zone, U.S. press outlets operated on the honor system. In other words, for stories written in the States, censorship was voluntary. Not so in Britain or the ETO. "We argued like fury with the censors," Cronkite recalled. "There were violent scenes going on all over the room."[36]

Reporters had to pick and choose their battles with censors. Cronkite always asked himself before submitting an article: Is this information something that *without doubt* the Germans know? Because if that was indisputably true, then perhaps it was worth feuding over with the censor. But if there was any doubt about the enemy's knowledge, then Cronkite and other reporters would censor themselves.

Censorship was bumpy, erratic, and often an embarrassment to the Four Freedoms the Americans were supposed to be defending. But, Cronkite recalled, "it worked with considerable smoothness, despite that."[37]

THE VAGARIES OF ALLIED CENSORSHIP were the last things on Private Andy Rooney's mind as he was ushered off the troopship *Orcades*. Lugging their gear, Rooney and his buddies in the Seventeenth Artillery trudged onto a packed train at the Liverpool depot.

They had orders to report to the U.S. Army base at Perham Down, a mushrooming camp near the village of Hampshire, not far from the Channel. "It was fun being in a strange country," Rooney recalled. "We were vaguely aware that there would be an invasion of France if the war lasted, but it seemed far off and we knew that the artillery would be a safer place to be than the infantry because the artillery never wades ashore with the first wave."[38]

Rooney's relations with the brass stayed rocky at Perham Down. One hard-ass upbraided Rooney for having the temerity to apply for Officer Candidate School—which, given Rooney's disdain for Army life, was indeed a bit of a head-scratcher. Still, the rejection stung Rooney so much he huffed out of his superior's office without saluting.

But Rooney was lucky: His contributions to the brigade newsletter were appreciated by a kindly lieutenant who recognized that Rooney's talents lay beyond firing a howitzer. The officer put Rooney in charge of the regimental band. Eventually the band job morphed into a more substantial task as regimental historian.

As scribe, part of Rooney's job was to examine the directives that came in from London and Washington. One day a memo arrived from Special Services urging qualified GIs to apply for possible reassignment to a newly revived Army publication, the *Stars and Stripes*. Rooney, with the lieutenant's encouragement, threw together a résumé that embellished his lowly internship at the *Knickerbocker Press* and a brief stint editing a Colgate University magazine. To Rooney's astonishment, their gambit worked: A few days later he returned from yet another confrontation with an officer to discover that orders awaited him. He was to report immediately to London to assume new duties at the *Stars and Stripes*.

Rooney knew he'd caught a break—but had no idea just how life altering those orders were. The twenty-two-year-old Rooney had stumbled into one of World War II's accidentally magnificent institutions.[39]

The *Stars and Stripes* traced its roots to the Union Army during the Civil War. It was exhumed in France during World War I, where it was edited in Paris by none other than Harold Ross. The future founder of the *New Yorker* was an absent-without-leave doughboy; the editing job may have saved him from doing time in the stockade.[40]

It was revived again in early '42 as U.S. troops began arriving in Northern Ireland; the brass recognized that GIs needed a morale boost. It started as a weekly with a modest staff of five. But as tens of thousands of American soldiers poured into the British Isles, the operation was moved to Soho in London's West End. Soon the *Stars and Stripes* became a three-times-a-week affair, then a daily with an eventual staff of more than 150 and a huge newsroom and printing press leased from the *Times* of London.

Rooney was just one of many great journalists who cut their teeth in Soho's editorial offices. Peter Lisagor of the *Chicago Daily News*, Don Hewitt of *60 Minutes*, and future Pulitzer Prize–winning cartoonist Bill Mauldin all learned their craft at the *Stars and Stripes*, as did dozens of other notables. At the Army's insistence, reporters and editors stayed active-duty military; many, including Rooney, were granted the rank of staff sergeant.

The paper's biggest fan was the Supreme Allied Commander; yet Eisenhower winced when, early on, it ran a series of overly rah-rah editorials. Instead of obsequious propaganda, Ike and his staff wanted something that had the feel of a hometown paper, complete with reasonably honest coverage of war developments (the two censors in the *Stars and Stripes* newsroom rarely killed stories[41]), local news, sports, and gossipy features about Hollywood and Broadway. Plus, of course, cheesecake photos of starlets. For every picture of Ike, there were dozens of scantily attired pinup girls like Betty Grable and Rita Hayworth.

Under the no-nonsense direction of Staff Sergeant Robert Moora, one of Homer Bigart's old bosses at the *New York Herald Tribune*, and Moora's deputy, Corporal (soon to be Sergeant) Bud Hutton, the former editor of the *Buffalo Evening News*, the *Stars and Stripes* became a must-read for GIs. It spawned field operations and separate editions all over the ETO and special issues for the Pacific Theater, as well.

The *Stars and Stripes* was full of characters who taught Rooney the ropes. The crusty Hutton, who looked and sounded like a character in *The Front Page*, became the first of Rooney's many wartime mentors.

Stars and Stripes' newsroom was like something out of central casting. It reeked of cigarette and cigar smoke; its floor was grease stained, littered with butts, soda bottles, half-eaten sandwiches, carbon paper, and rejected ledes torn with disgust out of Underwoods. Rooney loved every smelly inch.

The normally cocky Rooney was so green that when given an early assignment to cover the most mundane of stories—a service bowling tournament—he panicked, not knowing how to distill his notes into a simple who-won-and-by-how-much article. He got lucky, though. When he called to check in that night, the phone was answered by one of his pals on the night desk, not Moora or Hutton. His buddy jotted down the tourney information and volunteered to draft something for the next edition, sparing Rooney the humiliation of fumbling for a lede.

Despite the bumpy start, it didn't take long for Rooney to begin finding his rhythm. The cub reporter earned his first *Stars and Stripes* byline on December 8.

His breakthrough came in what became an archetypal Rooney profile: saluting the unsung grunts behind the scenes. His tribute to the men of the motor pool ran on page two, alongside a photo of a mechanic laboring under the hood of a jeep.

Datelined AN ORDNANCE MAINTENANCE UNIT IN ENGLAND, on December 7, precisely one year after Pearl Harbor, Rooney's article led with: "The Purple Heart may never be awarded to the grease monkey in olive-drab overalls who works seven days and nights a week to keep Army wheels rolling. But he is made of the same basic stuff that puts the men in the Flying Fortresses in the headlines day after day. The grease monkey is the unglamorous, backstage—and very necessary—human element of this war."[42]

Rooney had found his niche. Six days later he did a feature on B-17 technicians, men "who often work all day in a space that would make a telephone booth look like the waiting room of [the] Grand Central Terminal."[43]

The prep school kid from the elite college quickly became the *Stars and Stripes'* champion of "ordinary" guys. Rooney and Bud Hutton would become so infatuated with young air gunners that, together, they wrote a book about them.

IT TOOK HOMER BIGART MONTHS to convince his bosses at the *Herald Tribune* that he was the right guy to buttress the paper's two-person London operation. Thanks to the U.S. Navy's improved submarine surveillance, at least part of the U-boat hysteria had subsided when Bigart made his crossing in January 1943. Although Bigart never confirmed his exact convoy, given the timing it was almost assuredly SC 116, which departed New York on January 4, 1943, with a retinue of some sixty ships. Its flagship, ironically enough, was the USS *Arkansas*, the same battleship Cronkite had ridden to Scotland five months earlier.

Troopship convoys were now "no more eventful than a trans-Atlantic voyage at the height of the prewar June tourist rush," Bigart observed, more than a bit disingenuously, in his first article ever with a London date-line. With his ineffable touch at slipping the silly into the serious, Bigart told readers he was almost as fearful of mushy British food as U-boats. At the outset of the voyage, he planned to sleep either fully clothed, clutching his life preserver, or in a life raft, "winning the friendship of a plump seagull." Before the boat had even left the dock, Bigart claimed he was so unnerved that he drank all the brandy he'd hoarded to combat seasickness.

When he awoke on day two and discovered that, against all odds, he was still alive, he felt a patriotic surge, but then realized the lump in his throat "was a bit of undigested sourdough roll." After a few days at sea his shipmates "started grousing about the food, and then you knew that everything was normal."[44]

Enlisted men on a troopship were inclined to believe rumors that ran the gamut from enemy submarines lurking just off the bow and their ship taking on water to nefarious officers who unjustly threw men into the stockade and got to slurp beer while regular guys were stuck with soda pop.[45]

A hillbilly band of Texas GIs entertained Bigart's ship at night. Shooting craps and playing Ping-Pong were popular recreations. No one wanted to get too sweaty, though: the ship didn't carry saltwater soap, so the men took few showers.

Only a few select officers knew the boat's ultimate destination. Rumors were rampant that the convoy was headed toward North Africa. It wasn't until the eve of their arrival that unit commanders were told how to transport their men to American stations throughout the British Isles. That last night at sea, there was an eleventh-hour outbreak of paranoia. "Someone had it straight from the engineer that a big pack of submarines was trailing the ship. Another said the whole German Navy was loose in the North Atlantic—Major So-and-so heard it on the wireless," Bigart wrote.

Bigart's convoy steamed untouched into an unnamed harbor (almost certainly Liverpool), occasioning him to sheepishly tell readers, "You had crossed the submarine-infested Atlantic without sighting even a porpoise. A hell of a thing to have to confess to your grandchildren." As for his shipmates, they were just happy to be back on land.

"'When I get on shore,' said an infantry captain from Utah, 'I'm going to get a handful of dirt and eat it.'"

The story's clinching sentence was pure Bigart. Instead of waxing poetic about England's verdant landscape, he snapped, "The green fields looked like propaganda."[46]

It was fine for Bigart to poke fun at himself, but his fears were hardly exaggerated. In truth, there were still substantial "gaps" between Nova Scotia and Iceland in air support coverage of seaborne convoys. Two months later, two separate convoys (SC 122 and HX 229) that originated from New York by way of Halifax—the same route Bigart's group had taken—were attacked by three "rakes" of wolf packs. Twenty-two Allied ships and more than three hundred servicemen were lost.[47]

After that debacle, Allied planners demanded that the gaps be closed by carrier groups and long-range reconnaissance aircraft. As the war progressed, U-boats became less of a threat. Yet there had been plenty for Bigart to worry about beyond kippers and brussels sprouts.

CHAPTER 3

★

NORTH AFRICA'S LIPLESS KISS

In war, as in love, it is your first campaign that stays bone deep in your memory. And Tunisia was our introduction to the sweetheart with the lipless kiss.

—HAL BOYLE, 1950
HELP, HELP! ANOTHER DAY!

It was still pitch-dark when AP's Hal Boyle gingerly swung a leg over the side of the troopship and began inching down its boarding net. Boyle was heavily weighted: a volume of Emily Dickinson's poetry, without which he never went anywhere, strained an already-stuffed musette bag. The beloved portable typewriter he'd entrusted with an Army public relations officer would soon, to Boyle's horror, sink to the bottom of Fedala Harbor.

Heaving fifty feet below was a landing craft. Boyle, then thirty-one, was operating at a distinct disadvantage. Unlike the young men clambering over the edge, the beefy AP reporter had not been through anything resembling boot camp. He was brand-new to the war beat and not exactly in tip-top physical condition—unless repeated cigar stub removal and twelve-ounce curls could be counted as exercise.

Moreover, besides a bulky backpack, Boyle carried on his shoulders the burden of posterity: He knew from briefings that he would be covering the largest amphibious action in history and the first joint U.S. Navy–U.S. Army operation since the Spanish-American War. Having spent the last

72

couple of weeks crossing the Atlantic with the guys now knifing down the net, Boyle didn't want to embarrass himself. It must have amused Boyle, who never shied away from a good time, that his company's objective was Pont Blondin, a prewar playground that boasted a seaside casino and race-track. But croupiers and jockeys weren't waiting for them—heavily armed soldiers were.

It was eerily quiet. The only noise came from nervous officers hissing at them to keep mum. A few minutes before, the first wave of attackers go-ing in just north of Casablanca had surprised defenders and gotten to the beach virtually undetected. Boyle had heard only a few scattered shots. At that point, none of the ships in the U.S. flotilla had opened fire, nor had any of the "enemy" batteries along the four-mile-long beach. American forces, in fact, were under strict orders to fire only when fired upon. Allied plan-ners had hoped that the U.S. could get troops ashore in French Morocco with a minimum of bloodshed, perhaps even a laying down of arms by halfhearted mercenaries.

But as Boyle's landing craft joined others in motoring toward shore, "a bright searchlight stabbed the skies at Pont Blondin and then swept sea-ward, catching our assault wave. In a bright glare that dazzled the cox-swain, we ducked to the bottom of the boat," Boyle wrote in an article that took a week to reach the *New York Times* and other U.S. papers. Within seconds, machine gun fire from the beach raked Fedala Harbor. A Navy support ship on Boyle's port side retaliated, snuffing the searchlight.

"Then came a grinding crash as our landing boat smashed at full speed into a coral reef that has helped to win this shore the name of Iron Coast," Boyle wrote. "The craft climbed futilely, then fell back into the water."

Boyle and his shipmates were plunged into armpit-deep water. They tried to struggle onto the reef, but waves kept pummeling them. Their sixty-pound knapsacks made it doubly difficult. Gasping for breath, Boyle grabbed at an outcropping. Another soldier beat him to it; the GI lay there, exhausted, half submerged in water, as Boyle flailed for help. "Twice the surf pulled me loose and twice it returned me," Boyle wrote. "My strength was ebbing fast when another soldier pulled up the man before me and lent me a wet hand to safety."

It took Boyle a few minutes before he felt strong enough to stand. He looked around and "saw about me scores of dripping soldiers, their legs weary and wide-braced." His hands were so torn up by the spike-sharp coral that he couldn't type for days.

Boyle and a sergeant decided to rid themselves of their bulky life vests. Together they crept across a patch of coral the length of a football field, then waded through waist-high water to the beach. Boyle and his buddy suddenly realized they weren't alone.

"The way those soaked men, a few moments before so weary that they could barely stand, forgot their fatigue in seeing their objective is a never-to-be-forgotten example of soldierly fortitude," Boyle told readers. "Forlorn on a hostile coast, with much of their heavy equipment under water, they quickly organized and turned toward their assigned tasks when we had crossed the beach and flung ourselves beneath a covering grove of pepper trees."[1]

It didn't take long for enemy artillery to find the pepper trees. "There isn't much to tell about being under shellfire," Boyle wrote his mother two weeks later, "except that 10 minutes under it, with the shells hitting close enough to shower you with dirt, teaches you more about war than you could learn in a lifetime any other way."[2]

Boyle spent hours that morning crawling through muddy ditches. Seven artillery shells "hit close enough to have cut me down with splinters had I been standing." By that afternoon Boyle's landing party had dug foxholes. "We could lay there in comparative comfort and listen to the shells whistle by overhead," he wrote. In the evening an enemy fighter plane strafed the beachhead as Boyle was interviewing infantrymen; he and the others dove for cover. After an uneasy night's sleep, they were strafed twice more before breakfast.[3]

There was relatively little fighting around Pont Blondin on day two; Boyle was able to borrow a typewriter and dictate a couple of stories to a public relations officer since Boyle's hands were still scabbed. That night, Boyle and other correspondents hitched a ride to Casablanca and checked into a hotel. The next day they were surprised to learn that an armistice had been signed in their lobby.[4] French Morocco's feckless little war was over—at least in theory. The fighting farther east in French North Africa, however, would continue for seven more months.

Recalling his pal's near drowning, Boyle's AP colleague Don Whitehead wrote that Hal "was no Johnny Weissmuller either in face or form, [and] had barely managed to avoid becoming the first newspaper casualty of the invasion, a distinction which held no attractions."[5]

THE NORTH AFRICAN CAMPAIGN, CODE-NAMED Operation Torch, held few attractions for anyone. Over time, it became a testament to Allied resolve and what Boyle described as soldierly fortitude. But for much of its existence, the North African incursion was also a testament to ambivalent and absentee leadership, pedestrian planning, and slipshod communications and execution. Given how dysfunctional Torch was from its inception, it's remarkable how well America's fighting forces performed in French Morocco, Algeria, and Tunisia.

The U.S. Army came of age in North Africa. The men who skulked across the reef off Pont Blondin and splashed ashore at eight other African beaches on the Atlantic and the Mediterranean in November 1942 were, in the main, poorly prepared for combat. Most had not gotten anywhere close to the essential training they needed for amphibious and desert warfare. Yet a half year later those same tenderfoots helped trap more than a quarter million of Hitler's finest troops, forever puncturing the myth of the Wehrmacht's invincibility.

Torch became a testing ground not only for grunts in the field, but also for their commanders—Generals Dwight Eisenhower, George Patton, Lucian Truscott, Mark Clark, and Omar Bradley, among them—and for their commanders' commanders, the great Anglo-American alliance led by Prime Minister Winston Churchill, his Chief of the Imperial General Staff, Sir Alan Brooke, and Field Marshal Harold Alexander, as well as President Franklin Roosevelt and his top military advisor, Army Chief of Staff George Marshall.

North Africa is where Walter Cronkite burnished his reputation—but only by getting bum information and inadvertently leaving the field of battle. It's where Hal Boyle and Joe Liebling became lifelong friends—where Boyle, the Irish shanachie, established his signature column and where Liebling, the urbane stylist, encountered a corpse that became the genesis of his greatest war essay. It's where Andy Rooney and Homer Bigart narrowly averted an international incident while meeting the King of England and where Bigart prepared for his first amphibious assault. Finally, it's where Liebling, Boyle, Ernie Pyle, and a coterie of correspondents sipped black-market scotch on a seaside veranda, cheering on Allied warplanes as they attacked German fighters and bombers.

North Africa was undeniably a pivot point in American history.[6] But as eyewitnesses Boyle, Cronkite, and Liebling could attest, it was hell getting there.

AMERICA'S GROUND WAR AGAINST ADOLF Hitler was launched in the most improbable of places. At the insistence of Churchill and Brooke, the U.S. slugged not at the guts of the Third Reich, but at its extremities. After Germany captured France in the summer of 1940, Hitler cut a loathsome deal with France's Great War hero, Marshal Philippe Pétain. Pétain and other leaders of the Vichy puppet regime assured the Nazis that they would defend, with French troops, France's old colonial empire along the Mediterranean. In exchange, Hitler agreed not to "occupy" the South of France, although the Gestapo would still exercise brutal control.

To extend Joe Liebling's boxing metaphor, America's opening jab was thrown not at crack *Panzer* troops, but at a peculiar adversary. The French were not just the U.S.'s traditional ally, but also its historic partner in the democratic revolution that upended repressive monarchies in both hemispheres.

It was a bizarre first round in what became the most transcendent fight in history. Stalin, under siege from 225 German divisions gunning toward the oil fields of the Caucasus, wanted what amounted to a main event—a full-bore second front in the European Theater that would compel Hitler to divert troops and resources. But in truth neither North Africa nor any of the Allies' subsequent thrusts in the Mediterranean ever rose beyond the level of an undercard—an ancillary bout that had relatively little to do with the fight's outcome.

Ostensibly to avoid chaos in North Africa, the U.S. ended up making one deal after another with Fascist collaborationists—the very thugs that Roosevelt and Churchill had vowed to bring to justice. Watching the disquieting scene unfold from London, CBS Radio's Edward R. Murrow fumed: "Are we fighting the Nazis or climbing into bed with them?" After a few days in Algeria, Scripps Howard's Ernie Pyle somehow slipped this line past the censors: "We have left in office most of the small-fry officials put there by the Germans before we came. . . . Our fundamental policy still is one of soft-gloving snakes in our midst."[7]

Moreover, the U.S. committed the weight of its prestige to a part of the world where Great Britain had long vied with Germany and France for colonial supremacy. Much of the rationale behind the U.S. invasion was to prevent Germany from concentrating its forces against the British Eighth Army in northeastern Africa. But Churchill had sent His Majesty's finest to Egypt not to spread democratic freedoms, but to safeguard British dominion over the Suez Canal. Suez may have been a vital link to supplying Allied forces in the Pacific Theater, but it was also "Rule, Britannia's" lifeline to its still-potent empire in the Middle East, Asia, and the subcontinent.

The initial stage of the North African campaign was, in sum, the kind of surrogate war that most Americans abhorred. Confused and morally ambiguous, it reeked of the old order, of imperial powers butting heads in a remote part of the world. Yet the U.S. had little choice but to go along with Britain. Churchill was correct: the Nazis and their Italian coconspirators had to be forcibly ejected from North Africa so that the Allies could gain control of the Mediterranean sea-lanes, establish airfields, and begin, slowly, inexorably, chipping away at the Reich.

DESPITE ITS MANY DEFECTS, FROM a logistical standpoint, Torch was staggering—by far the biggest amphibious assault ever attempted. To work effectively, Churchill said that Torch's various movements had to "fit together like a jeweled bracelet"—and, almost miraculously, they did.

Hal Boyle and Walter Cronkite got to admire up close one of Torch's glittering gems—the oceanic transport of nearly forty thousand men and tens of thousands of tons of equipment. Five years after they had covered the New London explosion, the two Kansas Citians were billeted together in Norfolk, Virginia, for a week before the flotilla's departure.

Norfolk was so manic in the weeks preceding the launch of the Torch armada that merchants posted signs saying, NO DOGS OR SAILORS ALLOWED. Its streets were full of prostitutes and, it was feared, German operatives. To keep the enemy guessing as to where the U.S. and Britain would strike, Allied intelligence planted a series of ruses. One of them involved sending a group of correspondents to the Scottish Highlands to take lessons in skiing and cold-weather survival, then encouraging the reporters to file stories about their experience.[8]

Admiral Kent Hewitt, the commander of Task Force 34, is one of the war's unsung heroes. Hewitt not only oversaw the safe passage of a hundred vessels across the Atlantic and arrived at his precise destination eight minutes ahead of schedule, but also had to put up with the histrionics of one George Smith Patton.

Even senior military people had never heard of Major General Patton. But after Patton blistered enlisted men all over the Tidewater, dictated letters to his senior commanders that snarled, "If you don't succeed, I don't want to see you alive," and concluded a toast to the wives at a formal dinner party by chortling, "My, what pretty widows you're going to make!"[9] everyone knew who he was. His notoriety was such that when it came time to select GI password commands for Torch, planners chose "George!" to be followed by "Patton!"

What Cronkite called Patton's "cracked pipe" tenor was as far removed from actor George C. Scott's thunderous baritone as a voice can be; it was so effeminate that soldiers could barely wait until the general was out of earshot to do cruel impersonations.

Never subtle in issuing barbs, Patton told anyone who would listen—including the President of the United States—that Admiral Hewitt and the

Navy could not be counted on to deliver the men and matériel needed in North Africa. As was often the case, Patton was dead wrong.

Task Force 34 is among World War II's unheralded triumphs. Hewitt headed a magnificent fleet: thirty troop transports carrying tens of thousands of GIs, along with three battleships, seven heavy and light cruisers, thirty-eight destroyers, four submarines, one fleet, and four escort aircraft carriers stocked with more than two hundred fighters and dive-bombers and torpedo bombers, plus sundry minesweepers, tankers, and tugboats— not to mention a couple of dozen correspondents, two of whom were named Boyle and Cronkite. It was the most formidable American fighting force ever assembled.

Churchill's jeweled bracelet began long before Allied warships had to navigate the Strait of Gibraltar. The vessels in Task Force 34 left from a variety of eastern U.S. ports, including one as far north as Casco Bay, Maine. Other task forces left from ports in Great Britain. The ships originating in the U.S. set out on or around October 23, reconnoitering in mid-ocean.

Hewitt was in many ways Patton's temperamental opposite. Cronkite and other correspondents met with Hewitt four days before they shoved off. "[Hewitt] looks like anything but the commander of a tough amphibious force with a dangerous mission to perform," Cronkite wrote in his diary. "If he were in civilian life I would pick him as the manager of the lace department at Macy's."[10] A former professor of mathematics at the Naval Academy, Hewitt had been a young staff officer when the Great White Fleet, the pride of President Theodore Roosevelt, had circumnavigated the globe in 1907, delivering TR's not so subtle message about America's burgeoning power.

THE STATURE CRONKITE ACHIEVED WITH his *Wakefield*-burning-at-sea exclusive helped earn him United Press' berth as the Navy correspondent on the battleship USS *Texas*, a veritable twin of the USS *Arkansas*. On October 19, Cronkite flew from New York to Norfolk in a military transport, a converted DC-3, "and I do mean converted," he wrote. The plane's amenities had been ripped out, replaced by crude benches. Cronkite propped his feet on freight boxes as the plane made stops in Philadelphia and Washington before arriving in the Tidewater.

All the Navy told Cronkite was "You'll be gone for some time"[11]—and that once he registered at the Tidewater base, he couldn't leave. "The story is underway!" Cronkite ethused in a journal he began keeping October 15. Associated Press' Navy correspondent in Norfolk was John Moroso; International News Service was represented by John Henry. Security was so tight that reporters weren't even supposed to divulge to what ships they'd been assigned, but Henry couldn't help but brag that he'd been given the *Massachusetts*, a brand-new battleship. A newly christened battlewagon made for a better story than the creaky old *Texas*—or so the "heartsick"[12] Cronkite told his diary.

When Cronkite asked Moroso where he thought the armada was headed, the AP reporter guessed Africa. UP editor Harrison Salisbury, "a keener mind on affairs international," Cronkite confided, had correctly predicted Morocco in a conversation the previous week in New York. Cronkite noted that German radio propaganda was claiming that western Africa would be invaded and that its U-boat wolf packs were being transferred to the African coast—an assertion that didn't exactly assuage Norfolk's hysteria.

On Cronkite's second evening in town, Navy press liaison officers, decked out in dress whites, took Cronkite out for cocktails at the Norfolk Yacht and Country Club. His new friends offered to get him a date for the evening, but Cronkite, lonely for Betsy, declined. As he watched the officers dance and crack jokes, Cronkite couldn't help but wonder what they were thinking "in moments of periodic silence. 'How many of these guys will come back with me?' And, then, just as an afterthought, 'Well, what the hell, I wonder if I'll come back?'" Cronkite was surprised that his own existential musings began to mirror a typical sailor's: that somebody else would get it, but not him.[13]

Navy and Marine officers gave an amorphous briefing to reporters that hinted the operation would be the long-anticipated "second front" without identifying its objective or describing its interlocking parts. A Marine colonel called the maneuver the biggest of the war, surpassing that summer's invasions of Guadalcanal and Tulagi. Without disclosing much, an admiral made it clear that it was an amphibious action. "A landing operation!" Cronkite enthused in his diary. "What a terrific story, what an amazing assignment!"

It may have been an amazing assignment, but Cronkite soon learned there was a catch, at least in theory. Once Task Force 34 reached its destination, Cronkite the battleship correspondent was supposed to continue filing stories from the *Texas* about Navy operations, not jump ashore to cover the Army as it moved inland. Knowing UP wanted him on the ground, Cronkite hatched other plans.

"I had assumed (and I assumed that the Navy had assumed) that any red-blooded war correspondent was going to jump ship and stay where the action was," he wrote. So as the *Texas* zigzagged across the Atlantic in late October and early November, Cronkite made a point to befriend officers whom, he reckoned, would have shore responsibilities in the days following the initial assault.

In the meantime, Cronkite enjoyed the spectacle of watching Army men try to acclimate themselves to life at sea. "There may be nothing more amusing than the Army afloat, except perhaps the Navy ashore," he recalled. One of the propaganda ploys contrived by Army intelligence was to create an ersatz radio station that would broadcast pro-Allied messages to Moroccan soldiers and citizens, hoping to facilitate a quick surrender. Much to the amusement of the ship's crew, the Army had crammed their radio equipment onto the *Texas*.

Once the invasion started, the station's first job was to air a "we-come-in-peace" message recorded by President Roosevelt and converted into French. George Patton detested the idea of radio-fueled propaganda, disliked the conciliatory tone of the Roosevelt statement, and, as an ardent Francophile, deplored the way the remarks had been translated.

The Army's clandestine broadcast outfit went by the name Radio Maroc; it was run by a group of peacetime advertising and radio executives who, Cronkite noticed, were taking themselves and their Manhattan social standing way too seriously for the Navy crew's liking. One evening, as the battleship churned through rough water, a hatch located just above the quarters of the radio team was mysteriously left ajar. Seawater began cascading into their rooms. Convinced that the ship was foundering, the Army officers charged onto the deck, shrieking for everyone to head toward the lifeboats—a scene that doubtless gave the Navy men something to chuckle about for the remainder of the voyage.

To deceive Nazi intelligence, Hewitt's fleet steamed southeast, looking as if it were going to conduct a training exercise in the Caribbean. Fortunately no U-boat detected Task Force 34's easterly twist toward the Azores. German wolf packs were busily engaged a thousand miles north, where that same week Convoy SC 107, en route from Cape Breton to Liverpool, lost fifteen of its forty-two ships.[14]

On day two at sea, the task force's orders were unsealed: Journalists were briefed on "the whole story of our operation," Cronkite wrote. General Dwight Eisenhower, they learned, was in charge of a joint (but primarily American) invasion. Pointing to reconnaissance maps, charts, and photographs, Rear Admiral Monroe Kelly, the *Texas'* skipper, walked reporters through the planned three-pronged assault on Africa's Atlantic coast. "The scope of the movement absolutely startled me," Cronkite typed that night in his journal. "This is THE SHOW!"[15]

The next morning, just as the church service was getting under way, Cronkite's "show" got precariously close. A destroyer spotted something suspicious and dropped depth charges; Hewitt then ordered the carriers to dispatch their planes. It made for a tension-filled Sunday morning, but there was no U-boat attack. A sobering chart posted on the *Texas'* bridge purported to track enemy sub movements in and around the Azores.

Every night, Cronkite and his new friends gathered around the radio to listen to both legitimate news and the latest propaganda from Berlin and Vichy. Field Marshal Harold Alexander and General Bernard Montgomery had just launched their triumphant offensive against Rommel's forces at El Alamein in Egypt, pushing the Germans westward in the first move of the Allied pincer attack meant to trap the Axis host somewhere around Tunisia. Joseph Goebbels' propaganda mouthpieces, meanwhile, were claiming that the Allies would attack along the Moroccan shore—a bit of prescience that didn't make the officers rest any easier.

Just before reaching the African coast, Task Force 34 planned to break into three invasion armadas: the southern group would go to Safi, south of Casablanca; the main group, including Hal Boyle, went to Fedala, just north of Casablanca; and the northern group, with Cronkite, targeted Port Lyautey, twelve miles northeast of the Moroccan capital. Cronkite was told that the *Texas* would be joined off Port Lyautey by the cruiser *Savannah*; five destroyers; the *Chenango*, a onetime oil tanker that had been hastily transformed into a crude aircraft escort carrier; eight troop transports; and various cargo vessels. The *Chenango* was carrying seventy-seven P-40 fighter planes slated to be transferred to Port Lyautey as soon as its airstrip was captured.

The seaborne infantry's job, Cronkite wrote in remaining true to the Navy's admonition not to commit specific targets to print lest they fall into enemy hands, "will be to take an all-important ____ and silence a great _____ that, remaining in enemy hands, could jeopardize the venture. We also shall seize or bombard ____—and, as Admiral Kelly says, 'this is our meat,' an _____."[16] Among the blanks, as soon became apparent, was the airdrome located seven miles inland of Port Lyautey, some sizable artillery guns, and a garrison of about three thousand French, Senegalese, and Moroccan soldiers.

While quietly marking his twenty-sixth birthday on November 4, Cronkite must have wondered if he'd ever see another one. An unidentified plane "gave us a short fright" and rumors persisted that U-boats were lurking off the African coast.

A musical combo put on a boisterous show that buoyed spirits in the middle of continued foul weather. "I wondered what the militaristic Nazis would think if they could see our boys going into battle with a smile on their faces and 'Flat foot floogie with a floy-floy' on their lips?" jazz buff Cronkite wrote on his birthday.

On the evening of November 7, Admiral Kelly summoned Cronkite to his quarters. The battleship's crew at that point had still not been fully

briefed on their mission. Kelly planned on delivering remarks over the
ship's public-address system and wondered if Cronkite could compose
something inspirational.

Cronkite racked his brain but couldn't come up with anything more
fitting than what Kelly had already scribbled. The Navy and Army hoped
their men wouldn't need big pep talks. In fact, they hoped American soldiers and sailors wouldn't have to fight at all. At several strategic points
along the North African coast, Eisenhower sent either furtive messengers
operating under the cloak of darkness or French-speaking agents operating under a flag of truce to negotiate "diplomatic" solutions or foment mu-
tinies, depending on circumstances.[17]

On November 8, Port Lyautey invasion commander General Lucian
Truscott, acting on Eisenhower's orders, sent two emissaries to negotiate a
truce with the French commander. The mission failed when a Vichy sentry
machine-gunned the jeep carrying the two Americans and their white
flag. Both officers were awarded the Congressional Medal of Honor, one
posthumously.

Since Port Lyautey's garrison was guarded by fewer than three thousand defenders, Torch planners thought that pacifying it would be fairly
easy. Ironically, the fighting in and around the sixteenth-century fortress
that GIs facetiously nicknamed the Kasbah was as fierce as any in the
three-day Moroccan war.

Truscott, a forty-seven-year-old former horse soldier fated to spend too
much of the war under the thumbs of George Patton and Mark Clark,
made his share of mistakes in attacking Port Lyautey. Instead of having the
Navy level the garrison with concentrated fire, Truscott ordered a series of
infantry assaults from troops who'd never seen combat. The attacks proved
tepid and uncoordinated. Two hundred U.S. casualties later, they still
hadn't captured the fort. Truscott and his staff were appalled by the number of infantrymen who refused to fight or abandoned their weapons at the
first sign of trouble.

When French artillery located at both ends of Port Lyautey began firing
at the invaders at first light on November 9, the *Texas* responded all out,

unloosing its fourteen-inch guns in a spectacular barrage. Cronkite, gripping the bridge rail with both hands, was actually singed by flames leaping out of the massive barrels. As the salvo continued, the *Texas* staggered; some of its aging ceramic pipes burst. "It was as if, instead of disgorging the shells, she had been hit by them," Cronkite remembered.

Just then fighters appeared overhead. Convinced they were Vichy planes from Port Lyautey's airdrome, every antiaircraft battery on the *Texas* opened up. "Fortunately, none was hit," Cronkite recalled, "and a moment later a furious Captain Roy Pfaff was on the ship's public-address system.

"'Men, there is nothing worse in war than firing at your own men. We've been drilling on aircraft identification ever since we left Norfolk. There is no excuse for this. I'm going to find the man who gave the order to fire and I'm going to have him before the mast.

"'But, men, my God, if you're going to shoot at them, hit them!'"[18]

In the midst of this chaos, Radio Maroc was trying to try transmit President Roosevelt's message. The intensity of the concussions knocked it off the air. To the amusement of the Navy guys, it took a long while before the Army's station was operational. But as Hal Boyle pointed out in a piece published later that month, Radio Maroc did succeed in helping explain the Allies' cause to skeptical Moroccans.

On November 10, Cronkite filed his first eyewitness account of close-in combat—and in doing so, created his first war hero. Datelined SEBU RIVER,[19] PORT LYAUTEY, FRENCH MOROCCO, the article recounted the courage of a Navy lieutenant commander in getting his ship up the heavily guarded river and capturing the airdrome.

The officer's name was Steve Brodie, which also happened to be the moniker of an infamous daredevil in the 1880s who supposedly jumped off the Brooklyn Bridge for a wad of cash—and lived to squander it. Six decades later, "Steve Brodie" was still synonymous in America with machismo derring-do. Cronkite saw his opening.

"This Steve Brodie took a chance, too," went his minimalist lede.

The second paragraph drilled home Cronkite's theme: "But instead of jumping off a bridge, this Steve Brodie stood on the bridge of a stripped-down old American warship and pushed her through the mud of the shallow Sebu River to capture the Port Lyautey airdrome."

Censorship rules precluded Cronkite from identifying Brodie's ship, but it was the twenty-three-year-old destroyer USS *Dallas*, whose superstructure had been reduced by engineers specifically for the Sebu mission. Army ground troops had been bottled up for nearly two days in trying to assault the airfield. Now it was the Navy's turn to force its way inland. Using wire cutters, volunteer seamen attempted to sever the net that Vichy forces had planted in the river, but succeeded only in puncturing a hole.

Brodie and his crew of 122, including seventy-five commandoes, failed twice to penetrate the damaged netting, but tried a third time. The *Texas* was anchored at the mouth of the Sebu; Cronkite was standing near Admiral Kelly, who was getting constant updates from his lieutenant commander. "We're going to ram the net," Brodie reported, then a few minutes later announced, "We're through the net!" The *Dallas* navigated the rest of the Sebu, piled its commandoes onto rubber rafts, and within twenty minutes captured the airdrome.[20]

When it finally surfaced weeks later, Cronkite's article cracked front pages all over the country, including the *Kansas City Kansan*, the paper of record in Wyandotte County, across the Missouri River from Cronkite's adopted hometown. It annoyed Cronkite that the *Star* gave local guy Hal Boyle consistent exposure while ignoring his own wire copy. His letters back home constantly inquired if the *Star* was giving him bylines.

KANSAS CITY'S OTHER FAVORITE SON also used historical allusions to forge a hero in the fighting in and around Port Lyautey. A few days after the cease-fire, Boyle got a tip from Truscott's public relations officer that a direct descendant of Confederate naval legend Raphael Semmes, the captain of the raider *Alabama*, had helped blunt a French counterattack on the first day of the invasion. "A former Washington, D.C., attorney and tank commander saved an entire American landing force here from being thrown back in to the sea by leading six U.S. tanks against an overwhelmingly

superior French force and knocking out every one of 18 opposing machines," Boyle wrote.

Colonel Harry Semmes had come to the rescue on the evening of November 8 when Navy surveillance pilots spotted a French tank unit, accompanied by a regiment of infantry, heading toward Lyautey from Rabat,
twenty-five miles away. Semmes quickly off-loaded two more tanks, then
maneuvered to defend the beach. The French had ten-ton Renault tanks
that were creaky but packed a wallop. U.S. forces had new, light tanks suitable for amphibious action. Semmes' own tank, Boyle reported, was hit
eight times while putting four French tanks out of commission.

"If they had gotten through, we probably would have been driven back
in the seas," Semmes told Boyle. After the battle Truscott sought Semmes
out and congratulated him. "'Well, general,' [Semmes] came back, 'we just
kept pecking away at them.'"

Semmes wasn't the only American fighting man pecking away during
those seventy-two confused hours in Morocco. It was the shortest war in
American history—and the weirdest.

"I don't understand it," a private told Boyle. "All the French people
come out to clap and cheer us when we take a town. Nothing's too good for
us. But when we start to move on we have to fight like hell all over again at
the next town."[21]

ONCE VICHY FORCES AGREED TO the cease-fire on November 11, Cronkite
spent a couple of days ashore surveying artillery damage and talking to
Truscott's GIs about their first taste of combat. Seventy-nine had sacrificed
their lives; another 250 had been wounded.[22] Ironically, the P-40s slated for
the Port Lyautey's airfield never became the fighting force that Patton and
Truscott envisioned. More than a few planes were wrecked or damaged
upon landing; none saw action in the weeks that followed.

Cronkite wrote a number of follow-up stories about ground action and,
once approved by censors, relayed them, as agreed before the invasion,
to the British Royal Navy's transmitter on Gibraltar. By then German
U-boats had begun slipping past the destroyer cordon around the Moroc-

can task forces, unleashing torpedoes with alarming regularity—none of which Cronkite could report, of course. Between the ships scuttled by the French navy and the damage being inflicted by Nazi submarines, Port Lyautey Harbor wasn't easy to navigate.

An officer on the *Texas* told Cronkite, who'd been spending his nights on the ship, that it would be heading down the coast to reinforce Hewitt's main task force at Casablanca. So Cronkite, eager to report on Torch's primary thrust, stayed on board, since getting to Casablanca via jeep was extremely dangerous; rogue vigilantes were roaming around.

The *Texas* was heading west, all right, but it didn't stop at Casablanca. Instead, it steamed into open water and, along with a slimmed-down armada, charted a course back to Norfolk. Cronkite, dejected, was convinced his career as a war correspondent would ignominiously end once UP–New York got wind of how he'd miscalculated.

But a couple of days into the trip home it occurred to him that he might be the first U.S. correspondent to return from the North African war zone—a coup that might help UP forgive his gaffe. He shared his first-reporter-back epiphany with *Texas* chums, who were pleased at the prospect that Cronkite's stature might generate extra attention for their ship. By then, Cronkite had proudly filed thirteen stories on the task force voyage and invasion, most of them centered on the *Texas'* role. He started feeling better.

In midocean, Cronkite was called into Admiral Kelly's quarters and given bad news: The newer and faster USS *Massachusetts*, with INS' John Henry aboard, was a couple of days ahead of the *Texas* armada and headed back to its home port in Boston. Henry, Cronkite knew, had a big yarn: a firsthand account of the *Massachusetts'* dismantling of the French battleship *Jean Bart*. It was the worst of all worlds for Cronkite: Now he wouldn't be the first correspondent back, his screwup would be doubly glaring, and his competitor had a better story.

One of Cronkite's *Texas* buddies, a Navy pilot named Bob Dally, came up with an inventive solution. "If you can get the Old Man's approval," Dally told Cronkite, "I could fly you into Norfolk and probably save a couple of days. Maybe you could still beat the *Massachusetts*."

Admiral Kelly, enamored of more publicity for the *Texas*, liked Dally's idea. The minute the battleship ventured into air range, Dally and Cronkite climbed into an observation pontoon biplane, the smallest aircraft in the Navy. The plane was fired from a large catapult on a railway that ran the width of the ship. It was "as close to being shot out of a cannon as one could arrange without joining the circus," Cronkite kidded.[23]

Just as the seaplane neared Norfolk, Dally volunteered that they were dangerously low on gas. Dally plunked into Norfolk Harbor and deposited Cronkite at the dock with the tank virtually empty.

Security guards wouldn't let Cronkite near any phones, which was just as well because he learned that a Navy plane was about to depart for Floyd Bennett Field in Brooklyn. Minutes after the plane touched down, he managed to hitch a ride with a truck driver headed to Manhattan. With no advance warning, Cronkite strolled into the UP office in the *Daily News* building at 23 Park Place. It was like a scene in a hokey movie: every noise except the *tat-tat-tat* of the Teletype machines abruptly went dead. His officemates stared, disbelieving, as if seeing a ghost. Cronkite hadn't been heard from since Task Force 34 left Norfolk six weeks before. None of his dispatches from the *Texas* had gotten through. United Press—not to mention his wife and parents—had feared the worst.

Crusty editor Mert Akers, not prone to emotional displays, leapt from behind his desk and gave Cronkite a bear hug. "My God, Cronkite, you're safe!" Akers gushed. Then regaining his usual abrasiveness, Akers yelled, "And where in hell have you been?"

The Allied radio relay system set up before the invasion—from American warships and ground stations to the Royal Navy's transmittal center on Gibraltar, then, via Teletype, to the respective press outlets in the U.S.—had been a bust. Many of the transmissions didn't go through because of mechanical breakdowns. Even worse, the Gibraltar technicians had exercised favoritism, sending the reports of British correspondents back to the U.K. while brushing aside U.S. requests.[24]

Cronkite immediately asked about INS' Henry: had Henry's reports come across the wire yet? The answer was "no": Henry, apparently believing he was well ahead of any potential competitor, had taken a couple of days of rest and relaxation in Boston. Thanking the Almighty for his good fortune, Cronkite made a tearful call to Betsy, then jumped behind a typewriter. He had been smart enough to save carbons of all thirteen stories. With secretarial help, he reconstructed his accounts, consolidating them into four or five articles. Within hours, the stories hit the wire with an editor's proud note bragging that they were the first uncensored eyewitness accounts of the fighting in North Africa. Cronkite, competitive to the end, always took great delight in explaining how Henry had just sat down to compose the first of his North Africa stories when Cronkite's bylines came clattering across the wire.

UP wasted no time exploiting Cronkite's newfound fame. He was interviewed by CBS Radio and filmed a segment for Paramount News. Millions of American moviegoers in the late fall of '42—including Betsy—saw the black-and-white newsreel short that was introduced with the dramatic teaser: HE SAW IT HAPPEN!

The camera picks up the fully uniformed Cronkite pretending to bat out a story on his typewriter. Then he glances up, stops typing, and says in his gravelly baritone at that unmistakable cadence, "I've just come back from reporting the greatest assignment any American correspondent has had so far in this war. . . ."

Cronkite the Navy correspondent had gotten lucky twice over: with the *Wakefield* exclusive and now by being the first reporter back from Morocco. But both times he'd earned his good fortune. More importantly, he was earning a reputation as the kind of correspondent who would take serious risks to gain an edge on the competition. He woke up every day back then, he once remarked, determined to "beat the hell" out of AP.

THERE WEREN'T ANY NEWSREEL CAMERAS around on November 9, 1942, when Joe Liebling left England on a boat "in an atmosphere thick with fog and mystery."[25] For two weeks Liebling and other U.S. correspondents stationed in Britain had been on notice that they could leave at any instant for a new war zone. When news broke over the radio on November 8 that Allied troops had invaded French North Africa, it pained Liebling. The last thing the French devotee wanted to see was American infantrymen fighting Frenchmen.

Earlier in the war, Liebling had hoped to land a job with a big daily. But sticking with the *New Yorker* proved fortuitous: no newspaper editor would have let Liebling be Liebling like Harold Ross did.

En route to Africa, Liebling shared cramped quarters with a passel of American reporters, including Ernie Pyle of Scripps Howard, Red Mueller of *Newsweek*, Bill Lang of *Time* and *Life*, Gault MacGowan of the *New York Sun*, and Ollie Stewart of the *Baltimore Afro-American*. Liebling saw in Stewart a kindred spirit. "'Where do you hope we land at?' [Stewart] asked me. 'Someplace where resistance has ceased,' I told him. That established a perfect rapport." They were on a big troopship transporting Air Force personnel to the Mediterranean.

Two days before the ship departed, Liebling developed ill-timed gout. "There were 52 nurses who got a first impression of decrepitude that I never consequently had a chance to overcome, because each was immediately appropriated by three Air Corps officers," Liebling recalled. After eleven bumpy but uneventful days at sea, they docked at Mers El Kébir in Algiers, then traveled by jeep to Oran.

On Liebling's first night in Oran he witnessed a light air raid. But that was the only action he saw for the next few weeks. He spent the better part of a month training with the First Infantry Division, the men who had captured Oran after two days of fighting. "The First had many enlisted men from the sidewalks of the Bronx and Brooklyn, and rich New York accents had new charms for me in Africa," wrote Liebling.

"'Give da passwoy,' I once heard a First Division sentinel challenge.

"'Nobody told me nuttin,' the challenged soldier replied.

"'What outfitchas outuv?'

"'Foy Signals.'

"'Whynchas get on da ball? Da passwoy is "tatched roof."'

"'What is it mean?'

"'How do I know? Whaddaya tink I yam, da Quiz Kids?'"

Despite diction that seemed lifted out of a Bowery Boys short, or perhaps because of it, the Big Red One "looked and acted and talked like a good division even then," Liebling wrote.[26]

The rest of the U.S. Army, Liebling wasn't so sure about. He was appalled at the official Allied policy of coddling Vichy leaders and the Algerian plutocrats who happily embraced the Nazis' anti-Semitism. Under Vichy, Algerian aristocrats had imposed their own version of the Nazis' Nuremberg laws, robbing Jews of property and bank accounts and denying many of them the opportunity to hold jobs. Hundreds of innocent Jews and anti-Vichy Frenchmen who had put their lives on the line in backing the Allied cause remained in Algerian jails despite the "liberation."

To Liebling's disgust, the landowners lavishly entertained the top U.S. commander, General Lloyd R. Fredendall, seeking to persuade the high command that a stable Algeria depended on continued repression of Jews.

Most Algerians, they told Fredendall over rare wines, distrusted Jews as much as the Germans did. Many members of Algeria's ruling class were, in fact, brownshirts; their "*sturm* duds," as Liebling scorned them, had been secreted away once U.S. warships had appeared.[27]

Liebling surmised that turning a blind eye toward Algeria's treatment of Jews was a quid pro quo, part of the rapprochement that Eisenhower struck with Vichy strongman Jean Louis Darlan. Consummated after weeks of covert negotiations, the Darlan Deal, as it became known in the American press, called for North Africa's Vichy to remain in power in exchange for a laying down of arms and "cooperation" in the fight against the Axis. Darlan, an admiral in the French navy, had become rich carrying out Hitler's sordid agenda along the southern Mediterranean. In the words of one U.S. official, Darlan was "a needle-nosed, sharp-chinned little weasel."[28] At one point in their back-and-forth, an exasperated Eisenhower wished aloud for an assassin to bag the weasel.

For three days after the landings, Darlan defied Eisenhower, only cutting a deal when a combined German/Italian army, from their stronghold across the sea in Sicily, invaded Tunisia, signaling Hitler's contempt for Vichy's grasp of French North Africa. The Darlan pact was "not very pretty," declared the exiled leader of France's patriots, General Charles de Gaulle. "I think that before long the retching will take place."[29]

De Gaulle proved prophetic: the retching soon began in earnest. It wasn't just liberal commentators who denounced the ploy: Conservative papers editorialized against it, too. The Darlan Deal not only soured many Americans on the North African campaign, but also colored their perceptions of the officer who engineered it. Enabling Darlan hadn't been Eisenhower's idea; he and his aide-de-camp, Mark Clark, had merely carried out the wishes of London and Washington. Roosevelt and Churchill wanted the French armed services—especially its still-potent navy—neutered and believed that accommodating Darlan was the best way to achieve it. It depressed Eisenhower that his good name had gotten dragged into the morass.

Throughout the campaign, the Supreme Commander was forced to spend too much time working political levers and too little time worrying about battlefield exigencies. Ike was so consumed by political matters, in fact, that he didn't arrive on the front lines in Tunisia until Christmas Eve, which, by fiendish coincidence, was just hours before Darlan was assassinated.[30] Darlan was supposedly done in by a demented young Algerian. Joe Liebling and Hal Boyle, however, weren't the only Americans who suspected a broader cabal. Overnight, without benefit of a trial or collecting any evidence, a tribunal ordered the suspect executed. When news of Darlan's death reached headquarters, one U.S. officer was heard to exult, "Merry Christmas."

Boyle was in Algiers with the Allied press pack when the rumor hit that the Vichy leader had been murdered. Hal's colleagues scrambled off to the Allied public relations office. But Boyle, sensing that reporters would just get the runaround, hung back. With instincts honed from covering Kansas City street crime, he slipped across the road to where he knew Darlan's chauffeur belonged to a motor pool. Sure enough, Darlan's driver told Boyle that the admiral had been shot and killed.

Boyle had an exclusive on one of the biggest stories of the war to date. He ran back to his typewriter, rapped out his news flash, and raced it over to the censor in the public relations office. The nervous PRO didn't know what to make of Boyle's story; the youngster embargoed it for a couple of hours while he tracked down his superiors. By then the competition had confirmed the story, too, but Boyle's piece should by rights have been transmitted first, since he'd been at the head of the queue. "Bejeezus if the PRO didn't rule there should be a drawing among the agencies to see which story got first priority," reminisced Don Whitehead. "The AP boys screamed like demented banshees at this injustice but AP lost the draw and with it Hal's beat."[31]

The next day Boyle filed a piece that went as far as censors would allow in questioning the abrupt execution. "There was no official explanation… why [the accused] was condemned by a court-martial instead of being tried in civil courts," Boyle wrote.

AP and Boyle never got the kudos they deserved on the Darlan story. In a way, his exclusive-that-wasn't typified Boyle's experience in North Africa. Most correspondents enjoyed interviewing soldiers in the field, but Boyle soon made it an art form. He drove his jeep companions crazy by constantly jumping out to grab a few words with the men marching by.[32] GIs got a kick out of Boyle because he was wickedly funny and, like the feisty customers who had come into his old man's meat shop, could curse with abandon. Boyle filled one notebook after another with the conversations he had with soldiers.

Yet for all his regular-guy bonhomie, Boyle never became as celebrated as Ernie Pyle. At the outset of Torch, Boyle was, like Cronkite, just another wire service grunt, whereas Pyle had been a commentator of note for the better part of a decade. In 1934, the Scripps syndicate, delighted with a series of offbeat stories Ernie had penned while on a cross-country trip for its *Washington Daily News*, commissioned Pyle to travel the back roads of Depression-era America. Pyle's pieces on everything from his own hypochondria to Alaskan gold miners and the hobo who painted watercolors in a hovel behind the Memphis city dump were much admired.[33] Ernie took that same common-man approach to his early accounts of American fighting men in North Africa, soon becoming GI Joe's favorite reporter. Pyle put a human face on war, commiserating with officers and enlisted men fresh off the front lines or cracking wise with the beleaguered cook trying to keep a chow line fed. From day one, Pyle was careful to identify everyone's hometown and weave a heartwarming story about the GI's family and peacetime life. His column became an overnight sensation; every week, it seemed, dozens of papers began subscribing to Scripps.

Yet the irony is that Pyle didn't arrive in North Africa until two weeks after Hal Boyle, Walter Cronkite, and other reporters had risked their lives in landing operations. By the time Pyle waded ashore, the nearest fighting was hundreds of miles away. Moreover, Boyle had already established his own Everyman style and nonchalant rapport with infantrymen by the time Pyle got close to the front. Boyle thumbed rides in jeeps and tanks so often that he soon earned the nickname Hal the Hitchhiker.

The difference between them was that Pyle was a known commodity with a burgeoning national platform. Boyle, on the other hand, was still trying to establish himself. And he was handicapped by AP's insistence that he be identified as "Harold V. Boyle," a starchy byline that made him sound like anything but a regular guy. It wasn't until well into 1943 that AP finally granted the reporter's plea to become "Hal Boyle." Pyle, by contrast, became famous so quickly in North Africa that when entertainer Al Jolson came through on a USO tour, everywhere Jolson went he was asked if he knew "Ernie."

Pyle was only in his early forties but seemed much older. He was elfin and wan. Sallow-skinned, he barely weighed a hundred pounds and was almost never without a lit cigarette and a smoker's hack. Yet Pyle's veneration of the American fighting man was so widely admired and imitated, A. J. Liebling wrote after the war, that Ernie had "contributed a stock figure to the waxworks gallery of American history as popularly remembered. To a list that includes the frontiersman, the Kentucky colonel, the cowboy, and Babe Ruth, [Pyle] added GI Joe, the suffering but triumphant American infantryman."[34]

Ernie's notoriety came at a price. The more Pyle saluted the brave men in foxholes, the more his editors insisted on eyewitness accounts from the front. Being in close proximity to combat scared most journalists, but it absolutely petrified Pyle. War reporting, Liebling observed, was an "adven-

ture" for some correspondents and an "enthrallment" for the likes of Ernest Hemingway. But for Pyle it was "unalleviated misery." Artillery fire
left Hal the Hitchhiker as shaken as anyone—but Boyle was able to mask
it with jocularity and another tug on his flask. For Pyle, who suffered from
melancholia, it was harder.

Boyle and Pyle finally met, the Missourian remembered, at a seedy
Oran hotel, where Pyle lay on a bed "mopping his nose and gently cursing
the people who had reported that Africa was a warm country."[35] Hal got a
laugh out of Pyle by saying, "I'm writing for the people who look over the
shoulders of the people reading Ernie Pyle's column."[36] Throughout the
war, Boyle liked to refer to himself as the "poor man's Ernie Pyle"—a
phrase later expropriated by Hemingway.

IN THE MIDDLE OF HIS spate of stories about Darlan's murder, Boyle filed a
lighthearted piece about the arrival of the first batch of female nurses and
WAAC officers in North Africa. It was a fat pitch—and the female-obsessed
Boyle hit it out of the park. His story got nice pickup in the States, including the front page of the *Washington Post*.

"The appearance at the officers' mess of the young women had immediate repercussions," Boyle wrote. "When they first entered the long private
dining room, looking as neat and fresh in their military garb as a Monday
morning wash, all conversation halted momentarily. Heads of generals and
second lieutenants alike turned as if they were on the same pivot to watch
the women march a little self-consciously to their table. Gray-haired colonels, who usually gnaw their rations in grumpy austerity, dusted off their
military gallantry and shamelessly sabotaged officers of lesser rank to get
seats near the newcomers."

Two correspondents—one of them almost certainly Boyle—scored a
coup by getting all five WAAC officers out to dinner at a Tunisian restaurant. "Army Air Corps officers also were taken along after they begged to
join the party and pledged they would pay for the food, buy the wine, and
get the correspondents a free airplane ride home after the war.

"'Listen, if you'll fix me up with a date with that pretty little blonde—

the lieutenant with the dimples—I'll wrap you up a bomber right now,' said one flier, 'and what's more I'll give you a private hangar to keep it in.'"[37]

After seven weeks of being in a war zone, Boyle celebrated a "canned" Christmas at an airdrome along the Tunisian front. "We are having canned steak, canned peas, canned tomatoes, canned sweet potatoes, canned apricots, canned beets, canned biscuits, canned milk, and canned corn," a technical sergeant from Dallas said with a grin to Boyle.

Nineteen forty-two was over. As they ate their holiday rations, American soldiers were thinking they had endured some nasty moments. But North Africa's lipless kiss was just beginning.

CHAPTER 4

★

ANGRY METEORS IN TUNISIA

*If there is any way you can get colder than you do when
you sleep in a bedding roll on the ground in a tent in
southern Tunisia two hours before dawn, I don't know
about it.*

—A. J. LIEBLING, 1943
THE ROAD BACK TO PARIS

Early one morning in mid-January 1943, A. J. Liebling was trading barbs with ground crew grunts over breakfast alfresco at a hellhole of an airdrome near Thélepte in the southern Tunisia desert. The men were balancing plates of eggs on empty gasoline canisters when they heard the menacing buzz of approaching aircraft. Abruptly leaving breakfast behind, they sprinted for cover behind a knoll, with the porky Liebling leading the pack.

"They always faced eastward while they ate in the morning so that they could see the Messerschmitts come over the mountains in the sunrise," Liebling recalled. "This morning there were nine Messerschmitts. By the time I hit the ground on the lee side of the mound, slender airplanes were twisting above us in a sky crisscrossed by tracer bullets—a whole planetarium of angry worlds and meteors."[1]

The North African campaign in the first half of 1943 was full of angry projectiles. Liebling spent several weeks at Thélepte with a P-40 fighter squadron and A-20 bomber crews attached to the 47th Bombardment Group. The base got strafed so often at sunup, then again at sundown, that

Liebling and fellow correspondents, among them AP's estimable Noland "Boots" Norgaard, got used to dining in installments.

An Army Air Force major from northwestern Pennsylvania named Philip Cochran was so eerily prescient at predicting when raids would occur that it was as if he was "sensing when to hop on or off a guy who is shooting craps," the major told Liebling. It turned out that Cochran was already something of a known commodity before Liebling profiled him. Comic artist Milton Caniff had used Cochran as the inspiration behind his balls-to-the-wall aviator "Flip Corkin" in Caniff's popular strip *Terry and the Pirates*.[2]

Cochran was a favorite Liebling archetype: the bare-knuckled Irishman. A few weeks earlier, Cochran had defied orders and transferred his squadron to Thélepte, conducting what amounted, Liebling claimed, to a rogue war. North Africa was so chaotic that hell-raisers like Cochran were desperately needed—or so Liebling argued. "The situation [in North Africa] called for officers who were good at guessing, bluffing and guerrilla tactics," Liebling wrote, "and Cochran found himself in the spot he had dreamed of all his military life."[3]

Another controversial rogue warrior, Major General Terry de la Mesa Allen, the commander of Liebling's First Division darlings, also got the full A.J. treatment. As a young man, Allen had managed to get himself tossed out of West Point, the sort of puerile behavior that bad boy Liebling always viewed as strength of character. Liebling also liked the fact that the young Allen had boxed professionally, sometimes under an assumed name. The onetime pugilist possessed "shrewdness and dash . . . not acquired from textbooks," Liebling enthused.

It was true that the pugnacious Allen was beloved by many GIs. But it was also true that Allen was sloppy, undisciplined, and constantly at loggerheads with superiors—little of which was addressed in Liebling's fawning portrayal. A few months later in Sicily, Allen's handling of the assault at Troina was so cavalier that Omar Bradley felt compelled to relieve him.[4]

Liebling, the lefty subversive, loved to tweak right-wingers. In mid-March, outside the central Tunisia oasis of Djebel Berda, while the First Division's brass planned its next maneuver, Liebling was standing near

Allen's deputy, Brigadier General Teddy Roosevelt, Jr., as Army public relations magnate Lieutenant (later Captain) Ralph Ingersoll happened to wander by in the company of several engineering officers. Ingersoll, a good friend of Liebling's, was a onetime *New Yorker* editor and founder of the left-wing newspaper *PM*, the bane of Wall Street. Despite their political differences, Liebling had grown to admire General Roosevelt, whose political leanings were considerably more conservative than those of TR Senior— and miles removed from TR junior's distant cousin in the White House.

Ingersoll greeted Liebling, had a pleasant exchange with Roosevelt, and walked off. Once Ingersoll's entourage was out of earshot, Liebling couldn't resist.

"That was Ralph Ingersoll, the *PM* editor," Liebling informed Roosevelt.

"The general likes to descant on the thesis that all the prominent interventionists stayed safe at home while he, a hard-shell America Firster, went to war," Liebling wrote. "He stopped sharply. 'Hell,' he said, 'I always thought that man was a sonofabitch.'"[5]

One of the reasons Liebling the gourmand was taken with Roosevelt was that the general always went out of his way to cultivate the mess sergeant in every outfit. "He asks the sergeant, for instance, if the company has enough baking powder. The sergeant invariably says no, and Roosevelt leaves him with the impression that if he, Roosevelt, were Secretary of War, there would be enough baking powder."[6]

Liebling hooked up with Teddy, Jr., and the Big Red One in February of '43 and stayed with them through much of the ultimately victorious Tunisian campaign. The *New Yorker* writer called North Africa's scruffy terrain the Foamy Fields. Liebling saw a fair amount of action when the Fighting First finally began pushing east. Yet his only close brush with death came while still encamped at Thélepte, a few days after the Me 109 breakfast strafing.

"I have at last joined the large legion of Hairsbreadth Harries who have narrow escape stories to bore people with," Liebling wrote to an old New York friend. At noon on the day he was scheduled to leave Thélepte, Liebling had just loaded his gear and climbed into an idling jeep when cannon shells began exploding.

I leaped out of the jeep and lit running and somebody yelled "Down!" and I dived for the ground so hard I tore a lot of skin off my hands and knees and elbows and lay there wishing my ass didn't stick so far up in the air while the Messerschmitts made their first pass. . . . All I could think of was "Joe Liebling has been a nice guy and it's been a pleasure knowing him," and I was awfully sorry that I would never know how Liebling's life was going to come out.[7]

As the enemy fighters reorganized to make a second run, Liebling raced across the runway and piled into a slit trench. He lay there, face buried, until the attack was over. Liebling was amazed that he hadn't been hit: a series of shell craters "like the marks of a rake" were embedded just yards from the jeep.

THE FIRST DAY OR TWO of Hitler's reaction to the Allied landings in French Morocco and Algiers may have been sluggish, but he made up for it in a hurry. Nazi commandoes seized the Tunisian ports, while transport planes and ferries rushed tens of thousands of reinforcements across the Mediterranean from southern France, Sicily, and Italy.[8] Once the Vichy French capitulated, the Allies under Eisenhower (at least nominally: Ike never truly asserted control over the North African battle zone) began probing east toward Algeria's border with Tunisia while the British Eighth Army under Montgomery pushed west through the Libyan desert from Egypt.

The German high command's gambit meant that they now had the firepower to strengthen their grip on Tunisia and disrupt the Allies' pincer movement. It also meant Germany's onetime wunderkind, Erwin Rommel, whom Joe Liebling wrote had a "hypnotic influence" over Hitler, had time to reassemble his Afrika Korps in the remote mountains of Tunisia, plotting ways to bedevil the Allies.[9]

In the midst of these Nazi machinations, Churchill and Roosevelt met in mid-January under extraordinary security several hundred miles west in Casablanca. The photo opportunities were spectacular: Wire services ran shots of FDR visiting the Ninth Infantry, Churchill and FDR touring the countryside, and bitter French rivals Charles de Gaulle and Henri Giraud exchanging a sickly handshake at the insistence of FDR, who approached byzantine geopolitics with the same cheekiness he employed to paper over differences among Democratic Party chieftains.

At Casablanca George Marshall revived his plea for a cross-Channel assault in 1943 but was again rebuffed by Churchill. An aggressive assault on Sicily, the British PM argued, might knock Italy out of the Axis and reroute German divisions away from Stalin's front—and maybe away from northern France, too. Marshall dismissed Churchill's strategy as "periphery-picking."[10] But the Brits, FDR conceded—perhaps too happily—still had the upper hand. All parties agreed to invade Sicily once Axis troops were ejected from North Africa.

Churchill's claim that a sustained Mediterranean offensive would inflict a deathblow on Hitler was exaggerated—and FDR and Marshall knew it. But like his decision to light Torch, FDR made the correct call in overruling his chief. Churchill's analysis may have been off-base—and he had at least one eye focused on protecting Britain's possessions in the Middle and Near East—but the PM's conclusion was accurate: The Allies were nowhere near ready to launch a cross-Channel attack.

FDR, too, had a hyperbolic moment at Casablanca—and it was one that Allied field commanders would come to regret almost as much as Churchill's prevarications. At the concluding press conference, FDR stunned everyone by announcing that the Allies would accept nothing short of "unconditional surrender." Knowing it would play well with an American electorate still disgusted with the murky ending of World War I, FDR was consciously—and disingenuously—evoking General U. S. Grant's famous demand to the Confederate commander at Fort Donelson during the early days of the Civil War.

Churchill, who later admitted he was caught unawares, deftly endorsed FDR's pronouncement.[11] Omar Bradley wasn't the only Allied field commander who believed FDR's impetuous declaration was a mistake, emboldening the enemy and perhaps prolonging the war.

AFTER BEING CHASED THROUGH NORTHERN Libya by Montgomery in the wake of El Alamein, Rommel was reinforced by General Jürgen von Arnim's divisions across the sea. The combined Axis armies now more or less matched the Allied presence in North Africa. But Rommel and von Arnim knew that time favored the Allies. What they didn't know was that British Intelligence, now privy to the codebooks that fueled the Germans' compromised Enigma code, was reading their secret communiqués with Berlin.

Ultra machine intercepts told the Allies when enemy ships, oil tankers, and aircraft were heading toward Tunisia; German supply sources were blown up with such regularity that the enemy commanders understood they had to move quickly or be bled dry.

It helped Rommel and von Arnim that nasty weather and indecisive leadership undercut the Allied advance. A gloomy Eisenhower that winter wrote a friend that the Allied operations in North Africa "will be condemned, in their entirety, by all . . . War College classes for the next twenty-five years."[12]

In late January, the Germans struck, eventually capturing Faïd Pass and cordoning off eastern Tunisia. The big blow came on Valentine's Day when, as foretold by Ultra, Rommel launched a blitzkrieg reminiscent of Western Europe in the spring of '40: a vicious armored thrust toward the strategically critical Kasserine Pass in the Atlas Mountains, spearheaded by shrieking Stuka dive-bombers.

Rommel's prey was the American II Corps, green GIs commanded by General Fredendall, whom historians invariably describe as "weak" and "bombastic."[13] Fredendall talked tough but retreated into a reclusive lair when the firing started. "His 'command post,'" Omar Bradley wrote, "was an embarrassment to every American soldier: a deep underground shelter dug or blasted by two hundred engineers in an almost inaccessible canyon far to the rear."[14]

From his bunker Fredendall ordered a pair of counterattacks but both boomeranged. Besieged Americans, including Andy Rooney's old artillery regiment, the 17th, began surrendering and deserting en masse: Germans poured through the Kasserine Pass.[15] British officers, appalled by the spectacle, scornfully called GIs "our Italians."[16]

In early March, Eisenhower replaced Fredendall with George Patton, who at Ike's direction had been planning the coming invasion of Sicily. But the Supreme Commander smartly hedged his bets by appointing Bradley as Patton's deputy; Ike encouraged Bradley to keep one eye on the battlefield and the other on Patton. Patton was even more bombastic than his predecessor, but wouldn't have been caught dead in an underground dugout.

Despite its breakthrough, the Africa Korps lacked the firepower to exploit the opening. After annihilating Fredendall, Rommel turned north, hoping to split the Allied armies. Four days of wild combat ensued, with Americans rushing in fresh troops from Oran and the Army Air Force finally flexing its muscles. Eleven days after launching his offensive, the Desert Fox conceded defeat, retreating back through the Kasserine Pass and into the mountainous Mareth Line. He had lost a thousand men, but had killed, wounded, or captured six times that number.[17]

Suffering from nervous exhaustion, Rommel was told by superiors in Berlin to come home. Patton and his II Corps, joined by the British First Army, pressured the Afrika Korps from the north, winning a tank battle at El Guettar, while the British Eighth kept up its harassment from the south. The great American triumph of the North African campaign came at Hill 609 outside Mateur, which fell on May 1 after days of bloody fighting. Hill 609's capture, wrote Eisenhower, was "final proof that the American ground forces had come fully of age."[18] Within days, the Axis armies surrendered. More than a quarter million German and Italian soldiers were bagged in one swoop; another sixty thousand had been killed or wounded. Allied casualties in North Africa were almost as catastrophic: Some seventy thousand were killed, wounded, or captured.

Churchill's objectives, which had reluctantly become the U.S.'s, too, had been secured. The Axis had been kicked out of Africa, the Suez Canal was no longer threatened, and Germany was no longer poised to gobble up the Middle East.[19]

HAL BOYLE WITNESSED ALMOST EVERY decisive moment of the Tunisian campaign. The Ousseltia Valley in central Tunisia was a hundred miles or so south of the Mediterranean on the Eastern Dorsal plateau and some sixty miles northwest of the Kasserine Pass. Defense of the Ousseltia had been assigned to a Free French army of thirty-five thousand, but after a combined force of German and Italians suddenly surfaced, the Allied command hurried the First Division and other outfits to the valley. Boyle was there on January 23 with the 26th Regimental Combat Team when American bombers and ground artillery attacked an Axis stronghold.

"From high ground above the valley I could see through field glasses the columns of debris and smoke thrown up as 105-millimeter shells hit among the entrenched Germans," Boyle wrote. American artillerymen deliberately kept their shelling irregular so the enemy couldn't time an advance or retreat. When the "harassed Nazis" called in air support hoping the planes would draw fire from the hidden American batteries, the Americans responded in kind. Soon a bevy of P-40 fighters and A-20 bombers "chased [the enemy] from the skies." A few minutes after noon, Allied bombers unleashed a fierce pounding.

A Free French infantryman had been captured but managed to escape during the pandemonium caused by the Allied bombing. The bombing "threw them [the enemy] into great confusion," the Frenchmen told American officers, "and I managed to slip out of the ammunition truck in which they were holding me. A few seconds later that truck and another ammunition truck were hit and blown up by the plane's bombs."[20]

One Big Red One officer enthused that the joint air-artillery bombardment was one of the best-coordinated attacks of the North African campaign. Two other air raids were launched before dark that day, evidence of increasing Allied air superiority, Boyle maintained—an assertion he probably came to regret three weeks later when Stukas and Messerschmitts were scattering American troops all over central Tunisia. The *Post* headlined its article GERMANS BLASTED FROM STONGHOLD IN TUNISIA, a claim that didn't quite jibe with Boyle's next-to-last paragraph. Axis infantry, "despite the bombardment," had managed to infiltrate into the mountains west of the valley.[21]

Two days later, Boyle was still in the Ousseltia, this time riding in a jeep near the front lines with a twenty-five-year-old First Army captain from Long Island named William Byrne. Boyle was again impressed by how air and artillery strikes worked "in perfect unison" to thwart the enemy advance. His article was written in blow-by-blow diary form; it is excerpted here in its raw and unedited "cable-ese." It offers a revealing snapshot of life at the Tunisian front.

PRESS
VIA CABLE TO

ASSOCIATED PRESS
LONDON

Censored Boyles 12317—With American Army in Africa, Jan. 25, 1943—Jerry took it on lam today as American forces broke backbone of threatening German drive down Ousseltia Valley in best coordinated attack put on by Uncle Sam's boys since they came to Tunisia on detour to Berlin Paragraph

In one daylong All-American push which saw tanks artillery and infantry teaming in perfect unison Nazis were slapped back several miles to head of valley and doughboys grabbed and held mountain heights insuring allied control of road to Kairouan vital enemy supply link Paragraph

By eleven thirty a.m., Boyle was pinned down on a hillside by machine gun fire that zipped "like angry bees over our heads." The whining bullets made Boyle wonder if Mary Frances had paid his life insurance. It would have served her right if she hadn't, Boyle joked. Fifteen minutes later the

Missourian was likening artillery noise to the "murmurous sounds" of a Keats or Tennyson poem and wondering why he wasn't teaching English somewhere in the Ozarks.

Five hours later, Boyle was comparing the tumult of an enemy counterattack "to the sounds of ten thousand kids outside your window on the Fourth of July only these firecrackers are playing for keeps." As the fire grew ferocious, Boyle couldn't resist taking a quick look-see. "Just one quick glimpse," Boyle wrote in cable-ese, "and machine gun bullet has me biting sand and shooting backward on my belly like a crab stop Its pleasure to skin hands in such worthwhile cause Paragraph."

He ended the piece by observing that American soldiers were trying to end the war the only way they knew how: by ferreting out the enemy. "Tonight they will know neither food nor sleep dash only the terrible loneliness of clashing in battle in midnight blackness with foe stop Tomorrow some will be dead stop None will be defeated."[22]

How journalists such as Boyle and Norgaard had the poise to jot down names, ages, and hometowns with machine gun fire whizzing all around is remarkable—but they did it all the time. It's clear from the telegrams and letters Boyle was receiving from his bosses in New York that they were delighted with his impressionist style and nudging him to do more of it.

A week later, the peripatetic Boyle heard a story about a German soldier caught "roaring drunk" while pushing a stalled motorcycle up a road near Medjez el Bab in northern Tunisia. The soldier "had gotten muzzy on native wine and stolen the motorcycle. Somewhere along the road he had met with an accident. His face was bloody and the machine smashed and he was singing half to himself when an American patrol overtook him. Not at all displeased by capture, he submitted readily to a soldier who took the motorcycle while the others took away the singing and hiccoughing prisoner."[23]

A road incident that Boyle described for readers a few days later was less amusing. Sergeant Dan L. Mullis, a twenty-one-year-old antitank specialist from Georgia, found himself surrounded by German tanks moving through the Ousseltia. Several members of Mullis' outfit were killed; as the enemy approached, Mullis jumped into a ditch with fallen comrades and played dead. For a few minutes, his ruse worked but enemy soldiers in a passing half-track hauled him into custody. Halfway toward the rear, Mullis' German captor, "about thirty years of age and about one-half drunk," forced Mullis at gunpoint to show him how to operate the machine gun on a captured American truck, then made him join the German caravan. After subsisting for two days on bread and a little water, Mullis and other American prisoners were dumped into a truck with French captives. Three or four miles up the road, Mullis' truck was machine-gunned by Free Frenchmen hidden in the hills who had no idea that the vehicle contained Allied prisoners. One American and two French prisoners were killed; fifteen were wounded. The driver of the truck ran off; their German guard was mortally wounded. Mullis was fortunate: He escaped serious injury and eluded enemy patrols.[24]

When Boyle and other correspondents in northern Tunisia heard about Rommel's offensive in mid-February, they scrambled southward. Three days into the German drive Boyle filed an article that cracked the lead pages of the *New York Times* and *Washington Post* as well as the *Stars and Stripes*. "As one who has slept and eaten in the field for almost two months of steadily more successful operations with every branch of the American Army, I had my first opportunity to see how they reacted when the going really got tough," Boyle wrote.

To ensure that his piece would pass muster with censors, Boyle avoided panicky descriptions. Still, one can sense the battlefield chaos Boyle witnessed when he wrote, "As one who watched for three straight days as American tank men threw away their lives in a gamble to stem the onward avalanche of the German armored force, I for one, couldn't question the decision to withdraw. That's why German patrols roam the plains of the Sbeitla-Feriana Valley tonight."[25]

Just three months into being a war correspondent, Boyle had figured out ways to outsmart the censors. His third paragraph casts the retreat in upbeat terms yet makes it abundantly clear that it was a rout. "Out into the long valley and into the hills they marched and rolled on wheels— thousands of American soldiers fighting mad because they had to march backward toward New York instead of forward toward Tunis and Sfax." He also adroitly handled the fact that Rommel had essentially overrun Joe Liebling's pals at the Thélepte airdrome (barely two weeks after Liebling departed) by pointing out that all Allied planes had been flown to safety instead of writing that the Germans now had control over a vital airstrip.

Boyle ended the piece with a poignant vignette of French soldiers and American tankmen exchanging the V for victory sign, even as American tanks raced away from the advancing enemy.[26]

JOE LIEBLING AND HAL BOYLE must have encountered one another in the new mobile press camp that Army public relations had proudly deployed in midcampaign. For correspondents, the early days of Torch were a filing nightmare. They were supposed to submit their stories for transmission back home at Army message centers that tended to be poorly equipped and erratically staffed. When they learned that the message centers weren't reliable, reporters began giving carbons and oilskins willy-nilly to pilots, Army couriers, jeep and truck drivers—anyone heading toward the rear. If through some miracle an article reached Allied Force Headquarters, an Army wireless could, at least in theory, transmit the message back to the States. But even going through HQ didn't guarantee success.[27] It was driving reporters, their employers, and their PRO handlers up a wall.

Enter Brigadier General Robert McClure, the director of information services in the North African theater, and Lieutenant Colonel Joseph Phillips, the former managing editor of *Newsweek*. In early '43, the pair devised a mobile field press camp that became the template for future press operations in the Mediterranean and European theaters. Besides facilitating the gathering of battlefield news, it fed and housed correspondents, transported them to the front lines, and relayed their dispatches via Army teleprinters and air couriers to Allied HQ.

"As a result," Boyle wrote in early '43, "reporters who used to have to hunt for a foxhole out of the wind to spread their blankets for a night's sleep now are quartered in a small tent city which can accommodate up to 50 correspondents with cots, good Army food, a place to work and—at the moment—even a place to swim and sun themselves."[28]

Liebling and Boyle both befriended the bearded Jack "The Bear" Thompson of the *Chicago Daily Tribune*. Thompson told Boyle that the press camp had changed his own modus operandi so much it was "like hunting buffaloes in a place and coming back later and finding it in the middle of an oil boom."[29]

The press camp made their lives easier—but it didn't make gathering news any easier, Boyle told readers. Reporters spent much of their day "in open-air jeeps, riding sometimes 100 miles to reach a fresh battle sector. It is usually necessary to spend most of the day visiting various frontline units, interviewing soldiers on their experiences and learning at first hand the details and progress of the operation. In such positions correspondents are as exposed as the average soldier to battle injury and death. Then after collecting the news the correspondent must ride 100 miles back to the press headquarters, keeping a watchful eye out all the way for strafing enemy planes which like to pick off jeeps because they are easy targets. Before he can eat he often must sit down and write his news dispatch by wavering candlelight to make a deadline. After a cold dinner he is usually too tired then to do anything else but crawl into his bedroll."[30]

His piece lauding the new operation was a testament to Boyle-ian detail, listing the name and hometown of practically every jeep driver, mess cook, and motor pool mechanic. "Upon the broad shoulders of stocky Acting Sergeant Frank Lazio, 27, of 18 Independence Ave., Freeport, Long Island, falls the heaviest grief of the whole setup—the task each morning of putting 30 to 45 correspondents and photographers, each with his own idea of what part of the battlefront he wants to cover, into fourteen hardworking little jeeps. 'Sometimes I dream of heaven,' says Frankie, a former women's clothing designer in New York to whom everyone, correspondents, army officers and local Arabs, bring their troubles. '[Heaven] is a place with one thousand jeeps with self-filling gas tanks and self-repairing tires, and only five correspondents to put in them.'"[31]

BOYLE AND LIEBLING, TWO LITERATI who enjoyed slugging alcohol while ruminating over great books, or boxing, or women, became fast friends.

Liebling referenced Boyle in several pieces, expressing admiration for his pal's combat profiles and light writing touch. Boyle, for his part, loved Liebling's wry sense of humor. The *New Yorker* writer was with Boyle one day when, just as a German artillery shell exploded "with a fearful bang," someone offered Liebling a drink of water. "No, thanks," Liebling rejoined, "but would you mind throwing a little in my face?"[32]

Boyle recounted Liebling's quip in late April in the column he had begun calling Leaves from a War Correspondent's Notebook. Without consulting his AP superiors, Boyle started the column while still in Morocco in late '42. The title was meant to evoke another one of Boyle's poet heroes, Walt Whitman and his *Leaves of Grass*. Sometimes Boyle's feature was a collection of amusing anecdotes about soldiers' lives; at other times, it was a deadly serious look at the human cost of war. It proved enormously popular, not only with readers but with editors, too. One week in early '43 Boyle failed to submit a column and his editors dashed off a wire asking why. Between his round-the-clock combat reportage and his column, Boyle was the most prolific correspondent in North Africa. Ernie Pyle faced deadline pressures with his near-daily column, but Pyle never had the kind of hour-to-hour coverage responsibilities that Boyle experienced.

The Irish shanachie was never afraid to engage in a little showmanship for the sake of a good story. Two weeks after Rommel's breakthrough at Kasserine, Boyle hit on a column idea reminiscent of the peacetime Pyle: Hal would start hitchhiking in Tunisia and see how far he could get in twenty-four hours. His "thumb voyage" began in midafternoon when he was picked up by a weapons carrier tugging a thirty-seven-millimeter gun. It ended twenty-three hours and four hundred miles later when he was dropped off by a twenty-eight-year-old WAAC who was transporting a group of Army Air Force fliers in her jeep. Along the way he encountered artillerymen, medical officers, a black quartermaster sergeant who had a truck full of chewing gum, signal corpsmen, two British military policemen, a French civilian driving a fancy car, a C-47 pilot evacuating wounded GIs, and, finally, Sergeant Joan James of Brighton, Massachusetts, and her jeep full of flyboys.

"You start off in a jolting weapons carrier and four hundred miles later a pert brunette WAAC drives you to your journey's end in a jeep. What other country—even wide, bountiful America—has hitch-hiking like that?"[33] The *Kansas City Star* ran the column with a cartoon showing a grinning Boyle waving to Sergeant James.

BOYLE DIDN'T NEED TO HITCHHIKE to see George Patton. Sizing up George Smith Patton, Jr., became something of a Rorschach test for Mediterranean Theater of Operations (MTO) and ETO reporters. Andy Rooney saw Patton as a pathetic bully—an extension of the abusive officers he'd despised as an enlisted man. Rooney so disliked Patton that he was still hurling brickbats—and getting into a public pissing match with the general's survivors—six decades later. Homer Bigart saw Patton at his worst in Sicily and concluded he was bloodthirsty and megalomaniacal. Joe Liebling was offended by the way Patton and his Third Army glory-hogged their way through France in the late summer of 1944. Walter Cronkite, on the other hand, had a more tolerant view: Cronkite saw Patton at his best, rescuing the besieged 101st Airborne at Bastogne during the Battle of the Bulge in late '44.

But of our five principals, only Hal Boyle covered Patton extensively *before* he became an American idol. In fact, Boyle's early articles from North Africa helped forge the Patton mystique. Boyle saw a side of Patton that the others didn't: the savior of the demoralized II Corps. As Boyle put it a year later, "[Patton] took a defeated but still fighting American force after the Kasserine debacle, shook it back into shape, gave it confidence, and led it to victory at Gafsa and El Guettar."[34]

Indeed, as early as day four of the Moroccan operation, Boyle's bosses were requesting a profile of the prickly invasion commander who supposedly tough-talked Vichy into a quick submission. When a Darlan sycophant wielding a white flag approached Patton about negotiating a surrender, Boyle quoted the general as saying, "I will discuss an armistice when the troops in front of my troops lay down their guns! Not before!"[35]

Boyle was on hand as first Moroccan and then Algerian potentates fêted Patton in their palaces, giving the general a chance to flaunt his impeccable French and show off a chestful of medals. The AP reporter was close to the front lines on March 16 and 17 when Patton's troops surged toward Gafsa. Boyle described Gafsa as an Allied "victory," but in truth, the Axis forces, mainly Italian, fled before the attack was launched. "The Dagoes beat it" before he got there, a disgusted Patton told his diary.[36]

For Boyle, however, Patton's most affecting moment in North Africa came a few days later at El Guettar. Hollywood's depiction of El Guettar in the biopic exaggerated both Patton's role and the skirmish's importance in the North African campaign. In truth, it wasn't all that pivotal and it was fought, from the U.S. perspective, strictly on the defensive. American forces held the high ground and were smart enough not to leave it. Still, Omar Bradley called El Guettar "The first solid, indisputable defeat we inflicted on the German army in the war."[37] American GIs drove from the field a battle-hardened Tenth Panzer Division that had decimated Polish, British, and French troops.

But the real heroes at El Guettar, Bradley recognized, were the men defending Keddab Ridge that early morning: the Brooklyn Bums, the boys in the Big Red One. "The Hun will soon learn to dislike that outfit," Eisenhower gloated.[38]

Boyle was standing near Patton at El Guettar when the general got the news that his aide, young Captain Richard Jensen, had been killed. The artillery shell that struck Jensen came dangerously close to hitting Omar Bradley, too. Jensen was, Boyle explained to readers, Patton's "personal aide and member of a California family closely allied to the Pattons for three generations." [39] Patton sobbed when told the news and continued breaking down for days afterward. It became one of Boyle's most powerful memories of the war, a story he told numerous times to his wife, Frances, and daughter, Tracy.[40]

"CONFUSION IS NORMAL IN COMBAT" went a hoary military saying. Joe Liebling became so taken with the adage—and with the resilient First Division infantrymen who lived it day after day—that he used it as the title of a collection of his pieces on North Africa.

Late in the afternoon of Easter Sunday in 1943, Liebling and Boyle were riding in a jeep along *la piste forestière*, the dirt "foresters' track" that connected Cap Serrat on Tunisia's Mediterranean coast to villages two dozen miles inland. They were anxious to get back to the press camp before nightfall: Once the sun disappeared, their jeep would have to give way to two-and-a-half-ton supply trucks barreling down the blacked-out road. With tanks and troops clogging almost every inch, it would have been quicker to walk, Liebling concluded. There was plenty of time for Boyle to climb out of the jeep and buttonhole soldiers.

Boyle was chatting with passing GIs when his companion spotted a body lying by the side of the road. Liebling got out to inspect.

"A blanket covered his face, so I surmised that it had been shattered, but there was no blood on the ground, so I judged that he had been killed in the brush and carried down to the road to await transport," Liebling observed. He asked a sergeant, a "hawk-nosed, red-necked man with a couple of front teeth missing," about the corpse's identity.

"That's Mollie. Comrade Molotov. The Mayor of Broadway," blurted the sergeant. "Didn't you ever hear of him? Jeez, Mac, he once captured six hundred Eytealians by himself and brought them all back along with him. Sniper got him, I guess."[41]

So began Joe Liebling's tortured "Quest for Mollie," the story that consumed him for the rest of his life. When Liebling learned that most of the sergeant's improbable account was true—that Private Mollie had (more or less) single-handedly brought in hundreds of Italian prisoners and was indeed a slippery character from the shadows of Broadway, Liebling became obsessed with piecing together Mollie's story. Boyle, too, wrote about Mollie, but the story never haunted him the way it did his friend.

By happenstance a few weeks later, on board a steamer heading back to the States, Liebling ran into some wounded men from Mollie's company. No one seemed to know what his real name was, but everybody had a couple of Mollie stories.

A GI confined to a wheelchair remembered how irked Mollie had been to discover, upon arriving in North Africa, that he couldn't telegraph his racetrack bets to his bookie. "'Vot a schvindle!' That was his favorite saying—'Vot a schvindle!' He was always bitching about something. He used to go out scouting with [field] glasses, all alone, and find the enemy and tip Major [Michael] Kauffman off where they were," the disabled man told Liebling.

Mollie packed a stash of cash and wasn't shy about telling people it was illicit booty—that he'd gotten rich from some "racket." He supposedly never shot craps for less than fifty bucks a roll. But for Liebling, the clincher came when the writer learned that Mollie swore he never saluted an officer ranked beneath brigadier general or screwed a woman below an actress.[42]

At least in fervid imagination, Mollie became Liebling's kind of guy: a big-talking New York immigrant kid who, much like the writer's Bowery-bred old man, knew how to play street con. In memoriam, Mollie became Liebling's beau ideal: GI Joe by way of Damon Runyon.

A couple of pals on the troopship thought Mollie's real name had been something like Carl Warren. Whether Mollie or Warren, Liebling confirmed through his company commander, now Lieutenant Colonel Michael S. Kauffman, that the private had, in fact, been instrumental in the capture of more than six hundred Italian troops.

At dawn on March 23, 1943, in the hills surrounding Sened Station, a remote Tunisian rail depot, Mollie and an Italian-speaking buddy, Private First Class De Marco, watched as skittish Italian infantrymen began surrendering in singles and pairs. It occurred to Mollie and De Marco that others might be similarly persuaded. Bearing a white flag, they crawled up to the enemy trenches. With De Marco serving as translator, they managed to coax 147 enemy infantrymen down the hill. Once Mollie directed artillery fire to pound the enemy position, the remaining Italians got the message. Soon some five hundred other *soldati* were scrambling down the hill, hands held aloft. The incredulous Kauffman put Mollie in for a Distinguished Service Cross, but Mollie's record was too checkered. He had to settle for a Silver Star, which ended up being awarded posthumously.

Back in New York in the summer of '43, Liebling played a hunch that Carl Warren was Karl C. Warner, a private listed in the *New York Times* as killed in action in Tunisia. Liebling found Warner's sister, a Mrs. Ulidjak, living in a downscale tenement on East Eighty-eighth Street. "A thin, pale woman with a long, bony face and straight blond hair pulled back into a bun came to the apartment door," Liebling wrote.

Mrs. Ulidjak had heard a few weeks before of her brother's demise. She asked if he had been killed fighting Japs and seemed disappointed when Liebling told her no, that her brother was slain fighting Germans and Italians. Warner, it turned out, had been a Mollie pretense: Their family name was Petuskia. They were Russian immigrants who'd settled in coal-country Pennsylvania before moving to the city. When told of Mollie's heroics outside Sened Station, his sister, in the presence of neighbors of Italian descent, exclaimed: "Six hundred wops!"

Her brother had been a busboy and bartender at Jimmy Kelly's, a Greenwich Village nightclub. Mollie, it turned out, had been an outspoken union guy who looked out for fellow workers. When Mollie had had a little downtime, he chatted up well-heeled patrons. "The customers didn't seem to mind," a bartender told Liebling. "[Mollie] had a nice way about him."[43]

Mollie's old mates had howled when Liebling told them about the wad of bills that Mollie always had in his pocket in Tunisia. While working at Kelly's, he had been forever bumming money, but they had been so fond of him they didn't care.

Liebling loved New Yorkers who dreamed big and lived large. Mollie, Liebling wrote, was "fond of high living, which is the only legitimate incentive for liking money. . . . I lived with him so long that I once half-convinced myself he was not dead."

At one point Liebling became so infatuated with Mollie that he began writing a play about him until theater friends pointed out that "it is customary for the protagonist of a work of that nature to remain alive until the last act." Instead, Liebling ended up giving Private First Class Karl C. Warner a eulogy for the ages.

> When I walk through the East Side borderland between
> Times Square and the slums, where Mollie once lived, I
> often think of him and his big talk and his golf suit grin.
> It cheers me to think there may be more like him all
> around me—a notion I would have dismissed as sheer ro-

manticism before World War II. Cynicism is often the shamefaced product of inexperience.[44]

"Quest for Mollie" became a Liebling signature, an essay that, at least for a time, appeared in anthologies. The piece is dedicated to Boyle, Liebling's friend and Tunisian jeep mate. Had Hal been less affable and less keen to kibbitz with GIs, Liebling never would have spotted Mollie's corpse.

ANDY ROONEY HAD GOTTEN TO know Homer Bigart in early '43 on the trains going back and forth to East Anglia while covering the bombing war. Like every reporter who read Bigart's stuff, Rooney was awed by his friend's "incomparable" writing.[45]

Harrison Salisbury, the United Press editor, had arrived in London two weeks after Bigart. Salisbury first encountered the *Herald Tribune* reporter in an ancient University of London lecture hall that had been reconfigured as a press bullpen by the Ministry of Information.

"[Bigart] was alone, a slim, almost frail figure hunched over his Olivetti, slowly punching with two or three fingers, often pausing, often X-ing out words, often consulting notes, often looking out into space before resuming. He gave no sign that he saw me nor the oak-stained walls. . . . He was alone in the corridors of his mind."[46]

The solitary figure's reporting on air operations was so penetrating that peers knew instantly that Bigart was destined to achieve great things. Cronkite may have been the first to glimpse Bigart's genius, since the UP reporter read his friend and "rival's" copy almost every day for months as they went back and forth to Molesworth. In Salisbury's mind, Bigart became *the* war correspondent of the ETO.[47] Rooney, for his part, always regarded Bigart and Liebling as the two best reporter/writers operating in Europe, with Boyle not far behind.

Bigart and Rooney got a break from their coverage of the air war in late May 1943. Along with other correspondents, they were flown from London to Oran to witness King George VI's triumphant visit to Allied troops. The British brass pulled out all the stops; newsreel cameramen and photographers captured every moment of the king's interaction with Tommies and GIs, just three weeks removed from obliterating the Wehrmacht.

Bigart and Rooney were assembled at a British officers' club with fourteen other members of the press. Flustered PR advance men insisted that the reporters stand at awkward attention as the monarch made his way toward the receiving line.

"It is important to this story to remind you," Rooney wrote in his memoirs, "that both King George and Homer stammered badly. Both of them had great difficulty getting out their words."

The first correspondent the king singled out was International News Service's Bob Considine, the prominent sports columnist and author of the Doolitle raid account, *Thirty Seconds Over Tokyo*.

> "How ... how ... how ... da ... da ... do you ... you do?" the king inquired. "Who ... who ... whom ... da ... da ... do you ... rep ... rep ... repre ... represent?"
>
> And so it went for half dozen or more awkward exchanges. Finally His Highness reached Bigart.
>
> "How ... how ... are ... are ya ... ya ... you?" the king said, then moved on without lingering.
>
> Later, Homer, who always put everyone listening to him at ease with his sense of humor, said, "It's a ga ... it's a ga ... dodamn ... good thing, ta too. There ca ... could ... ha ... have ... ba been ... an inter ... international ... in ... incident."[48]

———

AFTER THE AXIS SURRENDER AT Bizerte, an impromptu victory celebration formed as Allied troops marched back toward the Mediterranean. Cheering Tunisians were lined up on both sides of the road. The scene reminded Hal Boyle of the torchlight parades that Boss Pendergast organized in Kansas City to rally the party faithful, with Boyle's old man proudly leading the pack.

Boyle happened to be riding in a jeep equipped with a loudspeaker. In midparade, probably after a few pulls on his flask, Boyle grabbed the microphone, stood up, and began chanting:

Vote for Boyle, son of toil!
Vote for Hal, the A-rab's pal!

The vast majority of his audience, of course, had no idea of what Boyle was yelling, but they were nevertheless tickled by his performance. "Vote for Boyle!" they parroted to the clueless British troops marching in Hal's wake.[49]

AFTER ENCOUNTERING MOLLIE, LIEBLING HOLED up at the Hotel Aletti in Algiers to organize his Tunisian notes. By Manhattan standards, the Aletti's amenities were crude, but after weeks of bunking in the field they seemed to Liebling like the Ritz. One could also "receive female visitors if they stood in well with the concierge," which was Liebling's euphemistic way of saying that if you hooked up with a lady of the evening, the Muslim clerk could be paid to look the other way.

Its milieu made the Hotel Aletti special—especially the view from the terraces overlooking the Mediterranean. "In the twilight, as we walked to our dinner, German planes would come like swallows out of Sicily, far away, and jettison their bombs before reaching the center of our magnificent antiaircraft display, like a beehive drawn in lines of orange tracer," Liebling recalled.[50]

He wasn't alone: Hal Boyle, Ernie Pyle, Jack Thompson, Boots Norgaard, John Daly of CBS, Don Coe of UP, Graham Hovey of INS, and John Steinbeck of the *Herald Tribune* were among the many U.S. correspondents who at one point or another that spring sipped black-market brandy on their Aletti verandas, watching Allied pilots duel with the Luftwaffe.[51]

"Then, in the dark after the third Armagnac," Liebling reminisced, "we would steal away to a place of enchantment called The Sphinx, where girls would act charades that graying members of the American Legion still dream of with nostalgia in Terre Haute."[52]

In its seven months, Operation Torch had run the gamut from Hal Boyle clinging to a coral reef in Morocco to Joe Liebling knocking back liquor on a hotel porch in Algiers. In between, the Allies had scored a bizarre but decisive victory over Adolf Hitler. For the first time, the Wehrmacht was on the run.

CHAPTER 5

★

BOMBING GERMANY WITH THE WRITING 69TH

Bomber bases were damn depressing places. Death was always in the air, even though the guys were trying hard to laugh and forget.

—Andy Rooney, 1995
My War

Andy Rooney had been in the wartime Army for nearly two years, yet until that instant had never seen a bullet fired in anger. Now, suddenly, as the B-17 *Banshee* cleared the Frisian Islands off the Dutch coast, thrumming toward Germany, a slew of Messerschmitts appeared out of nowhere, spitting orange-red death.

"Peeling out of the sun came shining silver German fighter planes, diving at one bomber in the formation and disappearing below the cloudbanks as quickly as they had come. They seemed tiny, hardly a machine of destruction, and an impossible target," Rooney wrote the next day, February 27, 1943, in a page-one *Stars and Stripes* story headlined HOW IT FEELS TO BOMB GERMANY. The piece ran with a head-and-shoulders photo of a grim-faced Rooney that was only marginally more flattering than the wanted-dead-or-alive mug shot taken a year earlier.

While in air combat, Rooney took the advice of crewmates and sat or stood on the heavy flak jacket that he'd been issued: Many airmen feared castration more than wounds to the chest. Rooney was crouched in the

Banshee's plastic nose, feeling claustrophobic as he craned his neck to spot enemy aircraft.

Two-thirds of the way across the North Sea, Rooney saw what he thought from his recognition training was an Me 109. "It whipped down through the clouds to our left," Rooney wrote. "From that time until three and one half hours later, when we were halfway home, no one had to look far to see German fighters." Rooney was amazed that *Banshee*'s crew could somehow follow the path of enemy fighters, calmly communicating over the intercom as their tormentors careered in and out of clouds.

"Here comes one at 2 o'clock, Elliot," Lieutenant Bill Casey, the pilot, told the top-turret gunner. "Get the son-of-a-bitch!" The gunner, Technical Sergeant Wilson Elliot of Detroit, was the only member left from *Banshee*'s original crew; the others, Rooney noted, had all been disabled or taken out of commission. And *Banshee* had been flying raids over the Third Reich for less than three months.

As it neared the U-boat pens at Wilhelmshaven, just north of Hamburg on the coast, the formation began to draw flak. "Deadly black puffs began to appear around us," Rooney wrote. "It seemed as though they were 'air mines' that were touched off as we came to them. A puff would appear to our right and then in quick succession a row of five more black splotches flowered out, each one closer as they caught up to us." After the mission, Rooney learned that the Germans had unveiled a deadly new antiaircraft weapon that day: "parachute flak" shrapnel that would be shot from cannisters on the ground, reach a certain elevation, then open its chute and explode.

Rooney marveled as pilot Casey toggled *Banshee* from side to side. "Lt. Casey zigged, and the puff appeared in the track of our zag. He was one jump ahead of the flak."[1]

Suddenly the zigzagging Casey's luck ran out. *Banshee* was rocked by a deafening hit. To Rooney, it seemed like the explosion took place six feet in front of the nose.

As the plane staggered, the Plexiglas appeared to Rooney to disintegrate. With shards of plastic spewing all around, Rooney watched bombardier Malcom Phillips, Jr., of Coffeyville, Kansas, fling his gloves over his eyes. It took Phillips a few seconds to recover from the shock and realize that he hadn't been hurt.

Rooney's eyes shot forward, fearing that he'd see the nose torn clean away. To his amazement, the damage seemed fairly minimal; the Plexiglas was intact, save for a jagged hole the size of a man's fist. Rooney watched as Phillips, on his first mission, violated a cardinal rule of high-altitude flying by taking off his gloves and trying to stuff the hole with them. Within seconds, the bombardier had lost feeling in his fingers; soon they were nearly frostbitten.

As his wits returned, it occurred to Rooney that despite the mayhem, the U.S. bombers had stayed together. From far above, Rooney was surprised to see farmers tending fields.

Navigator William H. Owens of Tullahoma, Tennessee, suddenly began struggling with a damaged oxygen tank. "I was healthy but helpless," Rooney confided.

Finally, the valve to Owens' air intake cut off completely; the navigator fainted, his head dropping on top of a fifty-caliber. Owens' face, Rooney wrote, took on the pallor of an "unlovely greyish purple."[2]

Pilot Casey got Rooney's attention and told him to come forward and grab an emergency mask from the cockpit. Rooney, who'd gotten a crash course three weeks earlier in oxygen maintenance, surprised himself by slipping the new mask around Owens' face with a minimum of fuss. Owens' head instantly jerked up. But now Rooney's own oxygen was running out as he stumbled back toward the cockpit. Casey nonchalantly grabbed an extra tank and hooked it into Rooney's mask. Within seconds, Rooney felt fine.[3]

As the U-boat base loomed on the horizon, Rooney watched the bomb bay doors swing open on the B-17 flying directly ahead. Above *Banshee*, he spotted a similar scene; the bombs seemed to be "hanging by some mechanical hairpin, waiting for the bombardier to push the tiny button that sends them to the target." His fellow air war correspondent Walter Cronkite remembered how agonizingly slow bombs fell. They seemed to "float" forever—so long that airmen in the planes below could read the graffiti the ground crew guys had scribbled: "To Hell with Hitler" or "Greetings from Mabel in Brooklyn."[4]

Rooney had packed a camera; despite unwieldy gloves, he was trying to get a picture of bombs falling. But he couldn't keep his hands still enough to get a decent shot. When *Banshee* released its payload, Rooney was surprised that he didn't feel more of a jolt.

As Rooney's group headed home, the tail gunner, Technical Sergeant Parley D. Small of Packwood, Iowa, reported that he'd seen a B-24 Liberator spiraling downward, one wing aflame. A few minutes later, Rooney saw three Junkers (Ju) 88s jump another crippled B-24 that had fallen out of formation. After a while, the Liberator disappeared from sight; Rooney couldn't be sure of its fate.

"After 20 minutes without sign of Jerry, things began to look more pleasant," Rooney wrote. Casey and the crew began singing over the intercom. As England came into view, the pilot told Rooney: "I'm an Irishman, southern Ireland, but that is still the best-looking damned little island I ever saw."

Rooney, another Irishman, was thrilled by the way *Banshee* buzzed the airdrome at Thurleigh, coming in at treetop level. When they hurtled to a stop, Rooney joined the crew in inspecting flak and fighter damage. *Banshee* had been hit in about ten different spots. There was a gaping tear a few feet from where tail gunner Small sat; the flak had seared a hole in a British penny that Small had tossed on the floor behind him. The crew had been lucky: the only wound they suffered was bombardier Phillips' frostbitten finger.

"*Banshee* had what the crew called 'a quiet trip,'" Rooney mused at the end.

His clinching sentence was classic Rooney, sharp and self-effacing: "I don't want to go on a noisy one."[5]

ROONEY, CRONKITE, BIGART, BOYLE, AND Liebling covered more than their share of noisy bombing missions. Rooney was on the air war beat almost from day one of the Eighth Army Air Force's operations in Britain, soon to be joined by Cronkite and Bigart. Liebling never covered the bombing war day to day, but some of his most memorable *New Yorker* pieces fêted airmen; Joe went on a B-26 mission over France in early '44. Boyle, for his part, filed dozens of pieces about bomber boys and fighter jocks; Hal went up a number of times in spotter and surveillance planes.

The bombing campaign against Nazi Germany is, in many ways, the most controversial, least understood, and least appreciated facet of the war in Europe. In part because it was so grisly and redundant, it tends to get overlooked. Yet dominance in the air ended up being, unquestionably, *the* decisive factor in the Allied victory over Nazi Germany. Ironically, it wasn't the damage that bombs inflicted on Hitler's cities, factories, and bases that swung the war in the Allies' favor. Instead, it was forcing the Luftwaffe to defend the Reich, then shooting down German fighters in such prodigious numbers that the Nazis couldn't possibly replace the pilots or machines. By mid-1944, Britain and the U.S. had destroyed so many enemy planes that the Allies had effective control of the air from the Irish Sea to the heart of the Reich.

Eisenhower vowed that when cross-Channel invaders saw planes in the air they could be secure in the knowledge that they were friendly; remarkably, Ike turned out to be correct.

It took two-plus years of intensive bombing and tens of thousands of Allied casualties to reach that point. Indeed, for an interminably long stretch in 1942, the only action against the Axis came in the Atlantic and in the skies over Europe. The Allies at that point had no continental army that could defeat the Germans, Churchill conceded. "But there is one thing that will bring [Hitler] . . . down, and that is an absolutely devastating, exterminating attack by very heavy bombers from this country upon the Nazi homeland."[6]

Churchill's air chief marshal, Arthur Harris, was known as "Bomber" Harris to Fleet Street reporters but "Butcher" Harris to British Royal Air Force (RAF) fliers because so many airmen died under his command.[7] Harris imposed what he called "area bombing," a euphemistic term that meant systematic nighttime raids of German cities. After the Cologne raid of May 1942 decimated six hundred acres of housing and damaged 350 factories, Harris was knighted. But as was so often the case in World War II, within weeks—if not days—the enemy plants were running at near capacity.

At the Casablanca conference in January 1943, Churchill and Roosevelt agreed to coordinate air attacks: Harris' RAF would attack German cities by night; General Carl Spaatz' USAAF would target defense installations by day.[8] In a top secret memorandum, the U.S. and Britain declared that the aim of the air offensive was to not only devastate Hitler's military and industrial power, but also to destroy his people's fighting spirit.

Yet the combined bombing offensive, for all its notoriety, didn't commence until mid '43. Early in the war, RAF had experimented with daylight bombing but switched exclusively to night attacks after suffering grievous losses. The Brits also soured on the notion of so-called "precision" attacks, preferring Harris' "area" technique.

American bombardiers and pilots, buoyed by the U.S. Navy–invented Norden bombsight, thought they could do their British counterparts one better. In the words of British historian John Keegan, "strategic bombing" combined three distinctly American characteristics: "moral scruple, historical optimism, and technological pioneering."[9]

In theory, strategic bombing was noble; in practice, it was something considerably less. The skies over the Third Reich—filled with clouds, smoke, flak, Focke-Wulfs, and Messerschmitts—proved far more daunting to precision bomb than the brilliant blue skies of the American Southwest, where the U.S. bomber boys had spent much of '42 and '43 rehearsing. The Norden bombsight itself, although a significant improvement over British technology, proved balky and overly complicated.[10]

As 1942 WORE ON AND the Eighth Army Air Force began to take root in and around London, American correspondents became smitten. For many, it was their only beat; they were determined to cover it with élan. Rooney later called the Eighth Air Force "one of the great fighting forces in the history of warfare. It had the best equipment and the best men, all but a handful of whom were civilian Americans, educated and willing to fight for their country and a cause they understood was in danger—freedom."[11]

When United Press editor Harrison Salisbury arrived in London in early '43, he was impressed by the former reporters, advertising executives, and Hollywood producers that were part of the Eighth's public relations machine. It was, in Salisbury's words, a "high-octane outfit"— professionals who knew how to manage the press for optimal effect.

"We were all on the same side then," Salisbury's UP colleague Cronkite recalled, "and most of us newsmen abandoned any thought of impartiality as we reported on the heroism of our boys and [the] bestiality of the hated Nazis."[12]

When the convoy that Cronkite accompanied in August of '42 arrived at Greenock, Scotland, it deposited the 820th Engineer Aviation Battalion and hundreds of tons of construction equipment. The engineers and their bulldozers made their way south to the flatlands an hour's drive or so north of London, where they immediately began building one airfield after another. East Anglia soon became "a mosaic of aerodromes five miles apart," remarked one British Air Ministry official.

Although quickly slapped together, each base was its own village, complete with a post exchange (PX), a movie theater, a baseball diamond, and separate clubs for enlisted men and officers. Apparently bottomless supplies of soda pop, candy bars, and cigarettes could be had on the cheap and sometimes gratis at the PX.

General Carl A. "Tooey" Spaatz came to London to take command of American air operations. Spaatz was a Great War hero who, in limited action, had splattered three of the kaiser's biplanes. He and his handpicked head of the Eighth Air Force, Brigadier General Ira C. Eaker, another one-time fighter jock, were convinced that the war could be won through the brute application of air power.[13]

The right kind of bombing, Spaatz and Eaker argued, would exact so much damage on the Reich that it would effectively preclude the need for sustained ground operations. Having witnessed practice runs in New Mexico and Arizona, Spaatz and Eaker also maintained that U.S. bombers could carry out daytime precision bombing without undue loss of life and machinery. Finally, they believed that their bombers could fly long-range missions, penetrating deep into enemy territory, without protection from fighter escorts.[14]

All three theories would be sorely tested—and found wanting.

———

ANDY ROONEY'S FIRST BYLINE ON a bombing raid story—what would become over the next eighteen months his stock-in-trade—came in the December 22, 1942, edition of the *Stars and Stripes*. It described the toughest U.S. bombing foray yet attempted, an attack on the huge Nazi airfield at Romilly-sur-Seine, not far from Paris. Although Rooney was not permitted to identify the bomb group or its airfield, he was with the 306th at Thurleigh (pronounced "Thir-lie") when the planes returned.

> Some of them came home on two engines, with gaping holes in their wings and fuselage; some of them flopped down to pancake landings because their controls had been shot up in the fiercest fighting of the air war over Europe; some of them slithered into home base on their bellies. Six of them didn't come back at all.
>
> But the Flying Fortresses and Liberators and their crews who fought their way to bomb the Romilly-sur-Seine Nazi air park there to smithereens and then fought their way home again had some of the war's best stories of sky combat to tell.
>
> The Forts told their yarns with mute scars in the bodies, with dead engines and shattered props—and with empty bomb racks and empty ammunition belts.[15]

Early in the war, northern France was full of well-stocked Nazi airfields; sixty or more German fighters harassed the Romilly-sur-Seine raiders from every direction. Thirty-seven Forts were lost or damaged that day—a figure that seemed staggering but proved minuscule as the war wore on.

ROONEY HAD BEEN SPRUNG free: He didn't have to worry about early morning reveille or snap barracks inspections anymore. He was more or less on his own in wartime London. It was love at first sight.

"The whole scene in London was a constant source of interest to any young American there," Rooney recalled. "Tens of thousands of Londoners routinely brought their mattresses, blankets, and burners with which to make hot tea down into the cavernous subway stations."[16]

It amused Rooney that SHAEF headquarters at 20 Grosvenor Square had four antiaircraft zeppelins tethered directly overhead. "They were designed to obstruct any low-level bomb run by the Luftwaffe, but in fact they made an obvious target of the headquarters building. HERE! HERE! HERE! the balloons shouted to the bombardier overhead," Rooney joked.[17]

The Bethnal Green tube station in the East End was one of Rooney's regular stops. On the evening of March 3, 1943, air raid sirens began blaring, with Rooney located several blocks away. As he jogged toward Bethnal Green's entrance he saw thousands of panicked people trying to jam onto its moving steps. Wary of such a big crowd, he wisely decided to take his chances aboveground. When the escalator malfunctioned, more than 170 people were crushed to death. Ironically, it turned out to be a false alarm: No Nazi bombs fell on the East End that night. War Ministry officials insisted that the location and number of fatalities be kept out of the press. Londoners learned their lesson; after the Bethnal Green tragedy, there was less pandemonium during raids. More and more Londoners stopped seeking shelter in the tube at all.

In addition to Rooney's Army pay, he was given a per diem to offset living expenses, so he could afford a more than occasional meal out. He and another *Stars and Stripes* staffer, photographer Dick Koenig, shared a basement hovel on Clarges Street in Piccadilly. An enterprising lady of the evening occupied the apartment directly overhead. Her creaky bedsprings caused Rooney and Koenig so many sleepless nights that they were forced to find a new place in Hyde Park. Their flat may have had an elegant address—11 Palace Court—but it was just a two-roomer. Its bathroom fixtures worked, however, which in wartime London was living in the lap of luxury.

ANDY ROONEY COULDN'T REMEMBER WHEN and where he met Walter Cronkite for the first time, but it was probably at the St. Pancras or Paddington railway stations, the central London depots where correspondents gathered to grab trains north to Bedford and the East Anglia airdromes. Cronkite was all business the first few times Rooney was around him, spare with small talk, a "tough, competitive scrambler" hell-bent on beating INS and AP.[18] It took a while for Cronkite's icy demeanor to warm, Rooney recalled. It helped that Rooney, as a *Stars and Stripes* guy, wasn't a competitor of UP's, per se. Rooney's broadsheet, in fact, turned out to be a steady UP and Cronkite customer.

Having taken three trips across the Atlantic in less than five months, Cronkite got settled in London during Christmastime '42. On the eve of his departure from New York, he sat down—twice—to write Betsy a farewell letter.

> *My very dearest darling:*
> *This isn't a fancy card at all but more than any card*
> *could ever say it must tell you "Merry Christmas." Wherever*
> *I am today, sweetheart, you know where my thoughts will be.*
> *They will be with you every second of the day just as if we*
> *were getting up together to go to our tree. . . .*

A few days later, on December 12, he tried again.

> *My very dearest darling:*
> *Thirteen is the number of days until Christmas. If I could*
> *just stay here that much longer to be with you. . . .*

Years later, in a handwritten note scrawled on yellowed stationery, Betsy explained to her children that both fragments were meant to be goodbye letters that "Daddy" never finished. Her parenthetical note ends: "He didn't get home again for two years."[19] It was actually closer to three.

There was little time for Cronkite to explore London when he first arrived; he was immediately thrust into war coverage, handling the two p.m. to ten p.m. (often later) shift five days a week, plus nine a.m. to five p.m. on Saturdays. He was essentially on call twenty-four/seven; his phone constantly rang in the middle of the night. Only on Wednesdays was he "off," but even then he often found himself going into United Press' cramped quarters in the News of the World building.

After UP's special stipend to new arrivals ran out after a couple of weeks, Cronkite found a "cell" at the Park Lane Hotel in Piccadilly. It was so tiny, Cronkite complained to Betsy, that "my knees and shins bruised severely with a fresh injury occurring every time I attempt to turn round."[20] For this he was paying the princely sum of eighteen shillings a day, about three bucks.

The Park Lane's chief attraction was the American Bar on its first floor; if late owls tipped the bartender, it sometimes stayed open past the mandatory eleven p.m. closing time. So some nights Cronkite could sip a watered-down beer or bourbon before collapsing into bed.

Fellow UP reporters Jim McGlincy, Bob Musel, John Parris, and Doug Werner were all bunking at the Park Lane and hanging out at the American Bar, too. In McGlincy's case, he was spending too much time at the pub, often drawing the owner's ire by insisting it stay open past midnight.

The blackout in a London winter night was near total: U.S. correspondents soon learned to carry a "torch" (flashlight) with them at all times.

On January 9, 1943, Cronkite wrote Betsy that he'd forgotten his torch the previous night. "Not having it was serious. In the first place, it was a pitch black nite and I stood [in] serious danger of tripping over a curb or running into a wall, or worse, completely losing my way—which isn't a darned bit hard to do even for the oldest Londoners."

Waving a torch, Cronkite explained, was the only way to hail a bus or taxicab. Cronkite was fortunate. After wandering around Fleet Street trying to grab the correct bus, he was able to whistle down a taxi. "Somehow we found each other in the pitch blackness. Thus ends the adventure of our rover boys and the blackout," he kidded.[21]

EARLY ON, THE ROVER BOY visited the white cliffs of Dover to profile the plucky antiaircraft gunners who tried to knock the Ju 88s and He 111s out of the skies as they began their bombing runs over the southeast of

England. Cronkite was perched in a sandbag bunker outside Dover as the battery began firing on a fleet of bombers that could barely be seen by the naked eye.

Amid the *ack!-ack!* a bespectacled man next to Cronkite shouted something that Cronkite couldn't quite make out.

"What's that?" Cronkite hollered back.

"I'm the best piano player in town!" the man bellowed.

That night, a bemused Cronkite shared the story with some locals at the village pub. "Oh, that's such-and-such," they told Cronkite. "He *is* the best piano player in town!"

In late January 1943, Betsy's nephew Bob, an Army lieutenant, got a two-day pass and came to London to see his uncle. Cronkite used Bob's stopover as an excuse to take a real day off and peruse the city.

The day began with Cronkite throwing open his windows at the Park Lane to show off London's infamous fog. Before sitting down to lunch, he and Bob stopped by an Army PX to pick up Cronkite's weekly rations: one can of orange juice; one can of tomato juice; one box each of vanilla wafers, chocolate cookies ("very much unlike," Cronkite was quick to tell Betsy, "the wonderful ones my wife makes"), and cheese niblits; one can of pipe tobacco (or five packs of cigarettes or three cigars, depending on tastes); one bar of soap; one pack of pipe cleaners; and sundry other items, all purchased for about a buck and a half.

Cronkite took Bob to the Army Officers' Club near Hyde Park, where for forty pence uniformed correspondents could get a decent meal in a pleasant setting. The wood-paneled bar downstairs had a fireplace and a piano.

Then uncle and nephew set off on a four-hour stroll through the scarred city. They ended their pilgrimage back at the Park Lane bar, where they bumped into some Navy pilots.

"I made the mistake," Cronkite laughed to Betsy, "of telling these guys that I thought I had perfect balance & if it weren't for the old color blindness would make a terrific flyer. To prove which I had to pull that little stunt of holding one leg straight out in front & kneeling on the other—you know, I did the stunt with great aplomb. But I'm still limping."[22]

CRONKITE LIMPED HIS WAY ONTO a lot of trains from London to East Anglia. In late '42 and the first few days of '43, there were just a couple of reporters covering the Eighth Air Force—but the trains got crowded in a hurry.

At the beginning, the press contingent consisted of the *Stars and Stripes'* Rooney, sometimes accompanied by colleagues Bud Hutton or Charles Kiley; Sergeant Denton Scott of *Yank* magazine, the periodical counterpart to the *Stars and Stripes*; UP's Cronkite; AP's Gladwin Hill (Cronkite's chief competitor and a wily journalist); the *New York Times'* Robert Perkins Post; and International News Service's William Wade. By the end of January they were joined by Homer Bigart of the *New York Herald Tribune* and Paul Manning of CBS Radio and later the Mutual Broadcasting System.

To alert reporters that a newsworthy raid was imminent, public relations officer Hal Leyshon came up with a novel system. Leyshon or aide Jimmy Dugan would give reporters a call using coded language. Lest enemy spies be eavesdropping, the PRO would say, "We've got a poker game in the works at my place," or "There will be a mail delivery tomorrow." Rooney remembered that it gave him the feeling "that I was part of a great conspiracy to save the world."[23]

The correspondents would meet at St. Pancras or Paddington or sometimes King's Cross and take the train north to a centrally located spot like Bedford or Cambridge. There, Army trucks would be waiting to transport them to one of several airdromes. Cronkite and Bigart, who knew each other a little from New York, soon became attached to the 303rd Bomb Group at Molesworth, and Rooney to the 306th Bomb Group at Thurleigh. Often the reporters spent a night or two or three in the barracks before heading back to London.

In February of '43, Cronkite and Bigart began bunking more than occassionally in the crude Nissen hut barracks at Molesworth. If they had a little downtime between deadlines, they'd borrow bicycles and pedal around the picturesque countryside. A Cronkite letter to Betsy described how parched he and Bigart had been after one midafternoon excursion, only to discover to their chagrin that the Cross Keys tavern didn't reopen for the evening until four o'clock.

But for every relaxed moment spent around an air base, there were a dozen brutal ones waiting for the bomber boys to return from a bloody mission. Correspondents settled into a ghoulish routine, interviewing pilots and crew members for potential profiles before they went wheels up. Then the reporters would hang around for the six or eight hours it would take for the planes to return, praying their interviewees were still in one piece and, after their debriefing with the base command, could join them for a beer and a raid recap.

Without divulging much, Leyshon and his deputies would provide generic information about each mission, identifying the target, its military value, the number of times that it had been bombed, and sometimes the mission's total bomb tonnage.

Much of it was educated guesswork; some of it bordered on outright fabrication, Cronkite later admitted. As the months went on and Allied bombing raids increased in size and frequency—some characterized as "light," some "medium," some "heavy," some "very heavy"—Cronkite and his counterpart at AP, Gladwin Hill, would engage in a machismo duel in guesstimating the total number of aircraft committed to that day's mission. U.S. papers wanted to print the wire service story that contained the most impressive number. So the stakes were high between AP and UP.

Cronkite would examine the scant information provided by the USAAF, consider whether the raid was being called "medium" or "heavy" or whatever, and, given recent history, estimate the number of bombers involved and stick it into a bulletin that would move over the UP wire. Then he'd go down to a Fleet Street tavern called the Bell Pub, order a gin and lime, and await the inevitable pas de deux with Hill.

Hill would walk into the Bell and shout at Cronkite: "How many?" Cronkite would throw out a number. Hill would stare disbelievingly, not sure if Cronkite was telling the truth or bluffing. Sometimes Hill would bolt back to the AP office to up the ante. Editors back home had no way of knowing, but when UP estimated that 575 heavy bombers had attacked industrial targets in Düsseldorf whereas AP cited 580, neither number may have been even in the ballpark.

But all that came later. On any given day in early '43, chances were roughly one in six or seven that U.S. airmen would not be returning from a mission. Too many surviving bombers, moreover, were forced to fire red flares out the pilot's window as, belching smoke and leaking oil, their planes careened to a stop. The red signal meant they had wounded aboard. Ambulances with doctors and nurses cramped inside or clinging to the running boards would screech down the runway, performing instant triage.

After weeks of filing heartrending stories, the reporters began clamoring to go along on a raid. "We were tired of going up to those air bases and interviewing young guys our age that had lost friends in battle and returning to the comforts of London that night," Rooney remembered. The correspondents were excited when the Eighth's top brass okayed their request, but a little flummoxed when told it would require intensive training. None of them had thought through that part.

NO ONE COULD QUITE REMEMBER which public relations maven at the Eighth's Grosvenor Square press headquarters dubbed the air beat reporters the Writing 69th. It might have been Cronkite's pal Leyshon, then a captain, or one of Leyshon's deputies, Joe Maher or Jimmy Dugan, or their boss, John Hay "Jock" Whitney, who doubled as a mogul at Twentieth Century-Fox and was the Air Force's self-appointed emissary to London's elite, or John "Tex" McCrary, a peacetime newsreel commentator and columnist for the *New York Mirror* who was engaged to the silky Jinx Falkenburg, a model and actress. Falkenburg, a leggy Chilean, possessed such beguiling beauty that she supposedly turned more heads in wartime London than Eisenhower's redheaded driver, Kay Summersby, or the Prime Minister's statuesque daughter-in-law, Pamela Digby Churchill. Cronkite's letters to Betsy often gossiped about Whitney (whom he liked), McCrary (whom he didn't—and Cronkite wasn't alone; Andy Rooney called

McCrary a "con artist."), Falkenburg (whom he ogled), and London's American expatriate social scene, to which the deadline-plagued Cronkite only peripherally belonged.

Its name parodied *The Fighting 69th*, a popular 1940 Jimmy Cagney–Pat O'Brien movie about the World War I exploits of the 69th Infantry Regiment. Rooney, Cronkite, and company liked to refer to themselves as the Flying Typewriters or, in more jaded moments, the Legion of the Doomed.

Only the eight men who'd been consistently covering the air war beat were invited to join the Writing 69th. When word reached UP's Salisbury that his charge Cronkite was among the invitees, Salisbury winced. "I was not happy about it," he recalled, "but a dozen elephants could not have kept Walter out of the B-17."[24] The same could have been said of Bigart and Rooney.

GLADWIN HILL, CRONKITE'S ARCHRIVAL, WAS a fine reporter but too often enamored of his own voice. A devotee of Great War press coverage, the Harvard graduate liked to share wearying stories about how certain correspondents had handled the earlier conflict. During one rambling Hill monologue, Cronkite recalled, "Homer [Bigart] leaned over, tapped him on the knee, and said, 'G-g-g-g-glad, if you're not d-d-damned c-c-c-careful, you're going to b-b-b-b-be the Gladwin Hill of W-w-w-w-world War Two.'"[25]

Robert Perkins Post of the *New York Times* had an even more patrician background than Hill. Just thirty-two, Post belonged to a Boston Brahmin clan that summered on Long Island and had social connections to the Roosevelt family. At St. Paul's School and Harvard, he earned high marks in creative writing. A poem he wrote while still at St. Paul's presaged his life and death.

> *As the clear sunset, brilliant, color-wild,*
> *Died in the West, so dies our near-run youth;*

> *As the clear after-glow lights up the Western sky,*
> *So may our age light up a darkening world.*[26]

Post got to glimpse the darkening world in a way he never imagined. Having joined the *Times* soon after graduating from Harvard, Post at a tender age became a White House correspondent. He earned the wrath of his family friend by having the temerity to ask President Roosevelt at a press conference in 1937 about FDR's intention to seek a third term—three years *before* the next presidential election. With his usual aplomb Roosevelt tried to brush it aside; when Post persisted, FDR sputtered, "Oh, Bob, go put on the dunce cap and stand in the corner!"[27]

Cartoonists and FDR detractors had a field day. In the summer of 1940, when FDR accepted the Democratic nomination for a third term, Post sent the president a telegram. "Who's the dunce now?" he twitted FDR.

Post was dashing in his Cambridge years, but by the late '30s had turned more than a bit beefy. He wore his hair slicked back, à la Jay Gatsby. And like any Fitzgerald protagonist, he was fixated on his own social standing and preoccupied by thoughts of his own demise.

The *Times* delighted Post by sending him to their London bureau. His byline graced many of the *Times*' best articles about the Blitz and the war's grisly beginnings.

"The sun rose red over London yesterday after one of the worst air raids that London has experienced," Post wrote in November 1940 after the horrific nocturnal bombing of Westminster Abbey and the Commons Chamber of the Houses of Parliament. "Weary and drawn after a night of horror and fire—a night that even women living alone spent in putting out incendiaries—London began to make a preliminary reckoning of what had happened. . . . It is perhaps not important to the historian that little shops have been blasted or that a street of little homes has been destroyed: but it is vital to men who own and work in those shops and live in those houses."[28]

One night a group of British Home Guardsmen barged into the *New York Times*' London offices wielding rifles and axe handles. A suspicious Londoner had complained that the *Times*' lights were violating strict blackout rules. "Lights?" Post responded when the guardsmen challenged him. "Oh, that's just our regular nightly signal to the Germans."[29]

Post may have had a quick wit, but he also possessed a dark side: He could be snooty and sullen. He smirked when telling colleagues that American GIs, upon finding out that he was a reporter, would naïvely ask if he could get an article about them into their hometown papers. How could they confuse the *New York Times* with some two-bit rag? Post would snigger. He had a rocky relationship with Raymond Daniell, the *Times'* London bureau chief. Post had been the interim head of the office before Daniell arrived; they quarreled over which reporters would get what assignments and jockeyed over who would get credit for scoops.

His wife, Margot, also came from an impeccable northeastern pedigree. After years of trying to join her husband in London, she was finally due to arrive in midwinter '43.

"WE DIDN'T REALIZE UNTIL THE top boys in the Eighth cleared the idea," Andy Rooney recalled of the Writing 69th, "that we'd have to attend gunnery school for a week. If we were going to go on a bomber in battle, we were told, we'd better know how to shoot a gun in case we got in trouble."[30] Hal Leyshon, who at one time or another had bought them all drinks (although in Rooney's case it was probably a root beer), was placed in charge of their preparation.

The Writing 69th's training began in earnest during the first week of February. Beyond the eight original correspondents, the "students" now included several photographers and famed Hollywood director William Wyler. Wyler's 1942 film *Mrs. Miniver*, about a London family enduring the Blitz, had just won the Academy Award for best picture. The director had joined the Army Air Force to film a documentary about the air campaign.

Wyler and his sound- and cameramen proved to be erratic pupils, not always showing up for class and feigning scheduling conflicts to skip—or, in one notable instance, Cronkite recalled, cheat on—the "exams" that punctuated each set of instructions. But Wyler and his team ended up

producing *The Memphis Belle*, a film about a B-17 crew finishing its allot-
ment of twenty-five missions that remains one of the finest documentaries
made during World War II.

The auteur's movie embellished the facts but was so powerful that when
it was screened for FDR in the White House, the president turned to the
director, a German émigré, and said, "Everyone has got to see this." They
did. Within weeks the film was being shown in thousands of theaters in
the U.S and Britain.

Members of the Writing 69th developed their own fraternity grip,
"which is not dirty," Cronkite assured Betsy, "but involves a military
secret. Remind me to show you when I get home."[31] They all felt "pretty
war-like" as they traipsed through Paddington Station wearing service
pants, galoshes, and mackinaws, with helmets and gas masks slung over
their shoulders. When they got to Bedford they were met by an Army
truck—for the first of many bumpy rides that week as they ricocheted from
base to base.

The reporters' regimen began at seven thirty in the morning and lasted
until ten thirty at night. They crammed three months' worth of training
into less than a week. On the first morning, at a combat crew replacement
school, there was a scheduling mix-up; the pupil/reporters ended up killing time at the Ping-Pong table. When they finally sat down in a classroom,
the orientation lecture was delivered by the school's commandant, an Air
Force colonel, who urged them to pay attention: Not only their asses were
on the line, but also those of ten crew members, not to mention the fate of
a million-dollar aircraft.[32]

At Bovingdon, a Hertfordshire RAF instructional base not far from
General Eaker's headquarters, the entourage was instructed in oxygen
maintenance, first aid, aircraft identification, and "ditching out," which
meant abandoning a plane by parachute or dinghy, Bigart explained to
readers of the *Herald Tribune* on February 8.

"It was during Lieutenant Alex Hogan's 'ditching out' lecture that some
of us felt like hopping the next train back to London's Paddington Station,"
Bigart joked. "The lieutenant is a pleasant lad from Starkville, Miss., but
his discourse was a bit grim."

What would happen, a reporter asked, if they ditched into the North Sea and an enemy plane swooped down to investigate? "'In that event,' Hogan tartly replied, 'merely tell them you're waiting for the R.A.F. and wave 'em on.'"

Lieutenant Hogan wasn't alone: other trainers gave the Writing 69th men equally unsettling counsel. One medical officer, Bigart wrote, painted an "unforgettable picture of what might happen to our fingers if we took off our gloves at 30,000 feet." Another urged them to constantly yawn and swallow after takeoff to relieve pressure on the eardrums. Since flatulence at a rarefied altitude could be painful and hazardous, he also prescribed avoiding gaseous foods such as beans, chips, and red cabbage, and to treat beer, Bigart wrote, "like the plague."[33] We're in England, for God's sakes, the reporters protested, what else are we supposed to eat and drink?

After a couple of days they were ushered onto a B-17 named *Johnny Reb*, which zoomed around the Midlands at twenty-five thousand feet. No-nonsense sergeants were bemused by the specter of these typewriter jock-eys fumbling with oxygen masks and parachute packs while squirming their beer bellies through *Johnny Reb*'s innards.

Cronkite made sure he got a prized seat in the Fort's plastic nose. "It was a real thrill," Cronkite told Betsy, "taking off in that spot—watching the ground roar past you as those great motors throbbed, and then the ground pulling away."[34]

"All survived" the shakedown flight, noted Bigart, "and there is noth-ing to report, aside from a faint buzzing in the head."

Their tutor in aircraft recognition was a Yorkshire native named Ber-nard "Benny" Hall. The RAF sergeant was an expert teacher, having flown some four dozen combat missions, a fourth of them over Germany. "But his Yorkshire accent was baffling at first," Bigart wrote. "He kept talking about 'edam position' until some of us began drawing outlines of a spher-ical Dutch cheese with wings. Later, it developed that he was referring to aircraft approaching from 'ead on.'"[35]

Cronkite remembered Hall's stirring, if barely intelligible, tribute to Britain's Hawker Hurricane fighter. "This 'ere," the RAF man said while displaying a silhouette on a domed ceiling, "is the 'Awker 'Urricane. A mighty nice aircraft. It helped our troops when Rommel had them on the run in the desert. It protected the boys getting out of Greece. And it was a big help in getting out of Norway. The 'Awker 'Urricane, as a matter of fact, was essential in all our defeats."[36]

Bigart and Cronkite's lighthearted commentary aside, their training was deadly serious. The reporters gulped when told that in the event their bombers were shot or forced down, enemy soldiers in the heat of battle would never be able to distinguish "correspondent" from "combatant." Learning how to return fire, therefore, was essential.

Yet the only one who could fire a rifle or pistol with any degree of accuracy was the *Times'* Post, who'd spent many a summer afternoon on Long Island shooting skeet. Even the cocksure Rooney, who'd gone through basic training, was a lousy shot.

Cronkite told Betsy that the group was given four "very tough examinations." He proudly reported that he'd gotten a ninety-eight on aircraft recognition, made the second-highest grade in the class on another test, "barely eked by" on a third, and flunked the final one, which was probably fifty-caliber machine gun assemblage. Cronkite had done better than most—and a lot better than William Wyler. Still, all of them, Wyler included, "graduated."

Given survival percentages, Bob Post reckoned late in their training, "one of us will not be here after the first mission." Post then needled, "It will probably be you, Homer [Bigart]. You're the Frank McHugh type, the silent, amiable guy who always gets it in the end."[37] McHugh, a '30s character actor, had built his Hollywood career around playing the best buddy who gets rubbed out near the final scene. Ironically, McHugh had a role in *The Fighting 69th* as one of Cagney's doughboy sidekicks. Sure enough, McHugh's character was gunned down in the trenches a few minutes before the credits rolled.

THE MACHISMO IMAGE OF THE Flying Fortresses had grabbed the public's imagination; naturally, all the reporters wanted to fly with the B-17s. "Come on," Air Force Major Bill Laidlaw, the PRO for the First Bomb

Wing, admonished them on one of their last nights of preparation, "one of you has to go with the Liberators (B-24s). Those guys deserve some recognition, too."

Laidlaw was getting heat from his bosses to score publicity for the Libs, since a batch of new B-24s had just arrived from the States. But the reporters wouldn't budge. A Laidlaw deputy, Second Lieutenant Van Norman, suggested they hold a lottery to determine who would fly what bomber. Cronkite and Hill staunchly refused, with the stuffy Hill braying, "I regret to inform you that my office has sent me here to cover the story of the B-17."[38]

After several minutes of stalemate, Bob Post raised his hand, cracked a weak joke about his newspaper not caring about headlines, and volunteered to ride in a B-24. Leyshon and Laidlaw were stunned that Post, never reticent in reminding people he represented the omnipotent *New York Times*, was the one that broke the impasse.

Post had already confided to his wife and friends that he'd had premonitions of death. He was assigned to *Maisie*, a B-24 flown by Captain Howard Adams of the 44th Bomb Group in Shipdham. The plane had been named after a series of B movies starring screen siren Ann Sothern, one of which, ironically, had been based on an A. J. Liebling story in the *New Yorker*.

The Writing 69th's orientation wrapped up February 9. For several days and nights they hung out in East Anglia, anxiously awaiting a thumbs-up that didn't come. One night they were all cramped together in the same barracks dead asleep when a member of the fraternity tripped over a chair on the way to the restroom. Within seconds the entire gang was up, convinced the mission was on, Cronkite related to Betsy. One of them even began shaving before they discovered there was no reason to be stirring hours before reveille.[39]

Eventually they returned to London, where they cooled their heels for another week and a half. The fateful call finally came on February 25, so they donned their galoshes and mackinaws again and scrambled back onto the train.

CBS' Paul Manning had contracted pneumonia and *Yank*'s Denton

Scott had received a conflicting order, but the other six were scattered at different air bases. At their respective preflight briefings in the early hours of February 26, the correspondents learned that their bombing target would be a Bremen factory that manufactured Focke-Wulf fighter planes. If that area of Lower Saxony proved cloud-covered, their fallback target would be the *Kriegsmarine* U-boat base at Wilhelmshaven on the North Sea. Both outposts were heavily fortified with antiaircraft batteries and uncomfortably proximate Luftwaffe bases.

The Eighth Air Force had been attacking enemy-occupied territory for seven months, yet the Writing 69th's sortie would mark just the third time that U.S. planes had bombed Germany proper. On January 27, four weeks before, the first U.S. bombing attack on German soil had been carried out against Wilhelmshaven. Although the Eighth Air Force had insisted that the American press trumpet the raid, in truth visibility had been poor: most of the U.S. bombers missed their targets by wide margins. More bombs fell on the village and in the sea than on Hitler's U-boat pens. The second U.S. attack against Germany had come against the coastal fortifications near the cities of Emden and Hamm; it, too, drew big headlines but had been largely ineffectual.[40]

OF NECESSITY, THE BOMBER FLEETS on the morning of February 26 took off in increments, beginning at 0830, then circled the south of England, waiting for others to join. Andy Rooney likened it in his *Stars and Stripes* piece "to a pickup football team on a Saturday morning. We grew in strength as we flew, until all England seemed to be covered with bombers." At the outset there were ninety-three bombers, but some twenty returned to England with mechanical or personnel issues, including the B-17 to which INS' William Wade had been assigned. That left five members of the Writing 69th still airborne: Cronkite, Bigart, Rooney, Hill, and Post.

The B-17s of the 305th led the way, followed by Bigart and Cronkite in the 303rd, then the 91st, then Rooney in the 306th, followed by the B-24 groups. Post, Captain Adams, and the 44th were in the most vulnerable spot in the formation, the back end, where the planes were known as "Rear-end Charlies." Enemy fighters liked to attack formations from behind. Eventually the entire U.S. flotilla climbed to twenty-nine thousand feet and stayed there for most of the flight over the North Sea.

Cronkite was with Captain Glenn Hagenbuch's crew in *S for Sugar*; Bigart with larger-than-life Arkansan Lewis "Hoss" Lyle in *Ooold Soljer*, the same officer destined to lead the 303rd's D-Day attack on the bridge at Caen.

At precisely ten twenty-two a.m., a German radar station on the Dutch island of Texel spotted the formation and sounded the alarm. Within eight minutes, they were under attack by Focke-Wulfs stationed at Deelen, Holland, and along the Frisian Islands. The deadly harrassment continued, almost unabated, for the next two-plus hours. At one point Hoss Lyle counted thirty-five fighters "darting in from all directions," Bigart wrote. Bigart put his machine gun training to use, manning one of the fifty-caliber waist guns on *Ooold Soljer*, but was racked with worry about accidentally hitting friendly planes. A few hundred aerial yards away in *S for Sugar*, Cronkite was in its Plexiglas nose, blasting away, conscience free, on the starboard fore-gun.

"I fired at every German fighter that came into the neighborhood," recalled Cronkite. "I don't think I hit any, but I'd like to think I scared a couple of those German pilots."[41]

The German skies were so cloudy that, as the formation arrived over Lower Saxony at 1100, the objective was switched from slightly inland Bremen to coastal Wilhelmshaven. The entire formation was forced to execute a sharp turn to bring the U-boat base into its bombsights.

"I could not quite make out our specific target for obliteration, the submarine pens, because at our altitude the installations along the Jade Busen (Jade Bay) seemed no bigger than a pinhead," Bigart wrote later that day. The street pattern of the old Prussian village, on the other hand, could easily be discerned from five miles aloft, he noted.

As they approached Wilhelmshaven Bigart watched in horror as an American bomber went "down in a dizzy spin." Only two parachutes opened.

Inside *Ooold Soljer* Bigart watched intently as the bombardier, Second

Lieutenant Reinaldo J. Saiz of Segundo, California, and the navigator, First Lieutenant Otis A. Hoyt, of Dawn, Missouri, zeroed in on the target. The reporter glanced back and for the first time in an hour couldn't see any Focke-Wulfs on their tail. "We had a good run and we were squarely over the town. I watched Saiz crouch lower over his sight. I heard him call 'Bombs Away!'

"Our salvo of 500-pounders plunged through the open bomb bay. From where I stood I could not see them land, but our ball turret gunner, Sergeant Howard L. Nardine, of Los Angeles, took a quick look back and saw fires and smoke."

Bigart was less concerned about fire on the ground than the flak exploding all around *Ooold Soljer*. "Nasty black puffs" were erupting as they barreled northwest over the sea. Soon enemy fighters were swarming again; this time, the 190s and 109s gave way to the twin-engine Me 110s, which seemed to Bigart to be preying on the crippled bombers desperately weaving in and out of cloud cover.[42]

Banshee, *Ooold Soljer*, and *S for Sugar* all made it back to England without incident, although as we've seen, Rooney's ship, *Banshee*, was pretty shot up.

Cronkite always claimed that thirteen American bombers were lost that day, but the actual count, according to research conducted by *The Writing 69th* author Jim Hamilton, was seven. One of them, sadly, was Bob Post's Liberator. After *Maisie* absorbed a mortal hit from an Me 109 over the outskirts of Wilhelmshaven, the crew of a companion B-24 spotted two streaming parachutes as the plane plummeted. Post never exited the stricken bomber. Later that day, his remains were found by German soldiers amid the wreckage.[43]

Back on the ground, Cronkite and Bigart rendezvoused by plan at Molesworth with UP's Harrison Salisbury, Hal Leyshon, fellow Air Force PRO Jack Redding, and an army censor, identified only in Salisbury's account as Colonel Gates. The news that Post's plane was missing hit everyone hard; the atmosphere in the windowless shed turned gloomy. Bigart couldn't be sure, but he wondered if the wounded bomber he'd seen spinning toward the ground outside Wilhelmshaven had, in fact, been Post's.

Ten of them jammed into Leyshon's sedan for the tense ride back to London. It was then that Bigart asked Cronkite if he'd drafted a lede and was incredulous to learn about his friend's "assignment to hell" construct. As the years wore on, Salisbury claimed to have fed Cronkite the "hell" line—an assertion missing in Cronkite's memoirs and three other detailed recollections of the mission and its aftermath.

But there's no doubt that once they got back to the Ministry of Information, Salisbury sat at Cronkite's elbow as the story took shape. Salisbury kept murmuring, "That's right down the old groove, Cronkite. Now you're cooking," Cronkite related to Betsy.[44]

"Actually the first impression of a daylight bombing mission is a hodge-podge of disconnected scenes like a poorly edited home movie," the grooved Cronkite wrote that night, "bombs falling past you from the formation above, a crippled bomber with smoke pouring from one engine thousands of feet above, a tiny speck in the sky that grows closer and finally becomes a Focke-Wulf peeling off above you somewhere and plummeting down, shooting its way through the formation."[45] Salisbury kept pounding Cronkite on the back as one paragraph after another poured out.[46]

Not only was Salisbury hovering, but also an anxious John Charles Daly of CBS Radio, who had arranged for the correspondent fresh off the Wilhelmshaven raid to appear on a live broadcast feed. The instant Cronkite pulled his copy out of the typewriter he raced off to the BBC studio that CBS was leasing.

Daly and his guest cobbled together a quick script for the radio program, but didn't get it in front of the censor until ten minutes before airtime, causing Daly palpitations.

"Even as Daly was setting up the circuit to NY and they were doing the old 'Hello, New York, Hello, New York. London calling, New York, London calling,' censorship called and said the script was okay," Cronkite told Betsy. They were on the air for only three minutes before the circuit failed, leaving Daly infuriated. Ten minutes later NBC used the same circuit and got its transmission through, which didn't make Daly any happier.[47]

Rooney also appeared on radio in the aftermath of the Wilhelmshaven raid, his first-ever broadcast interview. Expatriate American actor (and future Hollywood studio executive) Ben Lyon invited Rooney onto Lyon's BBC show, *London Calling*. Every "Well, Ben," and pause was carefully scripted.

"Well, Andy, suppose you give us some low-down on one of those raids?" Lyon asked Rooney as the reporter delivered pedestrian patter about the previous day's mission. The experience was so awkward that Rooney vowed he'd never again go on the air unless he'd personally written the copy—and never did. At least Rooney was well compensated for his troubles: the BBC gave him twelve quid, more than a week's pay at the *Stars and Stripes*.[48]

By the time Cronkite left the radio studio it was well past midnight. "I was horribly tired that night," he wrote Betsy. "We had been routed out at [it had been scratched out by censors but was clearly "Molesworth"], for our briefing and a spot of breakfast before taking off for Germany, and then [again censored] hours in a bomber at high altitude living on pure oxygen, standing up most of the time with 50 lbs. of heavy fur flying equipment and parachute on your back, and the general exertion of shooting guns and moving about keeping out of other people's way, is very tiring."[49]

Cronkite's UP story somehow got delayed in being transmitted to the States, so Glad Hill's AP piece got bigger pickup back home. But Cronkite's story hit huge in the British papers, which loved his repeated allusions to Hades and his evocative—if purplish—prose.

Walter, however, knew none of this when he got back to the Park Lane at five a.m. and collapsed. Four and a half hours later Salisbury was on the phone, asking Cronkite to come in to the office to write a tribute to Post, who'd been officially declared missing.

Once Cronkite finished his encomium, Salisbury insisted on treating Cronkite to a celebratory—and very liquid—lunch at the Savoy with UP deskman Bill Dickinson and Dickinson's fiancée, a society reporter with the *London Daily Mirror* named Hilde Marchant. Marchant was instantly recognized by the Savoy's maître d', who proceeded to treat the party like royalty. They were given a table with a stunning view of Waterloo Bridge and the Houses of Parliament.

Afterward, Cronkite begged off and "re-collapsed," he told Betsy, at the

Park Lane. At six thirty p.m. his phone rang; it was Salisbury again, ordering Cronkite to join the threesome for dinner at Jack's Club, a favorite
hangout of British and American correspondents. Then they were off to
watch jitterbugging at the Opera House in Covent Garden, a lavish theater
where Marchant had done stories about the U.S. dance craze sweeping
Britain. Again, they were greeted with open arms and whisked to a box
with an unobstructed view of the dance floor.

"Boy, has jitterbugging hit this land! Wow!" Cronkite enthused to Betsy.

They capped off the marathon party with a stop at the Cocoanut Grove,
a nightclub where they repeatedly toasted Cronkite's safe return. "As
usual," Cronkite laughed to Betsy, "everybody got drunk but Cronkite."[50]
For his entire life, he prided himself on his capacity to nurse alcohol and
worried about people—like his father, Jim McGlincy, and Hal Boyle—who
couldn't.[51]

The sober but bushed Cronkite was again rousted out of bed Sunday
morning by UP's London bureau, this time to respond to a story idea from
UP–New York. He then hustled over to the Officers' Club just before it
closed for lunch.

As he entered the club, he sensed heads turning in his direction. Soon
a palpable buzz filled the room. Walter Cronkite was no longer an obscure
wire service scribbler. He had, literally overnight, become Walter Cronkite,
famous war correspondent. Every Sunday paper in England, it seemed, had
played his Wilhelmshaven story on page one, under "great, glaring headlines," he told Betsy.

Suddenly everyone was deferring to him; even the Park Lane's "snooty
elevator boys who hadn't bothered saying hello before began ingratiating
manners, the teller at the bank where I cash my check bowed and scraped,
the telephone at the hotel rang all day with congratulations from some
persons I knew and more often not. . . . Honestly, it was the damndest
performance I've ever undergone."[52]

FOR THE SURVIVING MEMBERS OF the Writing 69th, the Wilhelmshaven
raid and its aftermath had been one big damndest performance. All

through training the hard-bitten reporters had kidded one another about the obligatory clichés they would use if a member of the Legion of the Doomed didn't come back. Now that the scenario was real, it didn't seem amusing anymore.

"This is the story of Bob Post of the *New York Times*—the story he cannot write today," Cronkite wrote on minimal sleep. "It's the story of a big lumbering bespectacled Harvard graduate who looked about as much like an intrepid airman as Oliver Hardy, but whose heart beat the same do-or-die cadence as the pilots and crew of the American bomber which he accompanied to doom somewhere over Wilhelmshaven."[53]

"A mission to Germany is a nasty experience," Bigart wrote in a reflective *Herald Tribune* piece a few days later. "Apart from the very real danger to life and limb, there is the acute discomfort of enduring subzero temperatures for hours at a stretch and taking air through an oxygen mask."[54]

Despite the danger and discomfort, Bigart told readers he'd like to go on another bombing mission. But Bob Post's death had horrified everyone from President Roosevelt (who sent a tender note of condolence to Mrs. Post) and *New York Times* publisher Arthur Sulzberger (who sent a what-the-hell-are-we-doing? cable to his London bureau chief Raymond Daniell) to Tooey Spaatz and Hal Leyshon. Despite the early bravado about keeping the Writing 69th together, permitting correspondents to go on combat missions would not become commonplace in the ETO until later in the war, when the Luftwaffe had been essentially neutered.

Bigart worried for the rest of his life that his erratic machine gun fire over Wilhelmshaven had somehow contributed to the downing of Bob Post's plane. He knew his fears weren't rational—but that didn't stop Homer from losing sleep. Bigart took his neurosis to the grave.

CHAPTER 6

✯

FALLING LIKE DYING MOTHS

*All the [American airmen] had to do, I thought, was
look around at each other and they would understand
that democracy was worth defending.*

—A. J. LIEBLING, 1942
THE ROAD BACK TO PARIS

Twenty days after the Wilhelmshaven raid, the Mighty Eighth unleashed an even bigger assault against the *Kriegsmarine*'s U-boat pens.
This time, the target was Admiral Dönitz' submarine yard at Vegesack, at
the mouth of the River Lesum, a few miles upriver from Bremen. And this
time, it was Molesworth's 303rd Bomb Group, the men Walter Cronkite
and Homer Bigart covered day to day, which was in the formation's lead
spot.

The one-hundred-plane phalanx was spearheaded by a B-17 from the
359th Squadron known as *The Duchess.* Its bombardier was Lieutenant
Jack Mathis, from San Angelo, Texas; its navigator was Lieutenant Jesse
Elliott, from Tallahassee, Florida. They were flying their fifteenth combat
mission together and were considered one of the better bombardier-
navigator tandems in the squadron, which is in part why they'd been entrusted with the formation's up-front position. They'd had a big evening
the night before: Mathis' older brother Mark, also an Eighth Air Force
bombardier, had come to Molesworth for a visit.

"We had a pretty routine trip to the [Vegesack] target," Elliott told UP's

Cronkite a day later. "Jack [Mathis] called out the altitude over the inter-communications system and we were humming along prettily until we ran into the fighters."[1]

The Duchess was still twenty-five minutes from the German coast when it got jumped. Suddenly there were so many enemy planes flitting around that they almost looked like Allied escorts, Elliott remembered thinking. The Germans had thrown everything at the attackers, Bigart explained. In addition to what Bigart called the "usual reception committee" of Fw 190s and Me 109s and Me 110s, there was a horde of twin-engine Ju 88s that kept their distance and flew parallel to the attackers, looking to pounce on crippled bombers.[2]

"They actually weren't so tough," Elliott told Cronkite. "It was just that there were so many of them. They weren't even coming in as close as usual, except for a few daring ones."

Mathis was doing what bombardiers had to do, performing simultaneous double duty, calculating the bombing run while jumping up to operate a machine gun in the nose. "He got plenty of shots in at the enemy fighters coming in head-on," Elliott said. "He really was beating out there, pouring on coal. He ran out of ammunition at least twice, and I remember him passing the ammunition three times."

The Duchess had warded off dozens of fighters and was just turning into its bombing run when flak erupted. It was exploding so close to the plane, Elliott explained to Cronkite, that first one wing, then the other, was being jerked up in the air.

"[Flak] was raining off the nose like hail off a tin roof and knocking the plane all around," Elliott said. "Jack was easy-going and the flak didn't bother him. He wasn't saying a word—just sticking there over his bomb-sight doing his job."

A minute later, Elliott heard Mathis tell the pilot that he'd opened the bomb bay doors. "Then [Mathis] gave instructions to climb a little more to reach bombing altitude. By that time we had settled down on the bombing run and Jack called up a couple of more technical directions to the pilot."

The Duchess was just seconds away from releasing its package when it was rocked by a barrage of flak. "One of the shells burst out to the right and a little below the nose," Elliott said. "It couldn't have been more than thirty feet away when it burst. If we had been much closer, it would have knocked the whole plane over."

Shrapnel ripped through the nose, shattering the Plexiglas, deafening the crew, and knocking Mathis and Elliott backward. "I saw Jack falling toward me and threw up my arm to ward off the fall, but by that time both of us were way back in the rear of the nose—blown back there, I guess, by the flak," Elliott said.

"I was sort of half-standing, half-lying against the wall and Jack was leaning against me. I didn't have any idea that he was injured. Without assistance from me, he pulled himself back to his bombsight. His seat had been knocked out from under him by the flak and so he sort of knelt over the bombsight, probably leaning on it, but I didn't know that at the time."

Part of navigator Elliott's job was to keep a flight log, so he glanced at his watch to record the exact time *The Duchess* released its load. "I heard Jack call over the inter-communications system, 'Bombs—'. But he never finished the phrase with the usual 'away,'" Elliott said. "The word just sort of trickled off and I thought his throat microphone had slipped out of place so I finished the phrase for him."[3]

There was a reason that Elliott stepped in to shout "away!" It was a hard-and-fast rule that pilots could not begin taking evasive action until the crew confirmed that their bombs had indeed been released. A moment later, Elliott glimpsed Mathis grabbing the handle to close the bomb bay doors. Just as Mathis pushed the lever, he fell backward.

"At first, I thought he was just getting back to his feet from that crouching position so he could carry on with other jobs," Elliott said. "But he didn't get up. He fell on his back and I caught him." Until that instant, Elliott admitted to Cronkite, the navigator hadn't realized that Mathis was seriously wounded. Mathis' right arm was a mangled mess, shattered above the elbow. Blood was gushing from his side and abdomen.

"'I guess they got you that time, old boy,' I remember saying, but then his head slumped over," Elliott said.

Jack Mathis was dead. But he hadn't died in vain.

"Following planes said the bombardier's salvos landed squarely in the

target area," Bigart wrote on the afternoon of the raid. Bigart's initial account, in fact, could not identify Mathis by name because his next of kin
in San Angelo had not yet been notified of his death.

Mathis' name was divulged two days later in a Cronkite article that ran
on page one in the *New York World-Telegram* and papers across the U.S.
and Britain. In DYING BOMBARDIER CARRIES ON, HITS THE MARK,
Cronkite told the remarkable story of the twenty-one-year-old officer who
had performed his duty until, literally, his last breath. Cronkite's lede was,
"The American bombardier who, though mortally wounded by antiaircraft
shrapnel, crawled back to his bombsight and sent his bombs crashing
squarely on the German U-boat yards at Vegesack was revealed today to be
First Lt. Jack Mathis, of San Angelo, Tex." Because the formation had been
led directly over the top of the target, the Eighth Air Force considered
Vegesack more successful than previous U.S. raids on U-boat bases.

Mathis had been enrolled at San Angelo Business College before the
war and was only three years out of high school. "If [Mathis] had seen [the]
incident in the motion pictures he might have laughed and called it 'Hollywood corn,'" Bigart wrote in his page-one tribute.

The coverage by Bigart and Cronkite made Mathis' martyrdom one of
the European war's most poignant moments. Readers on two continents
blinked back tears when they learned that Mathis' brother Mark was still
at Molesworth when Jack's body was carried off *The Duchess*. Four months
later, "for conspicuous gallantry and intrepidity above and beyond the call
of duty," Jack Mathis was posthumously awarded the Congressional Medal
of Honor.[4]

Mark Mathis was determined to avenge his brother's death. He asked
for and received a transfer to the 359th Squadron; on a couple of occasions,
he even got to serve as bombardier on the patched-up *Duchess*. Mark's
fourth combat mission was on a B-17 called *FDR*. After being repeatedly
attacked by German fighters, *FDR* went down in the North Sea. Seven
parachutes were spotted coming out of the plane, but no survivors were
ever found. Only a few degrees above freezing, the North Sea swallowed
up almost every airman who plunged into it without a rubber raft, Mark
Mathis included. Major Bill Calhoun, the 359th's commanding officer, said

five decades later that writing the second letter of condolence to the Mathis family was much tougher than the first.[5]

San Angelo's airport is now known as Mathis Field. Well after the war, a group of surviving Hell's Angels led by Calhoun gathered at the field to dedicate a plaque to the Mathis brothers. Calhoun's eyes glistened as he told the San Angelo Standard-Times, "They were great boys."[6]

THERE WERE A LOT OF great boys in the skies over the Third Reich—so many heroes, in fact, that it's hard to distinguish one from the other. They're all a blur. Therein lies the challenge of appraising the Allies' bombing war against Nazi Germany. Because no territorial ground was gained, it's hard for even serious students of the war to appreciate its import and nuances.

As reflected in the headlines of Cronkite, Bigart, and Rooney articles, the raids take on an almost numbing repetition. YANKS GO DEEP INTO GERMANY. HEAVIES RAVAGE COLOGNE. FORTS BATTER LORIENT, BREST. Behind the bold print was staggering human loss that Allied officials were loath to admit.

Every raid was carefully calculated, of course, part of a larger strategy aimed at gutting Hitler's capacity to make war. The targets were chosen by experts who agonized over intelligence reports, industrial data, and reconnaissance film and photographs, plus studied the sometimes sketchy information supplied by the Underground. Certain missions in certain weeks zeroed in on U-boat bases; others went after oil refineries or aircraft or other manufacturing facilities. The revenge-minded brass nicknamed such concentrated attacks "blitzes."

But little of this larger strategy could be shared with the press or public. General Eaker or General Spaatz would sometimes invite Cronkite, Rooney, Bigart, Hill, and other reporters into their offices, consult a map, and pinpoint objectives. The substance of the talks was almost always off-the-record, especially after first Cronkite, then Rooney, got into trouble in the spring of '43 for printing stories that hinted the Eighth Air Force was contemplating nighttime missions and perhaps altering its approach to strategic bombing. How the stories managed to clear censors was any-one's guess, but in both instances Colonel Jock Whitney and his PRO en-forcers threatened reprisals against United Press and the *Stars and Stripes*. The incidents, however, quickly blew over. Indeed, the vast majority of the Cronkite-Rooney coverage of the Mighty Eighth dealt solely with the blow-by-blow of raids, not larger strategic concerns. Even the great Bigart had trouble wrapping his arms around the bigger bombing picture.

The efficacy of the Allies' bombing war remains a contentious issue all these decades later, as does its morality.[7]

Both sets of critics miss the mark. Allied planners at the outset may have had inflated expectations for the combined bombing offensive, but they did a creditable job with incomplete information. They knew that ball bearings, for example, were integral to the German war effort. But so did Hitler and Luftwaffe *Reichsmarschall* Hermann Göring, which is why the industrial center Schweinfurt was so heavily ringed with Luftwaffe air-dromes and antiaircraft weaponry. Could Allied bombers have inflicted heavier damage on Schweinfurt's ball bearing plants? Absolutely, but only at a catastrophic loss of men and planes.

In *My War*, Andy Rooney dismissed the moral criticism of Allied bomb-ing tactics by explaining the origin of Britain's "area" bombing technique. It evolved, Rooney wrote, after German planes had viciously attacked Win-chester and Coventry, two historic sites that had little military value.

"For the British, Coventry wasn't just another industrial city," Rooney wrote. "It was rich with Shakespearean history, with the lore of Henry VIII and such legends as Lady Godiva's bareback ride through its streets. Cov-entry was dear to the British people and they never forgave the Germans for attacking it."

Allied air commanders were "too practical to have wasted bombs on churches and museums if they didn't think it would hasten the end of the war," Rooney wrote. "[They] wanted to show them what wanton destruc-tion was; they wanted to make them think about what Hitler had brought down on their heads."[8]

———

BY THE TIME THE MATHIS brothers died, the Allied high command had arrived at a tortured conclusion: The most effective way to undermine Nazi Germany's war-making capacity was to decimate the Luftwaffe. Wave after wave of bombers was sent over the Third Reich, luring enemy fighters out of their lairs. It was grisly stuff—not unlike General Ulysses S. Grant hurling thousands of men toward certain death at Spotsylvania and Cold Harbor. But just as Grant's gory assaults had broken the back of the Confederacy, so, too, did the air offensive hasten an end to the war in Europe.

Especially after late '43, when P-51 Mustangs and P-47 Thunderbolts were equipped with long-range gasoline tanks and could escort bombers deep into German territory, Allied airmen became sacrificial lambs. Day after day they clashed with the Luftwaffe, their superiors secure in the knowledge that the Nazis were certain to lose a war of attrition: Hitler and his henchmen could never replace lost pilots and planes. It was nasty business, but everyone from a ground crew mechanic to General Eisenhower recognized that it had to be done.

"OUR COVERAGE OF THE AIR war consisted mostly of interviewing the bomber crews as they returned from their missions," Cronkite wrote years later. "We watched them coming home from battle, most with at least some damage—a cannon hole here or there or the almost delicate lacework of holes left by a trail of machine-gun bullets."[9]

One of Cronkite's favorite B-17 pilots in the 303rd was a twenty-two-year-old from Redondo Beach, California, named Don Stockton. Cronkite met Stockton in February of '43, after he'd steered a shot-up and nearly tailless Fort back to Molesworth from a raid over France.

"[Stockton] was sitting on a table in the briefing room, a doughnut in one hand and a coffee cup in the other. His flying cap was pushed back on his forehead. His face bore red marks where the oxygen mask had been. It was dirty and sweaty, but it was broken in the middle by one of the biggest grins I ever saw."[10]

Cronkite thought to himself: "This bird isn't real; he is out of one of those slick magazine ads. Don turned out to be the realest man I ever met."

Stockton sported a stubborn cowlick and a "twenty-mission cap"—regular-issue USAAF headgear with the stiffening wire removed to affect a rakish (and slightly crumpled) look. The guy who left Stanford University for the then Army Air Corps after his sophomore year had been made a captain at twenty-one, but he never put on officers' airs nor pulled rank, Cronkite remembered. He loved buying rounds of beer for the whole gang and often arranged for the Cross Keys to send a keg over to the enlisted men's club.

Stockton had joined the corps with two buddies from California. All three had begun flying combat missions over occupied France in November '42, the early stage of the USAAF bombing operations. Within weeks, Stockton's two friends had been killed; Stockton figured his number would soon be up. So he sat for a handsome photo portrait and shipped it off to his parents.[11] Remarkably, by the spring of '43, he had completed twenty-three combat missions, which put him in rarefied company: Two more and he'd reach the threshold of twenty-five. He'd be home free.

For his twenty-fourth sortie, on May 14, 1943, Stockton was ironically assigned to *S for Sugar*, the B-17 in which Cronkite had made his maiden combat raid ten weeks earlier. The target that day was the U-boat base at Kiel. Just after Stockton and his crew delivered their payload, they were jumped by German fighters. A twenty-millimeter cannon shell pierced the cockpit and struck Stockton on the right side of his chest. It was a complete fluke: Stockton was the only member of the crew hit. But the shot killed Stockton almost instantly. He slumped over the wheel; the Fort went into a near-fatal dive before copilot John C. Barker and Engineer Roy Q. Smith were able to wrest control and fly the barely damaged bomber back to Molesworth.[12]

Cronkite was waiting on the Molesworth tarmac to congratulate his friend on number twenty-four and get the skinny on what had happened over Kiel. It appeared from Cronkite's vantage point to be a routine landing; to his eye, *S for Sugar* looked unscathed. He was surprised, then, to see a red flare burst from the cockpit and an ambulance rush out to the end of the runway. A crew member was placed on a litter, then the red-crossed vehicle headed toward the field hospital.

"The open truck that ferried the air crews around the base came rolling back toward the debriefing shack and, to my anxious but apparently hasty eye, all the crew seemed to be aboard. They drew closer and the scene changed drastically. There were only nine of them. . . . And to a man—or make that to a boy—they were crying uncontrollably."

When the crew told him what had happened, Cronkite began weeping, too. But later he pulled himself together to write an article called NINE CRYING BOYS AND A FORT. Cronkite always said it should have been called NINE CRYING BOYS AND ONE CRYING CORRESPONDENT.

Once Stockton was laid to rest at the Brookwood Cemetery outside Cambridge,[13] Cronkite vowed to visit the grave on Memorial Day, 1944—a year removed. But D-Day preparations chained Cronkite to London, of course, and he couldn't get up to East Anglia. Instead, he wrote his most moving article of the war, a tribute to his friend Don that took the form of a letter to his parents.

"Dear Mr. and Mrs. Stockton: This is to apologize for not keeping my promise," Cronkite's article began. "You did not know of my promise. I made it only to myself—and silently to Don in a way. I promised to go out to Brookwood Cemetery and visit his grave this Memorial Day. But the war—the one that cut that grand full life of his short at 22 years—interfered in carrying out that simple little gesture of tribute."

Young Stockton was one of the "pioneers," Cronkite wrote, who bombed the Reich without fighter escorts. Cronkite closed by telling his parents that "in the year that has gone by, Don still stands out as typical of all the things that are finest in our American fliers."[14]

ANDY ROONEY, TOO, WAS PAYING homage to all the finest qualites of American airmen. Rooney tried not to let on, but on those train rides he was absorbing as much as he could from the likes of Cronkite, Bigart, and Hill. It occurred to him that his mentors were successful because they were relentlessly inquisitive, never afraid to ask questions or follow different story threads.

After the first Schweinfurt-Regensburg raid on ball bearing plants in August of 1943, Rooney had plenty of questions. Everything about

Schweinfurt-Regensburg, where five dozen bombers perished, was tragic, including the raiders' return to East Anglia. Rooney was on the ground at Thurleigh "sweating them in," as the ground crew guys called it. Increasingly frantic radio traffic made it clear, Rooney wrote, "the ordeal wasn't over. There were dead and dying men on board half a dozen of the group's bombers."

One B-17 reported that its ball-turret gunner was trapped inside his plastic bubble underneath the plane. The gears that opened his bubble and allowed him to climb back into the plane's belly had been hit in combat and were completely jammed. Even worse, the Fort's hydraulic system was also inoperable. The only way the plane could get on the ground was via belly landing.

> There were eight minutes of gut-wrenching talk among the tower, the pilot, and the man trapped in the ball turret. He knew what comes down first when there are no wheels. We all watched in horror as it happened. We watched as this man's life ended, mashed between the concrete pavement of the runway and the belly of the bomber.[15]

Readers of the *Stars and Stripes* never saw Rooney's account of the gunner's gruesome end. Rooney was so shaken that he returned to London that night, unable to write about what he'd witnessed. "Some reporter," Rooney reprovingly wrote of himself a half century later.[16]

The death of the B-17 ball-turret gunner has become part of the air war's lore; it's been twisted, turned, and fictionalized over the years. President Ronald Reagan was fond of telling a version of the story whose roots appeared to come not from the circumstances surrounding the real tragedy, but from the movie *A Wing and a Prayer* starring Reagan's friend Dana Andrews.

MOVIES WERE AN IMPORTANT PART of the folkways of wartime England. Almost everyone with a few bob in his pocket went to cinema houses a couple of times a week. Cronkite, a movie buff from his days as a fill-in reviewer for the *Houston Press*, didn't get to see as many films as he wanted because he worked so many nights. An evening at a British wartime movie theater would begin with a group sing-along, followed by cartoons, the latest newsreels, a short or two, and the inevitable double feature.

The press back then was almost as celebrity conscious as today's media. When Hollywood megastars Clark Gable and Jimmy Stewart arrived in England in '43 to serve in the Eighth Air Force, it was huge news. There was an insatiable public appetite for information about how the two icons, both then signed to Metro-Goldwyn-Mayer, were getting along in Britain. Under pressure from their bosses back home, correspondents, including the supposedly above-it-all Cronkite and Rooney, fell over one another to see who could score the biggest scoop.

Gable, the King of Hollywood, was four years removed from his turn as Rhett Butler in *Gone With the Wind*. He was still grieving over the loss of his wife, Carole Lombard, the gifted actress who died in early '42 in a plane crash while raising money for war bonds. That summer, Gable rankled the suits at MGM by enlisting as a private. He was soon persuaded to accept a captain's commission by War Department officials, no doubt prodded by a still-irate Louis B. Mayer, who didn't want his meal ticket seen as a lowly enlisted man.

Gable went through an abbreviated training course as an air gunner and was asked by USAAF boss Hap Arnold to produce and narrate a recruiting film heralding gunners called *Combat America*.[17] In early '43, Gable arrived in Britain in the same Hollywood entourage as *Memphis Belle* director William Wyler and was assigned to the First Wing headquarters at Cheltenham, then eventually transferred to active duty with the 351st Bomb Group at Polebrook.

"I have a clear impression of how good [Gable] looked in his pinks [dress uniform] and it didn't occur to me at the time but I suppose they were tailor-made for him in London," Rooney remembered.[18]

Cronkite happened to bump into Gable on one of the star's first days at Cheltenham, getting a story that AP and INS didn't have. The two struck up a relationship.

"I'm having a helluva time these days with Clark Gable," Cronkite wrote to Betsy on May 18, 1943. "I think I told you that I had a clear beat with an exclusive on his arrival in this area and that finally even the public relations office was calling me to find out where he was.

"Well, since then pandemonium has broken loose. The poor guy when he talked to me that first day said he was rather sorry I'd stumbled into him because he wanted to be just another officer and do his part in the war effort and he knew that a lot of reporters around all the time were going to hinder him in that ambition. When the pub relations men heard that they clamped down the screws and now nobody gets near the guy—except by accident. So I spend half my time now trying to create an accident for myself and prevent one for the AP or INS."[19]

Gable was serious about avoiding the limelight. When Bob Hope came to Polebrook for a USO show, Hope asked for "Rhett Butler" to stand up and take a bow. Gable never budged and the guys around him refused to give him up.[20]

"It was considered good politics as well as good public relations to get Gable an Air Medal," Cronkite recalled. "So they picked five milk runs to the nearby coast of France, and he was decorated with all the hoopla that Air Force public relations could muster."[21] It's true that the Eighth Air Force didn't send Gable deep into the Reich, but his first mission was hardly a pushover. The plane got shot up and a shell narrowly missed wounding Gable.[22]

"Gable was a good guy," Cronkite wrote. "I thought he was just a little self-conscious about that Air Medal. He had good reason to be, but he was living the role assigned to him and doing it as graciously as possible."[23]

He may have been gracious to Cronkite, but Gable, traumatized by what he saw happening to fellow airmen, had some rough moments. "It's murder up there," he confided to a member of his film crew. "They're falling like moths. Like dying moths."[24] While visiting a hospital full of wounded fliers, an overcome Gable threatened to pummel a doctor he felt wasn't being sufficiently empathetic.[25]

The star's presence wasn't lost on the Hollywood-worshipping enemy in Berlin. *Reichsmarschall* Göring offered a $5,000 reward to any Luftwaffe

flier that shot down Gable's plane. Gable worried that, were he ever captured, Hitler and Göring would turn him into a circus freak, parading him
all over the Reich. "How could I hide this face?" Gable confided to a friend.
"If the plane goes, I'll just go with the son of a bitch."[26]

Combat America, Gable's film, was supposed to help the Army Air
Force recruit air gunners. But the AAF already had more than enough
gunners by the time the film was ready for distribution in late '43. The
documentary contains some gritty combat footage and revealing interviews with gunners, but doesn't come close to packing the wallop of Wyler's The Memphis Belle.

JIMMY STEWART, TOO, ENLISTED AS a private, just days after winning an
Academy Award for his memorable role with Katharine Hepburn and
Cary Grant in The Philadelphia Story. Stewart, by then in his midthirties,
had gotten a pilot's license after graduating from Princeton and owned a
little two-seater. Coaxed into B-17 school, he was lauded as a superior pilot
and became an instructor. But Stewart began itching for combat duty; in
the fall of '43, the Army Air Force finally relented, again incurring Mayer's
wrath.

Ironically assigned to a B-24 Liberator unit, the 445th Bomb Group out
of Tibenham, Stewart was dead set against publicity. For months he refused to pose for pictures and fought off an avalanche of interview requests. Only when the Eighth Air Force's public relations officers pointed
out that a little press attention would help the morale of squadron members did Stewart finally budge, allowing photographers and correspondents to cover a medal ceremony.

"I was reluctant to send a cameraman out in front of the line of men
receiving awards and singling out Jimmy Stewart to photograph but I suspect that, in this case, he must have been a little proud and only tentatively
reluctant to have his picture in the Stars and Stripes," recalled Rooney. As
Rooney studied Stewart's face during the awards ceremony, he couldn't
help but think, "Those don't look like lips that have kissed Lana Turner's."

Later in life Rooney wondered if thoughts of kissing Turner had ever come to Stewart, unbidden, while attacking the Reich.[27]

Lieutenant Colonel Stewart ended up flying twenty-one missions over enemy territory without ever losing a plane or a crew member and was promoted to operations officer for the 453rd Bomb Group, then made chief of staff for the Second Bomb Wing out of Hethel.

Stewart was so valued by crew members that on September 27, 1944, he was called back to Tibenham after his old unit absorbed the worst beating in the annals of American aerial warfare.

Twenty-five of thirty-five Liberators did not make it home from a mission over Kassel and Göttingen. After releasing their loads they were jumped by three of Göring's *Sturmstaffeln* ("storm squadrons"), special units of heavily armored Fw 190s. Some survivors were in such deep shock that they couldn't utter a word. Stewart intervened, quietly divided the men into small groups, and got them to share their grief—and discuss how such a debacle might be averted by future attackers.[28]

Stewart was "the kind of American that Americans like to think of as typical even though he was better than that," Rooney wrote.[29]

"IT WAS LIKE A DEATH in the family every time a crew returned and found that friends in another B-17 or B-24 hadn't made it," Rooney remembered. "Back in their Nissen hut, they found empty bunks and silence where friends had been that morning. The wife, the girlfriend, the mother stared out from the picture next to the bunk. The guys were gone. In all probability dead or, at very best, prisoners. No one mentioned the empty spaces at the breakfast table next morning."[30]

The tour of duty for bomber boys in '43 was twenty-five missions; after that, at least in theory, they'd be rotated off duty or sent home. Many crew members kept track of their progress on barracks' walls by marking each mission with a vertical line.

One day, Rooney was interviewing a young airman sitting on a bunk and spotted the markings behind him. Rooney congratulated him on having completed seventeen missions. "You're practically done," Rooney smiled. "No," the kid responded. "Those aren't mine. Today was my third."

"I didn't have to ask about the man who had carved the seventeen marks," Rooney wrote. "He never got back to carve the eighteenth."[31]

At the Thurleigh airdrome, Rooney's home base, American airmen "adopted" a three-year-old war orphan, nicknamed her Sweet Pea, and decorated the nose of a bomber with her painted palm print, hoping her mark would keep the plane safe.[32]

The bomber boys knew every guy who disappeared the way classmates in a small school know one another. "If you hear of someone who flew thirty-five or forty missions in a bomber, it was not from a base in the British Isles before D-Day," Rooney wrote. "No one made it that far."[33] In one of his first columns, Hal Boyle told the story of a pilot in the Mediterranean Theater who had a recurring nightmare about landing on top of the Rock of Gibraltar—with brakes that had gone out.[34]

MAINTAINING MORALE IN BOMBER CREWS became so thorny that the Eighth Air Force took up the British Air Ministry on its offer to make the RAF's rest-and-relaxation homes—known among the ranks as flak farms—available to American airmen. Homer Bigart filed a piece in late April '43 on the R & R spot for officers and followed up seven weeks later with a description of the respite home for air gunners.

Censorship rules, of course, prevented Bigart from mentioning either location. But the Air Ministry had established flak farms at resorts and estates all over England: at Ebrington Manor in Gloucestershire; at Eynsham Hall near Whitney; at Phyllis Court near Henley on Thames; and at Moulsford Manor and Bucklands Hotel at Wallingford, Oxfordshire.[35] Bigart's eclectic knowledge and his gift for tart tongue-in-cheek observation were on full display in both articles.

"A rest home, with breakfast eggs, mullioned windows, tiled baths, central heating, golfing privileges, a butler named Bunting, and fishing rights in a stream mentioned favorably by the late Izaak Walton, has been requisitioned by the Air Ministry and thrown open to tired pilots, copilots, navigators and bombardiers of the Eighth Air Force," was his lede in the April 29 piece that got wide pickup beyond the *Herald Tribune*. The estate, wrote the reporter, who had just spent weeks hanging around director William Wyler, "resembles a Hollywood version of the country diggings of a strictly upper-class Mrs. Miniver." Some of the estate's relics dated from the time of King Ethelwulf, the monarch whom, Bigart informed readers, had "sired" Alfred the Great.

Its main house was "a Tudor residence of mellowed red brick, surmounted by five squat gables, ornamented by heavily-carved woodwork. The broad terrace along the southern front slopes gently to a chain of ponds, bordered by high clumps of rhododendron. Along the west slope are hothouses enclosing peach trees, fig trees and grape arbors and the usual rock garden." Then, just to give his august portrayal a hint of American insouciance, Bigart slipped in: "For security reasons, there is no babbling brook."

The place had been open since early January, but Eighth Air Force officers had been reluctant to use it because of its "unfortunate psychiatric connotation." "'Rest home,' Bigart needled, "brought to mind long rows of metal beds, rocking chairs, and bearded medicos tapping guests on the knee to check their reflexes." Disconcerting connotation or not, the AAF guys were taking full advantage. Some "rests" lasted as little as four days; others as long as two weeks.

There was only one regulation at flak farms—and it was strictly enforced. If any officer was caught talking shop, he was fined two shillings, sixpence.[36]

The same rule was theoretically in effect at the other RAF rest home Bigart wrote about, but this one was off-limits to officers. It was strictly for noncom air gunners. "These gunners may fight only a few hours a month. Their battle is short and sweet—but as deadly and vicious as any land engagement ever fought in Tunisia, New Guinea, or Guadalcanal," Bigart told readers in mid-June '43.[37]

Several airmen who had just survived a bloody June 13 mission to Kiel and Bremen happened to check into the home on the day Bigart arrived. The B-17 *Shackeroo* had barely made it back over the North Sea from German skies when it was ambushed by three Messerschmitts.

"[The enemy fighters] must have made a suicide pact," a crew member told Bigart, "for they just didn't care what happened. We nabbed two of the three on the first blast, but they got the Fortress on our left, then the survivor made three direct passes at [*Shackeroo*]. His guns opened up with three other jolts in the number one engine, setting it afire."[38]

Twice more the enemy pilot attacked *Shackeroo* before a gunner got him, but the bomber was a goner. To lighten its load, the crew tossed out everything; the pilot took the machine down to wave-top level. Its engines were badly sputtering; the crew assumed the water crash position, moving into the radio compartment and piling their parachutes against the wall for extra padding.

"They were prone on the floor, each man's head on another's chest, legs straddled for the sickening jolt of a water landing," Bigart wrote. *Shackeroo* smashed into the sea at 100 miles per hour.

The pilot and copilot dove out the port cockpit window; the rest of the men plunged out the radio room hatch. "They were a green crew," Bigart wrote, "but they behaved like veterans," prying loose two rafts and propping two wounded men, the bombardier and the navigator, on the wing while they got the dinghies in place. Just before the plane sank, they managed to get the wounded officers onto a raft. The men of the *Shackeroo* were lucky: A B-17 flying nearby saw them going into the water and dropped a rubber skiff and an emergency radio, all the while dispatching an SOS to Britain.

It was midday and a strong current was pushing them back toward the German coast. Two planes appeared overhead; for a moment they thought they were a pair of Spitfires. But they were enemy Focke-Wulfs that must not have spotted them. By six o'clock the sea started running very heavy; the men had to bail furiously just to keep the rafts afloat. "The sunlight waned," Bigart wrote, "and the penetrating cold of the North Sea felt like an Arctic blast."

Teeth chattering, the men continued to drift. Sometime after nine p.m., they heard a distant drone. Soon they recognized the silhouettes of two RAF Boston bombers. The men shot up a red flare.

"One bomber dipped its wing and began hovering around like an anxious hen," Bigart wrote. "The other turned sharply and headed into the sun."

Another nerve-racking thirty minutes passed with the RAF bomber treading the airspace overhead, intermittently dropping smoke flares so it could keep track of the rafts' whereabouts. Had it not been within a few days of the summer solstice, the men of the *Shackeroo* would never have been rescued. There was just a flicker of sunlight left when the men heard the whirring of an approaching British torpedo boat.

The *Shackeroo* wasn't the only B-17 to go down in the North Sea following the Kiel-Bremen attack. A less fortunate Fort crash-landed a few miles west of *Shackeroo*'s position. Two of its crew members drowned before the survivors were pulled out of the water by an RAF seaplane.[39]

Kiel-Bremen was the bloodiest American raid of the war to date. The Eighth Air Force lost twenty-six of sixty bombers that day: 260 men gone in a matter of minutes. It was just the third day of the combined bombing offensive with the Brits; already losses were staggering, yet unescorted missions continued unabated through that summer.[40]

FOLLOWING THE NAZI SURRENDER IN North Africa, Joe Liebling spent five fitful months in the States. He lived at the Fifth Avenue Hotel in the Village, tracking down strands of the Mollie story and finishing the rest of his Torch articles for what became *The Road Back to Paris*. He also tried to figure out what to do with his estranged wife, Ann, who continued to require periodic hospitalization.

Liebling returned to London and his flat at the Flemings in the late fall of '43. By January, he began asking the Ninth Air Force to let him fly along on a bombing operation over his cherished France. "I wanted to fly one mission and write a story about it, and pretend to myself that I was a big man," Liebling wrote later.

It took weeks, but his request was finally granted in early March of '44. Liebling was told to show up at an Essex airdrome in the northeast of London; he was assigned to a B-26 Marauder crew whose pilot, Liebling noted with great élan, was a left-leaning bookworm who harbored ambitions to become a writer. The captain had nicknamed his ship *Typographical Error*.

The *New Yorker* correspondent arrived at Essex on a Tuesday in the midst of dreadful weather. For three days running, the squadron's raids were scrubbed. Liebling hung out in the officers' hut, swapping stories about politics and literature with the erudite young captain; he became fond of the crew guys who poked fun at the pair's high-minded discourse.

By Friday, though, Liebling was antsy about getting back to Flemings; he had a date with a WAAC officer he'd met at the hotel pub. Urged on by his new pals, he decided to take the noon train back to Piccadilly.

As Liebling packed his duffel, the men were lounging in their bunks. Before leaving the hut, he made a point to shake hands with each. He was struck by the strong grip of the wannabe writer.

A few nights later Liebling was at Flemings having a drink with a Ninth Air Force intelligence officer named Kobold. The lieutenant waited a bit to break the bad news: When the weather cleared the day after Liebling left Essex, the squadron's mission was green-lighted. *Typographical Error* was shot down a few miles into France; the entire crew was lost.

"They had all their bombs aboard," Kobold explained. Squadron mates spotted "one big hell of a cloud of smoke, and then parts of the plane falling out if it. No chutes—no time for them. The other boys brought back wonderful pictures of it. Poor bastards," he said.

Kobold was an "oldish lieutenant," Liebling noted, well overdue for promotion and not happy about it. He was "talking loudly, a little truculently, because he wanted a couple of B-17 pilots at the other end of the bar to hear him," Liebling wrote. "The heavy-bomber people sometimes talked as if they had all the losses; the lieutenant wanted to impress this pair. He never flew on operations himself."[41]

Liebling felt guilty about having missed the fatal mission, but even that, he thought, was an "ignoble" consideration. At Kobold's suggestion, he returned to Essex and eventually went up with another B-26 crew. The plane was dubbed *Roll Me Over* after the popular British jingle that was a staple of pub and cinema sing-alongs.

Curiously, Liebling chose not to write about his air adventure until war's end. Even more curiously, he decided to create a fictional personality to assume the role of war correspondent in the story. Liebling's account "was all true," he wrote in his introduction, "except that I made the chief character a more obvious fraud than I am, by lending him some of the characteristics of correspondents I disliked."[42]

It took some doing in late '45 to persuade *New Yorker* editor Harold Ross to add an element of fiction to straight journalism, but eventually Ross went along. They didn't know it, but the two of them were pioneering what would come to be known as New Journalism.

Liebling playfully called his creation Allardyce Meecham and gave him his own misshapen torso, skinny legs, literary pretensions, and weakness for food and drink. Meecham was supposed to be a New York drama critic who'd grown weary of newspaper colleagues bragging about their war exploits. Liebling's artifice was so devoted to left-wing causes that, back in the '30s, he'd gone so far as to attend "several cocktail parties" to raise money for Spanish freedom fighters. So Liebling had Meecham pull some strings, get fitted for a uniform at Abercrombie & Fitch, and, looking very fierce, loll around the lobby of the Algonquin for a few days, hoping to be spotted by well-connected friends before heading off to London.

Creating a blowhard like Meecham allowed Liebling to poke fun at himself and those correspondents who were prone to puffing themselves up, embellishing the dangers they found themselves in. Flying on a combat mission, Liebling wrote to Joe Mitchell that spring, "confirmed my opinion that the blood-and-guts correspondents are a lot of shit and just make that stuff up: there's nothing much to it unless you get hit and maybe nothing much to it if you do get hit either."[43] Meecham was also a way for Liebling to relate his own physical and emotional inadequacies without coming across as maudlin. He hinted to Mitchell that he'd gone on the B-26 raid out of respect for the airmen—many of them now dead—whom he'd befriended in North Africa.

No matter the motivation, Liebling's account of the B-26 raid on the enemy airfield at Montdidier in northern France remains among his most compelling wartime pieces. The account of the attack begins before sunrise, with Meecham nervously stirring in his cot, then fumbling around the blacked-out base, hunting for the mess tent.[44]

Meecham sat at the breakfast table with his *Roll Me Over* crewmates. He felt guilty about being repelled by the oily eggs and bacon until one of his mates commented, "This is pisspoor chow." After breakfast, the crew hoisted Meecham onto a weapons carrier that took them en masse to the preflight briefing.

The briefing itself, Meecham thought, was reminiscent of a compulsory college course. It was filled with airmen not paying much attention; most of the crews had been on multiple missions to Montdidier and knew its geography and defenses by heart. The final G-2 briefer reminded the men that the enemy had the approach to the Mondidier airdrome armed with six medium-sized antiaircraft guns.

While being transported to the cinder path that encircled the planes, the men in the troop carrier began singing a profane song whose first line was "How's your love life?" Liebling's alter ego put on a bulky flying suit over his AAF-issue pants and sweater, then watched airmen go through their rituals to ward off the cold, some rubbing hands, some stomping feet.

The chubby Meecham was relieved that it wasn't difficult to grab the metal stirrups on either side of the hatch to hoist himself into the plane. He was also thankful that he didn't have to crawl once inside the fuselage. "There's a hell of a lot of room in these [B-26] things. More than in a Fort," the bombardier said in motioning for his guest to sit near a pile of parachutes in a compartment behind the nose.

Once the propellers began revving they made such a racket that conversation became impossible, although a shouted monosyllable could be understood. Meecham had been told that the squadron had been armed with thirty hundred-pound fragmentary bombs. "We drop them on the runway and dispersal area to take care of planes and personnel," the bombardier calmly explained to Meecham through earphones. "Sometimes we carry a couple of big ones, but today frags." A fragmentary bomb packed less wallop than a five hundred pounder but spewed more shrapnel over a smaller area. In the late winter and spring of '44, tens of thousands of frags were dropped on enemy installations all over northern France.

After they got airborne, the pilot and copilot waved for Meecham to come forward to the cockpit, "and he did, scrunching his torso and hams down behind the [pilot's] seat, while his legs extended over behind the [copilot's]."[45]

Above the cloud cover, Liebling wrote in one of his ineffable similes, "the sky was as blue as the Bay of Naples on the wall of a spaghetti joint, and it was full of B-26s." The squadron was flying in its favorite configuration, "loose fives," a series of five-plane subgroups.

Meecham tried to count all the bombers within view. He got to sixty-seven before he realized it was hopeless; more kept appearing. The pilot plucked Meecham's elbow, signaling for him to look down. They were heading over the Channel, "which looked not blue but had, at its English edge, the color of a puddle of rain water glistening in sunlight. Then it became lead color."

All the attention was beginning to embarrass Meecham/Liebling: "the crew was treating him like a grandfather on a Sunday auto ride."

Montdidier was a village of four thousand in the Somme region north of Paris, the sacred ground that had proved so difficult for the *Boches* to conquer in the Great War. Now it had been under the heel of German oppression for four years.

The bombardier tapped Meecham on the shoulder and pointed out tiny dots on the horizon. Fearing they were enemy fighters, Meecham braced himself for onrushing Focke-Wulfs, but soon recognized that they were puffs of flak. He heard a new sound over the engines. It was a "sharp 'Pak!' like a champagne cork popping and then 'S-s-s' like half the wine in the bottle fizzing out. The 'Pak!' was the shell bursting, and the fizz was the flight of the fragments." At one point Meecham was startled when the pilot threw a hand up in front of his face, but no shrapnel penetrated the cockpit.

Soon the copilot was pointing forward: the B-26s up ahead were already dropping their frags. The bombs looked to Meecham "like chewing-gum nuggets out of a vending machine." Within seconds *Roll Me Over*'s frags were away, too—and suddenly the flak stopped. The bombardier began shouting. Through gestures Meecham asked if he'd landed his bombs on target. The bombardier answered by chortling and joining his thumb and forefinger: *Roll Me Over* had hit the bull's-eye.

Meecham was heartened when he glanced at the airspeed indicator in the cockpit and saw 330 miles per hour. There were no incidents on the way home, but it seemed to take five times longer than the trip out.

Back at Essex, as they climbed out of the plane, the pilot and copilot started muttering curses about their squadron mates' apparent inability to maintain a steady course. "What a ratfuck!" the pilot spat. When asked, the pilot explained that "a ratfuck was 'a rat race, but all bollixed up.'"

Meecham "felt unreasonably exalted. After all, he told himself reprovingly, he had only escaped from a danger that he had got himself into. And not a great danger, either, he thought. I didn't see one plane shot down. Still, he couldn't help thinking, pretty good for a dramatic critic."

Liebling threw everything—a novelist's eye, startling insights into wartime London, and his deep self-loathing—into the story's close. Meecham was still feeling euphoric when he got to the Chelmsford train station that afternoon. The train to London was packed, but when a group of American enlisted men spotted Meecham's war correspondent badge, they invited him to join them in their compartment.

"They were all Fortress men," Liebling wrote, "who, it appeared, had been on dozens of twelve-hour missions over Germany, from almost all of which they had returned with their ships aflame and three engines out. Meecham was ashamed to tell them he had been only as far as France that morning. By the time the train arrived at Liverpool Street station his exuberance was waning."

Feeling hungry, Meecham/Liebling stops in a fish restaurant, sits at the bar, and orders a dozen oysters. He wants to order a second dozen, but the barkeep tells him the Ministry of Food prevents them from selling more than eight bob worth to a customer.

"Meecham felt a certain resentment; he had half a mind to tell the man where he had been that morning. That would show him. But perhaps the man had a son in the R.A.F., so he would not be impressed. Or three R.A.F. sons, all killed in the Battle of Britain, so he would be pained by any reference to flying." Meecham/Liebling left the restaurant to hail a taxi. "He hoped his girl was in town and had no date for the evening. After all, this ought to impress her."[46]

AMERICAN B-26S HIT THE MONTDIDIER airfield several times in the windup to D-Day. So did British Lancashire and Halifax bombers. The Montdidier missions, in fact, were all part of Eisenhower's strategic bombing campaign, the Supreme Allied Commander's controversial insistence on making enemy fortifications in northern France and the Low Countries a bigger early-'44 bombing priority than bases and factories inside Germany. As Chester Wilmot revealed in *The Struggle for Europe*, Ike's demand that targets in Normandy and contiguous areas be repeatedly bombed set off one of the war's biggest internal squabbles.[47]

Siding with Ike was Omar Bradley, the commander of D-Day's U.S. seaborne infantry, and two of Churchill's leading air war advisors: Air Chief Marshals Sir Arthur Tedder and Sir Trafford Leigh-Mallory. On the other side was practically everyone else in the Anglo-American strategic bombing brain trust: Harris, Arnold, Spaatz, Doolittle, and Curtis LeMay—all of whom believed that the Allies were on the cusp of winning the war because Germany was being bled dry. Some even believed that bombing German oil fields would render superfluous a cross-Channel invasion—an absurd notion that nevertheless was given widespread currency.

Ike prevailed, but only after Churchill, Roosevelt, and Marshall were forced to intervene. In late winter, the Combined Chiefs of Staff agreed to place the air forces under Ike's operational "direction," but not quite control. The heavies were soon hitting rail marshaling yards and bases like Montdidier with brutal regularity.

As the years went by, nothing made Eisenhower prouder than discussing his role in softening enemy defenses in and around Normandy in the months leading up to the invasion. For a twentieth-anniversary documentary on D-Day, Ike told CBS News that he believed the strategic bombing campaign had made a huge difference in enabling the Allied invaders to gain a toehold in France. His interviewer was a newsman who'd covered the campaign up close, one Walter Cronkite.

———

On August 19, 1943, Andy Rooney wrote a tribute to the Eighth Air Force that commemorated its bombing campaign's first anniversary. The *Stars and Stripes* ran his piece as a special supplement; it was a good four times longer than the typical *Stars and Stripes* article. In it Rooney told a remarkable story that had occurred three weeks earlier. Staff Sergeant Tyre Weaver of River View, Alabama, a top-turret gunner, and Second Lieutenant Keith J. Koske of Milwaukee, a navigator, were on the crew of the B-17 *Ruthie II*. They were part of a July 26 Flying Fortress mission over Hanover, Germany, that ran into a swarm of Focke-Wulf 190s. One explosion of cannon fire killed the pilot. Another burst a few seconds later rocked the top of *Ruthie II*.

"Weaver fell through the [top-turret] hatch and slumped to the floor at the rear of the nose compartment," Koske told Rooney. "[Weaver's] left arm had been blown off at the shoulder and he was a mess of blood. I tried to inject morphine but the needle was bent and I couldn't get it in."

They were still four full hours away from England; there was no way, Koske reckoned, that Weaver could survive that long without serious medical help. He secured the gunner's parachute, wrapped the rip cord in Weaver's hand, and tossed him out over Lower Saxony, praying that Weaver would survive the fall and get decent care. "[Weaver] was really a stout fellow and seemed to know it was his only chance," Koske said.

When Rooney wrote his anniversary piece in mid-August, there had been no word on Weaver's fate. Koske and the other surviving crew members feared the worst. Weaver, his pals told Rooney, constantly talked about tinkering with his '33 Ford;[48] the heap was up on blocks in his parents' driveway in River View.

Rooney ended his piece with this homage to the bomber boys he knew so well: "The Eighth Air Force is a story of men necessarily buried under the damnably cold heap of statistics the Allies are trying to pile higher than Axis statistics. When the pile is higher the airmen can go home, and if that American kid was saved by a German doctor, maybe he can get a license to drive his '33 Ford with his one arm."[49]

Four months later, miraculous word arrived from Red Cross officials: Weaver had survived his ordeal and was being treated in a German prison hospital. A young German girl had seen Weaver's parachute thud into a field; defying the Gestapo's orders not to approach enemy fliers, she ran over to Weaver and realized he was seriously injured. She then ran to a nearby army post; two soldiers arrived and took Weaver, unconscious, to a local doctor.

After recovering, Weaver was sent to Stalag 17-B near Krems, Austria, the notorious POW camp that inspired a book, a play, and a fine 1953 movie starring William Holden and written and directed by the great Billy Wilder, an Austrian émigré.

Weaver's good fortune continued: A year later, he was repatriated in a prisoner exchange. As Weaver returned to Alabama *Life* magazine followed, running his picture on October 23, 1944; the photo showed Weaver grinning broadly, his left uniform sleeve neatly pinned at the shoulder.

He managed to do a lot more than just drive his Ford one-handed; he learned to pilot a plane with one arm, too. Weaver got himself elected tax collector of Chambers County, in part because voters loved the unusual way he campaigned: tossing out ELECT WEAVER leaflets as his two-seater zoomed overhead. His plane buzzed so low one day that it nearly clipped the steeple of the Chambers County Court House.

While waiting at a local bank one day, Weaver spotted a pretty teller and shrewdly hopped lines to meet her; two weeks later, he and Frances were married. They raised a family of seven kids and, eventually, twenty grandkids. Today an entire wall of the United States Air Force Enlisted Heritage Hall in Montgomery is devoted to the wonderful saga of Staff Sergeant Tyre Weaver.[50]

Weaver lived long enough to see the wall dedicated in his honor. He also lived long enough to be reunited with Keith Koske, the navigator whose quick actions had saved his life. Together with Gene Ponte, another member of the *Ruthie II* crew, they would chat every July 26, the anniversary of the fateful raid.

The story of the one-armed gunner who survived a parachute fall from five miles up was featured in the 1949 Gregory Peck film *Twelve O'Clock*

High and highlighted in *Ripley's Believe It or Not*—but the fictionalized accounts of Tyre Weaver's story don't do justice to the real one.[51]

Weaver was one of 9,300 USAAF airmen wounded in action in the ETO and one of twenty-six thousand American airmen captured by the enemy. Nearly twenty-four thousand American fliers were killed in action in the ETO.[52]

"I love Mr. Weaver's quote," wrote his daughter-in-law Brenda, the wife of Tyre's son Bob. It was an inscription that helped Sergeant Weaver get through his trials: "For you see, no matter what a man believes before the mission starts, after it's over he knows he's been in God's hands."[53]

CHAPTER 7

★

SICILY—DARKER THAN A WITCH'S HAT

On the outskirts of San Stefano a dead German lay by the roadside. His comrades had covered the body with a white shroud, but it had slipped from his face. His blond head was matted with blood and dust and he was staring open-mouthed at the blue Tyrrhenian Sea.

—HOMER BIGART, July 31, 1943
NEW YORK HERALD TRIBUNE

It was "hellish hot" that August night, Homer Bigart recounted, as nearly seven hundred Army commandoes, their faces blackened, piled from the transport vessel into DUKW assault boats. They were bobbing on the Tyrrhenian Sea seven miles behind enemy lines, poised to launch a clandestine attack on the Fifteenth Panzer Grenadier Division's stronghold at Brolo on the northern Sicilian coast. Looming beyond the rocky beach was the imposing specter of Monte Cipolla. In the forbidding blackness, the commandoes and the seven correspondents covering them—an esteemed list handpicked by the U.S. Seventh Army's public relations staff that included Bigart of the *New York Herald Tribune*, Tom Treanor of the *Los Angeles Times*, Jack Belden of *Time*, and Don Whitehead of Associated Press—could barely make out the mountain's 750-foot-high peak.

A few minutes earlier the raid's commander, Lieutenant Colonel Lyle A. Bernard of the Third Division's Second Battalion, had pinpointed Monte Cipolla on a map. "Take this objective," the thirty-three-year-old native of Highland Falls, New York, pleaded to the men gathered around him on the ship's deck, "and we'll be in Messina in a week."[1] They'd attack Brolo and Monte Cipolla in four waves of riflemen and artillerymen, spaced fifteen minutes apart, Bernard explained. Two companies led by Bernard would seize the summit, a mortar unit would be stationed midmountain, and the remainder would seek to control the valley. The ship wasn't alone: Second Battalion's transport was flanked by the light cruiser *Philadelphia* and six destroyers.

Forty tortuous miles east of Brolo, Messina was the island's last outpost; the toe of Italy protruded two and a half miles across the strait. Days before, the Germans had begun ferrying thousands of troops to the safety of the mainland, a massive retreat that went on for another week, inexplicably unmolested by the Allies.

Bernard may not have known at that point that the enemy was in the process of evacuating Sicily. But he knew all too well that his ultimate boss, Lieutenant General George Patton, the U.S. Seventh Army's commander, was obsessed with beating British commander Bernard Montgomery and Monty's British Eighth Army to Messina. Patton wasn't the only American determined to outrace the Brits to Sicily's northeastern edge. A BBC report given wide airing in Sicily that week suggested that Patton's boys had the easier go of it against mainly Italian troops in the western part of the island, while Monty's men had a tougher slog against Hitler's finest along the eastern coast. There was more than a smidgeon of truth to the charge, but it nevertheless got doughboys riled up.

Even the impassive Omar Bradley, Patton's deputy commander, was angling to outdo the Brits. "I confess that while no strategic purpose would be served by it," Bradley recalled in his memoirs, "I was equally anxious to beat Monty to Messina, if it were possible without recklessness or undue casualties."[2]

The problem, of course, was that "recklessness" and "George Patton" went hand in hand; moreover, Patton rarely gave "undue casualties" a second thought if they stood between him and a headline. And that early August morning, with seven top combat reporters poised to herald his latest bid for military genius, Patton saw his name in a lot of headlines.

Ironically, it was corps commander Bradley and Third Division head

Lucian Truscott who came up with the notion of tapping the small naval force docked at recently captured Palermo. Their scheme was to launch amphibious assaults to leapfrog German defenses, cutting off the enemy's means of escape along coastal road 113.[3]

With Patton bleating in their ears, Bradley and Truscott rolled out their first amphibious end run along Sicily's northern coast on the evening of August 7, 1943. Lieutenant Colonel Bernard's commandoes surprised the Germans by landing near Sant'Agata and San Fratello, some ten miles into enemy territory. Undetected, they sleuthed toward the Rosmarino River. That same night, in a choreographed move, Truscott's inland troops opened an offensive against Germans holding the hills between the Third Division's position and San Fratello.

The pincer movement confused the enemy—but only temporarily. Truscott and Bradley ended up disappointed with the mission's results. The Third Division regulars struggled to gain ground against armored troops. Bernard's battalion, meanwhile, got caught in the vise of a counterattack; it was trapped at the riverbank for the better part of two days before being relieved by another unit of Truscott's infantry.

Dog tired, their ranks depleted, the Second Battalion men were ordered by Patton just hours later to perform another amphibious miracle at Brolo.[4] Truscott, chastened by the Sant'Agata experience, was wary of ordering another seaborne incursion unless he was convinced his inland troops could crack the German line around Cape Orlando and quickly link up with Bernard. The Brolo raid had been scheduled to jump off on August 9 but Truscott pleaded for and got a twenty-four-hour reprieve, although it rankled Patton. Bradley and Truscott wanted a similar delay on August 10 to get the Seventh and 15th Infantry Regiments closer to Brolo. But this time Patton refused, irking Bradley, who felt that Patton was undermining his prerogatives as corps commander.

Patton chewed out Truscott several times by phone, then blistered him, as depicted in *Patton*, in person at Truscott's command post near Terranova, invoking Frederick the Great's maxim: *"L'audace, l'audace, toujours l'audace!"*

George Patton was good at preaching audacious courage when the lives of other men were on the line. But even Patton had twinges of guilt. He wrote in his journal that night: "I may have been bull-headed."[5]

BULLHEADED INDEED. "TWO AMPHIBIOUS OPERATIONS in three days is a nasty business, requiring more guts than are given the average man," Bigart observed. Not a reporter given to sentimental outburst, Bigart was so inspired by the commandoes' grit that his account of the August 7 raid imagined a postwar victory parade.

"There was one platoon in particular whose men should be remembered when they move down Fifth Avenue beneath the victory arch. They were the men of Lieutenant Jesse Ugalde, a twenty-one-year-old art student from Greeley, Col. Ugalde's platoon was the only one to reach the objective in the Agata mission. Cut off, they held the edge of San Fratello for thirty hours without food or water, harassing the enemy retreat and killing or capturing a score of Germans."

With barely a day's rest, Bernard, Ugalde, and their men now were greasing their faces for another nighttime attack. "They walked with the heavy tread of men half drugged by want of sleep," Bigart wrote.

The holds of the attack ships were brimming with tanks, half-tracks, and special amphibious trucks. DUKWs were marvels of American ingenuity, wheeled "duck boats" that could motor through waves, then drive onto a beach and into the fields beyond. To compensate for the men lost in the earlier raid, Bernard had been given a unit of Army Rangers. Bernard congregated his men at midnight, two and a half hours before H hour. Combat had wearied him, Bigart thought; Bernard looked much older than his early thirties.

Bigart described the pipe-smoking Bernard as "wiry," but photos taken the next day suggest that "wan" might have been a better adjective. With his men squatting in front of him, Bernard "told some jokes, unprintable here but suited to the occasion," Bigart wrote. "Faces relaxed."[6]

A battalion mate remembered that Bernard had two favorite expressions, which, for effect, he often spliced together: "Horseshit!" and "Get off the beach!" Out of affection his men dubbed him Horseshit Bernard.

"He was never satisfied with the speed with which we got off the beach," the friend recalled. "At the beginning of every critique, he would say, 'What I saw out there was a lot of horseshit! You were too slow getting off the beach! That's pure horseshit!'"[7]

As the men strained to hear Horseshit Bernard, a blare came from the foredeck. Some commandoes scrambled for cover alongside a hunk of tarpaulin; others jumped behind a mast.

"Then someone laughed, and the laughter spread uncontrollably," Bigart noted. "The cry that cleared the decks was 'Chow!'"

Bernard led his officers into the wardroom where they ate their snack while reviewing a map of Brolo and Monte Cipolla. Each officer had been assigned a series of specific tasks. A kid engineering lieutenant from Anoka, Minnesota, named Walter W. Wagner had a big job. Once he cleared the beach of mines and barbed wire—no small task—Wagner would be in charge of loading ammunition and supplies onto vehicles moving inland.

The officers studied their landing target, a five-hundred-yard tuft between the dry mouths of the Naso and Brolo rivers. Bigart joined them in examining air reconnaissance photos of a culvert beneath the railroad that hugged the coast. Bernard reminded his duck and amphibious tank drivers that the underpass was navigable—probably the best means to get inland in a hurry. He also stressed that the first two hundred yards beyond the beach were fairly flat, dotted with vineyards and lemon orchards. But once the invaders got beyond the road they would hit what Bigart called the "sheer slopes" of Monte Cipolla.

At one o'clock Bernard halted the briefing, lit his pipe, and lightened the mood by reading a letter written by his three-year-old daughter. Bernard's gentle blue eyes again turned serious.

"Amphibious operations are no fun—definitely," Bernard said. "It'll be darker than the inside of a witch's hat on that beach. And this time the Germans should be ready for us."

The first and second waves of attackers went below, boarded the duck boats, and waited. And waited. Ghostly blue lights made the moment even eerier, Bigart noted.

"Helmeted heads and rifles glistened in the semidarkness," wrote Homer's friend Tom Treanor. The men were allowed to smoke until the attack boats shoved off. A seasick soldier began retching. Finally, someone barked, "Kick over your engines!"[8]

A lone harmonica player began a mournful rendition of Cole Porter's "Night and Day."[9] The soldiers might not have known the lyrics by heart, but the reporters surely did. By the time they murmured "in the roaring traffic's boom," Bigart, Treanor, Belden, and Whitehead were no doubt anxiously scouring the shore for signs of enemy artillery.

Sounding like a flotilla of motorboats, the ducks circled for several minutes until what Treanor called "their little flock" had fully gathered. "Let's go, then!" Bernard bellowed.[10]

As they got under way, a GI sitting near Don Whitehead stage-whispered, "Why don't we do this more often?" drawing nervous chuckles across the water.[11] An orange quarter moon had gone down; the sky was now filled, Treanor noted, with "pitiless" stars. "The black mass of Monte Cipolla[12] blotted the stars directly ahead," Bigart wrote.

It took a bit longer than Bernard had reckoned to churn the two-plus miles to shore. It was 0243, thirteen minutes past H hour, before the first wave of ducks, hauling minesweepers, wire cutters, and a detachment of infantry, waddled across the pebbly beach. Bigart was in the second wave. From his perch on the DUKW, he breathed a sigh of relief that the initial attackers had "done their work without arousing the shore sentries."

Remarkably, for the second time in three days the Second Battalion caught the enemy napping, at least at first; Brolo's beach and adjoining fields were unoccupied. "Our duck scrunched through the sand and came to a gentle halt near the orchard rim," Bigart wrote. "A big gap had been cut in the barbed wire and we started running down a lane toward the hill."[13]

Their furtive dash—"Watch the fucking barbed wire!"[14] one GI warned—took them to the edge of the village. "Tense and breathless, we huddled in front of the first house in Brolo, our ears straining for the sound of enemy traffic," Bigart noted.

An enemy truck rumbled in the distance, then drove past, unsuspecting; the commandoes held their fire. "A minute later along came a small tan Italian car. Sixty rifles blazed and the [vehicle] burst into flames," Bigart wrote. Two men leapt out, screaming. One went down; the other kept running. "There he goes! Hit the bastard!" a GI shrieked.[15] There was another shower of bullets. "We could hear them whimpering for another ten minutes, then silence," Bigart wrote. One of the enemy soldiers had been killed; the other severely wounded.

Soon enough, they heard an ominous clanking. They assumed it was an enemy tank and dove behind a stone wall. It turned to be a less lethal half-track.

"Shoot, you stupid clown!" hissed an officer at a bazooka gunner. "'Can't,' drawled the soldier. 'Some of our men across the road are directly in the line of fire.'" The bazooka man waited until the half-track was fifty yards removed before cutting loose.

A dazed German soldier, probably wounded, stumbled out. He staggered over the stone wall, heading toward the murky figures he could see under a copse of trees. His last words before being shot by a dozen riflemen were "Herr Lieutenant!"[16]

By now the Germans in Brolo were wide-awake and scrambling. Within seconds an enemy machine gun started firing, sending a stream of red tracers over the attackers' heads and into the Tyrrhenian. The Americans began clambering up Monte Cipolla, until an enemy gunner spat at them from farther up the slope. "We pressed against the cliffside as bullets whined over our heads," Bigart wrote. "A spate of rifle fire silenced the gun. We heard no further shooting until dawn."

Sweating buckets in the oppressive heat, the raiders continued to climb, often reduced to all fours, hoisting themselves up the hill by grabbing shoots of grass and bushes.[17] They could hear trucks being unloaded on the beach instead of at the base of the mountain and instinctively knew something was wrong. The railroad underpass had proved too narrow; a precious half hour had been squandered while Lieutenant Wagner and his engineers rigged a ramp.

It seemed to take forever to the out-of-shape correspondents, but finally they crested the summit. To their astonishment they discovered eight slumbering Germans sharing the same blanket, oblivious to the bedlam seven hundred feet below. They tied up the Germans and spent the pre-dawn hours digging foxholes and trenches, then tried to catch some rest under a grove of olive trees.[18] At daybreak they spotted forty to fifty enemy troops in the valley making a beeline toward Brolo, but a U.S. machine gunner forced them back into the woods. The Germans soon retaliated by killing fifteen GIs bravely stringing phone wire uphill. Grenadiers also slaughtered twenty-two of the twenty-four mules the Army had requisi-tioned to haul ammunition and food up the mountain.

Whitehead happened to overhear Bernard mutter something about the "absolute confusion" that plagues amphibious landings.[19] No doubt Ber-nard peppered his remarks with a few well-chosen "horseshits," which Whitehead kept out of his journal.

Around 0800 Bigart heard Bernard predict that before long German artillery and tanks would begin zeroing in. "I'm going to ask the Navy for point-blank fire on the town." What Bernard didn't know was that the *Philadelphia* and its escorts, worried about daylight attacks from the Luft-waffe, had already vacated the beachhead. It took two and a half hours before the worried Truscott, who'd just learned that his inland troops had been stymied in their advance toward Cape Orlando and Monte Cipolla, prevailed on the *Philadelphia* to get back into range to fire at enemy en-trenchments.

The cruiser's guns kept the Germans at bay for a while. But again the ship turned back toward Palermo Harbor. By late morning the raiders' luck had run out. At 11:40, Bigart spotted a big enemy gun being mounted in an orchard east of town. Seventy minutes later, the reporters could see Ger-man soldiers hustling at the foot of the mountain, reconnoitering to coun-terattack. Mortar fire began plastering the hill.

"From a jutting crag atop the mountain we saw two Tiger tanks creep down the single street of Brolo," Bigart wrote the next day. "Almost simul-taneously a Tiger and a Mark IV tank crawled out from behind a bend in the coastal road west of our position. They looked like harmless little bugs as they scurried for the cover of a closer bend.

"Lying snug in a tuft of red-top hay, we felt no fear. We were 700 feet above the road, and height gives a deceptive feeling of confidence. We had yet to learn that the Germans could lift a storm of shrapnel to our ledge, ripping some of us to shreds before the day was gone."[20]

Stuffing his last tobacco into a pipe, Bernard again radioed Truscott for help. The Third Division head ordered the *Philadelphia* to resume its barrage; for forty brief minutes it did, but repeated Focke-Wulf attacks sent it hightailing west. "We'll catch hell this afternoon," Bernard solemnly predicted.[21]

They did. German mortar, artillery, and tank shells killed and wounded dozens, triggered fires that destroyed the hastily laid telephone wires, and cut off Bernard's communications down below with both his troops and naval gunfire observers.

"The sun beat mercilessly on our summit bivouac," Bigart wrote. "Dripping perspiration, we hacked slit trenches in the rocky soil beneath the almond trees."[22] They soon began running out of water, food, and ammunition. The reporters were so parched, they stood in line to stick their canteens in a slimy ditch "alive with wrigglers," Treanor reported.[23] But German artillery soon zeroed in on the spring, eliminating the raiders' only water source.[24]

At around four o'clock a cheer went up and down the mountain as seven American A-36 fighter-bombers zoomed over. But poorly directed pilots bombed Bernard's command post by accident, scattering GIs into their slit trenches and inflicting nineteen horrific casualties. Then, compounding their woes, the friendly planes bombed the commandoes' position farther down the hill, immobilizing their last four howitzers. A medic whose arm had been mangled in the air attack tried to amputate it with a pocketknife. The Germans began moving snipers and machine gunners up the slope; it looked like the enemy would storm the crest at any instant.[25]

His hands tied, Truscott ordered a reprise attack from the *Philadelphia*, which this time had to fight off a swarm of Focke-Wulfs as it fired a thousand shells in a fifteen-minute fusillade. Once the shelling stopped, Bernard sent word for the few survivors down below to join the men at the summit for what he felt sure would be their last stand. A few of Bernard's valley charges chose a different route, jumping into the Tyrrhenian and thrashing toward Palermo.

Enemy sharpshooters got close enough to knock out Bernard's only functioning radio; now the men of the Second Battalion were completely cut off and surrounded. Resigned to their fate, they dug deeper trenches, with Bigart, Treanor, and Whitehead furiously scraping, too. Bernard fortified his position by collapsing his rear and flank guards into a tiny perimeter. Most men by then were out of bullets. In toto, they had fewer than two dozen mortar shells.

Into the night and early morning, they braced themselves for the attack that would obliterate them. It never came.[26]

At first light they were startled to see American trucks and jeeps heading up the coast road. A few minutes later, an Army runner who'd pounded up the mountain informed Bernard, between pants, that the enemy had abandoned Brolo and was retreating toward Messina. Sure enough: Bernard trained his binoculars west and could see forward elements of the 30th Division coming to relieve him. Miraculously, the Second Battalion had again beaten the odds.

So had Bigart and the other correspondents, all of whom were lucky to be alive. "Well, we took a licking," Bernard told Bigart as they started down the hill. "We put the cork in the bottle but we couldn't hold it in."[27]

At about 0800, Bernard, his exhausted men, and the reporters gingerly worked their way "past the torn bodies of American and German dead," Bigart wrote. They reached the valley in time to see Patton's command jeep, its three silver-starred pennants streaming, shriek to a halt in front of a Messina road sign. With Patton was Senator Henry Cabot Lodge, the Massachusetts Republican whose bristly prewar isolationism had made him a darling of the America First movement.

Patton's public relations officers, the same execs who, at their boss' insistence, had arranged for the reporters to go on the Brolo raid, now contrived a photo opportunity. Without deigning to leave his vehicle, the general posed for pictures with Bernard. Patton stood in the back of the jeep, imperiously staring down at his valiant lieutenant colonel, while the telltale arrow in the backdrop pointed toward Messina. The picture ran in the *Herald Tribune* and scores—probably hundreds—of other newspapers back home.

With photographers, reporters, and a U.S. senator present, Patton felt obliged to make a little speech. "Only American soldiers can climb mountains like those," he effused, dramatically gesturing toward Cipolla with his swagger stick. Patton was full of it, of course. The Germans had been all over the mountain for months and could easily have recaptured it.

Patton's insistence on *l'audace* had triggered nearly 180 casualties—with little to show for them. Don Whitehead, like Bigart, was standing a few feet away from the general; he later wrote in his diary, "The whole tableau sickened me."[28]

Whitehead wasn't alone. Omar Bradley, a commander not prone to hyperbole, called Brolo a "complete fiasco."[29] The Germans suffered losses comparable to those of the Americans, but their line was never breached. Nor was the enemy escape route blocked or even impeded, although the raid may have accelerated their retreat. But the Germans weren't *that* harried; a few miles east of Brolo, they dynamited a hunk of the coastal road, making it tougher for Patton's men to pursue them.[30]

Bigart's lede, batted out in Brolo on no sleep, with Seventh Army tanks and trucks grinding past, was a thing of beauty, vivid and crisp without being maudlin.

"A tough and gallant band of Americans was relieved at 8 o'clock this morning on the thorny summit of Monte Cipolla, where it had made a last-ditch stand against encirclement and annihilation by the 15th German Panzer Division."[31]

Square that with the curious piece filed from afar by Hal Boyle that same day. Boyle was in a pack of reporters struggling to keep up with Patton's advance elements as they bulled their way up the coast. The story that Boyle got on the Brolo raid, undoubtedly spoon-fed by Patton's PROs, bore little resemblance to the terrifying reality experienced by his friends Whitehead, Bigart, and Treanor. THREE GERMAN TANK ATTACKS BEATEN

OFF IN YANK LANDING was the way the *Stars and Stripes* chose to flag Boyle's article. In Boyle's telling, "the Allied air forces bombed the German positions in a well-coordinated effort with the navy to help [the raiders] in every way."[32] Whatever puny air cover the raiders had received was hardly "well coordinated," especially since most of the ordnance fell on them, not the enemy. Bernard's men, moreover, might not have been inclined to characterize the Navy's role as helping them "in every way."

A staff officer also had the temerity to tell Boyle that the August 7 Agata–San Fratello raid had sparked a "collapse" in the enemy line—a spurious account to which Lucian Truscott and Omar Bradley would have taken strong exception.

Boyle did, however, finish with an accurate statement: "For many of these men it was their third landing on enemy shores. They smashed ashore to establish African beachheads last November and repeated their success last month on the southern coast of Sicily." But his piece ended with more unwitting fiction: "This second overnight sortie behind entrenched enemy positions illustrated anew the continuing close cooperation between the navy and army in reducing Germany's last shrinking rampart in the mountainous northeast corner of this island."[33]

HOMER BIGART STAYED IN THE shrinking rampart long enough to pick up another story of an American soldier cheating death. Two days after tempting fate on the summit of Monte Cipolla, Bigart filed a piece about the wild misadventures of Second Battalion Staff Sergeant Odell Tedrow of Rockport, Illinois.

Tedrow was a member of the battalion's medical detachment, Bigart noted in an article that was picked up all over the country. The sergeant's job upon hitting the beach in the early morning hours of August 10 was to help set up a field hospital near the railroad culvert. "At dawn, when the shooting began," Bigart wrote, "[Tedrow] set out with a stretcher party in search of wounded men."

Communications and picket lines were so slipshod that Tedrow and five other stretcher-bearers were under the impression that Brolo was in friendly hands. It wasn't. The six Americans stared, mouths agape, as they rounded a bend and came upon two swastika-bedecked German staff cars parked in front of a stone residence. Shots rang out; two of Tedrow's cohorts were hit; the other three threw their hands up to surrender. Tedrow dove between the cars and jumped into the unoccupied house.

Bigart must have realized as he interviewed Tedrow that he had a spectacular story; Homer gave it a nimble simplicity that Hemingway might have admired.

"Tedrow found himself in the kitchen. A door leading to the interior part of the house was locked and he looked about frantically for some place to hide. There was only the big oven. Tedrow got down on his hands and knees and crawled into it."

German soldiers barged into the house looking for him. Tedrow wedged himself deeper into the oven and held his breath. One German yelled, in English, "American swine!"

A few moments later, Tedrow heard car doors slam and glimpsed polished boots crossing the kitchen floor. It was an enemy colonel ordering the soldiers out of his headquarters.

Tedrow prayed that the colonel and his staff wouldn't want to bake anything for breakfast. Instead of preparing food, they were debating the merits of the German counterattack in and around Brolo.

It was stifling hot in the oven; soon Tedrow had swallowed all the water in his canteen. "A sharp prong was digging into his back," Bigart wrote. "He stood the agony as long as he could and finally, when the room emptied for a moment, he managed to squirm around and blunt the prong with his knife."

As the *Philadelphia* blasted away at various points, Tedrow felt the reverberations. He also heard the American A-36s drop their bombs on Monte Cipolla. The dwelling was made of impenetrable stone that was vulnerable only to a direct hit, Bigart pointed out.

Tedrow heard the Germans chuckle about the Americans' vulnerability. The Germans had driven the Americans out of the valley and were again directly linked to their front units five miles ahead. Tedrow could sense they were licking their chops about the prospect of reclaiming Cipolla.

At ten o'clock that evening, though, a motorcycle courier roared up with bad news: The Germans' inland line southwest of Brolo had been violated; a full-scale retreat to Messina was under way. Tedrow worried that the colonel would want to burn papers in the oven before heading east, but the sergeant's luck held. Bigart's close again had a Hemingwayesque feel: "The staff cars roared away. A sudden wave of fatigue overcame Tedrow and he slept until dawn. When he awoke American jeeps were passing the house. He emerged and walked stiffly to the road.

"In an orchard down the hill wounded men were moaning softly. They were his comrades, lying on cots beneath the trees."[34]

SICILY CONSIGNED A LOT OF men to cots. If North Africa was, as Hal Boyle called it, a lipless kiss, then Sicily was a joyless embrace, that moment when romantic illusion gives way to cold reality. The Brolo raid that came within a whisker of abject disaster was the Sicilian campaign in microcosm: so sloppily planned that it led to inevitable fratricide, but fought nonetheless with rousing valor.

When Supreme Commander Dwight Eisenhower visited Sicily three days into the invasion, he confidently informed his diary that the island would belong to the Allies inside two weeks. It ended up taking two and a half times that long for troops to go from Gela, Licata, Pachino, Cassibile, and other beaches in Sicily's south to its northeast crook: an area about the length of Vermont. For almost the entire campaign, German and Italian troops fought with one eye trained on the rear: Their strategy was to effect a steady retreat to Messina, where ferryboats awaited to transport them across the strait. To be sure, Axis troops dug in and fought hard. But the truth is undeniable: Had the Allied offensive been better coordinated, enemy troops not only would have been vanquished sooner, but also captured en masse instead of 120,000 of them slipping across to the mainland.

Sicily is where the rivalry between Montgomery and Patton became so toxic that it began costing men their lives. Patton had disquieting moments throughout the war, but Sicily is where he fell apart, where his behavior became an embarrassing albatross to Eisenhower. Ironically, it was in Sicily where Patton suffered the sort of nervous collapse he was so quick to scorn in others. It cost him his command and nearly cost him the rest of the war.

THE LARGER QUESTION, OF COURSE, is should Sicily have been invaded at all? Did Churchill and Roosevelt at Casablanca double down on a futile Mediterranean wager?

Just as he had in Operation Torch, George Marshall sought to rebut Churchill's argument that the Mediterranean offensive should be expanded to include the conquest of Sicily, code-named Operation Husky. Roosevelt was again forced to intervene, correctly overruling Marshall to side with the Brits. FDR's proviso, however, was to delay a go-ahead on the next Mediterranean push, a possible invasion of Italy's mainland, until the Allies sized up the enemy response in Sicily. The holdup irked Churchill, who'd been eyeing a bold march against Rome since America entered the war.

Churchill's hyperbole aside, there were compelling reasons for the Allies to control Sicily, chief among them the three dozen airstrips that the Germans had scattered throughout the island. Sicily also had a series of natural harbors that could be converted into naval bases, enabling the Royal and American navies to interdict enemy sea-lanes.

Launched during the second week of July 1943, Husky was an even more elaborate amphibious exercise than Torch had been nine months earlier. An armada of 2,600 U.S. and British navy ships left from ports in North Africa, England, and the U.S. Once more orchestrating the seaborne movements on the American side was Admiral Kent Hewitt, Walter Cronkite and Hal Boyle's favorite from the Torch convoy. Again, Hewitt delivered a logistical marvel, helping to land 160,000 Allied troops after the fiercest naval bombardment to that point in history on July 9 and 10. Hewitt was once more forced to host George Patton on his flagship, this time the USS *Monrovia*, a beefed-up troop transport.[35]

The Allies appointed Sir Harold Alexander, Churchill's darling, as overall coordinator of Sicilian ground forces, working under Eisenhower. Alexander was less hostile to Americans than his subordinate Montgomery, but still disdainful of the GIs' performance in Tunisia. Sir Harold ordered Montgomery and the Eighth to advance up rugged terrain on the eastern side of the island, which he knew from intelligence reports was defended by hardened *Panzer* units. Patton and the Seventh were assigned the "easier" path through Sicily's central and western hills against predominantly Italian troops. As the Brits surged toward Messina, Patton's primary job was to protect Montgomery's left flank.

It didn't exactly work out that way. Monty had a tougher go than he had anticipated. Plus he began to exhibit the maniacal cautiousness that would drive Eisenhower and Bradley to distraction.

SICILY GAVE HOMER BIGART HIS BAPTISM in ground combat. Reporter Tex O'Reilly, Joe Liebling's Citroën pal in the escape from Paris, had been the *Herald Tribune*'s featured frontline reporter during the Tunisian campaign. When it was clear in late spring '43 that the Allies would expand their Mediterranean push, O'Reilly telegrammed his bosses for help.

Bigart, thrilled to be closer to ground action, arrived from London in time to file reports on the damage inflicted on Sicilian air bases by the Northwest African Air Forces. Homer reported that for five successive days leading up to the invasion, the Gerbini airfield and its four satellite strips near Mount Etna—all of which the enemy had cleverly camouflaged—took merciless poundings from B-26s, B-17s, and B-24s.[36]

O'Reilly went ashore with the Seventh Army in Gela while Bigart stayed in Algiers. They soon switched, with Bigart covering Patton's thrust north and O'Reilly handling the official pronouncements from Allied headquarters.

Tex was blessed with a light and literate writing touch. It was O'Reilly,

Bigart's friend Betsy Wade believes, who first used Shakespeare's metaphor from *As You Like It* to define his risk-taking colleague. "Stay away from Homer," O'Reilly told a *Saturday Evening Post* correspondent in the fall of '43. "He's always trying to build his reputation at the cannon's mouth."[37]

It was in Sicily where the legend of Homer Bigart, at the mouth of a cannon, on the back of a mule, and in the craw of a censor, began to grow.

BIGART AND HAL BOYLE WOULD spend the next nine months together, often cheek-to-jowl, chronicling some of the war's bloodiest and most controversial fighting. After the Germans surrendered at Bizerte in May, Boyle stayed in North Africa, filing stories about how the Allies were gearing up for their next Mediterranean offensive.

Mimicking their pre-Torch subterfuge, Allied intelligence forced the German spy agency, *Abwehr*, to track down plenty of mis- and disinformation in the weeks before the Sicily landings. Boyle and other correspondents in Algiers were fed rumors that the Allies were heading toward other Mediterranean islands, Greece, or even Italy or France. Algerian Frenchmen were making bets on the invasion date, Boyle wrote on July Fourth. "Many were hopeful that Southern France instead of Sicily or Greece would be the target for landing operations."[38]

A British MI6 agent named Ian Fleming helped cook up an exotic scheme: phony papers claiming that the Allies would invade Greece and Sardinia were planted on a suicide victim disguised as a British officer. A submarine dumped the corpse in full uniform off the coast of Spain, where a fisherman plucked him out of the water. Fleming and MI6 sat back and watched with satisfaction as Ultra intercepts demonstrated that *Abwehr* had taken the bait. Thousands of German troops were transferred to Greece and Sardinia to defend assaults that never happened.[39]

At four in the morning on July 10, Bigart joined more than a hundred "weary, sweating" American and British correspondents at Allied Force Headquarters in Algiers. PROs ushered them into a room that previously had displayed a panoramic chart of the Mediterranean. Now the atlas had been replaced by a single topographical map featuring Sicily—and Sicily alone. The "more acute strategists," Bigart needled, "were able to deduce that the invasion, in its initial stage, was more limited than we had been led to believe. All their notes on the flora and fauna and on hotel accommodations in Sardinia, Corsica, Crete, and southern Italy could be for future reference."[40]

BIGART MAY NOT HAVE BEEN feeling much stress at that moment, but a hundred miles north, Boyle was engulfed by it. Boyle was positioned on the main deck of Admiral Hewitt's flagship, the *Monrovia*, moored off the shore of Gela. Standing on the deck immediately beneath Boyle was Seventh Army head George Patton, intently watching the action through his field glasses.

It had already been a long and loud morning; H hour for the first wave of invaders had come at 0245. It was Boyle's second amphibious landing, but unlike Morocco, this time he wouldn't be going in early; he would climb into an assault craft only *after* the beachhead had been pacified. The men tasked with capturing Gela were ordered to begin getting ready at midnight. As Boyle saw it: "Sweating, straining, cursing men began to lower the Higgins assault boats from giant cranes, and to load them with weapons. Silent as statues the infantrymen whose job it was to seize a bridgehead waited in dark lines to clamber down a swinging rope and wooden ladders to the pitching assault boats."

The attack craft circled around a rendezvous point until all the boats were ready to surge toward the beach. "Spray drenched the solders from head to foot as they knelt or stood with rifles clenched in hand," Boyle wrote.[41]

Enemy searchlights had been futilely sweeping the water in front of the fleet for hours. Now, suddenly, the assault boats were caught "in a shaft of dazzling light," Boyle wrote. The fifty-caliber guns on the attack vessels poured tracers at the searchlights but their bullets fell short. Then the big guns from the U.S. cruisers and destroyers opened up. Their shells went out in a great arc and "dropped seemingly as softly as a feather," Boyle wrote, but were deadly accurate. Within seconds, the sea "dissolved into darkness."[42]

Boyle could still see flashes of infantrymen leaping into waist-high water, wading ashore with rifles held high. An abrupt series of blasts that sounded to Boyle like a string of firecrackers detonated along the shoreline, sending up huge geysers of water. But the Italians had miscalculated; their electrically controlled mines did little damage. A few moments later there was such a big explosion onshore that it shook the *Monrovia*. At daylight they learned that the Italians, knowing that they were about to be overrun, had blown up Gela's only pier.

The men left on the *Monrovia* were anxiously leaning over the rails, ears cocked, as the first Higgins boat returned. "'Everybody safe ashore and the wops are scared as hell!' called the little navy coxswain. Then more cargo for the fighting troops was lowered, and he pulled away again," Boyle wrote. All morning long dinghies and barges ferried men and matériel to the beach. "In each boat was a crew of drenched, sleepless shivering boys, most of them from 17 to 20 years old. . . . If they failed, the army would fail."[43]

The Army didn't fail. But getting GIs off Sicily's beachheads proved daunting. Spearheading the assault at Gela was General Terry Allen's Big Red One, backed by several units of Rangers whose mission was to seize the Ponte Olivio airfield a few miles inland. Lucian Truscott's Third Division went ashore eighteen miles northwest of Gela at Licata. General Troy Middleton's 45th Division, freshly arrived from the States, went in a dozen miles southeast at Scoglitti.

As invasion day wore on, encouraging news began to filter in, Boyle reported. Hewitt had one of his officers post status reports in blue pencil on a lower-deck situation map, not far from where Patton and his staff were standing. "Landings successful. Progress OK," it indicated at dawn. An hour or so later word came in that the Brits on Sicily's southeastern side had also creased enemy beaches. "All assault landings successful," was scribbled in "jubilant" blue, Boyle noted.

Resistance was "light," Boyle wrote, but that was not entirely accurate.

The only piece of the battle visible from the *Monrovia* that first day was the haze of smoke and dust being kicked up by artillery units of the Big Red One as it muscled inland.

Boyle was by then a seasoned (and still generally sympathetic) observer of George S. Patton. The fiery general that morning "fretted like a firehorse to get to the beach. But he was chained to his communications on ship," Boyle wrote. Patton planned to go ashore late in the afternoon, but adequate radio and telephone connections had not been established.

The Seventh Army leader may have been concerned about communications, but not enough to actually initiate any with his Supreme Commander. Ike was stewing in Algiers, furious that Patton was keeping him in the dark, just as his underling had in the Moroccan invasion and later in the Tunisian campaign. Two days later, Eisenhower would thoroughly chastise Patton. It was the first of several dressing-downs Patton would get over the next few weeks; compared to what was to come, it was mild.

At dusk on day one, Boyle was chatting with a member of Patton's staff as they strained their eyes toward Gela's beach. "The whole thing seems like an anticlimax," the officer said. "We came here expecting a hell of a lot of trouble, and the Italians are folding up like an accordion. This doesn't seem like an invasion at all. It isn't even as exciting as some of our maneuvers have been."[44]

The first eighteen hours of the Sicilian campaign may not have felt climactic, but the folded accordion turned out to have some wheeze left in it. At 0900 on day two, as Patton departed the *Monrovia* with a newsreel crew for the Gela beachhead, he didn't know it, but he was stepping onto a beehive.

By then the Hermann Göring Panzer division and other Axis units in a ten-mile-wide swath had launched a surprisingly strong counterattack north of town, Boyle and his AP buddy Don Whitehead reported. The enemy move succeeded in pushing much of the Big Red One and elements of the 26th Division back toward the beach. First Division cooks, supply sergeants, and motor pool mechanics who had been organizing the beachhead found themselves pressed into a fight for their lives, staring down Nazi tanks.

A few miles northwest, the men of the 26th groveled for cover in lemon and olive groves south of the Ponte Olivio airfield. That airstrip, and several others in southern Sicily, changed hands in the next twenty-four hours before the Germans and Italians were overwhelmed by the new Allied troops landing by the hour.

The only thing that saved the Allied central front from collapsing on day two, Whitehead wrote, was the lack of coordination in the Axis' three-pronged drive.[45]

ALLIED PARATROOP UNITS HAD PLAYED only a peripheral role in the North African campaign. Sicily, planners vowed, would be different; they were determined to fully engage British airborne units and the American 82nd. Indeed, Patton's invasion strategy called for 3,400 paratroopers from the 82nd to jump a few hours ahead of seaborne troops, seize the high ground north of Gela, capture roads and bridges, and stifle any enemy counterattack.

But severe winds, poor visibility, erratic maps, and terrified Dakota transport pilots scattered men from the 82nd all over the island. Only about one in seven paratroopers landed anywhere near their drop zones.[46]

The Americans' password challenge for Husky was "George!" to be followed by the response "Marshall!" Members of the 82nd spent hours hissing "George!" into the darkness, only to be met with silence. Worse, no one had thought to clue in the Brits on the U.S. password—an oversight that led to several tragedies in the coming nights as American paratroopers, still disoriented, traipsed through territory now occupied by Monty's men.

But those accidental deaths paled in comparison to what transpired on the night of July 11, when twenty-three American paratroop planes were accidentally shot down by friendly fire because of slipshod communications. The official death count was 410, but that number was surely sugarcoated: the real toll was undoubtedly higher.[47]

But the most disquieting part of the entire episode is what happened the next day. Patton, who had witnessed the slaughter, must have believed that he could hide the unpleasant truth from Eisenhower—at least for a while. He chose not to brief Ike about it when they met face-to-face on

July 12. Even after Ike had skewered him for not keeping him abreast of critical developments, Patton stayed mum.

Eisenhower didn't learn of the Gela catastrophe until he arrived back at his command post a few hours later. Ike proceeded to tear off a biting message to Patton that attributed the incident to "inexcusable carelessness and negligence" and all but laid the whole matter at Patton's doorstep.[48]

Boyle likely didn't witness the disaster; by that point, at least according to his Associated Press colleague Joseph Morton,[49] Boyle was with Truscott's men north of Licata, as they battled to protect the Big Red One's left flank. But word about the tragedy spread through the island; it would not have taken long to reach someone with Boyle's antennae. The news may have been slower to reach Bigart, who was still in Algiers, itching to get on the northern side of the Mediterranean. Censors forbade any mention of the 82nd's heartbreak, of course, so it wasn't until after the war that the American public found out about it.

BIGART AND BOYLE SAW A lot of each other in Sicily. It varied from day to day, but they were essentially shadowing the same troops: the 45th Division most often, with occasional forays among the First, Third, 26th, Second Armored, and 82nd Airborne, all of which were advancing north by northwest along a front that mushroomed some thirty to forty miles. Most of the time Bigart and Boyle traveled by jeep or hitched rides on trucks or tanks. But like a lot of men and matériel in Sicily, they spent considerable time on the backs of barnyard animals.

The Allies had requisitioned thousands of mules and horses to help them transport supplies over the rugged Sicilian terrain. As troops pushed deeper into the hills, reporters would occasionally jump onto mules—a colorful happenstance that inevitably made its way into their accounts.[50]

Hal the Hitchhiker must have sprained his thumb in Sicily. On July 14 he was hustling north of Licata with the Third Division. Within a day he was east of Gela along Highway 115, keeping a watchful eye out for German fighter planes "who would find it a perfect avenue for strafing." Soon he encountered an Allied field hospital, jumped out of the jeep, and marveled at the preternatural calm of its workers. Army nurses, "pretty in their blue uniforms," were sitting on some grass near the tents. The nurses had landed in Sicily a few hours after the soldiers, Boyle explained, "without an outward sign of worry. They work harder than any other group in the Army and relax now only because casualties have been surprisingly light."[51]

Later that day Boyle bumped into hundreds of paratroopers from the 82nd. They were marching down the road in parallel rows toward a new bivouac area. "These troops, dropped by the thousands a few hours before arrival of the ground troops, *fell slightly short of their target*" (emphasis added). Despite the chaos, the paratroopers had rallied to knock out pillboxes and enemy strongholds, Boyle reported. The long, marching columns were headed by full colonels and other senior officers. Some of the paratroopers were pedaling bicycles that they had acquired along the way; others were riding bareback on horses that they had confiscated from Italian artillery batteries. Many troopers had stuffed green vines into their helmet rigging to make them harder to spot in the woods.

Farther up the road Boyle's jeep stopped to pick up a lone trooper, Private Mervin Golden of Tallassee, Alabama, who had somehow gotten separated from his squad. Golden worked in a cotton mill back home, Boyle wrote, and "was still a bit dazed by the great adventure." As he and other troopers had attacked a pillbox, a bullet grazed the rim of Golden's helmet.

"'From the time I took off from Africa that night everything seems like a dream,' [Golden] said in his soft southern voice. 'It still doesn't seem real. A few days ago all of us were playing in Africa. Now some of the boys are gone and some are wounded. But we did good and I enjoyed it. Yes, I enjoyed it. I'd like to make another jump.'"[52]

Not long after, Boyle managed to get himself a few miles farther southeast to witness the 45th's capture of Vittoria. Vittoria was the first sizable village that Boyle had come upon since Gela. He was impressed by the town's towering church spires and the classical statuary that adorned certain buildings.

The 45th had stationed a military policeman from Gilbert, Minnesota, to guard the town bank. On the afternoon of their second day in Vittoria,

Boyle asked the MP how long he'd been on duty. "Twenty-one straight hours without a break," he replied.

"Little children run out, hold their fingers up to their lips as if smoking and cry shrilly 'Cigaretti! Cigaretti!' Children seem to start smoking as soon as they quit nursing," Boyle noticed. "To the left of the road is a pillbox cleverly concealed as a cottage. The Italians have been very adept at camouflaging their coastal defenses."

They had also been adept at painting Mussolini's stirring slogans on the walls of buildings. One read: MANY ENEMIES, MUCH HONOR. Another declared: OUR DESTINY IS ON THE SEAS, now a cruel joke.

As American tanks and trucks rolled by, Vitorria's peasants would make "V for victory" signs with their fingers. "A few days ago they were holding up their palms in the fascist gesture," Boyle wrote. "Their hearts are in neither sign. All they really want is some food and peace and to be left alone. They are worn out with war and trouble, death, and high taxes. . . . The farm animals look better cared for than the women and children."[53]

His Vittoria impressions were shared in a remarkable ten-part "invasion diary" that AP proudly pushed across its wire. Installments were written from different spots; each contained Boyle's quirky insights and humor. After leaving Vittoria and the 45th, he rejoined the Third's GIs as they slugged northwest toward the coastal hamlet of Agrigento.

Boyle was in Agrigento on July 20, holed up with the men who had saved his life in Morocco, members of the Second Armored Division, when he wrote a letter to an Algeria-based AP editor named Hutchison about his immediate plans. Boyle's memo to the boss is a fascinating glimpse into the competitive and ethical considerations he faced practically every day.

The PROs of Patton's favorite armored unit had tipped off Boyle that it would be attacking the airdrome at Castelvetrano, some twenty miles up the coast. Boyle explained to "Hutch" that he'd done some "forecasting" in the article he'd attached, a guesstimate as to when the airstrip would fall into American hands. "The story should be okay," Boyle wrote, "if we move as scheduled, but appreciate it if you or Stan Gates [another AP colleague] will phone check G-2 in the morning to see that everything worked out as per the timetable before pushing it through signals."

Once in Castelvetrano, Boyle explained, he would write a follow-up story that he was planning to courier back to the PROs' office in Agrigento, "where they will probably send it your way if they can't find a way to get it out." Then, understanding that UPI and INS, AP's competition, would likely have reporters covering the division's offensive, he pleaded: "Please do all you can to get this one through."

Whatever copy he'd generate up north, Boyle told Hutchison, would be channeled through the Seventh Army's mobile "message center" to the PROs' office in Agrigento.[54]

In Agrigento Boyle talked to a GI who'd witnessed a grisly accident. The Italian unit that abandoned the coastal village left behind eight small tanks. Before the Third Division guys could disarm the tanks, "a small Sicilian boy crawled unobserved into one of them and began fooling with the mechanism," Boyle wrote. "[The boy] pushed a button and the gun went off with a roar."

A shell fragment wounded an Allied soldier; another "almost severed" the leg of a little Sicilian girl. "The lad who had caused all the trouble had to be lifted out of the tank by sympathetic soldiers. He was rigid with fright."[55]

A day earlier, Boyle had been with the 45th when it overran the central Sicilian crossroads of Caltanissetta. Patton and his entourage were lurking nearby; they decided to celebrate by lunching at a palace that had years before been commandeered by Mussolini's blackshirts and had, until a few hours earlier, served as the local Axis headquarters. "It looked like the dining room of King Looie the Fourteenth," a staff officer told Boyle. Patton and his staff, joined by other Allied officers, sat down at an elegant table laid with gold-plated silverware, exquisite porcelain, and an embroidered tablecloth. But the pièce de résistance turned out to be canned C rations— with toilet paper substituting for napkins.

The palace's spacious roof was later used to dry out a million dollars in gold seal American currency. The money had been in a safe that had gotten soaked during the Scoglitti landing. The 45th's finance officer, Lieutenant Colonel Ross N. Routh of Oklahoma City, surrounded the palazzo with armed guards and MPs, then directed a group of men to spread out the cash on the roof. "'It's an ill wind,'" Boyle kidded, "but the wind wasn't blowing that day."

Boyle concluded his Caltanissetta stories by invoking William Tecumseh Sherman's famous axiom: "As General Sherman observed, war is a long way from heaven."[56]

BIGART, TOO, WAS GLIMPSING HIS own corner of the netherworld. On July 19, day ten of the invasion, he joined the 45th as it skirmished along Highway 123 toward Palermo. In the Seventh Army's frenetic march, first to Palermo, then east along Highway 113 to Messina, the 45th was trailing the Third Division. Truscott's Third, at Patton's direction, was throwing a big left hook along the northwestern Sicilian coast. The 45th was countering with a diagonal punch at the island's midsection, while the First was jabbing up the right-center while protecting Montgomery's left flank.

It took Bigart and the 45th six days to catch up to the Third outside a coastal village about halfway between Palermo and San Stefano called Cefalù. On July 25, the 45th ran into resistance as the enemy briefly dug in along the town's limestone cliffs. "Shells from the enemy's mobile 88-millimeter all-purpose guns came whining across the hills. There were snipers in every crevice," Bigart wrote. With his field glasses, he could see two German Mark IV tanks duck behind a promontory a mile or so up the coast. "At that distance," Bigart wrote, "[the tanks] looked like black beetles squeezing through a narrow crack."

Along with the Stars and Stripes' Jack Foisie, Bigart was given the okay to check out the town once the enemy abandoned it. "We swept the surrounding hills with field glasses, found no hint of snipers and advanced cautiously," Bigart wrote. Cefalù consisted of about a dozen stone houses, all of which fronted the road. "A shell had opened the front of one house, baring the squalor of a typical Sicilian home. The inhabitants had fled."

Bigart and Foisie spotted a white flag being waved from a dwelling and assumed it was enemy soldiers wanting to surrender. Instead three middle-aged civilians emerged, grinning and flashing the V salute. The road was littered with debris left behind by fleeing soldiers: soap tins, shaving brushes, bags of biscuits, and bedrolls. "There was no sign of German dead, for the Germans are very diligent in disposing of their killed," Bigart wrote.

It somehow didn't seem like a real war, Bigart mused. "War is associated with mud, foul weather and hostile civilians. There is none of that here. The weather has been perfect and the civilian conduct exemplary."[57]

Later that same day the war became very real for Bigart. The retreating Germans turned to fight at Capo Raisigelbi, a few miles east of Cefalù. Bigart had completely caught up with Patton's advance elements. Soon he was "passing columns of [American] foot soldiers, hot and grim after a day in the foxholes just ahead."

Bigart, presumably still with the *Stars and Stripes*' Foisie, was in a jeep that was being driven by a GI. No one stopped them or discouraged the jeep from lurching ahead. About two miles east of the village they turned a corner and were nearly deafened by the roar of an American artillery battery.

"Our driver suddenly remembered a date he had in Palermo. We had gotten ahead of the infantry. An artillery major informed us dryly that the Germans were just around the bend. Our infantry had gone into the hills on a flanking mission, and there the main column was canalized on the narrow coastal strip between sea and cliff.

"We got out of there in a hurry. As we raced back for the shelter of the town, a shell stirred the dust 500 yards from the road and the blast reverberated from the great cliff of Cefalù. We had caught up with the war."[58]

Bigart stayed caught up. In fact, from that moment until the Japanese surrender ceremony on the deck of the USS *Missouri* twenty-six months later, he was almost never more than a bend away from the action.

THREE DAYS AFTER ACCIDENTALLY STUMBLING onto the howitzer, Bigart found himself flirting with another front line, this one seven or eight miles up the coast in a village called Castel di Tusa. It was Bigart's first up-close encounter with Nazi depravity.

At midmorning on July 28, Bigart was tailing a 45th Division patrol that had been ordered into Castel di Tusa to make sure that the Germans had completely pulled out. The GIs "bolted into the town, advancing in a stealthy half-crouch, from house to house along both sides of the coastal road," Bigart wrote. "The shell-pocked houses were empty, the dusty street deserted except for starving cats."

For the first time in many hours German artillery shells were not pummeling the town. "There was no sound," Bigart wrote, "but the dull roar of the Sirocco [Italian for "tropical gale"] carrying its stifling blasts of hot wind and dust through the mountain pass." As the patrol approached an abandoned railroad tunnel on the western edge of town, the Americans heard "an incoherent babble of voices and children wailing." Inside, they discovered three hundred townspeople, including scores of babies and small children. Abandoned by the town's Fascist leaders, who had "fled in panic before the American advance," the villagers had been huddled in the tunnel for six days, subsisting on meager rations. Many were starving, begging soldiers for food and water.

German artillery, the survivors told Bigart through a GI translator, had been "spitefully" shelling both ends of the tunnel to ensure that none of the townspeople could escape. Villagers blamed local Fascists for colluding with the Germans to keep them trapped.

The fighting around Castel di Tusa presaged the wicked warfare to come on the Italian mainland. "This narrow ribbon of dust will never be forgotten by the American and German soldiers who fought for three days in the citrus orchards and vineyards along the way," Bigart wrote in a separate article two days later.

Castel di Tusa's Fascist leaders made things even harsher by secreting themselves on cliff ledges where they could spot American troop movements coming from the south or west. The Germans had given the Fascists a radio to signal camouflaged gunners in Mosto three miles east. Between pounding the townspeople in the railroad tunnel and raining shells on the advance elements of the 45th and Third, the guns stayed busy for days.

Most of the Fascists got out when the Germans did, but the mayor and the town marshal remained. An American counterintelligence officer fluent in Italian jeeped into Castel di Tusa while it was still being shelled to arrest the two officials, locking them up in the *municipio* (city hall) near the church. Once the shelling stopped, a jeep-load of officials from AMGOT (the Allied Military Government of Occupied Territories) drove into the piazza and began restoring law and order. The AMGOT unit included a doctor from Philadelphia, a post office clerk from San Francisco, and an inspector from Scotland Yard.

London's erstwhile detective immediately walked over to the old Fascist headquarters, with Bigart trailing. A crowd of a hundred young men, many of them deserters from the Italian army, was loitering out front. The door was cracked open from the inside by a recently deposed Fascist potentate, giving Bigart the chance to display his gift for searing irreverence.

"Guiseppe Pollizzi is thirty-eight years old, a stout man with a comfortable paunch and a well padded posterior. Jowls hung from his face like the folds of an ill-fitting overcoat. His eyes were wide, brown and bovine and suited Guiseppe's present role of cowlike meekness."[59]

The next day, after Bigart and the 45th had inched their way another couple of miles up the coast, Homer found himself near "a crowded, filthy little town of 7,000" called San Stefano. The Axis forces had done a number on the village.

"They blew up bridges over a dozen deep gulches west of the town," Bigart wrote. "They planted thousands of tank and personnel mines in the dry flats of the San Stefano River. Hillside farms with their ponderous masonry made perfect pillboxes. Road blocks of solid concrete made the highway impassable for guns."

Because of these entrenchments, a frontal assault would have been foolhardy. "A reversion to frontier warfare was essential," Bigart informed readers. GIs in small clusters were forced to "shoot and scoot," à la John Wayne in a Western, up one ridge, then another. The slope of one hill was so severe that two mules died trying to haul heavy mortars to the summit. After capturing one village in a valley five miles southwest of San Stefano, the Americans had to endure "murderous artillery fire" from Germans holed up in the hills.

"That night, no one slept," Bigart wrote in a piece published a week later, on August 6. "Huddling under the stone arches of the village, the troops could see the sharp flashes of the German mortars an instant before the shells came down. A man who had lost his child in the bombardment went screaming through the street unmindful of the shrapnel that beat like rain against the cobbled road."[60]

It took days, but slowly the men of the 45th began closing in on San Stefano from the south, buttressed by elements of the Third moving in from the west. Many of the guys in the 45th were out of rations, but Sicily offered some of the finer foraging fields of the war: vineyards, olive and almond groves, and the occasional lemon orchard. At nine a.m. on July 31, the Germans finally deserted the village and began retreating down Highway 113, harassed by fire from the destroyer *Rowan*.

"Even then the town was precariously held," Bigart observed. "The long bridge across the San Stefano River had been demolished and in the dry bed of the river German personnel mines had been sown thicker than grass."

Bigart watched in horror as a battalion of men from a reserve unit advanced single file into a disguised minefield, suffering dreadful casualties. "The German mine is a vicious little instrument. It springs three to six feet into the air, exploding with a sharp retort similar to rifle fire. A half dozen of these shots had us leaping into a ditch," he wrote. Bigart and the GIs he was with thought they were under sniper attack. They froze until someone yelled, "Stay where you are: the whole damn river is mined."[61]

By the time Bigart got into San Stefano, the locals had already broken into Fascist headquarters for the obligatory defacing of Il Duce portraits. As Bigart's company resumed its march toward Messina, villagers showered them with grapes and figs; more importantly, they showed them a mine-free passage across the river.

HOW HOMER BIGART MANAGED TO repeatedly slip provocative copy past censors remains a mystery. Cronkite, Rooney, and Boyle witnessed both

Homer's play-dumb act, where his sometimes-affected stammer enabled him to pry information out of unsuspecting sources; and his cunning MO with censors, which apparently consisted of outwitting and outwaiting them.

Just before Bigart left for the Mediterranean, Cronkite watched as Homer sweated out his copy, then dueled with the censor over the appropriateness of certain references. When the sergeant finally okayed the piece, the stammering Bigart asked: "Wo-wo-wo-would you mi-mi-mind re-re-reading this to my off-off-office?"

The censor, Cronkite observed, "performed an almost impossible physical feat. He slouched upward, assuming a position nearly erect." "Why can't you read it?" the kid indignantly asked Bigart. "Da-da-da-dammit," Homer countered, "C-c-can't you s-s-see? I'm de-de-de-deaf!"[62]

In combat zone press tents, most reporters would compose their stories at night, usually in the presence of a young public relations officer or noncom who doubled as a censor. Once the correspondent finished typing his piece, he would submit it to the censor, who, under strict orders from superiors, would delete anything viewed as unduly "critical" of the Allied war effort or that might betray information useful to the enemy, such as the size or direction of a certain offensive.

Inevitably, arguments erupted over what the censor had deemed *too* disruptive or *too* revealing. Almost every night, one frustrated reporter or another would loudly defend his copy.

Invariably, Bigart would be the last reporter in the tent, perspiring over his copy. Fellow correspondents remembered how Bigart would stare into space, rhythmically tapping the space bar, cigarette ashes dripping, racking his brain for the right word or phrase. The censor, anxious to join his buddies for a beer, would get more and more annoyed as Bigart played his sly waiting game.

By the time Bigart finally got around to showing the censor his copy, the kid was tired of bickering. Bigart, no fool, would also tug on the youngster's heartstrings by playing up the stammer. Between the pity and the censor wanting to wrap it up, Bigart would often get his way.

A classic example is an article Bigart filed from amid north-central

Sicily's Peloritan Mountains on August 10, the same day he left for the amphibious assault on Monte Cipolla. The lede that somehow got past the censors was signature Bigart, jagged and taut.

"The Sicilian campaign is a month old. The final days of the slow and undramatic progress toward Messina, and of anticlimactic victories over the Axis forces still clinging to the northeast peninsula, will exasperate a lot of Americans who cannot understand why so powerful an Allied ground force with unlimited superiority cannot swiftly annihilate the German divisions."[63]

No reporter could insinuate big-picture considerations into an account of tactical combat like Bigart. His August 12 piece recounted the frustrations of infantry commanders, who lamented that a small number of enemy gunners could conceal themselves in Sicily's high country. A well-hidden machine gun nest could inflict lethal damage, holding up an offensive for hours, sometimes days, officers told Bigart.

"In such a country tanks are useless and emplacements for heavy guns are exceedingly hard to find. There is still the air force, but bombers must have a suitable target. Six Germans and a machine gun tucked away on a rocky crag of the Peloritan Mountains would be tough to liquidate from the air."[64]

The Allies moving across Sicily faced essentially the same challenge as the Japanese attacking Bataan in the Philippines, noted Bigart. The difference, of course, was that the Americans eluding the Japanese on the Bataan peninsula had no means of getting away, "where the Axis force can escape across the narrow Messina Strait. As far south as Taormina on the Ionian coast and as far west as Falcone on the Tyrrhenian, numbers of landing craft have been observed evacuating unessential German personnel."[65]

Bigart's passage has two noteworthy dimensions. First, if by August 10 reporters not only had deduced that the enemy was ferrying men across the strait but were also permitted to write about it, then why weren't Allied commanders able to muster a more formidable assault from air and sea to discourage it? Concerted attacks from surface ships and submarines might have impeded the evacuation. A steady barrage of heavy bombing attacks on both sides of the strait, moreover, could have destroyed the docks and the enemy's capacity to launch ferries.[66]

In their memoirs, both Eisenhower and Bradley kicked themselves for not cutting off the enemy's escape route. Indeed, while the Sicilian battle was still extant, Eisenhower confided to aides that history would never forgive him for letting huge numbers of German troops get away. Allied intelligence knew as early as August 1 that the enemy was plotting its escape from Siciliy.[67]

The second remarkable facet of Bigart's passage was its geographic literacy. Bigart was writing for the *Trib*'s upscale readership: cosmopolitan denizens of upper Manhattan and Westchester County. The *Trib*, as Betsy Wade likes to say, was proud to be a "writer's paper," a place that gave its reporters leeway without intrusive editing. It encouraged Bigart to show off his mastery of European culture and geography. Not bad for a guy who started out as a pariah in the *Trib*'s newsroom and never came close to completing college.

WAR ALWAYS BEGETS BARBARISM ON both sides, but Sicily is where the European conflict took an ugly turn. There were two separate instances in Sicily where American GIs executed large numbers of enemy prisoners; neither episode was properly prosecuted.[68]

Moreover, Sicily is where George Patton forever sullied his own legacy. On the afternoon that Lieutenant Colonel Bernard's raiders were hanging by a thread on Monte Cipolla, the man who sent them into harm's way was visiting the 93rd Evacuation Hospital near San Stefano. There, for the second time in a week, Patton confronted a soldier suffering the effects of battle fatigue. Patton slapped the private twice as he loudly ordered that he be removed. A reporter from the *London Daily Mail* followed Patton back to his staff car. The correspondent overheard Patton tell a doctor, "There's no such thing as shellshock. It's an invention of the Jews."[69]

Omar Bradley, Patton's deputy, was alerted about both incidents—and so, eventually, were various correspondents, including Hal Boyle and, almost assuredly, Homer Bigart. Reporters agreed to keep it quiet, as Bradley promised them the matter would be addressed with superiors—and that Patton would be duly punished.

Weeks later Patton's deeds finally became public when Washington columnist Drew Pearson ran a scathing column. It sparked calls for Patton's head. Before reassigning him, Eisenhower ordered Patton to apologize to both soldiers—and to his men at large. Before five separate audiences of GIs, Patton delivered profanity-laced "apologies" that left his bewildered men staring at one another, since he never explained what had triggered his appearance before them in the first place.[70]

BEFORE HOSTILITIES ENDED IN SICILY, Homer Bigart encountered another ghastly tunnel—this one even more pestilential than the one in Castel di Tusa. On August 18, while most reporters, including Boyle, were fixated on Patton and the Seventh having finally beaten Montgomery and the Eighth to Messina, Bigart was writing about the human tragedy he'd witnessed in a long tunnel at the end of the Via Protorolia. For many weeks, thousands of Messina's citizens had sought refuge in the underground warren to escape the wrath of Allied bombing and German guns across the strait.

"The siege claimed three more victims," Bigart wrote. "A seven-month-old baby starved, two old people died of dysentery. Their bodies lay somewhere in the black recesses, jostled by the crawling mass of the living. Not one of the survivors, estimated at 5,000, had the energy or will to drag the corpses out into the sun and to the cemetery up the hill. They were unmourned. People living in a black hole for months are not apt to waste pity on the dead."

A distraught doctor was pleading for the American liberators to give him disinfectants, iodine, bandages, anything that might alleviate suffering. The physician took Bigart inside the tunnel. "A swarm of black flies, sticky with filth, spread infection to every portion of the cave. Children were afflicted with malnutrition and scabies and looked almost as dirty as Arabs. Their parents quarreled and fought over scraps of food pillaged from stores."[71]

The rest of what was left of the city was only marginally less abhorrent. "This correspondent walked two hours in the heart of Messina and found fewer than a score of buildings unscathed and none habitable. From end to end, the Via Garibaldi was a wide lane of rubble between walls of blackened stone."[72]

Much of the Sicily that Homer Bigart and Hal Boyle saw in July and August 1943 was a wide lane of rubble. Five thousand Allied soldiers, nearly ten thousand Axis soldiers, and untold civilians perished on the island in the hellish summer of 1943. Yet compared to what was to come, the Sicilian campaign was a cakewalk.

CHAPTER 8

★

WHITE CROSSES ALONG THE
RED RAPIDO

*In my mind swam a picture of the stricken valley crossed
by the Rapido River beneath a terrible hill called
Cassino. If they put up a cross for every man killed or
wounded there, it would be a white forest.*

—HAL BOYLE, 1952
HELP, HELP! ANOTHER DAY!

Straining his eyes as he peered through the binoculars, Hal Boyle could
barely make out the two American soldiers tramping through the dank
gloom along the swollen river. It was cold and foggy, as it had been practically every day that benighted winter. Everything around the riverbed
reeked of death.

The two soldiers—David Kaplan, a thirty-year-old medical officer from
Sioux City, Iowa, and Arnold Fleischman, a twenty-year-old private from
Wood Haven, Long Island—were carrying a makeshift Red Cross banner
stretched between two sticks. "Amid a deathly silence," Boyle watched as
they "marched through battered no-man's-land to the brink of the bloody
Rapido River."

A rubber raft was supposed to be waiting. But in typical Army fashion, as Kaplan conceded later, there'd been a screwup. Kaplan and Fleischman were forced to scavenge their own vessel. There were plenty of choices:
the river's edge was littered with abandoned boats. They picked one that
wasn't too badly shot up, grabbed a discarded oar, and paddled their way

across the angry Rapido, making sure to keep the Red Cross banner in full view.

With thousands of pairs of field glasses trained on every step, Kaplan and Fleischman trudged another eight hundred yards through the mire. As they picked their way over corpses, they were careful to tread near exploded mine craters. Their theory was that the craters would mark a safe path through the muck, since the Germans weren't likely to place deadly explosives one on top of the other.

Eventually they came up against a barbed-wire barrier. After making Kaplan and Fleischman wait an uncomfortably long time, an officer from the 15th Panzer Grenadiers emerged from hiding. He was from the same Wehrmacht unit that at Brolo five months earlier had nearly martyred Homer Bigart. Kaplan and Fleischman later told Boyle that the German officer was wearing a crisply pressed uniform and freshly shined boots, which stood in stark contrast to their own filthy garb.

Private Fleischman's German was so impeccable that the enemy negotiator, impressed, asked where he had learned it. "In school," Fleischman fibbed, loath to admit he'd spent his childhood in the Fatherland. With Fleischman interpreting, both sides affirmed a three-hour truce to remove their dead and wounded.[1]

Did Hitler's surrogate appreciate the irony of the Americans sending soldiers of probable Jewish ancestry to negotiate the truce? Boyle, observing from the opposite bank of the Rapido, never got the chance to ask.

Once white flags were bared, some seventy-five American medics and litter carriers crossed the river to help Kaplan and Fleischman comb through the detritus. They were joined by a smaller contingent of Germans. One enemy soldier bummed a cigarette from an American private, proudly revealing in broken English that his brother had emigrated to Brooklyn before the war. Another German, perhaps a minion of Nazi propaganda chief Joseph Goebbels, took footage of the surreal scene with a motion picture camera. At one point the officer with the shiny boots eyed an Allied observation plane hovering nearby, sputtered "This is very unfair!" and demanded that the Piper Cub be grounded since it was violating terms of the truce. Kaplan ordered a runner to scurry across the river, but by then the plane had disappeared. A few minutes later a muffled burst of gunfire sent men from both sides sprawling—but it turned out to be from a distant German gunner at a different spot on the battlefield.

The Rapido was something out of Dante's *Inferno*. For more than a week, the two sides had been exchanging wretched artillery and machine gun fire. As they had done throughout Italy, the Germans had implanted thousands of mines. On the evening of January 20, in the chaos of the initial charge across the Rapido, a company of GIs from the 141st Infantry had stumbled into a minefield; one explosion followed another, each punctuated by chilling screams. Many bodies had been rotting for three or four days, some longer.

In the hours leading up to the truce, the Germans carried American corpses down from the hills sub rosa, lest U.S. medics deduce exactly where enemy troops were positioned. Working in concert, medics from both sides stacked the mutilated remains of some eighty bodies; virtually all belonged to the 141st.[2] Many of the riverbed victims had perished in the artillery exchange that signaled the beginning of the nighttime attack. Others had succumbed the following morning when the American high command, despite appalling losses and the attack's failure to gain any ground, ordered the assault renewed.

Hal Boyle had seen all manner of death and deprivation in North Africa and Sicily and during the push north from the beachhead at Salerno. But he'd never witnessed anything like the carnage along what GIs were now calling Purple Heart Valley. No one had. On top of the hundreds of deaths inflicted by mines and guns, scores of Allied soldiers drowned when the Germans dynamited upriver dams and levees, sending water rampaging down the Rapido and Garigliano.

The 36th Division had already been through hell in Italy, absorbing big losses on the Paestum beachhead, during the bloody crawl up the Sele Valley, and in the mountains surrounding San Pietro Infine. Its roots were in Texas as a National Guard outfit. The men proudly wore their Texas allegiance in the patches on their sleeves; a T was embedded in their unit's insignia. But so many "T-Patchers" had been killed and wounded that the division no longer had a dominant Texas flavor. Along the Rapido alone, more than four hundred men in just three regiments of the 36th had perished. One company sent into the hellhole lost all but 17 of 184 men.[3] The Rapido crossings were, in sum, a tragic—and utterly avoidable—reprise of Great War foolishness.

Ironically, the 36th's commander, General Fred L. Walker, was a World War I veteran who'd earned his stripes in July 1918 rebuffing a reckless German attack across the Marne River.[4] It's clear from Walker's bitter diary entries that he knew fording a stream against an enemy entrenched on high ground would be disastrous.

The 36th's gambit was supposed to be part of a coordinated series of assaults against enemy positions in the hills bordering the Liri Valley and its 1,300-year-old Benedictine abbey at Monte Cassino. But earlier flanking thrusts by the British 46th Division and a group of Free French Algerians and Moroccans had failed to dislodge the Germans; both Allied units were forced to retreat.

Without personally eyeballing the 36th's position, Lieutenant General Mark W. Clark, the Fifth Army's commander, insisted that the river attack go off as planned. Clark and the overall British commander, Sir Harold Alexander, wanted the 15th Panzer Grenadiers occupied so they could not be sent northwest to reinforce the beachhead at Anzio, where a big—but, as it turned out, not big enough—Allied amphibious end run was scheduled to take place on January 22.[5]

On January 23, three days after the 36th's assault, Boyle filed a story about the heroic actions of Staff Sergeant William C. Weber of St. Marys, Pennsylvania, a rifle platoon leader in the 142nd Regiment. Weber and another member of the 142nd, a private from Rockford, Illinois, named Harry W. Lund, dove into the frigid Rapido to save six companions who'd somehow survived the onslaught while stranded on the far side. Boyle caught up with Lund and Weber a few minutes after the dramatic rescue; they were shivering in a dugout on the "safe" side of the river.

"We figured the best way back after the situation became hopeless was over one of the [temporary] pontoon bridges not knocked out," Private Lund told Boyle. "We found the bridge all right, but it was half sunk in the middle of the river. I tied a rope around me and swam out and tied it to the bridge. Then we tried to pull it into position. We couldn't because one section was under four feet of water.

"I tied a piece of communications wire around me and set out again," Lund continued. "This time I tried to swim to the other side, but I was tired and might have drowned if the boys hadn't hauled me back. Then Sergeant Weber said he would try it."

"I took off all the clothes I could so I would not get waterlogged," Weber told Boyle. "I was out as far as I could—it was like somebody putting an icicle on your toe and running it up to your waist. But that current bothered me more than the cold water. There was also an awful undertow. I was never sure I would get over until I finally crawled out on the other side."[6]

GIs COULDN'T BE SURE OF much that winter: Visibility was so poor and the fighting so intense along the Rapido that, for weeks, Allied and German lines got confused. Early one morning in late January a captain from San Antonio named John Henning was on the far side of the river looking for the rest of his patrol. Armed only with his service revolver, Henning suddenly happened upon a Volkswagen jeep carrying a pile of enemy soldiers and dragging a seventy-five-millimeter gun.

Henning, a North Africa veteran "not exactly unacquainted with the working of the Teutonic mind," told Hal Boyle that he decided to try a bold bluff.

"Henning jumped into a crevice, and as the bouncy little volkswagon[7] with its cargo of Nazis rolled past, he suddenly called out: 'Halt!'"

The Germans rolled right past but hit the brakes when Henning yelled even louder. "Believing they were surrounded, they climbed off the volkswagon and gave themselves up." Henning knew he'd be overpowered if they realized he was all alone, so he called out for help; fortunately, two GIs were nearby.

"A few minutes later," Boyle wrote, "the crestfallen Germans were marching to a prisoners' camp, and their 75-mm gun was earmarked for an American ordnance dump."[8]

In Italy there weren't enough moments of semitriumph like Captain Henning's. On January 27, the day of the truce, Boyle interviewed Captain Kaplan and the team that had brought back some twenty-five bodies and four wounded men, one of whom happened to be a medic who'd been languishing for days. "When he was lifted into a litter, [the medic] grinned feebly and said: 'Look, I have got maid service—you can't beat this battlefield!'"

Within minutes of the truce's expiration, "both sides opened up with heavy, rolling artillery barrages," Boyle wrote. "This sector of the sanguinary Rapido River again became a 'no-man's-land.'"[9]

"SANGUINARY" WAS A FAVORITE ADJECTIVE of both Boyle's and Bigart's. It means "bloody," and there was no shortage of opportunity to use it in the Italy of 1943 and 1944. Italy was, as Ernie Pyle called it, a "tough old gut," pockmarked with one gory field after another. The insidious German strategy that Boyle and Bigart witnessed firsthand in Sicily—blowing up roads and bridges, falling back to high ground, turning and fighting, then slipping away to blow up more roads and bridges and falling back to even higher ground—was magnified on the mainland.

In Sicily, Albert Kesselring, the crafty commander of the Wehrmacht's Army Group C, was constrained by the geography of a small island. There were no such constraints up Italy's boot, where deep rivers and daunting mountain ranges provided the stuff of Confederate General James Longstreet's dreams: natural boundaries that could be fiercely defended.

Indeed, Italy's topography lent itself to the rearguard warfare at which the Germans had become expert, much to Hitler's dismay. Kesselring, Joe Liebling wrote after the war, was an anomaly: a Göring protégé who never became a fanatic Nazi, a onetime artillery officer who'd learned to fly at age forty-eight, and an early blitzkrieg proponent whose name later became synonymous with defensive warfare.[10] The *Generalfeldmarschall* and his officers studied south-central Italy's hills and streams and established a series of lines between Naples and Rome, collectively known as the Winter Line, to which they would retreat once Allied troops began pressing north.

The mountains beyond the Volturno River constituted Kesselring's first row of defense. A few miles north came the Barbara Line, followed by the Reinhard and Gustav (aka Hitler) Lines running in front of Monte Cassino. Anchored in the rugged central Apennines, the Gustav Line proved nearly impenetrable.

It was all by wicked design. Kesselring wanted his lines farther south to retard the Allies. He wanted the Gustav Line to wreck them.

Historians often compare the long-drawn-out battle for Italy to World War I's trench warfare. But Homer Bigart plumbed that analogy long before academics got ahold of it. Early in the campaign, Bigart drew parallels to Britain's ill-advised maneuvers in Turkey in 1915. And by late winter Bigart was writing the likes of: "It is a depressing experience to return from the Anzio beachhead, where front-line misery rivals World War [I] Flanders."[11]

Bigart's pointed reporting on the Anzio-Cassino stalemate earned him the enmity of Allied censors, chronic grumbling from Mark Clark and his deputy Geoff Keyes, and a stinging rebuke from Sir Harold Alexander. Allied commanders complained that skeptical reporting from Bigart and others was hurting troop morale and undermining the war effort back home.

But the irony is that the correspondents covering the war in Italy didn't come close to reporting its ugly truths. With men still fighting and dying, journalists such as Bigart, Boyle, and CBS' Eric Sevareid censored themselves. Had they accurately described the perils faced by Allied troops, there would have been a public outcry to stop the "senseless slaughter," Sevareid said after the war.[12] Boyle's coverage of Italy was less barbed than Bigart's; as always, it focused more on the grunts in the field than the dubious decision making of their bosses. But it was so human and powerful that it helped win Boyle a Pulitzer Prize.

Much of Italy's fighting evoked not just Great War despair, but also the cannibalism of Cold Harbor. Members of the 36th along the Rapido weren't the only Allied troops sent to almost certain death, much like U. S. Grant's men late in the Civil War. The GIs who dug in along the Volturno and places farther north "were living in almost inconceivable misery," Ernie Pyle wrote.[13]

Stars and Stripes cartoonist Bill Mauldin spent weeks trying to sleep in Italy's ubiquitous muck, but concluded that lying on rocks was more comfortable. "Rocks are better than mud because you can curl yourself around the big rocks, even if you wake up with sore bruises where the little rocks dug into you. When you wake up in the mud your cigarettes are all wet and you have an ache in your joints and a rattle in your chest."[14]

THE ITALIAN CAMPAIGN GAVE A lot of people aches in their joints. It's where Winston Churchill's great Mediterranean gamble finally fell apart. It's where Franklin Roosevelt should have listened to George Marshall and drawn the line with Churchill and the Brits. But FDR exercised the kind of commander-in-chief restraint that most commentators laud: He left the ultimate decision on the wisdom of invading the Italian mainland to his field commander, Eisenhower. In mid-July 1943, one week into what appeared to be a relatively "easy" invasion of Sicily, Ike green-lighted Operation Avalanche, and put his top deputy, Mark Clark, in charge of Italian invasion planning. Clark assumed command of what he would soon insist on calling—over the snickers of correspondents—"Lieutenant General Mark W. Clark's U.S. Fifth Army."

At that moment, the Churchill-Eisenhower logic seemed compelling: A quick Allied thrust would decimate the Italian army, keep German *Panzer* units back on their heels and away from northern France, and give the Allied bombing command better airfields from which to attack Nazi fortifications and oil fields along the Adriatic and points north.

Yet what Allied planners failed to grasp is that in both North Africa and Sicily, the Wehrmacht essentially fought with one hand tied behind its back. In the earlier Mediterranean campaigns, the German army had been hamstrung by long supply lines and Hitler's indifference to the area's geostrategic significance.

All that changed in September 1943 once Montgomery's Brits and Canadians came ashore at Reggio di Calabria on Italy's toe and a polyglot force led by Clark and the Americans landed two hundred miles north at Salerno. Italy, after all, was part of Hitler's *Festung Europa*, which of late had developed its first fissures. Germany's Eastern Front had begun to col-lapse; the Germans had just suffered an epic defeat in the tank battle at Kursk. Hitler didn't want another humiliation on the Reich's southern pe-rimeter. To buck up Kesselring, Hitler sent sixteen fresh divisions to Italy, insisting that the mountainous country be fanatically defended.

The Nazis were also zealous in punishing the traitorous Italians. Six hundred thousand Italian soldiers were marched at gunpoint into slave labor. Tens of thousands of other *soldati* were executed, along with incal-culable numbers of Italian civilians. As Allied troops grew nearer, scores of museums and precious Roman artifacts were ransacked or firebombed.

Hitler also abruptly ended Mussolini's "lenient" policies toward Jews. That fall, some twelve thousand Italian Jews were rounded up and sent to concentration camps. But the Italian people, led by valiant priests and nuns, effectively "hid" 80 percent of the country's Jewish population from the Gestapo. Had the clergy been discovered concealing Jews, they would have been murdered; many were anyway.

Kesselring had a clear objective and strategy: sucker punch the Allies up the peninsula, wage a war of attrition, and wait for an opportune mo-ment to expose and eviscerate the U.S. Fifth and British Eighth Armies.[15]

Alexander, Montgomery, and Clark had a much murkier objective—and no real strategy to speak of. When, on the eve of the Calabria landing, Montgomery asked his boss, Alexander, about the Eighth Army's geographic goal, Alexander shrugged and muttered something about getting as far north as Monty could manage—and never made it any less amorphous.[16] The linkup of Monty's and Clark's forces was also sloppily thought through.

Clark's plan for the Salerno invasion, moreover, contained a seven-mile gap between the British and American landing beaches—a flaw that proved nearly fatal and should never have passed muster. But the Supreme Com-mand was preoccupied with planning Operation Neptune, as the cross-Channel invasion was then code-named. Eisenhower tasked Patton, at the time doing penance as Sicily's occupation viceroy, with critiquing Clark's invasion plan. Patton looked at the seven-mile breach and predicted that the Germans would exploit it. Yet Clark, given too much latitude by Eisen-hower, never altered his plan.

The morass into which Italy degenerated was not Clark's fault—it had many parents, both British and American—but Clark took a bad situation and made it worse. As historian Chester Wilmot argued, Allied architects early in the war were desperately seeking a "blueprint" in the fight against Nazi Germany—and never found one in the Mediterranean. It wasn't until Normandy in the spring and summer of 1944, Wilmot maintained, that Allied planners finally devised a strategic design that worked.[17]

IRONICALLY, THE ALLIES STARTED THE Italian campaign brimming with confidence. Monty's September 3 (Operation Baytown) assault across the Strait of Messina had the feel of a country outing. Early on, the Brits and Canadians met only token resistance; Kesselring had deliberately abandoned Italy's toe to defend more forbidding ground north. Clark, slated to land at Salerno a week later, was so convinced that Axis troops would flee that he told a colleague the Fifth Army's offensive would be more "pursuit" than contested fight. When on the eve of the Salerno invasion Eisenhower announced that Italy had officially surrendered, many Allied soldiers rejoiced, deluding themselves into thinking that the Germans would never spill blood to "save" Italy.

Reprising their one-two approach in Sicily, *Herald Tribune* reporters Homer Bigart and Tex O'Reilly switched places at the outset. O'Reilly went in with the troops at Salerno while Bigart stayed back in North Africa to coordinate coverage at Allied headquarters. Bigart spent five weeks sifting through wire service cables and battlefront communiqués to file stories that consistently made the *Trib*'s front page. He didn't arrive on Italy's front lines until almost mid-October.

Hal Boyle, as he had at Morocco and Gela, steamed across the Mediterranean and Tyrrhenian with an invasion fleet inevitably headed by Admiral Kent Hewitt. "Mussolini's boasted '*Mare Nostrum*' (Our Sea) has become an Allied mill pond," Boyle wrote, perhaps too cockily, aboard a British-piloted troopship on September 12. "Crossing to Italy in a British and American invasion convoy was as uneventful as a trip by ferry from Manhattan to Staten Island."

Things quickly turned eventful. Although casualties were higher than anticipated, the initial Gulf of Salerno landings on September 9 and 10 went reasonably well. Within four days, some seventy-five thousand troops—about two-thirds of them British—had established a beachhead between six and ten miles deep along a forty-mile swath.

Boyle was several miles inland on September 13, a day that went so calamitously for the Allies it was forever branded Black Monday. Beginning just after dawn, Kesselring launched a series of counterattacks that threatened to push the Fifth Army back into the gulf. Boyle had somehow managed to get close to the front with members of the 12th Air Support Command, a unit whose mission was to rehabilitate captured airstrips—a task that would, over the next ninety-six hours, be the least of their concerns.

The next morning, Boyle was eating breakfast with about fifty men along the swampy bottomland of the River Sele at the extreme northern flank of the American invasion force. They weren't far from the infamous Tabacchificio Fioche, a tobacco factory whose imposing walls and tiny windows resembled a garrison's. Boyle's new buddies in the 36th Division and his old friends in the 45th would spend much of the next few days huddled around the Tabacchificio as control of the factory seesawed back and forth.

Hal was chatting with two PROs he'd gotten to know in North Africa, Lieutenant Louis Harris, a former reporter from Pontiac, Michigan, and Captain Jay Vessels, a prewar journalist from Minneapolis, when the first German artillery shell came crackling overhead. The three instantly dived into a prickly ten-foot-high blackberry bush. "They were the most comfortable thorns anyone ever laid on," Boyle wrote. Joined by others in the 12th, Boyle, Harris, and Vessels sought cover in those thorns for several hours.

U.S. howitzers and Navy guns soon matched those of the Germans. The menacing artillery barrage gave way to the rumble of tanks from the 29th Panzers. With thousands of infantrymen in tow, the enemy tanks were rolling down the Sele Valley toward the Tabacchificio. "Despite stiffening resistance, the heavy Nazi tanks bored forward in force," Boyle wrote. "Their whistling shells began shuttling a few feet over our heads and bursting somewhere near the sea with the terrific crack peculiar to German high-velocity artillery."

Kesselring's aim was to splinter the British troops in the northern part of the gulf beachhead from the American troops in the south. The Germans were attacking exactly where George Patton had predicted: in the crack between the two Allied forces.

None of the men in the 12th Air Support Command was equipped with heavy weapons. "All we have got to throw back at them is bedrolls," quipped Vessels. They had no choice but to "lie there and sweat it out," Boyle wrote.

The battle noise was excruciating: At one point that morning, the grenadiers had advanced so far down Highway 18 that they had practically reached Boyle's blackberry bush. Had the Germans continued pushing toward the sea, Boyle and his friends would have been, Hal wrote, "exposed like so many pins in a giant bowling alley."

Minutes later the cavalry arrived, in the form of an American air armada. Boyle goosed his neck outside the bush. "Dozens of A-36 Invaders and P-38 Lightnings suddenly swooped low out of sight," he wrote. The planes descended to what seemed to Boyle to be just a few feet off the ground. "We could hear their whining motors, thud of bombs, and rattle of machine guns and then they wheeled around the river bend, and rose triumphantly into the sky."

All of a sudden it was quiet—except for the huzzahs from the guys in the 12th. The German tank advance had been halted. Not long after, another cheer went up; a fleet of Mitchell medium bombers droned overhead. Boyle began counting but lost track at forty-two. "After passing us they tuned sharply inland and later we heard distant dull rumbles as they unloaded heavy bombs on German positions and supply lines," he wrote. "When they passed us on the return trip we were packing to pull out."[18]

BUT THEY WEREN'T PULLING OUT to chase Germans. Americans along the Sele were retreating to find what Boyle euphemistically called "more tenable shelter." Brits and Yanks all around the gulf were hunkered down amid ruins that one GI likened to the cover of a Latin textbook.

Assessing events from the other side of the Mediterranean, Boyle's friend Bigart called September 14 a day of "deepening crisis" for the Fifth Army. Salerno, the history devotee wrote, was beginning to "bear an ominous resemblance to the Gallipoli campaign in the Dardanelles in 1915." Just as the Australians and New Zealanders had in Turkey three decades earlier, Allied invaders at Salerno had spread themselves too thin and were vulnerable to both counterattacks and artillery fire.

"So far," Bigart wrote of the six-day Salerno invasion, "[the Allies] have been unable to wrest from the Germans the high ground that must be won, at whatever cost, if the bridgehead is to be saved."[19]

Not even the jaded Bigart realized how precarious the Allied bridgehead truly was. By then, Mark Clark had ordered his underlings to develop various withdrawal scenarios, a directive that caused teeth to grind at Supreme Headquarters and aboard Admiral Hewitt's flagship. For two days, Army and Navy staff officers agonized over the prospect of a Tyrrhenian Dunkirk until Alexander put an end to it, slapping his swagger stick while sputtering, "Oh, no! We *can't* have anything like that. Never do, never do."[20]

Worried that his image had been tarnished, Clark by September 16 was disingenuously telling correspondents that the situation at Salerno was "never desperate." Fortunately for Clark, that day things significantly turned in the Allies' favor when forward patrols from Montgomery's Eighth Army began linking up with Clark's Fifth.

After another series of counterattacks was rebuffed on September 17 and 18, the Germans began what Bigart called an "unhurried" retreat toward Naples, plugging mountain passes, mining roads and fields, and detonating bridges and culverts. Allied warplanes, mainly A-36 Invaders, inflicted horrendous damage on the German tank columns plodding north, but Kesselring was undeterred.

Naples was less than thirty miles away; the German commander wanted to buy time to demolish the city's harbor facilities so the Allies would be hard-pressed to convert it into a naval base.[21] Kesselring and the Gestapo decimated much more than Naples' port. Precious antiquities, museums, libraries—none of which had military worth—were torched as the Allies inched closer. By October 1, Naples had been virtually abandoned by the Nazis. There was still fighting in the streets, but it was mainly internecine warfare among Italian Partisans and youth street gangs, some of it directed at a common Fascist enemy but too much of it driven by fratricidal revenge.

HAL BOYLE WAS WITH THE 36th Division as it attempted to pacify a city that had turned primal. "Italian guerrillas and American soldiers, in a thrilling battle for the rooftops over crowded Neapolitan streets, shot it out for an hour with the last pocket of enemy resistance in Naples late today," Boyle wrote in a piece the *New York Times* subheaded HOSPITALS CROWDED WITH DEAD AND WOUNDED CHILDREN.

A week earlier, the Germans had tried to force some thirty thousand young Neapolitans into labor conscription, triggering a vicious response, which, in turn, elicited even more vicious reprisals and frenzied street fighting. Helmetless, their collars flung open, Naples' guerrillas "looked like something out of the French Revolution," Boyle thought. "They fired through holes in concrete rails bordering a hospital, where hundreds of wounded and unburied dead—victims of the week-long street fighting and German executions—lay. Two hundred dead men, women, and children— some dead for a week—lay alongside one of the walls of the hospital and on the other side were wailing survivors and 600 wounded persons. These were just a fraction of the toll."

General Clark thought that enemy soldiers had deserted Naples when an English-speaking Italian guerrilla approached the Allied command post to report that several dozen members of the Wehrmacht and some local *Fascisti* were holed up in an ancient temple. A spectacular firefight ensued, with doughboys side by side with vigilantes as they dodged from pillar to pillar. Most of the enemy holdouts were killed, but nearly three dozen ended up surrendering.

Boyle watched as American GIs tried to protect the Fascist survivors from an angry mob that spat on the prisoners and threatened them with knives and rocks. The rioters also begged for food and water. An aging grandfather proudly pointed out one youngster, whom Boyle estimated to be about twelve, and pantomimed how the lad had snuck up behind a German soldier and slit his throat.

The scene at the hospital was even more ghoulish. Weeping mothers were beating on doors and windows, desperate to see their wounded and dying children.

"An 8-year-old-boy lay with a rosary gripped in his hand, which almost covered the hole in his abdomen, ripped open by a German bullet," Boyle wrote. "Nearby was an old man who was so thin that one could circle his thigh with a finger and thumb. He had apparently died of starvation."[22]

Boyle asked someone at the hospital why so many young people were armed with carbines and automatic rifles. Once the Germans began looting Naples' treasures, the person said, members of the carabinieri, the Italian state police, plus disaffected *soldati*, began handing over weapons en masse. Soon the city devolved into a bloodbath.

The Germans had stolen or destroyed all of the Incurabili Hospital's supplies. Hospital officials had nothing left to treat wounds—no morphine, no serum, no bandages.

"Candles were lit in the shrine at one end of the room," wrote Boyle, "and serene-faced nuns moved about comforting the ill and wounded or helping care for their families."[23] Boyle interviewed Incurabili's head, a doctor named Giuseppe Marinelli, who told him that they didn't have enough carts to transport all the dead bodies to the cemetery. Marinelli and a prominent Neapolitan named Franco showed Boyle a pair of brothers, ages six and eight, guarded by their sixteen-year-old brother, whose head bore a wound from a German rifle butt.

"These boys' father was killed, and their mother was shot in the eye and the ten-year-old brother was killed," Franco said, adding, "This family will always have something to remember the Germans by."[24]

The AP columnist was among the first Americans in the hospital ward. Patients cheered, trying to kiss his hands as he walked by. One young woman thought Boyle was a physician and begged him to look at her mother's mangled arm. "The woman's face was turning visibly white with the pallor of death," Boyle wrote. When Marinelli explained that nothing could be done, the girl "made a sound like a shot animal and began rubbing her mother's hands."[25]

With its lurid description of persecuted Neapolitans reduced to drinking sewer water amid Nazi depredations, Boyle's article sparked tears and outrage throughout the U.S. It also caught the attention of his bosses in New York, who singled him out for praise, began preparing a Boyle portfolio for submission to the Pulitzer committee, and gave him a bump in salary—all the way up to $125 a week.[26]

Homer Bigart, too, witnessed Nazi depravity in Naples. He arrived at the front in the second week of October, in time to file stories about the sadistic ways that Kesselring had booby-trapped the city. One powerful time bomb had been concealed in a passage underneath an old artillery barracks. When the device detonated, it rocked the city, killing scores of civilians and some two dozen American GIs. Another time bomb had exploded in a Naples post office a few days before, with comparable casualties, Bigart revealed.[27]

IN THE MIDDLE OF THIS human suffering, Boyle still managed to find heartening stories—and find time to do them justice. In February, an Army Air Force PRO tipped off Boyle about a remarkable rescue of the 807th Medical Air Evacuation Squadron, among them thirteen nurses, who had gotten lost on the wrong side of the Adriatic and survived a miraculous two-month trek through harsh mountain terrain. Boyle raced south from Cassino to cover the squadron's tearful homecoming at an Allied air base. His story (headlined by the *Kansas City Star* STALKED BY PERIL: U.S. NURSES AND SOLDIERS SURVIVE 60 DAYS IN NAZI-INFESTED ALBANIA) got huge pickup.

"The dangerous game of hide-and-seek with the enemy started for nurses and soldiers when their big transport hospital plane crash-landed in the mountains of Albania [in] early November, after being lost in a thunderstorm and fired on by Nazi fighters," Boyle wrote. He had no idea when he wrote his lede that the nurses' ordeal had been anxiously followed by the White House and 10 Downing Street. FDR, in fact, was so caught up in the 807th's struggle that he requested daily updates from intelligence officers.

The 807th's saga began in Catania, Sicily, when their routine medical flight to pick up wounded at Baria on the Italian mainland went awry. Soon after takeoff, the C-53 transport got trapped in a violent thunderstorm; the pilots lost their bearings. After three hours of aimless flying they finally spotted terra firma, found an airfield, and tried to land on what they believed was friendly soil. As they went wheels down, however, the Iron Crosses on the planes parked on the runway told them that something was dreadfully wrong. By the time the pilots aborted the landing, tracer bullets were lacing into the fuselage.

With fuel now running low, they somehow shook off two Messerschmitts by flying in and out of clouds. The main pilot, Lieutenant Charles B. Thrasher of Daytona Beach, Florida, saw a field in the middle of a mountain range and crash-landed. The plane lurched nose first into a bank of mud, causing a toolbox to career through the plane's innards, bloodying several squadron members. They still had no idea where they were.

"As the party piled out in the pouring rain, a band of 15 or 20 *partisans* approached," Boyle recounted. "Where are we?" a member of the party nervously asked. "One who spoke a little English replied: 'This is Albania.' He warned the group that the hills were full of German troops."

Thrasher set the plane afire to prevent it from falling into enemy hands. The little party followed the Albanians to the leader's home, where they were fed corn bread. They stayed hidden for forty-eight hours before setting off on a three-day hike to a larger village.

"The villagers billeted the party in various homes, but one morning they were forced to flee to the hills as the Germans dive-bombed and shelled the town," Boyle wrote. In the frenzy of escaping into the mountains, three of the nurses got separated.

The main group wandered from one mountain village to the next, often getting caught in blizzards but somehow pushing onward. "While in one village awaiting help they were caught in the middle of a feud between pro-Nazi and pro-Allied natives. Nazi sympathizers shooting down from the surrounding hills fired on the Americans but no one was injured," Boyle wrote.

A few days later the local Resistance leader arranged for an Allied plane to rescue them. But as the plane attempted to land, it was fired upon by German troops. The rescue mission was scrubbed, breaking the hearts of the Americans. Their Resistance friends came up with an alternative escape plan—but it involved getting to a boat on the Adriatic.

So they proceeded to lumber for twenty-six harrowing hours to the coast, eluding German patrols along the way. "That night they waited tensely on the rocky shores as a single motorboat took them, a few at a time, out across the shallow waters to the waiting British launch," Boyle wrote. "It was after midnight until the last of the little group was aboard. With muffled motors the launch turned and the rocky shores of Albania faded into the night." The launch motored south to the safety of the Allied-controlled Mediterranean.

"As the rescue vessel neared its home port the nurses—feminine to the end—spruced up as best they could and dabbed on their last bits of lipstick which they had been saving for this moment," wrote Boyle.

Amazingly, the three nurses who got separated from the group in the Albanian mountains were also rescued and rejoined their unit a few days later.[28]

BOYLE'S FASCINATION WITH WOMEN WAS almost Liebling-like; even given the sexist tenor of the times, it bordered on the unseemly. His great pal and boss, AP's Wes Gallagher, wrote in January of '44 that Boyle talked about women nonstop, then impatiently waited for letters from his wife.[29]

That winter, after talking to several recently jilted doughboys, Boyle curiously chose to pen an article chastising women back home for being unfaithful to their men in khaki. Stop writing Dear John letters, Boyle lectured, because they're too devastating to the boys in the trenches. So many Mediterranean Theater GIs had been dumped that they'd formed their own organization, the Brush-off Club, Boyle noted.

The response from the distaff set was pointed—so pointed in fact, that

Boyle was forced to backtrack in a follow-up column. Boyle sheepishly acknowledged that the Rosie the Riveters were doing an extraordinary job back home under trying circumstances—plus most were keeping the home fires lit for their men. His piece also admitted that "Some of the boys in uniform have been playing traitor to Cupid, too."

Boyle tried to make amends by writing, "Well, girls, if your boyfriend in uniform has passed you up for another frill, cheer up—you can always become a 'WABOC'"—the Women's Auxiliary of the Brush-off Club. The WABOC, Boyle revealed, had been championed by a female reader in Santa Monica, California, one Irene M. Cozine, whose passion-filled letters were apparently not enough to prevent her soldier boy from taking up with someone else. "Perhaps the WABOC club members could hold a joint meeting after the war and burn our ex-sweethearts in effigy or something," Miss Cozine suggested. Her proposition, Boyle claimed, was immediately embraced by male founders of the Brush-off Club.[30]

THE FIGHTING AROUND SAN PIETRO Infine, the tiny hamlet tucked halfway up the southern slope of Monte Sammucro on the southeastern side of the Rapido, inspired as much literary and cinematic outpouring as any battle in the war. San Pietro is where Ernie Pyle wrote his posthumous tribute to Captain Henry Waskow, not only among the most celebrated pieces of war correspondence in American history but also the essay that helped propel Hollywood into filming Pyle's story, with Boyle playing himself in a cameo. The village is also where filmmaker John Huston created *The Battle of San Pietro*, one of World War II's finer documentaries, even if it did take liberties with the facts, deployed GIs dressed up in enemy uniforms, and required extra footage shot at mountain venues that were manifestly *not* San Pietro. Finally, San Pietro is where Bigart buttressed his reputation by writing a series of searing articles that captured the pathos of the Italian campaign.

Exactly one week before Christmas 1943, Bigart and his cohort from the Brolo raid in Sicily, AP's Don Whitehead, plus Farnsworth Fowle of

CBS Radio, followed a platoon of men from the 36th Division across a valley "littered with dead" below San Pietro.

"The battlefield was strangely still," Bigart wrote. "A thick haze lay stagnant above the pass and a wan sun bathed the scene in sickly light. There was not a sound except our own cautious footsteps as we crossed the pasture, still uncleared of mines."[31]

Near a forward aid station they encountered a medical officer from Oklahoma who'd been heroically evacuating wounded men within sight of snipers. He showed them a steep mountain path that the Germans had somehow failed to mine. The captain also warned that the enemy had thoroughly booby-trapped San Pietro and was still shelling the town from a distant mountaintop. Bigart's platoon came upon three dead Americans at the base of the path.

> One boy lay crumpled in a shallow slit trench beneath a rock. Another, still grasping his rifle, peered from behind a tree, staring with sightless eyes toward the Liri plain. A third lay prone where he had fallen. He had heard the warning scream of a German shell. He had dropped flat on his stomach but on level ground affording no cover. Evidently some fragment had killed him instantly, for there had been no struggle. Generally there is no mistaking the dead—their strange contorted posture leaves no room for doubt. But this soldier, his steel helmet tilted over his face, seemed merely resting in the field. We did not know until we came within a few steps and saw a gray hand hanging limply from a sleeve.

The platoon resumed its cautious advance near a creek bed along the path singled out by the medical officer. CBS' Fowle scrambled over a patch of barbed wire that the Germans had strung perpendicular to the creek. Whitehead was poised to do the same when Bigart suddenly shouted, "Watch out!"[32] The bottom strand had been booby-trapped; Bigart's eagle eye spotted a trip wire connected to a hidden Teller mine. It had been a miracle that Fowle hadn't set off an explosion that might have killed them all. Bigart's account, typically, did not acknowledge who sounded the warning, but Whitehead's description credited Bigart with saving the day.[33]

Immediately below San Pietro the platoon crept through a field littered with abandoned rifles and cartridge belts. Nearby were immense caves that the Germans had used as ammunition dumps and machine gun sites. On the other side of town were secret caverns in which scores of San Pietro families had sought refuge—and where young men had concealed themselves from Gestapo thugs looking for slave laborers.

The platoon began creeping up a cobbled alley. As they neared the village they came upon old Fascist slogans painted onto the cobblestones. STRAIGHT AHEAD WITH MUSSOLINI! one shouted.[34] Two charred Sherman tanks sat at the top of the alley, ghostly sentinels guarding an eviscerated town. The stench of dead mules and pigs overwhelmed the smell of battle.

"We passed the first house," Bigart wrote. "A rifle was in position near the doorstep. Looking within we saw an American man lying beneath a heap of straw." Inside were three other dead GIs. "Every approach to San Pietro, every ravine and sunken path offering shelter from machine-gun fire, had been covered by German snipers."[35]

San Pietro was "ghastly," Bigart wrote. Every dwelling around the tiny Piazza San Nicola was buried under five feet or more of rubble. Since the Germans had built their defenses in the heart of the town, "Americans had no choice but to beat the fortress to pieces," Whitehead maintained.[36] The village had been bombed from the air for three weeks and attacked from the ground by American—and now German—artillery.

A barefoot mother nursing her baby begged the Americans for food, but they had none. The Church of St. Michael was so decimated Bigart could barely read the prayer above its alcove: ST. MICHAEL THE ARCHANGEL: ALWAYS REMEMBER US, HERE AND EVERYWHERE. The choir loft dangled atop an altar that had all but collapsed.

Beneath a statue of St. Peter, Bigart and Whitehead noticed an inscription that the young mother translated for them: BY THE DEVOTION OF AMERICANS FROM SAN PIETRO. Many San Pietro emigrants had settled in

Syracuse, New York, she explained. Amid the wreckage was a figure of Christ whose head had been torn off; an arm of the Madonna of the Waters had also been severed. The village priest had vanished earlier that fall, apparently killed by the Gestapo.[37]

Bigart and Whitehead examined a nearby house that the Germans had used as an ammunition depot. Next door they discovered a batch of letters that had been written to an American soldier, who was now presumably dead or captured. Sitting on the table, inexplicably, was a baseball glove. Did the mitt belong to the unfortunate GI? Bigart never found out. Up the street they wandered into what they reckoned had been the enemy's command post. In it they found a copy of the December 6, 1943, edition of the *Völkischer Beobachter,* the Nazi party's propaganda sheet dating back to the days of Hitler's Beer Hall Putsch in Munich.

In another house, Bigart found two American medical aides dressing the wounds of San Pietro peasants. "One of the natives had retrieved a case of wine from the ruins and toasts were offered to the American victory," he wrote.[38]

IT MAY HAVE BEEN A VICTORY—but it came at great cost. In San Pietro Bigart sat down with Lieutenant Colonel Howard K. Dodge of Temple, Texas, a battalion commander with the 36th Division. Dodge's men were among the first to encircle the village; they had to withstand a furious nighttime German counterassault that lasted four hours. In the confusion of the first few minutes of the enemy surge, Dodge and the officers back at the regimental command post didn't know what they were up against. Over the telephone wire they heard a frontline infantryman groan, "My God, when are we going to get artillery support!"

"At first we thought it was merely the usual enemy patrol probing our position and we didn't dare to fire for fear of endangering our men," the colonel told Bigart. "But when the firing increased in intensity we ordered a barrage. It came within a few minutes and fell smack where we wanted it. It must have caught a lot of the Germans, for we could hear them hollering and moaning in a draw just beyond our lines."[39]

Three more times that early morning the Germans tried to crack Dodge's position. Each time they inflicted horrible casualties but were repulsed. An officer from Wilmington, North Carolina, named Henry C. Bragaw rallied his men when the Germans shifted their attack from the right of the American line to its center. Bragaw, a redhead who sported a huge handlebar mustache, was a horticulturalist by training. But he had little time to admire Sammucro's flora and fauna; he and his men had been on the front lines for days without a break.

Equally exhausted was a lieutenant from Waco, Texas, whose name— Rufus J. Cleghorn—sounded like something out of a Warner Brothers cartoon. Cleghorn was a barrel-chested former lineman for Baylor University. His platoon was the first to reach the mountain's summit.

"Exulting in battle," Bigart wrote, "Cleghorn clambered to the highest rock of Sammucro's pinnacle and howled insults at the Germans, pausing now and then to toss grenades. For variety, Cleghorn occasionally put his weight against a huge boulder and sent it rolling down the slope. He roared with laughter as the Germans attempted to dodge the hurtling boulders."

Bigart ended his remarkable three-thousand-word dispatch from San Pietro with one of his uncanny observations. "It is very cold these December nights on Sammucro's peak, and the uniforms and overcoats issued to the men were not too warm. Yesterday Army cooks carried warm combat suits to the troops and a can of Sterno to each man."[40]

JOHN HUSTON AND HIS SIGNAL Corps crew were probably issued warm coats and Sterno cans, too. They began filming their documentary two days before Whitehead and Bigart made their trek up Sammucro.

Positioned atop Monte Rotondo, Huston's cameras whirred as two platoons' worth of Sherman tanks began their arduous climb toward San Pietro. They didn't get far before German artillery began raining down; the American tanks retaliated with seventy-five-millimeter shells but soon found themselves overwhelmed. Four Shermans struck mines and were quickly disabled; three others absorbed direct hits from enemy antitank batteries.

Intent on capturing a triumphant moment for the American fighting man, Huston and his photographers were instead filming a debacle. In full view of the cameras, crew members from disabled tanks were either huddled on top of machines going backward or beating a hasty retreat on foot. Much blood had been spilled while no ground had been gained; Huston's first day of shooting didn't make for inspirational celluloid.

But Huston's cameras stuck around long enough to see American tanks actually scale Sammucro. Still, the director had to embroider battle sequences using GIs disguised as Germans, another village that pretended to be San Pietro, and a different mountaintop that masqueraded as Sammucro. Huston put together a fifty-minute film whose battle sequences were hailed as gritty and real—perhaps *too* gritty and real—but George Marshall's staff insisted it be chopped to a half hour. The Army liked it so much they used it as a training film. It was generally well received, although some critics thought the left-wing Huston had produced an antiwar polemic. Huston, who'd now seen the misery of combat up close, supposedly said that if he ever made a "pro-war" film he should be shot. Humphrey Bogart's favorite director, the auteur behind *The Maltese Falcon*, went on to make two other wartime documentaries for OWI and the Signal Corps.[41]

HUSTON, IT APPEARS, NEVER TOOK his cameras to the Anzio beachhead—which is a shame, because he could have filmed a saga of human failure and redemption more stirring than *The African Queen*. Bigart and Boyle, however, did cover Anzio. Bigart stayed there, without reprieve, for week after excruciating week; Boyle wasn't far behind.

An amphibious assault leapfrogging the Gustav Line and putting Allied troops just thirty-five miles south of Rome was Winston Churchill's answer to the bloody impasse along the Rapido. Like everyone else in the Allied high command, Churchill was disconsolate over the way the advance toward Rome had ground down. In the previous seven weeks, the Allies had inched forward only seven miles, incurring sixteen thousand casualties.[42] At that rate it would take another year to reach the ancient capital.

The Anzio plan was a hundred times bigger and more audacious than the raid on Brolo and Monte Cipolla—and a hundred times riskier. The lives of "only" seven hundred commandoes had been at risk at Brolo. And even if the Monte Cipolla raid had been completely snuffed, it would not have materially affected the outcome of the Sicilian campaign.

Anzio's stakes were much higher. Churchill, Alexander, and Clark were gambling with the lives of nearly fifty thousand men on top of the tens of thousands of soldiers stuck in the mountains south of Cassino. And without question, the success of the Italian campaign hung in the balance.

The aim of Operation Shingle, as it became known, was ambitious: Grab the Anzio beachhead, make a quick strike northeast to the Alban Hills, block Kesselring's escape routes from the Liri Valley by seizing Highways 7 (the ancient Appian Way along the Tyrrhenian) and 6 (the road leading northwest from Cassino), and capture Rome. In one fell swoop, went Churchill's fondest dream, the bulk of Italy would belong to the Allies and Kesselring's Army Group C would be destroyed.[43]

It wasn't that simple, of course. In contrast to the Gulf of Salerno invasion four months earlier, the initial stage of the Anzio landings went off almost without a hitch. "The first round," Bigart wrote, "went decisively to the Allies. The troops achieved a surprise landing on beaches practically undefended. Every break went to the Allies. The port of Anzio fell intact. There was an unusual run of fine weather—rough seas hindered the landing of supplies only two days. With negligible loss the initial objectives were taken quickly. . . . There was no confusion. It was nothing like Salerno."[44]

It may have been nothing like Salerno the first week, but during weeks two through nine, Anzio was much more dire. Encouraged by Alexander and Clark to consolidate his position before penetrating inland, invasion commander General John Lucas dug in on the beachhead, collecting additional troops and supplies and planning his next move.

Boyle stayed in Purple Heart Valley to cover the ill-fated Rapido crossings. Bigart, though, was one of just six Allied correspondents who went in with Lucas' invaders—and one of only two reporters who stayed on the Anzio beachhead for the duration.

The landing itself, as Bigart acknowledged, was fairly easy: The only

Germans they encountered on the beach were four drunken officers joy-riding in a car. Two hundred other enemy soldiers were quickly captured, many still wearing pajamas.[45] Anzio was a staggering logistical feat: By midmorning on the first day, thirty-six thousand men and nearly 3,200 vehicles had been unloaded. Only two German battalions stood between Anzio and Rome. The great Allied gamble appeared to be paying off. Still chastened by his experience at Salerno, however, the oddly passive-aggressive Clark urged Lucas not to "stick his neck out."[46]

Kesselring sensed the Allied indecisiveness; the German commander knew that geography would trump surprise. He may have been caught "dumbfounded" at Anzio, as Boyle put it, but by January 30, day eight, Kesselring's troops had cemented strong defensive positions to thwart advances from either the coast or from Cassino.

On that bloody Sunday, Kesselring's men were lying in wait as the Allies tried to break out of the beachhead by attacking Cisterna di Littoria on the Appian Way just twenty-four miles south of Rome. Two Army Ranger battalions—nearly eight hundred men—were at the point when Kesselring sprang his trap. Only six Rangers made it back to U.S. lines. The surviving prisoners were paraded through Rome and used as propaganda toys by Joseph Goebbels and his mouthpiece, Axis Sally.[47] An assault three days later at Carroceto was repulsed with similarly heavy losses.

Most of the Allied troops remained on the Anzio beach, huddled in tents, dodging unending artillery and mortar shells. Hospital tents seemed to draw particularly intense fire: A hundred medical professionals—including many nurses—were killed in the line of duty.[48]

One warmish afternoon Homer Bigart decided to take a break by paddling a raft around an inlet. In midexcursion, a Messerschmitt 109 appeared out of nowhere. Bigart began furiously scrambling toward shore. After strafing the beach, the enemy pilot dove at Bigart. Bullets ripped through the raft but somehow missed Homer.[49] Thus ended his recreational boating at Anzio. In combat, Bigart seemed to have nine lives.

Wrote a devastated Churchill of Anzio, "We hoped to land a wild cat that would tear out the bowels of the Boche. Instead, we have stranded a vast whale with its tail flopping about in the water."[50]

———

THE WHALE CONTINUED TO FLOP at Anzio and Cassino through the bleak winter of '44. In mid-February, Sir Harold R. L. G. Alexander (Bigart, probably out of spite, always on first reference used Alexander's full name and title, in all its initialed pretension) got in a pissing match with the correspondents covering the Anzio beachhead, chief among them the *Herald Tribune*'s prickly reporter. On Valentine's Day, Alexander ushered the Anzio press contingent into his tent and erupted.

"Alexander said he had been notified by superiors that stories emanating from the beachhead 'alarmed the people,'" Bigart wrote. Anzio reporters, Alexander claimed, had become unduly downcast. As a result, the high command was penalizing reporters by denying them access to radio facilities to file their stories through Allied press headquarters at Naples. Radio privileges would be restored only when reporters began following a stricter policy line, Alexander threatened.

"There's no basis for pessimistic rubbish," the British general scolded Bigart and the others.

Bigart's rejoinder was to publish an article demonstrating that his previous accounts were neither "pessimistic" nor "rubbish." The press' coverage of Anzio had been positive, Bigart pointed out, when there were positive developments to report, such as the unimpeded landing and the surprise achieved by the Allies.

But beginning with the late January–early February reversals at Cisterna di Littoria and Carroceto, "The initiative went to the Germans. We reported it.

"We tried to report that the situation was tense and critical. We still believe it was," Bigart wrote in a piece that took five days to clear censors and be relayed to the *Trib*.

Bigart then addressed the underlying concerns in a manner worthy of an essay in the *Columbia Journalism Review*. "Basically, the issue is this— shall the public receive accurate day-by-day reports of the changing fortunes of battle or shall we maintain an 'even tone,' speaking only vaguely of reverses?" Bigart argued that he and his five beachhead colleagues had been "exceedingly careful" not to publish information of military value to the enemy.

"But the quarrel is not over battlefield security," he wrote. Instead, the debate centered around the view of certain military advisors that American and British newspaper readers "do not yet realize that war involves risks, that the breaks do not always go to the Allies. They are afraid the public cannot stand the shock of bad news and that it must be broken to them gradually over long periods of time and preferably after some victory."[51]

Relations between the press and the Allied command in Italy remained acrimonious. Practically everything about the Italian campaign was full of anguish. Despite a lack of evidence that the Germans had occupied the abbey on the summit of Monte Cassino, Alexander and Clark ordered it destroyed by Allied bombers. The order came the day after Alexander excoriated the press. With no warning, four separate formations of B-17s decimated one of the world's great religious shrines, to no apparent military end. There was no more dismaying sight in World War II than the specter of the abbey's monks seeking refuge by marching toward the German lines.

Some fifty miles northwest, Allied forces remained bottled up at Anzio well into spring. In early March, Bigart was in a jeep behind a truckload of replacement doughboys as they headed toward Anzio. Six full weeks after the landings, the Allied position was still so vulnerable that any vehicle approaching the beachhead was exposed to deadly artillery fire.

"The green men must have had a premonition," wrote Bigart. "They had seen dead cows and sheep beside the road and they were crouching down to the floor of the truck when the first shells came in, rattling like a runaway coal truck."

The Germans undershot slightly, their misfires showering the truck with mud. Bigart's jeep came under attack, too, but his driver stomped on the accelerator; they wheeled around the truck and out of danger. Both vehicles made it safely to the beachhead.

"The terror faded from the faces of the new men. There always has to be a first time, but the men had not expected it so soon," Bigart wrote.

After they arrived at the beachhead, Bigart watched a no-nonsense platoon sergeant give the green GIs a demonstration on the proper method of digging a foxhole. The sergeant walked them over to a spot near some shell craters and ordered them to dig in for the night.

Thirteen months into covering the war Bigart had witnessed untold tragedies, yet had not grown inured to them. There was something exceedingly sad about watching these kids being thrown into battle in such a dismal setting. But rather than dwell on the young soldiers' anxieties, Bigart chose to describe the stark milieu.

"It was one of those grim March days that hold no hope of spring," he wrote. "The brown plain reached toward mountains still covered with snow. A raw wind marshaled steely bands of clouds across the sky and rippled the flooded fields.

"On such a day you expect death more than on bright days. You think that if only you can survive this day, then tomorrow will be sunny and you'll be one day nearer to the end of the war."[52]

Some sixty thousand Allied soldiers in Italy never saw another sunny day.

CHAPTER 9

★

THE BLITZ SPIRIT—LONDON AND
THE HOME FRONT

> *At midnight brawling London shuts up like a safe. The*
> *twisting roads become dark avenues of mystery, and un-*
> *less you have a flashlight along you are likely to lose*
> *your way and blunder from square to square and circle*
> *to circle until dawn.*

> —HAL BOYLE, MAY 23, 1944
> LEAVES FROM A WAR CORRESPONDENT'S NOTEBOOK

Walter Cronkite was grabbing a late Friday supper at the Grosvenor House near Hyde Park when the *ack!-ack!* barrage got uncomfortably loud. By February of '44 Londoners had become blasé about air raids. Piercing sirens still went off, triggering crisscrossed searchlights, sporadic antiaircraft fire from the sandbag bunkers all over town, and a smattering of bombs that, for the most part, failed to inflict much damage. It was nothing like the Blitz of '40, when tons of deadly ordnance struck almost every day and night, igniting fires throughout the city and forcing Londoners to flee underground inside tube stations.

A week earlier, in fact, Cronkite was watching actor Claude Rains in the film *Phantom of the Opera* when sirens began blaring and a defiant message was flashed on the screen: "An air raid warning has sounded. The performance will continue." Nobody left the theater to seek cover, despite the fact, Cronkite volunteered to Betsy, that the movie "stank—it just didn't jell."[1]

Several nights later, though, the noise enveloping the West End sounded more ominous. Cutting dinner short, Cronkite rushed out and goosed his neck to see a dozen or more glows from Nazi incendiaries.

Cronkite pulled out his torch and hailed a cab. The taxi took him to a neighborhood where two full blocks of apartment buildings were aflame. He got the attention of a female fireguard and asked if anyone had been hurt. Most of the flats had been vacant, he was told, but three older women had been evacuated and were being treated in an apartment across the street.

"I went over to have a look in on them," Cronkite told Betsy. "Here were these three old gals, all of whom looked to be in their nineties, with the few pitiable possessions they had saved stacked around them. There was no light in the parlor. It was lit only by the reflection of the three old ladies' burning flat across the street. But the three old ladies were huddled around a quart of Irish whiskey. And when I looked in one was just wiping her lips, laughing uproariously, and cackling: 'Gol blimey, if it ain't just like the good old days!'

"I guess that is the blitz spirit we read about. And the firemen here. I didn't hear them shout a single order. They went about the work with more calm, and about as fast, as a bunch of WPA workers digging a sewer. And this with magnesium incendiaries still burning in the streets beside them."[2]

Twenty-four hours later the Luftwaffe was at it again. Cronkite was on deadline that night, pounding out a story at UP headquarters about the Allied raids on Leipzig, Hamburg, and Braunschweig that had kicked off Operation Argument, a savage bombing offensive against German aircraft factories that had been nicknamed Big Week.[3] Perhaps Hermann Göring was determined to retaliate. Suddenly London was filled with the same wail that Cronkite had heard the night before.

He ran up to the roof of the News of the World building. Whole sections of London were already ablaze, "illuminating the skyline like a full moon," he told Betsy.

Cronkite hustled back downstairs and hollered for colleague (and roommate) Jim McGlincy to follow him. The two UP reporters ducked into a taxi and raced toward an industrial stretch of town where a conflagration was raging.

"It was no fun with the sparks whipped by a high wind, flying down the street like Fourth of July sparklers," Cronkite told Betsy. The embers were so fierce that McGlincy and Cronkite were forced to beat them off their coats and pant legs with gloved hands and hats. Between the bitter cold and the malevolent sparks it was impossible for the correspondents to take notes or conduct interviews.

The next day they learned that one of their UP colleagues had been bombed out of his flat. Other UP reporters, including Cronkite and Mc-Glincy, had experienced "narrow squeezes": Several incendiaries had fallen within a block or two of their apartment building on Buckingham Gate.

"Some fun!" Cronkite facetiously wrote Betsy. "We all had a little taste Friday night and again last night of what London went through in the blitz and an even smaller taste of what Berlin must be going through now. And believe you me, a taste is enough."[4]

SOME FUN INDEED. CRONKITE'S "LITTLE taste" of terror bombing ironically became known in London lore as the Little Blitz. Journalist-historian Chester Wilmot was in southern England during that stretch, billeted with paratroopers from the Sixth British Airborne Division. On nine separate nights in February and March of '44, Wilmot recalled, Göring's bombers hit London harder than the British capital had been hit in years.[5] But the Luftwaffe couldn't sustain the offensive. Göring had cobbled together a makeshift fleet of bombers from Nazi airfields in France. Once those planes were destroyed or damaged, few replacements were available. By mid-March, the Luftwaffe had again been reduced to ineffectual spot raids.

Thanks to forty thousand tons' worth of Allied bomb attacks over launch and construction sites, moreover, Hitler's scheme of a sky full of *Vergeltungswaffen* ("revenge") rockets raining down on England was running well behind, five full months away from realization.

On Thursday, February 10, 1944, Cronkite went along on a B-26 Marauder raid against what he explained to Betsy were "special military targets" along the Pas de Calais on the Belgian-French border. In truth, USAAF sources told Cronkite, the targets were secret Nazi rocket-gun emplacements. The 114 medium bombers were escorted for the entire mission by British Spitfires, which effectively discouraged the Germans from dispatching their own fighters. "The trip was about as exciting as a windy day in a Piper Cub," Cronkite complained to his wife. Only a couple of bursts of flak exploded anywhere close to Cronkite's formation.[6]

When he got back to London, censors forbade Cronkite from identifying the raid's objective, forcing him to stick, more or less, to the vagaries he offered Betsy. Still, Cronkite's piece was well received in England, landing on the front page of the *Daily Herald*, the *Daily Sketch*, and the *News Chronicle*.[7]

The article's pickup may have tempered his bosses' pique. UP's higher-ups were angry at Cronkite for violating an office "rule" precluding reporters from going on airborne missions. Cronkite quickly produced a two-month-old memorandum that gave him dispensation to participate in the B-26 raid—a blessing that UP boss Virgil Pinkley had apparently forgotten.

"I think that secretly they [his bosses] probably admired the initiative. At any rate, I hope so," Cronkite confided to Betsy.[8]

LONDON WAS FULL OF ADMIRABLE initiative in the winter and spring of 1944; still, it was a bizarre and, as Hal Boyle put it, "jittery" place.[9] The city was again under siege, but this time only peripherally from German bombs. Invading England in droves, however, were American servicemen and servicewomen.

When Cronkite, Rooney, and Bigart had first started covering bomber boys in early '43, there were just four USAAF air bases in Britain and fewer than fifty thousand servicemen. By the end of '43, both figures had more than quintupled—and that was just the beginning.

Newly arrived airmen looked around at all the airfields, Cronkite remembered, and declared England the "world's largest aircraft carrier." By the spring of '44, nearly six dozen airdromes had taken root and a million and a half American men and women were being housed in the U.K. And that didn't count hundreds of thousands of troops from the British

Commonwealth nations, plus France, Poland, Holland, Norway, and Czechoslovakia.[10]

Indeed, London was the makeshift capital of every country that had been dismembered by the Third Reich. The place was full of so much intrigue and innuendo, Joe Liebling wrote, that "lunch at Claridge's or the Ritz Grill resembled an Alfred Hitchcock film."[11] Things were so topsy-turvy that the heir to the Persian throne lived in the modest hotel room next to Liebling's.[12]

Shakespeare's scepter'd isle was bursting at the seams. London was a much different town than it had been in the nadir of the Blitz. Londoners still showed remarkable resilience. But they were numb from five years of war; by early '44, many had grown weary and claustrophobic. Twelve months earlier it had been rare to see American servicemen on leave in London. Now Yanks were on every street corner and in every pub—and not always exhibiting refined manners.

"The attitude of the British changed during the war. They got pretty damn tired of their island being weighted down by tens of thousands of these rather brash Americans," Cronkite recalled.[13] When Cronkite first arrived, British families would host U.S. servicemen in their homes for Sunday dinner, posting thoughtful invitations on bulletins boards at base PXs and places such as the Ministry of Information.

In early '43, Cronkite visited the home of a family who appeared to be trying to marry off a "not uncharming" daughter and were doubtless disappointed to see Cronkite's wedding ring. As a special treat for its American guest, the family had saved up ration points to buy a joint, the traditional Sunday entrée for better-off Britons.

A FEW MONTHS LATER, EDWARD R. Murrow, the CBS Radio commentator who had done so much in 1940 and '41 to build American support for Britain's cause, invited Walter Cronkite to lunch. Murrow had admired the UP reporter's coverage of the air war and was impressed by Cronkite's natural ease in front of a microphone. Cronkite had been a popular interview choice for Murrow's London boys; the aftermath of the Wilhelms-haven raid in February of '43 was one of several Cronkite appearances on CBS Radio.

Murrow asked Cronkite to meet him at the Savile Club, the tony May-fair restaurant. But London's elite haunts were unknown to the workaholic Cronkite, who thought Murrow had said "Saddle Club" and didn't want to embarrass himself by asking the broadcaster for directions.

Cronkite jumped into a cab on Fleet Street and instructed the driver to take him to the Saddle Club. "Don't believe I know it, governor," the cabbie replied. Cronkite had the cab pull over next to a phone booth; he called the UP office, where a colleague steered him toward the proper location on Brook Street.[14]

Feeling like a rube, Cronkite arrived late for his luncheon with the world's most celebrated American expatriate. Murrow, who could be prickly, was gracious. He surprised Cronkite by offering him a job as CBS' Russian correspondent. Murrow was calling back to London Cronkite's former UP colleague Bill Downs; he wanted Cronkite to replace Downs in covering Stalin's government in exile at Kuibyshev. CBS was offering Cronkite a king's ransom: $125 a week, plus "commercial fees" of some $25 almost every time Cronkite appeared on the air, which would be a lot. The CBS offer came close to tripling Cronkite's $57.50-per-week salary with UP. Yet Cronkite had been ambivalent about his broadcast experiences in Austin, Kansas City, and Norman.

"I thought it was kind of a schlock business compared to print," he remembered. "But I still thought, well, $125 and a chance to go to Russia, I probably ought to take it. So I accepted it, and I was going to give United Press a couple of weeks' notice, which, frankly, wasn't adequate in wartime."[15]

When Cronkite told his then boss, Harrison Salisbury, about Murrow's offer, Salisbury immediately countered with a $17.50 per week raise—unheard-of largesse at UP—and promised to arrange for the wire service's president, Hugh Baillie, to make his own plea. Sure enough, Baillie got through on the phone from New York that night—no mean feat in wartime

London—and "gave me a sales pitch like I never heard in my life," Cronkite recalled.

"I'm going to raise you $20 a week just to show my good faith," Baillie vowed. Cronkite inquired if the $20 was in addition to the $17.50 that Salisbury had offered—or part of it. There was a long pause. "No, no, this is on top of that," Baillie insisted—which may or may not have been part of UP's keep-Cronkite strategy, but was nevertheless now in its counteroffer.

Cronkite was in a position to pocket 95 bucks a week from UP—good money for a gumshoe reporter without a college degree.[16]

When Cronkite broke the news to Murrow, "he didn't take it too kindly," Cronkite remembered. Murrow didn't say it directly, but the inference was that Cronkite had used the CBS offer to leverage more money out of UP. "I hadn't meant to; it wasn't my intention when I accepted Ed's offer," Cronkite allowed. "But it worked out that way, and Ed had every right to feel that way about it."[17]

By mid-'43 Ed Murrow and his team were the hottest commodities in journalism—wordsmiths inventing a new medium. Murrow, the toast of the free world, wasn't used to people saying no—especially ambitious young reporters. Cronkite's clumsy turndown drove a wedge between them.

Although they would later spend fifteen years at CBS News as colleagues, Cronkite and Murrow were never close. Murrow and his "boys," Eric Sevareid and Charles Collingwood among them, tended to look down their noses at Cronkite, the wire service grunt who—heaven forfend!—actually cared about breaking news. The Murrow Boys weren't reporters so much as seers, urbane commentators who dined with prime ministers one day—and parachuted out of planes the next. Murrow and his minions didn't just write and read news: They dissected it, putting it into bold historical context, giving events a passion that print journalists—even Liebling and Bigart at their best—were hard-pressed to match. And as Collingwood would later demonstrate, the Murrow guys sometimes weren't above manipulating the facts for their own aggrandizement.

It wasn't until after Cronkite proved himself as CBS News' anchorman

in the early 1960s that the surviving Murrow men accepted him as a peer—
and even then it was grudgingly. Cronkite always admired the Murrow
Boys and what they meant to the evolution of journalism. But in the main
he felt their work should be labeled "opinion"—which is what happened
when Eric Sevareid, the quintessential Murrow protégé, became a regular
commentator on Cronkite's *CBS Evening News*.

ANDY ROONEY AND WALTER CRONKITE still saw a fair amount of each
other on the USAAF and SHAEF beats. But by early '44, they weren't sharing train rides up to East Anglia nearly as often. Allied censors, less fearful
of enemy infiltration, deemed that it was no longer necessary for correspondents to compose their air war articles at the Ministry of Information
in London—a move Cronkite likened to being given a new lease on life.

The edict left reporters like Cronkite and Rooney free to spend less time
commuting and more time at their offices and "home" bases: in Cronkite's
case, the 303rd Bomb Group at Molesworth, in Rooney's case, the 306th in
Thurleigh. They could go for several days at a stretch, spend quality time
with the airmen, write their stories, have them approved by censors more
or less on the spot, then phone their copy in to their home offices in London. The field phone connections were often dreadful. Even the simplest
words, Cronkite recalled, had to be loudly dictated—"Smith! 'S' as in 'Sam!'
'M' as in 'Mary!'"—usually in the presence of a young sergeant-censor eager to hit the local pub. Although late-war censors tended to be somewhat
less paranoid, there were still knockdown battles. By mid-'44, Cronkite's
UP protégé Collie Small had pretty much taken over the day-to-day Molesworth beat, freeing Cronkite to coordinate daily bombing coverage.

CENSORS WEREN'T THE ONLY ONES frequenting nightspots. By late '43 London had turned into a den of iniquity, a place only marginally north of
Sodom and Gomorrah.[18]

The city's ambience was surreal: bomb debris, the heavy fog off the
Thames, and the acrid smoke rising from thousands of chimneys com-

bined to give London the gothic feel of a bad Sherlock Holmes movie. Every afternoon and evening, swing bands could be heard throughout the city—young couples jitterbugging their cares away.[19]

The airmen whose everyday exploits Cronkite and Rooney commemorated were especially in need of the release that only London could provide. "They had been hauling regularly," Rooney remembered, and "had to take care of their physical needs."[20] The Eighth and Ninth Air Force guys would pile out of trains and instantly go prowling for female companionship; most weren't overly picky. "Good time girls" offered quickie "wall jobs" for eight bucks—and didn't lack for customers.[21]

Cronkite recalled the sex-ploits of the Piccadilly Commandoes, the professional hookers who worked blacked-out doorways and alleyways. "[W]e could hear the click of heels announce the arrival of a lady of the night. Wearing cheap perfume, she would run her hand along our pants leg." The prostitute's move was pecuniary, not prurient. By grabbing trousers, streetwalkers could tell whether the target was American or British or an enlisted man or an officer. "On that determination hung the price at which she would open the bidding," Cronkite laughed.[22]

Rooney wrote an amusing piece in April of '44 about Lady Astor, the Virginia-born firebrand who, well into her seventies, was a self-appointed ambassador to American troops in Britain. The former Nancy Langhorne had become the first female member of Parliament in 1919 and an outspoken Tory celebrated on two continents. She regularly visited London's canteens and clubs, sampling the humble cuisine and imploring the staff to take care of "her boys."

"Somewhat the same spirit of aggressive maternalism is put into operation when she encounters an inebriated GI on the street," Rooney wrote. "Without the formality of introductions she collars him, gives him a brisk lecture on the evils of rum, then, before he can figure out what is going on, piles him into a cab and sends him back to his billet." Lady Astor's "invariable gag" when she entered a canteen full of Yanks was to yell out, "Are there any rebels in the house?"[23]

Every day in early '44, thousands of "rebels" visited the Rainbow Corner in Piccadilly at the intersection of Shaftesbury and Coventry. Run by the American Red Cross, the Corner's basement had been decorated to evoke a small-town drugstore. Cokes could be had for a nickel; hamburgers went for a dime. A jukebox constantly blared Tommy Dorsey and Glenn Miller; almost every night, dances were held in the big upstairs ballroom.[24]

The hostesses who staffed air base auxiliaries and social clubs such as the Rainbow Corner often had to multitask: soothing the spirits of one lonesome GI while simultaneously fending off the drunken advances of another. With their exquisite hair and empathetic smiles, the young women came across, Rooney remembered, as "a sort of remote combination of Rita Hayworth–and-your-best-friend's-big-sister."[25]

THE YOUNGSTER WHO COULDN'T WRITE a coherent news article when he first joined the *Stars and Stripes* in late '42 had become in short order an accomplished journalist. Once Rooney learned to trust his writing instincts and editors Bob Moora and Bud Hutton loosened their reins, he began earning regular bylines. Rooney's accounts of bombing raids, coupled with his poignant profiles of USAAF airmen and support personnel and his entertaining features on life in London, soon made him one of the *Stars and Stripes'* most recognizable figures. The 1944 publication of *Air Gunner*, Rooney and Hutton's compilation of stories about courageous fliers, added to his growing stature.

He learned his craft from some of the best American journalists of his generation. Rooney watched Cronkite pry quotes out of airmen and cram the who-what-why-when-where of a bombing raid into a lead paragraph. He watched Bigart sift through a flood of data, then relate it without using a single cliché. Later in the war Rooney watched Boyle chat up half the doughboys in the First Army, juggle a dozen stories, and still meet every deadline. And over dinner at the Lamb and Lark Rooney got to pick Liebling's brain.

Above all, Rooney learned from his older colleagues what constituted "news"—and what didn't. In mid-'43 the *Stars and Stripes* sent Rooney to SHAEF headquarters, where General Eisenhower was scheduled to conduct a press briefing. Along with a dozen other reporters, among them fellow Writing 69th member Gladwin Hill of Associated Press, Rooney was ushered into a mahogany conference room. At the appointed hour, the doors swung open and there stood the Supreme Commander, every bit as engaging as Rooney had imagined. "[Ike] was somehow lovable, being, at the same time, competent and bumbling," Rooney remembered.[26]

Eisenhower made some staff announcements and touched on a few other topics, none particularly newsworthy, before Hill asked about the timetable for the invasion of the Continent. Ike hemmed and hawed in his rambling style, then finally allowed that the cross-Channel invasion was likely to take place "within a year."

Rooney returned to the *Stars and Stripes'* offices and dutifully began writing up Eisenhower's remarks in the order in which the general had delivered them. Just then Hill's story came crackling across the AP wire: "General Dwight Eisenhower announced today that the Allied invasion of France will take place within the year." Hill's story barely mentioned the other subjects that Ike had broached. It dawned on Rooney that the other announcements weren't news, but the Supreme Commander predicting the invasion timeline, however amorphous, was *big* news.

"These reporters were my teachers although they didn't know it. While I tried to act more like one of them than a student, I watched and listened carefully," Rooney remembered.

ROONEY DID MORE THAN WATCH and listen: he emulated his mentors, consistently putting himself in harm's way to get spectacular stories. Nine weeks after Cronkite watched B-26s bomb the Pas de Calais, Rooney went on another one of Eisenhower's preinvasion "shuttles"—a massive bombing raid that gave the Nazis' Channel wall "its worst pounding of the war," Rooney wrote.

"Fortresses and Liberators poured back and forth across the English Channel in a steady stream this afternoon, and there wasn't a moment almost up to dark that found the skies above the Channel free from the roar of the shuttling bombers or their escorts," Rooney wrote in a piece the *Stars and Stripes* played on page one.

Rooney had flown on April 20 in a B-17 piloted by First Lieutenant Carl N. Grending of San Leandro, California. At Ike's insistence, the USAAF threw everything it had at a forty-mile swath stretching westward from the Belgian-French border: heavy and medium bombers, P-38s, P-51s, and P-47s. Censors wouldn't let Rooney identify the objectives, but they were doubtless troop encampments, or bridges, or rail marshaling yards, or crucial highways—the tier one targets in Eisenhower's transportation plan.

"There was some flak, but it wasn't up to Nazi standard, and their fighters were conspicuously absent, at least in our area," Rooney wrote. Disappointed that enemy fighters had taken the afternoon off, badass P-47 pilots "crisscrossed the coastal area as long as their fuel held out, but no one would challenge them."[27]

No news outlet could challenge Rooney and the *Stars and Stripes* in covering preinvasion mobilization—and the way it was transforming the lives of the young Americans swarming all over Britain. As early as February of '44—almost five months before D-Day—Rooney was reporting on the extraordinary steps being taken to care for wounded invasion soldiers.

"The first complete air-evacuation group ever organized for the sole purpose of carrying wounded men is ready and waiting in England to transport thousands of Allied casualties a day from the invasion battlefields of the Continent to secure hospitals in the British Isles," Rooney wrote in a piece about specially equipped C-47s.

The magnitude of planning that went into medical evacuation, Rooney discovered, was stunning. Censors wouldn't permit him to pinpoint the number of evacuation squadrons now part of the Ninth Air Force, but did allow him to report that each squadron would be composed of thirteen C-47s, each capable of carrying eighteen litter patients on the stacked bunks built into both sides. At least one nurse and surgical technician had been assigned to each transport.

There was a serious element of danger in using aircraft to transport the wounded. Rooney pointed out that the Geneva Conventions expressly forbade attacks on hospital ships marked with the traditional red-and-white symbol; there were no such protections for planes, however.[28]

USAAF markings were part of a special three-week display at Selfridges department store on London's Oxford Street that Rooney wrote about in January of '44. Seven thousand people a day visited the exhibit, which public relations–conscious Eighth Air Force officials had organized to help Britons appreciate why their country had been turned upside down. The cockpits of B-17s and B-24s were re-created, along with the ball turrets and radar and radio compartments.

Four air gunners, each of whom had won the Distinguished Service Cross, greeted visitors. The sergeant-guides were amazed at how much English kids knew about the bombers.

Not long after the exhibit opened, Rooney noted, Technical Sergeant Rob Bryson, of Stockport, Iowa, watched a small boy walk in with his mother. She approached Bryson and asked if he might be available to speak with her son. "'You bet,' Bryson said, 'come over here and I can show it to you better.'

"The boy's mother hesitated a minute and then said, 'I'm sorry, but could you just explain? My son is blind.'

"Bryson spent half an hour with the twelve-year-old, taking him to every part of the exhibit and letting the boy touch every piece of equipment which to the average visitor was forbidden with 'Please Do Not Handle' signs."[29]

The boy told Bryson that he had a complete set of RAF model planes and had learned to identify them by feel. Bryson promised to get the youngster a B-17 model.[30]

AS THE WAR DEEPENED, so did Walter Cronkite's stress. He was chronically pooped, often working fifteen hours or more a day, shuttling among UP's offices, the Ministry of Information, East Anglia, and his Buckingham Gate flat. By mid-'44, he had a staff of four reporters working for him on the air war beat; still, it was Cronkite's job to synthesize their dispatches into one lead story about that day's bombing efforts. At one point, Cronkite learned he was being undercut by a cabal at UP–New York, which was crediting his copy to a different reporter. Here he was working around the clock—and he had to fight just to get proper acknowledgment!

He spent untold hours at the Ministry, hawking the communiqués that the Allied command issued three times daily: at ten thirty a.m., at five p.m., and at eleven thirty p.m. Often he had to cover all three announcements, writing his final story well after midnight. Once asleep, he would typically be interrupted two or three times a night by calls from UP's overnight desk guys, asking about this story or that or confirming information about past bombing campaigns that only Cronkite knew.

He spent months trying to get Betsy over to London, either as a UP or *Kansas City Star* reporter or as a new hire by another organization. At one point, with his UP boss Virgil Pinkley back in the States, Cronkite arranged for Pinkley to stop at Kansas City's Union Station on his way west so he could meet Betsy and conduct a job interview on the fly. The elaborate planning for the Kansas City rendezvous went on for weeks: Walter relayed to Pinkley that the redheaded Betsy would be wearing a certain hat and dress. But the station was so crowded when Pinkley's train arrived that the two missed each other.

The Cronkites were crushed. Neither the *Star* prospect nor the UP gambit went anyplace: The couple continued to pine for one another 4,500 miles apart.

Betsy never did get to London during the war—and Walter, alone among our five correspondents, never got a stateside vacation. In July '44, Cronkite finally screwed up the nerve to ask Pinkley for a respite. His boss was empathetic but after "beating around the bush," as Cronkite put it, made it clear that UP couldn't afford to let its star reporter get away that summer or fall; he was too valuable. Plus UP president Hugh Baillie was scheduled to arrive in London a few weeks hence; Pinkley didn't want the big boss to see UP's ETO operation without one of its (better compensated) luminaries.

Pinkley's decision was "so much malarkey," a bitter Cronkite wrote Betsy, but Walter was hardly in a position to defy him. Once Germany was defeated, UP-Europe would be so damned busy, Cronkite wrote, that there'd be no chance to get home for many months afterward.[31] Late in the war, a fatalistic Cronkite wrote to Betsy and urged her not to sit around waiting for him, but to go out dining and dancing with friends in Kansas City.

Mrs. Cronkite ended up becoming an editor and featured contributor to the *Hallmark Military News*, a weekly newsletter put out by the greeting card company that kept the home fires burning.

AS LATE MAY OF 1944 approached, the fifty-eight media professionals who'd been given invasion-day or immediate-aftermath assignments were told to "wander up" to an unmarked townhome at 38 Egerton Gardens in Knightsbridge near Brompton Oratory.[32] But they were warned to knock on the door solo, not show up in groups of three or four; bunches of uniformed correspondents might have stirred attention from German spies.

There was no placard outside to indicate that 38 Egerton Gardens had been commandeered by U.S. Army public relations, but inside the crowded flat a bevy of PROs under the command of Majors Jack Redding and Barney Oldfield was coordinating first-wave press relations, trying to square away the thousand-and-one details required to pull off such a massive undertaking.

Redding and Oldfield insisted that the media professionals swear an oath of confidentiality, fill out personal information forms including data on next of kin, keep Army PR apprised of their whereabouts at all times, pack a musette bag of bare essentials, and, as the pièce de résistance, directed that each reporter, photographer, radioman, and newsreel cameraman write his (or her) own obituary.[33]

William Stoneman of the *Chicago Daily News* balked when Oldfield parked him in front of a typewriter. When told that his archrival, H. R. Knickerbocker of the *Chicago Sun*, had filed a four-and-a-half-page obit listing every battle and skirmish he'd ever witnessed, Stoneman told the PROs to "just say I was all the places Knick was—and usually filed first, too." Acme photographer Bert Brandt gave Oldfield's staff formal "laying out" instructions. "Part my lips in a smile," Brandt said. "That's the way everyone would remember me. If they ever find me."

Ernie Pyle, who liked to make wan jokes about his own demise, wrote a bare-bones account of his remarkable career, then volunteered: "And when it becomes necessary to release this information, please inform my syndicate so it can break the news to my wife."[34]

ALAS, JIM MCGLINCY'S SELF-COMPOSED OBIT has not survived. But McGlincy was Joe Liebling's kind of guy: a tempestuous Irishman who wrote like a dream (Cronkite always said that his roommate had "the news in his head") but drank and fought way too much for his own good. Cronkite's letters back home were full of stories about McGlincy picking pub fights, ticking off the landlord, sleeping off hangovers, missing deadlines, and generally making himself persona non grata at the London UP bureau.

But Cronkite glimpsed a side of McGlincy that few others saw—and loved his wicked wit. Cronkite took care of his friend, rescuing him in bars, sobering him up, and making sure his copy got to the bosses.

McGlincy had a flair for funny features that put him almost in the same league as Hal Boyle. In the late fall of '43, Pinkley told McGlincy to check out what had become known as "Ladies, Excuse Me" dances—social gatherings where English lasses would entertain American servicemen on leave. They were labeled "Excuse Me" because they required constant cutting in by the girls.

"Wow, whatta assignment!" McGlincy exclaimed at the top of a piece played up by the *Stars and Stripes*. "Soft lights, sweet music, and waltzing women. . . .

"'Find out something about these "Ladies, Excuse Me" dances,' said the boss, who apparently had been hitting the phonograph needle again. 'How'd they start? What're they like?'"

So off McGlincy went to the Opera House in Covent Garden, the same place Cronkite had visited nine months earlier with Harrison Salisbury to celebrate Cronkite's scoop on the Wilhelmshaven raid. After being comped his thirty pence cover charge, McGlincy learned from an Opera House manager that the special dance had a long tradition in England. Since there were often more women than men at community dances, they decided that during certain songs, women could cut in on couples, say "Excuse me," and waltz away with the man.

Amid McGlincy's "vision of buck-toothed buffaloes with horn-rimmed glasses saying, 'Excuse me,'" the manager approached the orchestra leader to request the dance.

"I shuddered, gulped, and blanched," McGlincy wrote, "but before I could say, 'Look, chum, let's not carry this thing too far,'" they were announcing the dance over a microphone. McGlincy soon found himself on the floor with "a couple of thousand other people—not tripping lightly, just tripping."

His first partner was a blonde named Edna. "The conversation turned out to be a brilliant tirade of scintillating talk, consisting entirely of the questions (from her) 'Do you like it over here?' and (from me) 'How do you like Americans?' and the answers (from both of us) 'Yes.'"

Soon enough "a neat little number with black hair and big bright eyes" cut in. McGlincy suspected that the manager had sent her his way—but he wasn't objecting. "'Do you like it over here?' asked my new partner. Playing it safe, I said 'Yes' and followed right up with 'Do you like Americans?'"

She turned out to be named Vicki, a waitress at a Leicester Square eatery. McGlincy felt his heart melting and was just about to ask what Vicki was doing the next night when he "was seized by what felt like a vise but turned out to be a pair of arms hanging on a buxom, brown-haired girl with a lot of teeth."

As soon as McGlincy could free himself, he went looking for Vicki but found "the little vixen" cozily chatting with an American GI. It wasn't their first encounter, McGlincy realized: They were clearly an item.[35]

C'est la guerre.

AS THE WINTER OF '44 turned to spring, Omar Bradley ("Brad") and Dwight Eisenhower ("Ike") were contending with far weightier U.S.-Anglo relations. The cross-Channel invasion plan they'd inherited from an Allied team led by British general Frederick Morgan was well thought out in terms of location and timing, but woefully inadequate in what Ike called "wallop."[36] Eisenhower, the Supreme Commander, and Bradley, the commander of U.S. ground forces, effectively doubled the size of the initial seaborne assault force (from three divisions to five), demanded much heavier and broader naval gunfire and strategic bombing support, and insisted on the aggressive use of airborne troops.

After leaving the U.S.'s Italy operation in the unsteady hands of Lieutenant General Mark Clark, Ike and Brad met nearly every day in the Norfolk House on the east side of St. James's Square.[37] Ike and Brad had witnessed in Sicily the hazards of paratroop operations. The more they studied maps of Normandy and assessed intelligence reports of the Wehrmacht's deployment in northern France, however, the more convinced they became that it was imperative to land airborne divisions behind the beachheads. Without troopers from the U.S. 82nd and 101st and the British Sixth harassing enemy troops and seizing key arteries, it would be nearly impossible for the seaborne infantry to push inland, Bradley and Eisenhower believed. Allied paratroopers had to be in position to disrupt enemy counterattacks; without them, *Panzer* units and the other outfits the German field marshal Gerd von Rundstedt was holding in reserve would have an unbroken line to vulnerable beachheads.

THROUGHOUT THAT WINTER AND SPRING, St. James' Square would attract onlookers hoping to catch a glimpse of the famous American generals. One of the hangers-on was Joe Liebling, who would often take a workout jog through the square and nearby Hyde Park.

In November '43, Liebling had again crossed the Atlantic without benefit of military escort, arriving in Liverpool aboard a cramped Norwegian fruit ship. "My notion," he wrote a few years later, "was to get to England early in order to be sure of a good spot in the invasion. I did not want to get caught up in some ancillary theater and then not be able to transfer out in time for the main event, and as the lone correspondent of the *New Yorker* I had to fight my own campaign against red tape and the stuffy lay bureaucrats."[38] Liebling endeared himself to the *New Yorker*'s London correspondent, Mollie Panter-Downes, by bringing her dozens of nylons—a luxury impossible to find at Selfridges or Harrods.

When not beseeching SHAEF public relations officers for an invasion berth, Liebling enjoyed London's hedonistic charms. Again he found lodging at Flemings in Piccadilly. He got chummy enough with the blokes who ran Shepherd Market that he managed to sometimes score gulls' eggs and black-market seafood delicacies. He even re-created his Runyonesque life in the Big Apple by frequenting a back-alley bar called Toby's. It was a smoky joint that featured a raffish clientele who, despite a little distraction like a world war, still managed to find their way to the track.

Acting as if nothing had happened, he resumed his relationships with the two women he'd known in '42: a lady from Yorkshire and a Wren, a British servicewoman, from Nottingham. The fact that the Wren had been impregnated by somebody else didn't appear to daunt Liebling. The Yorkshire woman, whom Liebling snidely called "the canary" in letters to Joe Mitchell, convinced Liebling to write a story about the bomb damage in Hull, her hometown.

By early '44, Liebling had gone through two sets of gas masks and helmets and had ordered a new pair from Army PROs. He was so bored waiting month after month for the invasion that he thought about volunteering for Army Intelligence, but abandoned the idea when First Division commander General Clarence Huebner offered him the chance—if approved by the public relations staff—to go ashore on D-Day with the Big Red One. It didn't help Liebling's prospects of landing an invasion assignment that an old gout condition resurfaced, forcing him to gimp around London. His gout, his ample girth, and his thick glasses all made him look pathetic to the PROs handing out invasion slots.

Even Liebling's boxer-inspired workouts failed to put much of a dent in his belly. His overeating was becoming more compulsive. He constantly dined at an upper-crust restaurant off St. James's called Wiltons, whose wartime prices were obscene.

His *New Yorker* articles from London were an eclectic mix: a piece on a munitions factory that gave English laborers credit in helping to turn the tide; an irreverent profile of "Paddy," a Royal Air Force ace; and "V for Victory," a valentine to the British Broadcasting Corporation for its efforts in building morale and making the V symbol an inspiration to the Resistance movement throughout Europe. During the winter of '44 Liebling also went on his own "Eisenhower shuttle," the B-26 raid over the Nazis' Montdidier airdrome.

To his eternal credit, Liebling was determined to pay homage to the French Resistance. Awed by the forbidden French newspapers that were smuggled into England, he tried to piece together a definitive picture of the Maquis' (literally "underbrush") defiance, but given skimpy information, it was impossible. It amazed Liebling that some of France's underground papers had circulations of fifty thousand or more. Merely to be seen reading an outlawed circular was to risk torture or a firing squad. The courage it took to actually print one under the nose of the Gestapo staggered him.

Liebling would quiz any French expatriate he encountered, picking their brains about their countrymen's efforts to defy Hitler. The topic would become a recurring theme, Liebling's most passionate wartime cause. Eventually he compiled his essays on the Resistance into a collection he called *The Republic of Silence*.

AFTER EIGHT ENERVATING MONTHS IN Sicily and Italy, Hal Boyle finally got a break. Boyle owed his respite to Ernie Pyle, whose battlefield adventures were being turned into a United Artists movie, *Ernie Pyle's The Story of G.I. Joe*, starring Burgess Meredith as the intrepid columnist. Among the Pyle intimates slated to play themselves were Boyle and Don Whitehead of Associated Press; Chris Cunningham of United Press; Sergeant Jack Foisie of the *Stars and Stripes*, Bigart's buddy from Sicily; and Tom Treanor of the *Los Angeles Times*, the correspondent who had climbed Monte Cipolla with Bigart and Whitehead.

AP shrewdly gave Boyle and Whitehead a few extra weeks off to make speeches, do radio interviews, and generally beat the drum for the wire service's coverage of the war. To get home, Boyle ended up hitching a ride in Naples on a B-24 known as *The Blue Streak*, a bomber that was being retired in the Mediterranean Theater of Operations after a record 110 missions.

"She dropped half a million pounds of bombs on enemy objectives, sank a destroyer, a tanker, and a merchant vessel," Boyle wrote in a piece that ran on page one of the *Atlanta Constitution*. "During her 1,058 hours of combat her gunners brought down 23 enemy fighters. In her long career—she has used up 10 engines and twice been rescued from the junk heap—the big-bellied Liberator never lost one of her crewmen to German guns or German ack ack although her paint-peeling frame is pitted with 150 flak holes."[39]

Boyle and *The Blue Streak* arrived in Miami on February 20, 1944. It took the Liberator forty-five hours and eighteen minutes to make the 8,100-mile flight—not that Boyle was counting. They'd flown from Naples to Dakar, where they refueled and attempted to fix a balky electrical problem that had put the navigation system on the fritz.[40]

On the tarmac at Miami's 179th Street Airport, Boyle posed for pictures with the *Streak*'s passengers and crew. The photos moved on AP, thus serving both the wire service's and USAAF's interests.

By late winter '44, Boyle had become much more than "the poor man's Ernie Pyle": He was regularly outperforming the master, although he never achieved Pyle's iconic status. In any given week, Boyle put out at least twice and sometimes three times the amount of copy that came out of Pyle's typewriter. Boyle would feed AP spot coverage updates each day, then sit down almost daily to write Leaves from a War Correspondent's Notebook. His column typically ran in about half the four-hundred-odd newspapers that used Pyle's column in early '44; still, by any measure, Boyle's stuff got sensational pickup.

BOYLE FLEW FROM MIAMI TO New York, where he and Frances had a joyful reunion. They hadn't seen one another in fifteen months, since Boyle had left for the Operation Torch convoy.

As part of his publicity tour, on the evening of March 7, 1944, Boyle appeared as a guest on CBS World News' *Report to the Nation*, a program hosted by "noted foreign correspondent" Quentin Reynolds. The script has survived in Boyle's papers and demonstrates why print journalists, Cronkite and Boyle among them, were so wary of the broadcast medium. Cronkite's adjective, "schlocky," doesn't begin to describe the Reynolds–Boyle exchange. "Vapid" would be closer to the mark. Boyle's two most celebrated moments in North Africa—his Darlan scoop and his vote-for-Boyle silliness—were distorted and reduced to specious caricatures, complete with anti-Arab slurs.

Despite the contrived patter, Reynolds did ask Boyle meaningful questions about censorship, GI spirit, and Allied antipathy toward the Nazis. Boyle allowed that he didn't care much for censors but said they weren't vicious, "just capricious." When Reynolds asked about morale in Italy, Boyle said, "There's nothing wrong with morale when they're fighting but the boys are really aching to get home. Some of them have been away from home for two years."

When quizzed on how he felt about the Germans, Boyle mused, "Well, as you know most of the American soldiers in Africa were a lot sorer at Japan than they were at Germany, in the beginning. However, the Nazis have managed to gain equal footing with the Japs. Our kids see the death and desolation Germans leave behind when they evacuate a town. The sick and dying women and children, the stripped hospitals, the unnecessary misery. And of course, American soldiers have seen a lot of good friends fall under German bullets."

Boyle closed by urging folks at home to write to the men and women on the front lines. "Tell them all the news of what's going on at home and tell 'em you know what they are going through. . . . You have no idea what that sort of recognition means to a kid."[41]

The Reynolds program poked fun at the very thing Hal Boyle did so superbly: doggedly gathering information and telling stories about the human drama of war. Moreover, the real news—the Nazi atrocities that Boyle had witnessed in Italy—barely merited a mention. If that's how the great CBS conveyed wartime news under the portentous banner *Report to the Nation*, imagine what less reputable outlets were doing.

AFTER PAINTING THE BIG APPLE redder, Frances and Hal worked their way west on the train, stopping in Cincinnati so Boyle could do a radio interview and address a civic group. They spent more than a week in Kansas City, seeing Hal's mother, Margaret, and older brother Ed, who, as a thirty-two-year-old store proprietor, was the only Boyle boy not in uniform. Neil was an airman in North Africa; John an Army machine gunner who was wounded in the Pacific.

Margaret was at Kansas City's Union Station to give her son a "good Irish welcome," as the *Kansas City Star* put it. "Yes, it's sure good to be back," Boyle told the *Star* in a story that ran underneath a photo of Boyle *mère et fils* grinning from ear to ear. "We were out to a New York nightspot the other night and when we got ready to leave, the other fellow reached out and picked up the $44 check. Then I knew I was home—that's home when the other fellow reaches for the check."[42] Boyle's vacation included a lot of nights out at a lot of nightspots.

The Sunday, February 27, *Star* had run a front-page tribute to the war reporters and photographers that had ties to the Paris of the Plains. Boyle, of course, was featured, fêted by his boss Wes Gallagher: "[Boyle] has an unshaken faith in the American infantry and his idea of an ideal army is one with millions and millions of infantry, a couple of big guns, and an airplane. The airplane would be used only to carry his copy from the front."[43]

While in Kansas City, Boyle got to admire the scrapbook that his sister-in-law, Ed's wife, had lovingly kept since Hal climbed aboard his first troopship. Encased in a handsome beige cover with a soaring eagle on the front, the album was already crammed with four or five inches' worth of clips and mementos. By war's end, it would be close to two times that thick. The *Star* printed everything that moved on the AP wire with Boyle's byline, often playing it on page one, so Monica had plenty of material.

Boyle signed the first page of the scrapbook: "To my nephew, Edward Michael, and to his mother, Monica, who made this book. With love, Hal Boyle, March 15, 1944."[44]

Monica reminded Hal to keep an eye out for her little brother Jack, who was a radioman with a naval amphibious unit that had landed in North

Africa and Sicily. He's in England someplace, she told Hal. Maybe you'll run into him. Four months later, Boyle did.[45]

NEXT STOP FOR FRANCES AND Hal was Hollywood. Somewhere along the line, they were joined by dear friends Don and Marie Whitehead. Associated Press did a good job flacking the Southern California visit of their two star correspondents: The *Los Angeles Times* sent a reporter and photographer to Union Station as the Whiteheads and the Boyles disembarked on St. Patrick's Day, probably after a few club car toasts to the Old Sod. Despite the impasse in the mountains of Italy, the Fifth Army was "still killing a hell of a lot of Germans," Whitehead told the *Times.* "There'll have to be lots more fighting—and lots more casualties—before we win in that area."

Whitehead and Boyle told the paper they were looking forward to seeing their friend, *Times* reporter Tom Treanor, due in L.A. any day to read his part in the Pyle movie. Boyle explained that Treanor had been the first U.S. correspondent to make it to the summit of Cassino.

"Are we in the town [Cassino proper] right now, on this spot?" Boyle had Treanor asking the company commander at the fateful moment. When told they were, Treanor took one step toward the German lines, drew a line in the dirt with his boot, and said, "Now let's get the hell out of here! We've BEEN in Cassino!" Having accomplished his objective of being able in good conscience to dateline his story "Cassino," Treanor beat a retreat.[46]

WHEN NOT POOLSIDE WITH THEIR wives or on the United Artists' lot with Pyle, Meredith, costar Robert Mitchum, and director William Wellman, Whitehead and Boyle were hitting the hustings. On March 28, the pair addressed a crowded Hotel Biltmore Ballroom at a luncheon sponsored by the Advertising Club of Los Angeles. Sharing the Biltmore's lectern was *G.I. Joe's* producer, Lester Cowan.[47] Producer Cowan had eclectic tastes, having produced everything from the comedic farces of W. C. Fields to actress Mary Pickford's melodramas. Director Wellman, a World War I aviator, was also in the midst of a distinguished career, having started in the early '20s on silent pictures.

Cowan, Wellman, Pyle, and their military advisors—a list that nominally included Lieutenant General Lesley McNair—set out to capture the gritty realities of combat as endured by American GIs in North Africa and Italy. Fifteen minutes into the movie, the humiliation of the U.S. retreat at the Kasserine Pass was depicted.

Mitchum, playing a popular but tough officer, grabs a battle-fatigued GI by the shoulders and tries to shake him out of his daze. The film also graphically portrays the caveman-like existence that Allied soldiers lived for months at Monte Cassino.

Still, *G.I. Joe* is hamstrung by the same hackneyed story lines that plague other war movies: the outfit adopts a dog in Tunisia and (perhaps out of deference to the vote-for-Boyle story) nicknames it Ay-rab; a GI marries a nurse and promptly gets killed on patrol; a sergeant heartsick for his wife and baby boy flips out and has to be restrained before throwing himself at the enemy lines; and in midmovie Mitchum delivers the obligatory "It's quiet out there . . . too quiet" cliché. Cowan's production had a modest budget, relying on stock Army footage of artillery battles and firefights, so it has that bumpy quality of so many war films.

Nevertheless, Meredith is a likable and understated Pyle. Mitchum, who earned an Academy Award nomination for best supporting actor, is believable as Lieutenant-turned-Captain Bill Walker. The movie ends with a reenactment of the death of Captain Waskow, Pyle's most venerated column. Mitchum as Walker is killed and transported down an Italian mountain on the back of a mule. One by one, his men pay their respects, with Meredith-Pyle nearly distraught. But there's another battle to be fought; the men are ordered to move out. As Meredith-Pyle joins the outfit's march toward Rome, he narrates, "There's nothing we can do, except pause and murmur, 'Thanks, pal.'"

Ernie's reporter buddies are in the movie for only a few seconds. Whitehead, Boyle, and what looks to be Chris Cunningham of United Press are in a scene back at press headquarters when Pyle learns he's won the Pulitzer Prize. A big handpainted sign hangs over the headquarters door:

"Through These Portals <u>Pass Out</u> the Most Beautiful Correspondents in the World!"—a line that reflected Boyle's sardonic touch.

The boys greet Pyle with the "I-am-not-worthy" bow (think the palm tree scene near the end of *Mister Roberts*) and needle Ernie about going uptown on them. "I regret to inform you, Mr. Pyle," intones Whitehead in a Kentucky bourbon–honeyed baritone, "that you are no longer a noos-paper-man. You are now a dee-sting-wished journalist!" The lanky White-head and his Gable-like mustache steal the scene, but Boyle gets in a good line when Meredith-Pyle, feigning offense, asks why his colleagues opened the letter from the Pulitzer committee. "Well, it was marked 'private,' wasn't it?" Boyle retorts, before smirking and sticking a cigar back in his mouth.

Tom Treanor of the *L.A. Times* didn't make it, or at least his name didn't appear in the credits, but Foisie, Bob Landry from *Life*, George Lait from INS, Clete Roberts from the Blue Network, and Robert Reuben from Reuters were all acknowledged.[48]

BY ALL ACCOUNTS, THE REFUGEES from the ETO had a splendid time in Hollywood, hitting the hot spots. One night the gang autographed a menu from an L.A. restaurant and gave it to Pyle. Ernie kept that memento for the remainder of the war, proudly showing it to Boyle three months later in a press tent in Normandy. The whole California respite sounds surreal: a blur of parties for guys who'd been eating K rations in the mud of Italy for months, then trying to re-create the same deprivation on a movie lot.

Boyle put on fifteen pounds, two thirds of which he gained while bing-ing in Hollywood saloons, he told readers. "Leaving the United States to return to the war zone is like talking about heaven," Boyle wrote in a piece the *Star* published May 18. "Nearly everyone says he would like to go—but very few exceed the speed limit in trying to get there."[49]

Still, Boyle had no choice: AP was flogging his return to the ETO. Its star columnist's first eight pieces, the wire service vowed to subscribers, would compare life in preinvasion London to the America he just left.

Whenever and wherever the cross-Channel assault would take place, Boyle and his prolific typewriter would be there, AP assured customers.[50]

WHILE PYLE, BOYLE, AND WHITEHEAD were partying in Hollywood, the PROs in Major Jack Redding's outfit were sweating over the details of invasion press relations. Redding and his deputy, Barney Oldfield, had concluded that their outfit, coupled with the First Army's Publicity and Psychological Warfare unit, needed special invasion preparation, same as Allied troops. After scouting several locations, they settled on Clevedon in southwest England, across Bristol Channel from picturesque Cardiff, Wales.

There the young PRO-lieutenants destined to become so invaluable to reporters in French press camps—among them George Fuller, Bruce Fessenden, Sam Brightman, Jack Roach, and Roy Wilder, Jr.—were put through their paces, taught that their primary duty was to get stories and pictures back to London by whatever means necessary. Divided into teams of two, the PROs were equipped with special radio transmitters built into their jeeps, wire recorders, generators, and hand-keyed Morse code sets. They were also briefed on the schedule of Navy courier speedboats that would ferry messages to and from the massive communications complex on General Bradley's flagship, the *Augusta*.[51] Soon dubbed Redding's Rangers, the Clevedon men combined marching and calisthenics with elementary map reading and tent erection, plus learned to operate all the electronic equipment within their purview, much of which was new.[52]

BOYLE'S TRIP ACROSS THE ATLANTIC to Liverpool aboard a lightly armed freighter in a small convoy was uneventful: By May of '44 the U-boat threat had been all but eliminated. In midocean, though, Boyle came down with a strange virus, he told Frances, and spent half the voyage in his bunk. "I don't know what the devil was the matter with me. . . . All the time my stomach ached like hell. Maybe it was the change from a liquid (liquor) diet

to a solid food diet too suddenly."[53] Boyle's saloon-scarred innards eventually improved, but the convoy ran into ugly weather as they neared
England—and his stomach flip-flopped all over again.

In London, Boyle reunited with Whitehead, who'd beaten him there by
a couple of days. Along with Whitehead's friend Lieutenant Tom Siler, a
onetime AP sportswriter from Chicago, they found a three-room bunga-
low in Chelsea for $65 a month. Its address, Whitehead never tired of brag-
ging, was 1 Whitehead's Grove. The trio hired a woman in the neighborhood
to do their cleaning and ate shredded wheat when not scarfing down pub
food.

Bob Brunelle, London's AP bureau chief, kept Boyle "running ragged,"
insisting that Hal line up his invasion accreditation and collect his field
equipment and paraphernalia—all while churning out his column.

He may have been suffering the effects of excessive partying—but that
didn't stop Boyle from sampling London's nightlife. Taxis were allowed
three gallons of gas a day, only enough for about five hours' worth of cruising, and few buses ran after ten thirty p.m., he wrote on May 23. Since it
stayed light past eleven o'clock in late spring, "the wayfarer is always getting caught abroad at dusk with no way of getting back."[54] Getting a cab or
onto the proper bus was next to impossible, Boyle wrote. "Few officers
object to a moonlit stroll with a pretty girl through London's darkened
streets. It's not the walk to her door they mind—it's that long hike home
alone in the blackout afterward, when you bump into what you take to be
a lamppost and it objects with feminine stridency—'Ere, don't get fresh.
Mind your step, man.'"[55]

Exactly one week before D-Day, May 30, 1944, Whitehead talked his
buddy Boyle into going to a Soho restaurant to sample the house specialty:
horse steak. It gave Boyle one last chance before the apocalypse to flash his
humor.

"I thought I was hungry enough to eat a horse, but I wasn't," the son of
a butcher told readers. "Before I could swallow it visions of all the horses I
ever saw or heard of passed through my mind, and the piece of meat felt
like a lump of rock as it went down. I could see Black Beauty, Man o' War,
Old Dan Patch, and Traveler. I could see Tom Mix's Tony and the big, re-

proachful eyes of Frances, the old mare who used to pull our grocery wagon around a quarter century ago in Kansas City. My ears rang with hoofbeats, and something inside me said nay. (No pun.)"

Boyle looked at Whitehead contentedly chewing and accused him of being a traitor to the equine traditions of his native Kentucky. "Lissen," Don countered. "I used to lose quite a bit of money on these nags at the Derby. I'm just enjoying my revenge."[56]

ON MONDAY, MAY 14, WALTER Cronkite was having a late lunch at the Officers' Club, which had become so popular it now went by the trendy name Willow Run. As he was being seated, he heard a ruckus and realized that Boyle and Whitehead and other AP guys were just leaving. Cronkite tried to get Boyle's attention, but his fellow Kansas Citian was already out the door. But he did succeed in hailing Gladwin Hill and another original member of the Writing 69th, Paul Manning. Manning had just left CBS to become a "thrice-a-week" columnist for the McNaught Syndicate, Cronkite told his wife in a letter. The three commiserated over how difficult it was to get decent information out of the USAAF now that the bombing fleets were focused on invasion targets.

"Hill and I have been covering this air war so long we almost have ceased to be rivals—our problems are so similar," Cronkite told Betsy. "[Hill] is luckier than I, though, since his desk sees fit to let him fly on The Day—a thing which the UP insists I shunt off to one of the 'younger' men."[57]

By then, Cronkite, all of twenty-seven, had quite a staff of UP reporters working for him on the air beat: among them Collie Small, Doug Werner, Bob Richards and Ned Roberts. None of the "younger" guys ended up going wheels up in a bomber on "The Day." Nor did Glad Hill, who was destined to send the first "flash" that infantrymen had indeed landed in France. Ironically, the only one who ended up with a bird's-eye view of the whole shooting match—at least in theory—was Cronkite.

CHAPTER 10

★

CHERBOURG AND ST.-LÔ—UGLY FIGHTING AMONG DEAD CATTLE

> *Each [Allied soldier] who landed within the first twenty-four hours knew a small part of the story in intimate detail. . . . They knew the first names of ten who drowned, five who hung dead in the barbed wire off-shore and two who lay unattended, the blood draining from holes in their bodies. . . . That was about all they knew, and to many of the fighting men the Invasion seemed a hopeless catastrophe.*
>
> —ANDY ROONEY, 1962
> *THE FORTUNES OF WAR*

Staff Sergeant Andrew Rooney had never been around a hostile ground fight until he wheeled his jeep onto the Cotentin Peninsula west of Utah Beach on D-Day plus four. Rooney's previous brushes with Nazi bullets had come at twenty-five thousand feet in a B-17 and at twelve thousand feet in a B-26.[1] Now, having landed on the beach and "turned right and up," as he put it in a 2010 interview, he found himself constantly on his belly, diving for cover. Rooney learned in a hurry: After a couple of days on the Cotentin he could hear the rumble of big guns and distinguish American artillery from German.

The push north toward the port of Cherbourg was a bareknuckled brawl, Rooney soon discovered—an onslaught of air attacks, artillery exchanges, mortar barrages, and machine gun fire. More than a hundred thousand men—half of them doughboys from the Fourth, Ninth, and 79th

Infantry Divisions—were slugging it out on a slab of land smaller than Rhode Island. Field Marshal Rommel, knowing how essential Cherbourg was to the defense of Hitler's Atlantic Wall, demanded that its peninsula bristle with railway artillery, minefields, swollen streams, booby traps, camouflaged pillboxes, and subterranean forts. But most of Rommel's heavy guns along the Cherbourg waterfront had been encased in concrete with their barrels pointed seaward; now that the Allies were attacking from the south and rear, the guns were rendered useless. Still, there were plenty of smaller batteries that garrison commander Lieutenant General Karl-Wilhelm von Schlieben and the remnants of his 709th Division could call upon to savage the Americans. Every German soldier, moreover, had orders from *der Führer* to fight to the death.

Upon shadowing American tanks to the *Stars and Stripes'* temporary setup in the village of Carentan, five miles south of Utah, Rooney's first order of business was to clean the waterproofing off his jeep. It had taken him hours to lacquer its innards with thick grease; now it took him hours to de-lacquer it.[2]

While Rooney was scrubbing his vehicle's underbelly, enemy guns were pounding the tiny crossroads on the west bank of the Taute River. "Night and day German artillery poured shells in the thin strip of land we held," Rooney wrote. By June 12, the *Stars and Stripes* was forced to move its quarters five miles northwest to Ste.-Mère-Église.

A lot of Norman hamlets in the spring and summer of '44 would become hallowed: Ste.-Mère-Église—or St. Mare, as it was soon christened—was renowned for the church steeple from which wounded 82nd Airborne Division paratrooper John Steele hung from the cords of his chute for hours, playing dead. Steele was captured later that morning, but quickly managed to escape. His heroics became a permanent part of *The Longest Day* legend. Today, a uniformed mannequin, its parachute wrapped around the church steeple, pays homage to Steele.

The first decimated villages Rooney encountered as he scrambled to rejoin the Fourth Division infantrymen with whom he'd crossed the Channel were Valognes and Mountebourg, up the Cotentin from St. Mare.

The towns had been leveled by artillery fire from both sides and by American P-47 fighter-bombers that swarmed the peninsula, ready to pounce on any enemy target. Rooney was appalled by the wanton destruction, not comprehending that it was a harbinger of the entire campaign.[3]

Omar Bradley had hoped to take Cherbourg by D-Day plus four or five. But just as Caen to the southeast had proved an elusive objective for Bernard Montgomery and the British Second Army, the march to Cherbourg became chaotic for Bradley's able lieutenant, General J. Lawton Collins and his VII Corps. Every few yards, it seemed, there was another hedgerow to punch through, another machine gun nest to silence, another minefield to mark and sidestep. The Germans were fighting furiously; they knew that, given the Allies' utter dominance of sea and air, there would be no chance of a German Dunkirk, of their escaping Cherbourg via the Channel.

Collins had been handpicked by Eisenhower and Bradley for this moment. The forty-eight-year-old Collins had the one irreplaceable asset for which the Supreme Command was looking: combat experience. On Guadalcanal, Collins had moved his men with such speed that the press had dubbed him Lightning Joe; fortunately for Collins, the nickname stuck.

Operation Overlord, the D-Day master plan, called for Collins' VII Corps to strike directly at Cherbourg by moving north from just inland of Utah Beach. But it soon became apparent that large numbers of enemy troops were reinforcing the northern part of the Cotentin by slipping up its western periphery—and that the same area could eventually serve as an escape route if it weren't cut off. Bradley did what he did best: adapt his strategy. Collins' corps was sent west to lock down the peninsula's base.

By June 16, Collins' guys had battered their way through the Orglandes-St.-Sauveur region and reached the sea just east of Cherbourg.[4] The next day, GIs captured St.-Lô-d'Ourville and Barneville on the peninsula's western coastal road, ripping enemy defenses in two.[5] Still, the Germans held on. In Brix, a tiny village on the Channel, American troops stumbled upon a cache of unarmed V-1 rocket bombs and what they later deduced was a V-2 launch site.

With Rooney and AP's Don Whitehead among the correspondents

shadowing its advance elements, the Americans cracked Cherbourg's outer rim on Tuesday, June 20—D-Day plus fourteen. From a distance of some four miles, Whitehead and Rooney could hear a "thunder of explosions."[6] The Germans had begun their systematic demolition of Cherbourg's port facilities—the very scenario that Eisenhower and Bradley had wanted to avoid. The German dynamite was so deadly that it took nearly three months for Allied engineers to get Cherbourg's port back up and running. Against the distant roar of piers and buildings blowing up, the VII Corps crept forward, buttressed by air attacks from Marauders and seaborne shelling.

The Americans were also aided by hundreds of French patriots. Some were hard-core members of the Maquis, some were veterans of the Great War, some were just ordinary peasants desperate to rid their home of the Hun. An American officer told Whitehead: "They drifted in by ones, twos, and threes, begging us to let them help in the capture of Cherbourg. They know the country well and we see no reason why they couldn't help fight for their homes and country. They are in a weird assortment of uniforms, but they know how to fight."[7]

By June 21 the 314th Infantry had gotten close enough to cut off the Cherbourg–St.-Pierre-Église road east of town, tightening the noose. With the help of French scouts who'd watched the elaborate construction go on for years, the Americans also began to unearth a diabolical warren of tunnels, fortifications, and storage chambers. The Nazi genius for subterranean architecture (and other things) would become apparent as the war for Northern Europe went on—but it was at Fort du Roule in Cherbourg where it was first uncovered.

Fort du Roule was planted on a rugged promontory in the back end of Cherbourg. The Germans had taken the ancient Norman garrison and made it a near-impregnable bulwark. It dominated Cherbourg Harbor; the big guns protruding from its lower chambers were aimed seaward, but its upper floors had scores of mortars, artillery pieces, and automatic weapons encased in concrete pillboxes—all pointed landward.

It took many hours to control those sections of Fort du Roule visible to the eye. But that was just the beginning: now GIs had to root out the soldiers entrenched in the fort's subterranean lair. Collins' guys had barged into the underground city through a hidden entrance at the top of the cliff.

There they encountered something out of a Buck Rogers comic strip: deep tunnels holding immense quantities of food, ammunition, and supplies, enough to keep thousands of men going for months. The Americans also unearthed an ingenious electrical lighting system, automatically controlled ventilators and water mains, and a huge overhead crane that moved heavy equipment and armaments from one side of the complex to the other. The main tunnel connecting the underground chambers was a marvel of engineering: two hundred yards deep and thirty-eight feet high. Its corridors featured elongated shelves crammed full of foodstuffs and ammunition, all worth, Whitehead reckoned, many millions of dollars.[8] Although it had been wired with dynamite, the Germans had curiously chosen not to blow up their underground fort, perhaps because so many men were still in it when the Second Battalion guys stormed inside.

Rooney happened upon Fort du Roule on June 27, the same afternoon that Collins, in halting French, handed the city back to its prewar mayor at a ceremony on the steps of the bomb-wrecked city hall. The *Stars and Stripes* reporter followed a set of railroad tracks leading to a hillside entrance protected by an electronically controlled metal barrier. Rooney gingerly approached, sure that he'd see German soldiers surrendering.

He saw soldiers emerging from the tunnel all right, but they were American GIs, grinning broadly as they hauled out box after box of the spoils of war. Most of it was booze, an incredible cache of thousands of cases of brandy, rare wines, champagne, sherry, and liqueurs that the Germans had stolen from the French and stored inside their cliffside hideaway. The liquor had been discovered the previous day and immediately reported to General Collins, who put it under armed guard while the big brass determined what ought to be done with it. Bradley, who took a dim view of alcohol abuse and worried about the specter of drunken GIs staggering around Cherbourg, bucked the decision to Eisenhower, who decided the only fair thing was to divide the hooch among all the divisions that had waged war up the Cotentin.

Collins' lock on the liquor had been removed when Rooney arrived. Ecstatic GIs were loading their plunder onto trucks and jeeps. Rooney stared, incredulous: It was the first time he'd seen looting in action and the first time he'd heard "loot" used as a noun.[9]

Fort du Roule's alcohol was not the sort of swill that the average American grunt—or the average American reporter—knew much about. The correspondents taking it all in, Whitehead, Ernie Pyle, and INS' Clark Lee, among them,[10] spied Rooney, remembered that he had a preppie pedigree, and began hectoring him to pick out some noteworthy hooch. But Rooney, then a teetotaler, was useless.

Clearly the moment called for a connoisseur.

Word was sent down the line that Liebling was to report to Fort du Roule posthaste. Fortunately, the *New Yorker* writer was nearby, having spent much of the previous two days interviewing Resistance leaders in the now-very-public FFI, Forces *françaises de l'intérieur.* Liebling must have arrived beaming like the Cheshire cat; he was quickly hustled down a tunnel, trailed by a phalanx of thirsty correspondents. Liebling had the time of his life pointing to this case of wine and that batch of cognac.

The GIs needed the diversion: Capturing Cherbourg had required almost three weeks and cost twenty-two thousand Allied casualties.[11]

When Hal Boyle finally arrived in France to stay two days after Cherbourg fell, among the first stories he filed, no doubt tipped off by his reporter buddies, was on the booze of Fort du Roule. On June 28, he wrote: "Some American soldiers believe the decline of German potency in Normandy is attributable to the deadly virulence of the Nazi army's brand of cognac. . . . 'It's just bottled hangovers,' said one soldier. 'If the Germans drank that stuff regularly, it is no wonder we knocked them out of Cherbourg. We call it 'Hitler tonic.' One drink and you think you own the world.'"[12]

General Bradley was given a half case of champagne from the Fort du Roule stash that he saved until after the war. Years later, he broke it out to celebrate the christening of his grandson.

———

It was along the Cotentin where Andy Rooney got better acquainted with Joe Liebling. The two of them shared a room for three or four nights that late June in a three-story Cherbourg *maison* that had somehow escaped damage. Its stone facade was built almost on top of a narrow flagstone sidewalk not far from the heart of town.

The house's residents were fortunate. Many of the people on the Cotentin returned to find their homes "ruined or ransacked," Rooney noted.[13]

Although Rooney had been a devoted reader of the *New Yorker* since his teens, he wasn't all that familiar with Liebling's reputation. "All I knew about Joe was that he couldn't see very well and he was a gourmand who knew a great deal about food and boxing." Rooney soon witnessed first-hand Liebling's voracious—and oft-disturbing—appetites.

"I didn't learn as much as I should have from Joe," Rooney recalled. "He had such a strange and flawed personality that it didn't occur to me at the time that he was as good as he was. We talked at night as if we were equals."

Rooney got so comfortable in their ruminations, in fact, that he voiced his opinion that the quality of the *New Yorker* was going steadily downhill. "I don't know how I latched onto so fashionable a criticism about something I knew so little about," Rooney laughed a half century later. One particular night Liebling polished off a bottle of calvados, the fermented applejack that was the Norman equivalent of moonshine. Between slugs, Liebling shared with the twenty-five-year-old (and stone sober) Rooney the conviction that an artist should die at the peak of his obituary value. In what must have been an unsettling moment, Liebling volunteered that he was contemplating his own demise, since he felt he was cresting his own peak. Rooney was relieved the next morning when Liebling showed up for *le petit déjeuner*.

The *New Yorker* was hard to come by on the front lines, so Rooney didn't get to read much of Liebling's stuff. But after the war Rooney caught up with Joe's brilliant wartime essays.

"I cringe with greatly delayed embarrassment," Rooney wrote in his memoir, "at some of the things I said about writing and reporting in conversations with him."[14] Liebling not only loved lippy Irishmen, but also harbored a not so secret desire to be one himself. Joe no doubt enjoyed their conversations as much as Andy did.

LIEBLING AND HIS MILITARY-ISSUE GARB cut quite a striking figure in northern France. One First Division officer remembered: "The only Army pants big enough to button around the magisterial paunch left him with a vast, drooping seat behind a flapping void big enough to hold a beach umbrella. The legs of the pants were tucked into knee-high gaiters left over from the Spanish-American War, leading to a pair of thin-soled lounge-lizard civilian shoes."[15]

After LCI(L)-88 finished its postinvasion duties on D-Day plus five, Captain Bunny Rigg, with Liebling back on board after spending June 9 and 10 at Omaha Beach, returned to Weymouth to have the craft's ramp winch repaired. Liebling spent the better part of two weeks in London, assembling his notes for what became his *New Yorker* homage to the heroes of Easy Red.

Joe got back to Normandy on June 24 and immediately hitched a ride to catch up to the GI advance on Cherbourg, which at that moment was the most climactic action in northern France. "A battle lurches along until it comes to a series of grinding jerks, like a train entering a Long Island Rail Road station," Liebling wrote years later.

With his ability to converse in near-immaculate French (and even throw out Norman colloquialisms), Liebling took advantage of the delays to visit with members of the Maquis, the Resistance fighters who, now out in the open, referred to themselves as an army of liberation, the FFI. The FFI's symbol, displayed everywhere in Normandy, was steeped in French history: It was the *Croix de Lorraine*, the two-barred-cross insignia whose banner Joan of Arc had carried into battle and whose telltale ring was slipped to Paul Henreid's character, Victor Laszlo, at Rick's Café Américain in *Casablanca*. At its peak some 350,000 Frenchmen belonged to various Maquis units. General Eisenhower said after the war that the Resistance was worth fifteen divisions.

Painfully emerging through Liebling's reporting was the unspeakable truth about the Gestapo's treatment of the French during the Occupation. It was much worse than even Liebling had feared.

Any French citizen, even priests and nuns, thought to harbor Allied sympathies—no matter how peripheral—was subject to arrest and torture. Suspected Maquis leaders would have their fingernails torn out or their testicles crushed with a hammer. The pregnant wife of one Resistance leader was beaten so severely that she lost her baby.

A pair of middle-aged men Liebling met in a café had been thrown in jail for six months—with no reason given. "[The pair] presumed that an anonymous letter had denounced them as patriots," Liebling wrote. "They had at last been released, still without being told why they had been arrested. They didn't seem excited; they were slightly apologetic about even mentioning it, like Londoners in a pub diffidently exchanging bomb stories. After they had finished their reminiscences, [they] began to laugh. They slapped their knees, they bent double, they choked, they wiped their eyes, and finally one of them sputtered, 'And to think, we are rid of the bastards for good!' Then they all had another glass of wine."

The café's proprietress told Liebling that German soldiers would stagger in after curfew and demand liquor, threatening her and her family if she didn't serve them. She once had the temerity to tell a German that in her experience the British were decent people. Word reached Occupation authorities, who closed down her establishment for a month.

"A prostitute, sedately sipping an apéritif near the zinc bar, said, 'Once I called a German soldier a Jew just to make him angry. He reported that I had called Hitler a Jew. The Gestapo arrested me, and I had thirty-three days in prison on bread and water.'"

Throughout Normandy, FFI patrols perfected a hit-and-run technique on retreating Germans. *En enfilade*, Resistance fighters would lie in ambush, waiting for opportune moments to pounce. Every day, Allied commanders had to figure out what to do with the droves of prisoners that the FFI was herding through the woods.

Liebling interviewed a German doctor whose hospital unit had been overrun by a handful of lightly armed FFI guerrillas.

> I asked him if he thought the war was over, as far as Germany was concerned, and he said yes, the war was lost.

"Three million Germans have been killed or wounded to save Europe from Bolshevism," he said, assuming that martyred look which the Germans always used to put on when, as "reasonable men," they discussed the last war with the Americans they took for suckers. I could see a new myth—which would replace the "stab in the back" and "the English plot"—building up in the muddy, Teutonic mind, and I felt just like kicking the doctor in the seat of the pants.[16]

Liebling wasn't the only patriot in northern Europe looking to give Nazis and their collaborators a swift kick. As villages were freed that summer and fall, a fascinating ritual unfolded. Even as Allied infantrymen were flushing holdout snipers, crowds would gather to rough up the locals who had profited from the Occupation. German concubines had their heads shaved and were forced to run a gauntlet in the village square.

Prostitutes were curiously exempted from this public censure. Why? Liebling asked an FFI sergeant. "A prostitute is a prostitute and a German is a German, and each acts according to his nature," the Resistance fighter replied, shrugging.[17]

WALTER CRONKITE'S NATURE WAS TO be grumpy if chained to a desk. He spent much of June '44 annoyed at three things: the weather, which prevented him from seeing Normandy from the air early D-Day morning; the Army Air Force's public relations office, which in his mind had reneged on its promise of an invasion-day "exclusive"; and his bosses at UP, who insisted that he stay in London rather than cover the Allies' now-mushrooming ground operations in northern France.

On D-Day plus four or five, Cronkite finally got a chance to set foot on French soil. He and other reporters accompanied a delegation of engineers on an inspection tour of the Ninth Air Force's brand-new runway, Advanced Landing Ground A-1, at Grandcamp on the cliffs beyond Omaha Beach's Pointe du Hoc. The strip had been hastily patched together; pilots called the steel mesh sunk into the soggy soil "chicken wire."[18] It was more landing mat, Cronkite wrote, than true runway, but it was sturdy enough to handle fighters, liaison craft, and scout planes; in a pinch, it could be used by larger planes.

Cronkite filed a piece about the remarkable grace under pressure of USAAF engineers, then hung around the beachhead for another twenty-four hours, watching in awe as Omaha became an ersatz port through the massive Mulberries, the British-invented temporary harbors. He also watched in horror as Omaha's invasion-day victims continued to wash ashore. Cronkite wasn't pleased to be forced back to London.[19]

His fellow wire service reporter Hal Boyle was angry on D-Day, too, but mainly at the Army public relations staff that refused to make good on its commitment to take him to Normandy. Boyle was "so low he could crawl under the belly of an earthworm," he told Frances, joking that he and the other jilted correspondents were threatening mass hari-kari.[20] Because of the screwup on D-Day morning, Hal hadn't even been part of the official the-invasion-is-on announcement at the Ministry of Information.

It was Boyle's friend and superior Wes Gallagher who was among the select group of correspondents briefed by Allied public relations officials that fateful morning. Gallagher and his colleagues had been given exactly thirty-three minutes to file their stories at the Ministry; he crafted a 1,300-word gem and elbowed his way to the front of the high-ceilinged room. At the appointed hour, as Boyle related the next day, a British officer counted down from five, then shoved open the doors. Gallagher, Boyle wrote, was a "human torpedo"; he yelled "Gangway!" and lunged toward a hallway phone booth.[21]

Boyle, like Cronkite, got a brief and unsatisfying visit to Normandy. On June 9, he and other reporters were taken across the Channel for a one-day visit to the Omaha beachhead. Boyle's entourage, which must have included British correspondents, was also driven to Montgomery's mobile field headquarters, which at that point was three or four miles inland from the beachhead.

But Boyle, like Cronkite, was soon back in London, chomping at the bit, watching his pal Whitehead's copy from the Cotentin campaign race across the wire. At least Boyle knew that at some point soon, he'd receive a permanent assignment with ground troops.

Cronkite was slated to receive a permanent assignment, too—a job heading UP's bureau in Amsterdam once the city was liberated. It was an important job since the UP planned to coordinate much of its European war and postwar coverage through the Netherlands. Still, Cronkite kept hoping to latch onto a special airborne operation or be summoned to witness a decisive offensive. For months on end, neither happened. To make the situation even more frustrating, Cronkite's roommate Jim McGlincy, UP's perpetual screwup, by mid-June had been assimilated with troops in Normandy and was filing wonderful profiles and spot news reports. "I admit I miss the patter of [McGlincy's] little feet around the house," Cronkite wrote Betsy.[22]

WITH HIS ROOMIE GONE, CRONKITE moved from a top-floor flat on Buckingham Gate to a smaller interior apartment three floors below. It turned out to be a fortuitous switch; it may have saved Cronkite from injury when the "doodlebugs" began hitting London. Before summer's end, some 2,500 "robot bombs" would strike the British capital, killing nearly 5,800 Londoners.[23]

It's odd that a Nazi terror weapon—something that ended up inflicting twenty-three thousand casualties, virtually all of them British civilians, and damaging one hundred thousand English homes—was given such harmless-sounding nicknames. Even "buzz bomb" doesn't capture the two-ton V-1's viciousness.

The first drones raked southern England in the early morning of Monday, June 13, six days after D-Day. V-1s were the first of Hitler's vaunted *Vergeltungswaffen* weapons to actually become operational. Controlled by an automatic "gyro-pilot," the V-1s were the first jet-propelled aircraft in history. They didn't always strike where they were aimed—but that made them even more terrifying.[24]

Nazi propaganda chief Joseph Goebbels, whose radio broadcasts had been bragging ad nauseam about how Hitler's vengeance weapons would turn around the war, had a field day when the buzz bombs finally hit. German soldiers were told that all of London was aflame.

Some twenty-four hours after the first V-1 attacks, Cronkite attended a briefing by British officials. A big part of Britain's countermeasures, Cronkite wrote, was to use heavy and medium bombers to disable the rocket bombs' "take-off strips" along the Pas de Calais.[25] The buzz bombs typically traveled some three-hundred-plus miles an hour—fast, but not fast enough to evade antiaircraft fire or to elude Spitfires and Mustangs, which could toggle the V-1's wings and knock it off course.

On Sunday morning, June 18—day five of the buzz bomb hysteria— Cronkite had one of his closest shaves of the war. While still at his apartment at 11:20, he wrote Betsy that he had just rung for Charles, the building valet, to bring some coffee, when he heard an air raid siren coupled with the ominous *pssz-pssz* of an approaching V-1. He threw open his living room window and stuck his head out "to see what I could see." Since the flying bomb was approaching from his blind side, he couldn't spot it—but he did see many of the Guardsmen at the palace's Wellington Barracks craning *their* necks out doors and windows, trying to eyeball the phantom.

> Then I saw them duck back into the barracks and at the same instant the motor of the damned thing stopped. By that time we had begun to learn that we had five to fifteen seconds to get under cover between the motor shutting off and the explosion. I turned and started running like hell for the main corridor of the apartment building. I got through the tiny living room into the hall of my flat when the bomb hit. There was the terrible tinkle of falling glass like in an automobile accident only multiplied a thousand fold with the additional crumbling of plaster and ripping of wood. I felt like someone had slapped me hard on the back, and then shoved me but hard on the chest.[26]

Cronkite staggered but did not fall in the hallway. Dust and smoke were everywhere. The door of one nearby flat had been torn from its hinges; Cronkite worried that the door was going to become its own flying bomb.

It took him a few seconds to get his bearings. Soon he realized that although some windows had been blown out, the place was not going to collapse; outside and inside, he could hear people bellowing. Sirens had begun to blare.

Two hundred yards away at the Wellington Barracks, the scene was horrific. As if manipulated by Satan, the V-1's radio-directed jet engine had conked out directly over Guards Chapel; just as the choir was singing a Eucharistic hymn, the buzz bomb had nose-dived into the roof. Everything instantly collapsed: the ceiling, its concrete pillars and supporting walls, and the portico over the chapel's western door. Only the apse was somehow spared. The rubble was so thick that it took rescue workers days to locate all the bodies and body parts.

It turned out to be the most devastating V-1 attack of the war. One hundred twenty-one soldiers and civilians were killed; another 141 were seriously injured. Among the dead were several senior Allied army officers and their wives. The Bishop of Maidstone, who was presiding over the service, survived, as did the candles and silver cross that hung over the altar.[27]

Cronkite was still coughing up dust in the hallway when Charles, the "houseman," appeared. Though getting on in years, Charles insisted on dressing the part of the gentleman's gentleman.

"Are you all right, sir?" Charles asked. Without waiting for an answer, the valet vanished. Cronkite, tongue in cheek, told Betsy he was disappointed that Charles hadn't uttered the movie cliché, "You rang, sir?"

The V-1 demolition of Guards Chapel became a standard part of Cronkite's World War II repertoire, one of the half dozen or so stories he repeatedly told interviewers. Over the years, his facts got mixed up and the circumstances embellished. Charles became "George," and "Are you all right, sir?" became the bon mot that movie-buff Cronkite had hoped it would be: "You rang, sir?"

Maybe Cronkite inadvertently confused things or maybe he did it deliberately. Either way, Walter Cronkite was entitled to exaggerate his war stories a little, the same way any veteran is.

No exaggeration was needed to describe the chapel carnage. Surely Cronkite must have been the first reporter on the scene. He interviewed witnesses and rescue workers—knowing full well that censors would never allow him to use the material, at least not for a long while. It wasn't until weeks later when Churchill "sounded off and revealed all the secret details," as Walter told Betsy, that Cronkite was even able to mail a letter about the episode.

Despite the damage, his building stayed open until a second attack occurred a week later.[28] This time, Cronkite told Betsy, it was a "real daisy"—a flying bomb that smashed into a nearby structure. It came in the early morning, with Cronkite still in bed. All night long Cronkite had heard buzz bombs—or at least thought he had. Each time, he'd jump out of bed and sprint toward the hallway—as he had the previous Sunday morning during the barracks attack. Finally, exhausted by false alarms, he had fallen fast asleep.

"This one must have awakened me just before it hit because I remember in half sleep curling up in [a] tight ball, pulling covers over my head and clapping hands over my ears," he wrote Betsy. "Then it hit. All hell seemed to break loose."

The explosion was so devastating that it seemed like fifteen minutes before debris finally stopped falling. But in truth it was only a few seconds; the ceiling, to Cronkite's amazement, didn't cave. There were so many shards of jagged glass that Cronkite put on boots to exit the apartment. Miraculously, the only possession he lost was a bottle of hair tonic, which broke after it fell off the bathroom counter. His books and clothes were covered with soot—"but nothing that a little washing and cleaning won't fix," Cronkite wrote.[29]

WHILE HIS FRIEND CRONKITE WAS ducking doodlebugs in London, Andy Rooney was on the Cotentin eluding artillery fire. Once he headed southeast from Cherbourg, Rooney started angling to get what his confidant Joe Liebling already had: credentials to cover the day-to-day movements of the

First Army, which was still hunkered down in Normandy's hedgerow country. While Rooney waited for the PROs to process his request, he bunked at Grandcamp, in barracks next to the Ninth Air Force's A-1 airstrip that Cronkite had admired three weeks before.

Scores of P-47 Thunderbolts and P-51 Mustangs now called Grandcamp and its chicken wire runways home. Rooney marveled at the way the pilots would shriek overhead, touch down, rearm, refuel, grab something to eat, then head off on their next sortie. "For the P-47 pilots, zooming in with their eight machine guns blazing on a line of trucks bringing up ammunition and food, it was a vicious but satisfying business," Rooney wrote. "They made it impossible for the Germans to move anything on wheels in daylight hours. A P-47's firepower could turn over a heavy truck, cut a horse in half, knock the steeple off a church, or pierce the walls of a stone house and kill its occupants."[30] Normandy's church steeples were a constant target; the dirty deed had to be done, Rooney learned, because the enemy used anything above ground level as an observation post.

Rooney's roommate at Grandcamp was an Associated Press photographer named Bede Irvin, who filled their hovel with pictures of his wife, Kath. They weren't the only journalists around: a savvy Ninth Air Force public relations officer named Ben Wright, realizing that there were a lot of reporters and photographers without accreditation, like Irvin and Rooney, roaming around Normandy, provided them with food and shelter in exchange for an article or two or some pictures of Grandcamp's flyboys in action.

In late July and early August, Cronkite again got a quick glimpse at Normandy. Along with six other newsmen and two photographers, he flew in a military transport with an unnamed "very high ranking officer." The group spent two days touring the Cotentin, retracing the American advance from Isigny-sur-Mer through Carentan and Montebourg to Cherbourg.

"God, what desolation!" Cronkite told Betsy. "It is hard to imagine a town, say the size of Sedalia [Missouri], completely flattened. The towns just do not exist anymore. And everywhere convoys and the ever-present dust. Goggles like those worn in the desert are essential."

Cronkite was glad to be away from southern England and its omnipresent buzz bombs, at least for a few days. With the nearest German soldier a couple dozen miles away, things were quiet, the nighttime rest "heaven-sent." And in a commentary on London's putrid cuisine, Cronkite told Betsy that the Army field chow tasted damned good.[31]

Back in London, Cronkite waited for the momentous call that would bring him to the Continent for good. It turned out to be a far longer wait than he wanted.

HAL BOYLE GOT TO AN American marshaling camp outside a Channel port in the south of England seven days after D-Day. He was filing stories about the staggering amount of Allied personnel and equipment being ferried to Normandy. To stay dry, he spent the stormy night of June 22 stuffed into the seat of a supply truck, sans blanket, hankering, he told Frances, for his bunk and bunkmate on Waverly Place.[32] Five days later the Army finally deposited him at a Normandy beachhead. Like Rooney two and a half weeks earlier, Boyle immediately turned right and up.

Boyle was eager to see for himself the final stages of the Cotentin operation—and to sample some of Fort du Roule's liquor. On June 29 he caught up with the infantrymen in the Ninth Division as they rounded up the German holdouts at Cap de la Hague, eight miles northwest of Cherbourg. After Italy's depressing quagmire, Boyle was thrilled to be on the march. He hitchhiked his way to the front and watched the spectacle of the largest German surrender in the West since Tunisia thirteen months earlier.

As his ride pushed northwest through the now-liberated peninsula, Boyle passed hundreds of prisoners huddled in the rain; he then counted sixteen Allied trucks carrying scores of other enemy soldiers. The "fanatical Nazi" who commanded the Cap de la Hague garrison had lied to his men, Boyle learned, telling them that a counteroffensive would rescue them. A few days earlier, German commander von Schlieben had told Joe

Collins that, given Hitler's orders, he could not compel his officers and men to give up their arms.

The Nazis might have held out even longer if their liquor supplies hadn't run dry, "judging from the condition of a goodly number of prisoners," Boyle told readers. But besides cognac, the enemy had run out of ammunition, too.

Boyle quoted a public relations officer from Columbia, Tennessee, named Lindsey Nelson that Germans trapped in the upper reaches of the Cotentin became so desperate they began firing "star shells"—artillery casings without explosives embedded inside. The defanged shells made a "hell of a" hole but did not inflict any damage unless they happened to land directly on top of a trench, Captain Nelson told Boyle. "The only effect they had was to puzzle hell out of our infantry in their foxholes. They keep waiting for the real shells that never came."[33]

The onetime newspaperman with the hometown *Columbia Daily Herald* later joined the ETO press corps as a journalist with the *Memphis Commercial Appeal* and palled around with Boyle and company in three different countries. After the war, Nelson became a noted sportscaster and the eventual voice of the New York Mets and University of Notre Dame football highlights.

It had taken the better part of a month, but the Americans had finally silenced the railway artillery guns that had menaced so many GIs on the peninsula. Even after Cherbourg fell, the rail guns disrupted the work of Army and Navy engineers as they tried to salvage the port. Some 4,200 enemy soldiers, many of them burrowed into hideaways not unlike the Japanese on Saipan and Peleliu, became casualties in those final days on the Cotentin as the VII Corps mopped up with flamethrowers, grenades, and bayonets.

On July 1, Boyle spotted a German prisoner being interrogated in Cap de la Hague. "Standing straight as a ramrod, the tall blond said he was from Württemberg and was a Nazi sergeant and a party member." Through an interpreter, the sergeant shared with Boyle his view of American battle tactics. "Your American artillery is wonderful, wonderful and terrible," the enemy noncom said. "Why, it never dares attack without heavy preliminary artillery bombardment. If it was not for that artillery one of our machine gun crews could hold back a whole company of your infantry." The American interpreter let the prisoner's words soak in, then parried: "Well, sergeant, our way seems to get results. Wouldn't your soldiers like to have all that artillery supporting them, too?"[34]

BOYLE WAS DELIGHTED TO BE reunited with old chum Don Whitehead. At boss Wes Gallagher's direction, the AP duo was working in sync, divvying up assignments and making sure Normandy's best stories got covered. By early July, the Allied line ran west to east over some seventy miles, from the Cotentin through Bayeux to St.-Sauveur-le-Vicomte and the Gulf of St.-Malo. The British and Canadians in Bernard Montgomery's Twenty-first Army Group were on the eastern one third of the line; the American First Army under Courtney Hodges and Omar Bradley was positioned forty-some miles along the western front. The U.S. line bulged amid Caumont's marshlands and again in the Nazi-flooded swamps of Carentan and St.-Lô.[35] As Joe Liebling pointed out, the line ironically did not face east toward Germany, but instead aimed south and, in certain respects, west— an ironic twist of fate that a month later bedeviled George Patton.

The product of much back-and-forth politicking, the Allies had come up with a compromise, a bizarre chain of command. Eisenhower was the Supreme Commander, with Montgomery the overall Allied commander of invasion forces and Bradley the U.S. commander. But once troops arrived en masse in France, the arrangement called for Bradley to become commander of the 12th Army Group, a promotion that would make him Monty's coequal. It was a peculiar construct, rife with problems from the outset. Within weeks, it would prove untenable.

WES GALLAGHER AND FELLOW AP editor Bob Brunelle wired Boyle from London that Boyle was to concentrate on his column—and let colleagues worry about spot coverage. But Boyle continued to file multiple pieces— profiles, interviews, battle flashes, skirmish descriptions, and more—

virtually every day. His letters to Frances complained about the frustrations of covering a battlefield as complex as Normandy's and the energy it took to chase down infantrymen every day.

"We have been as busy as a flea in a dogshow the last few days, and I am not sure which is going to end first, me or the campaign," Boyle wrote on July 10.

> There is so much news to cover that it would take fifty newsmen for an agency to cover it all adequately. They won't allow us but two men with the First Army—Don and I—so we have to work as hard and as long each day as we can, writing everything we come across and let the rest go. I am so glad to be over here and working on this story that I don't mind the effort. I only hope I can keep up the pace. I don't have quite the same endurance I did when I started off in this business almost two years ago. Tunisia, Sicily and Italy have taken something out of me. Still I have been going from eight a.m. until one or two a.m. steady for two weeks and haven't collapsed yet—thanks to your vitamin pills and "hog" throat tablets.[36]

Boyle had plenty of accomplices with whom to share Frances' elixir, not the least of which was his drinking buddy Joe Liebling. The two of them picked up where they'd left off in Tunisia fourteen months before; Liebling couldn't wait to show his fellow gourmand the epicurean glories of France. In Barneville, a tiny Cotentin crossroads a dozen miles removed from the fighting at La Haye du Puits, locals had tipped off Liebling that the female chef at the Hôtel de Paris, though temperamental, was superb.

"She was a scrawny, enameled ex-soprano, whose extravagant circumspection inspired doubts about her past," Liebling wrote. To wangle decent wines, Liebling, Boyle, and other correspondents "had to pay her a bit of court." Robert Casey of the *Chicago Daily News* spoke no French but possessed matinee-idol good looks. Liebling put Casey to work sucking up to the chef. While sampling her appetizers, "Casey would roll his eyes and emit terrifying groans, representing passion, and I would order up the last bottles of Nuits-St.-Georges '37," Liebling recalled.[37]

On the weekend of July 8 and 9, Liebling, Boyle, and Casey piled into a jeep intent on sampling the Hôtel de Paris' delicacies. En route they bumped into a 79th Infantry Division intelligence officer. The officer was excited about the potential for a major breakthrough in that day's battle for La Haye and invited the three correspondents to witness history. La Haye du Puits was the place GIs had dubbed Hooey da Pooey; it was at the far western end of the U.S. line, almost to the coast. Its German occupiers, crowded by the sea, were staving off annihilation by putting up a hellacious fight.

"Casey and Boyle and I all felt it would be callous to tell the G-2 we were cutting his battle in order to eat *sole bonne femme* and *tournedos Choron*. We decided therefore, to attend the battle, but not until after lunch, when we would be in a better frame of mind for it."[38]

They washed down their four courses with two bottles of Burgundy, one white and one red, then drove south past summer villas on a blue-skied afternoon. Tank and jeep traffic was surprisingly light. "It was a little like going to Jamaica in time to have a bet on the third race, when most of the crowd had already gone through," Liebling wrote. As they neared La Haye, however, the roads became congested and the sound of battle was so loud they had to shout to be heard. At a Medical Corps clearing station they watched two combat-fatigued GIs grind their heads against a wall as they balked at getting into an ambulance.

With shells bursting nearby, the three of them gingerly drove around a bend in the road, then sought shelter in a big home—Liebling guessed it was a sanatorium—surrounded by landscaped grounds. The enemy had used it as a barracks and later a redoubt; the place stank, Liebling remembered.

"The German Army had two smells—one of sour cabbage, which permeated even its sweat-soaked blankets, and one resembling a blend of a camel house and raw ether, which attached even to fragments of shot down aircraft. I don't know yet what that one was, but it was known from Norway to Cyrenaica as the 'Boche smell.'"

The house had just been captured; it was full of dead German soldiers.

One of them was a tall man who'd dragged a wicker chaise longue onto a hillock in the garden. "There he had sprawled himself, binoculars in hand, to look about for likely places on which to call down fire. It was flat country, and even this slight elevation was serviceable. A fragment from an air burst [of artillery] had saved him the trouble of getting up."

As evening approached, the three friends followed infantrymen into the decimated streets of La Haye. "Street fighting, in my limited experience, is not particularly dangerous unless you want to fight personally. Observation is limited, and there is defilade everywhere. You sprint from shelter to shelter. Even while I was running, I felt that it was a game that did not in any way affect survival."

Liebling's skepticism notwithstanding, the three of them ran through and around smoking debris until they happened upon a company command post in a burned-out café. The commander was delighted to have such distinguished company, so they stuck around for a while, "rather at a loss for conversation, and then left, feeling that we had atoned for our good lunch," Liebling wrote.[39]

FIRST ARMY REPORTERS WERE RARELY at a loss for conversation that summer—and there was no shortage of fine meals, either. Along with Ernie Pyle, Bob Casey, and nearly two dozen others, by early July Rooney, Boyle, and Liebling were staying at a press camp set up by the First Army's public relations staff. None of the reporters could identify it in articles or letters, of course, but they were encamped at the Hamel estate outside the tiny village of Vouilly, a couple of miles southeast of Isigny-sur-Mer and some fifteen miles north of a strategic crossroads called St.-Lô. Rooney and the others enjoyed referring to the farm and its twenty-room stone manse as Château d'Hamel or Château de Vouilly, but the place was hardly in its heyday—upkeep hadn't been easy during the Occupation. Still, a picturesque poplar-lined lane led to a stone bridge over an ancient moat.

For five full weeks beginning in early summer, much of the Western world's press, including an incumbent and several prospective winners of the Pulitzer Prize, was bivouacked at Mme. Hamel's farm. The correspondents' tents stood next to a field that belonged to a herd of red-and-white steers, dozens of dairy cows, and hundreds of pigs. "If you have a little victory garden in the windows this summer, I can sell you all the manure you want," Boyle joked with Frances. "It's fresh and I can get it for you wholesale."[40]

Vouilly was the first of three press camps that First Army PROs established between Normandy and Paris. The PROs were indebted to Mme. Hamel because they'd approached her out of the blue about handing over her home and farm for an indefinite period of time—and she'd consented. At any given moment, there were two or three dozen reporters staying at Vouilly, bunking in one of six big tents pitched in the orchard beyond the old field kitchen.

Mme. Hamel's largest room included several long walnut tables and a series of smaller desks, which made for a superb makeshift pressroom. Censors were installed in an adjoining room. Reporters, therefore, had their dream scenario: one-stop shopping.

The tent nearest the château had six distinguished occupants: Hal Boyle of AP, Ernie Pyle of Scripps Howard, Hank Gorrell of UP, Jack Thompson of the *Chicago Daily Tribune*, Bill Stoneman of the *Chicago Daily News* and later the *Christian Science Monitor*, and photographer Bert Brandt of Acme Pictures. The six stayed together in the same setup through all the First Army press camps in northern France.[41]

Since retreating Germans had ransacked the place, the food situation for humans and animals alike was "pretty grim"—at least at the outset, Boyle wrote. Tired of Army rations, certain correspondents were deputized to scour the countryside for fresh eggs and vegetables. Naturally, Liebling and his silver French tongue were commissioned to procure a local chef. Before long the camp's cafeteria-style mess was producing suppertime swill "of a magnificence unparalleled in that thrifty countryside," Liebling recalled.

Joe insisted on such heaping portions for everyone that there were plenty of leftover scraps. Starved for years under the Occupation, Mme. Hamel's pigs had never had it so good. The same could be said for the correspondents. On those mornings when eggs and bacon were available, Pyle treated his camp mates to breakfast. Rooney called Pyle the press camp's "den mother."[42]

"The press-association boys constantly competed among themselves on a strict time basis, like milers," Liebling wrote. He recalled an unnamed United Press reporter (given the time and circumstance, it was almost assuredly Hank Gorrell, whom, Rooney recollected in 2011, could be a little thick and crabby) inside a tent at Mme. Hamel's, proudly reading a cable from London that may well have come from Virgil Pinkley.

"Beat nearest competitor one minute forty-five. Kudos, kudos, kudos!" the cable read. The UP reporter looked up from his dramatic reading.

"What does 'kudos' mean?" he inquired.

"It means they've decided not to give you a raise," cracked someone, probably Liebling.[43]

Liebling, by then in his late thirties, was in all likelihood the second-oldest correspondent at the camp, bettered only by Bob Casey. Mme. Hamel's farm would become a recurring Liebling milieu, a place that loomed almost as large in his imagination as the tony precincts of Long Island had loomed in Fitzgerald's. In the years to come, Liebling never tired of extolling the farm and its temporary and permanent occupants.

Mme. Hamel's guests lived a strange existence. After grabbing coffee or one of Ernie's breakfasts, they'd leave in twos and sometimes threes in jeeps driven by young PRO deputies to cover the action outside St.-Lô. The reporters' commute south became as routine, Liebling wrote, as a taxi ride from uptown to downtown Manhattan.

Rooney, who kept the same jeep from Utah Beach to the Rhine, often gave Boyle and Liebling a lift to the front. Boyle's boss Gallagher hated for his star columnist to be in the same jeep as a wire service competitor, so for Boyle, Gorrell's vehicle was out; so was INS' Clark Lee's. But the *Stars and Stripes* wasn't a competitor of AP; it was a customer—and Gallagher certainly wasn't worried about Boyle being "scooped" by Liebling's egghead weekly. On top of that, the three men enjoyed each other's company. When they got near the front, as artillery exchanges got louder and closer, his mates admired Rooney's gritty driving.

By early suppertime they'd return, looking to enjoy that evening's repast and a lively discourse about women, boxing, and dirty books. Or maybe they'd watch a movie in the tin-roofed shed behind the field kitchen. To abide by blackout rules, the Army had hung a tarpaulin on the back and sides of the shed.

Naughty limerick composition—at which Boyle had no peer—was another favorite pastime. The correspondents tried to stump one another with obscure and difficult-to-rhyme names. One night someone came up with Frank Gervasi, a *Collier's* reporter with whom Boyle and Liebling had served in North Africa.

Boyle, whose dirty poetry skills had been honed in late-night sessions at the Sig Ep house at the University of Missouri, no doubt took another slug and another tug on his cigar, and intoned:

> *There once was a whore from Bengazi*
> *Who slept with a frog and a Nazi*
> *A wog and a dog*
> *And a razorback hog,*
> *But she drew the line at Gervasi.*[44]

Andy Rooney once heard Boyle remark that the great thing about being a newspaperman was that you got to meet such fascinating people—most of them other newspapermen.

The evening bull sessions in Vouilly were invariably fueled by liquor. Not only did they still have some of the stash they'd commandeered in Cherbourg, but Mme. Hamel also had a basement full of fermented calvados that somehow the Germans had failed to snatch. Charmed by Liebling's appreciation of Norman culture, Mme. Hamel opened her cellar to Joe and his friends. Each night the reporters passed around jugs. A field kitchen spigot plugged into a cider barrel had been dormant during the Occupation; in honor of the Liberation, Mme. Hamel had it cranked up again, so the reporters had constant access to fresh hooch.

One of the Hamel sons walked with a limp. While in the French army in the summer of '40 he'd been taken prisoner. Months later, in blatant violation of the Geneva Conventions, he was forced to clear a minefield in Alsace-Lorraine and was wounded by shrapnel; six of his POW comrades were killed. His disability made him useless to the Third Reich, so he was freed to return to Vouilly.[45]

His mother, the proprietress, then in her early sixties, "looked like a proper chatelaine," Liebling wrote, "tall and straight, with a high forehead, a long, straight nose, bright-blue eyes, and white hair." For much of the Occupation, she'd put up with enemy soldiers camped on her property. The only reason that the Germans hadn't seized her estate is that she'd tricked them into believing that a child staying at the house was violently ill and contagious—a phony diagnosis "confirmed" by a friendly local doctor.[46]

Although Liebling wrote, perhaps disingenuously, that Mme. Hamel had no "direct contact" with the Resistance, at any given moment during the Occupation she had harbored between two and six young men evading forced labor. She and her family also defied the Gestapo by listening almost every night to the forbidden BBC.[47]

At one point in the summer of '44, Mme. Hamel shared with Liebling the Occupation "proclamations" that the conquering Germans and their Vichy puppets had foisted on Normandy. On August 17, 1941, some thirteen months into the Occupation, a German *Kommandant* had vowed vengeance for an act of sabotage his circular blamed on "Jews and Communists."

Her cavernous room, which the PROs and reporters had taken over with telephones, typewriters, walkie-talkies, and hookups to the wireless vehicles parked in the pasture, was bigger than the city room of the *Providence Journal and Evening Bulletin*, Liebling claimed. "Scores of millions of people in America had hung on the stories of the ugly fighting among the dead cattle, and every word had gone out through the mysterious wireless trucks on Madame's farm," Liebling wrote fourteen years later.[48]

The whole experience was "dichotomous," as Liebling called it in *Normandy Revisited*. Here they were, a dozen miles from some of the war's fiercest fighting, yet leading pampered lives. Despite the proximity of the Wehrmacht, there was little danger on Normandy's roads and next to none at the farm: By midsummer, the plane-strapped Luftwaffe had virtually stopped strafing runs; the Germans, moreover, weren't likely to waste precious artillery shells by lobbing them into Vouilly. It was the obverse of North Africa, when reporters kept tremulous eyes and ears on the horizon. At the Army's insistence, the press guys maintained a blackout during Normandy's short summer nights—but felt silly as they threw blankets over Mme. Hamel's windows.

At one point Liebling went into the village and bought a huge wheel of Camembert cheese at the little grocery-café. Camembert stunk to high heaven but was nevertheless considered a Norman delicacy. It was so obnoxious, in fact, that Liebling couldn't persuade any of his mates to partake, so he would melt a big chunk of it and stick his finger in the pot while lying on his cot, reading or scribbling notes. One night Ernie Pyle dug underneath Liebling's bunk and—in a gesture universally applauded by the Vouilly press camp brethren—tossed Joe's stinking cheese to the animals.

BRIGADIER GENERAL NORMAN COTA OF the 29th Division (soon to be commander of the 28th) had weightier matters than cheese to worry about in mid-July of '44. The soldiers of the German Third Parachute Division and other crackerjack German units were putting up a stout defense at St.-Lô, throwing everything they had at the famed Blue and Gray division and other U.S. troops. The Allied offensive had become so bogged down in hedgerow country—the *bocage*, as the Normans called it—that Eisenhower, Bradley, and Montgomery were worried that another stalemate like the one in Italy was taking root. But unlike in Italy, an impasse in Normandy would have had catastrophic consequences on the outcome of the war.

On Sunday morning, July 16, Liebling had spotted Cota north of St.-Lô, a mile or so short of the enemy right flank, near a decimated village called St.-André-de-l'Épine. Cota, eyes narrowed, was stopping GIs skulking away from the firing line.

"'Where are you going, boys?' I heard him ask a pair of stragglers, and they pulled up sharp when they noticed the star on the helmet of the

spindle-shanked, Roman-nosed old man alone in the road with his walking stick," Liebling recalled.

"'The lieutenant bugged out, sir, and we thought we might as well, too,'
one of them said.

"'Harses! Harses!' the General said in a non-Harvard New England
accent.[49] 'I haven't seen any lieutenant coming this way. Get up there before
he notices you've been away.'"

The two men that Cota shooed back to the front trenches weren't the
only GIs who'd grown weary of the carnage outside St.-Lô. For weeks on
end, their daily progress had been measured in yards, not miles. Normandy's hedgerows proved to be far more daunting obstacles than Allied intelligence had reckoned. Irregular in length and height, the hedgerows had
been designed two millennia before, during Julius Caesar's conquest of
Gaul, to mark property boundaries and keep Norman cattle from wandering. "Six to ten feet high and five feet thick, made of roots twisted around
dirt and stone, they were natural barriers to the movement of men and
machines," Rooney remembered. "German gunners leaned up against
them, their rifles poking over the top, their bodies protected. A tank coming down the narrow lane between two hedgerows separating fields on
either side was a sitting duck for an 88-mm artillery piece at the end of
the lane."[50]

PROBABLY THE ONLY AMERICAN IN Normandy in the summer of '44 who
actually called the ancient bushes "*bocage*" was Joe Liebling. Everybody
else, Rooney recalled, called them "god-damned hedgerows." One area two
miles by four miles in size in the Cotentin was dotted with some four thousand divided fields.[51] Liebling wrote in mid-July that "the struggle for orchards and pastures is disheartening because it is so repetitious. There is,
as Army men say, no observation in this country, which means that you
can't see an enemy position until you have taken the one in front of it."[52]

G-2's failure to appreciate the hazards of Normandy's hedgerows, historian Stephen E. Ambrose argued, proved to be the most glaring intel-

ligence shortcoming of the war. Omar Bradley and his deputies Chet Hansen and Monk Dickson spent years kicking themselves for not properly interpreting surveillance photographs. Few places in the world were better suited for defensive action. Besides the *bocage*, Normandy had myriad stone walls, rivers, streams, bogs, and swamps—some natural, some Rommel-made.

Andy Rooney remembered ghoulish scenes where American tankmen, trapped in the narrow lanes between hedgerows, would run over anything in their path, including the dead and wounded, regardless of uniform. Boyle and Pyle both filed pieces deploring enemy tactics in the hedgerows. The vegetation was so thick that German snipers could hide in it, even amid a retreat. Once an Allied squad had maneuvered past their position, the enemy riflemen would shoot Tommies and GIs in the back.

The unlikely American hero who ultimately figured out how to punch a hole in the hedgerows was a sergeant in the 102nd Cavalry Reconnaissance Squadron named Curtis "Bud" Culin. Culin had grown up in Cranford, New Jersey, where he had been an apprentice mechanic before the war. Hal Boyle caught up with Culin in the early 1950s, after Dwight Eisenhower had commended the ex-sergeant in Ike's memoir, *Crusade in Europe*. By then Culin was in his early thirties, an employee of Schenley Distillers, Inc., in New York City. Culin told Boyle the story of how he came to be an accidental inventor.

ATTACHED TO THE BLUE AND Gray Division, the 102nd Cavalry had come ashore after D-Day and immediately got bottled up in the hedgerows. "When our tanks hit [the hedgerows], it was like cracking into a stone wall," Culin told Boyle. "And if we tried to climb over them, the under belly of the tank was exposed. The German antitank guns [enemy bazookas were called *Panzerfäuste*] then could rip us open like sardine cans. Our own tank guns were pointed at the sky—useless. We couldn't defend ourselves."[53]

During the first few weeks of fighting, field commanders sent combat engineers out to the hedgerows with sticks of dynamite. But the gambit rarely worked—and engineers were getting picked off in alarming numbers. One day Culin's commanding officer called a meeting of the squad's noncoms and threw the floor open. Culin volunteered that he didn't know much about engineering, but had been impressed by the iron roadblocks that the Germans had implanted all over Normandy. Could Allied tankers put sharpened prongs of iron on their tank fronts and try to muscle through the hedgerows?

What the hell, the officer decided, it might be worth a shot.

"They tried it," Boyle wrote. "They welded four flanges to a crossbar, fixed it to a tank—and the 15-ton vehicle pitch-forked its way right through the nearest hedgerow."

Word of the 102nd's brainstorm quickly reached Omar Bradley, who'd been fretting for weeks over the Allies' lack of progress. Bradley insisted on a demonstration, loved what he saw, alerted the Brits, swore everyone to secrecy—and immediately ordered that six hundred Allied tanks be similarly equipped. In the weeks to come, Sergeant Culin's pronged tanks—dubbed Rhinos after their rhinoceros-like protuberances—would not only break through thousands of hedgerows, but also be instrumental in the Allies' breakout. Boyle's postwar piece quoted the Supreme Commander's accolade for Culin: "He restored the effectiveness of the tank and gave a tremendous boost to morale throughout the Army."[54]

EVERY DAY IN NORTHERN FRANCE, Boyle interviewed dozens of men like Bud Culin as he looked for stories of heroism and humor; inevitably, many of Boyle's tributes were posthumous.

Master Sergeant Joe "Shorty" Plotnick of Baltimore, Maryland, was another Mollie, a Russian émigré who enjoyed thumbing his nose at military discipline, was never shy about bragging about himself, and rarely left a poker game without pockets stuffed full of cash. All of five foot four, Shorty had been in the U.S. Army his entire adult life; twenty-six year earlier, he'd earned a Purple Heart in the trenches outside Château-Thierry. Plotnick never knew his age because there was no official record of his birth.

"He had put away enough buck privates' pay," Boyle wrote in the summer of '44, "so that he and his wife could afford more than C-rations any time he wanted to hang up his uniform."

The crusty Plotnick was an operations noncom with an armored outfit. "[Plotnick] had the reputation of eating young 'shavetails' for breakfast, and every man in the unit was fond of this sawed-off, gray-haired little man with the salty voice and the tough manner," Boyle wrote.

Shorty had hated the enemy long before he'd arrived for his first tour in France. "'Leave me tell you,' he said with a deeply serious look on his gnomelike face, 'I'll get those Germans!'" Boyle wrote.

Plotnick got more than his share of enemy soldiers—but one afternoon, as Boyle related, Shorty's luck ran out.

> "We'd just taken a town," said his company commander, Captain James Kuhns of Greensburg, Pennsylvania, "and Shorty and two other men heard there still was a German machine-gun nest giving us trouble in one of the buildings.
>
> "It wasn't the concern of the operations sergeant to knock it out, but you couldn't keep Shorty from going after those Germans. He was armed only with a pistol, but the two men with him had carbines. Shorty told them, 'O.K, I'll go out and draw their fire, and then you boys give it to them.' He edged out, but the Germans caught him with the first burst and mowed him down. He died before he knew he had located and wiped out that machine-gun nest. That was like Shorty—sticking his own neck out."[55]

Shorty Plotnick, Boyle made clear, stuck his neck out for a lot of guys. "'He was the best damn soldier in this division,' said Major Nathan M. Quinn of Spencer, Massachusetts.

"Shorty would rather have had that sentence over his grave than his own nameplate," Boyle wrote, "because when he was alive he proudly thought so, too. He knew he was the 'best damned soldier' in any division. He wouldn't have been Shorty if he didn't think so."[56]

All five reporters went on combat missions in the skies over the Reich. Bigart, Cronkite, and Rooney flew on B-17s, which drew ferocious flak as they neared their targets. Cronkite was aboard the B-17 *Shoo Shoo Baby* on D-Day morning over Caen, Normandy.

Rooney, Bigart, and Cronkite all covered the savage raids against Nazi munitions factories. On October 9, 1943, B-17 bombers attacked a Focke-Wulf 190 factory near Marienburg in East Prussia.

Rooney (*standing, left*) was a more cheerful soul after joining *Stars and Stripes* in London in late 1942. His articles saluted the unsung heroes behind the scenes of the USAAF's air war against the Nazis.

Rooney (*left*) poses with a crew from the *Mission Belle*, a bomber with the 385th Bomb Group, stationed in Great Ashfield, England. Rooney called air bases "damned depressing places to visit"; three-fourths of the U.S. airmen who flew on bombing missions in 1943 and the first half of 1944 became casualties of one kind or another.

Rooney stops to smell some flowers while leaning against heavy bombs stored at an airfield, probably at Thurleigh. He chose this photo as the cover for his memoir, *My War*.

The London edition of *Stars and Stripes* was essentially a USAAF journal from late 1942 through early 1944. Rooney's mentor and writing partner, Bud Hutton, is on the left, Andy's great pal Charlie Kiley in the middle.

Rooney, Cronkite, and Bigart never tired of extolling the heroism of air gunners. Rooney and his *Stars and Stripes* colleague Bud Hutton wrote a book about them.

A few weeks after the Battle of the Bulge, Brigadier General Clift Andrus took command of Liebling and Boyle's favorite outfit, the Big Red One, the Fighting First Division. Boyle (*left*) got an exclusive with the general on February 3, 1945.

A wrecked American glider from ill-starred Operation Market Garden, September 1944. Cronkite crash-landed in Zon, Holland, on a glider carrying 101st Airborne general Anthony McAuliffe.

Close-in street fighting in the war's final winter produced ghoulish scenes like this one in Deidenberg, Belgium, with German soldiers lying dead near an American tank.

Rooney snapped this shot of GIs being greeted by delirious Frenchwomen on the day of the liberation of Paris. The locale was probably the Place de l'Opéra, where the correspondents were holed up at the Hôtel Scribe or the Hôtel Le Grand.

Rooney took this photograph of German prisoners being paraded through the streets of Paris. A few moments later, a Parisian smashed a bottle over the head of one of the prisoners. Rooney wrote that he'd never witnessed such hatred.

Stars and Stripes "Continental HQ," probably in Rennes, France, in late summer 1944. Rooney's great exclusive on the liberation of Paris never reached Rennes—and never got into print.

August 25, 1944—the day Paris was liberated—was the happiest day in Francophile Liebling's life. Liebling and Rooney were among the first correspondents into the freed French capital. Boyle was not far behind.

Hal Boyle of the Associated Press (*left*), Ernie Pyle of Scripps Howard, Gordon Gammack of the *Des Moines Register*, and Don Whitehead (*right*) of the Associated Press pictured at Vouilly, Normandy, on the site of the First Army's press camp in July and August 1944. Rooney called Pyle the camp's "den mother." It rained continually that summer.

Just days after the liberation of Paris in September 1944, Hal Boyle (*left*) and Ernie Pyle exchanged notes on the veranda of the Hôtel Le Grand with the Opera House looming in the background. Boyle and Pyle were the most popular columnists in the European Theater. Pyle won a Pulitzer Prize in 1944; Boyle in 1945. Seven months after this photo was taken, Pyle was killed by a Japanese sniper.

All five correspondents witnessed the reprisals that would take place against collaborationist women once villages were liberated. Nazi concubines had their heads shaved; collaborationist leaders and militiamen were often executed on the spot.

SIGNAL CORPS

A month after D-Day, American infantrymen slug their way through what Joe Liebling and historians called the *bocage*. GIs, Rooney remembered, called them "god-damn hedgerows." The thick underbrush stymied the Allied advance for weeks.

COURTESY OF THE ANDY ROONEY ARCHIVES

Rooney took this shot of Major Tom Howie's corpse lying in state atop the debris in St.-Lô, France, on July 18, 1944, the day Howie was killed helping to liberate the Norman village. The three-week siege at St.-Lô caused some forty thousand American casualties; it was covered from its inception by Rooney, Liebling, and Boyle.

COURTESY OF THE ANDY ROONEY ARCHIVES

Rooney with his great *Stars and Stripes* buddy and D-Day partner Charlie Kiley. The two reporters were billeted with the Fourth Division in Bristol Harbour, landing at Utah Beach four days after D-Day.

SIGNAL CORPS

German soldiers are led out of a cavern in Cherbourg two and a half weeks after D-Day. The Nazi genius for underground architecture was uncovered during the Cotentin operation. Liebling, a connoisseur, helped fellow correspondents "liberate" particularly choice bottles of champagne and cognac.

From a distance, Cronkite, Liebling, Boyle, and Rooney all saw V-2 rockets like this one being fired from their launching sites in the Reich. Unlike the V-1, which could be heard as it approached, the V-2 struck with no warning and could set an entire city block ablaze.

A D-Day predawn briefing at Thurleigh, Rooney's "home" air base and the site of the 306th Bomb Group squad. Bigart and Cronkite covered the action at the 303rd base a few miles away at Molesworth. When they learned the invasion was finally on, men hooted and hollered.

A V-1 "doodlebug" like this one nearly killed Cronkite on Sunday, June 18, 1944. Instead of striking Cronkite's apartment building, it landed next door at the Guards Chapel at Wellington Barracks near Buckingham Palace. More than a hundred Sunday worshippers were killed—the worst V-1 attack of the war.

Rooney was always proud of this photograph that he took of intrepid St. Paul's Cathedral in London, which, despite merciless bombing and rocket attacks, was never destroyed.

Bigart carrying his bedroll and typewriter during the dispiriting Italian campaign of '44. For writing the truth, Homer and other reporters incurred the wrath of Allied commanders Sir Harold Alexander and General Mark Clark.

SIGNAL CORPS

Andy Rooney was one of the first correspondents on the scene when the bridge over the Rhine at Remagen was captured intact. When it collapsed on St. Patrick's Day 1945, this is the view Rooney saw from the bridge's eastern end.

Cronkite finally returned home to Kansas City in December 1945 after three years of covering the war. This photograph was probably taken on the porch of his mother's home. The following month he was back in Europe to cover the Nuremberg Trials.

COURTESY OF THE CRONKITE FAMILY

COURTESY OF THE ANDY ROONEY ARCHIVES

A *Stars and Stripes* reunion in the 1960s. Charlie Kiley is to Rooney's right. The great editor Bob Moora is directly across from Kiley. Bud Kane and Ben Price are to Rooney's left.

A mid-1960s reunion of the fabled "Writing 69th." Former USAAF media relations maven Hal Leyshon sits to Rooney's right; to Leyshon's right is former CBS correspondent Paul Manning. At the head of the table is former Associated Press correspondent Gladwin Hill, archrival of Cronkite (*standing*). Bigart sits to Hill's left. Two other former USAAF officials, Jack Milady and Jack Redding, sit in front of Cronkite.

On the fiftieth anniversary of D-Day, Cronkite helped dedicate this plaque at the site of the First Army's press camp in the summer of 1944, the Château de Vouilly in Normandy. Rooney, Liebling, and Boyle all spent five weeks as guests of Madame Hamel.

His encomium to the immigrant who died fighting the Germans for a second time is one of the pieces that earned Hal a Pulitzer Prize.

TWO DAYS AFTER JOE LIEBLING saw Norm Cota shoo the two skittish GIs back toward the front lines, Liebling glimpsed the general in action again. By Tuesday, July 18, the Blue and Gray men, along with regiments from four other divisions, had fought their way from the periphery of St.-Lô into the village itself. Cota was directing the Twenty-ninth's advance when Liebling saw the general grab at his cane-carrying arm: A German sniper had wounded him. "He shifted his stick to his other hand and stepped inside a gaping shop front while a medic put a dressing on the damaged member," Liebling wrote.

"Cota came out in time to see the correspondents departing as rapidly as possible," Liebling wrote, "and my last memory of that victory is of the laughing general waving his stick and yelling, 'Don't leave me now, boys! Don't leave me now!' The wound hurt worse later. When I next saw the General, he said, 'I was standing out there to give the boys confidence, but it didn't work out right.'"[57]

Cota's wound notwithstanding, a lot of GIs got an injection of confidence that day. July 18, 1944, proved to be pivotal in the fight to break out of Normandy's logjam. It was the day that St.-Lô finally fell. The strategic village was at the confluence of arterial roads from the south and east, through which the Germans might have been able to pour reserves to smother a breakthrough farther west. "Its capture," Liebling wrote, "was like a tourniquet on an elbow, permitting an operation on the forearm."[58]

The *New Yorker* writer used it as a metaphor, but hundreds of GIs outside St.-Lô were wearing real tourniquets. Liebling was almost one of them. On the morning of July 18, he remembered diving facedown onto St.-Lô's cobblestones to avoid sniper fire. He looked up "to steal a glance at the man lying in front of [me], noticing that his eyes were closed, like those of a girl waiting to be kissed."[59]

St.-Lô had frustrated Bradley and the American command since D-Day plus twelve when, Hal Boyle wrote, "the first surge from the beachhead spent itself."[60] North and west of St.-Lô a series of sloping ridges posed thorny obstacles to the Americans. The two longest slopes were both Nazi artillery strongholds that Allied intelligence officials branded Hill 192 and Hill 122 in reference to the number of meters their summits were above sea level.

In the previous three weeks, U.S. artillerymen had "pulverized" Hill 192 with a thousand tons of explosives, Boyle wrote, then watched as tactical fighter-bombers "knocked another 20 feet off the crest of the hill." Hill 192, Lieutenant Colonel Edward W. Wood told Boyle, "was a tough nut to crack with snipers and pillboxes operating almost every foot of the way." It gave the Wehrmacht a commanding view of the entire Norman battlefield, from the Vire River on the west to Caumont in the east, including every conceivable approach to St.-Lô.

Boyle was with the Second Division under General Walter M. Robertson on July 12 when, after eleven hours of miserable combat, the Americans finally uprooted enemy artillerymen from the crest of Hill 192. A ridge less than two hundred meters high had cost that division alone 1,253 casualties.[61] "Victorious American doughboys," Boyle wrote that night, "slept the sleep of exhaustion today in enemy positions by the bodies of German dead from whom they wrested control of this height."

The Germans had brought up so many mortars that GIs on the outskirts of St.-Lô were reduced to advancing on their bellies. St.-Lô had become "a miniature Stalingrad," Boyle remarked, a place with frantic Nazis retreating behind heaps of broken stone and mortar.[62]

Hill 122, a couple of kilometers closer to the village, had to be secured so that the Blue and Gray Division's sustained attack from the northeast could be carried out without harassment from close-in artillery. The still-green 35th Division under General Paul Baade drew the assignment. They fought their way up the slope with such élan that after the war Andy Rooney compared their bloody sacrifice to the Marine conquest of Tarawa eight months before. "We could not get the Germans off [Hill 122], and a lot of American boys lost their lives trying to climb it in the face of withering enemy fire from bunkers at its top," Rooney wrote.[63] The battle for Hill

122 went on, unflinching, day after day, before its occupiers finally crumbled at dawn on July 18, falling back into town to continue the fight.

"Correspondents—among them me—who entered [St.-Lô] shortly after the troops saw little," Joe Liebling wrote, "because they either hugged what they hoped would prove to be the lee of a wall or lay flat on their faces during their sojourn. The Germans, having been thrown out of the city, were reacting like a drunk who has been chucked out of a saloon and then throws a beer bottle through the window."[64]

July 18 was also the day that, some forty miles east, Bernard Montgomery launched Operation Goodwood, Monty's much-heralded, and eventually much-maligned, offensive to draw enemy attention to his front and away from Omar Bradley and the Americans.

It was also the day that Bradley put the finishing touches on his overhauled plan to break out of the hedgerows, dubbed Operation Cobra. Cobra was designed, as boxing maven Liebling appreciated, as the right cross that followed Goodwood's left jab. From the outset of Overlord planning in London months before, the Allied strategy had called for Montgomery and his Brits and Canadians to keep the enemy occupied in eastern Normandy while, from the west, Bradley and the Americans wheeled south and east, rocking Rommel and Rundstedt back on their heels. But the slow going in the hedgerows had delayed the Allies' one-two combination.

HAVING STARTED JULY 18 AT Mme. Hamel's farm, Liebling, Boyle, and Rooney were all within relative arm's reach. How Liebling and Boyle hitched a ride to the St.-Lô front that morning is not known. Rooney, however, recalls having escorted Liebling's Barneville restaurant coconspirator Bob Casey of the *Chicago Daily News*. Rooney held Casey, then the grand old man of Normandy correspondents, in awe; Casey was a longtime international affairs columnist who had written some twenty books about foreign policy and his travels abroad.

Once Casey and Rooney got within a mile or two of St.-Lô, artillery shells began thumping. When Rooney spotted Blue and Gray infantrymen joining men from the Big Red One and the Second and the Fourth Divisions and all locking horns with the Wehrmacht's Third Parachute Division, he couldn't wait to witness the action. "A fight between those [units] was the Super Bowl," Rooney recalled a half century later.[65]

Rooney steered the jeep past inert bodies and burned-out vehicles. By now the noise of the battle was alarmingly close. Rooney and Casey could see plumes of smoke shooting up from buildings smouldering in St.-Lô.

"I'm just going to walk down a ways," Rooney told his companion.

Casey laughed nervously, shook his head, and told Rooney to tell him all about it when he got back—if he got back.

"It was the mindless sort of thing you wouldn't do if you considered the risk, but I was interested, curious, and somehow oblivious to danger," Rooney remembered. "The thought of being hit never entered my mind."[66]

Dodging mortar rounds, Rooney jogged down a road that took him past several small farms. He encountered a group of GI's who had been left behind to secure the just-seized area. Most of the men were wearing the scarlet red patch of the 29th's 116th Infantry Regiment, which had been fighting virtually nonstop for days.

On July 17, one of the 116th's battalion commanders, Major Thomas D. Howie, a native South Carolinian who had been an instructor at the Staunton Military Academy in Virginia, had led a predawn raid that knocked a hole in the German line at the base of Hill 122 and succeeded in rescuing an American unit that had gotten cut off from the rest of the division.[67]

Now, twenty-four hours later, Howie and the rest of the 29th's staff officers were meeting with the big boss, Major General Charles Gerhardt. Gerhardt had a soft spot for Rooney, mainly because the gridiron buff had remembered that Gerhardt once quarterbacked West Point to a dramatic upset over Notre Dame.

Gerhardt could be a "tough old buzzard," Rooney wrote; reporters loved him because he was sassy and contrarian. Liebling recalled that Gerhardt once ordered the divisional band to play "Roll Out the Barrel" as his men departed a solemn ceremony in a cemetery. When a chaplain protested, Gerhardt explained that after paying homage to the fallen by playing funereal hymns, it was time to change the mood. Another time a reporter had asked why the Allies were so preoccupied with the capture of St.-Lô. "It's a catchy name," Gerhardt replied. "[St.-Lô] fitted well in head-lines, and the newspaper took to using it every day. After that, it became a morale factor, so we had to capture it."[68]

The morale-conscious Gerhardt was as fond of Major Howie as the men of the 116th. "After helping to relieve pressure on this [now-rescued] unit," Boyle wrote, "[Howie] then boldly launched another attack toward the hill which dominated the northeast entrance to the city." Howie drove his men hard, but he had a gentle heart; his guys loved him because he was never more than a step or two behind. Boyle, who'd been tailing the 116th on and off for a couple of weeks, called Howie a "tremendous soldier."[69]

At sunup on July 18, Gerhardt asked Howie for another miracle: to take St.-Lô that day "if you have to expend the whole battalion," Rooney re-called.[70] The major's last words to Gerhardt and the other officers at the 29th's briefing were "See you in St.-Lô."

It was Howie's concern for the welfare of his troops that cost him his life, Boyle wrote after the war. "Before hitting the ditch during a sudden German mortar barrage, [Howie] paused to see that his men were safe—and death took him, standing." Fragments from a shell that landed a few yards away pierced Howie's neck and chest. He died on the spot. Word was immediately relayed to Gerhardt.

The general ordered Captain Thomas D. Neal of Richmond, Virginia, to take an ambulance and drive Howie's body through the battered village. When Boyle first wrote about the episode, censors ironically allowed Boyle to mention Neal's name but not Howie's, pending notification of next of kin, or Gerhardt's, for fear that the Germans would seek vengeance on the 29th Division.

Boyle recalled years later that "Tom's body, still clad in full combat gear, was placed in an ambulance in the task force column." The AP columnist followed the grimy cortège as it navigated pockmarked roads, "past stricken trees whose limbs hung down like broken arms, past meadows where no birds sang, but bullets did. Churning clouds of yellow enveloped the vehicles, sweat grimed the faces of firing soldiers."

A sudden enemy artillery bombardment disrupted the column as it passed a cemetery. The ambulance was pressed into duty to transport wounded infantrymen. "Tom, lying on a stretcher, was transferred to a leading jeep," Boyle remembered. "The column trundled on. It smashed through the last ring of German defenders and entered the fallen city, a sea of flaming ruins."[71]

By now, Rooney, too, had caught up with the rolling elegy. "When I finally got down into the center of St.-Lô," Rooney recalled, "there was a knot of men by the side of the main church in town." Given the smoke and debris, Rooney couldn't tell, but it was the Église Notre-Dame, considered one of Normandy's Gothic masterpieces.

"The whole side of it had been knocked out and the rubble was piled high where it had fallen," Rooney wrote. "I hurried over and saw 10 or 15 soldiers lifting a flag-draped body laid out on a wooden door up the head of stone and mortar that been the side of the church. It would be accurate to say that St.-Lô had been leveled and the mound of stone and brick was the highest point in town. The soldiers were placing the body at the very top of the heap."[72]

In death, Boyle wrote," [Howie's] comrades had won for the major the last goal of his life—he was the 'first into St.-Lô.'"

Twenty-four hours later, as Rooney, Liebling, and Boyle accompanied the mop-up infantry squads into St.-Lô, Howie's flag-draped body was still there, "lying in state on an altar of rubble," Boyle wrote. "All the troops who went through St.-Lô that day, and there were many, heard of the young major and paid him tribute. Some doffed their helmets as they passed. Some knelt."[73]

SEVERAL MONTHS LATER ROONEY CAME back to Paris from the front and was surprised to receive orders to report to Lieutenant Colonel Ensley M. Llewellyn's office in the *Herald Tribune* building. Llewellyn was the officer in charge of the *Stars and Stripes*. After Sergeant Rooney saluted, he was confused when the boss handed him a small box and a certificate.

It was a Bronze Star, awarded per the official proclamation because Rooney had "penetrated to the heart of St.-Lô under small arms and open range artillery fire and gathered, without regard to his own safety, first hand descriptive materials for a complete and accurate story."

Rooney didn't know quite what to do. "I was simultaneously pleased and embarrassed. I knew that there were a lot of heroes in the war, and I knew I wasn't one of them." He thanked the colonel and shook his hand "as if he'd given me a diploma," Rooney remembered.[74]

Andy never mentioned it to any of his colleagues. Nor did Llewellyn.

In 1949, Boyle visited St.-Lô and its rebuilt place of worship and admired the monument the French had erected to commemorate Tom Howie's sacrifice. "The French people still deck the monument with flowers, and remember him in prayers," Boyle wrote.[75]

LIEBLING HURRIED BACK TO VOUILLY on the evening of July 18, eager to share the momentous news with Mme. Hamel and beat Agence Française correspondent André Rabache to the better calvados.

When Liebling arrived, Madame was sitting in her kitchen, entertaining several neighboring farmers. "'Madame,' I said proudly, for I wanted her to think well of the American Army, 'I come from St.-Lô. The city is ours! Now we can advance!'

"'I felicitate you, Monsieur,' she said. 'I am happy to hear it.'"

One of the neighbors also congratulated Liebling, mistakenly referring to him as *commandant* instead of *correspondant* (the French, for whatever reason, had trouble picturing journalists embedded with the military). But then the neighbor anxiously inquired about what would happen to the pigs.

"The pigs?" Liebling asked. He was still thinking about Cota, wrapping his wound while directing traffic.

"'Yes, *mon Commandant*, the young pigs who depend for their nourishment on the leftovers of the mess,'" the neighbor said.

Liebling, mystified, could only respond that perhaps the enemy would dig in south of St.-Lô—and that the press camp would stay rooted in Vouilly.

Mme. Hamel, turning a "disdainful eye" in her friend's direction, came to the rescue by volunteering that the pigs were already "well launched" and would do fine without the leftover haute cuisine. To celebrate St.-Lô's liberation, she poured calvados all around.[76]

The battle for St.-Lô had cost some forty thousand American casualties.

CHAPTER 11

✭

THE BREAKOUT—*MERCI! MERCI! MERCI!*

All the Germans in the area were trying to get out at once. The chief danger we faced was being trampled to death by escaping supermen while we slept.

—A. J. LIEBLING, AUGUST 1944

THE ROAD BACK TO PARIS

The culinary delights being served nightly at Mme. Hamel's press camp achieved such renown that chatter about them reached Omar Bradley's rolling command post. Bradley's mobile CP full of maps and troop disposition charts was, at that moment, stationed not far from Vouilly. A four-foot-high mahogany railing would soon cleave Bradley's expanded trailer, separating its lower half from its slightly elevated upper. The general's acolytes dubbed the wooden partition the Communion Rail.[1]

Since Bradley radiated the bearing of a kindhearted—if chronically demanding—vicar, the nickname fit. A decade after the war, Liebling described Bradley as "tall, bespectacled, and Missouri-speaking" and noted that the general often seemed to project "the pleased look of a Sunday-school superintendent announcing that the cake sale had brought in eleven dollars and fifty cents more than anticipated."[2] Bradley was so great a soldier, Liebling maintained, that "he never felt compelled to bark to prove it."[3]

The great soldier-vicar spent much of Thursday, July 20, poring over maps and contingency plans with his commander-bishop: Supreme Commander Dwight Eisenhower. Ike and Bradley devoted hours that day to reviewing Bradley's latest strategy to break out of hedgerow country, then Eisenhower returned to London. Bradley himself had been in England the day before, meeting with the joint Allied bomber command to plan the colossal bombing attack on which the offensive hinged.

On July 17, Bradley had chewed out General George Patton for bragging to the Third Army press corps about Patton's role in the forthcoming campaign. The press guys, in turn, couldn't help but brag about their a priori knowledge of the big operation to counterparts in the First Army press camp—all of which was a serious breach of security, ticking off Bradley no end. Patton blamed the mess on his overly aggressive chief public relations officer, Colonel Charles Blakeney, but it's hard to imagine that Blakeney had played up Patton's part in the plan without his boss' okay. Remarkably, Patton had not at that point been called into battle in Normandy and had been explicitly (and repeatedly!) ordered by Eisenhower, Bradley, and even Secretary of War Henry Stimson to keep his trap shut—yet was already in trouble for yakking out of school and trying to claim credit for a plan that wasn't his.[4]

Late on the afternoon of July 20, after Eisenhower had left for London, Bradley decided to sample Vouilly's chow for himself—and, while he was at it, clear up any misconceptions by giving the First Army correspondents a thorough briefing. If the press guys assigned to Bradley and Courtney Hodges were going to be covering the breakout, they should at least hear it described by its architect.

Bradley directed his personal aide, Major Chet Hansen, and his chief intelligence officer, Colonel Monk Dickson, to grab an easel and a map. The three of them hopped into Bradley's jeep and, its three-starred pennants flapping, motored toward Vouilly.

As it had been for much of the six weeks since the Allied invasion, the weather that evening was dismal—so dreary, in fact, that it was threatening to delay Bradley's offensive. The general's jeep no doubt stirred a commotion as, unannounced, it clattered up the dirt lane at Mme. Hamel's château. Reporters lounging in bunks or fumbling at typewriters must have jumped to their feet wide-eyed, tucking in shirttails as Bradley began greeting people.

"Why didn't you tell us you wanted to hold a press conference, General?" they protested. "We would have come over to your headquarters." In Liebling's recollection, Bradley chuckled and said that he didn't want to trouble such important people. But Liebling and other reporters deduced that there were legitimate security concerns behind Bradley's decision. If several dozen reporters and their drivers suddenly began traveling en masse toward Bradley's mobile CP, it might attract the attention of Vichy spies, who would conclude—correctly—that something big was up.

After being treated to a quick meal, Bradley, Dickson, Hansen, and their easel repaired to the shed and makeshift move theater behind the Hamels' detached field kitchen. Thirteen years later, when Liebling visited Mme. Hamel, Joe asked if she remembered the evening that the great General Bradley had come to visit.

"Yes," she recalled. "There were no movies that night."[5]

Instead of watching a Humphrey Bogart potboiler, reporters sat in the shed and witnessed an eyes-only briefing of the Allies' pending offensive. It was called Operation Cobra, Bradley explained, and was a modification of what had been planned all along to "stove in," as Liebling put it, Hitler's left wing in Normandy.

Bradley began by swearing everyone to secrecy, then prefaced his presentation with a typically self-effacing remark: "I may be sticking my neck out in predicting it," but this operation would effectively destroy the German Seventh Army. Using boxing imagery that delighted Liebling, Bradley proceeded to spell out the plan.

> General [Joe] Collins' VII Corps, so reinforced that it virtually constituted an army—four infantry and two armored divisions, I think—was to make the strike, amputating the arm that [General Charles] Gerhardt [of the 29th Division] had bound off. Then Patton's Third Army was to come into official being—it already existed incognito, behind the First Army line—and race through the hole south and west into Brittany. (The plan worked even better than that, of course, but a fighter starting a

combination of blows can't know in advance the other fellow's capacity to absorb them.)[6]

This was no mere feint, Bradley said, but a real haymaker: an all-out pummeling designed to flatten the Wehrmacht in northern France. The American breakout, Bradley said, was being carefully coordinated with Monty's renewed Operation Goodwood. If everything worked, Bradley's right hook and Monty's left cross would trap the enemy southeast of St.-Lô.

Pyle, Boyle, and Rooney were seated near Liebling in Mme. Hamel's shed that night, too. The four reporters had long admired Bradley and had seen the fruits of his leadership on two continents. But they didn't often get to see Bradley, logistician extraordinaire, in his element. It was only the third time that Liebling had watched Bradley deliver a lecture. The first occasion was in the spring of '43 in Béja, Tunisia, where Bradley, then the brand-new commander of II Corps, explained via maps how his army would ensnare the Nazis. The second came in February of '44 at Bradley's First Army headquarters in Bryanston Square, London. Without disclosing how or where, Bradley described the rationale behind D-Day—the way Allied seaborne and airborne troops would gain a toehold in *Festung Europa*.

Bradley's ascent through the ranks had been breathtaking—in less than a year and a half, he had gone from being an Eisenhower advisor without a portfolio to commanding the largest army in American history—but his demeanor hadn't changed. Liebling wrote that Bradley was the same "benevolent, pedagogical, and slightly apologetic" guy he'd always been.[7]

Professor Bradley may have lacked Eisenhower's charisma and Patton's prickliness, but he was long on substance. His presentation skills had been honed as a mathematics instructor at West Point, then under the exacting eye of George Marshall, as both a pupil and an instructor at Marshall's officers' training school at Fort Benning, Georgia.

In classic Fort Benning style, without consulting notes, that night Bradley walked reporters through a riveting overview of Cobra, citing from memory avenues of attack, key transportation arteries, the locations and strength of enemy troops, the likely German response, and how the Allies would seek to take advantage of different contingencies.

Pyle remembered Bradley pinpointing an area west of St.-Lô about five miles wide. "In that narrow segment we would have three infantry divisions, side by side," Ernie wrote later. "Right behind them would be another infantry and two armored divisions. Once a hole was broken, the armored divisions would slam through several miles beyond, then turn right toward the sea behind the Germans in that sector in the hope of cutting them off and trapping them."[8]

Bradley circumscribed a three-and-a-half-mile-by-one-mile rectangle south of the Périers–St.-Lô road and said that bombing and artillery fire would be concentrated there. A conventional artillery barrage or tactical bombing run would not be sufficient to dislodge the enemy. Instead, to kick off the assault, he was calling for something virtually unprecedented: a massive aerial bombardment from the "heavies." After the war, Liebling facetiously called Bradley's Cobra raid "the most impressive assemblage of air power ever up to then on view outside a Howard Hughes production."[9]

Pointing at the east-west highway, Bradley said he'd been adamant that Allied bombers use the road as a line of demarcation between friend and foe, keeping it as a compass point by approaching it from the west. The 366th Tactical Fighter Group, then stationed at Grandcamp, would lead the attack, dropping red smoke bombs to mark the enemy position. American troops would be pulled back some 1,500 yards—almost a mile—north of the road to give the heavies room to operate, Bradley said.

Bradley may or may not have disclosed that the day before (July 19), he had flown to England to meet with the joint bomber command brass at Stanmore, north of London. Bradley sat down with Air Chief Marshal Trafford Leigh-Mallory, pored over maps and weather forecasts, and got Leigh-Mallory's personal assurance—or so Bradley thought—that Allied bomber pilots would fly parallel to the road, then veer off south to drop their loads into the rectangle where the mechanized *Panzer Lehr* outfit and its lethal tanks lay concealed in the woods.

If Liebling, Boyle, Rooney, or Pyle, observers who knew firsthand the imprecision of airborne attacks, had qualms about Bradley's claims, there's no record that they broached them in Mme. Hamel's shed. Cobra would uncoil, Bradley promised, as soon as the weather cooperated.

As the briefing broke up, the correspondents stood in line to wish the general well, "like members of a congregation shaking hands with their minister," Liebling wrote.[10] The parishioners resolved to get as close to the front lines as public relations officers would allow so they could get what Pyle called "a worm's-eye view" of the aerial kickoff. But the weather stayed nasty—and Cobra wasn't launched for what turned out to be four long days.

IN THE SUMMER OF 1957, Liebling returned to the Château de Vouilly to thank Mme. Hamel for her hospitality during the war. The chatelaine was sitting outside under the shade of one of her poplars when Liebling arrived. Mme. Hamel greeted Liebling with a shout, telling him that she always knew that one day he would return.

"She rose," Liebling wrote, "a trifle heavier but even more impressive than I had remembered her, like a great, noble Percheron mare, white with age, getting up in a field."[11]

Mme. Hamel proudly showed Liebling scrapbook clippings about the château's role in the war. She also shared guest book inscriptions from Hal Boyle and Monk Dickson, both of whom had come back to Vouilly to pay their respects.

"To the good family of the Château de Vouilly," Dickson had scribbled, "which was the repository for a week of the secret of Cobra."[12]

WHEN COBRA FINALLY STRUCK, ITS first two bites proved disastrous, nearly poisoning the entire operation. On Sunday evening, July 23, Air Chief Marshal Leigh-Mallory flew in from Stanmore to eyeball the next morning's scheduled bombardment.

The weather was passable before dawn but soon turned ugly. By the time Leigh-Mallory unilaterally scrubbed the mission because of thick cloud cover, the tactical bombers in Normandy and some 1,600 heavies from different airfields in East Anglia had already taken off, armed to the gills. Bradley was aghast when most of the bombers came in due north, perpendicular to the Périers–St.-Lô road, not parallel from the west, as he had been promised. Still, for the most part, Leigh-Mallory's bombers pounded the correct targets that morning, even in a futile cause.

Joe Liebling was positioned with an artillery unit four miles behind the Thirtieth Division's jump-off spot. Once the smoke disappeared, he and other reporters couldn't understand why the armored units at the 30th spearhead weren't plunging ahead. It wasn't until later in the day that correspondents were told that Cobra had been postponed for twenty-four hours. And it wasn't until much later that they learned that some sixteen Allied heavies had tragically dropped their ordnance onto friendly trenches. The lead plane in that particular gaggle experienced mechanical problems with its bomb release; when the bombardier finally managed to unjam it, he dropped his load early—and the other fifteen bombardiers followed suit.[13] One hundred twenty-six members of the 30th were wounded by the misdirected bombs; some thirty were killed.

The awful accident and the slipshod coordination with bomber command did not deter Bradley from pushing forward with the planned attack once the weather cleared the following morning. After one more heated discussion on the evening of July 24, Bradley conceded defeat in his tug-of-war with Leigh-Mallory. It was too dangerous, the air brass argued, for the bombers to expose themselves to enemy antiaircraft batteries for that length of time by flying in on the parallel. The armada would again come in on the perpendicular and hope that the red markers from the 366th's P-47s would delineate the target.

This time there was no postponement in midmission. It was an awesome spectacle: No raid during the war, Andy Rooney wrote, called for so many planes to drop so many bombs in such a tiny area.[14] More than a thousand U.S. Eighth Air Force Forts and Libs and a comparable number of RAF Lancasters, Wellingtons, and Halifaxes, joined by nearly four hundred medium bombers and scores of P-47s armed with fragmentary bombs and a lethal new weapon known as napalm, came zooming in from the north. The P-47s dropped their red markers right in the heart of the enemy rectangle. When the heavies appeared, their bombs triggered such a deafening noise that each thud shook the curtains of the home a mile from the front that Bradley and Joe Collins were using as a forward command post.[15]

The impact was devastating. Within minutes, the *Panzer Lehr*'s forest had been reduced to a lunarscape; the strikes were so intense that afterward it was hard to distinguish the rims of bomb craters. So many trees were splintered that thousands of German soldiers were wounded by the wood that spewed from them. Thousands more were killed or deafened by the bombardment and the artillery barrage that immediately followed.

But as Rooney recalled, "Unfortunately for U.S. forces, there was a strong wind blowing from east to west. The heavy line of smoke and dust heaved into the air by the first wave [of bombers] was blown in a uniformly straight line directly west. Clouds of it obscured the new positions to which American forces had withdrawn."[16]

It all meant catastrophic confusion for the pilots, navigators, and bombardiers in subsequent waves. A disaster ensued that morning that was four times worse than the day before. There were three separate short-drop incidents, one of which nearly obliterated Ernie Pyle. The columnist was near the Fourth Division's leading edge; he heard something in the skies overhead that he'd never heard before: a "gigantic rattling noise as of huge ripe seeds in a mammoth dry gourd."

Pyle and everyone around him dove for cover, spreading out "like the cartoons of people flattened by steam rollers." He tried to squirm his way under a nearby wagon but gave up when bombs crashed too close.[17]

Nearly five hundred American soldiers were wounded in the short drops; more than 110 lost their lives, many of them in the 30th Division, the same guys who'd been hit the day before. One victim was the highest-ranking American Army officer killed in action during the war, sixty-one-year-old Lieutenant General Lesley J. McNair.[18]

McNair's body had absorbed a direct hit. His remnants had been thrown some twenty-five yards from the slit trench in which he'd taken cover; he was identified only by his three-starred shoulder patch and a scarred rifle butt that bore his initials. Since McNair's presence in France was a secret, he wasn't even afforded a burial with military honors. The short drops along the ill-starred Norman roadway turned out to be among the worst friendly-fire episodes of the war, in a league with Patton's paratrooper debacle in Sicily twelve months earlier.

Bede Irvin, the AP photographer and Boyle sidekick who'd shared a room with Andy Rooney at Grandcamp, was also killed by friendly fire on July 25. It took two days for the sad news to reach Rooney.

Rooney had left his barracks bag and some personal effects at Grandcamp, so in late July Andy returned. Irvin's belongings had already been shipped off to his widow in the States. He dejectedly sat on his cot, thinking about his pal Bede, wondering what Irvin might do if the situation were reversed. "My eyes stopped at the top of the four-drawer dresser Bede and I had shared. The picture! The picture of Margie that I had put there was gone! They had shipped my wife's picture along with Bede's possessions, back to *his* wife. When she unpacked them, she was going to be confronted by a picture of a pretty stranger that Bede had never mentioned to her."[19]

Rooney placed a series of "frantic" calls to AP in London. Irvin's effects were already en route, but were going through AP's offices in New York. He was able to have Margie's framed photograph removed before Bede's boxes were delivered to the grieving Kath Irvin.

Irvin was buried with full military honors at a cemetery in La Cambe, France, on what would have been his thirty-fourth birthday.[20]

LIEBLING WITNESSED THE COBRA BOMBARDMENT from the top-floor window of a Normandy farmhouse about five miles north of ground zero. Three ridges separated the farmland from Bradley's front line. Liebling watched squadrons of heavies zoom in from both sides, fly beyond the third ridge, and, unseen, release their bombs. "For two hours the air was filled with the hum of motors, and the concussions of the bombs that, even though they were falling five miles away, kept my sleeves fluttering."[21]

By then Liebling had hooked up with the headquarters battery of an artillery unit in the Big Red One. The unit's enlisted men were watching the aerial assault from the sloping ground underneath Liebling's window; they were rolling on the grass "with unsportsmanlike glee," Liebling wrote.

"Their emotion was crude but understandable. 'The more bombs we drop, the less fight there'll be left in them,' a soldier said, and, remembering the first bombs on Paris in 1940 and the bombings I have seen decent people undergo since then, I could not feel ashamed of the men's reaction."[22]

Liebling, Pyle, Rooney, and Boyle had all hoped, like their hero Bradley, that the four-mile-wide gap opened by Cobra's bomb carpet would immediately put the Germans on the run. But it didn't. A crestfallen Bradley had to report to Eisenhower on the night of the 25th that the Ninth Division had advanced only about a mile and a half, and the Fourth and the 30th approximately half that distance. Lightning Joe was at that point still bottled up. There was as yet no hole through which Patton and his Third Army tanks could surge.

But as Liebling could appreciate, that day's action was only the first exchange of blows. Within days, the enemy was back on its heels in a pell-mell retreat; the U.S. Army, cornered in hedgerows for nearly two months, was finally getting a chance to throw some haymakers.

THE DAY AFTER COBRA STRUCK, Hal Boyle wrote a story about Lieutenant Homer W. "Benny" Bennett, a reconnaissance pilot whose unarmed Piper Cub (fighter pilots dismissively called the Cubs Maytag Messerschmitts) was jumped by a covey of Focke-Wulfs—yet somehow survived. Bennett, from Sioux City, Iowa, and his observer, Lieutenant Edwin Maxey from Lincoln, Nebraska, were trolling over the crumbling enemy front at two thousand feet, pinpointing German gun and troop positions for artillery units.

"The first thing I knew," said Bennett, "eight Fw 190s were swarming around me, two coming directly toward me firing and a couple more from the sides. There was a terrific clatter from the engines and guns. I thought I was a goner."

Bennett had no choice but to do something bold. He turned his "grasshopper" directly into the flight path of the first two Focke-Wulfs, causing them to overshoot. "I did some dives, wingovers, and some other stuff that's never been named trying to get into the protection of our ack-ack batteries," Bennett told Boyle.

"[Bennett] slipped from beneath the nose of one overeager Nazi plane and it crashed into the ground and burst into flames," Boyle wrote. "The friendly ack-ack knocked down another German and then some wandering P-47 Thunderbolts pitched in on his side and sent the rest of the Nazis racing back toward Berchtesgaden [Hitler's Bavarian retreat]."[23]

Hermann Göring's Luftwaffe didn't often show up in northern France in the summer of '44—and when it did, its planes were usually manned by inexperienced pilots, which might explain how Lieutenants Bennett and Maxey lived to tell Boyle their tale.

Five days later Boyle encountered a group of Frenchwomen scavenging through the debris left behind by enemy soldiers fleeing the *Jabos*, the dreaded P-47s. "Farm wives and girls paw happily through the disordered and scattered personal effects left by the Nazis. They save everything from strings to bandages. From German uniforms they fashion clothing for themselves or suits for their children.

"But the prize discoveries in this harvest of ruin," Boyle wrote, "are long bars of precious laundry soap and fine pairs of leather shoes and rubber boots."[24]

The harvest of ruin was quickly spreading west, south, and east. Outside the German railway center at Rennes on August 3, Boyle heard about the exploits of a twenty-nine-year-old doughboy Hal began calling the Sergeant York of Brittany. By Boyle's reckoning, Private Donald McKay of Grand Island, Nebraska, had in the previous forty-eight hours killed six German soldiers, captured twenty-eight, and had twice been voluntarily led blindfolded to an enemy command post to plead with Nazi officers to give up.

Boyle arrived on the scene just as Private McKay was returning to the American lines outside Rennes after his second attempt to persuade the Germans to abandon their last-ditch efforts.

"They still want to make a fight of it," reported McKay to Lieutenant Colonel William Bailey of Danville, Virginia. "They can have a fight then," replied Bailey. "We will blow some sense into them."

A few moments later Boyle watched as artillery shells began thudding with deadly accuracy into the German redoubt, blowing a big enough hole in the line that Bailey's unit could muscle through. Rennes soon fell.

Later, Boyle sat down with McKay and got the blow-by-blow on the private's amazing day. McKay began sheepishly.

"I don't know how my commander is going to feel about all this," he said, acknowledging that he had no one to blame but himself for getting separated from his unit twenty-four hours earlier. "Yesterday, I was caught up in an acre of high grass by a German outfit. They were spraying bullets everywhere and I had to pick my spots and keep moving to keep from being killed.

"I picked off two of them with my rifle. Then I saw two Germans lying by a machine gun. I shot and hit one, breaking his back. That unnerved the other, an officer, and he stood up and waved a white handkerchief."

The Wehrmacht officer had no idea that McKay was by himself. So when McKay barked orders to have the officer and his men come out with their hands up, they obliged.

McKay was stunned when more than two dozen men emerged from the weeds, all yelling "*Kamerad*," which suggests that most were Eastern European conscripts. Suddenly a group of French Resistance fighters came running up and helped McKay disarm the enemy soldiers. McKay tied twenty-two pistols to a tent rope and gave them to the FFI guerrillas. He was marching the prisoners back toward the American lines when four of them abruptly made a break for it. But they stayed bunched up, making themselves easy targets. McKay killed three and wounded the other in the hind end.

He delivered his prisoners to the first substantial American unit he saw, then went off to find his company. Across the next field a French girl warned him that German soldiers were lurking close by, but McKay continued on. An enemy helmet suddenly came into view and McKay fired, his bullet pinging off the helmet. Someone with a German accent shouted, "Don't do that!"

McKay looked around and realized that he was surrounded. A dozen or more enemy soldiers had him covered from every angle.

"No shoot?" they hollered at McKay. "No shoot!" McKay answered.

Then the Nebraskan tried to argue with them to surrender, pointing out the futility of fighting on. They grudgingly agreed but said they had orders to fight to the death. When McKay volunteered to take the argument to their commander, they blindfolded him and marched him through their lines. The one English-speaking officer in the company wasn't there, however, so McKay agreed to come back in an hour, this time accompanied by an interpreter. The Germans escorted him back through their lines and McKay told them to wait there: he'd be back soon.

North of Rennes McKay found Lieutenant Colonel Bailey, who sent him back toward the front under a white flag, escorted by translator Art Kallman, a private from Erie, Pennsylvania. The pair was shot at a couple of times by sniping Germans but Kallman bellowed, in German, "Safe conduct!" and they proceeded without incident through the enemy position.

The same group of German soldiers that McKay had left an hour before were there to greet them. Again blindfolded, the two GIs were led to the German command post, which turned out to be in a dank basement three floors underground, the better to escape the constant artillery pounding and *Jabo* attacks. The enemy colonel opened the dialogue by asking why the Americans were there. Through Kallman, McKay urged the Germans to give up to avert "much bloodshed and death." The commander responded: "This is war." To which McKay rejoined, "But we will go through you." The commander conceded that the Americans were good soldiers but said that the Germans were better and were fully prepared to fight to the end. He complimented McKay and Kallman on their bravery before sending them back to deliver his defiant message.

As McKay, with Lieutenant Colonel Bailey nearby, finished relating his death-defying story to Boyle, the private expressed concern that his commanding officer would prosecute him for being a "straggler."

"'You stay with us,' said [Bailey] with a grin," Boyle wrote. "'I think we can fix things up with your commander.'"[25]

ANDY ROONEY AND HIS JEEP were in Brittany, shadowing Sherman tanks that belonged to the Third Army. Outside the walled medieval village of Vannes on August 3, Rooney uncovered an extraordinary story—but had to sit on it for two weeks. When the censors finally allowed the *Stars and Stripes* to publish Andy's piece, it must have delighted Joe Liebling.

A French paratroop battalion of 120 hardened commandoes had been dropped outside Vannes on D-Day eve. Their mission was to lay low, if possible, and arm and train Brittany's FFI, disrupting enemy communications and supply lines whenever possible. Twelve days after their drop, the battalion was holed up at a big farmhouse and barn near Puy-Maladroit, well behind enemy lines. Some four hundred FFI members were holed up with them.

The local German garrison commander became suspicious when Allied planes were spotted dropping parachutes of supplies around the farm. At four a.m. on June 18, a force of several hundred enemy soldiers, mainly unhappy Georgian conscripts, marched on the farm. The French paratroopers and their FFI compatriots were lying in wait with machine guns. They let the enemy close to within a few yards before opening up. "The withering burst cut the German ranks in two," Rooney wrote, "and the remainder retreated in disarray."

The garrison commander returned to the farm with a much stronger contingent—some three thousand men—and launched one attack after another. The battle raged all day and into the night as the Frenchmen fought off each assault. Before long, some five hundred Germans bodies were stacked up in a bloody circle around the farmhouse. Finally, sometime after midnight, the French paratroopers and their FFI compatriots took advantage of a lull to slip away, vanishing into the forests of "friendly Brittany," as Rooney put it.[26]

Although the Germans put big prices on their heads, the paratroopers remained undetected until early August when, with Vannes now under siege by the Americans, they suddenly materialized to fight side by side with GIs. By August 5, Rooney and the FFI were inside Vannes' ancient walls, toasting the French paratroopers.

JOE LIEBLING AND LIEUTENANT ROY Wilder, Jr., a First Army PRO, jeep driver, and hell-raising buddy of many a reporter, were also offering thanks in Brittany that week. For a month, Liebling had been extolling the pleasures of a certain bordello in Rennes, claiming that in the '20s, it had had no peer in France.

As their jeep approached Rennes in early August of '44, however, the pair got depressed: The city had been so flattened by bombs and artillery that almost no building had escaped damage. They feared the worst. But as the ninety-six-year-old Wilder related in 2011, as their jeep crept into downtown Rennes, Liebling practically jumped for joy: The brothel was not only intact, but open for business!

Liebling turned to Wilder and proclaimed: "The Lord takes care of the pure of heart."[27]

THAT SAME WEEK, BOYLE, TOO, unearthed a story of French defiance, this one a band of five youths operating undercover on the Cotentin Peninsula not far from Valognes. The five youngsters, some farmers, others students, escaped into the woods one night when a Maquis leader informed them that one of their fathers had been killed on a Resistance raid; as a reprisal, the Gestapo was rounding up the young men of Valognes and forcing them into slave labor.

For four months, the boys "played Robinson Crusoe," as Boyle put it, southeast of St.-Sauveur-le-Vicomte in the thick foliage known as the *bois de Limore*. After the night of June 5 the boys emerged to help lost Allied paratroopers and expose enemy strongholds, "which American guns promptly wiped out," Boyle wrote.[28] One GI mortar attack on a hidden enemy machine gun nest killed three German soldiers and forced the rest to flee. The boys bunked one night with members of an airborne outfit that had gotten disoriented.

Earlier, the boys had survived in the woods by trapping small game, mainly rabbits. They had found an old woodcutter's shed and spent cold nights there, although they didn't dare light a fire for fear of being discovered.[29]

Boyle interviewed a "freckled blond-haired boy of twenty" whom he called Pierre but never identified by his real name because the surviving members of the family feared retribution. Pierre's older sister and brother-in-law were both active in the Paris Maquis—and easy targets for the Gestapo in the still-occupied capital if Boyle even hinted at their identity. It was Pierre's father who'd been killed by the Germans while performing Resistance work. He was also the lad who had escorted fifty American paratroopers into a town on the Cotentin, then watched as weeping villagers gave them garlands of flowers. The GIs were embarrassed as Pierre led the liberators to the next enemy hideout across some marshland; once out of sight, they dumped their wreaths.

Joe Liebling, too, saw delirious Frenchwomen hand out flowers and bushels of kisses to GIs, some of whom were sheepish and others who didn't hesitate to lock lips. By early August Liebling was riding down the same road to Coutances and Avranches that he'd taken four years and two months earlier, when he'd escaped Paris in the company of Tex O'Reilly and Waverly Root, forlornly watching tens of thousands of refugees resign themselves to their fate.

But now he was moving in the other direction—and villagers by the thousands were flooding the roads to embrace their saviors.

"Last week, as four years ago, the road was choked with vehicles moving as slowly as a trickle of water through dust," Liebling told *New Yorker* readers in a letter dated August 4, "but this time, instead of autobuses and pitiful automobiles loaded with civilians, the traffic was half-tracks, empty ambulances, tank destroyers, two-and-a-half-ton trucks, the small, track carriers (called 'weasels') that take ammunition across country, and, scattered through all the heavy stuff, jeeps."[30]

Liebling, like every veteran of North Africa, marveled at the sudden impotence of the mighty Luftwaffe. Early in the war, Allied troops and reporters had constantly cast nervous eyes skyward, searching for marauding Messerschmitts like the ones that spoiled Liebling's breakfast at Thélepte. But by mid-'44, "soldiers grinned every time they heard an airplane motor," Liebling wrote.[31]

Even after the breakout, when there were spectacular triumphs at every point on the Allied front, Joe stayed loyal to his personal security detail: the boys in the Big Red One.

"Wherever the First was, the best story was sure to be," Liebling wrote. "Because it was the most thoroughly tested American division, it had to go into the trickiest places. This saved a reporter the trouble of trying to divine official intentions; while my colleagues stared helplessly at maps . . . I had only to stick to the First and the Great Riddle would come clear in due course."[32]

Divisional artillery commands were nicknamed "div artys." For most of that month, Liebling's First Division div arty hopscotched from one observation spot to the next, usually a tall farmhouse or dwelling that had somehow escaped destruction. In one five-day period, Liebling's unit moved to a different CP four times, including a couple of places that the Germans had occupied (and nearly wrecked) just a day or two before. Every div arty team had a switchboard, a set of maps, and a ton of communications gear. They would arrive at a new location, instantly set up their equipment, communicate with their bosses, quickly run through the calculations needed to establish a target, phone it to the guys manning the guns—and await the go-ahead to authorize firing.

That first week after the breakout, armored divisions and the infantries in their wake were moving so fast that there was almost no safe place to aim big guns. "It was an artillerist's nightmare," Liebling wrote. "[T]here was no place they could shoot without fear of hitting some of our own people." Corps headquarters had marked "no fire" zones in red on their situation maps; pretty soon all the maps looked like a big lipstick smear.

Artillerymen, Liebling observed, led a strange existence. A cribbage game would often break out at night, even when there were targets to fire at. The phone would ring, an officer would get up from the cribbage table, mutter "uh-huh" a couple of times, hang up the phone, then share something like, "Infantry patrols report some sort of Jerry movement at that road junction at 4124. Mediums can reach it." The officer would then grab a different telephone, bark the command, and return to the cribbage match. "Outside, in the night, twelve hundred pounds of high explosive [would] scream toward the dark crossroad twenty-five times, at short, irregular intervals," Liebling wrote.[33]

ON DAY FIVE OF BRADLEY'S offensive, Boyle and John MacVane of NBC found themselves in Hautteville along the Norman coast, caught in a traffic jam with members of an American armored unit. They were trying to chase the enemy, Boyle wrote, "like remorseless steel bloodhounds." It was a Saturday evening, and Boyle watched a priest who had been active in the Resistance lead a procession of villagers to a roadside shrine. Many of the women were dressed in black to mourn loved ones buried in 1940; the children were wearing their Sunday best.

"They grouped around the slender concrete pillar surrounded by a life-sized crucifix," Boyle wrote. "In the bar of the cross were stuck French, British, and American flags."

The priest led his parishioners in singing a hymn of thanksgiving to their liberators. A pair of French policemen whom MacVane and Boyle had given a ride joined in the chorus. As soon as the priest began offering his benediction, the GIs, who'd been observing in uncomprehending silence, took off their helmets and knelt in prayer. One of the gendarmes translated for Boyle: "We pray that these men who have left their land and crossed the sea to liberate us will return to the home in which they live with safety and with peaceful hearts."

As he spoke, the priest pointed to the figure of Christ on the crucifix. "Remember, you have known torture, too, for four years, but you held out, dear friends. Now that is ended, thanks to our allies, who have brought us liberation. It is for us now to sacrifice together until the war is ended."

The priest turned to the American soldiers, held out his arms, and said, "Goodbye. *Au revoir. Merci! Merci! Merci!*"

"[The priest] came over and shook hands with many of the tankmen and then returned to his parishioners," Boyle's column concluded. "They followed him in the setting sun across waving wheat fields to their homes. Soon the tank column started down the road to battle."[34]

AT THE SAME TIME, ON Liebling's fourth day with the div arty, Joe happened upon a farmhouse where a dead soldier from a Schutzstaffel (SS) division had been left behind—a sure sign that the Germans had bolted in a hurry, because they normally took care of their dead. By then Liebling had seen more than his share of decaying bodies—and he reveled in playing de Maupassant. The wannabe coroner-detective went in for a postmortem.

There was a typewritten form in one of the dead man's pockets that the soldier had filled out but apparently had not given his commander. It requested emergency leave to go home. Under "reason," the man had written, "Bombing deaths in family—urgent telegram from wife."[35]

Jumping from one abandoned French home to another gave Liebling more investigative opportunities. The retreating Germans, having ripped though every drawer and cupboard looking for food and liquor, left behind chaos. A family's history—photo albums, personal mementoes, church and school records—would be strewn all over the house by the time Liebling's div arty got there.

Most reporters would have ignored the clutter to trade slugs of calvados with the artillerymen or jump into a cribbage game. Not Liebling. With his affection for French culture and custom, he was able to piece together the lives of these uprooted families.

One family's young son had been a prisoner of war since the spring of '40, Liebling deduced after juxtaposing a 1915 baptismal notice with a 1940 leaflet describing how French families could communicate with loved ones now imprisoned in Germany. It was Liebling at his best, taking mundane details and making them magnificent.

————

UNLIKE A LOT OF JOURNALIST-HISTORIANS, Liebling never skewered World War II generals, even after the war when he could have settled scores with arrogant commanders who'd snubbed him. Joe found pointless the contentious debate, which continues to this day, over the action—or, more accurately, inaction—of the Allied high command in early to mid-August 1944. In Liebling's view, Eisenhower, Montgomery, and Bradley did the best job they could defeating an odious enemy; engaging in after-the-fact recrimination served no purpose. Andy Rooney, for his part, was resentful of "scholars" who rewrite history by arguing that the Allies squandered a big chance to end the war then and there.

Rooney, Liebling, and Boyle were eyewitnesses to the byzantine events that occurred in northern France that month. All three began August out west in Brittany as American armored units pushed toward the ports of Brest and St.-Malo, then moved south and east as General Bradley hustled his troops to exploit new opportunities.

By August 7, Boyle was with General Troy Middleton's U.S. Eighth Corps as it attacked the German sea supply base at St.-Malo. The next day, Boyle went up in a Piper Cub to survey the situation. "From this sky perch besieged St.-Malo can be seen billowing black and white smoke, stabbed with flashes of flame," he wrote. "American tanks and infantry advance behind a rolling artillery barrage and smash in street battles toward the port's fortress citadel, where the Nazis have barricaded themselves in a Stalingrad-like stand." In his two years of covering the war, it was one of the most spectacular sights he'd seen, Boyle told readers.[36]

In St.-Malo, Boyle was subjected to the same frustrating German defiance that Private Donald McKay had encountered in Rennes the week before: an obdurate German refusal to give up. Boyle and other reporters soon came to call the commander of the German holdouts, Andreas von Aulock, the Mad Colonel. Aulock, whom enemy prisoners described as a pathetic drunk, refused to listen to reason, despite repeated pleas. On August 10 Boyle filed a piece about how the beleaguered defenders of St.-Malo eventually had no choice but to shoot their officers so they could surrender and avoid annihilation.[37]

Prisoners told Boyle that they'd hoped the German counterattack at Mortain, launched on the nights of August 6 and 7 some forty miles east, would come to their rescue. It didn't come anywhere close, of course: Mortain was lunacy.[38] Had Hitler ordered a strategic retreat to the Seine, it would have given the battered Wehrmacht a natural barrier beyond which to regroup and make a creditable stand. Instead, *der Führer* sacked Field Marshal Rundstedt, who in Hitler's eyes had committed treason by advocating a withdrawal, and replaced him with Field Marshal Günther von Kluge, a more pliable sycophant. Erwin Rommel had been hospitalized on July 17 after being severely wounded by an Allied fighter-bomber, so von Kluge was operating without the two chief architects of the German defenses in Normandy. Hans Speidel, Rommel's chief deputy, was as appalled by Hitler's reckless strategy as von Rundstedt had been.

A cabal of German officers that included, at least peripherally, Speidel and Rommel attempted to assassinate Hitler on July 20 at *Wolfsschanze* ("Wolf's Lair"), *der Führer's* command outpost in East Prussia. Hitler barely survived the bomb blast, which killed four and wounded two dozen others.

Two weeks later, Hitler's stooge von Kluge was told to attack westward toward Avranches through the slim corridor between the See and Sélune Rivers. Hitler's stated objective was to drive a wedge between the Allied armies in Normandy and Brittany. He called it Operation Lüttich, after the Belgian battle where the Kaiser's forces had scored an early and decisive victory in the Great War.

The historic talisman didn't work. There was so much radio traffic between Berlin and von Kluge that the Ultra intercept teams at Bletchley Park and in northern France were able to predict the time and location of the German assault. Omar Bradley had the better part of three days to prepare a riposte, even confiding to Chet Hansen that the desperate Hitler had become the Allies' best ally.

Hitler sent the remnants of three and a half *Panzer* units, plus other underequipped outfits, against the U.S. 30th Division, the same GIs who two weeks earlier had been twice bombed by their own planes. The Germans fought gamely, ripping a hole in the 30th's line that ultimately proved too small to exploit. Bradley checkmated every move, hurling reinforcements and armaments into the fight that von Kluge didn't have. Patton's Third Army entered the Mortain fray, capturing Le Mans to the south on August 8, although its heroics weren't publicly acknowledged until midmonth.

At noon on August 9, the omnipresent Ninth Air Force struck again, its *Jabos* raining mayhem on von Kluge's mechanized units. The RAF's rocket-firing Hawker Typhoon fighter-bombers proved invaluable in the Mortain campaign, too, destroying dozens of tanks running out in the open. By August 13, the Germans had reversed course and were limping away.[39]

Suddenly Bradley was presented with the stuff of every commander's dreams: a panicked enemy on the run. The best-case scenario he'd broached three weeks earlier with the First Army press corps had actually come to pass: There was now a distinct prospect of linking up with the Canadians and Brits on the north and east and trapping the retreating Germans in a pocket. The meeting point for the entrapment was not far from where Bradley had anticipated, near the villages of Falaise and Argentan.

It would take sharp coordination between Patton's Third, wheeling north and east from Le Mans, with the British Second and the Canadian First, slugging south and west, having at last broken free from the outskirts of Caen. With Patton rapidly closing the gap, Bradley at that moment issued his most contentious order of the war, a move that, decades later, still draws the ire of many historians. The 12th Army Group boss called a halt to Patton's advance. Patton had, with his usual hubris, gone farther north than Bradley had directed, encroaching on territory that had been given to Montgomery's Twenty-first Army Group. Bradley's other ostensible reason for reining in the Third Army was that it had already outrun its supply lines. But Bradley surely feared a reprise of the friendly-fire debacle along the Périers–St.-Lô road two weeks earlier. The notorious "gap" was not closed until August 19—day six of the German retreat—when Canadian and Polish troops finally moved into the village of Falaise and the Americans captured Dreux.[40] Somewhere between twenty thousand and forty thousand German soldiers—estimates vary wildly—slipped through the pocket.

Andy Rooney was advancing with the 90th Infantry Division and arrived near Dreux in time to see firsthand the dismemberment of the German army. The *Jabos*, P-51 Mustangs, Typhoons, and Allied artillerymen did a murderously effective job in strafing the fleeing enemy.

"I've tried to compare what I've read in the history books to what I saw and there's no comparison," Rooney wrote after the war. "What do you historians want, anyway? In an area thirty miles long and twenty miles wide, 30,000 Germans were killed and 92,000 were taken prisoner. A lot of them were from the elite Fifth and Seventh Panzer Divisions. Is that a big failure?"[41]

Rooney's enemy casualty figures may be a bit inflated, but his view of Allied operations around Falaise in mid-August 1944 wasn't: a better name for "gap" would have been "trap," he always maintained. By the time Rooney got there, watching from nearby hills, the pocket had been stitched. When, under the cloak of darkness on August 20, several thousand Germans emerged from the Forêt de Gouffern near Chambois and tried to skulk out of the valley, Allied artillery decimated them. "It was a shooting gallery," Rooney remembered. "I can't believe anything in the war, including Stalingrad, was any worse for German troops." When the carnage finally ended, Rooney pointed out, the better part of the three dozen–plus enemy divisions in northern France had been "chopped up and sent into disorganized flight."[42]

On August 13 Hal Boyle was with the Fifth Division of Patton's Third Army as they pushed through Argentan on their way to Chartres. "From a wheat field overlooking Argentan," Boyle wrote, "I could see the vanguard of the great Nazi retreat try to stab its way through a bottleneck twelve miles wide between this town and the city of Falaise." Boyle called the Allied envelopment "a steel vise." Every enemy escape route was under heavy artillery fire, he wrote.

Through field glasses, Boyle watched an artillery unit "beat to pieces" a

German convoy. An Army captain named Albert G. Kelly from San Jose, California, was in constant radio contact with the P-51s circling overhead. As soon as Kelly received word via walkie-talkie that German tanks were trying to break through at the head of the valley near Carrouges, he got on the radio and dispatched the Mustangs. As the P-51s dove on the enemy tanks, the artillery and tank guys cheered.[43]

On the road toward the ancient city of Chartres, Patton's forward units found themselves mobbed by ecstatic villagers who "bombarded the grinning tankmen with roses and besieged them with wine," Boyle wrote. When they reached the walled city three days later, there was trepidation that its magnificent Gothic cathedral had been seriously damaged. Through his binoculars, however, Boyle could see the cathedral's tower looming over the city's rubble. The GIs sent into Chartres to mop up the remaining enemy snipers were told to use only small arms and aim their fire away from the church.

The cathedral had sustained only superficial wounds—some bullet scrapes, a few windows broken, but nothing that couldn't be fixed, Boyle noted. A priest and the head of the seminary took Boyle on a tour, proudly pointing out that at the start of the war, they'd had the foresight to hide the cathedral's precious stained glass.[44]

LIEBLING, WHO ALSO WAS CLOSE to the action, always thought the controversy about the Falaise Gap was much ado about nothing. In mid-August '44, he was still attached to the First Division artillery unit that was jumping almost daily to different reconnaissance posts. Among the correspondents in northern France at the time, the enemy's slipping away at Falaise wasn't considered a big deal. Only in the postmortem following the Battle of the Bulge, when it surfaced that some of the German soldiers steamrolling through the Ardennes had slipped Falaise's noose, did the issue become a cause célèbre. Omar Bradley inflamed the debate by somewhat second-guessing himself in his memoirs, intimating that perhaps he had been too cautious in the wake of the rout at Mortain. The three scribes on the spot—Liebling, Boyle, and Rooney—would have none of it. Nor does contemporary historian John McManus, who correctly calls Falaise a great, if flawed, victory.[45]

IN AUGUST BOYLE, AND TO a lesser degree Rooney, yo-yoed between covering Patton's Third Army and Courtney Hodges' First. Liebling, though, stayed exclusively with the First and its Big Red One; most nights Joe spent at the First Army press camp, wherever it happened to be. After the breakout, the camp moved from Vouilly about twenty miles southeast, to a muddy apple orchard outside Canisy. The boys were roughing it again: The palmy days of Mme. Hamel's bottomless spigot were over; the mess tent reverted to pedestrian Army chow.

Hodges' guys were moving so quickly that within a few days the press camp was uprooted to a shabby mansion farther south, on the periphery of Forêt de St. Sever, not far from Vire. By now the traveling carnival and their PRO roustabouts—Roy Wilder, Jr., and Jack Roach among them—had it down to a science: the tents were pitched behind the house, the wireless trucks and equipment were positioned out front, and the censors and reporters set up shop "amid the shards of elegance" of the formerly opulent château, as Leibling put it.

Liebling and his colleagues spent their days in hot pursuit of the best stories about the battered Germans and the brave troops chasing them. In the evenings, as they banged away on their typewriters, they had to carefully choose chairs; many in the St. Sever house would disintegrate if plopped in too quickly. Vire had been one of Liebling's favorite Norman haunts as a young man. Now he had to avert his eyes when driving through the town: It had been virtually annihilated. It broke Liebling's gluttonous heart that most of Vire's restaurants had been bombed out of business, since he'd been bragging about Vire's brasseries for weeks.

Within five days, however, Liebling and company were off to the First Army's next press camp, at a down-at-the-heels lake resort at Bagnoles de l'Orne. There, they actually got to stay indoors with something approximating running water. It was still Normandy, but steadily, irrevocably, Joe Liebling's road was leading back to Paris.[46]

ON AUGUST 15, 1944, AS Liebling, Boyle, and Rooney were fixated on events around Falaise, their old friend Homer Bigart of the *New York Herald Tribune* had finally set foot in France, albeit five hundred miles south. Bigart was covering the Allies' clandestine assault on the Îles d'Hyères islands, part of the long-debated and long-delayed Operation Dragoon—the invasion of southern France.

Churchill had never been enamored of attacking the Riviera; earlier that summer, in fact, the prime minister had pleaded with Roosevelt and Marshall to scrub the operation, claiming a second offensive in France was no longer needed to deliver a knockout blow. The prime minister for good reason was overruled: Dragoon hastened the German demise and liberated a swath of the occupied Reich that had been terrorized by the Gestapo.

Once Rome had fallen in early June, Bigart stayed in the Eternal City for several weeks, filing stories about war-ravaged Italy's struggles to recover from two decades of Mussolini. At one point Bigart was covering the interim Italian parliament's effort to "abolish" Fascism. When a government aide ran up to inform Bigart and other journalists that there had been a delay in the proceedings, Homer turned to his colleagues and cracked that the Italians probably needed more time "to p-p-put in the l-l-loopholes."[47] Thirteen months in the Mediterranean Theater hadn't dulled his mordant wit.

Nor had it dulled Bigart's appreciation for culture and antiquity. In a piece filed a week after Rome was redeemed, he pointed out that the Nazis may have been respectful toward the capital's art, but had senselessly ransacked museums a few miles south. Ironically, the Lake Nemi relics of the Emperor Caligula had been salvaged by Mussolini in 1929 but savaged by Il Duce's partners fifteen years later. Before retreating north, German soldiers torched galleries, lopped off the heads of ancient statuary, and confiscated or desecrated some of the most revered paintings in Italian history. When Bigart visited on June 11, all that was left of Lake Nemi's national museum was "a handful of ashes and some bronze nails."[48]

Three days later, Bigart told the story of two American air gunners who were among the fifteen Allied prisoners of war "enjoying asylum" inside the Vatican. Sergeants Anthony Brodniak of New Jersey and Bernard Scalisi of New Orleans had been on a bomber shot down over Viterbo in April. They managed to elude capture for a week as they snuck forty miles south to Rome. Finding the sanctuary of the Vatican was the dream of every shot-down flier and escaped POW in the Mediterranean; hundreds tried, but few got to experience it. Brodniak and Scalisi scaled the sacred venue's twelve-foot-high wall and were safeguarded by Vatican officials.

Bigart was told by Archbishop Testa that during the course of the war nineteen Allied soldiers had succeeded in making it inside the Vatican: eleven Britons, two Canadians, two Poles, one Australian, one New Zealander—and Scalisi and Brodniak. "They had a good time here," Testa told Bigart, smiling. "They walked in the Vatican gardens and got rations of cigarettes."[49]

On July 11, art aficionado Bigart was back, this time with a piece about how the Nazis had absconded with two paintings by Titian as well as Raphael's *Madonna of the Divine Love*. In all, a dozen canvases worth more than $3 million had been stolen from galleries from Naples to Monte Cassino. Members of the Hermann Göring Panzer Division, perhaps acting on orders from their art-loving (and thoroughly corrupt) namesake, were suspected of being the culprits. Bigart's source on art thievery was Major Ernest T. DeWald, who in peacetime served as a professor of art and archaeology at Princeton University. DeWald helped direct the Allied Control Commission on antiquities and monuments, a big job given the depth of Nazi thieving. There could be no doubt, DeWald told Bigart, "that the paintings were stolen by persons who knew just what they wanted." The price tag on the purloined treasures would be added to the Germans' postwar reparations bill, Bigart informed readers.[50]

BY MID-JULY BIGART HAD REJOINED Lieutenant General Mark W. Clark's belated push north. On July 18, the day that Liebling, Rooney, and Boyle watched St.-Lô fall, Homer reported on the Fifth Army's breakthrough behind the Renaissance city of Livorno, a key Tyrrhenian port. Buttressed by the "equally spectacular" Polish spearhead along the Adriatic, the Allies were now closing in on two of ancient Italy's gems: Pisa and Florence.[51] In the six weeks since the capture of Rome, the Fifth Army had progressed some one hundred miles. Yet beyond pushing ever farther north, nearly a year into the Italian campaign there was still no clear-cut military objective.

Eleven days after Livorno fell, Bigart was with New Zealand troops as they locked horns with the 15th Regiment of the Panzer Grenadier Division on the heights five miles southwest of Florence. After all those months of watching Field Marshal Albert Kesselring counterpunch, Bigart had developed an appreciation for his rearguard brilliance.[52]

It was evident that Kesselring was buying time; Florence and the guts of the Gothic Line would fall soon. When the line collapsed five days later, Bigart was with a South African regiment in the Eighth Army as they entered the City of Lilies. Bigart had been telling readers for months that the Nazis had declared Florence a "neutral" city; art devotees had hoped that meant Kesselring's forces would forgo wanton destruction. Those hopes were dashed on August 4, when Bigart revealed that, although the bejeweled Pitti Palace had escaped serious damage, the Germans had cruelly blown up five of the city's six ancient bridges.

The only bridge left intact, the professorial Bigart explained, was so narrow it could not have been used by Allied mechanized units. It was the Ponte Vecchio, the "Old Bridge," with its hoary jewelry shops. As the Allies fought their way to the banks of the Arno, the Germans detonated explosives on the five wider bridges, all of which dated to the thirteenth century.[53]

How Bigart managed to do his homework on these antiquities amid artillery and mortar fire is unclear. It's not as if there was a tour guide handing out brochures as the Germans strung their dynamite. But what's remarkable is the seamless way he was able to weave cultural and historical references into his combat narratives.

In one paragraph, he would define the heroes of that day's skirmishing, being careful to identify GIs by name and hometown. Then he would shift gears to explain how the present battle was linked to a larger Allied strategy, then juxtapose that with another historical allusion to Roman times or the First World War. It was all testament to Bigart's voracious appetite for learning, to his eclectic knowledge of just about everything, and to his infamous play-dumb act, the unending asking of questions.

ELEVEN DAYS LATER, BIGART took his act to another special amphibious operation, this one in the French Riviera—and it was almost as harrowing as the August 1943 raid on Monte Cipolla in Sicily. Dragoon planners determined that the German artillery garrison on the Îles d'Hyères, a trio of desolate islands that guarded the western approach to the invasion beaches, had to be silenced at the outset.

"Aerial reconnaissance had disclosed what appeared to be four medium coastal guns near a lighthouse on a bald knob," Bigart told readers. "No ship could the reach the western sector of the beachhead in safety as long as this battery was able to fire." Knocking out these coastal guns, Bigart wrote, demanded "an amphibious operation unusual for its emphasis on stealth rather than overwhelming firepower."[54]

Descendants of two gritty commando outfits, the U.S. Army's Darby's Rangers and the U.S.–Canadian Devil's Brigade, the raiders had trained long and hard at Lake Albano south of Rome and later at Santa Maria di Castellabate. In early August, the commandoes moved to their staging area off the island of Corsica. Bigart joined them there, watching them daub their faces with paint and charcoal, then noiselessly climb into the transport ships anchored three miles off the coast.

The *Herald Tribune* reporter settled in a small rubber boat as the commandoes silently paddled to the Île du Levant and its tiny sister island, Île de Port-Cros. They landed undetected.

"Long trained in mountain fighting, they scaled the rocky bluffs in darkness and, wrestling with the dense tangle of maquis undergrowth, emerged on a trail that brought them to the rear of strong enemy positions dominating the only beach available to landing craft," Bigart wrote.

Île du Levant was about a mile across; a thin dirt path up its spine linked the lighthouse and harbor to an abandoned penitentiary and to the remnants of a long-deserted nudist colony. It took Bigart's column two hours of "stumbling and groping" to reach the dirt track.

The commandoes were getting ready to launch their ground assault when "the sky went suddenly red," Bigart wrote. They learned later that a German patrol boat leaving its base at Toulon had struck a mine and exploded.

Incredibly, there was still no sign that the Germans had been alerted to their presence. "There had been a few nervous bursts from a machine gun on our left, but nothing at all from the direction of the main objective on our right," Bigart reported. "Toward dawn there was a lively chatter of small-arms fire and a few mortar shells came slamming down."[55]

As the sky began to brighten, the Allied commandoes captured their first prisoner, an ack-ack gunner from Poland who'd been forced into duty years earlier. The Pole gladly guided them to the dugouts where the German commander and most of his nineteen-man crew were still asleep.

The commander of Île du Levant was, curiously, a young lieutenant, Bigart noticed—not the caliber of officer who should have been in charge of a key coastal battery, although the lieutenant did have the wherewithal to toss a machine gun down a well so the Allies couldn't seize it intact. His artillery and antiaircraft crew consisted entirely of Polish conscripts; like their compatriot, they couldn't wait to throw their hands up.

Île de Port-Cros' mainly Canadian invaders had a tougher slog. An old French couple who lived inside the lighthouse were convinced that the Germans had secreted themselves in the island's caves. It turned out that the enemy soldiers, many heavily armed, had hunkered down in dilapidated cabins that belonged to the old nudist settlement, which in its heyday had spread across both islands. Four Devil's Brigade members were killed before HMS *Ramillies* was called on to provide a well-targeted rocket attack.

Within hours, Île de Port-Cros belonged to the Allies, too. A formidable threat to Dragoon had been eliminated.

DRAGOON WAS DUBBED THE CHAMPAGNE Campaign because the invasion was fought around Cannes and St.-Tropez and other exotic places in the Riviera. Today, it has been virtually forgotten, which is a shame because the Allied fighting was exemplary and the contributions of the Resistance were extraordinary.

Two days after he arrived on the French mainland following the raid on the Îles d'Hyères, Bigart interviewed a German prisoner, an *Oberstleutnant* from Koblenz. The two of them were gazing at an unnamed harbor—almost assuredly St.-Tropez—jammed full of Allied ships being unloaded.

"I have seen more American equipment in one day," the German officer told Bigart, "than of our own in the last six months. I have a relative in America, and if I had had enough money, I would have gone there, too."[56]

Bigart's interviewee was not alone. Many Germans fought hard in the south of France, but more than a few were as eager to surrender as the Polish conscripts on Île du Levant. The Allied invasion of some two hundred thousand men was headed by Lieutenant General Alexander "Sandy" Patch, a personal favorite of George Marshall.

Patch was chosen after Mark Clark's wobbly performance in Italy. Clark's military and political judgment remained dubious: He was as adamantly opposed to Dragoon as Churchill. Instead of attacking the south of France, Clark advocated an Allied invasion across the Adriatic onto the Balkan Peninsula, a view he must have known would exasperate his bosses. Patch's job was to drive a wedge in the German defenses in southern France, surging north through the Rhône Valley and linking up as quickly as possible with Patton's Third Army. On balance, Dragoon lived up to its name: It imprisoned thousands of enemy soldiers and helped implode German resistance on the western front.

After being stuck in Italy's muck for much of '43 and '44, it must have been exhilarating for Bigart to be on the move. "This afternoon I watched French troops march through a town which Americans had liberated a few hours before," he wrote on August 18. "The townspeople waved and cheered the Americans with genuine warmth, but the reception accorded the first French [unit] to enter the town was completely uninhibited. On the Boulevard Marshal Pétain—soon to be renamed—crowds alternatively wept and cheered as the column passed by. The gallery was mostly feminine, since every male over fourteen was out in the brush, armed with Luger pistols and tommy-guns and hunting Germans."[57]

As the Seventh Army slugged up the Rhône, Bigart became infatuated with the same story line that animated his colleagues in the north: the role of the French Resistance in wiping out the Nazis. In what amounted to Bigart's valedictory in the ETO, almost all of his final dispatches dealt with the implausible moxie of the Maquis turned FFI.

The Gestapo that summer had conducted a reign of terror in the south of France, rounding up anyone suspected of harboring Partisan sympathies. When word of the Riviera landings reached the Gestapo commandant in Marseille eighty miles north, he tortured and jailed hundreds of Frenchmen, putting them on a starvation diet while making hasty plans to evacuate the city. Bigart heard about the plight of the Marseille Partisans from their compatriots in Cannes. On August 20, he wrote that the Marseille prisoners had been rescued and released by an FFI band that stormed police headquarters once the enemy had abandoned Marseille for Vichy farther north.

The day before, Bigart had filed a remarkable story about Émile Mauret and his seventeen-year-old son, who along with ten other Partisans saved American troops from being ambushed. Four years earlier, in the spring of 1940, reserve lieutenant Mauret had watched the Maginot Line crumble. But now the roles were reversed: It was Mauret and his fellow FFI guerrillas who had the Nazis scurrying for cover.[58]

Émile and the FFI came to the rescue just outside their home village east of Toulon. An American outfit commanded by Major Clayton C. Thobro of Rock Springs, Wyoming, was probing down a village road. Unbeknownst to the Americans, two hundred yards from the hill, cleverly concealed on a wooded spur, eighty Germans lay armed with machine guns and two thirty-seven-millimeter antitank guns. A Sherman tank with infantrymen aboard was chugging precariously close to the enemy stronghold when young Mauret raced up on his bicycle to warn them. Émile followed a minute later on foot to reinforce his son's message. An American lieutenant, George E. Stripp of Newark, New Jersey, didn't understand French but was savvy enough to call a halt until an interpreter could be summoned. Once the translator arrived, the Maurets explained the danger to Stripp and his commanding officers; together they devised a plan to smoke out the Germans.

Young Mauret led the GIs through a concealed gully that brought them behind the German position. "Only two of the Partisans were armed and all they had were little .25-caliber pistols," Stripp told Bigart. "But they all took off, whooping and yelling after the Germans. I saw one kid shoot a German and grab the kraut's gun before he even stopped kicking. You never saw a more eager bunch of fighters. In a few minutes they had killed enough Germans so that all the Partisans had tommy guns and Lugers. Then they rushed the nearest gun and shot up the whole crew. They didn't have a casualty."[59]

Two days later, Bigart was with the Third Division as it entered Aix-en-Provence, at that point the biggest French city yet liberated in the Champagne Campaign. The city was "shimmering like a Cézanne canvas" in the morning sunlight, Bigart wrote, as American tanks rumbled through its ancient streets. "The boulevard leading down to the shuttered Casino was empty and deserted except for a smoldering Nazi truck which Partisans had fired last night. But by midmorning the street was swarming with people and every building flaunted the Tricolor," he wrote. Bigart watched a Great War veteran solemnly raise the Stars and Stripes while thousands of his countrymen sang the "Marseillaise."[60]

There hadn't been much singing the day before when the Germans blew up buildings, booby-trapped others, and tried to sabotage the town's power grid.[61] Earlier, when the Resistance had destroyed a pair of bridges north of Aix-en-Provence, the Germans had rounded up twenty-three suspects and tossed them in jail. A few days before the Americans arrived, Maquis leaders had developed an ingenious rescue plan: Two German speakers impersonating Gestapo officers strode menacingly into police headquarters and ordered the suspects released. Their ruse worked: The Partisans were turned loose.[62]

But Aix-en-Provence's "Vichy hoodlums," as Bigart called them, weren't done: They kidnapped, tortured, and shot eight suspected Maquis leaders, including the head of the local Communist party. The Partisans were machine-gunned in a field outside town, yet two men survived by feigning death.[63]

The back-and-forth reprisals were repeated twenty-four hours later in Marseille. By the time Bigart got into the heart of the city with the conquering heroes, most of the remaining Germans had already been imprisoned; they were forced at gunpoint to march past jeering crowds. "I saw four Partisans leading 40 Germans at rifle-point down a narrow alley, while thousands of spectators whistled and hooted," Bigart wrote.[64]

It turned out that Marseille's Partisans had been funded, in part, by wealthy American expatriates. One of them was Mrs. Henry Clews, formerly of Philadelphia, the widow of a prominent sculptor. "She is 63-years-old, wears ankle-length dresses and Queen Mary hats and rides a bicycle," Bigart told readers. A gardener who did work for Mrs. Clews and other wealthy American expats was a nighttime Resistance warrior, running what amounted to an "Underground rest home," Bigart wrote. Mrs. Clews and her American friend, Princess Alexandra Chica, the erstwhile Hazel Suger of Chicago, funneled money to Maquis leaders through the gardener.

The Clews villa was ransacked by the Gestapo, but somehow Mrs. Clews escaped suspicion. Her friend, the princess, wasn't as fortunate. The Gestapo imprisoned her for two weeks before the Riviera invasion. When she took ill in her jail cell, the Gestapo granted her request to be hospitalized. She got out in the nick of time: On August 15, the morning of the invasion, the Gestapo tossed all the hospital's political prisoners into a courtyard and shot them. Among the victims was a twenty-one-year-old pregnant woman.

A third American woman, Eleanor Pell, formerly of New York, was warned by Partisans that the Gestapo was hunting for her: she successfully hid in the woods for weeks, subsisting on whatever scraps Maquis fighters could spare.[65]

In Grenoble a day later, Bigart watched FFI leaders force German soldiers to dig up the remains of French citizens massacred two weeks before by the Gestapo. "There was a stench like that of rotted potatoes as the Germans clawed the earth from the bodies of three Maquis Partisans and six Poles and Czechs, deserters. Nearby in rough pine coffins, lay twenty-three Maquis youths removed from another pit two days ago."

Bigart interviewed a German noncommissioned officer, originally from Munich, who was part of the exhumation crew: "An ordinary German would not do a shameful thing like this," he told Bigart. "It's the business of the Gestapo and the S.S."[66]

The "business" of the Gestapo, the SS, German regulars, and the Vichy militia got more feverish as Bigart and the Seventh Army surged farther north. The last article that Homer Bigart wrote in the European Theater of Operations was datelined Lyon, France, September 4. The *Trib*'s page-one header was ALLIES SWEEPING BEYOND LYON IN PURSUIT OF NAZIS. His lede was pure Bigart: literate and penetrating.

> We crossed the Rhone River into the center of Lyon yesterday on a slender thread of concrete hung from bank to bank after the Germans had blown up the middle span of the Pont Wilson. Like a column of purposeful ants on a twig, workers from the industrial quarter of La Guillotiere crawled over the span, intent on slaughtering the small bands of Joseph Darnand's Vichyite militiamen still holding out on the roofs of big department stores near the Place de Commerce.

In midwar, Vichy strongman Darnand had taken a personal oath of allegiance to Hitler; he was made a full major in the Waffen SS. Darnard cofounded the Milice, the genocidal vigilante outfit that by the summer of '44 claimed thirty-five thousand members across the south of France. The Milice fought viciously up and down the Rhône—even *after* their German protectors had fled.

Having dodged mortar fire in snaking across the Rhône with the Partisans, Bigart tailed them into Lyon. The scene was nightmarish.

"There is nothing more blood-chilling," he wrote, "than street fighting between undisciplined trigger-happy civilians. Units of the regular [French] army were in town, but mostly the mopping-up of Fascists had been left to the townspeople. It seemed like a good idea, because Lyon required a blood purge. It was here that the Gestapo and Darnand Fascists perpetrated their worst excesses. Months of festering hatred needed a release."[67]

One Vichy militiaman who'd killed a French soldier minutes before dropped his revolver and tried to blend in with the Patriots mobbing the streets. A female Partisan spotted him, shrieked to warn the others, and began chasing him as he frantically bounded away. Eventually he was thwarted by a succession of locked doors.

"He turned to the crowd and, seeing no hope of mercy in their snarling faces, collapsed on the stoop," Bigart observed. "Someone bashed his head with the metal handle of a Sten gun. He lay moaning, while an officer brushed the crowd aside and drawing his revolver, administered the coup de grace."[68]

Bigart would soon leave to record the final throes of a different conflict—but one every bit as brutish. The difference in the Pacific Theater, though, was that Bigart no longer got to witness joyous scenes of liberation or the persecuted rising up against their oppressors. Instead, Bigart wrote about the debilitating grind of soldiers jumping from rock to rock, dueling a suicidal foe that should have surrendered years earlier.

The *Herald Tribune*, with considerable fanfare, announced that Bigart would become a featured correspondent in the Pacific. Ironically, the one reporter best equipped to capture the military and geographic import of the Allied sweep across northern France never got the chance. Bigart's best work was devoted to covering World War II's forgotten campaign, the Allies' rudderless advance up the Italian peninsula. No dysfunctional conflict ever had a better Boswell.

AS THEIR FRIEND BIGART WAS pushing his way up the Rhône Valley, Liebling, Boyle, and Rooney were watching Omar Bradley administer a coup de grâce of his own. On Monday evening, August 21, 1944, they hustled to see Bradley conduct another press briefing. It was convened near the general's headquarters in Laval, an hour's drive or so from the First Army's press camp at Bagnoles de l'Orne. Bradley had chosen Laval to park his trailer because it overlapped the zones of the First and Third Armies, both of which he commanded.

Since Bradley's briefing would not end until after dark and the correspondents didn't want to be caught traveling on a blacked-out road with speeding supply trucks, Liebling's colleagues entrusted him with booking them hotel rooms along the way to Laval. Naturally, Joe booked the coziest setup for himself and his PRO driver (and fellow babe-hound), Lieutenant Roy Wilder, Jr., a colorful Carolinian known as "Chitlin."[69] Joe and Chitlin's hotel was in Ernée, a charming spot that had been spared artillery damage. Ernée sported a brasserie that might, the boys figured, hold certain attractions later in the evening.

The Third Army's correspondents would be on their own that night, which was fine by Liebling. A feisty and not always friendly competition had sprung up between reporters covering the First and Third. Rooney, Boyle, and Liebling resented the way the Third's correspondents, fanned by Old Blood and Guts' PROs, embellished Patton's exploits. To hear the Third guys tell it, Liebling joked, Patton's men were already on the outskirts of Vienna.[70]

SHAEF's original plan was to bypass Paris. The capital had no intrinsic military value; planners, moreover, were worried that seizing Paris would overstrain Allied supply lines. But Free French leaders persuaded Eisenhower, Bradley, and Montgomery that Paris and its inhabitants had to be protected from Nazi carnage.[71] It turned out that the German occupation of Paris, although harsh, was less malevolent than in other places.

"[Laval] was the most cheerful briefing I had yet attended," Liebling wrote, acknowledging that Bradley had proven prescient at his Vouilly conference thirty days before. Bradley began by smiling and volunteering that he knew they all wanted to find out when the Allies would be getting to Paris. The most important objective was to destroy von Kluge's army; the next was to secure Paris in as intact a condition as possible. Bradley's deportment stood in cool contrast to Mark Clark's grandstanding in Rome ten weeks earlier.

Pointing to a map, Bradley said the First Army's Fourth and 28th Divisions would hopefully force the German garrison to pull out or surrender without much of a fight. "A Third Army correspondent said that General Patton had bet him five dollars the Third would be in Paris before the First," Liebling recalled, "and General Bradley remarked that he might just take it into his head to tell General Patton to go someplace else." The Missourian assured reporters that, in any case, no Allied army would be making a rush for Paris.

Bradley had what psychiatrists call a "therapeutic personality," Liebling wrote. As the correspondents stood in line to pay their respects, Liebling remembered a colleague—it sounds like Hal Boyle—saying, "General, I'm always glad to see you, because you always make me feel good."[72]

Secure in the knowledge that the City of Light would not be freed anytime soon, Liebling and Wilder drove back to Ernée, hoping a couple of *belles femmes* would be frequenting the café. Sure enough there were; Joe and Roy spent much of that night and most of the next day pursuing them. Alas, they struck out—or so, years later, Liebling claimed.

When Liebling and Wilder returned to the press camp in Bagnoles de l'Orne on Wednesday afternoon, August 23, they were flabbergasted. The place was almost deserted: Rooney, Boyle—everyone—was gone. Only a couple of PROs were left—and they were hurriedly packing up equipment.

"Where is everyone?" Liebling asked. His heart sank when he learned there'd been an unexpected breakthrough; all the correspondents were, at that moment, gunning toward Paris. The new press headquarters would be at the Hôtel Scribe, near the Place de l'Opéra.

Liebling was seething: The liberation of Paris had been his obsession for more than four years—and now, because of his own sybaritic stupidity, he was going to miss it! Wilder later confided in Andy Rooney that Liebling was so upset he actually shed tears.[73]

Joe ran upstairs and stuffed his things into a sleeping bag, then groveled for a ride. Wilder was in the doghouse; Roy and his jeep had already been reassigned. But Liebling was in luck: First Lieutenant Jack Roach, a former press association reporter from Philadelphia, was available. Roach had somehow wangled a Chevrolet sedan that had belonged to a German officer. If they hurried, Liebling promised Roach, they could still catch the best of the celebration—even if Paris had already been freed.

So the two of them set out for La Ville Lumière, hoping they could get there that night if the roads stayed clear. After a couple of hours it hit them that they hadn't brought any food. But as they passed a stretch with a lot of military traffic, they discovered that an Army Quartermaster Corps outfit was handing out K rations in an inspired way. A black soldier stood atop a moving two-and-a-half-ton supply truck that would pull alongside jeeps and vehicles and dump boxes of food into the backseat. With visions of Paris dancing in his head, Liebling pretended the K rations were caviar and smoked partridges; he savored every morsel.

As they passed through a village crowded with excited townspeople, Liebling recognized African-American *Stars and Stripes* reporter Allan Morrison trying to flag a ride. Morrison had endeared himself to Liebling two weeks earlier when both reporters were covering the siege at St.-Malo. The German commander was "loaded," Morrison told Liebling and the other press guys. "When he finishes his last bottle of sauce, they'll run up a white flag." They did.

Liebling and Roach relayed to Morrison the word they'd heard in Bagnoles de l'Orne: that Paris was on the verge of collapse and that the other First Army reporters were probably partying in the city by now. Morrison, who'd been near the front for days, was immediately skeptical. Roach responded by saying that the rumor *had* to be true, otherwise he and Liebling would have run into their buddies on the road someplace. Morrison remained unconvinced.

"Maybe some prison-camp paper in Germany is going to have a hell of a staff," Morrison cracked.

Liebling closed his eyes and hearkened back to a boyhood fantasy of being Confederate cavalry commander J. E. B. Stuart, galloping toward a raid behind enemy lines. But the porky Liebling was no cavalryman and the Chevy sedan was hardly a horse.

Soon they noticed that they were alone on the road—suspiciously alone.

"If we keep on going, we're bound to meet someone," Liebling volunteered.

"That is exactly what I am afraid of," replied Morrison.

Not long after, they ran into two GIs in a jeep, who told them they could find the Seventh Armored Division camped for the night off a side road up ahead. There they learned from the tankmen at the spearhead of the American assault that they were now as close to the front lines as anyone. Ironically, they found out later, they were actually *ahead* of the other First Army correspondents, whose caravan had taken a wrong turn that afternoon.

Liebling, Morrison, and Roach stayed near the leading edge of the American advance the next day, Thursday, August 24, as it ground ever closer to Paris. They spent that night in the village of Montlhéry, sixteen miles southwest of the capital. It was on the road to Orléans, the same thoroughfare that Liebling and tens of thousands of others had taken in shame four years earlier, going in the opposite direction.[74]

Too wound up to sleep, Liebling was awake before dawn. It would be the greatest day of his life; he wanted to relish every moment. At the top of the tallest hill in Montlhéry stood the Tower, an ancient lookout that had been built on a medieval moat. With ruthless efficiency, the Nazis had slapped a listening post on top of the relic. The Germans were gone, but their eyesore remained.

Liebling climbed the hill and was squinting toward Paris when he heard an American voice shout, "Good morning!" A Signal Corps officer was standing on the Tower's platform, gesturing for Liebling to come up. "Neither voice (Philadelphia, perhaps) nor lieutenant (five ten, pale under a black stubble, serious mouth) was distinctive, but he was a man I won't forget," Leibling wrote.

The lieutenant told Liebling that he'd been up in the Tower since the day before, tasked with monitoring enemy movements. There hadn't been movements to monitor, at least none that the lieutenant could see. But he had enjoyed looking at Paris through his powerful Signal Corps binoculars.

"God, I just can't take my eyes off it!" the officer gushed. "Come over here and I'll show it to you." Offering Liebling his field glasses, he guided Joe over to the platform's northern edge.

"Paris was there, all right—there in the same place I had left it four years, two months, and fifteen days before," Liebling wrote.

The lieutenant unrolled a map, but proudly informed Liebling that he didn't need to refer to it anymore. He now knew Paris' iconic landmarks by heart.

"Now, over here," he went on, pointing to the Dome of the Invalides, "is the Opera House. Once you get that clear, you have your orientation.

"And over there," he continued, pointing now to the Opéra, "is the City Hall—you know, the Chamber of Deputies. Isn't it beautiful?"

"It's beautiful," I said, and meant it.

The lieutenant got the Eiffel Tower right. "I suppose you know what that beautiful white church is up on the hill?" he next said, swiveling my elbow into line with Sacré-Coeur. I was going to name it, but something warned me not to, so I shook my head.

"Why, it's Notre Dame, of course!" he said, and I was glad that I had kept my mouth shut.

"I can't wait to get down there," the lieutenant said. "It's the most beautiful city in the world."

I thanked him from the bottom of my heart. I hope he made it.[75]

CHAPTER 12

✭

RESCUING THE KITTEN—
PARIS REDEEMED

I had never been to Paris, and I was unaware that I was
about to experience three of the most eventful days of an
eventful life. It's better if you don't know you're going to
be in on history.

—Andy Rooney, 1995
My War

As the C-47 taxied out to the runway, the noise from its propellers was
so piercing that Walter Cronkite stuffed scraps of tissue in his ears.
By midsummer '44, Cronkite had squeezed aboard almost every kind of
Allied warplane. In the weeks following D-Day, the wannabe pilot had
even finangled space on two transports that shuttled VIPs from London to
the Ninth Air Force's makeshift air base at Grandcamp.

But until Wednesday afternoon, August 16, 1944, Cronkite had never
sat shoulder to shoulder among grease-faced paratroopers, helmet and
parachute pack securely strapped, ready to pounce into the Third Reich.
Cronkite's letter to Betsy the night before had hinted that he was going to
be part of a pivotal operation.

"I am writing tonight from an airbase somewhere in England," his mis-
sive began, spoofing the furtive dateline required by censors.

> Soon I will be leaving on an assignment that is back down
> the ole groove, something of the type of February, 1943,

that you will remember. Well, not exactly like that, so don't try to gather too much from that feeble bit of information. By the time you get this letter, you probably will know all about it. At any rate, I hope so.

What I want to say though, darling, is that there is considerable danger involved in this job. I don't feel that I am unnecessarily worrying you by reporting that, inasmuch as it will all be over before you ever get this note.[1]

By alluding to "assignment" (from his signature lede), "back down the ole groove" (from his letter eighteen months earlier describing editor Harrison Salisbury's typewriter-side cheerleading), and "February, 1943" (the date of the Writing 69th's famous foray), Cronkite was employing code, telling Betsy that he was about to go wheels up on another dramatic mission along the lines of the Wilhelmshaven raid, his original "assignment to hell." But by volunteering that it was "not exactly like" his previous duty, he hoped that she would deduce that he was going on a paratroop jump.

The only other American newspaperman assigned to the big mission, Cronkite told Betsy, was AP's Bill Boni. That week, Boni and Cronkite had both been given minimal training in airborne warfare. Neither had made an actual drop, but at least they had jumped off a platform, practiced landing and rolling, gotten reasonably comfortable with the bulky equipment, and learned how to gather a grounded chute.

When UP boss Virgil Pinkley, after being tipped off by SHAEF officials in early August, offered the airborne slot to Cronkite, Walter leapt. "As perhaps you have been able to read between the lines of my too infrequent letters, I have been in terrible doldrums since D-Day, with everyone else in action and my sitting by on the SHAEF desk," Cronkite told Betsy. "Now at last, I am getting into the show and with a splurge that may prove bigger than any correspondent has had since the original landing."[2]

It's clear from his letter that covering the bombing war from the ground in England hadn't cut it. In Cronkite's mind, he hadn't made enough of a "splurge" since his days as a charter member of the Writing 69th. His reputation as a war correspondent needed a jump start—or so he was convinced. The parachute jump into France would be a career maker, the story of a lifetime; after being cooped up for so long, Cronkite couldn't wait.

Knowing how worried Betsy would be, he tried to buoy her spirits by joking about how the USAAF guys wouldn't let him or Boni buy any rounds of drinks—which was fine by Cronkite, since he'd forgotten to grab English currency as he left London and only had a couple hundred dollars' worth of U.S. traveler's checks.

"I'll write again, honey, just as soon as I can," his V-mail ended. Knowing it might be the last time they'd ever share sweet nothings, Cronkite closed with: "Meantime, darling, remember that I love you very, very much. . . . Forever, Walter."[3]

CRONKITE COULDN'T TELL HIS WIFE, but he was on the cusp of becoming one of the first Allied correspondents to enter still-occupied Paris. Boni and Cronkite had been invited to cover a remarkable operation that the Allied command had code-named Transfigure. SHAEF's strategy was to throw a dagger into the backside of retreating Germans, divide and disrupt the enemy line of defense, and accelerate the capture of the French capital.

On August 2, Supreme Commander Eisenhower had authorized the creation of the First Allied Airborne Army, which at that point combined elements of the U.S. 101st Airborne Division, the Polish First Independent Parachute Brigade, and the British 52nd (Lowland) Division, a specially trained infantry outfit that could be rushed into battle via transports once an airstrip had been captured.

"Transfigure" was apt because it described the First Allied Airborne's mission: to fundamentally alter the battle configuration in northern France. If Transfigure caught the enemy napping, planners hoped it might not only hasten the liberation of Paris, but also end the war in Europe that much quicker.

The operation's immediate objective was an enemy air base near the Forêt de Rambouillet, some thirty miles west of Paris. The 101st and the Polish First would parachute and glider in en masse, overpower the relative handful of German troops defending the airstrip, and pave the way for the Lowlanders to be flown in, some on transports, some on gliders. Together, the Allied troops would create a fissure pointing toward the River Seine that might cause the entire German line to disintegrate.

The "go" order for Transfigure officially came down at 0845 on August 16.[4] At one point the C-47 carrying Cronkite taxied out to the runway—where it and many more like it sat for four long hours before the mission was postponed for a day. It was pushed back another day on August 17, yet another twenty-four hours on August 18, and finally scrubbed for good late on Saturday August 19.

Cronkite was crushed, but Eisenhower and his brain trust had good reason to forgo Transfigure. By the time the paratroop planes were revving on August 16, the First and Third Armies were moving eastward so quickly that they'd almost reached the western edge of the Rambouillet Forest. The 12th Army Group was picking up such huge chunks of territory that Hal Boyle told Frances that its camp followers were suffering "travel fatigue."[5]

When Dreux fell on August 19, Transfigure was rendered moot; the village had been one of the First Allied's paratroop targets. The German line was collapsing so quickly that the airborne operation was no longer needed to foist extra pressure on Paris' defenders. After nearly a week of on-again, off-again drama, the men of the First Allied Airborne were told to stand down and await further orders: The Supreme Command still had big plans for them.

On Sunday, August 20, Cronkite commiserated with Betsy that the mission's cancellation was "one of the bitterest disappointments of my life." Her husband still couldn't share details, but if the operation had come off, he "probably would have been the first American correspondent into Paris, although I might have had to share the honor with Bill Boni of AP," he wrote.[6]

Cronkite didn't bother to mask his dejection. "So here I am back at the same old stand in the same old slough of despond which has been growing deeper and blacker ever since D-Day left me standing on the platform holding the sack." He was worried that his "doldrums" were hampering his productivity—and that Pinkley had grown disenchanted. On top of that, he was worried about the cost of an eventual move to Amsterdam; he fretted that he and Betsy wouldn't be able to afford life in the Netherlands.

To escape the V-1s, he had moved to a more expensive flat, which was forcing him to further drain their bank account, "and that is too damned depressing for words," he wrote. None of his clothes fit anymore; he'd lost so much weight he looked "like hell." His old Bostonian wingtips were so beat-up that soon his "corns would be showing."

All those eighteen-hour days, all those frontline communiqués he had to turn around on a dime, all those god-awful train rides to cover dead and dying airmen had taken their toll on the twenty-seven-year-old Walter Cronkite. He was so down he was taking out his frustrations on his wardrobe and wallet and in letters to his adoring wife.

It may have been classic sublimation, but to Cronkite, there was no respite in sight. As if his letter hadn't been gloomy enough, he saw fit to inform Betsy that it would be "many, many months perhaps stretching beyond a year" before, realistically, they could see one another.

"Maybe I won't mail this," he meekly volunteered in the last line. "If I do, forgive me."[7]

He did and she did. Their marriage lasted another sixty-one years.

Yet it would be another month, and several more bitterly false starts, before Walter Cronkite and the men of the First Allied Airborne Army would be called into action. When they were, the least of their concerns was beat-up shoes.

AT THE MOMENT CRONKITE WAS bemoaning his fate, his friend Hal Boyle was hurtling toward the very places into which Walter was supposed to be parachuting: Dreux and Rambouillet. Boyle's jeep had to move to the side of the road to accommodate the Red Ball Express, the vaunted transportation supply chain that kept the tanks and trucks of the 12th Army Group rolling.

More than three quarters of the twenty-three thousand drivers and quartermasters in the Red Ball Express, named after railroad slang for a fast freight, were African American. Many of the six thousand trucks in the Express had yanked their governors so they could motor at higher speeds. Every day and night for weeks, the Express rolled virtually nonstop on blacked-out roads, the driver and the GI riding shotgun switching places literally on the move so that precious time was saved.[8]

As enemy lines crumbled, Express drivers began rounding up German stragglers. Small groups of Aryan supermen had been hiding "in caves and woods like the old Quantrill raiders in Missouri and Kansas after the Civil War," Boyle wrote in a piece that ran in the *Baltimore Afro-American*. Under the cloak of darkness the holdouts would try to escape along roadways—only to be corralled by their racial "inferiors," who would jump out of their trucks, M1 carbines in hand. Red Ball Express trucks would often arrive at the front with a mixed load of supplies and prisoners.

"Our platoon has taken about 70 prisoners while bringing up food and ammunition to the front," one member of the Quartermaster Corps, Sergeant Edwin Kelly of Richmond, Virginia, told Boyle, "but to tell you the truth, we'd rather not take them prisoners—we'd rather fight until we can get it over with."[9]

All five correspondents wrote pieces heralding the contributions of black soldiers to the war effort, but it's a testament to the deep-seated racism of the day that none of them—not even the outspoken Liebling—published commentaries during the war that directly deplored the second-class treatment of African-American soldiers. Only after the war did Liebling and the others condemn the U.S. for its hypocrisy on racial matters.

BLOWING THE WHISTLE ON THE enemy's racial hatred, however, was a different matter. On August 19, in the village of St.-Mars-le-Brière near Le Mans, Boyle encountered a group of some 220 Russian female prisoners of war. Ranging in age from fifteen to seventy-four, they had been taken captive in Leningrad and forced into slave labor. At gunpoint, the women were often forced to work fifteen hours a day fixing bomb-damaged railroad tracks.

They were confined to a filthy camp surrounded by barbed wire. "Only one Russian woman—a doctor—accepted the German invitation to retreat with them," Boyle revealed.[10] The other women stayed inside the camp to be freed by their Allies. Upon greeting the Americans, many of the women asked to be sent to frontline units so they could fight their Nazi tormentors, Boyle noted.

The next day, Boyle heard the legend of a local Maquis leader who'd blown up many of the tracks that the Russian women had been forced to repair. He was named, curiously enough, Patrick O'Neill. The O'Neills had left Ireland two centuries earlier and settled on farmland southwest of Paris. The bizarre juxtaposition gave Boyle a chance to flex his brogue and pay homage to his ancestry.

"Sure and wouldn't you be knowing," Boyle's amusing lede went, "that the leader of 5,000 French Maquis who have been playing hob with the Germans for two years has a name as Irish as Paddy's pig. The Gallic Robin Hood goes by the Emerald Isle moniker of Patrick O'Neill and he doesn't care if the Germans know it."

A graduate of St. Cyr, the French West Point, O'Neill had been wounded twice during the Nazi blitzkrieg in '40 but never captured. In '41 and '42, O'Neill was living quietly along the River Loire with his wife and three young children. Appalled at how the Gestapo was enslaving young Frenchmen, O'Neill joined the Resistance in midwar; before long, he headed what was believed to be the largest Maquis chapter in France.

O'Neill's men gave him, Boyle wrote, "strict obedience." Three hundred of O'Neill's guerrillas were killed by the Germans, many of them executed in cold blood. When the Gestapo uncovered a house in the woods that was being used as a hospital for O'Neill's men, they burned it to the ground, incinerating the seventeen wounded Resistance fighters inside.

"We do not forget these things," O'Neill told Boyle. O'Neill and his men fought with such fearlessness that they'd earned the respect of American GIs, Boyle said. The next day, Boyle relayed a story he'd heard from Corporal Don Cass of Waterloo, Iowa. Cass and his squad of men had some Germans cornered in an Orléans house and were cautiously moving in when six members of O'Neill's band pulled up in a car.

"As soon as they learned that there were Germans in the house, they ran right up and went into the building," Cass told Boyle. "A few seconds later they came out with the Germans collared. You should have seen the expressions on the faces of some of our boys at that way of operating."[11]

Wherever O'Neill went in those glorious days, Boyle wrote, he was cheered by awed and grateful French citizens.

BOYLE AND ROONEY HEARD A lot of villagers cheering as, on August 22, with Liebling and Wilder still on their spree in Ernée, the First Army press corps headed toward its interim camp at the Hôtel du Grand Veneur in the village of Rambouillet. Monk Dickson from General Bradley's staff spent much of the next two-plus days briefing the press guys on the Allied progress toward Paris.[12] It was just a matter of time before the capital fell, Dickson said, although reporters soon picked up on the political machinations transpiring with the French and the British. Montgomery's troops were almost as well positioned as Bradley's to strike at Paris—and Monty desperately wanted the credit. After much back-and-forth, with bruised feelings on all sides, it was determined that the honor of being the first Allied troops into Paris would fall to French brigadier general Jacques-Philippe Leclerc and his Second Armored Division.

The rapprochement with Monty and Leclerc wasn't the only politicking going on outside Paris. Andy Rooney and other First Army reporters resented the way that certain international correspondents and Third Army arrivistes barged into the Grand Veneur and began encroaching on the First's turf. By day two in Rambouillet, tensions were running high as reporters jockeyed for scraps of information. Things got so crowded at the hotel that latecomers were forced to spread out sleeping bags on the dining room's straw floor.

It was in that modest eatery, Rooney recalled, where "one of the great unchronicled skirmishes of World War II took place."[13] One of the combatants was an American literary icon—and the moment forever soured Rooney's view of him.

Ernest Hemingway had, by that point, degenerated into self-caricature. Decked out in a Canadian tanker's jacket and the tricolored armband of the FFI, often sporting a .45 ostentatiously strapped to his side, Hemingway was running what amounted to his own private war. The novelist had arrived in Rambouillet well ahead of the press contingent. To accommodate his party pals and the FFI vigilantes he supposedly was "commanding," Papa had booked ten rooms at the Grand Veneur.

Apparently not all of those rooms were occupied on the evening of August 23 when Bruce Grant of the *Chicago Sun* arrived. When his request for a room was turned down, Grant, who stood six foot four and, as a one-time city editor, took guff from nobody, went looking for Hemingway. He found the writer loudly holding court at the hotel bar for a rapt audience of hero worshipers.

Grant informed Hemingway that it was rude to hoard all those rooms when guys were being forced to bunk on the dining room floor. Hemingway, who was, to no one's shock, already in his cups, took exception. Voices got louder; Hemingway jumped off his barstool, fists coiled, to confront Grant. AP photographer Harry Harris, no bigger than a flyweight, stepped between Grant and Hemingway as Rooney and other reporters gathered 'round, hoping for adolescent fisticuffs. Even Ernie Pyle popped off the dining room floor to take in the action.

Although being restrained by Harris, Hemingway still wanted a piece of Grant. The writer stormed out the lace-curtained French doors that led to the Grand Veneur's courtyard. Ten seconds or so passed before Hemingway suddenly reemerged, bellowing at Grant, "Well, are you coming out and fight?" Cooler heads prevailed. Reporters went back to figuring out how they were going to crack Paris.

"You should never meet one of your heroes," Rooney related. "I had greatly admired Hemingway when I read *A Farewell to Arms* and *The Sun Also Rises* but after that night in Rambouillet I laugh whenever I think of him."[14]

The vainglorious Hemingway would continue to give Rooney and friends plenty to chuckle about in the days to come.

THE EVENING BEFORE THE SILLINESS with Hemingway and Grant, sad news had arrived at Rambouillet. Tom Treanor of the *Los Angeles Times* had been killed when his jeep collided with an American tank near Mantes-Gassicourt.[15] It was the sort of accident that happened all the time, though it was rarely reported.

Tall and handsome, Treanor had been a popular member of the MTO and ETO press corps, Hal Boyle observed, due in no small measure to his willingness to stick his neck out—both in combat and around fussbudget censors and PROs. Like Bigart, Treanor had done so much homework he had become something of a European cultural savant. After the war, Treanor planned to make the Continent his beat—and bring his wife and children over to share the experience.[16]

Treanor was Bigart's accomplice at Monte Cipolla, Boyle's buddy at Monte Cassino, and Rooney's and Liebling's pal at St.-Lô. After all those incredibly close scrapes, he was done in by a highway mishap. His two companions in the jeep both survived with minor injuries. After the accident, Treanor, still conscious and unaware of the severity of his injuries, kept telling doctors to hurry so he could finish his story.[17]

TREANOR WAS A GREAT FRIEND of "Beachhead Don" Whitehead, so it's a double tragedy that he didn't live long enough to see what Boyle called "one of the war's outstanding news beats." Boyle and the rest of the press contingent were milling outside the Grand Veneur early Thursday afternoon, August 24. A dust-covered jeep pulled up and Whitehead's lanky exterior stiffly climbed out. Whitehead's face, Boyle wrote, was "streaked with perspiration as he ambled unhurriedly toward the hotel's lounge, which had been converted into a press room."

"Where you been, Don?" asked a correspondent sitting on a bench.

"Paris," Whitehead replied without fanfare.

Whitehead was immediately surrounded by reporters, all peppering him with questions. How? Where? How far into the city? Why'd you leave?

He returned a couple of parries, then waved off his questioners and sat down at a typewriter. Forty-five minutes later, he emerged with a 1,600-word account of his remarkable experience.

"It was the first eyewitness story of one of the most dramatic days of the war," Boyle wrote. When Whitehead's story, having navigated censors, reached the U.S. the following afternoon, it caused a sensation, with bells ringing on wire service machines all over the country.

"Whitehead got his beat through a combination of forethought, good luck and drive," Boyle revealed. Several days before, Whitehead had arranged for a French-speaking driver, a jeep, and a small reconnaissance plane. His driver was an Evanston, Illinois, sergeant named Adrian Pinsince, who was fluent in French and, Whitehead said, the "best scrounger I ever met in the Army"—high praise indeed.[18]

Instead of joining the flood of correspondents trying to enter Paris from the west, Whitehead on August 23 chose a different path, hooking up southwest of town with a French armored column that was probing north on the Grand National highway in the tiny village of Bures-sur-Yvette. Whitehead had been tipped off by one of Pinsince's French sources that it was Brigadier General Leclerc's outfit. The French continued pushing toward the city that afternoon and evening but were stopped by enemy shelling at Longjumeau.

Whitehead and Pinsince spent the night in a farmhouse but were up before dawn to jump back in with Leclerc's men. While the column was stalled near a garage in Longjumeau, Pinsince overheard a mechanic say that he'd just gotten off a telephone call with a friend in Paris. It had not occurred to Whitehead that the capital's telephone system might still be functioning. Surely the Germans could not have been that sloppy, could they have?

Whitehead told Pinsince to pull over and find a phone. With the translator's help, he placed a call to "Anjou 74-60," the American Embassy in Paris. One "Mrs. Blanchard," who identified herself as the embassy's housekeeper, answered.

"Who is calling?" she inquired in English. When Whitehead told her he was an American reporter trailing the French Second Armored Division, she uttered, *"Mon Dieu!* Where are you?"

Firefights were raging throughout the city between the FFI and the remaining German soldiers, Mrs. Blanchard told Whitehead. Four days earlier, a group of Germans had attacked the embassy, shooting a guard and ransacking the place. Soon after, she and the rest of the staff had barricaded the embassy; there had been no further assaults.

"Mon Dieu!" Mrs. Blanchard repeated. "I hope the Americans move in tomorrow. I am carrying an American flag with me wherever I go. We aren't allowed to fly the flag now, but I hope the Americans will let me help hoist the flag the first time it is flown."[19]

After bidding au revoir to the housekeeper, Whitehead and Pinsince rejoined Leclerc's column. As they reached Porte d'Orléans on the near side of the Seine, they were held up by a mined road and antitank fire. Once the column resumed, a prickly French officer invoked de Gaulle *and* Leclerc in informing Whitehead that no noncombatant would be permitted to enter the city. Whitehead pondered the situation for a few moments, switched places with Pinsince, and, in full view of the martinet, jammed the accelerator.

At precisely nine fifty-seven a.m., Whitehead told Boyle, the jeep passed through the gates of Paris. They were promptly mobbed by hysterical Parisians, who crammed every lane despite the threat of snipers.

"The streets were like a combined Mardi Gras, Fourth of July celebration, American Legion convention, and New Year's Eve in Times Square, all packed into one," Whitehead wrote later that day.[20] Whitehead swung the jeep behind one of Leclerc's tanks, hoping it would provide better cover. But at one point the gunfire got so intense that he and Pinsince were forced to jump out and hide behind a small wooden shed. After fifteen minutes, with bullets still zinging all around, they decided that the shed was no safer than the road. Many of the snipers, Whitehead learned, were German soldiers disguised in civilian clothing or members of the Milice, the despised Vichyite militia. Men and women wearing the Tricolor were going from house to house, pointing to rooftops and windows, smoking them out.[21]

Whitehead stayed inside the city limits for about an hour before reversing course and heading to Rambouillet. But he was there long enough to claim a "Paris" dateline—and return to the Grand Veneur a conquering hero.

Walter Cronkite wasn't the only American correspondent who had aspired to be the "first one into Paris." There had been hundreds groveling for the honor—and several who later claimed it. But only Don Whitehead had truly earned it.

LIKE HIS FRIEND BOYLE, WHITEHEAD may have done some foreshadowing from time to time, anticipating certain events; most journalists did. But Boyle and Whitehead had the integrity not to issue a story until being certain that its assertions jibed with the facts on the ground.

Not so correspondent Charles Collingwood and CBS Radio, which accidentally went live with a Collingwood story on August 24 that described in detail Paris' liberation, with explicit accounts of jubilant crowds celebrating outside the magnificent landmarks that the dashing Murrow protégé knew almost as well as Liebling. Collingwood had marked his story "hold for release." But there was a mix-up at CBS-London; in his zeal to get the jump on NBC and the BBC, anchor Richard C. Hottelet read Collingwood's bulletin on the air—more than a half day *before* Collingwood had set foot in Paris and well before it could be declared "liberated."[22]

In an episode that marred Murrow's legacy in London, the phony story was aired repeatedly before CBS issued an embarrassed correction. Murrow always defended Collingwood, but it was slipshod journalism at best—and outright fabrication at worst. It inevitably raised questions about the veracity of other Murrow Boys' stories from across the conflict.

If "Bonnie Prince Charlie," as he was known, was chagrined, it was short-lived. The next day, the date of the *real* liberation of Paris, Collingwood was spotted by fellow correspondents drinking with Ernest Hemingway at an outdoor café. Surrounded by a bevy of adoring females, Papa and the Bonnie Prince were toasting the FFI—and, likely, themselves.

The Murrow Boys weren't the only U.S. correspondents who got into hot water while trumpeting Paris' redemption. Cronkite's longtime roommate, UP reporter Jim McGlincy, had his press credentials stripped for a month by Major Jack Redding and the 12th Army Group brass. On day one of the liberation, McGlincy and five other reporters, Larry LeSueur of CBS, Paul Manning of Mutual, Seaghan John Maynes of Reuters, and Robin Duff and Howard Marshall of the BBC, sidestepped PRO strictures by using Radio Nationale de France to transmit their stories—uncensored and unapproved.[23] McGlincy had a knack for getting into trouble, especially when Cronkite wasn't around to help him.

The situation inside and outside Paris was in such a state of flux that Omar Bradley's deputies, on the fly, held another press briefing at the Grand Veneur first thing on August 24. Rooney, Boyle, and the other reporters heard Chet Hansen and Monk Dickson confirm reports that thousands of Free French fighters were fomenting insurrection. The street fighting between Resistance members and the Miliciens—unleashed just as the craven Vichy leaders were fleeing to Belfort—was said to be particularly bitter.[24]

It took days before the Miliciens threat was snuffed out. G-2 reports, said Hansen and Dickson, indicated that just eleven thousand or twelve thousand Germans were left—many of them administrative personnel believed to be on the verge of cracking. Mrs. Blanchard, the embassy housekeeper, had been right: Men and women wearing the Tricolor had forced the enemy to abandon big chunks of the city and were winning gun battles all over town. The Paris police, whose loyalties had been called into question, were now fighting side by side with the Maquis. The battle for the heart of town, the Île de la Cité around Notre Dame, was especially heated.

Leclerc and the sixteen thousand men in the French Second Armored Division, already at the city's gate, would indeed spearhead the Allied assault, Bradley's guys confirmed, followed quickly by General Raymond Barton's Fourth Infantry, with the 102nd Cavalry Group at the point and the 28th Infantry not far behind.

Andy Rooney smartly recognized that the best story might come by catching up to the French—not by waiting for the guys in the Fourth or 28th as nearly all of his colleagues were doing. General Charles de Gaulle, Eisenhower's designated French leader-in-waiting, was in Rambouillet, too, intent on basking in the glory—and deflecting at least some of it away from his rival Leclerc.

———

NOT SUPRISINGLY, THE ROAD TO Paris was perilous that morning, Rooney remembered. At pivotal spots amid the hills, the enemy had secreted pill-boxes. Tanks and eighty-eight-millimeter artillery pieces were camouflaged in the woods.

Rooney's jeep was well back in the procession when artillery fire erupted. He jumped out of the jeep so quickly he forgot to grab his helmet. Bent over, he ran into a field on his right. The French tanks in front of him fanned out and began firing at a concrete-and-steel bunker perched in the hills. Feeling exposed, Rooney hustled down an embankment, hoping to gain better cover behind a stone wall.

After a minute or two, Rooney realized that there was someone else hunkered alongside the wall. Crouching about twenty yards away was a guy wearing a familiar green Canadian tanker's jacket and a leather-brimmed officer's cap.

The fellow turned to Rooney and barked, "There's another one right over the hill," meaning another artillery bunker.

Suddenly Rooney recognized who it was: the frustrated pugilist from the night before! "Jesus," Rooney remembered thinking, "here I am behind a stone wall with Ernest Hemingway." Rooney couldn't help but chortle over the "ridiculous" specter of being pinned down with the world-famous novelist turned romantic guerrilla fighter. "You could tell he was having the time of his life playing war," Rooney wrote.[25]

Hemingway inched closer to Rooney and pulled out a makeshift map. Papa's FFI contacts had pinpointed the location of all the German strongholds bordering Paris. Gesturing toward the map, Hemingway told Rooney, "We're going to be here for a while." A half hour or so elapsed before Hemingway could get back to his French-operated half-track and Rooney could return to his jeep.

By late afternoon on August 24, the midportion of the two thousand vehicles in Leclerc's column had reached the cobblestone streets of St.-Cloud on the near side of the Seine; its forward elements, as Don Whitehead had experienced, had already penetrated the north side of the river. Ecstatic Parisians showered the men surrounding Rooney with wine, cheese, and cakes. Rooney used his Albany Academy–honed French to ask one family to borrow its bathroom, where he struggled with the peculiar invention that is the French toilet. He traded a couple of boxes of K rations for a half loaf of bread, some cheese, and a bottle of unlabeled red wine. In honor of the august occasion, the teetotaling Rooney quaffed the wine— and enjoyed every drop.

That part of the column spent the night in St.-Cloud, its vehicles still strung along the roadside in front of the bridges. Rooney's jeep was squeezed between two Sherman tanks; he curled up in the passenger's seat, fearing that if he left the jeep to find a more a restful spot, the column might leave without him—and he'd lose his big story. His nap was interrupted a couple of times by small-arms fire that seemed to be coming from up ahead.

When they moved out that morning, Rooney saw what had happened: Two big German troop trucks had tried to make a break for it over the river. It was a "slaughter," Rooney remembered. The Germans had been so badly shot up that nearly three dozen of them were lying dead, "their blood still dripping through the grillwork into the Seine." Andy Rooney's introduction to the City of Light was the image of enemy corpses grotesquely splayed over a bridge.[26]

TWO OTHER CORRESPONDENTS WHO HAD wandered away from the journalistic pack on the push into Paris—the *New Yorker*'s Joe Liebling and the *Stars and Stripes*' Allan Morrison—navigated the sixteen miles from Montlhéry on the 25th to arrive by early afternoon, despite the pandemonium. Liebling had braced himself to see his darling city going up in smoke. To Joe's astonishment, Paris appeared more or less unmolested.

After the war, Liebling was not surprised to learn that Hitler had ordered General Dietrich von Choltitz, Paris' military governor, to torch the capital. When von Choltitz balked, Hitler court-martialed him from afar. "Since Leclerc [through the FFI] sent von Choltitz a warning that he would hold him personally responsible for any damage to the city," Liebling cracked years later, "it is possible that the German preferred the *in absentia* kind of trouble."[27]

As driver Jack Roach's Chevy crawled through the Porte d'Orléans, the procession was suddenly greeted by hundreds of bicyclists who were openly defying their oppressors by pedaling out to greet the troops. They were almost all women, a spectacle that made Liebling weep. "[T]o make a woman truly beautiful, liberate her," he wrote. "She visibly exudes a generalized good will that makes you want to kiss her."[28] More than a few *femmes* bussed Liebling, Morrison, and Roach that day. An older woman insisted they decorate the Chevy with a Tricolor banner. The homemade bunting was "big enough to drape a hearse," Liebling recalled.[29]

Roach was eager to report for his public relations duties at the Hôtel Scribe near the Opéra. But as they approached the intersection of the Avenue de l'Observatoire and the Boulevard du Montparnasse, they stopped for a few moments to get their bearings and determine if the path to the Scribe was safe. Liebling had never been enamored of that particular neighborhood, but it looked gorgeous to him that afternoon. "Any liberated place acquires a special charm," he wrote, "like a kitten recovered from the town dump."[30]

As they idled the Chevrolet to figure out their next move, they heard reports that the Germans were about to officially surrender—and practically around the corner! The ceremony was supposed to take place, they were told, in a waiting room at the Gare Montparnasse train station.[31]

The three flashed credentials and gained entrance to the nondescript rail shed where Leclerc, American General Leonard T. Gerow of V Corps, von Choltitz, and a dozen of the *Kommandant*'s staff officers waited for Charles de Gaulle's belated arrival. Von Choltitz was a "worried, fat little soldier," Liebling noted; his sycophants wore dress uniforms with flat-visored caps and impeccably shined boots, which contrasted with the mud-stained appearance of Leclerc and Gerow.

The imperious de Gaulle was making Leclerc wait, no doubt causing his adversary to grind his teeth. Liebling glanced up to see two more American correspondents—both of whom happened to be old friends from New York—jogging down the train platform: the sports scribe turned fiction writer Paul Gallico, then writing for *Vanity Fair*, and Harold Denny of the *New York Times*.

Denny looked at the faces in the crowd and quickly realized that he was the only American correspondent from a daily paper. "When Denny spotted the Germans, he reacted like a redbone hound to a tree full of raccoons," Liebling wrote. "He saw that he had a scoop of historic dimensions."

The *Times'* man fired up a cigarette, pulled out his typewriter, ran his hands through his hair for inspiration, and started banging away, the sound of his keys rattling around the depot. He was so excited that Liebling swore that at one point he actually yelled, "Boy!"[32]

When de Gaulle finally arrived, striding down the platform with his usual stiff-backed pomposity, he had the look, Liebling thought, of a "poker player hauling in his first big pot of the evening and trying not to show how good he feels."[33] Free French leaders, worried that the U.S. State Department would play the same disingenuous game it had played in North Africa with Darlan, were delighted that de Gaulle participated. To the FFI and its many Communist members, de Gaulle was far preferable to any number of Fascist French enablers the U.S. could have chosen, Liebling noted.

The surrender ceremony itself took only a few minutes and was remarkably bereft of ritual. Sirens blaring, von Choltitz and company were whisked away to captivity in French army jeeps.

Roach had to hustle Denny's exclusive through the censors and out over the wire, both of which were at that moment being set up at the Scribe. Sadly for Denny, the *Times* never got his big beat; somewhere along the line there was a mechanical problem.

Since Morrison had reportorial duties in the streets of Paris, Liebling was solo again. Joe grabbed his sleeping bag/valise out of Roach's Chevrolet and checked into the Scribe, intent on savoring an evening for the ages.

BY THEN, HAL BOYLE AND Andy Rooney, too, were being overwhelmed by celebrants. On liberation's eve, Boyle conducted an informal poll and determined that American GIs were "about equally divided on what they preferred to see first—the Eiffel Tower or a bottle of chilled champagne in a French bar."[34] Within his first few hours in the city, Boyle did both, hiking all the way to the top of the Tower and quipping, "I understand now why Paris fell so easily to Allied troops. The Germans were just too plumb worn out from climbing the Eiffel Tower to defend the city."[35] The editors of the *Kansas City Star* were so delighted with the hometown boy's treatment of the French capital's emancipation that they ran it in huge print on page one of that Sunday's edition.[36]

On his last night at Rambouillet, Boyle had gotten approval from Major Barney Oldfield, the acting PRO of the 12th Army Group, to mail home the enemy contraband that Hal had picked up in the sweep across France. A typewritten note, dated August 24, acknowledged that Boyle's stash did not include explosives or firearms. Among other items, Boyle had squirreled away a Nazi canteen, a gas mask, and a helmet.[37] Much more was to come: Boyle had an eye for swag. Toward the end of the war, his collection would include plenty of "forbidden" firearms.

Rooney by midafternoon on August 25 was wading through a sea of humanity down the Avenue Clichy near the Arc de Triomphe. People "shouted with joy, they laughed, they hugged, they kissed, they threw flowers, they held out champagne," he remembered. As Rooney's jeep got closer to the Arc de Triomphe, the mood turned darker. German prisoners, hands clasped on their heads, were being paraded by the FFI and French regulars. Most Parisians displayed restraint and restricted their protests to catcalls and obscenities. But Rooney watched a burly Frenchman smash a wine bottle over the head of a helmetless German soldier, a moment of bloody vengeance that triggered other vigilantism.

"The occupational forces were spit on, punched, and hooted at as enthusiastically as the French crowds had cheered us," Rooney recalled. "I'd never seen hatred so deep."[38] The Parisians called the German women in uniform *souris grises*, "gray mice," and treated them, Rooney observed, with almost the same level of derision.[39]

Rooney had a fabulous story and visions of it being splashed all over page one. Now the trick was to get it back to Rennes—a couple hundred miles west—where the *Stars and Stripes* had set up its interim field office.

He found a French army message center whose English-speaking officer assured Rooney he could get his copy back to the First Army's old press headquarters at Rambouillet, where it could be relayed to Rennes. Rooney also bumped into an American Piper Cub pilot who'd been tasked with ferrying documents from the front line to rear-echelon headquarters. Fortuitously, the pilot was headed toward Rennes; he took a carbon copy of Rooney's article and promised to personally deliver it to the *Stars and Stripes* office.

So Rooney was feeling good about getting his copy in print when he waded back into the mob gathered around the Place de l'Opéra. In the middle of the bedlam he ran into Larry LeSueur of CBS; Rooney was delighted when Larry invited him to share a few of his liberation experiences on the air. CBS was borrowing the French Radio Nationale microphone at the Tuileries near the Louvre—the hookup that got LeSueur crosswise with the Army brass. Rooney, perhaps unaware that he was violating the rules, did a three-minute interview. It was one of only a handful of times during the war that Rooney appeared on a radio broadcast and his first time ever on CBS.[40]

If anything, the party in the streets was getting more frenzied now that day was heading toward evening. Rooney didn't recognize anyone at the Scribe but spotted his pal Ernie Pyle, beatifically smiling at the throng from a second-floor veranda at the Hôtel Le Grand.

Rooney squirmed through the crowd. Joined by several other reporters, Pyle was chuckling at the amorous goings-on. "Ernie's language was refined compared to that of many of the correspondents, but he looked down that day, as French girls threw themselves with wild abandon at American boys, and said, 'Any GI who doesn't get laid tonight is a sissy.'" Pyle's quip was mild stuff, but when Rooney related it fifty-one years later for an ABC News documentary, never dreaming that the producer would actually use it, it stirred controversy among feminist and gay rights activists.

That night Rooney tried to check into the Scribe but was intercepted by Major Jack Redding, the big boss PRO, who unilaterally decided that as active-duty military, Sergeant Rooney did not qualify as a "correspondent"—a novel argument, given Andy's nonstop duties in the line of fire for two and a half months. The officious Redding went on to become President Truman's postmaster general and the public relations head of the Democratic National Committee—but that didn't make Rooney like him any better.

When Rooney learned the next morning that his article never made it to the *Stars and Stripes,* he was doubly pissed.[41] It turned out that the grasshopper pilot, after taking off from an open field near the Bois de Boulogne, was forced down with engine trouble. And the copy somehow didn't get through the French message center, either. Rooney's *Stars and Stripes* colleague Bud Kane, who'd followed the Fourth Division into Paris that afternoon, got a less colorful story onto page one. A half century later, Rooney echoed Cronkite's Operation Transfigure frustration in remembering his Paris strikeout as "the single most disappointing event in my three years as a war correspondent."

But Rooney would have plenty of opportunities to write about liberated Paris. The fun was just beginning.

HAL BOYLE, AMID DAY THREE of *la Libération,* managed to get to the Louvre. He asked a curator if the Germans had destroyed any precious treasures. Just one, Boyle was told: a 4,500-year-old mummified Egyptian sheep.

"It was torn to pieces yesterday," Boyle explained, "by a frantic [enemy] soldier in the basement as he sought shelter during the panic caused by gunfire between rooftop snipers and French patriots marching in the great liberation day parade."[42] As the wild gunplay began, 750 German prisoners were being guarded in the Louvre's courtyard. They begged their FFI captors for protection and were rushed into the museum, where stray bullets smashed dozens of windows. Once the shooting died down, the guards combed the basement and discovered six German soldiers hiding among the Egyptian sarcophagi. Another enemy soldier had ripped open a wall panel and wormed his way into the ancient sheep mummy. The *Chicago Daily Tribune* headlined Boyle's piece MUMMY SAVES NAZI.[43]

The Louvre wasn't the only building in the line of fire. Led by de Gaulle and Leclerc, the parade on August 26 courted disaster. Given the number of holdout SS snipers, desperate Vichy militiamen, and trigger-happy French regulars and FFI fighters—not to mention the possibility of the Luftwaffe suddenly showing up—a massive demonstration on the streets of Paris at that point was a monumentally bad idea.

Boyle, Rooney, Liebling, and everyone else in Paris worried that there would be assassination attempts on de Gaulle and his Free French followers. It happened in midparade.

De Gaulle got out of his vehicle to acknowledge the cheers as the parade reached the Place de la Concorde. Rooney was in his jeep trying to keep up. Suddenly there was a "staccato crackle of gunfire from the direction of the massive columns of the Hôtel de Crillon or, possibly, from the roof of the U.S. Embassy next to it."

Everyone near Rooney dove for cover, many of them trying to get behind tanks and trucks. Unlike his moment with Hemingway two days earlier, this time Rooney remembered to grab his helmet as he tore out of the jeep. The problem was that no one was absolutely sure from where the fire was coming, so they didn't know how to protect themselves. Mothers grabbed children and sought cover in doorways. People began scrambling underneath trucks, tanks, and jeeps, praying the vehicles would remain still. It was a terrifying few moments. Rooney kept his head down, so he missed the specter of de Gaulle standing erect, facing his would-be assassins without so much as a flinch—or so the legend goes.

Things seemed to be calming down when there was a second burst of fire, triggering another manic scramble. With that, "every French tank in the square, several hundred I suppose, turned their guns toward the Crillon and started blasting away at its facade," Rooney recalled.[44]

Hal Boyle, also hugging the ground in the Place de la Concorde, wrote that day that "thousands of men of the French forces of the interior were pouring rifle, machine gun, and pistol fire at the bordering rooftops."[45] The firing quickly spread, Boyle noted, from the Arc de Triomphe to the Hôtel de Ville to Notre Dame.

Rooney watched a dozen French commandoes race toward the Crillon to clean out the snipers. People stayed under cover for another ten or fifteen minutes before the procession resumed. Several spectators were killed; dozens more were wounded. "Paris today is like a big league Tombstone, Ariz., in the palmiest days of that wild west town," Boyle wrote on August 26.[46]

DESPITE MORE THAN OCCASIONAL FLYING bullets, the parading in Paris didn't stop. Nor did the partying. There wasn't much coffee or food in Paris that week, but there seemed to be limitless supplies, Boyle remarked, of champagne, cognac, wine, and chocolate truffles.[47] On August 29, the smooched-up and generally hungover men of the Fourth and 28th Divisions marched with all the other liberating troops down the Avenue des Champs-Élysées. Since the GIs—almost to a man—would soon be whisked back to the front after their four-day divertissement, they relished every step. Again, millions of Parisians gathered to give thanks.

Boyle positioned himself not far from the Arc de Triomphe so he could take in the panorama of the Americans marching down the world's most famous boulevard. Looking up and down the parade route, he couldn't help but notice that many of the "men" wearing FFI colors were barely in their teens. Much of the Resistance had been carried out by children, he wrote, with good reason: Many of their parents had been killed in the line of duty or executed by the Gestapo.

On August 27, the bodies of fifty French policemen and members of the FFI were exhumed from mass graves in three places around the city. Days before they had been murdered by assassination squads of the Waffen SS. A Frenchman who'd been forced to serve on the burial detail but managed to escape told Boyle that his group had been ordered at gunpoint to dig their own burial pits, then made to dance around until exhausted while the SS troops, for entertainment, fired at their legs. When the dancers collapsed, the storm troopers put pistols to their heads and pulled the triggers.[48]

Boyle's column the day before had been on a lighter topic: the things that American soldiers would never forget "the first time they saw Paris." The capital had "lived up to every man's expectation as the most beautiful city in the world, and its daughters, too, were the most beautiful in France, especially after Normandy's muscled sisters, many of whom are patterned after their own native, bulky hedgerows." Boyle spotted one white-haired French lady walking Paris' streets with a small stepladder. "Whenever she came across a parked jeep she set up the ladder, climbed up to the third step and kissed the boys sitting in the back seat," he wrote.[49]

There's a good chance Boyle was insinuated among adoring women at the August 29 parade when the police motorcycle bore down on him. He probably never saw it coming. Boyle may well have had his back turned, jotting notes, when a gendarme on a motorbike lost control and plowed into him. Boyle was tossed high in the air and landed squarely on his back. Badly bruised, he was unable to get up for several minutes. An ambulance was summoned. Before being taken to the hospital, he managed to grind out a story by hand and get it to a colleague. It turned out he had torn several ligaments in his back, although X-rays probing for a more serious spinal injury proved negative.

He was hospitalized for three days and took it easy for another week or so after that—the first real break he'd had since arriving in England before D-Day. The correspondent who had barely escaped drowning off Casablanca and eluded bombs, shells, and bullets in North Africa, Sicily, Italy, and halfway across France was almost done in by an accident far flukier than the one that had killed his friend Tom Treanor.

U.S. CORRESPONDENTS FELL INTO A serendipitous cash windfall on August 26—perhaps the luckiest break any group of reporters have gotten anywhere at any time. Charles Wertenbaker, a correspondent with *Time*, had been tasked by the home office to inspect the Paris bureau that the magazine's employees had abruptly abandoned in June 1940. The Nazis had stormed into the capital so quickly that *Time*'s staff had not had the chance to safeguard $100,000 in American currency that had been stuffed into a concealed office safe. Back in '40, Henry Luce's bean counters in New York had claimed it as an insurance loss.

Wertenbaker managed to get into the old *Time* office on the first day of the liberation. He assumed that the Gestapo, which had ransacked almost every business in Paris, had uncovered the safe and everything in it. To his astonishment, the safe was intact and the one hundred grand was sitting there, undisturbed.

He cabled his bosses and asked what to do with the money. "Dispose of as you will—insurance company already paid off," Wertenbaker was counseled the next day.[50]

Word spread like wildfire. Wertenbaker started handing out hundred-dollar bills to reporter buddies as if they were lollipops.

Captain Bunny Rigg, Liebling's D-Day hero, the skipper of LCI(L)-88, managed to score a two-day pass and bummed a ride from England to France on a C-47. Rigg found Liebling at the Scribe just as news about Wertenbaker's boon was hitting; together they hustled over to Wertenbaker's room. Despite Liebling's well-documented disdain for *Time* founder Luce's brand of politics and journalism, Wertenbaker bankrolled them. In truth, as Liebling later pointed out, any American in Paris in August and September 1944 didn't need a lot of dough to have a good time. It was almost impossible in those heady days, Liebling remembered, for an American to pay for a drink or a bottle of wine. Ernie Pyle had been right: There was virtually no need for any American to *pay* a woman for sexual favors. Joe and Bunny used their wad to treat some ballerinas to a big night on the town.

Not long after Liebling and Rigg collected their cash, Ernest Hemingway barged into Wertenbaker's room, demanding a big stake for him and his FFI posse. Wertenbaker, with a straight face, informed Hemingway that he'd gotten bum information; there was no such cash. A red-faced Papa stormed out, muttering well-chosen epithets.

Hemingway's grandstanding had finally caught up to him. "I wouldn't give that son-of-a-bitch the sweat off my balls," Wertenbaker snarled.[51]

Papa wasn't staying at the plebeian Scribe. He and his Resistance pals repeated their Grand Veneur ruse at the Ritz. FFI guerrillas were literally standing guard at the Ritz on August 25 when photographer Robert Capa walked up. "Papa took good hotel," one of them told Capa. "Plenty of stuff in cellar. You go up quick."[52]

TIME'S OFFICE WASN'T THE ONLY place that the Gestapo had inexplicably overlooked. The *New York Herald Tribune*'s old printing press at 21 rue de Berri was also in surprisingly good shape, thanks to a Frenchwoman who had hidden its vital parts from the Germans. When her old American colleagues arrived, she presented her gift with what Cronkite heard was a coquettish swish of the skirt. It took only a week to get the old *Trib* facility up and running; the *Stars and Stripes* soon began publishing the bulk of its ETO infantry editions there.

Jimmy Cannon, the Gotham sports columnist who wrote in the same guttural cadence as his hero, Damon Runyon, had been with the *Stars and Stripes* for a year when he arrived in Paris late that summer. Cannon, Rooney remembered, immediately began reprising his Runyon bit in Paris, collecting quotes from GIs that sounded suspiciously like the railbirds at Belmont Park. Rooney enjoyed Cannon's style but Bud Hutton, the no-nonsense editor, abhorred it and distrusted its practitioner.

Cannon came to Paris with a clear-cut objective: to hustle a transplanted New York showgirl named Gay Orloff. Gay was the sort of "prototypical dumb blonde," Rooney remembered, "[that] Jimmy would have invented for his column back in New York."[53] Orloff had been Lucky Luciano's squeeze before the notorious gangster was sent up the river to Sing Sing. To endear himself to Miss Orloff, Cannon pretended that he'd been up to the big house to visit Luciano, claiming that the mobster had turned his jail cell into a veritable shrine: Her pictures were everywhere, including the ceiling, so Lucky could gaze up at her as he drifted off to sleep. Then, to make himself a more attractive catch, Cannon assured Orloff that Luciano had big plans for their lives together when Lucky got out of the joint—twenty-five years hence. "Gay was not the kind of girl," Rooney dryly observed, "who looked forward to the day she'd be starting her life at age sixty."[54]

Cannon's reverse psychology may have been working on Orloff until it was revealed that New York governor Thomas Dewey had pardoned Luciano. The racketeer buster was sending his old foe to Italy, hoping that

Lucky's Mafia connections might help free Allied prisoners still being held in the mountains north of Rome. But to let bygones be bygones, the governor had given Luciano the okay to stop in Paris to visit his old friend Gay Orloff. Cannon immediately packed his duffel bag and returned to the front, where his life, Rooney commented, would be less endangered.[55]

MACHINE GUNS AND ARTILLERY WERE still rumbling after dark on August 25 when Joe Liebling headed out from the Scribe to celebrate the greatest day of his life. The firing "seemed part of the summer night, like thunder," Liebling wrote. "There was no menace in the sound, and if it were not for plaques on the walls of houses in various parts of Paris that now commemorate the deaths of Frenchmen on that very night, I would find it difficult to believe there was real combat on the evening of my stroll."[56]

He walked down to the Boulevard du Montparnasse where, a few hours before, he'd watched von Choltitz surrender. Liebling was looking for a favorite restaurant haunt, the Closerie des Lilas, that was little more than a hole-in-the-wall. The place was blacked out, but Liebling peered through a window and could see a blue night light glowing. He banged on the door and shouted, *en français*: "It's an old customer! An old customer! An American! An American!" After a dozen bleats, the door opened a crack; the *patron* smiled and shook Liebling's hand. There were no customers, only the man's family and a waitress.

Hoping it would enhance his prospects of being fed, Liebling began reminiscing about the wonderful evenings he had enjoyed at the Closerie des Lilas in the old days. It worked. The waitress brought out a steaming terrine of potato soup. As Liebling dug in, the man's wife apologetically said there would "only" be an omelet and a salad to follow. "The *patronne*, it was plain, had never sampled a K-ration," Liebling wrote.

As they listened in the distance to the last throes of the Nazi subjugation of Paris, the man brought out a bottle of Bordeaux and said with a fiendish grin: "A lot of good it will do them."[57]

The Bordeaux made everyone wax sentimental. Soon the proprietor was telling Liebling that in the darkest days of the Occupation, he had squirreled away a flask of Pernod and a bottle of scotch to break out when the Germans were finally given the boot. He gave Liebling his choice. Joe went with the Black and White, knowing that he could drink more whiskey than a sweet liqueur.

They toasted Lafayette and de Gaulle, the FFI, and every Tommy and GI who'd set foot in France. Liebling drank enough to begin lamenting lost love. "A chagrin of love never forgets itself," the waitress mused. "You must not make bile about it."

When they drained the scotch it was time to say *bonne nuit*. Liebling wrote that he "took an effusive leave and went out in the dark street. The bars that I had passed earlier were still busy, but I had no inclination to enter. Any further drinking that night would have been a letdown."[58]

Joe Liebling's road to Paris had finally, magnificently, ended.

Seven days later he got to fulfill his dream, submitting to the *New Yorker* a letter from liberated Paris.

"For the first time in my life and probably the last," his wondrous lede went, "I have lived for a week in a great city where everybody is happy."[59]

CHAPTER 13

✦

GASPING COUGH—CRASHING
INTO HOLLAND

*Not the landing itself but the twelve days of almost con-
stant shelling and bombing afterward really frightened
me. That I plainly admit and if I can help it I have no
intention of ever getting back within range of artillery
again.*

—WALTER CRONKITE, OCTOBER 3, 1944
LETTER TO BETSY

Once the lead C-47 cut its towrope, the glider carrying Walter Cronkite,
Brigadier General Anthony Clement McAuliffe, and a dozen other
101st Airborne staff officers began bucking over Holland's flatlands. Everywhere Cronkite looked he could see white-striped gliders—dozens of
them—poised to crash-land in the fields just west of the Meuse River outside the Dutch village of Zon. Suddenly the sky blackened with antiaircraft
bursts; as his glider plummeted, Cronkite could hear artillery fire.

September 17, 1944, was a perfect afternoon for an airborne invasion:
the wind was calm and the skies were overcast enough to make it tougher
on enemy gunners. CBS' Edward R. Murrow was also flying with American paratroopers—not in a glider, but in a C-47 paratroop transport whose
pilot would return Murrow to London. To make his report crackle for listeners, Murrow had brought along a tape recorder.

"You can probably hear the snap as they check the lashings on the static line," Murrow's report went. "Tracers are coming up! . . . We're throttling back! . . . Every man is out now! I can see their chutes floating gracefully down. Near a windmill next to a church. They're like nothing so much, as I said a minute ago, as khaki dolls hanging beneath a green lampshade."[1]

Murrow's future CBS colleague Cronkite, at that moment in Dutch airspace a few miles south, wasn't conjuring up similes. Cronkite had somehow been under the impression that glider flight would be soothing. Sure, the landing might be rough; from the air, he had seen remnants of gliders splintered all over Normandy. But to be snuffed out while gliding might be a good way to go to heaven, he recalled thinking, "no roaring engine, just a nice silent glide into eternity."[2]

It was all a misnomer: the last thing gliders did was "glide." Canvas-skinned American Waco gliders were held together by flimsy aluminum tubing. "The canvas cover beat against the aluminum," the eighty-year-old Cronkite remembered in 1996, "and it was like being inside the drum at a Grateful Dead concert."[3]

Every bump while on a glider felt like a violent jolt. Cold air rushed in; the noise was so deafening that troopers had to communicate through shouts and gestures. Once freed from the towrope, glider pilots knew they were dead ducks to German gunners. They wanted to get on the ground pronto, so they pointed the nose downward and plunged, hitting the turf almost as vertically as horizontally. Many gliders crumpled on impact; pilots would deliberately crash the nose into the ground to get the troops out quicker. "If you ever have to go to war, don't go by glider," Cronkite the daredevil volunteered later.[4]

The Cronkite-McAuliffe craft thudded into a mucky potato field, flipping over and breaking up as piles of dirt came pouring in. Helmets came flying off; men grabbed the first ones they saw in the manic scramble to get away from artillery fire. If McAuliffe yelled his soon-to-be-trademark "Nuts!" Cronkite missed it.

A pair of American gliders had, seconds before, collided in midair; as Cronkite got his bearings, the sky was raining guns and human beings. Cronkite hurried toward what he'd been told in a premission briefing was the rallying point—a drainage ditch on the periphery of the landing zone. After a few moments, he glanced behind and discovered a string of enlisted men from other gliders following him.

> One of them shouted: "Hey, Lieutenant, are you sure we're going in the right direction?" I shouted back that I wasn't a lieutenant; I was a war correspondent. With a full GI vocabulary of unrepeatable words he advised me, rather strongly, that I was wearing a helmet with an officer's big white stripe down its back. It was the only chance I had to lead troops in the whole war. I didn't do badly. The drainage ditch was that way.[5]

Enemy artillery fire along that stretch of the Meuse and its Wilhelmina Canal didn't last long. Within minutes of "Cronkite's platoon" rendezvousing next to the gully, a squadron of P-51s bore down on the German gun positions. Within Cronkite's eyesight the Mustangs dove on four enemy batteries, knocking them out.

Just as he had three months earlier over the Channel and Normandy, Cronkite anxiously scanned the skies. But at least at that point in Holland, even with enemy air bases practically next door, there were no German planes in the air.

CRONKITE HAD BEEN ON THE periphery of ground combat in Morocco and Normandy but never in the thick of it. Until September 16, the day before the Holland mission, he had steeled himself to arrive on the Continent via parachute. After the disappointment of Operation Transfigure, Cronkite and the First Allied Airborne Army had on eight separate occasions gone on alert, he told Betsy. Several times, Cronkite had scrambled to an East Anglia airfield, reacquainting himself with his equipment and rehearsing the drop and roll, only to have the mission scrubbed at the last instant because Allied ground troops were moving too rapidly. The First Allied

Airborne's landing targets kept on getting swallowed up by onrushing Tommies and GIs.[6]

But the Holland campaign was different. Christened Operation Market Garden, it was the brainchild of Bernard Law Montgomery and his able lieutenant, General Miles C. Dempsey. Monty may have been ultracautious in the trenches, but his plan for Market Garden was, as Chester Wilmot put it, "bold and unorthodox"[7]—perhaps *too* bold and unorthodox. Monty's scheme was to springboard the Allies over the Rhine and into Germany's industrial heartland, the Ruhr Valley, long SHAEF's ultimate aim.

To muscle into Germany, Monty urged Ike to authorize an airborne drop—code-named Market—against a series of bridges on five different waterways in Holland, including the Rhine (the Dutch called it the Rijn) farther north, along the German-Dutch border. If it worked, as Wilmot maintained, Monty could cut in two the German defenses in Holland, outflank Hitler's Siegfried Line entrenchments, and create what Monty called a potent "pencil thrust" into the Ruhr.[8]

The refortified First Allied Airborne Army—the U.S. 82nd and the 101st Airborne, the Polish First, and the British First Airborne—were tasked with seizing and holding the bridges for four, perhaps five days while the armored British XXX Corps—code-named Garden—rolled north through a narrow corridor in Holland. Once linked, the Allied units would turn east and push into Germany. Cronkite and the 101st were assigned five of the southernmost bridges in and around Eindhoven, just below Zon on the Meuse.

Eisenhower, fearing a stalemate, was desperate to penetrate deep into Germany ahead of cold weather. In early September '44, SHAEF was still hopeful that Germany would surrender before year's end. The Wehrmacht, after all, was in panicked retreat on both its western and eastern fronts. Ike and Bradley decided not to use precious space on supply trucks to send winter coats and gloves to the men at the front. The brass was gambling that thicker clothing wouldn't be needed.

Another factor that argued for Market Garden, at least in Eisenhower's mind, was the gutsy performance of Allied airborne troops in Normandy.

Despite being scattered all over northern France the night before D-Day, the paratroopers had succeeded in achieving their objectives—and then some. The horrific airborne casualty figures that Leigh-Mallory and others had predicted had not materialized. Eisenhower had created the First Allied Airborne Army six weeks earlier to handle the exact exigency that Monty and Dempsey were now outlining.

Ike earlier had wanted to use the First Airborne to try to leapfrog the Maastricht–Aachen perimeter—but Bradley, closer to the action, rejected it as too risky. The special airbone unit was Ike's creation—and after all the frustrating, on-again, off-again moments of the past month, the Supreme Commander was determined to deploy it.

Ike green-lighted Market Garden on September 10—just seven days before it was scheduled to jump off. That didn't give airborne officers much time to plan a drop more complicated than D-Day's. Nearly 1,500 C-47 transports and five hundred gliders were scheduled to take off from two dozen different British airdromes in two gigantic streams, each escorted by more than 1,200 fighters. Before that a thousand Allied heavy and medium bombers would soften up antiaircraft defenses en route to the Netherlands and around the key bridges. In all, twenty thousand paratroopers would be dropped or glided into Holland, almost all in broad daylight. It was the first time the Allies had attempted a big paratroop drop in daytime.[9]

THIS TIME, CRONKITE AND EVERYONE was assured that "the party was on." The Market Garden party stayed on even *after* G-2 unearthed evidence— including surveillance photographs—that SS *Panzer* units were now stationed precariously close to Allied drop zones. And the party stayed on even though the drop zone for the northernmost British paratroopers was changed at the last minute, to one fully ten miles from their objective, the bridge over the Maas at Arnhem.

Cronkite knew nothing of the plan until the morning of September 16, when he got a call from a PRO inviting him to come along on "that picnic we'd been talking about." As instructed, he showed up at 20 Grosvenor

Square dragging his full combat regalia. There to his surprise was Stanley Woodward, Homer Bigart's colleague at the *New York Herald Tribune*, one of America's most prominent—and pretentious—sports columnists. Cronkite had never met Woodward but knew him on sight. Brand-new to England and war reporting, Woodward was playing "foreign correspondent" to the hilt, decked out in ridiculous pink trousers and oxford shoes that made him appear even more out of shape than he was.

The only reason that Woodward had shown up at 20 Grosvenor was that he'd intercepted a phone message at the *Trib*'s London office intended for its regular airborne beat guy, Ned Russell, who was on assignment in Paris. Woodward didn't have a clue about the "picnic" to which Russell had been invited; he was beginning to get surly with PRO staffers when Cronkite tugged at his elbow, whispering that he'd explain everything once they were in the car heading to Newbury, the 101st's headquarters forty miles west of London. When Cronkite volunteered to the *Trib*'s sedentary columnist that, in all likelihood, they would be parachuting behind enemy lines, "[Woodward] was astounded. He stared long and hard at me through his bottle-thick glasses."[10]

The officers of the 101st were in prejump party mode when Cronkite and Woodward got to Newbury. They plied Woodward with alcohol as he regaled them with stories of sporting legends. Cronkite drifted away and was delighted, in middebauch, when the 101st's commander, General Maxwell Taylor, decided to hold an impromptu briefing. Cronkite tried to find Woodward in the bar, came up empty, and assumed that the PROs had come to their senses and told the chubby windbag that he couldn't go to Holland.

The next day, outside Zon, after watching the P-51s pulverize enemy batteries, Cronkite went looking for a wooded area beyond the rallying point where company headquarters was supposed to be situated. Part of the HQ setup was a radio that Cronkite could use to transmit his stories. He almost stumbled over a flabby fellow lying prostrate at the end of the gully.

His helmet was pushed back on his head; although unhurt, he was writhing. Suddenly Cronkite realized who it was.

"Stan?" Cronkite asked. "Is that you, Stan?"

Woodward peered at Cronkite through bloodshot eyes, "the picture of a man with a raging hangover.

"'Nobody told me,' he mumbled, 'that it was going to be like this.'"

The night before, Woodward, dead-ass drunk, had apparently passed out. His new pals decided to have some fun. They replaced his pink trousers with standard-issue khakis that were so small they wouldn't close at the fly. Instead of a belt, Woodward's pants were held up by a hunk of rope. And they jammed on a jacket so tight it split at Woodward's shoulders. After all that, they poured him into a glider. Woodward may not have come to until the glider was airborne.

Once sober, Woodward turned out to be an okay correspondent and a decent companion, although his paunch and poor eyesight proved to be hindrances. At one point, Cronkite and Woodward crossed the canal on a raft; Woodward needed a shove on the derriere to scale the slippery far side of the canal wall.[11]

The 101st's immediate objective was the Zon bridge over the Wilhelmina. But with Cronkite just upstream, the Germans blew it up, forcing American engineers to slap together a temporary span. U.S. troopers had to cross the canal in rafts made from empty fuel tins. Despite the strong enemy resistance, the 101st achieved most of its mission, capturing four bridges in and around Eindhoven and holding on while British armored units came up from the south. A few miles north at Nijmegen, the 82nd had a rougher go, but was able to capture intact two more bridges and clear most of the road north.

But the British First Airborne at Arnhem was plagued by Murphy's Law. The towropes carrying thirty-odd gliders full of armored jeeps and other essential equipment broke. Three battalions were forced to advance on foot; it took them four full hours to reach the Maas. All of which gave the *Panzer* units time to get into position.

Another impediment to Allied troops was the jubilant Dutch. After more than four years of occupation, the people of the Netherlands couldn't contain themselves. Despite still-lurking Wehrmacht snipers, they raced out to greet their liberators, brandishing orange flags and tossing tulips.

The only "wound" Cronkite sustained in three years as a war correspondent was a scrape inflicted by a wayward batch of flowers. Whenever the sniping would start back up, the tulip throwers would retreat to their attics.

IT WAS CRONKITE'S FIRST EXPOSURE to on-the-ground combat reporting. As he related to Betsy that fall, he found the experience jarring. Under the best of circumstances, it was difficult to put day-to-day skirmishing into perspective. Under circumstances like those that existed during Market Garden—sketchy information, agitated commanders, ever-changing battle lines, and a campaign that quickly turned sour—it was next to impossible. Cronkite found himself mimicking Hal Boyle by profiling the human side of GIs caught in battle. It's apparent from Cronkite's letters that he worried his "mediocre stuff" wasn't up to snuff.

The UP correspondent clearly wasn't Bigart when it came to gauging the import of a given battle. And his features on grunts at the front weren't as poignant or amusing as Boyle's. But those same criticisms could be leveled at almost every other reporter in the ETO, including Andy Rooney.

Cronkite's early dispatches with an Eindhoven dateline were too rosy, full of stirring accounts of how U.S. paratroopers had ousted the enemy from the lower Meuse and were on the verge of linking up with British tankmen driving north.[12] They stayed "on the verge" for days on end. When it finally happened, Eindhoven's narrow roads and wily German defenses made a rapid advance through the Dutch corridor tough—a thorny reality that the 101st's censors would not have permitted Cronkite to address. Yet even a week into the campaign, when it was clear that Arnhem would stay in enemy hands and that much of the Dutch corridor remained impenetrable, Cronkite, prodded by Allied PROs, was writing wishful pieces that the Germans were fighting what amounted to a holding action to preserve their escape route into Germany. In truth, despite the Allied paratroopers' courageous efforts, they hadn't dislodged the enemy.

It should not have been hard for Cronkite to spot Market Garden's defects. When the first English patrol arrived near Eindhoven, Cronkite watched 101st deputy commander Brigadier General Gerald J. Higgins

greet a cheeky English lieutenant. Higgins' engineers were busily rebuild-
ing the canal bridge that the Germans had destroyed on day one. But just
upstream was a smaller span, still in German hands. Buttonholing the
young Brit, Higgins began laying out a strategy to seize the bridge.

"I say, General," the lieutenant replied, "you know my chaps have been
going since dawn and we haven't had our tea yet." Cronkite watched an
incensed Higgins fumble for a wrench attached to the side of the lieutenant's jeep, intent on bullying the youngster into action. But at that instant
the Germans blasted the bridge.[13] Higgins' menacing gesture had been rendered moot.

A day later the forward elements of the XXX Corps arrived in Eindhoven, a "bumper-to-bumper parade," Cronkite recalled, that crowded the
north-south thoroughfare and crammed the village's narrow streets. At
dusk that night, the Luftwaffe suddenly appeared, strafing the exposed
British column. "The ammunition trucks turned all of Eindhoven into a
display of deadly fireworks," Cronkite remembered.

As the dive-bombers struck, Cronkite was in a jeep with his old UP pal
from Kansas City, bespectacled CBS Radio correspondent Bill Downs, the
reporter that Murrow had wanted Cronkite to replace in Russia. Cronkite
and Downs were driving near the Philips Electric works complex when
bombs began falling. They jumped out of the jeep and vaulted over a tall
fence into a park. There they huddled behind chopped-down trees as
bombs pounded all around. Neither knew how, but they became separated.

With incendiary fires raging, Eindhoven looked sickeningly familiar to
Cronkite: London during the Little Blitz. Cronkite knew about the Luftwaffe's dastardly "butterfly" bombs that tended to lodge in trees and bushes
before detonating. So as he went looking for Downs, he had one eye peeled
on the limbs overhead and the other scoping the ground for mines.

Cronkite decided to get out of the woods and go back to the jeep. When
he retraced his steps, he was astounded to find that the fence over which
he and Downs had scrambled was more than seven feet tall. Without an
adrenaline surge like the one he'd had earlier, Cronkite couldn't possibly
climb it. He had to find a downed tree whose trunk was close enough to
the fence to use as a makeshift stepladder.

Downs was nowhere to be found. Cronkite even checked Eindhoven's bomb shelters; no one had seen him. In one shelter a Dutch family with sobbing children spotted Cronkite's uniform and began pressing him about when the bombing would stop—which, of course, he couldn't answer. He went back to the jeep, found Downs' tape machine, and recorded a heartfelt tribute, praying someone would find it—and, eventually, Downs' body, too.

Then Cronkite hitched a ride to Brussels, where he hoped to find a warm bath, better wire facilities, and more malleable censors than the 101st's tight asses, which barely let reporters acknowledge that the division was in Holland and cramped their time on transmitters.

Cronkite found a room at Brussels' Hôtel Métropole and, still dirty head to toe, decided to toast his departed friend with a quick drink at the bar. "There stood Downs," Cronkite recalled, "immaculate in a clean dress uniform.

"'Damn, Bill, I spent all that time at risk of life and limb from those mines yelling for you, looking for you, and you just up and left me there.'"

Downs' excuse was that, after a few minutes of rasping "Cronkite! Cronkite!" it occurred to him that his friend's name sounded disconcert-edly like the German word for "sickness." If any enemy soldiers encoun-tered Downs, "They would have figured I was sick and hustled me off to a hospital in Berlin." Cronkite couldn't help but laugh.[14]

A few days later Downs and Cronkite were back in Holland with the 101st, which was fighting off another German attempt to regain control of the highway north of Eindhoven. In the midst of lethal mortar fire, Downs and Cronkite leapt into a ditch.

"We had been there a while when Downs, lying behind me, began tug-ging at my pants leg. I figured he had some scheme for getting us out of there, and I twisted my neck around to look back at him," Cronkite re-called.

"Just think!" Downs hollered. "If we survive them, these will be the good old days!"[15]

Sometimes the Germans would succeed in seizing a section of Dutch turf—only to forfeit it a few hours later after a bloody counterattack by Allied troopers.

A night or two after his gully episode, Cronkite and his jeep driver were on that same stretch when they heard the oncoming *clank-clank* of tank treads. As far as Cronkite knew, there weren't any friendly armored units in the area. So they pulled the jeep off the road and tried to stay very still. Five German tanks thumped past, with several drivers shouting greetings.

"They apparently assumed we were German. They rumbled on and we breathed again," Cronkite recalled.[16]

Cronkite's best early dispatch from Zon-Eindhoven came six days after the initial attack. Eleven members of the 101st were rescued on September 23 after having spent nearly a week behind enemy lines, successfully concealed by Dutch Partisans. Private John Kessel of Detroit told Cronkite that ack-ack had hit the motor of his glider's towplane just seconds into Dutch territory on September 17. "The pilot immediately climbed the ship as fast as he could to give us altitude to try to make a landing. These two pilots gave their lives to do that, [because] that plane crashed a minute later. We all landed, but were quite a few miles from the other gliders and were completely cut off."

Among the eleven troopers were two airmen who had survived the crash of Kessel's towplane. Four other troopers were from a glider that had managed to sever itself from a damaged C-47. Another survivor jumped from another burning tow ship; the others were crewmen from wayward gliders and planes.[17]

Soon it became apparent that they were surrounded by the enemy. Dutch Resistance fighters hid them in dense woods, bringing them milk, beer, and food. At one point, they were almost ensnared in a firefight between British paratroopers and a German company dug in not far from their hideout. After the skirmish, a German patrol came within a few feet of where Kessel and another trooper, Private Kitterman of Indiana, were cloaked in the woods. "He and I were so quiet I don't think our hearts were beating," Kessel told Cronkite.

On day five, a Partisan leader said he'd snuck through enemy lines and reached a British company. Help would be coming tomorrow, the Resistance head promised. The next day the eleven troopers were escorted to safety by six British Bren gun carriers and an unarmed Red Cross jeep.[18]

———

ON DAY THREE of MARKET Garden, Cronkite heard about an amazing—and lifesaving—piece of Yankee ingenuity from Lieutenant Colonel Ned Moore of Guthrie Center, Iowa.

Moore and his twelve-man patrol were reconnoitering a Wilhelmina Canal bridge. Along with two bazooka specialists, Moore got separated from the rest of his unit when a Tiger tank and a small detachment of enemy soldiers abruptly surfaced. The bazooka men fired at the enemy tank and missed; one of them fled in panic. Moore and Private J. J. McCarthy slid down the canal bank and toward a shed where they hoped to hide. Just then, the Tiger blew up the building, the flames shooting sky-high.

"Afraid the Germans would spot their silhouettes, Moore recalled a kid stunt and made a donkey head with his hands against the flickering flames from the house. 'The fire threw the silhouette of the donkey, as big as a house, right in front of the tank,'" Moore told Cronkite.

The German patrol chose not to investigate the "mule" on the side of the road. At which point McCarthy asked Moore what they should do. "We lie low," Moore whispered.[19]

A few minutes later a different bazooka unit knocked out the Tiger. Moore and McCarthy made their way to safety. Cronkite's donkey piece got huge pickup in the States, cracking page one of the *Atlanta Constitution* and being reprinted in the *Stars and Stripes*.

THREE WEEKS LATER THE BATTLE for Holland was still raging; the Allies' hopes for a quick thrust into the Ruhr had been thwarted. Much of the fighting west of the Rhine that fall took on the veneer of World War I—the very thing the Supreme Command had feared most. Operation Market Garden, in fact, had been designed to avert the ugly stalemate now taking root along the long stretch from the North Sea to Luxembourg and below.

Cronkite spent several days in early fall shadowing the U.S. Seventh Armored Division, the British 11th Armored, and the British Third Infantry in southeastern Holland. The Allied thrust was part of Operation

Aintree, a hastily patched-together offensive aimed at holding on to the narrow salient between Eindhoven and Nijmegen and uprooting the German bridgehead west of the Meuse. Aintree, named after a British racecourse, turned out to be Market Garden in microcosm: bold but naïve planning, extraordinary heroism, and an eventual withdrawal.

"For five days last week," Cronkite wrote in a piece picked up by the *Stars and Stripes* on October 16, "500 Americans and 800 Germans fought in a bloody miniature of World War I in a tiny boot-shaped wood near the crossroads town of Overloon. For 120 nightmarish hours, Americans and Germans with fixed bayonets chased each other from foxhole to foxhole and from tree to tree. They fought without quarter day and night, in sunlight and driving rain."[20]

Overloon has been largely forgotten but was among Holland's bloodiest clashes. Despite heavy losses, Overloon was eventually captured by Allied troops. The village of Venray was the next Allied target, but the Germans had flooded and mined the area surrounding Loobeek Creek. Overloon-Venray was Market Garden's only big tank-on-tank clash, with Montgomery's forces losing dozens of tanks they could ill afford. The advance toward the Meuse was postponed, in large measure because the Allies could not replace men and matériel sacrificed in Overloon's forest.[21]

Cronkite probably had to retreat to Brussels and its more pliable censors to get the following lines approved: "The boot-shaped wood had been a trap. Ostensibly, it was held light by a German labor battalion. . . . The 500 [Americans] infiltrated and met a hail of death. Three mounds of dirt turned out to be pillboxes, and the clearing beside the wood, through which the tanks had planned to roll in a flank movement, turned out to be alive with mines. The Americans were immobilized on the edge of the wood and then German artillery and 'moaning minnies' (huge rocket mortars) blasted their hastily-dug positions. The 'labor battalion' turned out to be fanatical German SS troops."[22]

Overloon-Venray was grisly stuff: For five successive nights, grenades and potato mashers were tossed back and forth at point-blank range. Cronkite's *Stars and Stripes* piece concluded with: "As the lieutenant-colonel commanding the battalion ordered the withdrawal over his 'walkie-talkie,' two Germans appeared out of a bush five feet away and ordered his surrender at gunpoint. Before the colonel could reply the Germans crumpled under the fire of Americans in the next foxhole. The colonel summed up the battle with, 'We killed a lot of Germans.'"[23]

The Brits and the Yanks had indeed killed a lot of Germans—but at horrific cost, with little territorial gain to show for it. Twenty-five hundred Allied soldiers died in and around Overloon in October 1944.

GEORGE PATTON WAS NEVER INVOLVED in Market Garden's planning or execution. But by then Patton was far from the only U.S. commander suspicious of Bernard Montgomery's motives and modus operandi. By September of '44 the rivalry between Montgomery, head of the 21st Army Group, and Omar Bradley, head of the 12th Army Group, had become a full-blooded feud. Bradley had grown weary of Monty's petulant-child act, not to mention his recurring tendency to go hors de combat. Monty's unwillingness to press what appeared to be his advantage at Operation Goodwood and at other moments in northern Europe perplexed Bradley and Eisenhower. At the September 10 conference where Monty sold Ike on Market Garden, he got so peevish that, in midmeeting, Ike had to grab his knee and scold, "Steady, Monty. You can't talk to me that way. I'm your boss."[24]

Despite Monty's rudeness, Ike approved the incursion into Holland—a move that left Bradley scratching his head. Eisenhower should have listened to his West Point classmate. Even if Market Garden had gone like clockwork, the chances of it attaining Montgomery's dreams were slight. Bradley wanted Monty to concentrate his resources on capturing the Schelde estuary between Antwerp and the North Sea. As long as the Germans maintained control of the Schelde, Antwerp's ports would be useless.[25]

WES GALLAGHER, HAL BOYLE'S BOSS at AP, ordered him into Holland three days after the initial parachute drop. Boyle, his back still aching from its collision with the motorcycle cop in Paris three weeks earlier, bumped into an extraordinary story as he hitchhiked into the Netherlands. On the French-Belgian border on September 2, an unnamed major general mobilized a group of just ten Americans and held up a heavily armed Nazi column for fifteen critical minutes while U.S. Shermans maneuvered to launch an ambush. Panicked by the Allied advance, the Germans were trying to push through the French village of Marchiennes and get back behind friendly lines.

The major general and a colonel had just greeted a Second Armored Division that rumbled through Marchiennes when a villager ran up, crying, "*Les Boches! Les Boches!*" The general sent a messenger after the tankmen, then "quickly organized his little army, deploying them to cover every route into town." The colonel happened to be a former national champion marksman; he and the tommy gun–wielding general took cover behind posts in the middle of town.

Boyle wrote: "The Nazi column was met by a stream of harassing small arms fire from four directions. The startled Germans, swearing and mystified by fire which they believed came from a far larger force, began shooting as the vehicles jammed up."

The tiny American force emptied their ammunition clips—rifles, carbines, and tommy guns—then slipped away before the Nazis wised up. The major general's plan worked, Boyle observed. "The Germans reorganized their column and swept on through the town and ran right into the flaming guns of waiting American tanks. The Nazis were cut to pieces before they knew what had happened to them."[26] Thanks to the quick-thinking major general, all but one of the enemy tanks, trucks, and half-tracks was destroyed or disabled. Some three hundred of the 470 soldiers in the German unit were killed in the ambush. Sixty were captured; only seventy or eighty escaped. No Americans were lost in the firefight, Boyle reported; the only casualty was an FFI fighter.

On September 16, Boyle was near Romorantin, France, when twenty thousand Germans, weary of the constant strafing from P-47s and P-51s, surrendered en masse. Most members of the "lost column," as Boyle called them, had been stationed in the south of France—some as far south as the Spanish border.[27]

One Nazi asked Boyle if American prison camps had whiskey. Another inquired if he could take a correspondence course at Harvard.

"I watched for more than two hours the long and sorry columns which told more vividly than words the plight of dying German military might," Boyle wrote. "There were no rumbling panzers, no motorized blitzkrieg. Only the slow, tedious plodding of tired horses and tired men, the gasping cough of badly worn trucks.

"'You defeated us only because you had better matériel,' said one. Oberleutnant Ben Wise, former South American steel exporter, said: 'It is destiny.'

"Always the excuse—never an admission that Germany is beaten because she just didn't have the stuff on the ball," Boyle wrote.[28]

Along with other Allied correspondents, Boyle had been shown a captured document in which Berlin had directed all German officers—except "expendable junior officers"—to save their own lives in battle so that Hitler's thousand-year Reich would have the leadership necessary to wage the next war.

"The junior commanders," Boyle wrote, "have been nominated to die a hero's death to spur the flagging troop morale while their superiors save their own skins in emergencies." The chilling order had been issued in the waning days of the Battle of France when desertion was becoming commonplace. "Noncommissioned offices were instructed to ferret out dissident soldiers and put them in the front-line posts," Boyle noted, "where they would be killed or send them back home on leave where the Gestapo or S.S. (Elite Guard) officers could arrest them."[29]

HAVING JUST FILED ARTICLES HERALDING the Reich's imminent collapse, it must have been jarring for Boyle to size up the situation in Holland. The Germans on the business end of Market Garden were not saving their own skins by retreating behind the Rhine. Five days into his visit to the Netherlands, Boyle must have realized that he couldn't write about triumphant Allies on an inevitable march to victory, so he went back to his tried-and-true formula: American GI's fascination with a foreign culture. "The national salute by Hollanders to every jeepload of American soldiers is 'Hello, boys,'" Boyle wrote. "Gone is that preliminary period of doubt and uncertainty when troops met with almost blank stares or covert 'V' signs."

"No country has been more of a surprise than that section of Holland now occupied by the [Americans]. Its wooded hills and green farmlands full of grazing black and white cows and neat brick towns look more like a corner of rural Pennsylvania than the land of dikes. In dress these people differ little from those the troops left behind in the small towns of America.

"Somehow most of the soldiers thought that all parts of Holland were full of quaintly attired folks and whirling windmills."[30]

IN THE FALL OF '44, the *Stars and Stripes* sent Andy Rooney to the land of whirling windmills, too. But not before the kid reporter had finished the First Army's sweep across France and actually stood on German soil—if only briefly. On September 3, Rooney filed an amusing piece from "Somewhere in France" about how a bunch of First Army Texans had corralled a couple hundred fine German saddle horses that had been abandoned by the Wehrmacht.

"The main trouble with the outfit was that none of the horses understood 'whoa' and 'giddap' and none of the brand-new cavalrymen knew how to say 'whoa' in German," Rooney kidded. One private confused his horse by naming it "Jackson," Rooney noted. "The name 'Jackson' held no significance whatsoever for the horse."

While the Texans went joyriding on German dobbins, the "Eastern boys," Rooney wrote, "picked themselves out maybe a neat-looking German amphibious jeep complete with 'propeller' or [a] command car" and, while awaiting orders, spun donuts in an orchard.[31]

Eleven days later, Big Red One GIs were hardly joyriding as they cracked the Siegfried Line near the border village of Roetgen—a coup that drew front-page treatment in the *Stars and Stripes* and most U.S. papers. The Germans had engineered their defenses to "funnel" invaders into tight spots that would leave them vulnerable to attack.

One of those traps, Rooney explained, invited invaders to attack a deep

gorge dotted with thousands of concrete tank obstructions. Six-foot trian-
gular obstacles ran fifty feet deep through the gorge. An armored task force
led by Third Armored Division lieutenant colonel William B. Lovelady
was "mousetrapped" in the gorge on September 13, some three and a half
miles onto German soil.

The Germans tried a clever ruse. They left abandoned artillery guns
and pillboxes on the road into Roetgen "to make it look," Rooney wrote,
"like they had made a hasty retreat. The German antitank and self-
propelled guns opened up on the column from three sides when the tanks
and half-tracks came into the town and knocked out several before they
were wiped out by our artillery and tanks."[32]

The lead American Sherman, driven by Second Lieutenant Paul Bear of
Reading, Pennsylvania, was instantly disabled by *Panzerfäuste*. Bear's tank
mate, Private Wesley White of Belleville, Illinois, jumped out and dragged
a wounded comrade to safety.

Residents of Roetgen feared retribution. Almost every house in the village, Rooney noted, hung a white bedsheet of surrender. Many civilians,
told by their country's soldiers that they'd be shot on sight, sought refuge
in haystacks, barns, or the woods. Those villagers that remained clasped
trembling hands over their heads.

When it became apparent that the Americans were there not to brutal-
ize but to liberate, the children of Roetgen came out of hiding and began
asking GIs for gum and candy. "Kids of all nations seem to be internation-
alists, minus fear or hate," Rooney wrote. "Some German mothers dragged
waving children from the streets."[33]

Rooney's piece ended with a poignant moment of irony. A U.S. medical
officer, Captain Jack Blinkoff, who had studied in Bonn before the war, was
asked by a German farmer if it was all right to kill one of the farmer's pigs.

"Go ahead, kill the pig," Blinkoff replied in German. "Why ask me?"

The farmer explained that the Nazis would exact severe punishment on
any German civilian who slaughtered animals without a license.

Four days later Rooney was still inside Germany, saluting the first
Americans who had breached the Fatherland's defenses. After all the talk
about the "impervious" border barrier, First Lieutenant Bob Kolb of Pa-

ducah, Kentucky, "took his company through it without a casualty."[34] Kolb's infantry unit helped open the floodgates for armored units that were now "pouring" through the gap, Rooney observed.

The first American scout who slipped through the "vaunted line" was Private First Class Alvin O. Kenyon of Seattle. Soon Kolb's entire company was across, followed quickly by an armored unit with tanks and M10 (artillery) support. Rooney was one of the first American correspondents to eyeball the Siegfried Line's obstacles.

"In the hilly country of the border, roads run through the valley, and the Germans placed the fortified concrete igloos [pillboxes] in positions which commanded the only possible entry for vehicles. On both sides of the roads, concrete 'dragon's teeth' extend for miles, preventing tanks from rolling over the open country between the road networks.

"'We knocked out about 15 or 20 pillboxes, I guess,' Kolb said. 'Our M10 fired at some of the them from about 20 yards and blasted them wide open.'

"There was no artillery at all in any of the pillboxes Kolb's company encountered. Most of the outdated fortifications had gun positions built for nothing bigger than the old German 47-millimeter antitank gun," Rooney's piece concluded.[35]

ROONEY DIDN'T KNOW IT, BUT he was chronicling the apex of the Allied advance in 1944. Given the fierceness of the German stand along the Rhine and the supply difficulties of sustaining the Allied offensive, Eisenhower's thrust had run out of steam.

Hitler's empire in September '44 was a fraction of its size two years earlier. In the east, the Russians had recaptured half of Latvia and Lithuania, close to two-thirds of Poland, Romania and Bulgaria, and were beginning to zero in on eastern Germany. In the West, almost all of France and Belgium had been liberated; a few select American units like Rooney's friends in the Second Battalion had pounded their way past the Siegfried Line. But Eisenhower and Bradley knew that unless something dramatic happened, they would be hunkering down on the western side of the Rhine for the winter.

That something dramatic did not happen in Holland. Rooney was sent to Maastricht, Holland, on September 21 and the next day unearthed a remarkable story about how the resourceful Dutch had preserved many of the world's artistic masterworks, including memorable canvases by Rembrandt, Vermeer, Van Gogh, Rubens, and Van Dyck.

"In the far recesses of a mountain cave where the Dutch villagers cart horse manure in which to grow mushrooms are 800 of the world's finest paintings," went Rooney's lede.[36]

The paintings had been secretly moved from museums in Amsterdam and Rotterdam at the outbreak of the war and hidden all over the Netherlands. In April 1941, under the noses of the Nazis, the works were transferred to a climate-controlled vault built into a subterranean cavern near Maastricht. The cave was ingeniously designed, Rooney observed. On one side of the hill, workers dragged heavy carts full of manure through a series of winding passages to the mushroom beds. On the other side, cleverly disguised steel doors guarded the art treasures.

Inside the metal doors, the Dutch had designed a gauntlet of five steel barricades, each guarded by a gendarme. In the art room itself, the temperature was controlled at 15 degrees centigrade; each painting was mounted on a specially designed steel rack. Rembrandt's *Night Watch* was attached to a special drum because the canvas was too big to be mounted on a rack. The drum was turned daily so the canvas wouldn't lose its shape.

Rooney noted that the canvases, many of them painted in the sixteenth and seventeenth centuries, were in "perfect" condition. Somehow, despite Hermann Göring's twisted obsession with magnificent art and bootlicking sycophants looking to ingratiate themselves with *Herr Reichsmarschall*, the Nazis never found the Dutch treasure trove. Allied troops now stood guard over the cavern to ensure that any enemy commando raid would be thwarted.[37]

PLAYING DEFENSE IS ABOUT ALL the Allies could muster in Holland after Market Garden bogged down. The Allies ended up sustaining more casualties in Holland—some seventeen thousand in all—than they suffered on D-Day's beaches.[38]

Market Garden may have backfired, but that didn't dilute Walter Cronkite's affection for the Netherlands and its people. "I'm absolutely in love with Holland—what I've seen of it, and even the residents of that portion claim that it is the ugliest section of the country," he told Betsy in a letter on October 3.[39]

On Friday, September 29, Cronkite had gone to Brussels for some R & R with a couple of *Yank* correspondents. They somehow managed to acquire a captured *Wasserwagen,* an amphibious Volkswagen jeep, and decided— what the hell!—they'd hit Paris for the weekend. Cronkite had never been to Paris, so he was thrilled.

About six o'clock that night, thirty miles north of the capital in the middle of the Compiègne Forest, the "damned car," as Cronkite put it, broke down. The threesome had talked their way into going southwest on a highway that the military police had restricted to northeast-bound supply traffic. So now Cronkite had to hitchhike the "wrong" way, yet still got to the next town, where he told the MPs where they could find his stranded buddies.

He got to Paris about ten thirty that night, filthy from exhaust grime, and collapsed at a Red Cross officers' club at the Hôtel Edouard VII on the Avenue de l'Opéra. The next morning, he stopped by UP's Paris office, where a colleague named Sam Hales took him to the USO's Rainbow Room at the Hôtel de Paris, a replica of its famous forebear in London. For lunch they headed over to the press headquarters at the Hôtel Scribe, which Cronkite enjoyed so much he had dinner there, too.

Cronkite played tourist all day, taking a horse-drawn carriage down the Boulevard des Capucines and the Champs-Élysées. At one point he sipped a couple of cognacs while watching Parisians and American soldiers parade past.

"Paris appears unaffected by war," he told Betsy. "The women are the most fabulously dressed people I have ever seen, complete with silk stockings, cosmetics (of which there are few in England), beautiful clothes and insane hats and shoes. And all carrying long, rolled parasols with lace frills or leading dogs as insane as the hats." Then in words that would have delighted Joe Liebling, Cronkite wrote, "Many dressed like that pedal by on bicycles with their skirts up to their thighs. Most disturbing!"[40]

He and his correspondent pals allowed themselves to be disturbed by other leggy sights that evening as they went to Montmartre to take in the much-anticipated reopening of cancan dancing at the Bal Tabarin. Cronkite was surprised that the Bal Tabarin was not the sophisticated theater that he had imagined but rather a "glorified Coney Island dime-a-dance joint." Paris was bereft of liquor but there were endless supplies of champagne, so that's what everyone drank that night, he told Betsy.

Cronkite was now covering the British Second Army out of Montgomery's back-of-the-line setup in Brussels—and not thrilled about it. The dream of covering an Allied army surging into the Ruhr had given way to the reality of settling in behind a static line.

He wrote Betsy that he "felt like a damned baby" in Brussels. Cronkite was kicking himself for not having stuck with French at the University of Texas. It was "lonely and discouraging" to be a daily newspaperman without being able to read daily newspapers, he wrote.[41]

Twice a day he would attend British Second Army briefings and, much like his experience at the Ministry of Information in London, write up the newsworthy communiqués for the UP wire. But in truth, by October there was little in the way of significant movements of troops.

A FEW DAYS BEFORE CRONKITE took in the cancan, Hal Boyle wrote a story that the Allied high command had dreaded: The Nazis' fierce stand after two months of backpedaling had come as a shock to Allied soldiers.

Boyle talked to dozens of grunts every day. "'Once we drive them back to their own country they'll come to their senses,' has been the thought and consolation of most soldiers ever since invasion day last June," Boyle wrote. "'Then we'll have a walkway parade to Berlin and the war will be over. They will never fight in their own country.'

"But they are. And it's making the American soldier angrier, tougher, and more eager to smash through to Berlin every day. Many of these combat troops have been overseas for two years or more and secretly had hoped their reward for a quick victory might be to return home by Christmas. Now they realize that is an outside chance, and they are uncomfortably aware of the possibility that the European war may well last through a cold and forlorn winter."[42]

Sergeant J. D. Peel from Geneva, New York, told Boyle that, "The American dogface is a poor hater." But Peel and the other men in his outfit were appalled by the apparent willingness of German leaders to drag their country down with them. "If they had an honorable leader among them," Peel said, "he would give up and save his country."[43]

German prisoners were telling interrogators that, were it up to them, the war would already be over. "They are all afraid of the SS officers and the Gestapo and they say [SS head] Heinrich Himmler himself is running the army," Boyle told readers. "They all say they are sorry that Hitler wasn't killed." Enemy prisoners were also jaded about the Goebbels boast of "secret weapons" that would turn the tide of war. "Don't kid us about those secret weapons," Boyle quoted one prisoner. "We know such talk is silly." The cynicism was in striking contrast to the "pugnacious faith" Boyle consistently heard from captured members of the Wehrmacht in Normandy.[44]

A FEW DAYS AFTER INTERVIEWING the prisoners in early October, Hal Boyle spent time at Spa, Belgium, the old vacation spot that had lent its name to the mineral-waters-resort craze of the nineteenth century. Along with several other First Army correspondents in Spa, Boyle was photographed cavorting atop a bed in which Kaiser Wilhelm had spent a nervous night before fleeing to Holland as the German lines crumbled in the fall of 1918.

Two bodies down the Kaiser's bed from Boyle was a horn-rimmed-glasses-wearing UP reporter named John Frankish, who had just arrived in the ETO a few weeks earlier. The reporters didn't bother to untie their combat boots as they mugged for the camera. Walter Cronkite didn't know his UP colleague well but had helped show the young University of Southern California grad the ropes when Frankish[45] was getting acclimated in London before being assigned to ground troops. One night at Cronkite's flat, much to the host's dismay, Frankish and another UP reporter got into a bottle of bourbon that Cronkite had been saving for a special occasion.[46] Even when not fueled by liquor, Frankish had a wicked sense of humor; like Joe Liebling, he was a dead-on mimic.

As October turned toward November, Boyle had a columnist's prerogative: He continued to shuttle from Holland to Belgium and from France to Luxembourg—wherever the best Allied human interest story was. Cronkite settled in Brussels to sift through Montgomery's self-aggrandizing statements, while their new friend Frankish stayed closer to the U.S. front lines near Belgium's Ardennes Forest.

Andy Rooney that fall stayed with the First Army but spent a lot of time editing stories at the *Stars and Stripes*' offices in Paris. In late October, the paper sent Rooney back to Brittany, where, remarkably, the Germans were still holding out, nearly five months after D-Day.

"Five hundred miles behind the bitter battle for the Siegfried Line and the plains of the Rhine, there is a milder war, a war almost forgotten," Rooney wrote."[47] Two south Brittany peninsula ports that the Germans had converted into U-boat lairs, St.-Nazaire and Lorient, remained uncaptured, despite near-constant artillery and bombing attacks. They were the last German outposts left in France in late '44; between them, some fifty thousand near-starving enemy troops were hunkered down.

Many of the enemy soldiers had operated antiaircraft batteries with such ferocity that Allied pilots had nicknamed St.-Nazaire Flak City.[48] Back in August, General George Patton's Third Army had been tasked by Omar Bradley with seizing the Brittany ports, part of Bradley's insistence on keeping Allied supply lines fully open. But once Patton realized that the enemy had dug in along the coast—and that martial glory lay elsewhere— he pulled up stakes. Eleven weeks later, the Allied "siege" consisted of one lone American tank outfit supported by FFI troops. The ragtag army encircled each port to ensure that there was no enemy breakout. Something of a bizarre rapprochement had settled in: No serious Allied effort had been launched in weeks to try to uproot the enemy; the Germans, in turn, only made halfhearted efforts to return artillery fire, although on occasion a gunboat would zoom up the Loire, fire a few rounds, then disappear.

By then, American and French soldiers had struck up friendly relations with young ladies in Brittany, who would bring wine and bread to the trenches. On weekends when the Allied boys could get passes, impromptu parties would break out.

In mid-October, a "small scrap" transpired when an American patrol ran into a German squad. When they reached the battlefield under a Red Cross banner, German medics had more wounded than they had estimated; they were short two litters. A German medical officer talked his American counterpart into "loaning" him two litters, with the proviso, Rooney noted, that the stretchers would be returned twenty-four hours later to the same spot.

> Next day the U.S. medic returned, but the German officer didn't show up. Instead he sent a man with a note: He was very sorry he had not showed up with the litters but could he please, because of the acute litter shortage on the German side, keep the two U.S. litters?
>
> The American, annoyed at being stood up in his rendezvous with the German medic, returned an indignant note. Certainly the Germans could not keep the two litters. Who did the German officer think the U.S. quartermaster was supplying, anyway? The following day the German office humbly returned with the two borrowed litters.[49]

BOTH SIDES NEEDED TOO MANY litters that autumn as the fighting inside the Hürtgen Forest and outside Aachen, Metz, and other places became bitter. Over the holidays, Rooney got the same break that Boyle had gotten the previous spring and Cronkite sorely needed—a trip home. The *Stars and Stripes* had instituted a rotation system to give their ETO correspondents a respite. Rooney spent almost two months back in the States, mixing reportorial duties with joyous R & R time with his wife, Margie, and friends.

Along with old pal Bob Ruthman, Margie and Andy headed out in late November to see friends at Colgate. A blizzard that killed dozens along northeastern highways that weekend nearly proved fatal to them, too. Stranded in a roadside snowbank, they were beginning to panic when they spotted the flashing light of a wrecker, which took them to safety. They never did make it to Colgate.[50]

Rooney did, however, make it to the *Stars and Stripes'* East Forty-second Street offices, where he got to file several sports-related articles, including a piece trumpeting West Point football coach Earl "Red" Blaik's prediction of victory (which proved to be correct) in the 1944 Army-Navy game.

On Rooney's second day in New York, he happened to bump into an old Army friend, an intelligence officer, at Grand Central Station. "In an excited subway whisper," Rooney's acquaintance related an astonishing story: The day before, Election Day, radar screens had detected the Germans launching a missile aimed at New York from a U-boat several hundred miles out into the Atlantic. East Coast air defenses had been scrambled. Rooney's friend saw the projectile on the radar screen. It was traveling some 250 miles per hour when it disappeared off the screen, either falling short of its target or shot down by an alert pilot. The Nazi threat had not come as a complete shock, Rooney's friend said. War planners had long feared that Hitler would use one of his *Vergeltungswaffen* weapons against the continental U.S. It was not outside the realm of possibility that German scientists could arm a U-boat with some variation of a V-1 buzz bomb or a V-2 rocket.

Staff Sergeant Rooney by then was a savvy reporter: he knew what to do with a hot tip. That same afternoon, he went out to Mitchel Field, the USAAF's stateside headquarters on Long Island, under the guise of wanting to do an article on pilot training. He worked his way up the chain of command to a colonel. Rooney pitched him on the training story, which the colonel okayed. Then Rooney nonchalantly mentioned the previous day's episode as if it were common knowledge and asked if the colonel had heard "any more dope" about it.

In a piece published in *Harper's Magazine* in March 1947, twenty-two months after V-E Day, Rooney described what happened next.

> The colonel jumped up from behind his desk, closed the door, and looked around the office as though it might have been wired.
>
> "Look," he said, the way colonels said *look* to sergeants, "where did you hear this silly story? Don't ever repeat it." He was trying to shout at me in a whisper. "Now get of here and don't say a word about it to anyone. It isn't true. I don't know a thing about it. I don't even deny it."[51]

The next day's *New York Times* was fascinating, Rooney thought. On page nineteen, an "obscure little story" with a Washington dateline quoted a War Department spokesman. Although officials were not issuing a warning, German attempts to attack New York City "are entirely possible," the article said. The same issue of the *Times* mentioned that Navy Admiral Jonas H. Ingram, a key strategist who was soon named commander in chief of the Atlantic Fleet, had been unexpectedly called to Washington.

Rooney returned to Mitchel Field a day later and was surprised to see the hangar and tarmac crowded with fighter planes. It looked to Rooney as if most of the fighters stationed on the East Coast had been transferred— literally overnight—to Hempstead.

He kept after the story, traveling to Washington in hopes of interviewing Major General Clayton Bissell, the Assistant Chief of Staff of G-2 Intelligence. One of Bissell's aides, a colonel, gave Rooney a brush-off not unlike the one he'd gotten at Mitchel Field. There was absolutely nothing to this story, Rooney was told—but it would be his ass if he breathed a word of it. "It was the same vigorous 'non-denial,'" Rooney told *Harper's* readers in March of '47.

Despite Rooney's best efforts to pin down something tangible and get it past censors, the story lay fallow—at least for the next few weeks. On

January 8, 1945, however, Admiral Ingram lent credence to Rooney's information by giving a press conference while aboard his command ship. Ingram curiously volunteered, "It is not only possible, but *probable* that both New York and Washington would be the target of robot bomb attacks 'within thirty to sixty days.'" Such an attack would not inflict much damage, Ingram assured. "It would certainly cause casualties in the limited area where the bomb might hit, but it could not seriously affect the progress of the war."[52] Then the admiral added: "There is no reason for anyone to become alarmed. Effective steps have been taken to meet this threat."[53]

Once Ingram's statement hit the wires and radio airwaves, train and bus stations suddenly became crowded with people trying to get out of New York and D.C. The Navy quickly issued an emphatic, if curious, denial. "There is no more reason now to believe Germany will attack us with robot bombs than there was November 7, 1944," the Navy Department statement said. Why the peculiar wording and why the gratuitous mention of Election Day? Rooney wondered.

After Rooney returned to Europe in early '45, he was too busy to pursue the story. But following V-E Day, Rooney was sitting in the Paris bureau of the *Herald Tribune* when it occurred to him that, since censorship had been lifted, the story about the Nazis' rumored attempt to bomb New York would make a compelling now-it-can-be-told feature.

The *Stars and Stripes* trumpeted Rooney's story on page one on May 15 under the header NAZIS TRIED TO BOMB N.Y.—BUT FAILED. The piece got good play on the wires and was boxed on the front pages of several New York dailies. The War Department, naturally, issued another refutation, denying any knowledge of the episode.

There the story sat, undisturbed, for more than a year until Rooney returned to Germany as a civilian correspondent for *Holiday*. He was spending a few days at Wannsee, a resort lake outside Berlin, when he got acquainted with a former German submarine officer. The German was fluent in English, having spent two years before the war studying medicine at Columbia University.

Rooney chatted with him about several topics, winning his confidence, before broaching the New York rumor. "As a matter of fact," the former

U-boater proudly informed Rooney, "mine was one of the freighter subs in the Atlantic which was refueling the smaller subs lying off the coast of America."

Ramps had been constructed on the decks of "several" German submarines; New York and Washington, he said, had both been targeted.

"I have heard from my friends that they launched the first projectile before they were caught but they don't know what happened to it," he told Rooney, before speculating that the attacking U-boats had been "immobilized" by radio beams that somehow disrupted their electric motors. "They [the U-boat crews] couldn't move and they were all captured alive," he said.[54]

Nearly another full year passed before Rooney filed his *Harper's* article. The magazine piece was triggered by a conversation Rooney had in the winter of '47 with a friend who'd served as a USAAF air traffic controller at Mitchel Field in November '44. Out of the blue the controller and his colleagues were directing "frantic" traffic over and around Long Island. "All [the onetime controller] knew," Rooney wrote in his *Harper's* piece, "was that the fighter pilots were directed to be on the lookout for pilotless robot planes flying toward New York."

Rooney told readers in early '47 that he'd pretty much given up on ever getting a straight story out of U.S. military officials. His article ended with "I'd like to know the real answer."

HAL BOYLE KNEW NOTHING ABOUT Nazi submarine sleuthing off the Long Island coast in the fall of '44. He knew all about the German stand outside Aachen and Metz, however, and was hearing firsthand about Nazi atrocities from bitter French, Belgian, and Dutch citizens. "People know how to hate along the border," Boyle wrote in a column in mid-October. The newly liberated could not fathom why Allied troops weren't being as ruthless with the German populace as the Nazis had been to them when "Hitler was in his heyday," as Boyle put it.[55]

One fall morning the AP columnist was driving toward the front with Captain Harry Volk of Cleveland Heights, Ohio, when they stopped in the Belgian village of Aubel, a few kilometers west of the German border.

Stretching their legs, they spotted a charming confectionary store and decided to buy some pastries. The proprietress, Mme. Lardinois, a lovely mother of three, insisted that the Americans stay for lunch. She prepared a feast of local delicacies that Boyle said tickled "palates weary of the sterile monotony of regular rations." They also enjoyed a bottle of red wine and homemade cookies.

After the dishes were cleared, Mme. Lardinois explained to Volk and Boyle how she had become a widow—and why she would always despise the Nazis. To Boyle's amazement, her eyes remained dry and her voice never cracked.

Her husband, Joseph, a handsome man with a black mustache, had been a grocer in Aubel when Hitler's storm troopers poured across the border in May 1940. The Lardinois family bundled themselves into their car and, along with other villagers, headed toward Brussels and safety—or so they hoped.

There were no Belgian or French troops in their caravan, nor were there any military vehicles. But that didn't stop forty Nazi fighter planes from diving on them. With everyone shrieking, Joseph got his wife and kids out of the car and into a roadside ditch. Four more times the planes came back. On the third pass, Joseph was wounded in the shoulder and chest, the bullets puncturing his lungs. Once the fighters left, Joseph was able to get back into the car and get to the next town. But there were so many wounded locals from that attack and others that Joseph didn't receive treatment for six hours. He died later that day.

"Much as I grieve for my husband, I feel sorrier still for the young mother who tried to run to safety with her baby in her arms," Mme. Lardinois told Boyle. "One bullet struck her child in the head and scattered its brains all over her. I will never forget the sounds that that young woman made."[56]

Boyle's column ended with Marie Jose, one of the Lardinois boys, telling him and Volk: "You Americans are too easy with the Germans now. You really don't know them. You will live to regret your kindness."[57]

———

NEITHER AACHEN NOR METZ WAS all that far from Aubel—and the Germans were being anything but kind to Allied invaders. The fighting in and around both cities that fall was fierce, inflicting thousands of casualties as the Allied advance stagnated. Nazi units that hadn't stopped to fire in weeks were suddenly laying down lethal artillery torrents. Boyle wrote from First Army headquarters on October 18 that the Germans defending Geilenkirchen, ten miles north of Aachen, were counterattacking virtually every day and tossing down "the heaviest barrage" along the barely breached Siegfried Line.[58] The next day Boyle likened the GIs' experience in the Aachen-Geilenkirchen corridor to climbing into the ring with Joe Louis. Except, Boyle wrote, foot soldiers couldn't always see their adversaries.

"'It's the guy you never see who gets you' is the first rule of street fighting," Boyle wrote after "sweating out sniper bullets from every doorway, window-ledge and rubble heap" in Aachen.[59]

The stalemate along the German-Belgian border precipitated the primal combat in the Hürtgen Forest. It was a fifty-square-mile stretch of woodland just east of the Rhine that was so primeval sunlight could barely penetrate. Boyle spent days shadowing the Third Armored and the Ninth Infantry as they attempted to push forward in the Hürtgen, stymied by enemy soldiers squatting in pillboxes and calling down presighted artillery fire. Many of the German shells had fuses designed to detonate at treetop level—a tactic that proved more devastating than the explosive itself. Thousands of First Army GIs were hurt or killed by splintered limbs. The best way to survive an artillery onslaught in the Hürtgen was by hugging a tree.[60]

A few weeks later, as Boyle and Cronkite learned firsthand, there weren't enough trees in the Belgian forest to save all the GIs in jeopardy from the biggest enemy counterattack of the war. And even if there had been, it would not have done them much good.

CHAPTER 14

★

GRAY PHANTOMS AND MURDER FACTORIES—THE BULGE TO BUCHENWALD

This new battle for Belgium is cowboy and Indian war-
fare on a grand scale. It is the reverse of our own victory
over the retreating Germans in this small country last
September.

—Hal Boyle, Christmas Day, 1944
Leaves from a War Correspondent's Notebook

The jeep carrying the Associated Press' Hal Boyle and *Time*'s Jack Belden slowed to a crawl as it approached the Belgian crossroads of Malmédy. At any moment, the correspondents feared, a Tiger tank would come roaring out of the woods, its turret grinding as the barrel swiveled to take dead aim.

For the two reporters, throwing their hands up and yelling, *"Korrespondent! Nicht schiessen! Nicht schiessen!"* would be futile. On day two of the Germans' lethal counteroffensive, it was distressingly clear that Hitler's legions were taking few prisoners.

Boyle and Belden spent much of December 17, 1944, wrapped in towels and blankets, trying to stave off the bitter cold as they scoured the woods for signs of enemy armor. The winds of the Ardennes Forest were so frigid, Boyle recalled a decade later, that Belgian farmers put woolen covers on the backs of cows.[1] Between the vicious cold and ugly rumors that Nazi tanks were everywhere, it made for a long day in the jeep. The pair kept passing wide-eyed American GIs trudging through the ice and mud, anxiously peering over their shoulders. For Boyle, it brought back memories of the panicked retreat he'd witnessed twenty-two months earlier in Tunisia's Grand Dorsal Mountains.

Waffen SS units led by fanatical Nazi Joachim Peiper's Blowtorch Battalion had come blasting through the Ardennes, spreading terror as they battered the American lines. One advance enemy unit got so deep into Belgium that it eventually overran General Courtney Hodges' headquarters in Spa—and with it, the First Army's press camp. Hodges narrowly evaded likely capture and execution—and so did the correspondents. Most reporters jumped into the retreat caravan stumbling west toward Brussels. But Boyle and Belden somehow managed to point their jeep back toward the front.

As the pair neared Malmédy, they had no way of knowing that earlier the same day at Five Corners, a crossroads on the outskirts of the village, Peiper had ambushed and massacred, in cold blood, nearly a hundred members of Battery B of the 285th Field Artillery Observation Battalion. To keep *Standartenführer* Peiper, one of Hitler's favorite henchmen, from wreaking even more havoc, American troops had chopped down two big trees to block a road near the village.

Belden and Boyle were barely out of their jeep when told the bone-chilling story. The two reporters were led to a small group of shivering GIs huddled at a clearing station; they were Battery B men who had somehow escaped the slaughter.

Hal Boyle was, by happenstance, the first daily newspaperman on the scene of the most appalling combat atrocity perpetrated in the European Theater. He may well have been surprised when Army PROs not only okayed his story, but encouraged him to tell it in gory detail; the Army wanted the world to learn about Nazi brutality. Frontline orders were issued that day, in fact, that no SS prisoners were to be taken for the next week.[2]

Sitting in a hovel, the Allies' front caving in around him, no doubt blowing on his fingers to keep them warm, Hal Boyle fashioned one of the most heartrending stories of the war. Millions of Americans learned of the Malmédy Massacre from his AP account. Here's how the *Kansas City Star* played Boyle's story on page one.

KILL GI WOUNDED

Nazi Tank Force Brutally Mows Down 150 Helpless American Prisoners
Survivors Sob in Rage
Only by "Playing Dead" Did a Few Escape Murder by the Germans
Herded into a Field Lacking Heavy Weapons, Yank Unit Is Overpowered by Enemy Armor

---

by HAL BOYLE

An American Front-Line Clearing Station, Belgium, Dec. 17 (Delayed)

Weeping with rage, a handful of doughboy survivors described today how a German tank force ruthlessly poured machine-gun fire into a group of about 150 Americans who had been disarmed and herded into a field in the opening hours of the present Nazi counteroffensive.

"We had to lie there and listen to German noncoms kill with pistols every one of our wounded men who groaned or tried to move," said T-5 William B. Summers of Glenville, W. Va., who escaped by playing dead.

The bloodbath had begun, Summers told Boyle, when a German officer pulled out a pistol and, point-blank, emptied it into a group of prisoners. Within seconds the Germans were slaughtering the whole unit with machine guns mounted on half-tracks and armored cars. The only recourse for Summers and his mates was to flop down and play dead.

"They were cutting us down like guinea pigs," Private William F. Geem of Elizabethtown, Pennsylvania, told Boyle. "Then those German noncoms began walking around knocking off our wounded. I kept my head down, but after they had emptied their pistols I could hear them click fresh cartridges in their hands while they were re-loading."[3]

The bodies of the eighty-four men executed in Malmédy were not re-covered until the 30th Division pacified the area a month later. Engineers were forced to use metal detectors to find corpses buried under piles of snow.[4]

Malmédy, sadly, was far from the Blowtorch Battalion's only massacre in the Ardennes. That same day, in fact, Peiper's men murdered nineteen GIs who'd surrendered at Honsfeld and later shot fifty disarmed Americans at Büllingen. The next day, December 18, Peiper executed 130 Belgian civil-ians in the village of Stavelot, including forty-seven women and twenty-three children. Their only "crime" had been to harbor American troops.[5]

"Like gray phantoms the crouching German infantry slithered through the woods," Boyle wrote a decade after the Battle of the Bulge. "Then came the coughing roar of endless panzers, their path lit by the artificial moons of giant floodlights."[6]

SS men were so venerated by the Reich at that point in the war, Boyle reported, that after one firefight in early December, German burial units scooped up only the bodies of dead SS soldiers. "Regular" soldiers were left to rot—and eventually to be interred by the Allies.[7]

WALTER CRONKITE WAS IN BED at his apartment in Brussels early on the morning of December 16 when the phone rang. UP-Paris was calling to say that the Germans appeared to be on the march along the Luxembourg-Belgium border. They wanted Cronkite, then still attached to Montgom-ery's army, to check things out and get back to them. Cronkite was supposed to be traveling to Paris that day—a trip he hoped to extend through the Christmas holidays, perhaps to meet up with his old roomie Jim McGlincy. (McGlincy's new best gal, an Irish lass, was a "volunteer" with the Catholic Women's League, an ironic happenstance that should induce "loud, cynical laughter," Walter joked with Betsy.) But a reunion with McGlincy in Paris was now by the boards.

No sooner had Cronkite hung up than UP's First Army correspondent Jack Frankish was rapping on the apartment door. Frankish looked a mess: unshaven, splattered with mud, and, not surprisingly under the circumstances, "considerably shaken," Cronkite remembered.[8]

"This goddamn thing is real," Frankish told Cronkite. "We have a headlong retreat."[9]

When reports hit of enemy tanks steamrolling toward Spa, Frankish had no choice but to join the flight to the rear. Now he wanted to get back to the fighting as soon as possible but needed Cronkite's help to get his story out.

Frankish gave Cronkite a quick blow-by-blow on the German surge; the two of them cobbled together a piece for Walter to run through the traps. Then Frankish jumped back into his jeep and managed to get back to the front, driving upstream against a deluge of men, jeeps, and trucks.

Ironically, despite their yeoman effort, Frankish's dispatch never made it onto the wire. That morning, Cronkite sent word to his bosses in Paris that he, too, would be heading toward the action.

Only after Cronkite departed did he learn the office had sent a return cable: "Communications difficult," it read. "Can you coordinate coverage of front?"

The message was absurd. "Hell," Cronkite remembered, "communications weren't difficult, they were nonexistent."[10]

Rather than buck the "maelstrom," as he put it, Cronkite consulted a map and navigated side roads to reach Namur, Belgium, a few miles west of the now-reeling American line. U.S. military police guarding a Namur intersection demanded that Cronkite repeat the password.

"I didn't have any goddamned idea what the password was," Cronkite recalled. But he sweet-talked his way through the checkpoint and got to Luxembourg City a few hours later.

When the full depravity of the invading Germans came to light, Cronkite realized how fortunate he'd been. Peiper and other Waffen SS hit men had trained and equipped squads of English-speaking soldiers—roughly two thousand men in all. They had American jeeps, uniforms, dog tags, rifles, grenades, and—because so many real GIs had been captured so quickly at gunpoint—often the password command and response. It soon reached the point where American soldiers could not trust the password exchange to identify friend from foe.

MPs and others began asking any "American" unit they encountered questions like, "Who won this year's World Series?" "How many home runs did Babe Ruth hit in his best year?" And hearkening back to junior high geography, "What's the capital of Nebraska?" Detained at a checkpoint, three-star General Omar Bradley nearly met his maker when he mistakenly identified Chicago as the capital of Illinois.[11]

Cronkite was fortunate that he'd run into a kindly MP—and not a hard-ass or, far worse, one of Peiper's stooges.

The UP reporter was stunned by Luxembourg City's eerie calm; the city dwellers seemed oblivious to the threat raging a few miles away. Cronkite checked into the Grand Hôtel Cravat—a move that proved fortuitous when Patton's Third Army started moving north; suddenly Luxembourg became crowded with Allied correspondents.

"For the rest of the Battle of the Bulge," Cronkite wrote a half century later, "several of us who were fast enough to get ensconced [at the Cravat] commuted from that fur-lined foxhole to the war each day, suffered through the snowstorms and the terrible cold that were bedeviling our troops, and returned each night to a bottle of champagne, a hot bath, and a warm bed. We got out of our warm beds and put on all our old clothes and got in the open jeeps and went out to battle, and came back to champagne and hot baths every night. If Episcopalians are supposed to suffer guilt from such selfish indulgence, I'm afraid I missed that day at Sunday school."[12]

All the Sunday school prayer in America could not have saved the First Army; much of its front line had disintegrated. Patton had already volunteered to wheel his Third Army north to rescue the 101st Airborne under siege at Bastogne, Belgium.

Cronkite got reassigned to the Third, which set up its press camp in a tiny schoolhouse in Esch, a crude coal-mining hamlet just outside Luxembourg City. Patton's press operation may have been in grimy Esch, but the general himself chose to reside at the Cravat—as, ironically, did Patton's boss, Omar Bradley. So Cronkite was staying in the right place to get the latest dope.

The Army gave Cronkite a driver who would escort him by jeep to Esch every morning in time for the ten a.m. press briefing. Third Army PROs would inform Cronkite and other correspondents about the previous night's action. Then the reporters would determine what sector of that day's anticipated fighting they'd like to cover. "Once you made up your mind, you told the press officer, 'I want to go to such and such,'" Cronkite recalled. "He either said you could or you couldn't go."[13]

Patton would not let jeeps in his command put up their windshields because the sun's reflection might attract German snipers. So Cronkite would wrap himself in blankets, scarves, goggles—anything that might help ward off the frigid winds as his jeep bounced from skirmish to skirmish.

At one point in a village south of Bastogne, Cronkite's jeep was part of a caravan that found itself swept up in a street firefight. Cronkite leapt out and ducked into a doorway. A GI armed with a carbine was shielded inside the door. Every few moments the plucky youngster would pop out and take a quick potshot.

Cronkite smelled a story. "What's your name?" Cronkite shouted. "What's your hometown?"

The kid yelled a reply over his shoulder, keeping a wary eye out.

"And what's your unit?" Cronkite yelled back, still scribbling.

"Hell, Mr. Cronkite," the kid replied, "I'm your driver."

Later that same day, Cronkite's helmet popped off while riding in the jeep. The helmet bounced into a minefield pocked with warning signs. So Cronkite continued on, helmetless—which, in George Patton's world, was a serious breach of conduct. Cronkite's misfortune thickened; Patton's jeep appeared a few minutes later.

One of Patton's toadies, a colonel, challenged Cronkite about his helmet. Cronkite explained that: a) his helmet had rolled into a minefield; b) he wasn't about to risk life and limb to go get it; and c) he wasn't a soldier, he was a war correspondent.

"Stay as you are!" the officer barked, and returned to Patton's jeep.

"We watched [the officer] gesticulate, pointing to the field and then raising his arms in the universal sign for 'what can I do?' hopelessness," Cronkite wrote decades later. "Whereupon Patton uttered a single word that might have been an expletive well known among the troops. The colonel climbed in and they drove on."[14]

PATTON'S EXPLETIVE, WHATEVER IT MAY have been, accurately described the Allies' situation in mid- to late December 1944. A few weeks before, there had been exultation at the prospect of ending the war before the holidays. Now generals were being forced to flee in the face of an enemy onslaught. And thousands of American GIs—many of them as green as the kids from the Kasserine Pass two years earlier—were being trampled.

One week Boyle was flipping deep into his notebook to write about GI sign painters (one painter claimed to have created seventeen thousand placards in Normandy alone: "Booby Trap!"; "Mines Cleared!"; "Supply Route," etc.)[15] and Fritz, a German shepherd of suspect loyalties who made himself a nuisance by peeing in foxholes.[16] The next week Boyle was writing about SS assassination squads roaming unchallenged through the Ardennes and petrified GIs helpless to stop oncoming tanks.

The debate still rages seven decades later. Wasn't the collapse at the Bulge avoidable? Shouldn't Eisenhower and Bradley have seen it coming?

In truth, Eisenhower and Bradley knew their defensive line in the Ardennes was vulnerable. A few days before the German countersurge, Bradley met in his headquarters with a group of American newspaper editors. Bradley stood before a map and reviewed the entire Allied line, conceding that its weakest point was in the Ardennes. The 12th Army Group head called his Belgium-Luxembourg alignment a "calculated risk."[17] But the Germans, now once again led by the shrewd Field Marshal Gerd von Rundstedt, would be foolish to launch an attack in such a dense forest with poor visibility and poorer roads, the Allied command believed.

"We were all wrong, of course—tragically and stupidly wrong," Bradley wrote. "After the experience of Mortain, it should have occurred to at least one of us that as we pushed Germany to the wall, Hitler might very well do something crazy and desperate again. That was his style."[18] It was also Hitler's deluded style to relive moments of Teutonic triumph: The Ardennes had not only been Hitler's main blitzkrieg route in 1940, but also the Kaiser's path to glory early in the Great War.

Ultra intercepts, moreover, may have given the Allied command a sense of false security. All those months of being able to read German intentions and adjust their responses accordingly had made the Allies sloppy. At Mortain, Hitler had telegraphed all of his moves through radio signals that were easily intercepted. On the eastern periphery of the Ardennes, however, Hitler amassed four armies of forty divisions, spearheaded by seven armored units—and did it all with abject radio silence. It was a staggering coup—one that Bradley and Eisenhower did not believe Hitler capable of launching.

Sustaining an ambush through the Ardennes, crossing the Meuse, and going all the way to the port of Antwerp—the ultimate objective—was even crazier than attempting to counterattack after the Allied breakout in Normandy. But Hitler was psychotic: Just how psychotic would become tragically apparent in the months to come.

HAL BOYLE CHRONICLED HITLER'S DELUSIONS from the front trenches. On December 20, two days after Peiper murdered 130 local villagers, Boyle filed a piece from Stavelot that captured the heartache Allied soldiers were feeling. Boyle was with an American engineering outfit forced to blow up a bridge across the Amblève River to keep it from being exploited by Nazi tanks.

"It was the first bridge ever blown up by Capt. James Rice and his men," Boyle wrote.[19] Rice had been compelled to operate under the cloak of darkness because enemy troops were just across the river, intently watching every move. A German machine gun raked the bridge when Rice's squad had appeared earlier in the day; they were forced to retreat. Once it turned dark, Rice and his men crept back down to the river's edge and snuck three fifty-pound boxes of dynamite under the structure and set four thirty-second fuses.

"After we had run one block and dived into a building, that bridge blew up like a Roman candle. It was a beautiful explosion—knocked out windows for three blocks," Rice told Boyle.

The next day, still in the Stavelot area, Boyle wrote a piece about how a medic, Private Theodore Watson of Brooklyn, had smoked out eight German spies. Dressed in American uniforms, two jeeps full of Peiper-trained SS men had passed through several checkpoints. The German impersonating a captain spoke in impeccable, friendly English, sharing smokes with exhausted MPs.

But by the time they reached Watson's position near the front, the enemy's smooth veneer was gone. "Like all sons of Brooklyn, [Watson] takes nothing at its face value," Boyle wrote. Watson noticed that the jeep occupants were fidgeting, nervously craning their necks toward the German lines, obviously looking for something. The medic discreetly moved closer to eavesdrop and overheard a heavy German accent mutter, "Where is it?"

Watson figured they were looking for a German tank that was supposed to be heading through the American lines at that moment. "They're Germans!" Watson yelled to the GIs in nearby foxholes. "Shoot them! They're Germans!"[20]

Several GIs began firing as all eight Germans took off, running "like deer" toward their lines. Only one of the Germans was hit, but he was dragged to safety. To Watson's chagrin, all eight escaped.

His coverage of the Bulge was Boyle at his best. Flitting from one section of the front to the next, interviewing GIs on the fly, he memorialized their stories of courage and desperation. Every day during the Bulge, Boyle filed two or three pieces, often more. All of them painted a portrait of American officers and GIs knocked on their heels but scrambling to punch back. Not unlike Bigart's coverage of the Italian campaign, Boyle's reporting from the Ardennes makes for a dramatic first draft of history.

By Christmas Day, the Bulge's tide had begun to turn—and not just because the Third Army was on the cusp of relieving Bastogne. Boyle enjoyed a holiday repast—complete with turkey and cranberry sauce—in a small village outside Stavelot with Major Hal D. McCown of Ruston, Louisiana. McCown told Boyle the remarkable story of how he'd been taken prisoner by the Germans on December 21 when the major, his radioman, and an orderly were bushwhacked by an enemy patrol. "They were cutting grass above our heads with those machine guns," McCown told Boyle.[21]

McCown and some 140 other Americans were being held in a pen just inside the German line at La Gleize across the Amblève River. On Christmas Eve, the prisoners' total food ration consisted of two dog biscuits and a couple of small nips of cider. But McCown and the other American prisoners were lucky: The SS officers who interrogated them slammed their sidearms down on a table for effect—but chose not to use them. The German commander, not a member of the SS, took a shine to McCown. He expressed hatred of the Russians because, he said, Soviet soldiers took no prisoners—which, given his countrymen's behavior of the previous week, was the height of gall.

"He was worried about our attitude toward the SS troops," McCown told Boyle, "and wanted to know if we regarded them as criminals and gangsters, and he wanted to know if we also regarded Hitler and Himmler in this light."[22]

On December 24, when a combination of the 291st Engineer Combat Battalion, the 825th Tank Destroyer Battalion, and forward elements of the 30th Division pushed back beyond the Amblève, McCown and the other American captives were thrilled to witness a conflagration: At five-minute intervals, the eight-hundred-man German contingent torched more than 150 of their own tanks (including, McCown was pleased to observe, sixteen prized Tigers), half-tracks, and trucks rather than let them fall into American hands.

McCown and the others were forced to retreat with the German column, marching steadily without rest. But Christmas Eve night, after several brushes with American patrols, a firefight suddenly erupted. McCown and others slipped away undetected, then raced toward friendly lines, shrieking, "Don't shoot! Don't shoot!"

The major told Boyle: "'My wife would be proud of my waistline now. I'll never be so small again.'

"And he took another helping of turkey."[23]

On the day after Christmas, Boyle interviewed thirty American medics who hid for a half day in a church while SS troops methodically murdered captured American jeep and truck drivers. "We could hear the Nazi tank commander stopping our trucks and ordering the drivers and helpers out," Sergeant James W. Colella of Rochester, Pennsylvania, told Boyle. "Then we would hear shots. The next morning we saw the bodies of our men lying where they had been killed."

At one point during the night, an SS officer, under the mistaken impression that the church was occupied by German troops, opened the door and yelled into the darkness: "Is everything all right?"

A medic who happened to be fluent in German answered, "Everything is all right." Satisfied that things were under control in the church, the SS officer returned to the street to resume killing unarmed Americans. The next morning, the SS troops were driven from the village by American infantrymen.[24]

Boyle identified neither the young lieutenant nor the village, but at some point in late '44 or early '45, an American intelligence officer was being housed by a Belgian family: a mother, a father, and their gorgeous college-aged daughter. It was love at first sight for the lieutenant, who had designs on bringing the young lady back to America. But try as he might, he couldn't woo the girl or her parents. When he started to bring food to them, though, the parents warmed, at least a little. But he still wasn't getting anyplace with the girl.

He couldn't understand why the young lady, a skilled pianist, would play Schubert and Bach so vigorously. Finally, one night he heard voices coming from the basement. The lieutenant went down the stairs to investigate and discovered the girl of his dreams canoodling with an enemy soldier who had apparently been hiding. Suddenly everything became clear: The lieutenant had been in the home of German sympathizers. His romantic plans dashed, he had no choice but to arrest the soldier and turn the family in for harboring the enemy.[25]

THERE WAS NO TURKEY AVAILABLE for Walter Cronkite on Wednesday, December 27, although he'd more than made up for it two days earlier. On December 27, Cronkite had tried to reach besieged Bastogne along the north-south Arlon Road with three other correspondents: Cornelius Ryan of the *London Daily Telegraph*, Norman Clark of the *London News*, and Joseph Driscoll of the *New York Herald Tribune*. They kept on running into artillery and mortar fire; even after they sought refuge in the command post of Lieutenant Colonel Creighton W. Abrams, Jr.'s 37th Tank Battalion, shells from German 88s burst all around.

Abrams' CP was in a farmhouse just south of Bastogne that had been decimated by an earlier round of artillery. But the kitchen fireplace still functioned and there was enough of a wall for Abrams to tack up a map of known enemy troop locations in the area. The entire world had been transfixed by the gallant stand of the "battered bastards of Bastogne," Cronkite's mates from Market Garden, the 101st Airborne.

Even at Abrams' CP, none of them—including the lieutenant colonel and his staff—could feel safe: U.S.-German "lines" existed only in theory. Tiger tanks and hit squads were lurking everywhere.

So when an American jeep pulled up next to the farmhouse, there was no guarantee it was friendly. The vehicle, much to their relief, turned out to be carrying Cronkite's old friend, Major General Maxwell Taylor of the 101st. Taylor two days earlier had been in Washington, D.C., at the request of General Marshall, who wanted Taylor's input on future airborne missions.

The major general was still sporting the dress uniform he was wearing when word reached him that his men had been surrounded at Bastogne. On December 22, Taylor's protégé and temporary successor, General Anthony McAuliffe, had issued his defiant response—"Nuts!"—when the German commander demanded the 101st's surrender.

Taylor took a series of cargo planes from Washington to Paris, then on the morning of December 27 hopped a smaller craft to Luxembourg. There he talked with Eisenhower's Chief of Staff, Bedell Smith, intent on getting permission to take a glider or parachute into Bastogne. Smith relayed good news: The Fourth Armored Division was finally poised to break through. If Taylor could get to the front, he could ride into Bastogne with the Fourth's 37th Tank Battalion.

When Taylor finally arrived at Abrams' CP, he sorely needed a briefing. Out of earshot of the reporters, Abrams gave him a quick rundown, then Taylor came back outside and climbed into his jeep.

In *A Reporter's Life*, Cronkite has Taylor addressing him individually and inviting him to go along on the push into Bastogne. Other accounts, including one referenced in John Eisenhower's *The Bitter Battle*, Ike's son's history of the Bulge, have Taylor inviting all the reporters present to follow him north.

"The story would have been great—first correspondent into Bastogne," Cronkite recalled.

> On the other hand, how would I get the story out? There was no communication link from Bastogne, and in the days before I had my story on the wires, those correspondents monitoring military communication on the outside would be reporting the drama.
>
> That's the excuse I gave to Taylor, and tried to explain to myself. But I knew the truth—and I suspect he did: Taylor's drive to Bastogne could well have been a suicide mission. A lot of glory, perhaps, for a career officer; simply a sad footnote for a war correspondent.[26]

Cronkite made the right call in turning down Taylor: A reporter unable to relay his story wasn't worth much to a wire service. Forty-eight hours earlier, however, Cronkite had been with a super-macho "correspondent" who would not have hesitated to take up Taylor's offer, especially since the writer didn't have to worry much about deadlines—or about the facts, for that matter.

Ernest Hemingway and his wife and fellow *Collier's* correspondent, Martha Gellhorn, plus Cronkite's UP colleague Collie Small, were among the revelers at a Christmas gathering at the Cravat. Of all the depressing holidays he had spent in Europe, Cronkite told Betsy, Christmas '44 was "the worst ever, I think." The surroundings weren't unpleasant, he admitted, calling Luxembourg "as lovely as a postcard." But "the fact I was alone again without you made it almost unbearable."

They had a big turkey dinner featuring copious amounts of liquor. "We had some eggnog and everyone but old hardworking Cronkite who had a fistful of mediocre stories to do, got pretty well pied," Walter told Betsy. "I had a few drinks and filed my last story about midnight after which I was so tired I just collapsed into bed."[27]

Cronkite wrote the letter to Betsy on December 27, just hours after declining Taylor's offer to go into Bastogne, so he might have been especially down on himself. Still, he couldn't shake the blues that had plagued him for months. He was working "like a dog," he told Betsy, but "not doing particularly well at it." Since UP's Small and Bob Richards were in the Belgium-Luxembourg sector, Cronkite's own presence had been rendered "unnecessary," he complained. Plus, he told Betsy, the other fellows—his acolytes—were better at writing combat stories than he was. Both Small and Richards can right [*sic*] my sort of stuff better than I can—and that ain't good for the old morale."[28]

ANDY ROONEY'S RESPITE IN NEW York was plenty good for *his* morale. He not only was reunited with Margie and old friends, but also got the tip on the rumored German attempt to bomb New York. Plus the *Stars and Stripes* gave him the chance to craft several Once Over Lightly columns, the chatty feature that, for years, had been a staple of the paper's sports coverage.

On January 3, Rooney wrote a column that paid homage to the prominent athletes who'd been killed in service to their country. "It's a sad fact that the death in combat of great American sports figures who have been in the national spotlight has done a great deal towards making the public conscious of the great toll the war is taking."[29]

Among the sports figures who had perished, Rooney wrote, were Marine Captain Charlie Paddock, the onetime fastest sprinter in the world;

Navy pilot and Heisman Trophy winner Nile Kinnick of the University of Iowa; miler Lou Zamperini (who later turned out to be alive, having survived a POW camp); some forty minor-league baseball players; and no fewer than 131 professional boxers.[30]

THE NUMBER OF PRIZEFIGHTERS WHO had made the ultimate sacrifice was surely not lost on boxing aficionado Joe Liebling. After Paris was liberated in late August of '44, Liebling spent several weeks in the French capital, interviewing members of the Maquis and compiling notes for what became *La République du Silence*, his bilingual compendium of stories from and about France's courageous underground press during the Occupation.

In the company of a photographer with the newly organized French War Crimes Commission, Liebling also traveled to central France, a region known as the Côte-d'Or, to research the massacre that had taken place on August 21, 1944, in the village of Comblanchien. Liebling talked to surviving villagers and pieced together a chilling story. A company of enemy soldiers from a troop train that had been sidetracked at Comblanchien joined with Germans from other detachments to form a spontaneous vigilante mob. They terrorized the town, torching homes and shops and butchering any local they encountered.

The soldiers were neither members of the Waffen SS nor trained by the Gestapo; they were just bitter and scared kids. "I think it was because they were so frightened," one man who had witnessed the German genocide that night told Liebling. "It is unimaginable how frightened they were."[31]

It was also unimaginable to Liebling that his successor as the *New Yorker*'s ETO correspondent would be killed in the line of duty—but it happened. In the fall of '44, David Lardner, the son of sportswriter Ring Lardner, one of Liebling's childhood heroes, took Liebling's place as the magazine's First Army correspondent. Extremely nearsighted, Lardner had been rejected for military duty, but was determined to get to the front as a reporter. It ran in the family: Lardner's older brother James had been killed covering the Spanish Civil War for the *New York Herald Tribune*; another older brother, John, covered World War II in North Africa and Europe for *Newsweek*.

Lardner had only been at the front for a matter of weeks when, on October 19, he and two other correspondents, one of whom was Richard Tregaskis of International News Service, author of *Guadalcanal Diary*, decided to see for themselves the devastation surrounding the German city of Aachen. Navigating through the rubble, the reporters asked their jeep driver to take a shortcut. Although American engineers had planted wooden stakes with brightly colored tape to mark mines, the jeep nevertheless ran over an explosive. The shrapnel killed Lardner but barely injured the others.

Liebling was racked with guilt, somehow convinced that, had he been in Aachen, he would have been able to warn David of danger. Lardner's family elected to keep David's remains interred at the Henri-Chapelle War Cemetery in Belgium.

Joe Liebling went back to the States before the Bulge hit. Among other things, he put the finishing touches on "Quest for Mollie" and wrote the first of his many Wayward Press columns for the *New Yorker*.

IT MAY HAVE BEEN A minor miracle that Hal Boyle avoided David Lardner's fate, given the number of times he came within a hairsbreadth of German armor in the Ardennes. On December 28, the day after Bastogne was relieved, Boyle inspected Hitler's high-water mark, the deepest point of German penetration into Belgium. It was just three miles short of the Meuse River, near the village of Celles.

"Here on the raw cold soil of Belgium . . . is spread some of the ghastliest carnage of the European war," Boyle wrote. "Destroyed in four days of unceasing battle which kept the American armies from being chopped in half, the human and steel wreckage of the German panzer army lies in frozen ruin over miles of Belgium's fields and woodland."[32]

Some 1,200 German prisoners had been taken, but untold hundreds more had been killed or wounded, Boyle reported. He walked the battlefield and counted sixty-three smoldering enemy tanks and 177 vehicles damaged or captured.

"It is a sight to sicken any pageant loving human who is taught only the glory of war and never the price of defeat. That price is spread everywhere on this wintry landscape of torn flesh and bomb and shell blasted guns," he wrote.

Twenty-five months of covering combat hadn't dulled Boyle's poetic sensibilities. "A light snow lies on crisp fields and ice sheathed roads. It has collected in little ridges and around the blackened yellow bellies of burnt-out German tanks and wheels of silent breech-blown German guns. It goes unheeded on [the] spent chill faces of German soldiers stretched in death's perpetual frost."[33]

DEATH'S PERPETUAL FROST SPREAD EVERYWHERE in Belgium. On December 23, it hit correspondent Jack Frankish, Cronkite's UP colleague and Boyle's First Army counterpart. Two months earlier the wire service rivals had been photographed frolicking with other reporters on Kaiser Wilhelm's bed in Spa. Now Boyle sat down to write a tribute to his friend.

Not many Americans were done in by the Luftwaffe late in the war but, sadly, Jack Frankish was. He and other American correspondents, including Liebling's Manhattan buddy Harold Denny of the *New York Times* and George Hicks of the Blue Network, were temporarily holed up at a hotel in Chaudfontaine, Belgium.[34] Frankish had come down with a fever that made him laryngitic; ailing, he'd skipped the chance to go to the front that day to coordinate UP's coverage from the press setup at the hotel.

Without warning, four enemy dive-bombers attacked Chaudfontaine's railway station. Frankish and the other reporters ran outside onto a gravel path to investigate. They got there in time to see the bombers make a second run. Frankish spied a plumeting bomb and tried to race back into the hotel. But it was too late: The bomb hit less than twenty feet away; the shrapnel struck Frankish in the back just short of the doorway. He was instantly killed—as were three GIs in the 113th Cavalry Group. Hicks and Denny suffered only superficial wounds, as did twenty other soldiers.

"A bespectacled reporter with a likable grin, [Frankish] was popular in the press corps," Boyle wrote. "Frequently, after a day's work was done, he would entertain his colleagues with dialect stories."[35]

A graduate of the University of Southern California, Frankish had been a fraternity brother of Rod Dedeaux, a Trojan shortstop destined to become a legendary coach at USC and mentor to many future major leaguers. One of the two children that Jack Frankish left behind, a son named Brian, became a movie producer. Young Frankish ended up producing the baseball epic *Field of Dreams*. By sheer coincidence, Frankish hired Dedeaux to make the movie's baseball scenes more authentic. When Dedeaux heard Frankish's last name, he asked about the identity of Brian's father. Brian related the story. Dedeaux smiled and said, "Your dad was one of my best friends."[36]

BELGIUM STAYED A MESS LONG after the immediate threat of the Bulge ebbed. Lines between friend and foe continued to be bollixed up.

In late January, Boyle told the story of First Sergeant Percy L. Imbody of Perkiomenville, Pennsylvania, the noncom with "the million dollar fist." Imbody was in a frontline trench at five thirty a.m. when he heard an "American" voice shriek, "Hold your fire! Hold your fire!" A commotion was going in front of Imbody but in the darkness he couldn't quite make out what it was.

When he moved up to investigate, he realized that a German soldier had grabbed a member of Imbody's platoon and was using the GI as a human shield to bludgeon his way through the American lines. Before Imbody could sound the alarm, another Nazi soldier grabbed him.

"That was bad judgment," Boyle wrote. The two brawled near an abandoned German tank. Imbody, a husky welterweight, had a right hand the size of a ham, Boyle noted. The sergeant coldcocked his tormentor, splattering him against the tank, then rescued his buddy when the other German, wanting no part of Imbody, lit out toward the Rhine.[37]

When the weather cleared, troops of every nation were surging toward the Rhine: The bridges that spanned the river were the real prizes. If they

could somehow be seized intact, the path into Germany's industrial heartland would be made that much easier. Thanks in no small measure to Hal
Boyle's reporting, the *Kansas City Star* and many other U.S. newspapers
charted the Allies' progress to and over the Rhine.

On March 3, Boyle was in Neuss, not far from Düsseldorf, as three
historic bridges were blown up by Nazi engineers just as the U.S. 83rd Infantry was preparing assaults. "The destruction of the bridge was in itself
an admission by the German high command that the battle for the Rhine-
land has been lost and that the legendary river which every Teuton loves
again has become the western frontier of a rapidly shrinking Reich," Boyle
wrote.[38]

Three days later, forty kilometers or so downriver from Boyle, Andy
Rooney got to witness the Reich shrink a little faster. Rooney was with a
pack of other correspondents on the Rhine near Cologne. There they witnessed a bloody confrontation between the Shermans of the Third Armored Division and Tiger tanks desperate to keep the Americans at bay.
In Cologne the correspondents had unearthed their biggest cache of liquor
since encountering the underground delights of Fort du Roule in Cherbourg eight months earlier. The stash had been discovered beneath the
wine cellar of the Hotel Excelsior: endless cases of champagne and cognac
from all over Europe.

While their colleagues were sampling the Excelsior's booty on the afternoon of March 7, Rooney and Howard Cowan of Associated Press got
one of the hottest tips of the war: Twenty miles farther south, at Remagen,
the Ludendorff Bridge, one of prewar Europe's busiest railroad spans, had
miraculously been captured while still standing. Cowan and Rooney were
told that GIs were already heading across the bridge.

They jumped into Rooney's jeep. With all the tanks on the road, it took
more than an hour. But when they got there and looked around, they were
thrilled to discover that they were the first reporters on the scene.

There were so many American soldiers atop the trestle that "it looked
like the George Washington Bridge across the Hudson at rush hour,"
Rooney remembered. If he could figure out a way to get his scoop back to
the *Stars and Stripes*' headquarters in Paris, he knew he'd have one of the

best stories of the war—an exclusive that might help ease the frustration of the failure to get his liberation-of-Paris story in print.

Rooney and Cowan learned that German engineers had lashed powerful explosives under the bridge, intent on detonating them as soon as the Allies got close. But U.S. specialists, in a moment of still-unsung heroism, rappelled under the bridge, defusing by hand most of the explosives as German soldiers a few hundred yards away were desperately hitting their detonators. Some of the dynamite went off—but not enough to knock down the bridge.[39]

IT WAS A FORTUITOUS MOMENT for SHAEF, too. Omar Bradley, unexpectedly, was able to push thousands of troops across the Rhine, slamming a dent in the German defenses, forcing a debilitating enemy pullback, and causing such tumult that Hitler again cashiered *Generalfeldmarschall* Gerd von Rundstedt—this time for good.

Bradley was especially gratified. Capturing the bridge at Remagen gave him the chance to revive the "two-thrust" assault into Germany that he had been advocating for months. In the wake of the Bulge, Montgomery in early '45 had persuaded Eisenhower to cede American troops to Monty's Twenty-first Army Group. Monty wanted the main thrust onto German soil to come from the British position in the north. By early March, Ike had incensed Bradley by assigning much of the American First Army as part of Monty's "reserves" for Operation Plunder, the Brits' long-delayed northern offensive.

All that changed, however, with the news from Remagen. "Hot dog, Courtney!" Bradley exulted when Hodges called him with the news about the Ninth Armored Division's seizure of the Ludendorff Bridge. "Shove everything you can across it. And button up the bridgehead tightly."[40]

Ike was having dinner with his airborne generals, Matthew Ridgway, James Gavin, and Maxwell Taylor, when Bradley called with the remarkable bulletin. "It's the best break we've had," Ike said. "To hell with the planners. Sure, go on, Brad, and I'll give you everything we've got to hold that bridgehead."[41] Bradley immediately began plotting a full-blooded right hook.

ROONEY HAD MORE THAN A ringside seat to watch Bradley's right hook take shape; he was inside the ropes—and he stayed there for more than a week. With all the planes and trucks heading from the bridgehead back to Paris, Rooney was almost guaranteed that his multiple daily dispatches would get through. The Ninth Armored Division's PRO, Charles Gillett, was savvy enough to recognize a PR bonanza; Gillett helped Rooney every way he could. On day one, Gillett arranged for Rooney and Cowan to get across the bridge, even though the Germans were still taking potshots from the hillside on the opposite bank. Rooney remembered crouching and running across the span, being careful that his boots didn't slip into the six-inch gaps between slats.

Every hour seemed to bring a different enemy response; the artillery fire never abated, but it came from different spots amid the hills along the eastern edge of the river. At several points, the Luftwaffe attacked the bridge, sometimes launching dive-bombs, sometimes strafing, hoping the weakened structure would collapse.

Anticipating that the bridge would eventually be rendered useless, American engineers performed another miracle by constructing a long pontoon bridge two hundred yards upstream. Rooney jogged across the new span twice, each time ducking as German artillery raked the Rhine. "[The shells] fell like huge raindrops into still water," he wrote, "exploding, for reasons I don't understand, as they struck the water."[42]

For days on end Rooney remained at Remagen, hustling to stay on top of the story as other correspondents began to arrive. The world was engrossed by the specter of the bridge that refused to die—but the story was constantly plagued by misinformation. Reporters who weren't there were writing that the original bridge had been completely rebuilt, or that the railway span had been closed down in favor of the new pontoon bridge.

Rooney's coverage in the *Stars and Stripes* turned out to be one of the few consistently accurate accounts of what was going on at the bridgehead. Every day the span got creakier—but every day, thousands of troops and hundreds of vehicles would make it across.

Finally, on day ten of the drama, St. Patrick's Day, 1945, the inevitable happened: The bridge collapsed. Rooney was interviewing GIs on the western side of the Rhine when there was a "great grinding roar" as the middle part of the span gave way. Rooney raced to the river's edge, cursing himself for not having brought his camera. Then he spotted an engineer with a camera strapped around his neck.

Rooney introduced himself to the man, who turned out to be Marcus Hoffman from San Francisco. Had Hoffman taken before-and-after pictures of the now-downed bridge? He had, he told Rooney. If Hoffman would permit Rooney to send the roll of pictures to Paris, Rooney promised to get him free glossies—plus arrange a nice photo credit in the *Stars and Stripes*. Hoffman agreed but only reluctantly, since that particular roll also contained personal shots of guys in his unit.

The *Stars and Stripes* editors back in Paris couldn't believe their good fortune. Andy's copy the next day was featured along with Hoffman's wonderful photo of the bridge half-submerged in the Rhine. SHE'S UP, the caption read on the upper left; SHE'S DOWN, it read on the upper right.

Alas, by the time the glossies got back to Remagen, Hoffman's unit had moved on—and Rooney couldn't track him down. For decades, a guilt-ridden Rooney kept the Remagen pictures in a file drawer, swearing one day he'd get them back to Hoffman. That day came in 1995, when Rooney recounted the story in the original edition of *My War*. One thing led to another, and soon Hoffman, still alive and still living in San Francisco, had tracked Rooney down—and Rooney air-expressed the pictures to him. After fifty years, Rooney again could sleep with a clear conscience, he joked in the next edition of his book.[43]

THREE WEEKS AFTER THE BRIDGE collapsed, at about nine o'clock on the evening of April 11, Rooney was typing up some notes in the dining room of a dilapidated hotel in Weimar that the First Army was using as a press camp. There was no one else around when his pals Hal Boyle of AP and Jack Thompson of the *Chicago Tribune* suddenly burst in.

"Here were two experienced newsmen who had seen everything in a lifetime of reporting and they were in an uncharacteristic state of high excitement," Rooney remembered.[44]

The usual MO for reporters with a big scoop was to keep their mouths shut and quietly type their stories. But Boyle and Thompson were so overwhelmed by what they had seen that they had to share it with a friend. Two days earlier, Boyle had been among the first reporters on the scene when U.S. troops liberated a ghastly Nazi camp at an insane asylum near Limburg. It was a "murder factory," Boyle had written, a place where sadistic guards tortured slave laborers and where as many as twenty thousand Jews, political prisoners, and Gypsies had been executed.[45]

But Limburg paled in comparison to what Boyle and Thompson had seen outside Weimar at a camp called Buchenwald. That morning Boyle and Thompson had driven south of the First Army lines and met up with the Third Army's Sixth Armored Division. Some tankmen told them a harrowing story about a death camp they'd unearthed that morning, one littered with thousands of skeletons. They drove over to Buchenwald to investigate.

As Thompson and Boyle typed their stories, they would hand Rooney each completed page.

> They described the bodies, piled like cordwood, in open graves. They told me of having seen the house in which Ilse Koch, the camp commander and so-called Bitch of Buchenwald, lived. They described the lampshades there that they had been told were made of human skin.[46]

Boyle and Thompson told Rooney more than enough information for Andy to compile his own story. But Rooney decided that in good conscience he could not file a piece without seeing the nightmarish scene for himself. The next day Boyle's account of Buchenwald's liberation ran on page one of the *Stars and Stripes* and hundreds of other papers back home.

"That's the way it should have been," Rooney recalled. "Hal was one of the best."[47]

Rooney, remembering the Allies' Great War propaganda about phony "atrocities" committed by the Central Powers, wasn't the only correspondent that spring skeptical about reports of Hitler's genocidal camps. When he got to Buchenwald, and two weeks later to the horrific slave labor camp at Thekla, Rooney felt ashamed that he'd ever doubted the reports—and even more ashamed that he'd ever flirted with pacifism. His left-wing Colgate professor had been dead wrong: Any peace was *not* better than any war.

George Patton, Rooney's bête noire, in one of his finer moments of the war, ordered his men to round up Buchenwald's villagers and force them to see what they'd pretended not to see for all those years.

Rooney walked through Thekla with Frederick Graham, a reporter with the *New York Times*. Graham and Rooney were struck by the contrast between the prim and gardened cottages in the village, just a few hundred yards away, and the lurid scene inside the camp's barbed wire. When Thekla's SS guards had realized that U.S. troops were rapidly descending on the camp, they herded three hundred prisoners into a hut, doused it with gasoline, and set it on fire. Somehow, a few dozen men, literally on fire, "clawed their way out of the burning barracks," as Rooney put it.

> The burned and blackened bodies of about sixty men were hanging in contorted positions from the needle-point barbs of the wire. When one part of the body burns, the skin and muscles contract and the body, in death, lies warped like a board left out in wet ground in the sun. A few—the lucky few—had bullet holes through them.[48]

Rooney and Graham walked into the village. "The people of Thekla said that to us endlessly. 'We didn't know.' They said it until we felt like kicking them down the street and into the compound themselves. If they didn't know, which seemed impossible, they should have known."[49]

Hal Boyle had hundreds of similarly infuriating conversations with German citizens who professed ignorance of Nazi wrongdoing. In the war's waning days, Boyle became fascinated with Hitler Youth and *Volksgrenadier* units, the children who marched to certain death or committed suicide rather than capitulate.

"They have been taught to be hard and cruel and ruthless—and as a class they are," Boyle wrote from Saxony. "There is more hate in the eyes of these knee-pant legions than in all the army's millions of trained soldiers."[50]

Three weeks earlier Boyle had written Frances. "Well I told you so," he began. "This bloody-by-Jesus business is getting over fast, and I don't think it will be many weeks before I can accept your invitation to return home and spend a couple of months having breakfast lunch and dinner in bed."[51]

He and his pal Jack Thompson had eaten dinner the night before with their "favorite general," Omar Bradley. They toasted the Third Army's penetration over the Rhine with steak and potatoes and pineapple ice cream; Bradley and Boyle doubled up on dessert. "Being made one of the really big shots of the war hasn't changed [Bradley] essentially a bit," Boyle told Frances. "He seems as modest and capable—and I guess as homely, too—as he did back in Tunisia and Sicily."

Hal and Thompson hung around Bradley's place until nearly midnight, shooting the bull. "I suppose that will teach [Bradley] never to invite us back again," Boyle joked. A few days later Boyle wrote to Frances that he'd been holed up at the Dreesen Hotel in Bad Godesberg, where he got to gambol on a bed in which *der Führer* had slept during his deceitful talks over the annexation of Czechoslovakia eight years earlier with British prime minister Neville Chamberlain. Boyle and the other press guys "liberated" a wondrous wine cellar, carting up several cases of sweet Rhine wine, which inflicted a horrible hangover, Boyle confided.

He also confided that the deeper they got into enemy territory, the more he sensed the hatred felt by the German people. Boyle was still busy, he told Frances, responsible for both spot coverage and for his near-daily column. If he concentrated strictly on the column, he'd have to give up his accreditation at the front, he explained, which was something that at this point in the war, Boyle was loath to do.[52]

Boyle was outside Torgau along the Elbe River on April 27 when units of the First Army's Fighting 69th Division hooked up with Soviet troops. Captured German soldiers told Boyle that they had been ordered to shoot only Soviets, not Americans. By then, Nazi infantrymen were streaming west, surrendering in droves to the oncoming Americans and praying not to be ensnared by Russian patrols, where they would have been executed on sight. Hal stayed with the First long enough to witness the victory party thrown by General Alexei Zhadov of the Red Army's Fifth Guards on April 30. A Russian military band greeted General Courtney Hodges and his First Army staff with the "Star-Spangled Banner," followed by the Soviet anthem. Zhadov presented Hodges with a plaque the Fifth Guards had been given by Premier Joseph Stalin. Hodges reciprocated by giving Zhadov a battle-stained flag the First had carried across Western Europe.

It was Hal Boyle's kind of bash: a drunken brawl with a lot of sentimental singing. After the obligatory toasts saluting Allied solidarity, Russian female soldiers began bringing in heaping trays of sausages, suckling pig, and various fish delicacies, all leavened with champagne, cognac, and vodka. Male and female Russian folk dancers and singers entertained until all hours. Only at dawn did they "call quits," as Boyle put it. The last revelers—the Russian performers joined by a couple of hearty American lads—were "twined around three leftover bottles of vodka in one corner of the room" as Boyle reluctantly exited the premises.[53] After weeks of covering apocalyptic scenes in concentration camps and the ritualistic suicides of the Hitler Youth, it must have been a relief for Boyle to cover an event that had the feel of Sig Ep parties at the Columbia Log Cabin tourist camp.

On May 1, the day before Hitler killed himself in the *Führerbunker* in Berlin, Boyle wrote about a lone American infantryman who had singlehandedly captured more than two hundred enemy soldiers. Sergeant Hubert Baine of Norfolk, Virginia, a member of the Ninth Infantry's 39th Regiment, was on a patrol through some "fluid" (meaning an undetermined enemy presence) woods outside the village of Henrode when a young girl got his attention.

"There's a German soldier in the woods over there who wants to surrender," the girl said.

Baine followed her through the forest. Suddenly, out from some shadows stepped a Nazi general, who stiffly came to attention, raised his right arm, clicked his heels, and barked, "Heil Hitler!"

"I was kind of confused at that point," Baine told Boyle. "So I just tossed him back an offhand GI highball."

After the awkward exchange, the German general, who must have been unfamiliar with American insignias of rank, asked Baine if he was an officer. "Yes," noncom Baine fibbed. The nearest 39th Regiment officer was miles away; Baine didn't want to gum up the works over niceties.

The general yelled a command toward the woods; out came scores of enemy infantry, each with hands up. None appeared to be armed nor eager to escape.

Baine figured that some of the soldiers might change their minds, so he briskly marched them toward Henrode, where the 39th was bivouacked.

Similar scenes were happening all over as German soldiers moved away from advancing Russians. That same day Boyle interviewed a corporal from Georgia who had encountered a German colonel adamantly refusing to surrender to anyone of inferior rank.

"Suh, if you don't cut out that damned foolishness," the kid said, "we are mighty apt to bury you right here," and gestured toward a ditch alongside the road. With a flamoyant gesture, the colonel handed the corporal his saber.[54]

ANDY ROONEY EXPERIENCED HIS OWN scare accepting the surrender of a German infantryman. He was alone in his jeep in late March near Paderborn, the village where Wernher von Braun and his team of scientists perfected the V-1 and V-2 rockets, when an enemy soldier suddenly appeared, alone, a rifle in his upraised hand. The unarmed Rooney didn't know what to do: If he sped up, he could be shot in the back; if he slowed down, he could get shot in the front.

Rooney gambled that the soldier wanted to surrender. He did. The soldier turned out to be as scared as Rooney was. Affecting a menacing look, Rooney grunted to the German to dump his rifle in the back. The soldier offered no resistance. It was only after Rooney had shifted the jeep into second gear that he realized his captive still had a pistol strapped to his waist.

"All he had to do to have a jeep of his own and an American uniform to wear—with a bullet hole in it—would have been to shoot me," Rooney recalled. "My mother told me never to pick up hitchhikers."

Again mustering bravado, Rooney demanded that the soldier hand over the sidearm. Andy took the gun—it turned out to be a .32 caliber semiautomatic—back to the States with him as a souvenir.[55]

Boyle, too, had a close shave in the eleventh hour of the war. Hal and Jack Thompson spotted a cache of captured paraphernalia that had been dumped in a roadside quarry. They thought it curious that no GIs were around to guard the weapons. But they couldn't resist the chance to grab more loot on top of the contraband they'd already collected. Boyle and Thompson had picked out a couple of sporty handguns and helmets when they noticed a pair of armed German soldiers staring down at them from the rim of the quarry. Like Rooney, they put on their toughest-looking faces and told the Germans to drop their weapons. They did.

Sadly, many of Boyle's wartime mementoes were sold after his death by his daughter, Tracy. Tracy's decision to barter her father's keepsakes caused friction with her cousins that contributed to her estrangement from the family.[56]

On Tuesday, May 8, 1945, the banner headline on the front page of the *Stars and Stripes* read:

It's Over
Over Here

Two reporters got page-one bylines that morning. Charles Kiley, Andy's buddy from Bristol Harbour in early June of '44, was in Reims to cover the actual surrender ceremony. Kiley's lede was classic *Stars and Stripes*, strictly meat and potatoes: "The Third Reich surrendered unconditionally to the Allies here at Gen. Dwight D. Eisenhower's forward headquarters at 9:41 a.m. Monday."

Unlike Associated Press' Edward Kennedy, Kiley and the *Stars and*

Stripes actually adhered to the embargo that the Allies had attached to the surrender story—a delay to allow the victorious governments ample time to announce the news. Sixty-five years after Kennedy jumped the gun, Rooney was still steamed about it. Kennedy always claimed it was inadvertent, but his detractors are legion.

Rooney, for his part, somehow managed to be in the French Riviera when General Alfred Jodl, representing the new (and instantly deposed) *Führer*, Admiral Karl Dönitz, signed the surrender papers. Yet Andy got a page-one byline interviewing suddenly triumphant and, presumably, well-tanned doughboys. American GIs were in one of the world's great resorts, yet when told the news about Germany quitting, one of them fumed: "Good! When do we leave this hole and go home?" Which is how the *Stars and Stripes* chose to headline Andy's piece.

"Soldiers who read it, who heard the announcement over the BBC or who got the news second-hand from a usually reliable friend, were happy but generally undemonstrative," Rooney wrote of V-E Day. "There was very little dancing or hugging by frontline soldiers in the area. They quietly talked over what it meant among themselves.

"At MP headquarters the sergeant on the desk, Julius Lavontiev of Perth Amboy, N.J., said, 'We're going to lock this place up tonight and let 'em tear the town down.'"[57]

Where Hal Boyle was that week the towns had—literally—been torn down—but not out of jubilation. Boyle was several hundred miles northeast of Rooney when the news hit that Hitler had committed suicide.

"There is little exuberance, little enthusiasm, and almost none of the whoop-it-up spirit with which hundreds of thousands of men looked forward to this event a year ago," Boyle wrote.

"It has been a long and bloody trail—the 800-mile march from the beaches of Normandy in less than eleven months. It has drained much from the men who made it—much from their bodies and much from their spirit. They are physically and emotionally tired."

One apprehension drove almost every soldier, Boyle noted: "Will I be sent to the Pacific?"[58] Most of them weren't, but Hal Boyle was.

The *Kansas City Star*'s headline on May 7, 1945, in huge print was:

Germany Surrenders; London V-Day Tuesday

BOYLE GOT WORD THAT HE'D won the Pulitzer Prize a few days later when he stopped at the First Division's command post after a quick trip to Prague with Cy Peterman of the *Philadelphia Inquirer*. Captain Maxie Zera, a First Army PRO, offered "congratulations" to Boyle in his nasal Bronx accent.

According to Don Whitehead, who got it secondhand, the exchange went something like: "Congratulations for what?" Boyle asked.

"Winning the Pulitzer Prize," Zera volunteered.

"Aw, horsefeathers!" Boyle replied, although given Hal's propensity for colorful language, his response was almost certainly more graphic.

"No, it's true," Zera said, showing Boyle a copy of that day's the *Stars and Stripes*.

"They must have made a mistake!" Boyle protested.[59]

But it was no mistake. No reporter ever worked harder or more resourcefully or moved more readers. Boyle was honored for his 1944 work in Italy, France, and Belgium, but in truth the medal dated back to the moment Boyle grabbed onto the coral reef in Fedala Harbor, Morocco, in November 1942.

It didn't take Boyle long to get home for a quick break before he was sent to the Pacific. Soon after V-E Day, Boyle sat down for a radio interview with Roy Potter of NBC. For two and a half years, Potter told listeners, Boyle had been living and marching with American combat troops. The Potter interview had none of the contrived schmaltz that had tainted Boyle's 1944 interview with Quentin Reynolds of CBS.

After his thirty-month assignment to hell, Hal spoke from the heart. He also spoke for his four friends and for every ETO correspondent.

> All I can remember with any feeling of pride in this whole sorry business of war is the courage and fortitude of the men who fought it.

Certain battle units I remember best, not because they were the finest but because I lived with them and shared a few of their dangers. But I don't think the nation . . . will ever forget the First, Second, or Third armored divisions, or the First, Second, Third, Fifth, Ninth, 34th, 36th, or 45th infantry divisions, or the 82nd and 101st airborne divisions. There is a roll call of honor from Casablanca to Bastogne to Prague.

But of them all, I think the best symbol of the American army overseas is the Fighting First infantry. We call them the "Brooklyn bums" but they came from every state in America. They have fought their way many more miles against more Germans than any unit in the American army.

They left their dead by the hundreds in Tunisia, Sicily, France, Belgium, and Germany. And when the final surrender came, they were still killing Nazis. Their battle achievements dwarf their losses.

But you can't forget those soldiers who died on the rough, long road of victory. We can reconvert our war factories for peace—but how can we ever reward those lost, magnificent men?[60]

Fortunately for Boyle, the war in the Pacific was virtually over by the time he got there. Hal didn't have to witness the sacrifice of more magnificent young Americans. All he had to deal with was a dismembered Japan and the dawning of the atomic age.

EPILOGUE

★

A Good Age

War, being the ultimate competition, often calls forth qualities a man has never had occasion to see in himself before. He accomplishes physical feats he did not know his body was capable of, and thinks of things with both an ingenuity and a depth that were not called for in peace.

—Andy Rooney, 1962
The Fortunes of War

Every Allied reporter on the deck of the USS *Missouri* that epochal Sunday morning noticed that the head of the Japanese delegation limped as he struggled with an artificial leg. But only a writer with the acuity of Homer Bigart could turn the foreign minister's disability into a metaphor for Japan's abject defeat.

"Japan, paying for her desperate throw of the dice at Pearl Harbor, passed from the ranks of the major powers at 9:05 a.m. today when Foreign Minister Mamoru Shigemitsu signed the documents of unconditional surrender," Bigart wrote from atop Tokyo Bay.

"If memories of the bestialities of the Japanese prison camps were not so fresh in mind, one might have felt sorry for Shigemitsu as he hobbled on his wooden leg toward the green baize-covered table where the papers lay waiting," Bigart observed. "He leaned heavily on his cane and had difficulty seating himself. The cane, which rested against the table, dropped to the deck of the battleship as he signed."[1]

On Sunday, December 7, 1941, Homer Bigart had been an anonymous grunt on the city beat of the *New York Herald Tribune*. By Sunday,

September 2, 1945, Bigart had become a journalistic giant, a newspaperman held in awe by editors, peers, military PROs, and thousands of dis-
cerning readers back home.

One of the many ironies of World War II journalism is that Bigart's
Pulitzer was awarded for his coverage of the Pacific Theater, which was not
nearly as gripping as his descriptions of the predawn commando raids on
Monte Cipolla and the Îles d'Hyères, nor as poignant as his portrayals of
the bloody debacles at Anzio and San Pietro.

The war in the Pacific was different, Bigart and his friend Hal Boyle
both discovered: cannibalistic in one sense, eerily impersonal in another.
Still, the two reporters witnessed plenty of history in the final stages of the
war against Tojo and the Rising Sun. Bigart covered the assaults on Iwo
Jima and Okinawa, the rescue of the Allied prisoners at Los Baños in the
Philippines, and was among the first reporters allowed into Hiroshima a
month after the atomic blast. Boyle arrived at the Pacific front only days
before the *Enola Gay* took off; nevertheless, Hal was one of the few reporters in Germany for V-E Day and in Japan for V-J Day.

In his first dispatch from the Philippines in mid-November 1944, Bigart wrote,

> This correspondent, coming from the European fronts,
> has been impressed by the weakness of the Japanese artil-
> lery, and the failure of the enemy to employ mines with
> anything like the diabolical thoroughness of Field Mar-
> shal Albert Kesselring's army in Italy. . . . Here you can
> drive right up to the front line in broad daylight without
> drawing a storm of artillery or getting blown sky high by
> Teller mines. And that is precisely why more correspon-
> dents have been killed here than in any comparable period
> in the European theater.[2]

One of those correspondents killed in the Pacific was Ernie Pyle, another Pulitzer winner. Pyle was picked off by a sniper on the island of Ie

Shima off the coast of Okinawa, six days after President Roosevelt died. Between FDR and Ernie, millions of Americans thought they had lost dear friends.

With Shigemitsu's signature the most horrific conflict in history, a conflagration that had raged on six of the world's seven continents, mercifully came to a close. Every few seconds for six years someone somewhere in the world was killed—some sixty million people in all. For every soldier snuffed out in the line of duty, three innocents perished. Four hundred thousand Americans died, fifty-one of whom were reporters.

Bob Sheets, who piloted Cronkite across the Channel on D-Day, remarkably survived another fourteen combat missions. Before war's end, he was promoted to major, then lieutenant colonel, and, having reached the threshold of thirty-five raids, was given command of the 427th Bomb Squadron. After the war Sheets went back to Oregon, used the GI Bill to finish his business administration degree in Eugene, married his sweetheart Colleen, and spent a career as an accomplished executive in the export-import industry. His last job, ironically, was for a company based in Japan. For decades Sheets commanded an air reserve unit; well into the 1970s he led weekend drills at the 403rd Air Base in Portland.[3]

In the early 1990s, Sheets sent Walter Cronkite an amusing note telling the legend that had the pilot known his surprise D-Day passenger was going to become famous, he would have had Cronkite autograph something. Cronkite responded by scribbling on a photo taken that auspicious morning: "To Captain Bob Sheets: With a lifetime of gratitude for getting us back! Walter Cronkite." Colleen and Bob had six kids and six grandkids. Bob suffered a stroke in 1996 and passed away four years later.[4]

Back in early 1944, Second Lieutenant Jack Watson, Sheets' coconspirator in the Yankee Stadium flyover, had gotten a telegram from New York Mayor La Guardia. His Honor had read a Cronkite-authored story about how Watson single-handedly piloted back to England a badly shot-up B-17. "All is forgiven," the mayor had wired. "Congratulations. I hope you never run out of altitude." Watson had responded: "Thank you, Mr. Mayor, and it can't be too soon for me. We'd sort of like to go back together someday and drop in on the Rose Bowl game."[5]

Coast Guard captain Bunny Rigg, who deposited Carusi's Thieves on Omaha Beach despite murderous fire, was awarded the Silver Star and the Legion of Merit.[6] Carusi also won a Silver Star to go with the Purple Heart he had earned on the evening of D-Day plus one on Easy Red. His Thieves won the Croix de Guerre from a grateful French government. After recovering from his wounds, Carusi went back to practicing law in the nation's capital. He died in 1987 at age eighty-two.

In peacetime Rigg became the editor of *Skipper* magazine, a mainstay of the Annapolis Yacht Club, a three-time winner of the prestigious Bermuda yacht race, and a founder of the annual hundred-mile sailing competition around Chesapeake Bay. Bunny and his wife, Marjorie, built a handsome colonial on Meredith Creek near the bay. Almost no one in Annapolis knew that Bunny was a D-Day hero.[7] Like so many of that generation, he never talked about the war. Rigg passed away in 1980, thirty-six years after he ordered Joe Liebling topside while their landing craft plunged toward Omaha Beach.

ALL FIVE OF OUR CORRESPONDENTS witnessed far too much of what Bigart called bestiality. But only Cronkite among the five covered in detail the ultimate exhumation of bestiality, the Nuremberg trials.

Cronkite missed the opening of the trials. En route to Germany in early December 1945, he was diverted by UP to cover what proved to be George Patton's fatal automobile accident in Luxembourg. The maniacal commander who had survived Great War tank battles in the Meuse-Argonne, amphibious assaults in Morocco and Sicily, and Luftwaffe attacks on two continents was ironically done in by a wayward truck driver. Boyle later wrote of Patton's burial marker at Hamm, Luxembourg, which, out of deference to Patton's rank, was moved away from the graves of ordinary soldiers: "His real monument was ruthless personal honesty. He believed that people, being what they are, made war inevitable."[8]

By January Cronkite was in Nuremberg, studying the faces of loathsome criminals who also believed in the inevitability of war. Cronkite was soon to be joined—at last!—by Betsy. After three years of heartache, the Cronkites were finally together in Europe. Betsy was credentialed to cover the trial for UP.

Every day the Cronkites sat in the Palace of Justice's second-floor courtroom, a few feet away from Hermann Göring and the other Nazi swine.

The defendants sat before eight judges—two each from the United States, the Soviet Union, France, and Britain. Cronkite and other reporters could barely contain their contempt for Hitler's enablers.

"I wanted to spit on them," Cronkite wrote. "I wouldn't spit on the street, but now I would spit on them, to show, subconsciously, I suppose, that I thought them lower than the dirt on the street."[9]

Cronkite had not covered with his own eyes the liberations of Auschwitz and Buchenwald and Hitler's other concentration camps. But now he watched, in horror, one Signal Corps film after another documenting Nazi atrocities. Almost as appalling as the film footage, Cronkite remembered, was the testimony from innocent-looking people who had contributed to the extermination of millions. The boss of Auschwitz, Rudolf Franz Ferdinand Höss, described in clinical detail the operation of gas chambers.

When Höss was asked if he felt any guilt, Cronkite recalled that the Waffen SS henchman replied, "Don't you see, we SS men were not supposed to think about these things. . . . It was something already taken for granted that the Jews were to blame for everything. We were all so trained to obey orders that the thought of disobeying an order would never have occurred to anybody."[10] Each day brought a harrowing new glimpse into Nazi depravity.

For nine of those days, Hermann Göring was on the witness stand, badgering, tormenting, and—in the view of Cronkite and other trial observers—outwitting the chief prosecutor, U.S. Supreme Court Justice Robert Jackson. Göring, a slick operator despite his heroin addiction, used his testimony, at least in Cronkite's eyes, to provide the next generation of Nazi leaders with a road map. Without a flicker of remorse, Göring acknowledged Hitler's gaffes, in effect telling young Nazi adherents, "Here's how *not* to do it next time."

It infuriated Allied reporters that Jackson, a capable jurist but an inexperienced prosecutor, let Göring get away with it. It also incensed them that the architect of the Nazi terror bombing of London managed to swallow a cyanide pill just hours before his appointment with the gallows. Nuremberg should have been Göring's moment of reckoning. Instead, on too many days it had the feel of *der Reichsführer* getting the last laugh.

Every night in Nuremberg eateries, Betsy, Walter, and their friends debated the moral underpinnings of the trial and whether it was prudent for the Allies to be prosecuting Nazis for "crimes against humanity." It was, of course, but that didn't make Göring's antics any easier to take.

One of Cronkite's searing memories of Nuremberg was going to the Luitpoldhain, the hundred-thousand-seat Nazi showcase where Albert Speer organized worshipful Nazi rallies and director Leni Riefenstahl filmed her chilling *Triumph of the Will*. In early May of '46, Nuremberg's mayor had asked special permission to use the arena for a prayerful gathering on the first anniversary of Germany's surrender. Immense marble and brass bowls stood at each end of the stage. As the solemn ceremony got under way, the mayor noticed that some youngsters had climbed into the bowls.

Cronkite recalled: "The mayor's first words—the first German words spoken in the stadium since the fall of Nazism—were 'Will the children please come down from the sacrificial urns.'"[11]

ANDY ROONEY WASN'T AT THE Luitpoldhain that day, but he, too, covered the trials—but only briefly—while on assignment with *Holiday*. It was the first time Rooney had ever had the chance to study the *Nuremberg Laws on Race and Citizenship*, the 1935 polemic that empowered Hitler to persecute people of Jewish ancestry. Rooney, with Thekla's blackened corpses still fresh in mind, was horrified to learn how methodically the Nazis had instituted racial hatred.

"The fiendish quality of this aspect of genocide seems important to know because it is, in part anyway, an answer to the mystery 'How could they have done it?'" Rooney wrote decades later.[12]

It's a question that dogged all five correspondents. They had seen what happens when an independent press and people abdicate responsibility and cave in the face of ignorance and intolerance. Each came back determined in his own way to make American journalism better: more inquisitive, more worldly, more informed. Joe Liebling always called America's press the "weak slat under the bed of democracy." Following the war, the slat became more resilient, one of the traits that made the U.S. the envy of the world. But in recent years, the American media has sadly reverted to its prewar pettiness and greed. Cronkite, Rooney, Bigart, Boyle, and Liebling didn't let us down; the generation that succeeded them did.

ROONEY ALWAYS MAINTAINED THAT THE war never consumed him the way it did other correspondents. Anyone who has read Andy's lovely *My War* or his keen *The Fortunes of War* or been touched by his Memorial Day commentaries is entitled to reach a different conclusion.

Metro-Goldwyn-Mayer wanted to make a movie of Rooney and Bud Hutton's *The Story of the Stars and Stripes*; regrettably, the project ran out of money. As a freelance journalist and later a writer for *Arthur Godfrey's Talent Scouts* in the golden days of CBS television, Rooney went to great lengths to pay homage to World War II veterans. A piece of footage that survives from the old Godfrey show features the star saluting Rooney for Andy's efforts on behalf of former GIs.

Not many TV writers from the '50s got to dine with *New Yorker* legends E. B. White and James Thurber, but Rooney did. His friend and mentor Joe Liebling once invited Rooney to join the famous humorists for lunch. Rooney, who had idolized White since he was a kid, spent the entire meal pinching himself.[13] The two Andys, bemused, listened as Thurber and Liebling tried to one-up one another. Liebling's idea of a perfect meal, Rooney concluded, was one in which Joe got to gorge himself and where everyone at the table fawned over his writing. But that was okay; in Rooney's view, Liebling's stuff was worth fawning over.

Rooney may have revered White and Liebling, but his own writing reflected more of the regular-guy sensibilities of Pyle and Boyle. When Rooney moved on to CBS News and its public affairs vehicle, *The 20th Century*, he was lead writer on a series of prime-time documentaries on World War II. Rooney took his research and turned it into *The Fortunes of War*—a superb examination of four pivotal battles: Stalingrad, Tarawa, Normandy, and the Bulge. To commemorate the thirtieth anniversary of Franklin Roosevelt's death, Rooney wrote the script for a CBS documentary called *FDR: The Man Who Changed America*. Rooney's old man must have rolled over in his grave.

Ironically, Andy Rooney didn't become an on-air commentator until he was almost sixty. In '78, when *60 Minutes*' debate segment, Point/Counterpoint with liberal Shana Alexander and conservative James J. Kilpatrick, took a summer respite, CBS looked for a replacement. Anchor Walter Cronkite urged the higher-ups to give his old crony a chance. A Few Minutes with Andy Rooney proved to be among the most popular commentary segments in television history, winning millions of new viewers for *60 Minutes* and becoming a staple for three decades. Rooney appeared in various fortieth- and fiftieth-anniversary World War II documentaries, even narrating a series on the air war, something he covered virtually every day from late 1942 to mid-1944.

Ever the curmudgeon, Rooney bristled (or at least pretended to) when journalist-historian Tom Brokaw labeled Andy and his World War II contemporaries "the greatest generation" any society has ever produced. Good-natured jousting went on between them for years. "I've joked I'm willing to put an asterisk by [Rooney's] name, excluding him from the accolade," Brokaw wrote in the foreword to the paperback edition of *My War*.[14]

The pistol that Rooney took off his "prisoner" collected dust for the better part of three decades until Andy's then-teenage son, Brian, hectored his dad about firing it. So while in upstate New York one weekend they grabbed an old clay planting pot, stuck it on top of a fence post, and moved a few yards away. Brian got the first shot with the .32 caliber. It misfired: nothing happened. Then it was Andy's turn. Brian jokingly cowered behind his father as Andy took aim. There was a ferocious *bang*!; the kick was so abrupt that it caused Andy to lurch into Brian. The two of them howled laughing for a good twenty seconds, then looked up. The clay pot was history; Andy had scored a bull's-eye. All that Writing 69th training had finally paid off.

Rooney's tender fealty to the people who shot guns for real and sacrificed their lives in the struggle against Fascism belied his protests. "They were all my age," Rooney wrote. "I think of the good life I have lived and they never had a chance to live. They didn't give their lives. Their lives were taken."[15]

HAL BOYLE, TOO, DEVOTED MUCH of his career to World War II remembrance. While still in Europe in early '45, Boyle and Jack Thompson of the *Chicago Tribune* tried to solicit bids on a book called *Breakout* about the Allied sweep across France.[16] Sadly, nothing came of it, because there would have been some great stories—and some great storytelling. Nor did anything come of a proposed book that Boyle wanted to write in partnership with former *New York Times* editor and Columbia University and New York University journalism professor John Tebbel. The book was to be a compendium of Boyle's wartime articles and letters to Mary Frances.[17]

Boyle was such a big name that when he arrived home from Europe on June 3, 1945, aboard the troopship *Monticello*, reporters and photographers greeted him. He obliged the shutterbugs by tossing his duffel over a shoulder and flashing his Irish bartender's grin.[18]

Hal became AP's globe-trotting columnist, writing under the banner Marco Polo. Before it was all said and done, the butcher's kid from Kansas City had visited more than sixty countries.

When the Korean conflict erupted, Boyle reprised his grunts-in-the-foxholes column, joining old pal Don Whitehead in Seoul. Boyle's writing in Korea was so good it earned him several awards, including a medal from the Veterans of Foreign Wars. The VFW prize meant as much to Boyle as his 1945 Pulitzer because it was presented by General Omar Bradley. "There are few men who understand the American soldier and how he feels as well as you," Bradley told Boyle from the dais. "There are even fewer who can write about him with such interest, such understanding, such compassion."[19]

Boyle came back to his apartment on Waverly Place in Greenwich Village and again became a daily columnist for AP. His column owed as much to Groucho Marx as it did to Walter Lippmann. Sometimes Boyle's column addressed weighty foreign policy issues; more often, he wrote about the silliness and frustrations of everyday life.

Hal was fond of quoting Horace Greeley's credo that "Journalism will kill you, but it keeps you alive while you're at it."[20] His MO from the war never changed: He still hunched over his typewriter, bemoaning his fate while muttering to himself as he munched cheap cigars and candy bars. The one thing that had changed was the exposure Boyle's column was getting. At its apex in the '60s, his column ran in some eight hundred papers across the country—more than double his pickup from '44 and '45. Yet despite all his commercial success, the Boyle bank account remained slim, no doubt drained by his fondness for nightlife.

In late 1962 AP sent Boyle to Vietnam, hoping he could re-create his magic. Even in Vietnam's early days, however, the war never lent itself to the kid-next-door salutation that made Boyle's work so popular. Colleagues in Saigon and Da Nang would wager that Boyle could never sober up and meet his deadlines—but he almost always won the bet.[21]

After a few frustrating months, Boyle realized it wasn't meant to be. He returned to New York to resume his Manhattan pub crawling—Pat Moriarty's place and Toots Shor's joint were favorite haunts—and write columns about his crazed Irish family or the chatter being bandied about the office watercooler.

One night he was out barhopping to all hours. The next day his co-revelers asked how Frances reacted when he finally got home. "I don't know," he deadpanned, "she hasn't gotten to the verb yet."[22]

On occasion the World War II press guys would get together to reminisce, usually at Bleeck's saloon. Boyle, Rooney, and Bigart, who liked his gin martinis, were sometimes joined by Liebling and even Cronkite on occasion.[23]

Cronkite took care of his fellow Missourian, arranging for Boyle to pick up extra cash by appearing on CBS News' Sunday morning program *Face the Nation*. For three decades, Boyle had been the more accomplished of the Kansas City journalist boys who made good; now Cronkite was by far the bigger name, even though Boyle ended up earning more bylines than anyone in AP's history.

Sadly, Frances died young after a short illness in 1968; Boyle's drinking, never light, got heavier. When Boyle got the Irish guilts and felt the need to dry out, he would take a few days off and visit Don and Marie Whitehead, vowing not only to go on the wagon, but also to lose a few pounds while he was at it. Invariably, though, Hal would look heavier when Don drove him to the airport. Marie would later find candy bar wrappers stuffed in a pillowcase.[24]

In 1973 Boyle was diagnosed with amyotrophic lateral sclerosis. He faced his fate with typically buoyant humor. In his last column in February 1974, Boyle wrote:

> Only two nice things can be said about [the disease]. It doesn't affect the mind and it is more fatiguing and un-comfortable than painful.
>
> The irony of it to me is that after surviving three wars without a scratch I come down with an ailment that on the average strikes only one out of every 100,000 people.
>
> I guess this is the place to express my deeply felt thanks to all the readers who through all the years made the journey with me and shored up my spirits with kind letters of cheer, suggestion, and criticism.
>
> See you later.[25]

They were the last words Hal Boyle wrote for publication. Two months later, three days after being given what *New Yorker* writer Calvin Trillin called "the rare Irish pleasure of attending his own wake,"[26] Boyle died of a massive heart attack.

Besides Kansas City native and Boyle devotee Trillin, among those attending Hal's premortem gathering was Boyle's old war buddy Wes

Gallagher, who by then had graduated to become AP's president and general manager. Boyle's final column, Gallagher wrote in notes that accompanied the piece, "was low-keyed and self-deprecating, reflecting eloquently the inner strength and courage of one of the finest journalists of our time."[27]

No shortage of encomiums came Boyle's way. Right after the war, Indiana University, Pyle's alma mater, appointed Hal its first Pyle lecturer. The Overseas Press Club of America named an annual reporting award after Boyle. Friends and colleagues, moreover, established a scholarship fund in his honor at Hal's alma mater, the University of Missouri School of Journalism. They were wonderful tributes, but none could match the letter Boyle received in July of 1945 from Mrs. Cary Hart of Topeka, Kansas.

> *Dear Mr. Boyle:*
> *I have wanted to write to you for a long time and thank you for the comfort and cheer your splendid articles gave me.*
> *I have a son in the 137th Regt, Co. B. in Germany, and during the crossing of the Rhine and the terrible fighting through Germany, I never missed a word that you wrote, always looked for your article first in the K.C. Star.*
> *To me, you are just as fine and tender a writer as Ernie Pyle. You will never know the good your writing did for me.*
> *May God keep you safe in the Pacific, I will be waiting for your articles again. I have a son in Marseilles, France, who runs an M.R.U. (records) machine, so you know I am praying the War will soon be over.*
> *Thank you again for the comfort you gave me.*[28]

———

HOMER BIGART'S WRITING DIDN'T APPEAL to readers' emotions so much as to their intellect. Bigart's dispatches—whether filed from Palestine or the Greek civil war or the Korean conflict or the Cuban revolution—continued to challenge readers. In January 1951, as Bigart departed Korea, *Newsweek* called him "the best war correspondent of an embattled generation."[29]

Harrison Salisbury, who never stopped admiring Bigart, said his future fellow *Times* man had an "eye as precise as Goya's."[30]

Spurred by a rivalry with his *Herald Tribune* colleague Marguerite Higgins, who was every bit as feisty and fearless as he was, Bigart's writing in Korea was in the same league as his 1944 work in Italy. Homer persisted in covering war from the cannon's mouth, taking risks that left other reporters dumbfounded. He and Higgins ended up sharing a Pulitzer with four other correspondents for their collective work in Korea.

Bigart, no misogynist, nevertheless tormented Higgins in every way he knew how; no shrinking violet, she returned the favor. When Homer was told that Higgins was pregnant, he supposedly muttered, "Oh, g-g-good. Who's the m-m-mother?" When the baby was born, Bigart allegedly inquired if Higgins had eaten it. Homer's great friend and confidante Betsy Wade once asked Bigart which of the two stories was true. "Yes," Homer replied.[31]

In 1955, when the *Herald Tribune* began to sputter, Bigart reluctantly moved to the *New York Times*. But his heart always stayed with the *Trib*. Wade called the *Trib* "a writer's paper"; it was the place that had hung with Bigart through thick and thin. In truth, the stiff-necked *Times* never gave Bigart the latitude to share his tart observations. Wade, who edited much of Bigart's stuff at the *Times*, always had to be on the lookout for the acidic barbs he'd slip into his copy, just to see if the pooh-bahs were paying attention.

It is a telling commentary on Vietnam that both of the Pulitzer Prize–winning correspondents sent to cover its early skirmishing—Hal Boyle and Homer Bigart—detested it and asked to be removed as soon as possible. Bigart became a mentor and hero to the young reporters cutting their teeth in Saigon and Da Nang—among them, Peter Arnett, Malcolm Browne, Neil Sheehan and, eventually, David Halberstam. In a 2011 conversation Sheehan remembered Bigart peppering a dissembling officer with questions, then punctuating his interview with: "Do y-y-you really think we're that s-s-stupid, C-C-Colonel?"[32]

When Bigart first arrived in Vietnam, Sheehan followed him around for a few days to get a feel for how Homer approached a story. Neil tagged along on helicopter assaults into Vietcong hamlets, listening as Bigart asked the same questions, over and over again. The whole exercise seemed pointless.

"Jesus Christ, Homer, we spent two days walking through the rice paddies and we don't have a story," Sheehan complained.[33]

Bigart raised an eyebrow. "There's no story?" he challenged Sheehan.

"Well, what is it?" Sheehan countered. "What do you mean?"

"You don't get it, kid. They can't do it. It doesn't work," Bigart rasped. "It doesn't work anymore."[34]

Bigart had seen in a matter of days what it took U.S. officials years to admit. Vietnam became for Bigart the Italian campaign redux, a rudderless conflict with murky objectives, run by commanders much too preoccupied with their PR images—and with telling their bosses what they wanted to hear instead of what they needed to hear.

Homer's first marriage ended in divorce; his second wife passed away in 1969. His third marriage, to children's book author Else Holmelund Minarik, proved happy. Gone was the pasty insecure guy with the nervous stammer and the chain-smoking jones.

Bigart in middle age became something of a dapper sophisticate, almost always impeccably turned out, sporting stylish suits, fedoras, and horn-rimmed glasses. Somehow in midlife he even managed to curb his stammering.[35] He assumed a desk near the front of the *Times'* newsroom and became (at least a little) less owlish; he enjoyed playing éminence grise. When introduced as a "Pulitzer Prize winner," he was invariably quick to say with a grin, "*Two-time* Pulitzer Prize winner," spoofing the pretentiousness of it all but still reminding listeners that, yes, he had won journalism's most prestigious award *twice*. He earned other press honors, a George Polk Award, a Meyer Berger Award, and an Overseas Press Club Award. Although he professed to hate war it continued to animate him; Bigart developed a passion for the American Civil War, collecting books and mementoes and combing battlefields.

Over the years Homer became the *Times'* go-to guy on big assignments, covering Israel's trial of SS war criminal Adolf Eichmann, Mississippi during the awful Klan-retaliation days, and later in the '60s, touring riot-torn cities and college campuses. Bigart was such a stickler for truth-telling that eight different countries did what the First Earl of Tunis, Sir Harold R. L .G. Alexander, had wanted to do in Italy: tossed Bigart out or banned him from coming back.

Homer retired in 1972 and a year later was given a *More* magazine journalism medal, coincidentally named in honor of A. J. Liebling. The award was presented by, among others, Homer's Vietnam protégé David Halberstam "for four decades of single-minded attention to his craft, persistent skepticism toward all forms of power and tenacious pursuit of social injustice long before such reporting became fashionable."[36]

In retirement, Homer and Else moved to a farm outside West Nottingham, New Hampshire. He returned to his reclusive ways, rarely leaving the property and avoiding the lecture circuit and J-school forums. Sadly, he never wrote a book on his war experiences or anything else. Without daily deadline pressure, he couldn't write—or so he claimed.

When in the '80s writer Karen Rothmyer and the Columbia University Press did a book on Pulitzer winners, the prize committee had no forwarding address for Bigart; some assumed he had passed away. Rothmyer found him in West Nottingham, a gracious white-haired gentleman still blessed with a devastating wit, trying to press a glass of gin into her hand.[37] Bigart's own drinking became so heavy that Else began cutting his gin.[38] Maybe the martinis helped Bigart ward off nightmares about accidentally shooting down Robert Perkins Post over Wilhelmshaven.

He died at eighty-three after a difficult bout with cancer. Whenever Rooney or Cronkite talked about Bigart they grew wistful, always referring to him as a dear friend, wickedly funny and irreverent, the quintessential newspaperman. In their youth, they had shared the same disheartening beat and flown in the same formation over Hitler's Germany. There had been a lot of nights together at places like the Cross Keys in Molesworth and the Savoy and the Bell Pub and the Lamb and Lark in London.

On November 22, 1963, Bigart was in the *Times*' newsroom when the tragic story came across the wire. He dutifully filed the assassination article assigned to him; early that evening, he went out for a somber drink with colleagues. At one point he excused himself to call his wife from a phone booth in the bar. His coworkers had been struck that day by Bigart's composure. But as Homer talked with his wife in the glass booth, his friends saw the toughness dissolve: Bigart was weeping.[39]

THE EVENTS OF THAT HIDEOUS weekend in Dallas made Bigart's friend Walter Cronkite a national icon, the rock on whom America leaned in moments of crisis. It was more than just his Midwestern decency; underneath the comforting presence viewers could sense Cronkite's steely resolve.

One of the reasons Cronkite could stay so calm is that he'd seen worse. He'd sweated in smoking B-17s at Molesworth, watched entire London blocks go up in flames, and seen the fear in children's eyes at a Dutch bomb shelter.

Walter Cronkite had seen the world fall apart—and be put back together again.

Like his performance for UP during the war, his success at CBS News was hardly preordained. It's not as if Cronkite showed up in the late '40s and owner William Paley snapped his fingers and said, "There's our anchorman!" It took more than a decade of sweat equity, of internecine dueling with Edward R. Murrow and his boys—not to mention some fairly degrading moments on the air—before Cronkite took the helm of the CBS Evening News.

An early critique from Andy Rooney was one of the reasons Cronkite developed such an avuncular on-air persona. Writer Rooney watched Cronkite rehearse one day and said, "Why are you yelling at me?" After that, Cronkite toned down his voice and relaxed his body language. It worked: viewers were drawn to him.

As late as 1964, however, there were still CBS executives convinced the network's ratings would improve with someone other than Cronkite anchoring. Office politics didn't faze Cronkite; he figured he'd just go back to UP. Yet just four years later, Cronkite had become such an important part of our societal fabric that when he editorialized against U.S. involvement in Vietnam, President Lyndon B. Johnson flipped off his television set, turned to aides, and said, "If I've lost Cronkite, I've lost America."

Throughout the '60s and '70s, Cronkite was infatuated with America's space program. NASA's astronauts reminded him of the flyboys he'd loved in East Anglia, the hell-for-leather daredevils that part of him had always wanted to be. But when writer Tom Wolfe spotlighted the Mercury astronauts' wild-ass ways in the book and movie *The Right Stuff*, Cronkite took exception. Sure military airmen were a little crazy; they'd have to be to climb into those crates, Cronkite believed. But Wolfe never saw what Cronkite did during World War II: their imperishable courage.

If Cronkite became the most trusted man in America, it was because he'd seen Americans at their best; in his own mortal way, he spent the rest of his life trying to live up to those qualities. Fortunately for the rest of us, he took us along on his journey.

It was Cronkite's affection for servicemen and servicewomen that drove him to be so active on World War II legacy projects. He wrote forewords for a dozen or more books, consented to interviews for scores of others, and narrated another dozen or so documentaries: some for CBS in the '50s, '60s, and '70s; some for the Discovery Channel as part of his *Cronkite Remembers* series; and, in his twilight years, two remarkable films produced by British documentary maker Alastair Layzell, *City at War* and *Legacy of War*.

D-Day Plus 20 Years, featuring Cronkite interviewing General Eisenhower in London, Portsmouth, and Normandy, was CBS News at its best: provocatively written and gorgeously filmed with a stirring score courtesy of Aaron Copland. Early in the filming, as the crew was getting footage of Ike crossing Omaha Beach, a group of French schoolchildren happened to stroll by, escorted by nuns. There's a marvelous moment when the former President of the United States and Supreme Allied Commander patiently waits for the group to pass, greeting each nun with that electric smile and nodding, "Sister . . . Sister . . ."

At another point Cronkite was planning to drive a jeep along the beach at Omaha while interviewing Ike about the seaborne invasion. But Walter and producer Fred Friendly agreed that since Eisenhower was giving Cronkite the tour it would be more appropriate—not to mention more compelling from a television point of view—to have Ike do the driving.

"General, you drive, don't you?" Cronkite gently inquired.

"Of course I drive," Eisenhower snapped, as if Cronkite had somehow challenged his manhood.

Mamie Eisenhower and Betsy Cronkite were watching from a nearby bluff. Mrs. Eisenhower turned to Betsy and said, "My dear, your husband has never been in greater danger. Ike hasn't driven in 30 years."[40] Between Eisenhower's rustiness and the old jeep's temperamental clutch, it took several minutes before Ike and Walter stopped lurching.

At the end of the piece Cronkite asked Eisenhower to put D-Day into perspective. "Well," Eisenhower said as he cleared his throat, "it's almost unreal to look at [Normandy's beaches] and remember what it was like. But it's a wonderful thing to remember what those fellows twenty years ago were fighting for and sacrificing for, what they did to preserve our way of life. Not to conquer any territory, not for any ambitions of our own. But to make sure that Hitler could not destroy freedom in the world."

The documentary concluded with a revolutionary moment for 1964: a sweeping helicopter shot of the cemetery at Colleville-sur-Mer, with Omaha Beach framed in the background. It cost Paley and Friendly a bundle, but it was worth it, especially when accompanied by Copland's "Simple Gifts" from *Appalachian Spring*.[41]

A year later, Eisenhower joined Cronkite for a special on the twentieth anniversary of V-E Day. CBS News again used the occasion to showcase something momentous: It arranged for Ike's old ally and rival Bernard Montgomery to appear in London via the Early Bird satellite.

Cronkite kicked off the segment by introducing Eisenhower, who barely slipped in "Hello, Monty," before the Britisher launched into a self-glorifying soliloquy. While Monty was bloviating, Ike disgustedly muttered, "Son of a bitch!" The hookup to London was so crude and the microphone so balky that Ike's epithet, which surely would have caused an international uproar, went unnoticed.[42]

In the 1990s Cronkite participated in various World War II fiftieth-anniversary celebrations. One of the most poignant was presenting an Overseas Press Club plaque to the Château de Vouilly for hosting the First Army press corps in the summer of '44. Mme. Hamel's grandson James, who was conceived during the German Occupation but born four months after *la Libération*, accepted the honor.[43]

A decade later, while contributing to *City at War* and *Legacy of War*, Cronkite got to visit places in the U.K. he hadn't seen in decades. He worshipped at the rebuilt Guards Chapel at Wellington Barracks, reading aloud the names of the victims of the V-1 attack. He dined at the Savoy and toasted his correspondent pals. He flew on a restored B-17 at Duxford. He toured the old barracks at Molesworth and admired the new stone memorial saluting the men of the 303rd Bomb Group, including Congressional Medal of Honor winner Jack Mathis, the mortally wounded bombardier who died before he could yell, "Bombs away!" Alas, there wasn't time to have a beer at the Cross Keys.

Perhaps most memorably, Cronkite paid his respects to Captain Don Stockton and other fallen airmen at the Cambridge American Cemetery and Memorial, the beautiful grounds donated to the U.S. by a grateful Cambridge University. Cronkite held it together at Stockton's gravesite, beaming at the memory of his old friend killed by a cruelly random cannon shot. At the Tablets of the Missing, though, the monument to the hundreds of American fliers lost forever, the imperturbable Walter Cronkite broke down. The microphone picked up the ninety-year-old murmuring, between sobs, about the unfairness and tragedy of it all.[44]

Andy Rooney was supposed to be among the eulogists at Cronkite's memorial service at St. Bartholomew's Church in July of 2009. Using a cane, Rooney hobbled to the lectern.

"You get to know someone pretty well in a war," Rooney began, his voice choked with emotion. "I just feel so terrible about Walter's death that I can hardly say anything. He was such a good friend. Please excuse me—I can't." Trembling, Rooney was helped back to his pew.

There were a lot of Cronkite intimates at St. Bartholomew's, some dating back several decades. But even those old friends viewed Cronkite the way most Americans did: as the broadcaster who defined television journalism.

Rooney was the only one who knew Walter Cronkite before he became *Walter Cronkite*. When he thought of his friend, Rooney saw himself: a

twentysomething kid scared witless about climbing aboard a bomber or
shadowing an infantry patrol but doing it anyway, because it was his duty—
and because it paled in comparison to what soldiers did, day after day.

In his mind's eye, Rooney could see what no one else could: the young
Cronkite staring out a train window on the ride back from East Anglia.
Cronkite had been just like Rooney was, lonely for his wife and heartsick
about the young men he'd chatted with that morning who hadn't returned
from the Reich that afternoon.

JOE LIEBLING NEVER DID FIND another D-Day. "The times were full of cer-
tainties," Liebling reminisced in the early '60s in the foreword to *Mollie
and Other War Pieces*. "We could be certain we were right—and we were—
and that certainty made us certain that anything we did was right, too. I
have seldom been sure I was right since."[45]

Sometimes Liebling felt ashamed that he harbored a "deplorable nostalgia" for the war. He went back several times to visit old haunts in London, Normandy, and Paris. Joe was fortunate to get to Vouilly in time to
share some calvados with Mme. Hamel before she passed on.

Of all his brilliant postwar writing, few things equaled his tributes to
Omar Bradley, both in the pages of the *New Yorker* and in the introduction
to Bradley's 1951 autobiography, *A Soldier's Story*. No Manhattan-centric
essayist ever resented the parochialism of Middle America more than
Liebling. Yet Bradley, the archetypal small-town provincial, was Joe's hero
for life.

Prizefighting—the obsession that made Liebling so popular aboard
LCI(L)-88 at the Weymouth Pier in early June of '44—continued to fasci-
nate him. His anthology of boxing pieces, *The Sweet Science*, has long been
ranked at the top of American sports books. Writer Pete Hamill, who edited
2008's *Liebling: World War II Writings*, met Joe only once, at a Floyd Pat-
terson bout. Hamill was greeted with a chuckle and a big fleshy handshake.

By then Liebling had become a hero to the New Journalists, among
them Hamill, Gay Talese, and Tom Wolfe. In gauging the impact of
Liebling's writing in a 2011 interview, Hamill quoted Ezra Pound's con-

viction that "literature is news that stays news."[46] By Pound's standard, then, virtually everything Liebling touched from 1935 on was literature.

At the Rome Olympics in 1960, Liebling helped introduce to the world a young boxer named Cassius Clay. Many journalists at the time were put off by Clay's racial defiance and brashness, but Liebling saw a kindred spirit and a genius.

Through his monthly Wayward Press essays, Liebling picked up postwar where he left off pre-, skewering money-hungry and narrow-minded media moguls. "Freedom of the press is guaranteed only to those who own one," he famously wrote. He was particularly scornful of the publishers and columnists who contributed to the anti-Communist hysteria. There's no record that he punched out any of them at Bleeck's—but no doubt he wanted to.

He finally divorced Ann, who later made good on her tragic threat to commit suicide. His second marriage was bumpy, too, ending in divorce. But his third marriage, to Pulitzer Prize–winning fiction writer Jean Stafford, proved happy. They traveled widely, often to London and Paris to relive Joe's younger days.

Liebling never got control of his gluttony, nor did he try very hard. He died young, not yet sixty, but a bit too old to have achieved the goal he shared with Andy Rooney in Cherbourg in '44: expiring while at the peak of his obituary value.

Joe didn't know it, but the *Mollie* collection was his World War II valedictory. Before 1963 ended, he would be dead. Among the last things Joe wrote on the war was the book's dedication. It was inimitable Liebling, lithe and sharp:

To many men who would now be in their forties.[47]

"Most people like to live in a good neighborhood," Liebling once mused. "I like to live in a good age."

He did. So did his four friends.

ACKNOWLEDGMENTS

✫

It was said of Joe Liebling that he took history personally. My Georgetown University buddies—Kevin Clark, Jerry McAndrews, Jim Smith, Tom Davis, and Jerry Towle—take history personally, too. When political figures or cultural icons pass from the scene, our e-mail exchanges tend to be so personal, in fact, that they border on the, well, snarky. But when Walter Cronkite passed away in July 2009, our comments were reverential. Therein lay the genesis for this book. I figured if our gang felt that way about Cronkite and his generation of journalists, then at least a few other people did, too.

As I was finishing the manuscript, it occurred to me that we respect Cronkite the way ETO correspondents venerated General Omar Bradley— and for essentially the same reason. There was a fundamental Missouri decency about both men. Hal Boyle and Harry Truman had it, too. They made us feel good about being Americans.

It takes a village to write a book. Two other Hoyas, Jim Clark and Ed Towle, provided literary counsel and encouragement. So did old friends and fellow writers Bill Scheft, Larry Tye, Paul Dickson, and Tim Wendel.

Esteemed World War II historians John McManus and Don Miller also generously gave of their time early in the process.

As always, David Kelly at the Library of Congress was invaluable, plus he put me in touch with the Library's military history specialist Ron Katz. Jeff Flannery in the Library's Manuscripts Division helped, too. The folks in the Library's Newspaper and Current Periodical Room were, as always, terrific, as were the people who run the Library's *Stars and Stripes* collection.

The same holds true of the professionals at the National Archives' College Park facility, the Newseum in Washington, the Smithsonian's National Portrait Gallery, the National World War II Museum in New Orleans, and the Harry S Truman Library and Museum in Independence. Jean Prescott at the Mighty Eighth Air Force Museum in Savannah, and Terry Foster at the U.S. Army Heritage and Education Center in Carlisle, were great, too. Ninety-six-year-old Roy Wilder, Jr., the legendary PRO dubbed "Chitlin'," told wonderful stories about Joe Liebling, Hal Boyle, and Andy Rooney.

Special acknowledgment goes out to Don Carleton, Ashley Adair, and the rest of the staff of the Dolph Briscoe Center for American History at the University of Texas at Austin, the home of the papers of both Walter Cronkite and Andy Rooney. The same goes for Harry Miller and the other archivists at the Wisconsin Historical Society on the campus of the University of Wisconsin–Madison, the home of the papers of Hal Boyle and Homer Bigart. Ditto for Ana Guimaraes, the head of reference services at the Rare Book and Manuscript Collections, and the rest of the staff at Kroch Library at Cornell University, the home of A. J. Liebling's papers.

The folks at the four branches of the Fairfax County (Virginia) Public Library that I visited in the course of researching the book were helpful, too. So were the Brits at the Churchill War Rooms, the Wellington Barracks, and the Imperial War Museum in London, as well as the Imperial War Museum at Duxford in East Anglia. Huge thanks go out to Arthur Brookes at the Cambridge American Cemetery, my impromptu photographer; Anthony Lewis at the Normandy American Cemetery, my "John Murphy" researcher; and Frances Peel, the proprietress of the Cross Keys tavern in Molesworth, where I hoisted a couple of John Smith Bitters to the memories of Walter and Homer. The beautiful little museum in Ste.-Mère-Église is one of my favorite places in Normandy, as is the now-bed-and-breakfast Château de Vouilly, where James Hamel and Gilbert Gallez were wonderful hosts and conscientious correspondents.

"Helpful" doesn't begin to describe the friends and families of the five principals. The Cronkites, Nancy, Kate, and Walter III (Chip) and Chip's son (and soon-to-be, with his Hamilton College professor Maurice Isserman, chronicler of his grandfather) Walter IV, were supportive every step of the way. Chip went above and beyond the call of duty in helping me track down people and things, including a rare copy of UP president Hugh Baillie's WWII memoirs, not to mention the 1964 CBS News documentary *D-Day Plus 20 Years*, which I loved as a kid and is even better as an adult. Cronkite family friends and former CBS News colleagues Sandy Sokolow and Marlene Adler could not have been more generous with their time and observations. British documentary maker Alastair Layzell and his lovely wife and coproducer, Anne, were insightful, too.

The same is true, of course, of Mr. Rooney himself, who, in his early nineties and still sharp as a tack, sat down with me twice for extended interviews. Mr. Rooney sadly passed away in November of 2011, just as I was finishing the manuscript. Sure, he was crotchety but he was also wickedly funny and incisive. His deputy Susie Bieber dug up all kinds of information and allowed me the run of Mr. Rooney's WWII files and photographs. Andy's daughter Emily and son, Brian, were also terrific, as was Andy's college roommate, former CBS colleague and friend for life, Bob Ruthman. Mr. Ruthman was hospitalized at Mr. Rooney's memorial service and tragically died a few weeks later.

If there's a most valuable player award for research on this project it goes to Ed Boyle, Hal's nephew. Ed packaged up one of the Boyle family's treasures, the scrapbook that his mother, Monica, kept during the war of Hal's articles in the *Kansas City Star*, and allowed me to use it for a year. It was an invaluable resource; I'm indebted to the Boyle family for entrusting me with it. Hal's daughter Tracy also spent time with me on the phone early in the project. Former AP–Kansas City reporter Paul Stevens generously compiled a batch of clips and background information on Boyle. AP-NYC archivist Valerie Komor was great at tracking down leads and gave me the run of her operation.

Betsy Wade and her husband, Jim Boylan, great friends of Homer Bigart, were gracious hosts twice in New York. A decade ago, Betsy pulled together some of Bigart's best war correspondence in the deftly titled *Forward Positions*. She helped unearth a lot of information about Homer and provided marvelous insights. So did Homer's old colleague from Vietnam, the Pulitzer Prize–winning journalist and historian Neil Sheehan.

Pete Hamill performed a great service three years ago when he compiled and edited A. J. Liebling's World War II writings for the Library of America. Pete generously gave of his time via phone and e-mail.

One regret is that my old friend and longtime boss Jody Powell, President Carter's distinguished press secretary, never got a chance to read this book. Now *there* was a guy who took history personally. He once chewed me out for not appreciating the geographic nuances of the North African campaign.

The sweetest thing about researching the book was coming in contact with the family members of the war heroes that the five reporters saluted. Colleen Sheets and Sally Sheets Wiggins, the widow and daughter of pilot Bob Sheets, were wonderful. So was Brenda Weaver, the daughter-in-law of Andy Rooney's hero, the one-armed miracle, Sergeant Tyre Weaver. So were Sunny Smith and Lester Trott, the Annapolis Yacht Club friends of Bunny Rigg that my old friend, sailing buff Brian Sailer, helped to locate.

Friends and neighbors Pat and Mike McNamee performed much-appreciated research. Mike almost sprained his wrist operating microfilm machines in tracking down Bigart's *Herald Tribune* clips.

Brent Howard, my editor at New American Library, exhibited the patience of Job. He and his team were a delight to work with.

The final thanks for this project, though, go to Elizabeth and our beautiful Triple As: Allyson, Andrew, and Abigail. Having the chance to walk Omaha Beach with them made it all worthwhile.

BIBLIOGRAPHY

✫

UNPUBLISHED SOURCES

Adler, Marlene, former assistant to Walter Cronkite, Jr. Interviewed by phone and e-mail, 2010–2011.

Atkinson, Rick, World War II historian. Interviewed in 2009–2010 by e-mail.

Bieber, Susie, deputy to Andy Rooney. Interviewed in New York, March 2010 and April 2011, and by phone and e-mail, 2009–2011.

Boylan, James, husband of Betsy Wade and friend of Homer Bigart. Interviewed in New York and via e-mail through Betsy, 2010 and 2011.

Boyle, Ed, Jr., nephew of Hal Boyle. Interviewed by phone and e-mail, 2010–2011.

Boyle, Hal, letters to his wife, Mary Frances Young Boyle, from North Africa and Europe, 1942–1945, part of Boyle's papers at the Wisconsin Historical Society.

——, draft manuscript for *Dear Mary: The Letters of a War Correspondent*, an unpublished book, part of Boyle's papers at the Wisconsin Historical Society.

——, World War II scrapbook compiled by his sister-in-law, Monica Murphy Boyle, and generously lent by her son Ed, Hal's nephew.

Brookes, Arthur, guide at Cambridge American Cemetery and Memorial. Interviewed by author in Cambridge, July 2011, and by e-mail, July–August 2011.

Carleton, Don, executive director, Dolph Briscoe Center for American History, University of Texas at Austin, Cronkite chronicler, and archivist of Cronkite: Eyewitness to a Century at the LBJ Library, University of Texas at Austin. Interviewed in Austin, May 2010, and by phone and e-mail, 2010–2011.

Chitwood, Dana, friend of the family of Sergeant Tyre Weaver. Interviewed by phone and e-mail, February 2011.

Cronkite, Kate, daughter of Walter Cronkite, Jr. Interviewed in Austin, May 2010, and by phone and e-mail, 2009–2011.

Cronkite, Nancy, daughter of Walter Cronkite, Jr. Interviewed by e-mail, 2009–2011.

Cronkite, Walter, Jr., November 1995 script treatments for Discovery Channel's *Cronkite Remembers* documentaries (drafted by Mary Dore, the Cronkite Ward Company).

——, 1942 shipboard diaries, USS *Arkansas* and USS *Texas*, in personal papers, Dolph Briscoe Center for American History, University of Texas at Austin.

——, 1942–1945 personal correspondence from Europe to his wife, Betsy Maxwell Cronkite, and his parents, in Cronkite's personal papers, Dolph Briscoe Center for American History, University of Texas at Austin.

Cronkite, Walter III ("Chip"), son of Walter Cronkite, Jr. Interviewed in Washington, D.C., November 2010, and in New York, April 2011, and by phone and e-mail, 2009–2011.

Cronkite, Walter IV, son of Chip, grandson of Walter Cronkite, Jr., and his grandfather's future chronicler. Interviewed by e-mail 2011.

Fields, Dana, Associated Press reporter, Kansas City. Interviewed by phone and e-mail, March 2010.

Flannery, Jeff, manuscript specialist, Library of Congress. Interviewed by phone, November 2011.

Foster, Terry, researcher, U.S. Army Military Research Center, Carlisle Barracks, PA. Interviewed in Carlisle, May 2010, and by e-mail, 2010–2011.

Frankish, Brian, son of former United Press reporter Jack Frankish, colleague of Walter Cronkite. Interviewed by phone and e-mail, 2010–2011.

Isserman, Maurice, professor at Hamilton College and future Cronkite chronicler. Interviewed by e-mail, 2011.

Gallez, Gilbert, archivist, Château de Vouilly, Normandy. Interviewed at Vouilly, July 2011, and by e-mail, 2011.

Gesas, Tracy Boyle, daughter of Hal Boyle. Interviewed by phone and e-mail, 2010.

Hamel, James, grandson of Mme. Hamel, proprietress, Château de Vouilly, Normandy. Interviewed at Vouilly, July 2011.

Hamill, Pete, Liebling devotee and editor of Liebling World War II collection. Interviewed by phone and e-mail, 2011.

Hamilton, Jim, Writing 69th historian. Interviewed by e-mail, January 2010.

Katz, Rod, military history specialist, Library of Congress. Interviewed by e-mail, November 2009.

Kelly, David, researcher, Library of Congress. Interviewed in Washington, D.C., November 2009, and by phone and e-mail, 2009–2011.

Komor, Valerie, archivist, Associated Press. Interviewed in New York, April 2010, and by phone and e-mail, 2010–2011.

Layzell, Alastair, and wife, Anne, British television documentary producers. Interviewed in London, July 2011, and by e-mail, 2011.

Lewis, Anthony, interpretive guide, Normandy American Cemetery. Interviewed at Colleville-sur-Mer, July 2011, and by e-mail, 2011.

Liebling, A. J., letters from Europe to his mother, sister, and friend Joe Mitchell, 1939–1944, part of Liebling's papers at Cornell University.

——, various unpublished draft articles and research fragments written in Paris and London, 1939–44, part of Liebling's papers at Cornell University.

MacArthur, John, president and publisher of *Harper's Magazine*, friend of the Cronkite family, and devotee of Cronkite's London roommate and United Press colleague Jim McGlincy. Interviewed by phone and e-mail, 2010–2011.

McManus, John C., World War II historian and professor at the Missouri University of Science and Technology. Interviewed in St. Louis, March 2010, and via e-mail, 2010–2011.

Miller, Donald, World War II historian and professor at Lafayette College. Interviewed by phone and e-mail, 2010–2011.

Miller, Harry, reference archivist, Wisconsin Historical Society. Interviewed by e-mail, March 2010.

Peel, Frances, proprietress of the Cross Keys, Molesworth, Cambridgeshire, U.K. Interviewed in Molesworth, July 2011, and by e-mail, 2011.

Pereira, Andréa Nunes, sales associate, United Press International. Interviewed by e-mail, October 2009.

Prescott, Jean, research specialist, Mighty Eighth Air Force Museum. Interviewed by e-mail, March 2010.

Romeiser, John B., professor, University of Tennessee, and biographer of AP correspondent Don Whitehead. Interviewed by e-mail, 2011.

Rooney, Andy. Interviewed in New York, April 2010 and April 2011, and via e-mail though his deputy Susie Bieber, 2010–2011.

Rooney, Brian, son of Andy Rooney. Interviewed by phone and e-mail, 2010–2011.

Rooney, Emily, daughter of Andy Rooney. Interviewed by e-mail, 2010.

Ruthman, Robert, college roommate and onetime CBS colleague of Andy Rooney. Interviewed by phone and e-mail via his son Chris, 2009–2011.

Sheets, Colleen, widow of Captain Robert Sheets. Interviewed by phone, 2010–2011, and via e-mail through her daughter, Sally Sheets Wiggins, 2009–2011.

Sheets, Robert, private World War II diary. Provided by his daughter, Sally Sheets Wiggins, 2010.

Smith, Sunny, and Lester Trott, Annapolis Yacht Club friends of Captain Bunny Rigg. Interviewed by phone, April 2011.

Sokolow, Sandy, former CBS News producer and friend and colleague of Walter Cronkite. Interviewed by phone and e-mail, 2010–2011.

Stevens, Paul, retired Associated Press reporter in Kansas City and admirer of Hal Boyle. Interviewed by phone and e-mail, March 2010.

Trillin, Calvin, friend of Hal Boyle and fellow Kansas City–bred humorist. Interviewed by e-mail via his assistant, 2011.

Wade, Betsy, colleague and chronicler of Homer Bigart. Interviewed in New York, April 2010 and April 2011, and by phone and e-mail, 2010–2011.

Weaver, Brenda, daughter-in-law of the late Sergeant Tyre Weaver. Interviewed by phone and e-mail, February 2011.

Weaver, Tyre, the one-armed USAAF miracle. Personal wartime correspondence and diary fragments, generously provided by his daughter-in-law, Brenda Weaver, February 2011.

Wiant, Susan E., daughter and biographer of former United Press reporter Toby Wiant, a colleague of Walter Cronkite. Interviewed by phone and e-mail, February 2011.

Wiggins, Sally Sheets, daughter of Captain Robert Sheets. Interviewed by phone and e-mail, 2010–2011.

Wilder, Roy, Jr., former First Army public relations officer and great friend of Joe Liebling, Andy Rooney, and Hal Boyle. Interviewed by phone and correspondence, 2011.

PUBLISHED SOURCES

Books

Alexander, Larry. *Biggest Brother: The Life of Major Dick Winters, the Man Who Led the Band of Brothers.* New York: New American Library, 2005.

Allen, Frederick Lewis. *The Big Change: America Transforms Itself: 1900–1950.* New York: Transaction, 1993.

Ambrose, Stephen E. *Band of Brothers: E Company, 506th Regiment, 101st Airborne from Normandy to Hitler's Eagle's Nest.* New York: Touchstone, 1992.

———. *Citizen Soldiers: The U.S. Army from the Normandy Beaches to the Bulge to the Surrender of Germany.* New York: Simon & Schuster, 1997.

———. *D-Day: June 6, 1944—The Climactic Battle of World War II.* New York: Simon & Schuster, 1994.

———. *The Victors: Eisenhower and His Boys: The Men of World War II.* New York: Simon & Schuster, 1998.

———. *The Wild Blue: The Men and Boys Who Flew the B-24s over Germany.* New York: Simon & Schuster, 2001.

Arnett, Peter. *Live from the Battlefield.* New York: Touchstone, 1994.

Associated Press. *Breaking News: How the Associated Press Has Covered War, Peace, and Everything Else,* with a foreword by David Halberstam. New York: Princeton Architectural Press, 2007.

Atkinson, Rick. *An Army at Dawn: The War in North Africa, 1942–1943.* New York: Henry Holt and Company, 2002.

———. *The Day of Battle: The War in Sicily and Italy, 1943–1944.* New York: Henry Holt and Company, 2007.

Ayres, Travis L. *The Bomber Boys: Heroes Who Flew the B-17s in World War II.* New York: New American Library, 2005.

Baillie, Hugh. *Two Battlefronts.* New York: United Press Associations, 1943 (generously provided by the Cronkite family).

Bernstein, Mark, and Alex Lubertozzi. *World War II on the Air: Edward R. Murrow and the Broadcasts That Riveted a Nation.* Naperville, IL: Sourcebooks, 2003.

Booth, T. Michael, and Duncan Spencer. *Paratrooper: The Life of Gen. James M. Gavin.* New York: Simon & Schuster, 1994.

Boyle, Hal, comp. *Help, Help! Another Day!* New York: Associated Press, 1969.

Bradley, Omar N., and Clay Blair. *A General's Life.* New York: Simon & Schuster, 1983.

Breur, William B. *Unexplained Mysteries of World War II.* New York: John Wiley & Sons, 2008.

Brokaw, Tom. *The Greatest Generation Speaks: Letters and Reflections.* New York: Random House, 1999.

Buell, Hal. *We Were There: Normandy.* New York: Black Dog and Leventhal Publishers, 2001.

Cloud, Stanley, and Lynne Olsen. *The Murrow Boys: Pioneers on the Front Lines of Broadcast Journalism.* New York: Houghton Mifflin, 1996.

Conn, Stetson, general ed. *United States Army in World War II.* Washington, D.C.: Center of Military History, 1964.

Cowley, Robert, ed. *No End Save Victory: Perspectives on World War II.* New York: G. P. Putnam, 2001.

Cronkite, Walter. *A Reporter's Life.* New York: Alfred A. Knopf, 1996.

Cronkite, Walter, and Don Carleton. *Conversations with Cronkite.* Austin: Dolph Briscoe Center for American History, 2010.

D'Este, Carlos. *World War II in the Mediterranean*. New York: Algonquin Books, 1990.

Dunnigan, James F., and Albert A. Nofi. *Dirty Little Secrets of World War II*. New York: William Morrow and Company, 1994.

Edwards, Bob. *Edward R. Murrow and the Birth of Broadcast Journalism*. New York: Turning Points/John Wiley & Sons, 2004.

Ellis, John. *Brute Force: Allied Strategy and Tactics in the Second World War*. New York: Viking, 1990.

Ferrari, Michelle, comp. *Reporting America at War*. New York: Hyperion, 2003.

Gallez, Gilbert. *Château de Vouilly During the Battle of Normandy, June and July 1944*. Normandy, France: Self-published, 2009.

Garrison, Gene, with Patrick Gilbert. *Unless Victory Comes: Combat with a World War II Machine Gunner in Patton's Third Army*. New York: New American Library, 2004.

Groom, Winston. *1942: The Year That Tried Men's Souls*. New York: Atlantic Monthly Press, 2005.

Hamill, Pete, ed. *Liebling: World War II Writings: The Road Back to Paris, Mollie and Other War Pieces, Uncollected War Journalism, Normandy Revisited*. New York: Library of America, 2008.

Hamilton, Jim. *The Writing 69th: Civilian War Correspondents Accompany a U.S. Bombing Raid on Germany During World War II*. Marshfield, MA: Green Harbor Publications, 1999.

Hart, B. H. Liddel. *History of the Second World War*. New York: DeCapo Press, 1970.

Hohenberg, John. *Foreign Correspondence: The Great Reporters and Their Times*. New York: Columbia University Press, 1964.

Hutton, Sgt. Bud, and Sgt. Andy Rooney. *Air Gunner*. New York: Ferris Printing Company, 1944.

Jeffers, H. Paul. *Command of Honor*. New York: New American Library, 2008.

——. *Onward We Charge: The Heroic Story of Darby's Rangers in World War II*. New York: New American Library, 2007.

——. *Taking Command: General J. Lawton Collins from Guadalcanal to Utah Beach and Victory in Europe*. New York: New American Library, 2009.

Jordan, Jonathan W. *Brothers, Rivals, Victors: Eisenhower, Patton, Bradley, and the Partnership That Drove the Allied Conquest in Europe*. New York: New American Library, 2011.

Keegan, John. *Six Armies in Normandy*. New York: Viking Press, 1982.

——. *The Battle for History: Re-fighting World War II*. New York: Vintage Books, 1996.

——. *The Second World War*. New York: Viking, 1990.

Kluger, Richard. *The Paper: The Life and Death of the New York Herald Tribune*. New York: Alfred. A. Knopf, 1986.

Knightley, Phillip. *The First Casualty: From the Crimea to Vietnam: The War Correspondent as Hero, Propagandist, and Myth Maker*. New York: Harvest Books, 1975.

Landstrom, Russell. *The Associated Press News Annual: 1945 (Volume I)*. New York: Rinehart & Company, 1945.

Liebling, A. J. *The Republic of Silence*. New York: Harcourt, 1947.

MacDonald, John. *Great Battles of World War II*. New York: Smithmark, 1986.

Manchester, William. *The Glory and the Dream: A Narrative History of America, 1932–1972*. New York: Michael Joseph, 1973.

McIntyre, Ben. *Operation Mincemeat*. New York: Crown, 2010.

McManus, John C. *Alamo in the Ardennes: The Untold Story of the American Soldiers Who Made the Defense of Bastogne Possible*. New York: New American Library, 2008.

Miller, Donald L. *Masters of the Air: America's Bomber Boys Who Fought the Air War Against Nazi Germany*. New York: Simon & Schuster, 2006.

—— (original text by Henry Steele Commager). *The Story of World War II*. New York: Touchstone, 2011.

Nichols, David, ed. *Ernie's War: The Best of Ernie Pyle's War Dispatches*. New York: Random House, 1986.

Oldfield, Col. Barney. *Never a Shot in Anger*. Santa Barbara: Capra Press, 1956.

Pogue, Forrest C. *Diaries of a World War II Combat Historian*. Lexington, KY: University of Kentucky Press, 2001.

——. *George Marshall: Ordeal and Hope, 1939–1942*. New York: Viking, 1996.

Pulwers, Jack E. *The Press of Battle: The G.I. Reporter and the American People*. New York: Ivyhouse Books, 2003.

Remnick, David, ed. *Just Enough Liebling*. New York: North Point Press, 2004.

Romeiser, John B., ed. *Beachhead Don: Reporting the War from the European Theater, 1942–1945*. New York: Fordham University Press, 2004.

Rooney, Andrew A. *The Fortunes of War*. Boston: Little, Brown and Company, 1962.

Rooney, Andy. *My War*. New York: Public Affairs, 1995.

Ryan, Cornelius. *A Bridge Too Far*. New York: Simon & Schuster, 1974.

——. *The Longest Day: The Classic Epic of D-Day*. New York: Simon & Schuster, 1994.

Salisbury, Harrison E. *A Journey for Our Times*. New York: Carroll & Graf Publishers, 1983.

Sevareid, Eric. *Not So Wild a Dream*. New York: Atheneum, 1976.

Sokolov, Raymond. *Wayward Reporter: The Life of A. J. Liebling*. New York: Harper & Row Publishing, 1980.

Steinbeck, John. *Once There Was a War*. New York: Viking, 1958.

Tobin, James. *Ernie Pyle's War: America's Eyewitness to World War II*. New York: The Free Press, 1997.

Voss, Frederick S. *Reporting the War: The Journalistic Coverage of World War II*. Washington, D.C.: Smithsonian Institution Press for the National Portrait Gallery, 1994.

Wade, Betsy, comp. and ed. *Forward Positions: The War Correspondence of Homer Bigart*. Fayetteville, AR: University of Arkansas Press, 1992.

Ward, Geoffrey C., and Ken Burns. *The War: An Intimate History*. New York: Alfred A. Knopf, 2007.

Wiant, Susan. E. *Between the Bylines: A Father's Legacy*. New York: Fordham University Press, 2011.

Willis, Clint, ed. *The War: Stories of Life and Death from World War II*. New York: Adrenaline, 1999.

Wilmot, Chester. *The Struggle for Europe*. London: Reprint Society, 1952.

Wouk, Herman. *Inside, Outside*. Boston, Little, Brown, & Company, Inc., 1985.

Magazines, Journals, Specialty Publications, and Web Sites

The AP World (Associated Press members newsletter)
The AP Inter-Office (Associated Press members newsletter)
Atlantic Monthly
The Blue Pencil (Los Angeles journalism newsletter)
Collier's
Columbia Journalism Review
Commonweal
Editor & Publisher
Harper's

Holiday
Life
Literary Digest
Look
McCall's
Michigan War Studies Review
National Review
New Republic
News Workshop (New York University Department of Journalism newsletter)
Newsweek
New Yorker
The Quill (AP newsletter)
Quill & Quire (Canadian journalism review)
Reader's Digest
Saturday Evening Post
Saturday Review
The Scene (Colgate University magazine)
Sigma Phi Epsilon Journal
Time
www.airfieldinformationexchange.org
www.ajr.org/article.asp?id=1543
www.ap.org/wallofhonor
www.archive.org/details/battle_of_san_pietro
www.dogfacesoldiers.org
www.history.army.mil
www.history.army.mil/books/WWII/Utah11
www.91stbombardmentgroup.com
www.sanangelotexas.org
www.6thbeachbattalion.org
www.taphilo.com/history/8thaf
www.texasmilitaryforcesmuseum.org/36division/archives.htm
www.303rdbg.com
www.uboat.net
www.warsailors.com
www.westendatwar.org.uk
http://en.wikipedia.org/wiki/Greenock_Blitz
http://en.wikipedia.org/wiki/First_Allied_Airborne_Army

Newspapers

Albany Times-Union
Atlanta Constitution
Baltimore Afro-American
Baltimore Sun
Boston Globe
Chicago Daily Tribune
Chicago Sun
Chicago Times
Des Moines Register
Detroit News
Kansas City Kansan
Kansas City Star
London Daily Mail (U.K.)
London Times (U.K.)
Los Angeles Times
Manchester Guardian (U.K.)

Miami Herald
Newark Evening News
New York Herald Tribune
New York Times
New York World-Telegram
Oakland Tribune
Philadelphia Bulletin
Philadelphia Inquirer

Providence Journal
San Francisco Chronicle
Seattle Times
St. Louis Post-Dispatch
Stars and Stripes
Washington Evening Star
Washington Post

Broadcast

CBS News, producer. *Air Power: The Riveting Stories of World War II Air Combat.* CBS News series rereleased in 2008; hosted by Walter Cronkite.

——. *World War II with Walter Cronkite: War in Europe.* CBS News series rereleased in 2003; hosted by Walter Cronkite.

Child, Rob, and Associates, producer. *Silent Wings—The American Glider Pilots of World War II.* Released in 2007; narrated by Hal Holbrook and featuring Andy Rooney and Walter Cronkite.

Friendly, Fred, producer. *D-Day Plus 20 Years.* CBS News documentary with General Eisenhower released in 1964; narrated and hosted by Walter Cronkite.

Gable, Clark, producer. *Combat America.* U.S. Signal Corps documentary, 1943–1944.

Huston, John, director. *The Battle of San Pietro.* U.S. Signal Corps documentary, 1943–1944.

Layzell, Alastair, producer. *City at War: London Calling.* Colonial/Independent production released in 2004; narrated by Walter Cronkite.

——. *Legacy of War.* Colonial/Independent production released in 2007; narrated by Walter Cronkite.

Polin, Daniel B., producer, with Kenneth Mandel, producer and director, and Ken Lewis, director. *George Marshall and the American Century.* Great Projects Film Company Inc., 1994.

Russell, William D., director, with Bernard Girard, director. *You Are There: World War II Begins.* CBS News series rereleased in 2004; hosted by Walter Cronkite.

Wellman, William, director, and Lester Cowan, producer. *Ernie Pyle's The Story of G.I. Joe.* United Artists, 1945.

Wyler, William, director. *The Memphis Belle*, U.S. Signal Corps documentary, 1943.

ENDNOTES

AUTHOR'S NOTE

1. Interview with Anthony Lewis at Colleville, July 2011; plus e-mail from Anthony Lewis, August 2011.

PROLOGUE

D-Day for All Their Lives

1. War diary of Major Robert Sheets; plus interviews with Colleen Sheets and e-mails from Sally Sheets Wiggins, 2010–2011.
2. Ibid.
3. 303rd Bomb Group History (www.303rdbg.com/missions.html).
4. *Shoo Shoo Baby* is not the B-17 *Shoo Shoo Shoo Baby* (three "Shoos") that's on permanent display at the National Museum of the U.S. Air Force in Dayton, Ohio. A different bomber, Bob Sheets' *Shoo Shoo Baby* (two "Shoos") was scrapped at the end of the war.
5. www.303rdbg.com/missions.html; plus referenced in the documentary *Legacy of War*.
6. Ibid.
7. Interviews with Andy Rooney, 2010–2011; plus *My War*, pp. 91–92.
8. Letter from Walter Cronkite to Betsy Maxwell Cronkite, August 20, 1944.
9. Ibid.
10. Letter from Walter to Betsy, July 9, 1944, although it may have been misdated.
11. Walter Cronkite and Don Carleton, *Conversations with Cronkite*, pp. 51–52.
12. Walter Cronkite, *A Reporter's Life*, p. 99.
13. Ibid., pp. 88–89.
14. *Cronkite Remembers* documentary, Discovery Channel, Volume 1.
15. Cronkite, *A Reporter's Life*, p. 78.
16. Letter from Walter to Betsy, February 12, 1944.
17. Various letters from Walter to Betsy, 1943–1944.
18. Sheets' diary. (Parenthetical note: Billy Southworth, Jr., the son of 1943 St. Louis Cardinals' manager Billy "The Kid" Southworth, Sr., was a pilot in the 303rd Bomb Group stationed at Molesworth. Small world.)
19. www.303rdbg.com/missions.html.
20. Slang expression used in Cronkite's letters to Betsy.
21. Cronkite–Salisbury story referenced in Miller, *Masters of the Air*, p. 139.

22. www.303rdbg.com/missions.html.
23. Miller, *Masters of the Air*, p. 7.
24. Rooney, *My War*, pp. 82–85.
25. Cronkite, *A Reporter's Life*, p. 103.
26. Letter from Walter to Betsy, May 14, 1944.
27. Barney Oldfield, *Never a Shot in Anger*, p. 65.
28. "On maneuvers" was the euphemism used by PROs to describe those correspondents who in the spring of 1944 were assimilated with troops girding for the invasion. It was meant to throw off the enemy in case reporters were under surveillance.
29. Cronkite and Carleton, *Conversations*, p. 58.
30. Cronkite, *A Reporter's Life*, pp. 103–4.
31. Script notes from producer/writer Mary Dore's treatment for *Cronkite Remembers* documentary, Discovery Channel, in Cronkite's personal papers.
32. Cronkite, *A Reporter's Life*, p. 104.
33. Cronkite and Carleton, *Conversations*, p. 58.
34. Stephen E. Ambrose, *D-Day*, p. 241.
35. www.303rdbg.com/missions.html, no. 172.
36. Ibid.
37. Dore notes.
38. Cronkite, *A Reporter's Life*, p. 104.
39. Pete Hamill, ed., *Liebling: World War II Writings*, p. 476.
40. Ibid., p. 461.
41. Letter from Don Whitehead to Liebling biographer Raymond Sokolov, Kroch Library, Cornell University.
42. Hamill, p. 825.
43. Ibid., p. 827.
44. Ibid., p. 846.
45. Raymond Sokolov, *Wayward Reporter: The Life of A. J. Liebling*, pp. 163–64.
46. Hamill, p. 460.
47. Sixth Naval Beach Battalion History, www.6thbeachbattalion.org.
48. Hamill, p. 473.
49. Hamill, p. 841.
50. Hamill, p. 474.
51. Ibid.
52. Ibid., pp. 474–75.
53. Ibid., pp. 475–76.
54. Interview with Andy Rooney, April 2011.
55. Rooney, *My War*, p. 146.
56. Rooney, *My War*, p. 156.
57. Don Whitehead column in *AP World*, Summer 1947, in Boyle's personal papers.
58. Letter from Hal Boyle to Frances Boyle, June 9, 1944.
59. *Atlanta Constitution*, June 9, 1944.
60. Betsy Wade, *Forward Positions*, pp. xiv–xv.
61. Richard Kluger, *The Paper*, p. 370.
62. Wade, p. 48; plus *New York Herald Tribune*, June 6, 1944.
63. Referenced in reviews of Atkinson's *Day of Battle*, amazon.com.
64. Eric Sevareid, *Not So Wild a Dream*, p. 414.
65. Geoff Ward and Ken Burns, *The War*, p. 207.
66. Hamill, p. 476.

67. Ibid., p. 477.
68. Ibid.
69. Ibid.
70. Ibid., p. 482.
71. Ibid., p. 488.
72. Ibid., p. 489.
73. Cronkite, *A Reporter's Life*, p. 104.
74. Cronkite and Carleton, *Conversations*, p. 59.
75. Cronkite, *A Reporter's Life*, p. 104.
76. Cronkite interview for CBS News documentary narrated by Charles Kuralt.
77. Cronkite and Carleton, *Conversations*, pp. 59–60.
78. David Nichols, ed., *Ernie's War*, pp. 277–78.
79. AP, Boyle column, July 15, 1944. (Endnotes marked "AP" are clips that come from Boyle's papers at the Wisconsin Historical Society; they're carbons of his original pieces. The dates, when available, reflect Boyle's date of submission, not of publication.)
80. AP, Boyle column, July 5, 1944.
81. Rooney, *My War*, p. 157.
82. Ibid., pp. 157–58.
83. Ibid., p. 158.
84. Wade, p. 9; plus *New York Herald Tribune*, February 27, 1943, p. 1.
85. Wade, p. xv.
86. Peter Arnett, *Live from the Battlefield*, p. 186.
87. *AP Inter-Office*, article by Ed Kennedy, in Boyle's personal papers.
88. Cronkite, *A Reporter's Life*, p. 99.
89. Rooney, *My War*, p. 133.
90. Hamill, pp. 822–23.
91. Ibid.

CHAPTER 1

Early Impressions

1. Quoted in Sokolov, p. 20.
2. Hamill, p. 20.
3. David Remnick, *Just Enough Liebling*, p. xx.
4. Letter from Katherine Sergeant White to Raymond Sokolov, Liebling's papers, Kroch Library, Cornell University.
5. Referenced in Remnick, p. xvii.
6. Letter from Roy Wilder, Jr., to Raymond Sokolov, Liebling's papers, Kroch Library, Cornell University.
7. Letter from Katherine Sergeant White.
8. Quoted in Sokolov, p. 9.
9. Ibid., p. 54.
10. Ibid., p. 61.
11. Referenced in Herman Wouk's novel *Inside, Outside*.
12. Quoted in Sokolov, p. 135.
13. Ibid., p. 13.
14. Hamill, p. 516.

15. Referenced in Sokolov, p. 15.
16. Taken from photo caption in Wade's *Forward Positions*, prior to p. 185.
17. Referenced in Kluger, p. 363.
18. Referenced in Wade, p. xx.
19. Referenced in Kluger, p. 364.
20. *Washington Post*, November 10, 1935, "Mr. Wolfe Listens," p. SM10.
21. Quoted in Kluger, p. 364.
22. Rooney, *My War*, p. 92.
23. Ibid., p. 16.
24. Referenced in a Brian Rooney–Andy Rooney "interview" in *The Scene*, a Colgate University magazine, Spring 2010, provided by Brian Rooney and Bob Ruthman.
25. Letter from Bob Ruthman to author, July 22, 2010.
26. Ruthman letter.
27. Interview with Bob Ruthman, April 2010.
28. Rooney, *My War*, p. 32.
29. *Newark News*, January 24, 1944.
30. *Newsweek*, November 19, 1957.
31. Quoted in photo caption, Boyle's *Help, Help!*, opposite p. 64.
32. AP Boyle column, believed to be June 17, 1943.
33. Ibid.
34. Article by Don Whitehead, *AP World*, Summer Issue 1947.
35. Letter from Hal Boyle to his mother, April 30, 1943.
36. Boyle note in personal papers, undated.
37. Referenced in *Sigma Phi Epsilon Journal*, circa 1945, in AP archives, New York.
38. Believed to be from the *Columbia* (MO) *Daily Tribune*, in AP archives, New York.
39. Letter from Hal Boyle to Frances Boyle, June 9, 1944.
40. Letter from Hal to Frances, August 29, 1943.
41. Interview with Kate Cronkite, May 2010.
42. Cronkite, *A Reporter's Life*, p. 31.
43. Cronkite and Carleton, *Conversations*, p. 12.
44. Ibid., p. 17.
45. Cronkite, *A Reporter's Life*, p. 73.
46. Hamill, p. 21.
47. Sokolov, pp. 94–95.
48. Ibid., p. 125.
49. Ibid., p. 127.
50. Hamill, p. 59.
51. *New Yorker*, April 27, 1940.
52. Letter from Liebling to his mother, May 14, 1940.
53. Letter from Liebling to his mother, May 29, 1940.
54. Letter from Paris, *New Yorker*, May 18, 1940, pp. 36–40.
55. Letter from Liebling to his mother, June 5, 1940.
56. Sokolov, p. 140.
57. Ibid.
58. Ibid., p. 141
59. Ibid., pp. 141–42.
60. Remnick, page xx.

61. Ibid., page xxi.
62. *New Yorker*, February 22, 1941.

CHAPTER 2

"All Sorts of Horrors"—Crossing Torpedo Junction

1. Quoted in Wade, p. xxi.
2. *Kansas City Star*, September 1, 1944. (Many of Boyle's *Kansas City Star* references come from the scrapbook kept by his sister-in-law, Monica Murphy Boyle, who did not record the dates the articles appeared in the newspaper. When available, the dates listed come from Boyle's dateline, which generally was a day or two before the articles were actually published.)
3. Wade, p. xx.
4. Chester Wilmot, *The Struggle for Europe*, p. 17.
5. AP Boyle article, November 7, 1942.
6. Wilmot, p. 18.
7. Quoted in Miller, *The Story of World War II*, p. 167.
8. Rooney, *My War*, p. 41.
9. AP Boyle article, November 7, 1942.
10. Ibid.
11. Rooney, *My War*, p. 42.
12. www.uboat.net.
13. Referenced in Dore's 1995 *Cronkite Remembers* script notes.
14. Cronkite and Carleton, *Conversations*, p. 34.
15. Cronkite, *A Reporter's Life*, p. 81.
16. Cronkite and Carleton, *Conversations*, p. 33.
17. Interview with Charles Kuralt, CBS News documentary.
18. Cronkite, *A Reporter's Life*, p. 81.
19. Hamill, p. 212.
20. Cronkite, *A Reporter's Life*, p. 82.
21. Cronkite uniform on display in LBJ Library museum exhibit, University of Texas at Austin.
22. Dore interview notes.
23. Cronkite and Carleton, *Conversations*, p. 34.
24. Cronkite USS *Arkansas* diary, August 1942.
25. Ibid.
26. http://en.wikipedia.org/wiki/Greenock_Blitz.
27. Cronkite and Carleton, *Conversations*, p. 36.
28. Cronkite told Don Carleton that the Dieppe controversy occurred after he'd taken a second trip to London in the summer of 1942. But Cronkite must have been mistaken: The Dieppe debacle happened during his maiden trip.
29. Statistic referenced at Imperial War Museum exhibit in London.
30. September 12, 1942.
31. Ibid.
32. Ibid., September 10, 1942.
33. Cronkite, *A Reporter's Life*, p. 83.

34. Ward and Burns, *The War*, p. 166.
35. Cronkite and Carleton, *Conversations*, pp. 36–37.
36. Ibid.
37. Ibid.
38. Rooney, *My War*, p. 44.
39. Ibid., pp. 48–56.
40. www.memory.loc.gov/ammem/sgphtml/sashtml/history.html.
41. Miller, *Masters of the Air*, p. 121.
42. *Stars and Stripes*, December 8, 1942, p. 2.
43. *Stars and Stripes*, December 14, 1942.
44. Wade, pp. 5–7; also *New York Herald Tribune*, January 19, 1943.
45. *Stars and Stripes*, July 10, 1943, p. 2.
46. Wade, p. 7; also *New York Herald Tribune*, January 19, 1943.
47. www.warsailors.com.

CHAPTER 3

North Africa's Lipless Kiss

1. *New York Times*, November 16, 1942, p. 1.
2. Letter from Hal Boyle to his mother, November 28, 1943.
3. Ibid.
4. Ibid.
5. *AP World*, Summer 1947, article by Don Whitehead.
6. Rick Atkinson, *An Army at Dawn*, p. 3.
7. David Nichols, *Ernie's War*, pp. 64–65.
8. Atkinson, *An Army at Dawn*, pp. 33–41.
9. Ibid., p. 102.
10. Cronkite USS *Texas* diary, October–November 1942, in Cronkite's personal papers.
11. Cronkite and Carleton, *Conversations*, p. 38.
12. Cronkite *Texas* diary, October 20, 1942.
13. Ibid.
14. www.warsailors.org.
15. Cronkite *Texas* diary, October 24, 1942.
16. Ibid.
17. Atkinson, *An Army at Dawn*, pp. 42–43.
18. Cronkite, *A Reporter's Life*, p. 85.
19. Cronkite spelled it "Sebu" in his dispatches; the river's name is generally spelled "Sebou" today.
20. *Kansas City Kansan*, November 28, 1942, p. 1.
21. AP Boyle article, datelined November 9, 1942.
22. Atkinson, *An Army at Dawn*, p. 147.
23. Cronkite, *A Reporter's Life*, p. 89.
24. Ibid., p. 90.
25. Hamill, p. 217.
26. Ibid., pp. 217–18.
27. Ibid., p. 222.
28. Atkinson, *An Army at Dawn*, pp. 251–52.

29. Ibid.
30. Ibid., pp. 251–58.
31. Article by Don Whitehead, *AP World*, Summer 1947.
32. Calvin Trillin tribute to Boyle, *New Yorker*, April 1974, reprinted in *Kansas City Star*, May 2, 1974.
33. Nichols, p. 8.
34. Hamill, pp. 751–52.
35. John Hohenberg, *Foreign Correspondence: The Great Reporters and Their Times*, p. 358.
36. *Atlanta Constitution*, December 12, 1943, Pyle's column, p. 5D.
37. *Washington Post*, December 24, 1942.

CHAPTER 4

Angry Meteors in Tunisia

1. Quoted in Sokolov, pp. 154–55.
2. Ibid., p. 155.
3. Ibid.
4. Bradley, *A General's Life*, p. 195.
5. Hamill, p. 301.
6. Ibid.
7. Sokolov, pp. 156–57.
8. Miller and Commager, *The Story of World War II*, p. 162.
9. Hamill, p. 765.
10. Ward and Burns, *The War*, p. 72.
11. Miller and Commager, *The Story of World War II*, p. 162.
12. Ward and Burns, *The War*, p. 76.
13. Miller and Commager, p. 163.
14. Bradley, *A General's Life*, p. 128.
15. Ibid.
16. Ward and Burns, *The War*, p. 78.
17. Miller and Commager, *The Story of World War II*, p. 163.
18. Ibid., p. 164.
19. Ibid.
20. *Washington Post*, January 27, 1943, p. 8.
21. Ibid.
22. An abbreviated account of this article appears in Boyle's *Help, Help!*, pp. 54–56; this account, however, is taken from Boyle's raw AP copy, datelined January 25, 1943, in his personal papers.
23. *Washington Post*, February 3, 1943, p. 2.
24. *Washington Post*, February 8, 1943, p. 3.
25. *Washington Post*, February 20, 1943, p. 2.
26. Ibid.
27. AP Boyle article, January 3, 1943.
28. Ibid.
29. AP Boyle article, April 13, 1943.
30. AP Boyle article, April 1, 1943.

31. Ibid.
32. *Kansas City Star*, datelined March 2, 1943.
33. Ibid.
34. AP Boyle article, November 10, 1943.
35. Ibid.
36. Atkinson, *An Army at Dawn*, p. 434.
37. Ibid., p. 443.
38. Ibid.
39. AP Boyle article, November 10, 1943.
40. Interview with Tracy Boyle Gesas, March 2010.
41. Hamill, p. 327.
42. Ibid., p. 333.
43. Ibid., p. 341.
44. Ibid., p. 342.
45. Rooney, *My War*, pp. 91–92.
46. Wade, *Forward Positions*, p. xi.
47. Ibid.
48. Rooney, *My War*, pp. 120–21.
49. *AP World*, Summer 1947, article by Don Whitehead.
50. Hamill, p. 344.
51. *Atlanta Constitution*, December 12, 1943, Ernie Pyle column, p. 5D.
52. Hamill, p. 345.

CHAPTER 5

Bombing Germany with the Writing 69th

1. *Stars and Stripes*, February 27, 1943, p. 1.
2. Ibid.
3. Ibid.; plus Rooney provided historian Don Miller with a detailed account of the Wilhelmshaven mission, *Masters of the Air*, pp. 114–17.
4. Cronkite interview with Charles Kuralt, CBS News documentary.
5. *Stars and Stripes*, February 27, 1943, p. 1.
6. Miller, *Masters of the Air*, p. 5.
7. Ward and Burns, *The War*, p. 115.
8. Ibid.
9. Quoted in Miller, *Masters of the Air*, p. 258.
10. Rooney, *My War*, p. 132.
11. Ibid., p. 78.
12. Miller, *Masters of the Air*, p. 121.
13. Miller and Commager, *The Story of World War II*, p. 257.
14. Miller, *Masters of the Air*, pp. 6–7.
15. *Stars and Stripes*, December 22, 1942, p. 1.
16. Rooney, *My War*, p. 67.
17. Ibid., p. 68.
18. Ibid., p. 91.
19. Unfinished letter(s) in Cronkite's personal papers, December 1942.
20. Letter from Walter to Betsy, January 9, 1943.

21. Ibid.
22. Letter from Walter to Betsy, January 25, 1943.
23. Rooney, *My War*, p. 90.
24. Miller, *Masters of the Air*, p. 115.
25. Cronkite, *A Reporter's Life*, pp. 96–97.
26. Hamilton, p. 2.
27. Ibid., p. 14.
28. Ibid., p. 20.
29. Ibid., p. 18.
30. Miller, *Masters of the Air*, p. 114.
31. Letter from Walter to Betsy, February 6, 1943 (Note: Rooney had no recollection of any "grip.")
32. Ibid.
33. *New York Herald Tribune*, February 8, 1943.
34. Letter from Walter to Betsy, February 6, 1943.
35. *New York Herald Tribune*, February 8, 1943.
36. Cronkite, *A Reporter's Life*, p. 98.
37. Hamilton, p. 51.
38. Ibid., pp. 53–54.
39. Letter from Walter to Betsy, February 6, 1943.
40. Hamilton, p. 67.
41. Cronkite, *A Reporter's Life*, p. 99.
42. *New York Herald Tribune*, February 27, 1943, p. 1.
43. Hamilton, pp. 71–75.
44. Letter from Walter to Betsy, March 8, 1943.
45. *New York World-Telegram*, February 27, 1943, p. 4.
46. Letter from Walter to Betsy, March 8, 1943.
47. Ibid.
48. Rooney, *My War*, p. 135.
49. Letter from Walter to Betsy, March 8, 1943.
50. Ibid.
51. Interviews with Chip and Kate Cronkite, 2010–2011.
52. Letter from Walter to Betsy, March 8, 1943.
53. Quoted in Hamilton, pp. 117–20.
54. Wade, pp. 13–14.

CHAPTER 6

Falling Like Dying Moths

1. *New York World-Telegram*, March 20, 1943, p. 1.
2. *New York Herald Tribune*, March 18, 1943, p. 1.
3. *New York World-Telegram*, March 20, 1943, p. 1.
4. www.303rdbg.com.
5. www.sanangelotexas.org.
6. Ibid.
7. Miller, *Masters of the Air*, pp. 460–68.
8. Ibid.

9. Rooney, *My War*, p. 87.
10. Cronkite, *A Reporter's Life*, pp. 94–95.
11. *Oakland Tribune*, June 1, 1944.
12. *Oakland Tribune*, May 31, 1943.
13. After the war, Stockton's grave was transferred to the Cambridge American Cemetery and Memorial, where it remains today. The author visited Stockton's grave on July 12, 2011.
14. *Oakland Tribune*, June 1, 1944.
15. Rooney, *My War*, p. 100.
16. Ibid.
17. Miller, *Masters of the Air*, p. 118.
18. Rooney, *My War*, pp. 76–77.
19. Letter from Walter to Betsy, May 18, 1943.
20. Miller, *Masters of the Air*, p. 119.
21. Cronkite, *A Reporter's Life*, p. 97.
22. Miller, *Masters of the Air*, p. 119.
23. Cronkite, *A Reporter's Life*, p. 97.
24. Miller, *Masters of the Air*, p. 119.
25. Ibid., p. 139.
26. Ibid., p. 119.
27. Rooney, *My War*, p. 77.
28. Miller, *Masters of the Air*, p. 351.
29. Rooney, *My War*, p. 81.
30. Ibid., p. 101.
31. Ibid.
32. Miller, *Masters of the Air*, p. 227.
33. Rooney, *My War*, p. 84.
34. *Washington Post*, December 27, 1942.
35. Ibid.
36. www.airfieldinformationexchange.org.
37. *New York Herald Tribune*, April 29, 1943, p. 1.
38. *New York Herald Tribune*, June 20, 1943, p. 1.
39. Ibid.
40. www.91stbombardmentgroup.com.
41. Hamill, p. 433.
42. Ibid., p. 430.
43. Quoted in Sokolov, p. 162.
44. Hamill, p. 441.
45. Ibid., p. 443.
46. Ibid., pp. 446–47.
47. Wilmot, pp. 222–23.
48. Rooney's original article referred to Weaver's jalopy as a '37 Ford; it was actually a '33. Weaver's buddies got it wrong.
49. *Stars and Stripes* (special supplement), August 19, 1943.
50. E-mail from Dana Chitwood, February 2011.
51. www.americainwwii.com/stories/stalag17b.html.
52. www.taphilo.com/history/8thaf.
53. E-mail from Brenda Weaver, February 2011.

CHAPTER 7

Sicily—Darker Than a Witch's Hat

1. *New York Herald Tribune*, August 16, 1943, p. 1.
2. Bradley, *A General's Life*, p. 389.
3. Ibid.
4. *Stars and Stripes*, August 13, 1943, p. 2.
5. Atkinson, *Day of Battle*, p. 163.
6. *New York Herald Tribune*, August 16, 1943, p. 1.
7. www.dogfacesoldiers.org.
8. *Los Angeles Times*, August 16, 1943, p. 1.
9. Atkinson, *Day of Battle*, p. 163.
10. *Los Angeles Times*, August 16, 1943, p. 1.
11. Atkinson, *Day of Battle*, p. 163.
12. Bigart's original article referred to the mountain as "Crioli" but it is now commonly referred to as "Cipolla."
13. *New York Herald Tribune*, August 16, 1943, p. 1.
14. Atkinson, *Day of Battle*, p. 163.
15. *Los Angeles Times*, August 16, 1943, p. 1.
16. *New York Herald Tribune*, August 16, 1943, p. 1.
17. *Los Angeles Times*, August 16, 1943, p. 1.
18. Ibid.
19. Atkinson, *Day of Battle*, p. 163.
20. *New York Herald Tribune*, August 16, 1943, p. 1.
21. Atkinson, *Day of Battle*, p. 164.
22. *New York Herald Tribune*, August 17, 1943, p. 1.
23. *Los Angeles Times*, August 16, 1943, p. 1.
24. *New York Herald Tribune*, August 17, 1943, p. 1.
25. Carlo D'Este,*World War II in the Mediterranean*, p. 73.
26. *New York Herald Tribune*, August 17, 1943, p. 1.
27. Ibid.
28. Atkinson, *Day of Battle*, p. 164.
29. Bradley, *A General's Life*, p. 197.
30. Atkinson, *Day of Battle*, p. 164.
31. *New York Herald Tribune*, August 16, 1943, p. 1.
32. *Stars and Stripes*, August 13, 1943, p. 2.
33. Ibid.
34. *Washington Post*, August 17, 1943, p. 3.
35. Miller and Commager, *The Story of World War II*, pp. 214–15.
36. *New York Herald Tribune*, July 9, 1943, p. 1.
37. Wade, p. 16.
38. AP Boyle article, July 4, 1943.
39. Macintyre, *Operation Mincemeat*, pp. 148-49.
40. *New York Herald Tribune*, July 10, 1943, p. 1.
41. AP Boyle column, July 10, 1943.
42. Ibid.
43. Ibid.
44. Ibid.

45. *Stars and Stripes*, July 17, 1943.
46. Atkinson, *Day of Battle*, p. 78.
47. Ibid., pp. 107–9.
48. Ibid., p. 112.
49. *Atlanta Constitution*, July 15, 1943, p. 17.
50. Wade, p. 16.
51. AP Boyle column, July 23, 1943.
52. Ibid.
53. Ibid.
54. AP Boyle memo, July 20, 1943.
55. AP Boyle column, July 24, 1943.
56. Ibid.
57. *New York Herald Tribune*, July 31, 1943, p. 1.
58. Ibid.
59. Ibid., August 3, 1943, p. 1.
60. Ibid., August 6, 1943, p. 1.
61. Ibid., August 7, 1943, p. 1.
62. Cronkite, *A Reporter's Life*, pp. 96–97.
63. *New York Herald Tribune*, August 12, 1943, p. 1.
64. Ibid.
65. Ibid.
66. Atkinson, *Day of Battle*, pp. 164–68.
67. Ibid., p. 167.
68. Ibid., pp. 116–19.
69. Ibid., p. 167.
70. Ibid., pp. 167–72.
71. *Washington Post*, August 22, 1943, p. M14.
72. Ibid.

CHAPTER 8

White Crosses Along the Red Rapido

1. *Los Angeles Times*, January 30, 1944, p. 9; and AP Boyle article, datelined January 27, 1944.
2. Ward and Burns, *The War*, pp. 158–59.
3. www.texasmilitaryforcesmuseum.org/36division/archives.htm.
4. Atkinson, *Day of Battle*, p. 331.
5. Ward and Burns, *The War*, pp. 158–59.
6. *Chicago Daily Tribune*, January 25, 1944, p. 4; and AP Boyle article, datelined January 23, 1944.
7. "Volkswagon" was Boyle's spelling.
8. *Atlanta Constitution*, February 1, 1944, p. 6.
9. *Los Angeles Times*, January 30, 1944, p. 9; and AP Boyle article, datelined January 27, 1944.
10. Hamill, p. 763.
11. *New York Herald Tribune*, March 27, 1944, p. 1.
12. Miller and Commager, *The Story of World War II*, p. 236.

13. Ward and Burns, *The War*, caption, p. 152.
14. Miller and Commager, *The Story of World War II*, p. 225.
15. Ibid., pp. 217–21.
16. Atkinson, *Day of Battle*, p. 180.
17. Wilmot, *The Struggle for Europe*, p. 102.
18. *Chicago Tribune*, September 17, 1943, p. 6.
19. *New York Herald Tribune*, September 16, 1943, p. 1.
20. Atkinson, *Day of Battle*, p. 231.
21. *New York Herald Tribune*, September 28, 1943, p. 1.
22. *New York Times*, October 3, 1943, p. 1; plus the *Chicago Tribune*, October 3, 1943, p. 1.
23. *Atlanta Constitution*, October 3, 1943, p. 6D.
24. *New York Times*, October 3, 1943, p. 1.
25. *Atlanta Constitution*, October 3, 1943, p. 6D.
26. Note from AP to Boyle, in Boyle's personal papers, October 1943.
27. *Baltimore Sun*, October 11, 1943, p. 2.
28. *Atlanta Constitution*, February 17, 1943, p. 1.
29. *Kansas City Star*, January 14, 1944.
30. *Los Angeles Times*, December 5, 1943, p. 23.
31. *New York Herald Tribune*, December 20, 1943, p. 1; also in Wade, pp. 25–34.
32. John Romeiser, ed., *Beachhead Don*, p. 84.
33. Ibid.
34. Atkinson, *Day of Battle*, p. 279.
35. *New York Herald Tribune*, December 20, 1943, p. 1.
36. Romeiser, p. 85.
37. Atkinson, *Day of Battle*, p. 279.
38. *New York Herald Tribune*, December 20, 1943, p. 1.
39. Ibid.
40. Ibid.
41. www.archive.org/details/battle_of_san_pietro.
42. Atkinson, *Day of Battle*, pp. 290–93.
43. Ward and Burns, *The War*, p. 155.
44. *New York Herald Tribune*, February 19, 1944, p. 1; plus Wade, pp. 35–37.
45. Ward and Burns, *The War*, p. 161.
46. Ibid.
47. Ibid., p. 162.
48. Ibid., p. 164.
49. Kluger, pp. 369–70.
50. Quoted in Ward and Burns, *The War*, p. 164.
51. *New York Herald Tribune*, February 19, 1944, p. 1; plus Wade, pp. 35–37.
52. *New York Herald Tribune*, March 9, 1944, p. 1; plus Wade, pp. 38–40.

CHAPTER 9

The Blitz Spirit—London and the Home Front

1. Letter from Walter to Betsy, February 12, 1944.
2. Ibid.
3. Miller, *Masters of the Air*, pp. 260–66.

4. Letter from Walter to Betsy, February 12, 1944.
5. Wilmot, p. 228.
6. Letter from Walter to Betsy, February 12, 1944.
7. Ibid.
8. Ibid.
9. AP Boyle column, May 23, 1944.
10. Miller, *Masters of the Air*, p. 216.
11. Hamill, p. 151.
12. Ibid., p. 152.
13. Cronkite and Carleton, *Conversations*, pp. 52–53.
14. Ibid., *Conversations*, p. 62.
15. Ibid., pp. 62–63.
16. Ibid., p. 63.
17. Ibid., pp. 63–64.
18. Miller, *Masters of the Air*, p. 217.
19. Ibid., p. 218.
20. Ibid., p. 216.
21. Ibid., p. 219.
22. Ibid.
23. *Stars and Stripes*, April 2, 1944, p. 1.
24. Miller, *Masters of the Air*, p. 217.
25. Ibid., p. 226.
26. Rooney, *My War*, p. 94.
27. *Stars and Stripes*, April 21, 1944, p. 1.
28. *Stars and Stripes*, February 29, 1944, p. 2.
29. *Stars and Stripes*, January 15, 1944, p. 2.
30. Ibid.
31. Letter from Walter to Betsy, August 6, 1944.
32. Oldfield, p. i.
33. Ibid.
34. Ibid., p. 65.
35. *Stars and Stripes*, December 1, 1943, p. 3.
36. Bradley, *A General's Life*, p. 226.
37. Hamill, p. 829.
38. Quoted in Sokolov, p. 161.
39. *Atlanta Constitution*, February 21, 1944, p. 1
40. *Kansas City Star*, February 24, 1944, p. 1.
41. CBS World News script, Report to the Nation, March 7, 1944, in Boyle's personal papers.
42. *Kansas City Star*, March 1944 (not certain of exact date).
43. *Kansas City Star*, February 27, 1944, p. 1.
44. Monica Boyle scrapbook, 1942–1946.
45. E-mails from and conversations with Ed Boyle, Jr., 2010–2011.
46. *Los Angeles Times*, March 18, 1944.
47. *Blue Pencil*, issue number 37, March 1944, in AP archives, New York.
48. *Ernie's Pyle's The Story of G.I. Joe*, United Artists, 1944.
49. *Kansas City Star*, May 18, 1944.
50. AP memoranda to customers, in Boyle's personal papers.

51. Oldfield, p. 75.
52. Ibid., p. 42.
53. Letter from Hal to Frances, May 13, 1944.
54. AP Boyle column, datelined May 23, 1944.
55. Ibid.
56. AP Boyle column, May 31, 1944.
57. Letter from Walter to Betsy, May 14, 1944.

CHAPTER 10

Cherbourg and St.-Lô: Ugly Fighting Among Dead Cattle

1. Rooney, *My War*, p. 163.
2. Ibid., p. 160.
3. Interview with Andy Rooney, April 2011.
4. Romeiser, p. 149.
5. Ibid., p. 151.
6. Ibid., p. 145.
7. Ibid., p. 146.
8. Ibid., p. 159.
9. Rooney, *My War*, p. 164.
10. Letter from Don Whitehead to Raymond Sokolov, in Liebling's papers at Cornell.
11. Ward and Burns, *The War*, p. 226.
12. *Kansas City Star*, June 28, 1944.
13. Rooney, *My War*, p. 166.
14. Ibid., pp. 166–68.
15. Remnick, p. xxi.
16. Hamill, p. 679.
17. Ibid, p. 674.
18. Ward and Burns, *The War*, p. 224.
19. Cronkite and Carleton, *Conversations*, p. 59.
20. Letter from Hal to Frances, June 29, 1944.
21. *Kansas City Star*, June 7, 1944.
22. Letter from Walter to Betsy, June 12, 1944.
23. Ward and Burns, *The War*, p. 226.
24. Miller, *Masters of the Air*, p. 297.
25. *Kansas City Kansan*, June 17, 1944.
26. Letter from Walter to Betsy, June 9, 1944 (almost certainly misdated; probably meant "July 9").
27. www.westendatwar.org.uk.
28. Cronkite could not remember the exact address of his flat on Buckingham Gate. When he returned to London to tape the *City at War* documentary, he did not recognize the specific building. At least one account on the Internet identifies Cronkite's flat as part of the old Queen Anne's Mansions near Buckingham Palace, but the author was not able to confirm that.
29. Letter from Walter to Betsy, June 9, 1944 (almost certainly misdated; probably meant "July 9").
30. Rooney, *My War*, p. 172.
31. Letter from Walter to Betsy, June 9, 1944 (almost certainly misdated; probably meant "July 9").

32. Letter from Hal to Frances, June 23, 1944.
33. *New York Times*, July 2, 1944, p. 6.
34. *Los Angles Times*, July 2, 1944, p. 7.
35. Hamill, p. 894.
36. Letter from Hal to Frances, June 29, 1944.
37. Hamill, pp. 894–95.
38. Ibid.
39. Ibid., pp. 896–900.
40. Letter from Hal to Frances, July 12, 1944.
41. Rooney, *My War*, p. 185.
42. Ibid., p. 92.
43. Hamill, p. 881.
44. Rooney, *My War*, p. 185.
45. Hamill, p. 498.
46. Interview with James Hamel and Gilbert Gallez at Vouilly, July 2011.
47. Hamill, p. 499.
48. Ibid., p. 881.
49. Liebling, who prided himself on being able to deduce where people came from after hearing them speak, was wrong on Cota; the great commander was a Main Line Philadelphian.
50. Rooney, *My War*, p. 172.
51. Ward and Burns, *The War*, p. 230.
52. Hamill, p. 505.
53. Hal Buell, *We Were There: Normandy*, p. 151.
54. Ibid., p. 152.
55. Ibid., pp. 205–6.
56. Ibid.
57. Hamill, p. 872
58. Ibid., p. 873.
59. Ibid., p. 790.
60. AP Boyle article, datelined July 12, 1944.
61. www.history.army.mil.
62. *Washington Post*, July 15, 1944.
63. Rooney, *My War*, p. 178.
64. Hamill, p. 872.
65. Rooney, *My War*, p. 179.
66. Ibid.
67. *Kansas City Star*, July 19, 1944.
68. Hamill, p. 873.
69. Buell, p. 52.
70. Rooney, *My War*, p. 180.
71. Buell, p. 53.
72. Rooney, *My War*, p. 180.
73. Buell, p. 53.
74. Rooney, *My War*, p. 181.
75. Buell, p. 53.
76. Hamill, p. 877.

CHAPTER 11

The Breakout—Merci! Merci! Merci!

1. Jonathan W. Jordan, *Brothers, Rivals, Victors*, caption following p. 366.
2. Hamill, p. 946.
3. Ibid., p. 885.
4. Jordan, p. 357.
5. Hamill, p. 886.
6. Ibid., pp. 885–86.
7. Ibid., p. 945.
8. Quoted in Miller and Commager, *The Story of World War II*, p. 318.
9. Hamill, p. 945.
10. Ibid., p. 947.
11. Ibid., p. 880.
12. Ibid., p. 885.
13. Jordan, p. 358.
14. Rooney, *My War*, p. 183.
15. Jordan, p. 359.
16. Rooney, *My War*, p. 183.
17. Quoted in Miller and Commager, *The Story of World War II*, p. 320.
18. Hamill, p. 360.
19. Rooney, *My War*, p. 184.
20. www.ap.org/wallofhonor.
21. Hamill, p. 511.
22. Ibid., p. 512.
23. *Kansas City Star*, July 26, 1944.
24. Ibid., July 31, 1944.
25. Ibid., August 3, 1944.
26. *Stars and Stripes*, August 17, 1944, p. 2.
27. Interview with Roy Wilder, Jr., August 2011.
28. AP Boyle column, Number 47, July 1944.
29. Ibid.
30. Hamill, p. 511.
31. Ibid., p. 512.
32. Ibid., p. 825.
33. Ibid., p. 515.
34. *Kansas City Star*, datelined July 30, 1944.
35. Hamill, pp. 515–17.
36. *Kansas City Star*, datelined August 8, 1944.
37. *Atlanta Constitution*, August 11, 1944, p. 1.
38. Ward and Burns, *The War*, p. 246.
39. Miller and Commager, *The Story of World War II*, pp. 324–25.
40. Wilmot, p. 467.
41. Rooney, *My War*, pp. 187–88.
42. Ibid., p. 188.
43. *Kansas City Star*, datelined August 13, 1945.
44. Ibid.
45. Interview with historian John McManus, March 2010.

46. Hamill, pp. 908–30.
47. Interview with Betsy Wade, March 2010.
48. *New York Herald Tribune*, June 13, 1944, p. 1.
49. Ibid., June 15, 1944.
50. Ibid., July 12, 1944.
51. Ibid., July 19, 1944.
52. Ibid., July 13, 1944.
53. Ibid., August 4, 1944.
54. Ibid., August 17, 1944.
55. Ibid.
56. Ibid., August 19, 1944.
57. Ibid., August 20, 1944.
58. Ibid.
59. Ibid., August 22, 1944.
60. Ibid., August 23, 1944.
61. Ibid.
62. Ibid.
63. Ibid., August 24, 1944.
64. Ibid.
65. Ibid., August 28, 1944.
66. Ibid., September 2, 1944.
67. Ibid., September 4, 1944.
68. Ibid., September 5, 1944.
69. To protect the guilty, Liebling referred to Wilder as "Chitterling" in his postwar account of their pre–Paris liberation maneuverings.
70. Hamill, pp. 946–47.
71. Ward and Burns, *The War*, p. 256.
72. Hamill, p. 946.
73. Rooney, *My War*, p. 199.
74. Hamill, pp. 968–70.
75. Ibid., p. 971.

CHAPTER 12

Rescuing the Kitten—Paris Redeemed

1. Letter from Walter to Betsy, August 15, 1944.
2. Ibid.
3. Ibid.
4. http://en.wikipedia.org/wiki/First_Allied_Airborne_Army.
5. Letter from Hal to Frances, August 11, 1944.
6. Letter from Walter to Betsy, August 20, 1944.
7. Ibid.
8. Miller and Commager, *The Story of World War II*, p. 328.
9. *Baltimore Afro-American*, August 26, 1944.
10. *Washington Post*, August 22, 1944, p. 2.
11. *Kansas City Star*, datelined August 21, 1944.
12. Rooney, *My War*, pp. 198–99.

13. Ibid., p. 199.
14. Ibid., p. 200.
15. Romeiser, p. 203.
16. *Los Angeles Times*, August 23, 1944, p. 2.
17. Romeiser, p. 203.
18. Boyle AP article, datelined August 25, 1944.
19. Romeiser, p. 207.
20. Ibid., p. 208.
21. Ibid., p. 209.
22. Stanley Cloud and Lynne Olson, *The Murrow Boys*, pp. 316–18.
23. Oldfield, p. 111.
24. *Atlanta Constitution*, August 28, 1944, p. 5.
25. Rooney, *My War*, p. 205.
26. Ibid., p. 209.
27. Hamill, p. 974.
28. Ibid., p. 978.
29. Ibid., p. 974.
30. Ibid., p. 986.
31. Ibid.
32. Ibid., p. 987.
33. Ibid., pp. 986–87.
34. *Kansas City Star*, datelined August 25, 1944.
35. AP Boyle column, datelined August 27, 1944.
36. *Kansas City Star*, datelined August 28, 1944.
37. Oldfield authorization note in Boyle's personal papers.
38. Rooney, *My War*, pp. 212–13.
39. Ibid, p. 213.
40. Ibid., p. 214.
41. Ibid., p. 216.
42. *Chicago Daily Tribune*, August 29, 1944, p. 3.
43. Ibid.
44. Rooney, *My War*, p. 222.
45. *Atlanta Constitution*, August 28, 1944, p. 5.
46. Ibid.
47. *Kansas City Star*, datelined August 28, 1944.
48. *Los Angeles Times*, August 30, 1944, p. 2.
49. *Kansas City Star*, datelined August 28, 1944; plus AP Boyle column datelined September 1, 1944.
50. Sokolov, pp. 172–73.
51. Ibid.
52. Miller and Commager, *The Story of World War II*, p. 327.
53. Rooney, *My War*, p. 224.
54. Ibid.
55. Ibid., p. 225.
56. Hamill, p. 990.
57. Ibid., p. 991.
58. Ibid., p. 992.
59. Ibid., p. 522.

CHAPTER 13

Gasping Cough—Crashing into Holland

1. Mark Bernstein and Alex Lubertozzi, *World War II on the Air: Edward R. Murrow and the Broadcasts That Riveted a Nation*, Murrow audio on CD.
2. Cronkite, *A Reporter's Life*, p. 110.
3. Ibid. (Cronkite became friendly with Grateful Dead drummer Mickey Hart late in life and enjoyed surprising people with rock concert references.)
4. Cronkite and Carleton, *Conversations*, p. 64.
5. Cronkite, *A Reporter's Life*, p. 111.
6. Letters from Walter to Betsy, October 3, 1944, and October 9, 1944.
7. Wilmot, p. 542.
8. Ibid., p. 555.
9. Ward and Burns, *The War*, p. 267.
10. Cronkite, *A Reporter's Life*, p. 110.
11. Ibid., pp. 111–12.
12. *Kansas City Kansan*, September 20, 1944, p. 2.
13. Cronkite, *A Reporter's Life*, p. 112.
14. Ibid., pp. 113–14.
15. Cloud and Olson, p. 228.
16. Cronkite, *A Reporter's Life*, p. 114.
17. *Chicago Daily Tribune*, September 25, 1944, p. 6.
18. Ibid.
19. *Atlanta Constitution*, October 2, 1944, p. 1.
20. *Stars and Stripes*, October 16, 1944, p. 3.
21. http://www.godutch.com/newspaper/index.php?id=291.
22. *Stars and Stripes*, October 16, 1944, p. 3.
23. Ibid.
24. www.socyberty.com/history/the-battle-of-the-bulge.
25. Bradley, *A General's Life*, p. 328.
26. *Washington Post*, September 21, 1944, p. 3.
27. *Los Angeles Times*, September 24, 1944, p. 10.
28. Ibid.
29. *Kansas City Star*, datelined September 20, 1944.
30. Ibid.
31. *Stars and Stripes*, September 4, 1944, p. 5.
32. Ibid., September 15, 1944, p. 1.
33. Ibid.
34. Ibid.
35. Ibid., September 20, 1944, p. 1.
36. Ibid., September 26, 1944, p. 1.
37. Ibid.
38. Ward and Burns, *The War*, p. 274.
39. Letter from Walter to Betsy, October 3, 1944.
40. Ibid.
41. Ibid.
42. *Kansas City Star*, datelined September 24, 1944.
43. Ibid.

44. Ibid., September 29, 1944.
45. Cronkite mistakenly referred to Jack Frankish as "Fleischer" in his memoir and in various interviews.
46. Letter from Walter to Betsy, May 18, 1944.
47. *Stars and Stripes*, October 25, 1944, p. 1.
48. Ibid.
49. Ibid.
50. Interview, e-mails (via his son Chris), and correspondence with Bob Ruthman, March–April 2010.
51. *Harper's Magazine*, March 1947, p. 274.
52. Ibid., p. 275.
53. *Stars and Stripes*, May 15, 1945.
54. *Harper's Magazine*, March 1947, p. 276.
55. AP Boyle column, October 10, 1944.
56. Ibid.
57. Ibid.
58. *Atlanta Constitution*, October 18, 1944, p. 1.
59. AP Boyle column, October 19, 1944.
60. Ambrose, *Citizen Soldier*, pp. 167–73.

CHAPTER 14

Gray Phantoms and Murder Factories— The Bulge to Buchenwald

1. Boyle, *Help, Help!*, p. 69.
2. www.historylearningsite.co.uk/malmedy_massacre.htm
3. *Kansas City Star*, datelined December 17, 1944, p. 1.
4. www.historylearningsite.co.uk/malmedy_massacre.htm
5. Ibid.
6. Boyle, *Help, Help!*, p. 70.
7. *Kansas City Star*, datelined December 4, 1944.
8. Cronkite, *A Reporter's Life*, pp. 116–17.
9. Cronkite and Carleton, *Conversations*, pp. 68–69.
10. Cronkite, *A Reporter's Life*, p. 117.
11. Miller and Commager, *The Story of World War II*, pp. 339–41.
12. Cronkite, *A Reporter's Life*, p. 117.
13. Cronkite and Carleton, *Conversations*, p. 70.
14. Cronkite, *A Reporter's Life*, p. 120.
15. *Kansas City Star*, datelined December 4, 1944.
16. Ibid., datelined December 1, 1944.
17. Bradley, *A General's Life*, pp. 351–55.
18. Ibid., p. 351.
19. *Kansas City Star*, datelined December 20, 1944.
20. Ibid., datelined December 21, 1944.
21. Ibid., datelined December 24, 1944.
22. Ibid.
23. Ibid.

24. *Atlanta Constitution*, December 28, 1944, p. 10.
25. *Kansas City Star*, September or October 1945 (no dateline appeared with the scrapbook clip, but it ran in the *Star* while Boyle was assigned to Hong Kong after the war).
26. Cronkite, *A Reporter's Life*, p. 121.
27. Letter from Walter to Betsy, December 27, 1944.
28. Ibid.
29. *Stars and Stripes*, January 4, 1945, p. 6.
30. Ibid.
31. Hamill, p. 543.
32. *Kansas City Star*, datelined December 28, 1944.
33. Ibid.
34. E-mail from Brian Frankish, April 2010, plus AP Boyle article, December 23, 1944.
35. *Kansas City Star*, datelined December 23, 1944.
36. E-mail from Brian Frankish, April 2010.
37. *Kansas City Star*, February 1, 1945.
38. Ibid., March 3, 1945.
39. Rooney, *My War*, pp. 251–55.
40. Bradley, *A General's Life*, p. 406.
41. Ibid., p. 407.
42. Rooney, *My War*, p. 252.
43. Ibid., pp. 255–56.
44. Ibid., p. 264.
45. *Kansas City Star*, datelined April 9, 1945.
46. Rooney, *My War*, p. 265.
47. Ibid.
48. Ibid., p. 268.
49. Ibid.
50. *Kansas City Star*, datelined April 4, 1945.
51. Letter from Hal to Frances, March 24, 1945.
52. Ibid.
53. *Kansas City Star*, datelined April 27, 1945.
54. Ibid., datelined May 1, 1945.
55. Interview with Brian Rooney, May 2010.
56. Interviews with and e-mails from Ed Boyle, Jr., 2010.
57. *Stars and Stripes*, May 8, 1945, p. 1.
58. *Kansas City Star*, datelined May 4, 1945.
59. Article by Don Whitehead, *AP World*, Summer 1947.
60. *Kansas City Star*, datelined May 14, 1945.

EPILOGUE

A Good Age

1. Wade, pp. 84–85; also *New York Herald Tribune*, September 2, 1945, p. 1.
2. Ibid., p. 56; also *New York Herald Tribune*, November 15, 1944.
3. Interviews with Colleen Sheets and Sally Sheets Wiggin, 2010–2011.
4. Ibid.
5. www.303rdbg.com.

6. ww.6thbeachbat.org.
7. Interviews with Rigg friends Sunny Smith and Lester Trott from the Annapolis Yacht Club, April 2011.
8. AP Boyle column, June 11, 1947.
9. Cronkite, *A Reporter's Life*, p. 125.
10. Ibid.
11. Ibid., *A Reporter's Life*, p. 128.
12. Rooney, *My War*, p. 272.
13. Interview with Andy Rooney, April 2011.
14. Rooney, *My War*, p. xiii, foreword by Tom Brokaw.
15. Ibid.
16. AP telegram, January 1945, in Boyle's papers.
17. Boyle-Tebbel proposal, undated (but probably 1946), in Boyle's papers.
18. *Kansas City Star*, datelined June 3, 1945.
19. Boyle, *Help, Help!*, p. 16.
20. *New York Times* obituary of Boyle, April 1974.
21. Arnett, p. 118.
22. Calvin Trillin's April 1974 *New Yorker* tribute to Boyle, reprinted in the *Kansas City Star*, May 2, 1974, p. 20D.
23. Interview with Andy Rooney, April 2011.
24. Don Whitehead tribute to Boyle, undated (but clearly spring 1974), published as a bylined column, clip courtesy of Ed Boyle, Jr.
25. Quoted in *New York Times* obituary of Boyle, April 1974.
26. Trillin, April 1974 *New Yorker* tribute to Boyle.
27. Quoted in *New York Times* obituary of Boyle, April 1974.
28. Personal correspondence in Boyle's personal papers.
29. Quoted in Wade, p. xvi.
30. Ibid.
31. Ibid, p. xxiii.
32. Interview with Neil Sheehan, May 2011.
33. Karen Rothmyer, "The Quiet Exit of Homer Bigart," *American Journalism Review*, Fall 1991, www.ajr.org/article.asp?id=1543.
34. Ibid.
35. Interview with Betsy Wade, March 2010.
36. Photo caption in Wade, following p. 182.
37. Rothmyer.
38. Interview with Betsy Wade, March 2010.
39. *New York Times* obituary, April 17, 1991.
40. Cronkite and Carleton, *Conversations*, p. 165.
41. *D-Day Plus 20 Years*, CBS News documentary, 1964.
42. Cronkite and Carleton, *Conversations*, pp. 166–67.
43. Gallez, *Château de Vouilly*, p. 24.
44. E-mail from Alastair Layzell, August 2011.
45. Hamill, p. 313.
46. Interview with Pete Hamill, July 2011.
47. Hamill, p. 310.

INDEX

★

Timothy M. Gay is the author of *Satch, Dizzy & Rapid Robert: The Wild Saga of Interracial Baseball Before Jackie Robinson* and *Tris Speaker: The Rough-and-Tumble Life of a Baseball Legend*. His essays and op-ed pieces on American history, politics, public policy, and sports have appeared in the *Washington Post*, the *Boston Globe*, *USA Today*, and many other publications. A graduate of Georgetown University, where he majored in American history, Tim lives in Virginia with his wife and children.